Routledge Handbook of Diaspora Studies

The word 'diaspora' has leapt from its previously confined use – mainly concerned with the dispersion of Jews, Greeks, Armenians and Africans away from their natal homelands – to cover the cases of many other ethnic groups, nationalities and religions. But this 'horizontal' scattering of the word to cover the mobility of many groups to many destinations, has been paralleled also by 'vertical' leaps, with the word diaspora being deployed to cover more and more phenomena and serve more and more objectives of different actors.

With sections on 'debating the concept', 'complexity', 'home and home-making', 'connections' and 'critiques', the *Routledge Handbook of Diaspora Studies* is likely to remain an authoritative reference for some time. Each contribution includes a targeted list of references for further reading. The editors have carefully blended established scholars of diaspora with younger scholars looking at how diasporas are constructed 'from below'. The adoption of a variety of conceptual perspectives allows for generalization, contrasts and comparisons between cases.

In this exciting and authoritative collection over 40 scholars from many countries have explored the evolving use of the concept of diaspora, its possibilities as well as its limitations. This *Handbook* will be indispensable for students undertaking essays, debates and dissertations in the field.

Robin Cohen is Professor Emeritus of Development Studies and Senior Research Fellow, Kellogg College, University of Oxford. He writes on globalization, development, migration, creolization, diasporas and identity. His books include: *Frontiers of identity: the British and the others* (1994), *Global diasporas: an introduction* (2008), *Encountering difference: diasporic traces, creolizing spaces* (2016) (with Olivia Sheringham) and *Island societies* (2017). He is currently writing an intellectual history of key intellectuals at eight universities where he has held academic appointments and, with Nicholas Van Hear, developing a solution to the problem of mass displacement using the notion of 'Refugia'.

Carolin Fischer is a post-doctoral researcher at the University of Neuchâtel, Switzerland. Her current work examines how migrant descendants experience, interpret, appropriate and modify otherness in their everyday lives. In 2015 Carolin completed a doctorate in Development Studies at the University of Oxford. Her doctoral thesis is about the lives and civic engagements of Afghans in Germany and the UK. During her time at Oxford, Carolin worked as a research and teaching assistant at the Centre on Migration, Policy and Society (COMPAS), the International Migration Institute (IMI) and the Refugee Studies Centre (RSC). Carolin's areas of interest are identity formation, inter- and intra-group dynamics and forms of civic and political engagement in the context of migration and mobility. Her recent work has appeared in *Ethnicities*, *The Journal of Intercultural Studies* and *Global Networks*.

Routledge Handbook of Diaspora Studies

Edited by Robin Cohen and Carolin Fischer

LONDON AND NEW YORK

First published 2019
by Routledge
2 Park Square, Milton Park, Abingdon, Oxon OX14 4RN

and by Routledge
711 Third Avenue, New York, NY 10017

Routledge is an imprint of the Taylor & Francis Group, an informa business

© 2019 selection and editorial matter, Robin Cohen and Carolin Fischer; individual chapters, the contributors

The right of Robin Cohen and Carolin Fischer to be identified as the authors of the editorial material, and of the authors for their individual chapters, has been asserted in accordance with sections 77 and 78 of the Copyright, Designs and Patents Act 1988.

All rights reserved. No part of this book may be reprinted or reproduced or utilised in any form or by any electronic, mechanical, or other means, now known or hereafter invented, including photocopying and recording, or in any information storage or retrieval system, without permission in writing from the publishers.

Trademark notice: Product or corporate names may be trademarks or registered trademarks, and are used only for identification and explanation without intent to infringe.

British Library Cataloguing-in-Publication Data
A catalogue record for this book is available from the British Library

Library of Congress Cataloging-in-Publication Data
A catalog record has been requested for this book

ISBN: 978-1-138-63113-7 (hbk)
ISBN: 978-1-315-20905-0 (ebk)

Typeset in Bembo
by Swales & Willis Ltd, Exeter, Devon, UK

Printed and bound in Great Britain by
TJ International Ltd, Padstow, Cornwall

Contents

Contributors ix

    Diaspora studies: an introduction 1
    Robin Cohen and Carolin Fischer

PART I
Exploring and debating diaspora **11**

1 Diaspora before it became a concept 13
   Stéphane Dufoix

2 Diaspora studies: past, present and promise 22
   Khachig Tölölyan

3 Key methodological tools for diaspora studies: combining the
   transnational and intersectional approaches 31
   Anna Amelina and Karolina Barglowski

4 The social construction of diasporas: conceptual development and
   the Rwandan case 40
   Simon Turner

5 Diasporas as social movements? 47
   Sharon M. Quinsaat

6 Performing diaspora 55
   Alpha Abebe

7 Embodying belonging: diaspora's racialization and cultural citizenship 63
   Taku Suzuki

8 Music, dance and diaspora 71
   Ananya Jahanara Kabir

9	Diasporic filmmaking in Europe *Daniela Berghahn*	79
10	Writing in diaspora *Zuzanna Olszewska*	86

PART II
Complex diasporas — 95

11	Making and 'faking' a diasporic heritage *Marc Scully*	97
12	Translanguaging and diasporic imagination *Zhu Hua and Li Wei*	106
13	Multi-religious diasporas: rethinking the relationship between religion and diaspora *Dominic Pasura*	113
14	Homelessness and statelessness: possibilities and perils *Barzoo Eliassi*	120
15	Diaspora and class, class and diaspora *Nicholas Van Hear*	129
16	Working-class cosmopolitans and diaspora *Pnina Werbner*	138
17	Transversal crossings and diasporic intersections *Amanda Wise*	146
18	Intersectionalizing diaspora studies *Marie Godin*	154
19	Bridging the mobility–sedentarism and agency–structure dichotomies in diasporic return migration *Nanor Karageozian*	163

PART III
Home and home-making — 171

20	Unravelling the conceptual link between transnationalism and diaspora: the example of hometown networks *Thomas Lacroix*	173

21	Deportees as 'reverse diasporas' *Shahram Khosravi*	181
22	Diasporicity: relative embeddedness in transnational and co-ethnic networks *Takeyuki (Gaku) Tsuda*	189
23	Moral comforts of remaining in exile: snapshots from conflict-generated Indonesian diasporas *Antje Missbach*	197
24	Islamic schooling and the second generation: a diaspora perspective *Hannah Höchner*	206
25	Diaspora and home: interrogating embodied precarity in an era of forced displacement *Divya P. Tolia-Kelly*	214
26	Diasporas and political obligation *Ilan Zvi Baron*	223

PART IV
Connecting diaspora   231

27	Diaspora and religion: connecting and disconnecting *Giulia Liberatore and Leslie Fesenmyer*	233
28	Digital diasporas *Mihaela Nedelcu*	241
29	Diaspora politics and political remittances: a conceptual reflection *Lea Müller-Funk*	251
30	Postcolonial states, nation-building and the (un)making of diasporas *Jen Dickinson*	260
31	The plasticity of diasporic identities in super-diverse cities *Tamsin Barber*	268
32	Displaced imaginations, bodies and things: materiality and subjectivity of forced migration *Sandra H. Dudley*	276
33	Disconnecting from home: contesting the salience of the diaspora *Gijsbert Oonk*	284

PART V
Critiques and applied diaspora studies — 291

34 Using pragmatism to approach 'diaspora', its meanings and political implications — 293
Carolin Fischer and Janine Dahinden

35 Why engage diasporas? — 302
Alan Gamlen

36 Diaspora mobilizations for conflict: beyond amplification and reduction — 311
Maria Koinova

37 Diaspora and development — 320
Ben Page and Claire Mercer

38 Diasporas and the politics of memory and commemoration — 328
Khatharya Um

39 At home in diaspora: the Babylonian Talmud as diasporist manifesto — 336
Daniel Boyarin

40 Diasporas building peace: reflections from the experience of Middle Eastern diasporas — 345
Bahar Baser and Mari Toivanen

Index — *354*

Contributors

Alpha Abebe completed her doctorate in International Development at the University of Oxford in 2016. Her research examined the ways in which people of Ethiopian descent construct a diasporic identity and engage with Ethiopian development initiatives through a mutually constitutive process. She has spent several years as an international and community development practitioner, with a focus on youth engagement and education. Alpha is also a photographer of people, landscapes and mundane objects. With J. Saha, she has published 'Points of origin: a visual and narrative journey' in N. Sigona, A. Gamlen, H. Kringelbach and G. Liberatore (eds) *Diasporas reimagined: spaces, practices and belonging* (2015).

Anna Amelina is a Professor for Intercultural Studies at the Institute for Philosophy and Social Sciences, Brandenburg University of Technology Cottbus-Senftenberg. Her main research areas include transnational migration research, studies on social inequality and intersectionality, social protection and care, cultural sociology and qualitative research methods. Her recent publications include *Transnationalizing inequalities in Europe: sociocultural boundaries, assemblages and regimes of intersection* (2017); *An anthology of migration and social transformation: European perspectives* (co-edited with K. Horvath and B. Meeus, 2016) and *Methodologies on the move: transnational turn in empirical migration research* (co-edited with T. Faist and D. Nergiz, 2013).

Tamsin Barber is Senior Lecturer in Sociology at Oxford Brookes University. Her work analyses constructions of identity and belonging, primarily among the Vietnamese diaspora in London. Her publications include 'Achieving ethnic authenticity through "return" visits to Vietnam: paradoxes of class and gender among the British-born Vietnamese', *Journal of Ethnic and Migration Studies*, 2017; *'Oriental' identities in 'super-diverse' Britain: young British-born Vietnamese in London* (2015) and 'Chinese, Japanese or "Oriental"? Vietnamese passing in "super-diverse" London', *Identities: Global Studies in Culture and Power*, 22 (4), 2014. Her current research includes the emerging East Asian youth identities and social spaces in urban Britain and the changing significance of race and ethnicity in 'super-diverse' contexts.

Karolina Barglowski is Junior Professor of the Sociology of Migration at the Institute of Sociology at Technical University Dortmund (Germany). Previously, she worked at Bielefeld University, where she obtained her PhD in 2016, University of Duisburg-Essen and the Max Planck Institute for the Study of Religious and Ethnic Diversity. Her research and teaching focuses on social inequalities, European migration, qualitative methods and cultural sociology. Her recent publications address issues of intersectionality in transnational spaces, European mobility regimes and transnational methodology. They include 'Coming out within transnational families: intimate confessions under Western eyes', *Social Identities* (2017) (with Anna

Amelina and Basak Bilecen); 'Migration pressures and opportunities: challenges to belonging within the European Union's mobility regime', *InterDisciplines: Journal of History and Sociology*, 2016; and 'Approaching transnational social protection: methodological challenges and empirical applications' in *Population, Space and Place* (2015) (with Basak Bilecen and Anna Amelina).

Ilan Zvi Baron is Associate Professor, School of Government and International Affairs at Durham University, where he is also the co-director of the Centre for the Study of Jewish Culture, Society and Politics. He has published on international relations theory, identity and security, dual loyalty, the Jewish diaspora's relationship with Israel and the international cultural politics of Israeli cuisine. His most recent books include *Obligation in exile: the Jewish diaspora, Israel and critique* (2014), published by Edinburgh University Press, and with Manchester University Press, *How to save politics in a post-truth era* (2018). He has held visiting posts at the University of British Columbia, and the Hebrew University of Jerusalem.

Bahar Baser is Research Fellow at the Centre for Peace, Trust and Social Relations, University of Coventry, and Associate Research Fellow at the Security Institute for Governance and Leadership in Africa, Stellenbosch University, South Africa. Her research interests include ethno-national conflicts and political violence, conflict resolution, third-party mediation, migration and diaspora studies. Her publications include *Diasporas and homeland conflicts: a comparative perspective* (2015), *Migration from Turkey to Sweden: integration, belonging and transnational community* (co-edited 2017) and *Authoritarian politics in Turkey* (co-edited 2017). Her research has been funded by the Swedish Institute, the Italian Foreign Ministry, Coventry University and the Newton Fund-National Research Foundation (South Africa).

Daniela Berghahn is Professor of Film Studies in the Media Arts Department and Director of the Humanities and Arts Research Institute at Royal Holloway, University of London. She has widely published on post-war German cinema, the relationship between film, history and cultural memory and transnational cinema. Her extensive work on migrant and diasporic cinema in Europe has been supported by the Arts and Humanities Research Council of Great Britain. Daniela's publications include *Head-on* (2015), *Far-flung families in film: the diasporic family in contemporary European cinema* (2013), *European cinema in motion: migrant and diasporic film in contemporary Europe* (co-edited with Claudia Sternberg, 2010) and *Hollywood behind the wall: the cinema of East Germany* (2005). Building on her work on diasporic and transnational European cinema, she is currently working on a new project that explores exoticism in contemporary transnational cinema.

Daniel Boyarin is Professor of Talmudic Culture, Departments of Near Eastern Studies and Rhetoric, University of California, Berkeley. His books include *Socrates and the fat rabbis* (2009), *The Jewish Gospels: the story of the Jewish Christ* (2012) and *A traveling homeland: the Babylonian Talmud as Diaspora* (2015). He is currently passionate about Hebrew as a diasporic language, diaspora nationalism and doubled consciousness.

Robin Cohen is Professor Emeritus of Development Studies and Senior Research Fellow, Kellogg College, University of Oxford. He writes on globalization, development, migration, creolization, diasporas and identity. His books include: *Frontiers of identity: the British and the others* (1994), *Global diasporas: an introduction* (2008), *Encountering difference: diasporic traces, creolizing spaces* (2016) (with Olivia Sheringham) and *Island societies* (2017). He is currently writing an intellectual history of key intellectuals at eight universities where he has held academic appointments and, with Nicholas Van Hear, developing a solution to the problem of mass displacement using the notion of 'Refugia'.

Janine Dahinden is Professor of Transnational Studies at the University of Neuchâtel, Switzerland. In her work, she specializes in issues of mobility, migration, transnationality, ethnicity, social networks, culture and gender. She applies qualitative methodologies, social network analysis and quantitative comparative surveys. She was a member of the board of directors of the Swiss Forum for Migration and Population Studies between 2005 and 2006, and she has largely published in German, English and French in a wide variety of journals such as *Ethnic and Racial Studies*, *Journal of Ethnic and Migration Studies*, *Global Networks*, *Journal of International Migration and Integration*, *Ethnicities*, *Social Politics*, *Diversities*, and the *Journal of Intercultural Studies*.

Jen Dickinson is a Senior Lecturer in the Department of Applied Social Sciences at the University of Winchester. Her research interests revolve around postcolonial theory as applied to citizenship, diaspora and migration in sub-Saharan Africa. Before joining the University of Winchester, she worked as a Teaching Fellow at St Andrews University and a Lecturer at the University of Leicester. Her publications include 'Chronicling Kenyan Asian diasporic histories: "newcomers", "established" migrants, and the post-colonial practices of time-work', *Population, Space and Place*, 22 (8), 2016; 'Articulating an Indian diaspora in South Africa: the Consulate General of India, diaspora associations and the practices of collaboration', *Geoforum*, 61, 2015; and 'Decolonising the diaspora: neo-colonial performances of Indian history in East Africa', *Transactions of the Institute of British Geographers*, 37 (4), 2012.

Sandra H. Dudley is Head of the School of Museum Studies, University of Leicester. She works on refugee and museum settings in Southeast Asia and South Asia, and has interests in exile and displacement; objects, materials and collections; and the uses of philosophy in anthropological and museum theory and practice. Her books include: *Displaced things: loss, transformation and hope amongst objects in Burma and beyond* (2018), *Museum objects: experiencing the properties of things* (edited, 2012) and *Materialising exile: material culture and embodied experience among Karenni refugees in Thailand* (2010).

Stéphane Dufoix is Professor of Sociology at the University of Paris Nanterre. He has published on exile politics, diasporas, French national identity, globalization and, more recently, the epistemology of social sciences in times of globalization and the prospects of world sociology. His publications include *Diasporas* (2008) and *The dispersion: a history of the word diaspora* (2017). He is co-editor, with Vincenzo Cicchelli, of the Doing Global Studies series at Brill; he is working on an historical sociology of the concept of globalization; and is writing a book about world sociology.

Barzoo Eliassi is Senior Lecturer in Social Work at Linnaeus University and a research associate at the International Migration Institute at Oxford University. His research area engages with ethnic relations, social policy, social work, statelessness, citizenship and multiculturalism in Middle Eastern and West European societies. Eliassi is the author of the first international book on Kurdish diaspora in Sweden: *Contesting Kurdish identities in Sweden: quest for belonging among Middle Eastern youth* (2013) and co-edited a special issue on Kurdish diasporas in the *Nordic Journal of Migration Research*. In 2015, Eliassi was nominated by and offered a Canada Research Chair (Tier 2) by York University (Canada) in Migration and Mobilities.

Contributors

Leslie Fesenmyer is an anthropologist and ESRC Future Research Leaders Fellow at the Centre on Migration, Policy and Society (COMPAS) at the University of Oxford. She is the author of several recent and forthcoming publications on migration, place-making, kinship, home and Pentecostalism in the Kenyan diaspora, including '"Assistance but not support": Pentecostalism and the reconfiguring of relatedness between Kenya and the United Kingdom' in J. Coles and C. Groes-Green (eds) *Affective circuits* (2016).

Carolin Fischer is a post-doctoral researcher at the University of Neuchâtel, Switzerland. Her current work examines how migrant descendants experience, interpret, appropriate and modify otherness in their everyday lives. In 2015 Carolin completed a doctorate in Development Studies at the University of Oxford. Her doctoral thesis is about the lives and civic engagements of Afghans in Germany and the UK. During her time at Oxford, Carolin worked as a research and teaching assistant at the Centre on Migration, Policy and Society (COMPAS), the International Migration Institute (IMI) and the Refugee Studies Centre (RSC). Carolin's areas of interest are identity formation, inter- and intra-group dynamics and forms of civic and political engagement in the context of migration and mobility. Her recent work has appeared in *Ethnicities*, *The Journal of Intercultural Studies* and *Global Networks*.

Alan Gamlen is the Director of the Hugo Centre for Migration and Population Research and an Associate Professor of Geography at the University of Adelaide in South Australia. Alan's research focuses on human migration and ethnicity, with special interests in the governance of international migration, diasporas and transnationalism. He is author of some 50 articles, book chapters and working papers on these topics, appearing in a range of journals including *Political Geography*, *Progress in Human Geography*, *Transactions of the Institute of British Geographers*, and *International Migration Review*. He is the Founding Editor-in-Chief of the journal *Migration Studies*, published by Oxford University Press.

Marie Godin is currently a research officer at the Oxford Department of International Development, University of Oxford. Her research interests are in migration and development, with a focus on diaspora engagement, gender and participation in peace-building and (post)-conflict reconstruction. Her recent publications include 'Breaking the silences, breaking the frames: a gendered diasporic analysis of sexual violence in the DRC', *Journal of Ethnic and Migration Studies*, 2017, and 'Theatre and photography as new contentious repertoires of Congolese women in the diaspora: towards another politics of representation of rape', *African Diaspora*, 2016.

Hannah Höchner is a postdoctoral researcher at the University of Antwerp and teaching fellow at the Université libre de Bruxelles. Her research seeks to shed light on the diversity and dynamism of Islamic schooling practices in contexts of ongoing social change. Her doctoral thesis, which she completed at the Oxford Department of International Development, offers an anthropological and participatory study with young Islamic school students in Kano in northern Nigeria. Her current work includes Muslim immigrant communities in the West and their relationships with their homelands. Connecting diaspora and transnationalism studies with the study of change within religious schooling practices in Muslim societies, she explores the involvement of the diaspora within Senegal's religious education sector.

Ananya Jahanara Kabir is a Professor at King's College London. She is a literary and cultural historian with interests spanning music, dance, film, the visual arts, academic discourse and literature, and invested in examining what these forms of cultural production can tell us about global modernity. Her publications include *Territory of desire: representing the Valley of Kashmir* (2009), shortlisted for the 2010 European Society for Studies in English Prize, and she co-edited *Postcolonial Approaches to the European Middle Ages: Translating Cultures* (2005, paperback re-issue 2010) and *Beyond borders: South Asian women artists respond to conflict*, a special issue of *South Asian Popular Culture*, April 2011.

Nanor Karageozian is an Assistant Professor and the Director of the Department of Armenian Studies at Haigazian University, Beirut, Lebanon. Her doctoral research at the University of Oxford – made possible by the financial assistance of the Calouste Gulbenkian Foundation, Lincoln College in Oxford, Luys Foundation, Open Society Foundations, and the Oxford Department of International Development – examined the immigration to and long-term settlement in post-Soviet Armenia of Armenians from various well-established diasporic communities. She serves as an ex-officio member of the *Haigazian Armenological Review* editorial board.

Shahram Khosravi is Professor in Anthropology at Stockholm University. His research interests include anthropology of Iran and the Middle East, post-deportation and border studies. He is editor of *Post-deportation: ethnographies of what happens after deportation* (2017) and author of *Precarious lives: waiting and hope in Iran* (2017) and *The 'illegal' traveller: an auto-ethnography of borders* (2010). Khosravi currently is working on two research projects. One is on what happens to young Afghans after deportation from Europe, and the other one is a study of undocumented migrants' waiting in Sweden. It focuses on their experiences of time and how their 'irregular' status is articulated while waiting.

Maria Koinova is Reader in International Relations at the University of Warwick and Principal Investigator of the European Research Council project on 'Diasporas and Contested Sovereignty'. She is the author of *Ethno-nationalist conflicts in post-communist states* (2013), 'Sustained vs. episodic mobilization among conflict-generated diasporas', *International Political Science Review*, 37 (4), 2016, and 'Beyond statist paradigms: socio-spatial positionality and diaspora mobilization in international relations', *International Studies Review* (2017). Her research interests span international relations and comparative politics, and focus on how ethno-national diversity impacts on the political development of conflict and post-conflict societies.

Thomas Lacroix is a CNRS research fellow in geography and associate director of Migrinter, University of Poitiers. He is also associate editor of the journal *Migration Studies*. He is author of *Hometown transnationalism: long distance villageness among North African Berbers and Indian Punjabis* (2016), *Migrants, l'impasse Européenne* (2016) and *Les réseaux marocains du développement* (2005).

Giulia Liberatore is Leverhulme Early Career Fellow at the Centre on Migration, Policy and Society (COMPAS), and Bryan Warren Junior Research Fellow at Linacre College, University of Oxford. She has a PhD in anthropology from the LSE, and is currently working on an ethnographic project on female Islamic leadership and guidance in Britain. Her most recent book is entitled *Somali, Muslim, British: Striving in Securitized Britain*, published in 2017 with Bloomsbury as part of the LSE Monographs in Social Anthropology series.

Claire Mercer is Associate Professor of Human Geography at LSE. She works at the interface of human geography, African studies and development studies. Her early research developed a geographical critique of the concept of civil society. Drawing on ideas from postcolonial studies, this work recast the discussion of civil society in Africa in terms that emphasized the diverse social and political work done by civil society actors such as non-governmental organizations and diasporic home associations. Subsequent research has been concerned with the relationship between the African diaspora and the African continent. This research places Africa at the centre of questions about diaspora. Her publications include: 'Middle class construction: domestic architecture, aesthetics and anxieties in Tanzania', *The Journal of Modern African Studies*, 2014; 'African home associations in Britain: between political belonging and moral conviviality', *African Diaspora*, 2010 (co-authored with B. Page); *Development and the African diaspora: place and the politics of home* (2008) (co-authored with M. Evans). Claire is currently working on new research on the middle classes, domestic architecture and suburban space in Tanzania.

Antje Missbach is a senior research fellow at Monash University, Melbourne, and also a member of the Centre of Indonesian Law, Islam and Society at the Melbourne Law School. She is the author of *Troubled transit: asylum seekers stuck in Indonesia* (2015) and *Politics and conflict in Indonesia: the role of the Acehnese diaspora* (2011). Her research interests include diaspora politics, transit migration and people smuggling in Southeast Asia.

Lea Müller-Funk is postdoctoral fellow at the Department for Politics and International Relations at Oxford University, and an Associated Postdoctoral Researcher at the Centre de recherches internationales at Sciences Po Paris. Her core research interests include migration, transnational politics, and media in the contemporary Arab world. Her interdisciplinary PhD in political science and Arabic studies was given an Award of Excellence of the Austrian Ministry of Science, Research and Economy for the year 2015/2016. Her publications include 'Diaspora mobilizations in the Egyptian (post)revolutionary process: comparing transnational political participation in Paris and Vienna', *Journal of Immigrant and Refugee Studies*, 2016; 'Inventing an Egyptian transnational nation: homeland politics in the Arab Spring Uprisings between migration processes, diasporic policies and political opportunity structures', in Elena Ambrosetti, Donatella Strangio and Catherine Wihtol de Wenden (eds), *Migration in the Mediterranean* (2016); and 'Transnational politics, women and the Egyptian Revolution: examples from Paris', *Mashriq & Mahjar: Journal of Middle East Migration Studies*, 2014.

Li Wei is Chair of Applied Linguistics and Director of the UCL Centre for Applied Linguistics at University College London. He is Fellow of the Academy of Social Sciences, UK. His research interests are in the diverse field of bilingualism and multilingualism. His recent publications include *Translanguaging: language, bilingualism and education* (with Ofelia Garcia, 2014), which won the 2015 British Applied Linguistics Association Book Prize, and the *Cambridge handbook of linguistic multi-competence* (with Vivian Cook, 2016).

Mihaela Nedelcu holds a PhD in sociology, and she is Associate Professor at the Sociology Institute, University of Neuchâtel, Switzerland. She pioneered in the field of migrations, and information and communications technologies (ICTs), and her work – on e-diasporas, highly skilled migrations, transnational families, ageing migrants, e-borders, among other subjects – questions the impact of digital technologies on migration processes through a cosmopolitan lens. Among numerous publications on these issues, she authored the book *Le migrant online: nouveaux modèles migratoires à l'ère du numérique* (2009) and co-edited the special issue 'Migration and ICTs: "being together" and "co-presence" in transnational families and communities', *Global Networks*, 2016.

Contributors

Zuzanna Olszewska is Associate Professor in the Social Anthropology of the Middle East at the University of Oxford. She specializes in the ethnography of Afghan refugee writers and intellectuals in Iran and the Afghan diaspora, as well as subjectivity, self-formation and cultural production. She is the author of *The Pearl of Dari: poetry and personhood among young Afghans in Iran* (2015) and numerous articles on Afghans in Iran and beyond, and translations of Afghan poetry. She is currently undertaking a digital ethnography of social media use in the global Afghan diaspora and its affective relationship with the crystallization of Afghan national or other identities, and discourses about women's and minority rights. She has previously worked on return migration to Nepal, and the Chechen diaspora in Central Europe.

Gijsbert Oonk is Associate Professor of African and South Asian History at the Erasmus School of History, Culture and Communication, Rotterdam, in the Netherlands. He is honorary research affiliate of the Centre for Indian Studies in Africa (CISA), University of the Witwatersrand (Wits), Johannesburg. He is a global historian whose research and teaching activities are in the fields of global history, migration, citizenship and diasporas. He has published extensively in this field. See, for example: *Settled strangers: Asian business elites in East Africa 1800–2000* (2013). He published a widely acclaimed biography of a South Asian business family, *The Karimjee Jivanjee family: merchant princes of East Africa, 1800–2000* (2009). He also edited the book *Global Indian diasporas: exploring trajectories of migration and theory* (2007). In that volume, the contributors critically review the concept of diaspora. (The volume is free and available as an open access publication.)

Ben Page is Reader in Human Geography and African Studies at UCL. His early work focused on infrastructure development and paying for water in Cameroon. It extended critical work on water privatization to historical questions around the social and political consequences of the commodification of natural resources. More recent research has been in the field of international migration and development, focusing particularly on the development work of African diaspora associations and individuals. His publications include: 'Engaging the African diaspora in the fight against malaria' (co-authored with R. Tanyi) in A. Christou and E. Mavroudi (eds), *Dismantling diasporas: rethinking the geographies of diasporic identity, connection and development* (2015); 'Fear of small distances: home associations in Douala, Dar es Salaam and London', in A. Datta and K. Brickell (eds), *Translocal geographies: spaces, places, connections* (2012); and 'Why do people do stuff? Reconceptualizing remittance behaviour in diaspora-development research and policy', *Progress in Development Studies*, 2012 (co-authored with C. Mercer). Ben's current work looks at the impact of international migration on house-building and everyday life in Cameroonian suburbs.

Dominic Pasura is a Lecturer in Sociology at the University of Glasgow, UK. His research interests include global migration, African diasporas, religion, transnationalism, migration and development. Dominic has published widely in peer-reviewed journals and edited books. He is the author of *African transnational diasporas: fractured communities and plural identities of Zimbabweans in Britain* (2014). He is the lead co-editor of the academic volume *Migration, transnationalism, and Catholicism: global perspectives* (2017).

Sharon M. Quinsaat is Visiting Assistant Professor in Sociology at Grinnell College in Iowa, USA. She studies collective behaviour and social movements, migration, and race and ethnicity from a global and transnational perspective. She has published her research on diaspora mobilization, US immigration discourse, multilateral trade negotiations, and anti-free-trade

Contributors

campaigns in edited volumes and peer-reviewed journals such as *Ethnic and Racial Studies*, *Mass Communication and Society*, *Sociology Compass* and *Asian Survey*.

Marc Scully is Lecturer in Psychology at Mary Immaculate College, Ireland, and was previously at the Department of Social Sciences, Loughborough University. He is currently researching how individuals use narratives of the past to authenticate local, regional, national and diasporic identities. Among his publications are: 'Becoming a Viking: DNA testing, genetic ancestry and placeholder identity', *Ethnic & Racial Studies*, 2016 (co-authored with S. D. Brown and T. King); 'Emigrants in the traditional sense? Irishness in England, contemporary migration and collective memory of the 1950s', *Irish Journal of Sociology*, 2015; and 'The tyranny of transnational discourse: "authenticity" and Irish diasporic identity in Ireland and England', *Nations & Nationalism*, 2012.

Taku Suzuki is Associate Professor in International Studies and the Director of the International Studies Program at Denison University in Ohio, USA. He is an anthropologist whose research interests include transnational migration, diaspora, collective memory and citizenship. Dr Suzuki has conducted field research in Bolivia, Okinawa/Japan, the United States, and the Commonwealth of the Northern Mariana Islands, and has authored a monograph, *Embodying belonging: racializing Okinawan diaspora in Bolivia and Japan* (2010). His current research examines memory work among the Okinawan repatriates from the Mariana Islands in the western Pacific, a former Japanese colonial territory, who have made annual pilgrimages to the islands for the last 50 years to console the spirits of those who had died on the islands during the Second World War.

Mari Toivanen is an Academy of Finland Postdoctoral Researcher (2015–18) at the University of Turku, Finland. She holds a PhD degree in social sciences from the University of Turku, and is an affiliated member of the School for Advanced Studies in Social Sciences in Paris. Her research interests include political activism and mobilization, diaspora politics, Kurdish diaspora and identity, second generation, as well as broader themes such as politics of belonging, nationalism and immigration. Her publications include 'Politicized and depoliticized ethnicities, power relations and temporality' in *Ethnic and Racial Studies*, 2017; 'The politics of genocide recognition: Kurdish nation-building and commemoration in the post-Saddam era' in *Journal of Genocide Research*, 2017; and 'Gender in the representation of an armed conflict: Kurdish female combatants in French and British media', in *Middle East Journal of Culture and Communication*, 2016. Her current research deals with the political and civic participation of Kurdish diaspora communities in Finland and France, and their transnational engagements towards Kurdistan in the context of the Syrian civil war and the political unrest in Turkey.

Divya P. Tolia-Kelly is Associate Professor of Cultural Geography at Durham University. Her research collaborations over 20 years have been with artists, curators, museums and archivists, and have contributed to scholarship on landscape, black heritage, visual culture, material culture, race and affect, visual methodologies. Her current research aims to develop approaches to Syrian refugee heritage futures; this connects with her research on material cultures, identities at museums and exhibition spaces. Her three key preoccupations are: (i) How do we decolonize the exhibition spaces of national cultures? (ii) What would a truly internationalist approach to art history/cultural heritage look like? (iii) How do we create archives for those experiencing forced mobility, migration and *culturecide*? Dr Tolia-Kelly is currently writing a research monograph entitled *An archaeology of race at the museum*, based on an exhibition of the same name.

Khachig Tölölyan is one of the pioneers of the field of diaspora studies and the founding editor of the award-winning *Diaspora: A Journal of Transnational Studies*, which he has been editing since 1991. His research addresses the theoretical underpinnings of diaspora studies as well as the concrete realities of the contemporary Armenian diaspora, of which he is a member. He is interested in the mobility of populations and cultures, and asks how the increasing level of migration and dispersion brings new populations to the West, how these dispersions become ethnic, or transnational, or diasporic, and how these in turn reshape the literature, culture and politics of the nations/states that host them. World literature, in particular global Anglophone fiction, is increasingly part of his recent research.

Takeyuki (Gaku) Tsuda is a Professor of Anthropology in the School of Human Evolution and Social Change at Arizona State University. He received his PhD in anthropology in 1997 from the University of California at Berkeley, and was Associate Director of the Center for Comparative Immigration Studies at the University of California at San Diego. His primary academic interests include international migration, diasporas, ethnic minorities, ethnic and national identity, transnationalism and globalization, ethnic return migrants, and the Japanese diaspora in the Americas. His current research examines Japanese Americans across the generations and the extent to which they remain connected to their ethnic heritage. He is the author of *Strangers in the ethnic homeland: Japanese Brazilian return migration in transnational perspective* (2003) and *Japanese American ethnicity: in search of heritage and homeland across generations* (2016). He is also editor of *Diasporic homecomings: ethnic return migration in comparative perspective* (2009).

Simon Turner is Associate Professor at the Centre for Advanced Migration Studies, University of Copenhagen. He works on forced displacement, diaspora, conflict and humanitarianism in the African Great Lakes region and on Europe. Presently, he is engaged in a project on anticipating violence in the Burundi conflict, and another project on 'carceral junctions' in European refugee policies. He is the author of *Politics of innocence: Hutu identity, conflict and camp life* (2010), the editor of *Diasporic tensions: the dilemmas and conflicts of transnational engagement* (2008) and the co-editor of *Agents of change? Staging and governing diasporas and the African state* (2013).

Khatharya Um is Associate Professor in Asian American and Asian Diaspora Studies at the University of California, Berkeley. She works on Southeast Asian and Southeast Asian American studies, refugee migration, transnational and diaspora studies, post-colonial, conflict and post-conflict studies, and genocide studies. Her recent publications include *From the Land of Shadows: war, revolution, and the making of the Cambodian diaspora* (2015); *Southeast Asian migration: people on the move in search of work, refuge and belonging* (2015); and 'Representation of violence and the violence of representation: the Tuol Sleng Memorial and the politics of memorialization in post-genocide Cambodia' (forthcoming). Her current projects concern women in conflict and post-conflict communities, and on what she terms 'refugitude'.

Nicholas Van Hear is Deputy Director at the Centre on Migration, Policy and Society (COMPAS) and a Fellow of St Cross College, University of Oxford. With a background in anthropology and development studies, he works on forced migration, conflict, development, diaspora, transnationalism and related issues, and has field experience in Africa, the Middle East, South Asia, North America and Europe. His books include *New diasporas: the mass exodus, dispersal and regrouping of migrant communities* (1998), *The migration–development nexus* (2003), and *Catching fire: containing forced migration in a volatile world* (2006). His main theoretical and conceptual contributions have been on force and choice in migration; migration and development;

diaspora formation and engagement in conflict settings, including post-war recovery; and migration and class. He is currently developing research on the interplay between geopolitical shifts, mobility, immobility and political mobilization.

Pnina Werbner is Professor Emerita of Social Anthropology, Keele University. She is author of *The making of an African working class: politics, law and cultural protest in the manual workers' union of Botswana* (2014) and of *The Manchester migration trilogy: the migration process* (1990/2002), *Imagined diasporas* (2002) and *Pilgrims of love* (2003). She has edited several theoretical collections on hybridity, cosmopolitanism, multiculturalism, migration and citizenship, including *Anthropology and the new cosmopolitanism* (2008) and *The political aesthetics of global protest: beyond the Arab Spring* (2014). She currently holds a Leverhulme Emeritus fellowship on 'The changing *kgotla*: the transformation of customary courts in village Botswana'.

Amanda Wise is Associate Professor of Sociology at Macquarie University. Her research interests include materialities, civilities and 'sensibilities' of urban life in diverse cities; multiculturalism and 'lived diversity' (especially 'everyday multiculturalism'); race and inter-ethnic relations; cultural attachments to and formations of place, especially in relation to multicultural cities; national and cultural identities; diasporic, transnational and migrant communities; labour mobility in and from Asia; and experiences of low-wage migrant labourers in Australia and Asia. She is co-editor of *Everyday multiculturalism* (2009) and author of *Exile and return among the East Timorese* (2006). She has published extensively on various aspects of 'everyday multiculture' in Australia and Singapore.

Zhu Hua is Professor of Applied Linguistics and Communication, Birkbeck College, University of London. Her main research areas are multilingual and intercultural communication in a number of contexts including diaspora and family. Among her recent publications are *Exploring intercultural communication: language in action* (2014), *Crossing boundaries and weaving intercultural work, life, and scholarship in globalizing universities* (2016, with Adam Komisarof) and *Research methods in intercultural communication* (2016). She is book series editor for *Routledge studies in language and intercultural communication* and *Cambridge key topics in applied linguistics* (with Claire Kramsch).

Diaspora studies
An introduction

Robin Cohen and Carolin Fischer

We start with an instructive story of an intellectual dispute.

On 26 January 1961, a student newspaper at McGill University, Montreal, reported that the then famous British historian, Arnold J. Toynbee, had suggested that the Israelis' treatment of the Arabs in 1947 was comparable to the murder of six million Jews by the Nazis. As Toynbee's biographer, McNeill (1989: 246), records, this marked the moment when Toynbee's sky-high reputation collapsed, at least in American eyes. It should be explained that Toynbee was no ordinary historian. He was the author of *A study of history*, covering the fate of 26 civilizations in 12 volumes, published in batches over 27 years (1934–1961). He was, perhaps is, the only historian to feature on the cover of *Time* magazine, on 17 March 1947. He was the ultimate sage, whose words dripped with authority, knowledge and wisdom. After the student newspaper account was published, Toynbee was immediately challenged to a public debate by the Israeli ambassador to Canada where, McNeill (1989: 246) reports, their differences were 'firmly but politely' explored.

However, this debate was shadow-boxing. The heart of the matter was that Toynbee had, as early as 1934, dismissed Jews as a surviving 'fossil' emerging from an extinct Syriac civilization. As the march of his 26 great civilizations proceeded, living fossils, like the Jews, Nestorians or Parsis, could survive in the nooks and crannies of colliding civilizations but – so it was implied – they were relatively insignificant. This riled a vocal section of the Jewish diaspora. A book-length attack by Maurice Samuel (1956) was sardonically titled *The professor and the fossil* while, even in 2007, 22 years after Toynbee's death, an angry (if superficial) article in the Israeli newspaper *Haaritz* was headlined 'This is how we ruined Toynbee's theory' (Sheleg 2007). As Dufoix (2017: 149–51) explains in his magisterial history of the word 'diaspora', Toynbee developed and changed his views on diasporas substantially after 1960. He submitted variously that established states would give way to dispersed communities (that is, diasporas), that diasporas were the wave of the future, that Judaism was uniquely placed to expand its precepts to a universal vision, and that he meant nothing offensive by the word 'fossil', which simply referred to the social cement that bound people together in the absence of a home country. All this elaboration of his views cut no ice. In Zionist circles, Toynbee was effectively dismissed as an anti-Semite, while his civilizational approach was decisively rejected by nationalist historians in many countries. It is only now, with a renewed interest in global perspectives, that Toynbee's many works are being hauled off dusty shelves and studied anew.

Inferences

Without seeking to rehabilitate him tout court, we draw four inferences from our story about Toynbee.

First, those living in diasporas do not necessarily agree with the characterizations of them drawn by external observers, however learned or scholarly. There may be a significant difference between diaspora as a category of self-identification as opposed to diaspora as a category of external classification. Moreover, 'they', the subjects (sometimes they are now called 'subalterns'), can make their voices heard. In other words, the tension between the emic (the perspective of the subject) and the etic (the perspective of the observer) matters. Etic classifications of a perceived group as diaspora are based on a combination of certain defining features. Conversely, as an emic category of self-identification, the notion of diaspora is imbued with emotionally laden meanings that are intertwined with the specific history and experiences of the population in question. Even where a diaspora's history is somewhat invented, this rarely dents the passion of conviction. To capture the emic perspective, we pay considerable attention in this volume to bottom-up, rather than top-down, approaches to diaspora.

Second, there is often a tension between nationalism (and more concretely the nation-state) and diasporas. For Toynbee, nationalism was an anathema, a view he derived partly from collecting witness statements of the murderous attacks by Ottoman forces on Armenians during the period 1915–17. Now, nation-states often attempt to reach out to 'their' diasporas, as Gamlen's account in this volume documents. In many cases, though, the nominated diaspora either historically predated anything resembling a nation-state or does not unanimously identify with the country of ancestral origin. The imputation of 'ownership' or primacy of nation-state over diaspora is often challenged, as a number of our contributors suggest. More saliently, when conflict erupts in the nation-state, the diaspora can either exacerbate or ameliorate the violence. Again, in some cases, a diasporic view can even question the legitimacy of the state, as Boyarin's chapter in this volume on the Jewish diaspora indicates – making him, a Talmudic scholar, an odd ally of Toynbee. Of course, there are also many cases of more benign interactions between states and diasporic members, with development aid going from diasporas to families, communities and hometowns, while offers of engagement in terms of voting rights, cultural outreach and practical support move from states to diasporas.

Third, the assumed relationship between nation-state and diaspora misconceives the ways in which identities are forged and draws on two limited assumptions. On the one hand, it builds on the idea that persons naturally belong to a specific nation-state. On the other hand, it holds that those belonging to but living outside their country of citizenship are prone, even obliged, to feel a sense of loyalty towards it. Critics of methodological nationalism have attacked such nation-state-based epistemologies for conflating territory, identity and belonging (Wimmer and Glick Schiller 2002). As a result, these precognitions ignore the existence of multiple layers of identity among those forming part of a diasporic population. Rather than assuming that those perceived members of diasporas necessarily identify with their (ancestral) country of origin, it is more pertinent to raise the question 'what do people identify with?' and to acknowledge that there may be additional or alternative links.

A fourth inference we can draw from the Toynbee debate focuses on the potency and future of diasporas. Are diasporic ties likely to be weakened as countries of settlement increasingly demand cultural conformity, social integration and exclusive political fealty? The tension between transnational or, more specifically, diasporic ties and local integration has been intensely discussed by migration scholars in recent years. These debates draw attention to the dynamic perceptions of changing relations between the 'us' (the native citizens) and the 'them' (the migrant others) and their political implications. Several contributions to this volume explore how changing relations between societies and their others affect the formation and engagement of diasporas as well as for the 'politics of diaspora', meaning state actors' attempts to govern diasporic populations on their territory. The future of diasporas is also being questioned in the light of increasingly mixed global migration flows and the arrival of forced migrants at destinations across the globe. The growing heterogeneity of migratory movements may be significant with regard to its implications for dynamics among migrant groups themselves as well as the relations between established and new immigrants and their societies of settlement.

Rather than a state being able to enforce conformity, are diasporas likely to provide a continuing challenge to nation-states, as Toynbee suggested, not on their own (as he seems to imply), but together with assertive global religions, the continuing rise of global corporations and transnational social movements (supporting, for example, feminism, human rights and the environment)? All these social entities are 'power containers' in their own right and may contest what Giddens (1987) called the territorial or bordered power container, that is, the nation-state. The idea that diasporas constitute a challenge to the nation-state is often conflated with the fear that diasporas may pose a security threat. Such fears have gained currency in recent years as assumed links between international migration and domestic security featured prominently in public debates and political decision-making. This is paradoxical. On the one hand, the authority of nation-states is perceived as threatened as domestic populations and regimes are being undermined by diasporic invaders. On the other hand, the assumption that representatives of certain nationalities are potentially more threatening than others fuels nation-state-based epistemologies, thus reinforcing the conflation of culture, identity and belonging.

Background themes

Naturally, the four inferences we derive from Toynbee's story do not by any means cover the rich array of contemporary diasporic themes. Indeed, this would be unlikely given that the idea of diaspora has gained traction in many spheres of knowledge and social life. The word has become highly fashionable and has leapt from its previously confined use – mainly concerned with the dispersion of Jews, Greeks, Armenians and Africans – to cover the cases of many other ethnic groups, nationalities and religions. But this 'horizontal' scattering of the word to cover the mobility of many groups to many destinations has been paralleled also by 'vertical' leaps, with the word 'diaspora' being deployed to cover more and more phenomena and serve more and more objectives of different actors. The word has graduated to the status of a concept, and now has an established niche in university curricula as 'diaspora studies'. Some even suggest that diaspora is 'a theory'.

Despite the proliferation of uses, it is something of an exaggeration to say that 'diaspora' is, in itself, a theory. We are happy enough at the more modest expression 'concept'. But what makes a good concept? Gerring (1999) suggests the qualities needed are eight-fold – familiarity, resonance, parsimony, coherence, differentiation, depth, theoretical utility and field utility. Diaspora does well on most of these criteria, but it would be difficult to say it is either especially parsimonious or particularly coherent. Indeed, the explosion of use of the word 'diaspora', led Brubaker (2005: 1), in a much-quoted article, to complain that as the term has proliferated, its meaning has been stretched to accommodate the various intellectual, cultural and political agendas in the service of which it has been enlisted. This has resulted in what one might call a '"diaspora" diaspora' a dispersion of the meanings of the term in semantic, conceptual and disciplinary space.

Brubaker's lament was written in 2005, when Google yielded a score of one million hits for the word. By October 2017, the word 'diaspora' yielded 159 million hits. It is a moot point whether this is evidence of conceptual success or failure? While the depth, resonance and several other criteria of a good concept remain, coherence and parsimony have been traded for imagination, audaciousness and strategic use. For many represented in this Handbook, the exchange has been well worthwhile. Concepts that are too precise become too prosaic, obvious and boring. Nor should they be confined and tethered by one historical experience or sacrificed to political wilfulness.

Much of the recent scholarly work on diasporas is based on an ever-growing corpus of case studies, which provide us with insights into diasporic ways of being across the globe. However, we thought it rather unchallenging simply to proliferate the number of studies of this or that diaspora in this or that country. Another strand of written work has emerged in more practice- and policy-oriented contexts. It mainly revolves around forms of diaspora involvement in countries of origin, including the development of strategies aimed at generating diaspora support. Politics and development are the primary areas of (desired) diaspora engagement. Rather than drawing on a wealth of examples to show that diasporas exist and do or should do things, our Handbook adopts an explicitly conceptual perspective. It seeks to revisit debates and themes that have emerged in conjunction with the study of empirical research on diasporas and diaspora politics. We sought contributions that allow generalization, contrasts and comparisons between cases.

Exploring and debating diaspora

Our contributors in Part I of this book have sought to chart a map of how the concept of diaspora emerged and how it debouched into different epistemological and experiential spheres. Dufoix, who has written an authoritative history of the word, focuses here on the period before diaspora formally entered a social science vocabulary some 70 years ago, demonstrating that the word had already morphed from a religious to a secular word, from a negative to a positive inflection, and from a restricted use to multiple usages. For his part, Tölölyan shows how diaspora has become a synecdoche (a part representing the whole) for all forms of dispersion, how the diasporic subject has been elevated in status compared with the objective study of diasporas, and how the central notions of home and homeland (discussed fully in Part III of this book) have become attenuated. A further challenge to another basic building block of diaspora, the idea that solidarity and trust are normally framed in terms of an ethnic bond, is provided by Amelina and Barglowski. Pointing to the internal heterogeneity of diasporas, they argue that differences based on gender, class, race and sexuality need to be welded to the core notions, thus making the idea of a diasporic community more contingent, more fluid and more open to negotiation between the relevant social actors.

Perhaps the most fundamental disruption to earlier approaches to diaspora has been to deploy the optic of social constructivism in diaspora studies. As Turner suggests, this privileges such questions as: *how* are diasporas made, *who* makes claims to be part of a diaspora, and *what* claims are made on behalf of a diaspora? The result is a 'battleground' of claims and counterclaims for rights and forms of recognition. Quinsaat also advocates the use of a social constructivist approach, with the specific recommendation that diasporic mobilizations can be analogized, as some earlier scholars had suggested, to the mobilization of social movements.

In one way or another, the remaining chapters in Part I concentrate on how social actors activate, express, mobilize or condition a diasporic consciousness. Abebe shows how performative and creative art can crystallize sentiments of loss, loneliness and nostalgia, so crucial to the expression of a diasporic sensibility. This insight is amplified in Kabir's chapter on how music and dance found their expression between civilizations, by Berghahn's account of how filmmaking in Europe has been transformed by exilic and diasporic filmmakers, and by Olszewska's analysis of diasporic writing. For his part, Suzuki describes how diasporic identities in new places of belonging have become embodied in complex processes of racialization and cultural citizenship.

Complex diasporas

As suggested earlier, one of the most important shifts in diaspora studies is to de-emphasize group solidarity and cohesiveness in favour of recognizing internal complexities – including multi-ethnic, multi-faith, multi-lingual, multi-cohort, multi-mobile and hybrid diasporas. The contributions gartered in Part II explore these different dimensions of diasporic complexity.

Focusing on the individual diasporan, Scully examines to what extent she or he exercises agency when constructing authentic diasporic heritage in relation to people and places. He also sheds light on concomitant meanings of nation and belonging. Hua and Wei also engage with diasporic subjectivity and sense of belonging in the context of identity construction, but situate their contribution in the context of applied linguistics. In so doing, they illuminate the links between language choice and diasporic imagination, with a particular focus on translanguaging practices.

Religion, as Pasura reminds us, constitutes another centrepiece of diasporic identity and complexity. He emphasizes the need to study the relationship between religion and diaspora at various levels, such as the structural and the discursive level, and urges us to pay attention to the history and context-related changeability. History and historical variability also feature importantly in Eliassi's elaboration of the narratives of homeland and belonging across different generations. His focus on forced migration and statelessness, moreover, unpacks the links between home, belonging, alienation and political otherness.

Adding yet another layer to engagements with diasporic complexity, Van Hear examines the dynamic interplay between migration, diaspora and class. He shows how socio-economic and spatial mobility may combine to shape both diaspora formation and diaspora engagement. Subsequently, Werbner further extends reflections on diaspora and class by drawing on working-class cosmopolitans to dismantle assumptions of a homology between class position and transnational subjectivity. While Werbner specifies the value of the concept to working-class and everyday cosmopolitanism, Wise illuminates the transformative effects of everyday practices – transversal crossings – that occur in situations of lived difference. Her focus on transversal crossings enables Wise to illuminate their transformative effects on diasporic 'roots' and thus transcend primordial identity claims. Transversality also plays an important role in Godin's contribution, in which she moves gender to the forefront and argues for the need of a 'transnational intersectional approach' to unpack the complex system of power relations that shapes the experiences and positionalities of men and women in the diaspora. Finally, Karageozian elaborates on the multiple facets of diasporic return migration. She draws attention to the role temporal and local elements play in shaping endeavours, experiences and outcomes of long-term diasporic return projects.

While all contributors to this section of the book highlight a particular facet of diasporic complexity, implicitly or explicitly they show that some aspects – including gender and class – are cross-cutting and therefore particularly important to further explore with regard to their implications for, and effects on, the expression of a diasporic consciousness and identity.

Home and home-making

Part III turns to the question of home, a theme that has traditionally been a crucial defining feature of diaspora. At the heart of the older versions of diaspora was the idea of homeland. However, the assumption that an identification with or an orientation towards a homeland constitutes an important binding tie among members of diasporic populations has at least two caveats. First, the idea of a homeland builds on an imagined natural connection between people, culture and territory. As such, a homeland often represents a subject of external ascription rather than self-identification. It therefore entails a danger of slipping into essentialist reasoning, as scholars like Anthias, Brubaker and Clifford have powerfully pointed out. They remind us that peoples' relation to an (ancestral) homeland should be approached as a puzzle rather than a given fact, because the levels and types of connection may differ markedly.

Second, the suffix 'land' was there to signify that an actual territory was the object of diasporic longing and return. To be sure, the gender of the homeland was contested. Was it a 'fatherland' or 'motherland'? The former was associated particularly with the Netherlands and Nazi Germany and with extreme masculinity. Blood was shed for the 'Vaterland'. The latter, as in Bharat Mata (Mother India) or Mother Russia, was associated with a comforting female bosom in which one could find peace and security. Homelands were also sanctified and mythologized over time, especially when populations had been dispersed and new settlers had arrived. The attempts by Israeli settlers to legitimatize their occupation of the Palestinian West Bank by evoking the historical kingdom of Judea and Samaria shows the potency and danger of claiming or reclaiming homelands.

While movement, home and group solidarity arguably remain at the heart of the concept, each of these spheres of meaning has been stretched in new and thought-provoking directions. In particular, homeland as a concrete entity with some historical geographical reference point has given way to 'home', 'home-making' and other looser forms of connection and belonging to natal communities and places. The contributions to Part III unpick different forms and levels of relations to 'home' and shed light on a variety of conditions in which these relations are maintained. Lacroix draws on his comparative work on hometown transnationalism in different geographical contexts to discuss a theme that has been salient in the context of diaspora studies for some time: the relationship between transnationalism and diaspora. The transnational lens he adopts yields insights to the way diasporic groups construct ties to their 'homes' through engagement in grassroots practices, businesses or associations.

For his part, Khosravi adopts a more critical take on ideas and notions of home in what he calls 'the contemporary age of mass deportation'. He coins the expression 'deportspora' as an umbrella term for those exposed to multi-dimensional precariousness following their forced return to an assumed home. Notwithstanding its exposure to force and coercion, the 'deportspora' should also be acknowledged as a space of agency and defiance, which brings to light the potential ambiguities of home. Tolia-Kelly anchors her reflections on conceptualizations of diaspora and home in a similar thematic context: the current Syrian refugee crisis. Observed conditions of precarity that derive from a lack of rights and recognition lead her to argue for the need of new grammars and theories of diaspora migration and concomitant ideas of home in a precarious world.

Returning to a more classical understanding of diaspora, Tsuda proposes to frame conditions where dispersal goes hand in hand with connections to an ancestral homeland and co-ethnics across the world as 'diasporicity'. He uses the concept both as descriptive and analytical tool to examine why different groups have different levels of diasporicity, arguing that diaspora constitutes a relative condition of diasporicity. In her contribution, Missbach sheds light on imaginings and constructions of, and relations to, home in conditions of conflict. Drawing on findings from research among Indonesian immigrant communities, she shows how idealized images of home can lead to a point of no return and thus perpetuate life in the diaspora. While Missbach illuminates politicized idealizations of home, Höchner explores points of contact between migration, diaspora and Islamic education. To this end, she discusses how the availability of Islamic education abroad and how diasporic demands for Islamic schooling affect wider religious educational landscapes and new meanings of (ancestral) homes across Muslim societies. Finally, Baron adopts a theoretical lens for examining political obligations as a binding tie between diaspora and home. He explores how the complex geography of diaspora identity and identification yields to – sometimes conflicting – normative commitments to people and place.

In many different ways, the contributions to this section demonstrate that home and homeland are imbued with different meanings, which shape diasporic relationships with place and people. Moreover, different meanings of and relations with the home inform the way individuals engage with, or disengage from, their (ancestral) place of origin, real or imagined.

Connections

Connections to home or homeland are widely assumed to be the most important ties to members of diasporas. These connections are discussed by Müller-Funk under the rubric of 'political remittances', a notion cognate to the early idea of economic remittances and the more recent idea advanced by Levitt (1998) of 'social remittances'. Our contributor does not wish to foreclose on the question of whether political remittances are 'bad' or 'good'. They simply give agency to migrants, who may act in unexpected ways. This cautious view of the direction of diasporic interventions in homeland politics is echoed in Baser and Toivanen's study of the Middle East. As they correctly point out, diasporas are 'stakeholders in virtually every conflict on earth today'. They have been important in the peace process in the region, but diasporas are internally fractured and can connect to social actors on the ground in ways that can also create dissent and distrust.

Despite the validity of continuing to examine homeland links, there are multiple other links that connect people across borders and across different regions of the world. Having explored different forms and levels of homeland relations, we dedicate the rest of Part IV of this volume to what Clifford (1994: 306) calls 'lateral connections'. These connections, he argues, derive not only from the tropes of homeland and return, but also from the ongoing history of displacement and migration, and sequential sites of adaptation and resistance. Lateral connections are maintained to specific persons or groups of persons (like families, clans and hometowns) living elsewhere and at levels below the ethnic group as a whole. Of course, this is not a novel phenomenon, but the key difference between earlier and contemporary practices is that letters and slow journeys, often to one place, have now been replaced by rapid travel, multiple visits, telephony and the internet. We now observe a multitude of ways in which oceanic distances are 'shrunk', and cultural memories and family ties are invented or reinforced through digital means. As Nedelcu argues, the density and configuration of digital networks connecting people in virtual spaces make specific territorial connections less salient. Even where the forms of connectivity are less technologically driven, as Dudley maintains, a connection to homeland might be borne by cultural memories, the regeneration of sensory experience and treasured material objects carried from place to place.

In contrast to lateral connections at a scale beneath that of the collective ethno-national groups are connections across and above conventionally defined diasporic spaces. Perhaps the most complex intersections are those between diasporas and religion, insightfully discussed in the contribution by Liberatore and Fesenmyer. There are, of course, a limited number of cases where diasporic identities are nominally congruent with religious identities (the cases of Jews, Parsis and Sikhs come to mind), though there are many secular people who nonetheless self-characterize as being members of these groups. However, even where the religious and ethnic lines do not coincide, as Liberatore and Fesenmyer make clear, diasporas can be cemented, activated and maintained through religious adherence. Even more important are the many cases where religious ties are held in a complex holding pattern somewhere above the level of the diasporic groups. Thus, many Somalis and Syrians may be Muslims, just as many Italians and Filipinos may be Catholics, but how national and religious identities connect and overlap and become mutually reinforcing or mutually contradictory will be situationally specific.

Conclusion: critiques and applied diaspora study

As we have argued, moving beyond its original inflections concerning the self-dispersion of religious communities and the forced dispersion of certain peoples, diaspora studies also now covers mobility of all sorts. Various typologies (for example, victim, imperial, labour, deterritorialized, cultural, refugee and trade diasporas) have usefully been developed, but these categories have failed to prevent the continual invention of even newer 'adjectival' diasporas – including incipient, queer, generational, gendered, mixed, post-colonial, and many others. Typologies of all sorts can only go so far. By their very nature they fail to capture the internal diversity of diasporic populations, which has always existed but is further reinforced as human mobility turns into an increasingly multifaceted phenomenon which, in turn, prompts attention, concerns, debates and engagement with diasporic questions to an unprecedented degree.

The contributions gathered in Parts I to IV of this volume reveal that diaspora studies constitutes a rich but also controversial field of inquiry. Controversy revolves mainly around the epistemologies that are at the heart of conceptualization of diaspora as well as empirical research on diasporic populations. In our final section, Part V, we depart from our major theme of theoretical elaboration in two directions. The first is to give recognition to the sceptics and critics who resist or contest the very idea of diaspora or think its explanatory power has been exaggerated. Scholars in any field need to hear voices of their opponents, if only to make their own arguments more nuanced and sophisticated. The second is to recognize that some scholars of diasporas have accommodated themselves to practical working definitions of the idea and have moved to applied fields. This is particularly evident in the study of the role of diasporas in development and conflict management and the study of the ways in which states have sought to engage 'their' diasporas.

Oonk is the first in Part V to raise a sceptical voice by stressing that home is not a natural calling. He launches a plea to acknowledge the experiences of those who move – sometimes more than once – and disconnect from their homeland, on the one hand, and those experiencing 'home' as an unwelcoming place, on the other hand. The dismantling of naturalizing categorizations also forms the centrepiece of Fischer and Dahinden's call for an approach based on 'Jamesian pragmatism' to unpack the meanings and political implications of diaspora. Boyarin joins the round of sceptics, though in a special sense. His re-interpretation of the Babylonian Talmud sets a counterweight to conventional Zionist narratives, because he reads it as a text that questions the hegemony of the land of Israel as ultimate Jewish destination, thus legitimizing permanent exile, rather than return, as the Jews' divinely ordained and normal condition.

While these sceptical reflections largely pertain to the conceptual underpinnings of diaspora, the remainder of the contributions critically revisit key fields of applied diaspora studies. Gamlen reviews and evaluates the main arguments for and against diaspora engagement policies. Two chapters on, Page and Mercer add some sector-specific observations to his argument. They show how the global development industry has been attempting to incorporate diasporas into mainstream development interventions, and how such attempts have produced a highly instrumental notion of diaspora.

With the aim of deepening the existing research agenda, Koinova revisits understandings of diaspora mobilization in conflict and post-conflict settings. To this end, she draws on insights from transnational social movements, foreign policy lobbying and sociospatial dynamics. The impacts of conflict also feature centrally in Baser and Toivanen's contribution, which shows that conflict-induced diasporas from the Middle East engage in multiple forms of action to influence policy-making 'at home' and in the country of residence. Against the backdrop of their observations, Baser and Toivanen urge future researchers not to accept diaspora involvements as a fact but to scrutinize forms, impact and conditions of engagement more closely. Um adds another facet to elaborations on diaspora and conflict. She argues that post-conflict moments are imbued with fears and trauma, which amplify the way memories inform exile as well as notions of past, present, place and identity.

As editors of *The Routledge Handbook of Diaspora Studies*, we wanted to achieve an authoritative take on the idea of diaspora and its evolution. Yet, as we have acknowledged, our wriggling semantic fish is difficult to hook, net and fillet. The lateral explosions of meaning of the word, covering many aspects of belonging, identity and solidarity, have proved difficult to capture. We have been open to the many attempts to deconstruct the purity of the term in order to understand the internal complexity of diasporic populations and how they variously express their diasporic sensibilities. Because we have favoured bottom-up, emic expressions of diasporic practices, our authors have shown how the conventional building blocks of a definition of diaspora – dispersion, homeland orientation and a shared group identity – are, at best, a simplification, a starting point. Sometimes, though not always, inspired by a social constructivist perspective, the younger generation of scholars have remade the world of diaspora studies by questioning many core assumptions. For some doubtful scholars, this will prove an exercise in futility and lead to the endless attenuation of the basic idea. For others, including those who always resisted seeing historic diasporas in simple terms, the new perspectives and preoccupations represented in this collection show the continuing heuristic and mind-expanding value of diaspora studies. We hope you, the reader of the Handbook, concur in the latter view.

References

Brubaker, R. (2005) 'A "diaspora" diaspora', *Ethnic and Racial Studies*, 20 (1), 1–19, doi: 10.1080/0141987 042000289997
Clifford, J. (1994) 'Diasporas', *Cultural Anthropology*, 9 (3), 302–36, doi: 10.1525/can.1994.9.3.02a00040
Dufoix, S. (2017) *The dispersion: a history of the word 'diaspora'*, Leiden: Brill.
Gerring, J. (1999) 'What makes a concept good? A criterial framework for understanding concept formation in the social sciences', *Polity*, 31 (3), 357–93, doi: 10.2307/3235246.
Giddens, A. (1987) *The nation-state and violence*, Berkeley: University of California Press.
Levitt, P. (1998) 'Social remittances: migration driven local-level forms of cultural diffusion', *International Migration Review*, 32 (4), 926–48, doi: 10.2307/2547666.
McNeill, W. H. (1989) *Arnold J. Toynbee: a life*, Oxford: Oxford University Press.

Samuel, M. (1956) *The professor and the fossil*, New York: Alfred A. Knopf.
Sheleg, Y. (2007) 'This is how we ruined Toynbee's theory', *Haaretz*, 24 January, available at: www.haaretz.com/print-edition/features/this-is-how-we-ruined-toynbee-s-theory-1.210993.
Toynbee, A. J. (1934–61) *A study of history*, 12 volumes, Oxford: Oxford University Press.
Toynbee, A. J. (1960) 'Pioneer destiny of Judaism', *Issues*, 14 (4), 1–14.
Wimmer, A. and N. Glick Schiller (2002) 'Methodological nationalism and beyond: nation–state building, migration and the social sciences', *Global Networks*, 2 (4), 301–34, doi: 10.1111/1471-0374.00043.

Part I
Exploring and debating diaspora

1
Diaspora before it became a concept

Stéphane Dufoix

Although the concept of a *diaspora* has been recognized in the social sciences for about 40 years, its preconceptual history is much longer and not very well known. Despite some thorough studies devoted to either the whole period (Dufoix 2017) or only a part of it (Baumann 2000; Edwards 2001; Krings 2003; Tromp 1998; Van Unnik 1993), a few factual errors keep being transmitted from text to text, thus impeding an accurate vision of the different processes that uses of the word have undergone historically. First, *diaspora* is undoubtedly a Greek word (διασπορά) encompassing the idea not only of 'dispersion' but also of 'distribution' or 'diffusion', and, as such, does not carry a negative connotation. Second, in Greek it has never been used to describe Greek colonization in the Mediterranean. Third, it is not a translation of the Hebrew words *galuth* or *golah*, meaning 'exile' or 'community in exile'. In this chapter, I address the evolution of the uses of the word from its Greek origins to the mid-1970s when it started to become an academic concept.

A religious word

The first occurrence of the noun 'diaspora' can be found in the Septuagint, the translation into Greek of the Hebraic Bible, in the third century BCE. Contrary to a widely held view, the 14 appearances of the word 'diaspora' in the Septuagint are not translated into a specific Hebrew word; the Hebrew words *galuth* or *golah*, which mean 'exile' or 'banishment', were not among the list of words translated as *diaspora*. In fact, the uses and meaning of *diaspora* in the Septuagint should be understood in a theological sense. *Diaspora*, then, does not indicate an historical dispersal, such as the Babylonian exile of Jews in the sixth century BCE, but describes the divine punishment – dispersal throughout the world – that would befall the Jews if they failed to respect God's commandments. Not only does the word refer to a theological, eschatological horizon, and not an historical situation, but the dispersal, as well as the return of the dispersed, is a matter of divine, and not human, will. The Jews could be dispersed and finally reunited at the end of time because they were the 'Chosen People'.

Certain historical events gave the threat of dispersion a form of reality from the first century CE onwards. The Roman destruction of the Second Temple of Jerusalem in CE 70 and its repercussions, such as the repression of the Bar-Kokhba uprising in CE 135, gradually made Jewish dispersion out of Palestine a real and terrestrial phenomenon. Consequently, the Jewish rabbis assimilated their current exile from the Holy Land (*galouth*) into the fulfilment of the curse in Deuteronomy. The meanings of *diaspora* and *galouth* were thus confounded, but since Judaic Rabbinism aimed to restore the superiority of the Hebrew language, the word *diaspora* itself was withdrawn from the Jewish lexicon. Beside this, the rise of Christianity created competition between the two religions. In the New Testament, the term *diaspora* referred to members of the Christian Church being exiled from the City of God and dispersed across the Earth. The condition of dispersion was understood as the very proof of their being the Chosen People. Christian writers eventually abandoned *diaspora* in the second century CE, limiting its use to the Jewish dispersion as an exemplary curse for their sins. As a result, the word 'diaspora' acquired a negative connotation.

From the third century CE onwards, Christianity gradually abandoned Greek in favour of Latin. In the Vulgate (fourth century), we generally find the noun *dispersio* or conjugated forms of the verb *dispergere* being used to translate *diaspora*. Yet, Greek remained the language of the eastern part, and this linguistic division entailed different uses of the Bible, with the Vulgate progressively becoming the western Bible and the Septuagint remaining that of the east. It is therefore not surprising to see authors from the eastern part of the Roman Empire using *diaspora* not only in the second (Justin Martyr, Clement of Alexandria), third (Origen) and fourth centuries CE (Athanasius, Eusebius of Caesarea, Basil of Caesarea, John Chrysostom, Gregory of Nyssa) but also later, in the fifth century (Cyril of Alexandria, Theodoret). Of the 271 mentions of *diaspora* in the Thesaurus Linguae Graecae, as many as 134 (slightly fewer than half) are attributable to only nine authors, all of whom were from the eastern half of the Roman Empire. The usage of the term can be attested until the end of the Byzantine Empire. There are several references to *diaspora* in the texts of Gennadius Scholarius, who became ecumenical patriarch of Constantinople in 1454, the year following the fall of the city to the Ottomans. These show a variety of meanings ranging from the 'diffusion of the gospel in the entire world' to that of the 'dispersion of men'.

A new religious meaning emerges in the eighteenth century with the rise in Germany and diffusion abroad of the Protestant Moravian Church, also known as the Unity of Brethren. From its base in Herrnhut (Saxony), members of this Church were sent to countries in Europe – the other German states, the Netherlands, Denmark, Sweden, Norway, Switzerland, France and Great Britain – where they influenced early Methodists, as well as the United States, where the conversion of the natives became one of their principal tasks. In the mid-eighteenth century, another aspect of the evangelizing mission, officially known since the mid-nineteenth century by the (capitalized) name 'Diaspora', developed in parallel, and its reach was limited to the European continent. It implied missionaries keeping in touch with various evangelical missions in other countries (Schweinitz 1859: 66–8). In this case, 'Diaspora' is not the name of the dispersion but the official name of the link, for in the Moravian Brothers' lexicon, the 'Diaspora mission' signifies both the maintenance of the link and the statistical addition of all members living abroad in the 'continental province'. This mission and its name spread beyond the limits of the Unity of Brethren to become a policy of support for Protestant minorities. In 1843, this policy was institutionalized, with the creation in Frankfurt of an organization named Evangelische Verein der Gustav-Adolf-Stiftung (Evangelical Association of the Gustav-Adolf Foundation), usually called Gustav-Adolf-Werk (GAW), which set itself the goal of organizing assistance for these minorities (Röhrig 1999). The reference to the religious concept of Diaspora, considered here as a dispersed geographical condition calling for the maintenance of a link between the dispersed communities, is constant. In 1838, this conceptualization of the 'Protestant Diaspora' as a minority in Catholic countries was taken up and inverted by German Catholics through the intermediary of the Ludwig Missionary Association (Ludwigsmissionsverein) and, particularly, following the creation of the Boniface Association (Bonifatiusverein) in 1849 (Röhrig 1993).

The Jewish debate

While *diaspora* is undoubtedly linked to Zionism, the association is more complex than commonly believed. Zionism emerges geographically in the *diaspora*, but it finds its political specificity in the refusal of the *diaspora* (*shlilat ha-galuth*) as a condition to create a state within the borders of which Jews could feel safe. The publication of Herzl's *Der Judenstaat* (Herzl 1917) in 1896 and the holding of the first Zionist Congress in Basel in 1897 both mark the beginnings of a new political programme that insists on the necessity to hasten the creation of a haven for the Jews. This contradicts the main religious principle that only God can organize the return of the Jews to the Holy Land at the end of time. On the one hand, *diaspora* (*galuth*) is the sign of the Jewish election. On the other hand, it is nothing but the weakening of the community and the risk of being exterminated.

The rise of Zionism entailed a great debate about the future of the Jews and about the solutions to be found. An active role was played by two Jewish figures, the Russian historian Simon Dubnow and the Russian thinker Asher Ginsberg, better known under the pen name of Ahad Ha'am. Dubnow defended the idea of a Jewish autonomism in which the preservation of the diaspora could be linked with the citizenship of Jews in the countries in which they lived. The most emblematic presentation of this perspective is to be found in an 1898 article (Dubnow 1958: 109):

> The Jews as inhabitants of Europe since ancient times demand equal political and civic rights; as members of a historic nationality united by a common culture, they demand as much autonomy as is appropriate for any nationality that strives to develop freely. If these two demands are satisfied, the patriotism of the Jews in all the different countries will be beyond doubt. The Jew who lives a life of peace and quiet in his fatherland, can well be an English, French or German patriot and can, at the same time, be a true and devoted son of the Jewish nationality, which, though dispersed, is held together by national ties.

For Ahad Ha'am, dispersion had spoiled the Jewish nation. It therefore needed to rejuvenate itself, less through the intermediary of religion than through that of Jewish culture. It was this latter that would be reborn in Palestine, in the context of a 'Jewish colony', which would, in time, become 'the centre of the nation' (Ha'am 1962: 78). This vision opposed religious orthodoxy by according a pre-eminent place to culture in the maintenance of unity; it opposed political Zionism by privileging the role of the nation over that of the state; it opposed assimilation by emphasizing the national existence of the Jews; and finally, it opposed the maintenance of Jews in a single diaspora by stressing the necessity of regenerating a national culture threatened by impoverishment. Ahad Ha'am's response to Dubnow's affirmation of the *diaspora* was that the latter corresponded to the 'position of a lamb among wolves' (Ha'am 1959: 270).

The creation of the State of Israel in 1948 opened a new era. As a Zionist state, it soon insisted on the need for every Jew to practise *aliyah* ('going up' to the homeland), and early Israeli governments were tough on Jewish organizations that upheld the right of Jews not to return, as did the American Jewish Committee (Feldestein 2006). This state of tension between Israel and the Jewish diaspora lasted until the late 1960s. The situation in the Middle East, as much as Israel's victory, considered 'miraculous', in the Six Day War in 1967, led to a different type of relationship between Israel and Jews around the world. After 1967, a singular relationship of

Stéphane Dufoix

Table 1.1 The four meanings of *diaspora*

Exile	Community
Eschatological horizon	Trans-state link
Historical and political horizon	Centre–periphery link

recognition emerged between these two entities, which bestowed a new meaning on the word *diaspora* and which was manifested in Hebrew through the adoption of the term *tfutsoth* – literally meaning *dispersion* – in place of *galuth*. Consequently, a form of link was established with a given state that did not imply possessing the nationality of that state: it was a type of belonging that was not a legally constituted status and that went beyond the exclusively juridical link that tied an expatriate – a citizen of one country living on the territory of another – to a state that recognized him or her as such and whose legitimacy the person in question also recognized.

The complexity of the meanings of *diaspora* in Jewish history can be organized according to two axes: the first separates conceptions founded on exile from those founded on community. In the first case, *galuth* calls for a return that must occur in time, be it eschatological in the case of Judaic Rabbinism or political in the case of Zionism; in the second, *galuth* is separated from the question of a return and calls for the constitution of links in space, either without a state in the case of diasporism, as Dubnow for instance proclaimed it, or with a state (or a centre according to Ahad Ha'am) as we can see in the recognition of *tfutsoth*. Four different meanings of *diaspora* thus coexisted, whose emergence is not simultaneous but historically stratified (see Table 1.1).

The first scholarly uses

From the first decades of the twentieth century onwards, several general processes characterize the evolution of *diaspora*: first, secularization, that is, the extension to nonreligious meanings; second, trivialization, namely the widening of the spectrum of relevant cases; and third, but only later, formalization, or the establishment of criteria that allow the shift to occur from a definite to an indefinite category with its subtypes.

Simon Dubnow's 1931 'Diaspora' entry in the *Encyclopaedia of the social sciences* marked a fundamental milestone in extending the term to other populations and to the academic world. The first paragraph (Dubnow 1931: 126) is rather eloquent:

> Diaspora is a Greek term for a nation or part of a nation separated from its own state or territory and dispersed among other nations but preserving its own national culture. In a sense, Magna Graecia constituted a Greek diaspora in the ancient Roman Empire, and a typical case of diaspora is presented by the Armenians, many of whom have voluntarily lived outside their small national territory for centuries.

For the first time, *diaspora* is understood as a category with different instances. That this entry was included in an important publication allowed for its further use. The American sociologist Robert E. Park took it up a few years later, applying it to the members of different Asian groups living far from their countries, but adding a geographical dimension: 'there are, at the present time, between 16,000,000 and 17,000,000 people of Asiatic origin living in the diaspora, if I may use that term to designate not merely the condition but the place of dispersion of peoples' (Park 1939: 28). American sociologist Rose Hum Lee, who trained in the sociological tradition of Chicago and whose doctoral thesis was devoted to the Chinatowns of the Rocky Mountains, presented a conceptualization of diaspora that drew on Dubnow but that she limited to the Jewish case, insisting on the fact that the dispersion of the Chinese people differed from that of the Jewish people (Lee 1949: 422). Yet, in her 1960 book on the Chinese in the United States, she uses the word *diaspora* several times and always in the context of the Chinatowns, which she describes as 'communities in diaspora' (Lee 1960: 56).

Such an extension of the possible cases of *diaspora* is also visible in the work of the British historian Arnold J. Toynbee. When the first volumes of his monumental *A study of history* were published in the 1930s, his use of the word was associated with the idea of the fossilization of a civilization, mostly the Jewish one. Thirty years later, in the twelfth volume, he reconsidered his prior judgement, acknowledging the cohesive function of *diaspora*, and suggesting that the Jewish diaspora was not exceptional and that its characteristics were to be found among other populations (Toynbee 1961: 111–17). In 1972, when revising his whole work, he (Toynbee 1972: 65–9) goes as far as writing that:

> The accelerating improvement in means of communications of all kinds may do more to promote the creation of diasporas by facilitating it than the Assyrian war-lords were ever able to do by force. In a society that is 'annihilating distance', world-wide diasporas, rather than local national states, look like 'the wave of the future'. The transformation of the world into a cosmopolis favours social organization on a non-local basis.

Elsewhere, Toynbee (1965: 81–2) had even hoped 'to see the number, size and importance of the world's diasporas increase in size as never before'.

People heard him, for a non-conceptualized usage of *diaspora*, open and often without much continuity, started flowering between the 1940s and 1970s in fields such as geography, history and anthropology. However, even when these uses became cumulative in a subfield, they hardly spread across disciplines. The appearance of the word in the academic lexicon helped to open the space of usage, but without leading to an accumulation of references. Beside the Chinese, Indians, Greeks and Armenians, it was possible to find growing references being made to the Dominicans, the Irish, the Koreans, the Hungarians, the Finns, the Ukrainians, the Québécois, the Croats, the Polish and the Puerto Ricans as diasporas, yet without any single definition of what a diaspora was.

Diaspora as a motto

The growth in the uses of the term *diaspora* is not just associated with the logic of academic diffusion, but has also benefited from a change in its semantic charge from negative to increasingly positive. In this respect, from the mid-1960s onwards, it became more and more popular in some social circles eager to display their identity as both irreducible to the boundaries of a nation (because of its dispersed condition) and united by a common heritage, ancestry, civilization, language, ethnicity and race. This trend was especially current among groups of people in America who insisted on being recognized for their specificity rather than merely discriminated against or condemned to assimilation. The case of the African Americans is emblematic of this tendency.

Until quite recently, scholars all agreed that the first written occurrences of the expressions 'African diaspora', 'black diaspora', and the use of *diaspora* to describe the situation of blacks living outside Africa, date from 1965 (Irele 1965; Shepperson 1966). In fact, as some scholars have already suggested though not demonstrated (Edwards 2001), both the idea and the words themselves occurred earlier. They were often used explicitly to draw the analogy between Jewish history and black history, or to note the existence of discrimination that both groups faced in the countries in which they lived. In *American civilization and the negro*, first published in 1916, the African-American thinker and doctor Charles Victor Roman raised the question of the future of blacks in Africa and the American South. He wrote that 'the slave-trade was the diaspora of the African, and the children of this alienation have become a permanent part of the citizenry of the American republic' (Roman 1921: 195). Soon afterward, in 1917, the analogy between blacks and Jews was drawn on the Jewish side. On 29 May 1917, a Yiddish newspaper, the *Jewish Daily Forward*, made the connection between the race riots that erupted in East St Louis, Illinois, on 28 May 1917 and the Kishinev pogrom in 1903, during which more than 50 Jews were killed.

> The situation of the Negroes in America is very comparable to the situation of the Jews . . . in Russia. The Negro diaspora, the special laws, the decrees, the pogroms and also the Negro complaints, the Negro hopes, are very similar to those which we Jews . . . lived through.
>
> *(quoted in Diner 1977: 75–6)*

Despite these two occurrences, the word *diaspora* was rarely used to describe people of African origin. It was not until the 1950s and 1960s that its usage became more common in academia. We find it in the texts of English-speaking historians of Africa like Colin Legum (1962: 14) and Basil Davidson (1964: 38), and of French scholars and intellectuals like the French ethnologist and great Haiti specialist Alfred Métraux (1951: 21), or the French psychiatrist and writer Frantz Fanon. In *The wretched of the Earth*, Fanon (1961: 148) described 'the Negro diaspora' as the 'tens of millions of blacks spread over the American continents'. It seems that a distinction needs to be established between the sporadic British or French academic or militant uses of the term in the 1960s, including those of Irele (1965) and Shepperson (1966), and the development of an actual self-description as a *diaspora* by fractions of the African-American population. From the late 1960s, academic and non-academic publications using the term *diaspora* to refer to black people residing outside Africa started to multiply in the African-American community. This use was characterized by its looseness and by the absence of any real reflection on its origins or Jewish flavour. The term *diaspora* provided black people with a name for themselves. It served as a reminder of their historical tragedy and, by emphasizing the connection and the return (spiritual and intellectual if not physical), as a positive way of recovering a sense of unity with Africa. This emphasis established the existence of continuities, or survivals, between black people living outside Africa and their African origin. This was all the truer for those fractions insisting more on blackness than on the achievement of civil rights (for a deeper analysis, see Dufoix 2017, chapter 5). The quest for black pride and the will to recover their lost history led to the constitution of the discipline of Black Studies in American universities in the late 1960s (Rojas 2007). The term *diaspora* – along with other words such as *ebonics* – was inherently part of a new lexicon that aimed to give positivity to a previous stigma, seen for instance in John Paden and Edward Soja's (1969: 437) report on the African experience:

> What has been the imprint of the Afro-American community on the modern culture of the Western Hemisphere? This question, which is the basis of all 'Afro-American Studies' programs can only be posed in brief in this lecture. Yet it is clearly related to 'African Studies', for this black 'diaspora', transplanted from Africa primarily by force, consists of nearly a third of the world's black people.

The scholarly–activist mix characteristic of this development was not limited to academic circles, but made its way into popular black magazines such as *Negro Digest* and *Black World* (the latter launched in 1970). To create an Institute for African American Studies in Atlanta, Vincent Harding, head of the department of history and sociology at Atlanta's Spelman College, wrote an open letter to black students in the North. He told them 'it will need millions of dollars, the best staff from every part of the African diaspora, students who are ready to take care of business, and it must have continuous exposure throughout the black community' (Harding 1969: 13–14). Though barely conceptualized, by the mid-1970s *diaspora* had become a social and political motto, a rallying cry that could be used in a positive way and, as Saint Clair Drake's (1975) seminal article clarified, one progressively dissociated from the Jewish prototype.

Proto-definitions

Apart from Dubnow's, there was no general or widely discussed academic definition of *diaspora* until the late 1970s; the social science literature contained only a few attempts that were rarely cited or adopted. The first author bold enough to go beyond mere analogy and to propose an actual definition seems to have been the French geographer Maximilien Sorre, who gradually transformed his supple use of the word into a geographical concept. In *Les fondements de la géographie humaine*, he used it in a sense close to 'number of emigrants' for three populations that had hitherto not been referred to in this way – 'the Japanese diaspora was smaller than the Chinese diaspora. Likewise the Hindu diaspora' (Sorre 1947: 279). Twelve years later, he made it the name of a particular space, occupied by 'national minorities in a foreign land', who enlarge the national space 'as long as they maintain their original links with the mother country' (Sorre 1957: 95). The reference to minorities is also found in the work of British anthropologist Maurice Freedman – a specialist on the Chinese family inside and outside China, about which he used the phrase 'Chinese diaspora' (see Freedman 1966). In his earlier research on the Jewish community in Great Britain, Freedman (1955) established parallels with other communities, for he assumed that the supposedly unique character of the Jews was a fallacy and that an analysis of the relationships they maintained with their social environment was required within a sociology of race relations. In this respect, Freedman (1955: 236) proposed a conceptual definition of a *diaspora* based on the existence, outside the borders of the countries to which they claimed to belong, of communities working to maintain their cultural specificity in the countries in which they found themselves:

> There are other 'diasporas', notably those of the Chinese and the Indians, in which it is common to find the overseas sojourners accused of trying to maintain an *imperium in imperio*, of fostering a separatist educational system, of breaking the loyalty of citizens to the land of their birth by stimulating the use of a foreign language and by inculcating the political and cultural values of a nation across the seas.

Other attempts, as in the cases of 'trade diaspora' and 'diaspora nationalism', were more circumscribed. In the late 1960s, Abner Cohen, a British social anthropologist of West Africa, proposed using the concept of 'trade diasporas' or 'commercial diasporas' to refer to the spatial organization of the trading peoples of West Africa, such as the Hausa, Mandé or Dyula. Having evoked the economic organization of the Hausa as 'a far-flung diaspora, which consists of a network of localized Hausa communities' (Cohen 1969: 9), he reintroduced the concept later in the year at an international seminar on the development of African trade in West Africa since the nineteenth century, which took place in Freetown in December 1969. In his paper, Cohen developed the idea of 'commercial diasporas' to describe 'a nation of socially independent, but spatially dispersed communities' (Cohen 1971: 267). Although criticized by the conference participants, other scholars in the field of African economic and social history, such as Paul Lovejoy (1973) and Philip D. Curtin (1984), soon appropriated the concept.

If not the first to link national *minority* to *diaspora* (see Macartney 1934: 57), the Australian political scientist Kenneth Minogue was probably the first explicitly to associate *diaspora* with *nationalism*. He defined *diaspora* as the scattered members of an ethnic group wishing to return to its historical or claimed homeland (Minogue 1967: 13, 106). Four years later, Anthony D. Smith elaborated a typology based on Minogue's work, which distinguished three forms of nationalism – territorial, mixed and ethnic. Here, Smith saw 'diaspora' as a rare subcategory of the ethnic type characterized by a search for greater cultural autonomy. As he put it, 'the only mode of ensuring the survival of the culture and its bearers is through evacuation of communities to a territory outside the hostile areas' (Smith 1971: 222), with the classic cases of this type being Garveyism, Zionism, the Lebanese, Liberians, Greeks and Armenians.

If the secularization of the term *diaspora*, multiplication of its possible occurrences, and growing academic use were undoubtedly prerequisites for its more general conceptualization, it did not automatically or immediately result in systematic attempts to provide academic definitions, for these began only from the late 1970s onwards.

References

Baumann, M. (2000) 'Diaspora: genealogies of semantics and transcultural comparison', *Numen*, 47 (3), 313–37, doi: 10.1163/156852700511577.
Cohen, A. (1969) *Custom and politics in urban Africa: a study of Hausa migrants in Yoruba towns*, Berkeley: University of California Press.
Cohen, A. (1971) 'Cultural strategies in the organization of trading diasporas', in C. Meillassoux (ed.) *L'évolution du commerce africain depuis le xixe siècle en Afrique de l'Ouest*, Oxford: Oxford University Press, 266–81.
Curtin, P. D. (1984) *Cross-cultural trade in world history*, Cambridge: Cambridge University Press.
Davidson, B. (1964) *The African past: chronicles from antiquity to modern times*, Boston: Little Brown.
Diner, H. R. (1977) *In the almost promised land: American Jews and blacks, 1915–1935*, Westport: Greenwood Press.
Dubnow, S. (1931) 'Diaspora', in E. R. A. Seligman and A. Johnson (eds) *Encyclopaedia of the social sciences, volume V*, New York: Macmillan Company, 126–30.
Dubnow, S. (1958) *Nationalism and history: essays on old and new Judaism*, Philadelphia: Jewish Publication Society.
Dufoix, S. (2017) *The dispersion: a history of the uses of diaspora*, Leiden: Brill (French edition 2012).
Edwards, B. H (2001) 'The uses of diaspora', *Social Text*, 19 (66), 45–73, doi: 10.1215/01642472-19-1_66-45.
Fanon, F. (1965) *The wretched of the earth*, London: MacGibbon & Kee (first French edition 1961).
Feldestein, A. L. (2006) *Ben-Gurion, Zionism, and American Jewry, 1948–1963*, New York: Routledge.
Freedman, M. (1955) 'Jews in the society of Britain', in M. Freedman (ed.) *A minority in Britain: social studies of the Anglo–Jewish community*, London: Vallentine Mitchell, 199–242.
Freedman, M. (1966) *Chinese lineage and society: Fukien and Kwangtung*, London: Athlone Press.
Ha'am, A. (1959), 'The negation of diaspora', in A. Herzberg (ed.) *The Zionist idea: a historical analysis and reader*, Garden City: Doubleday, 270–7 (first published 1909).
Ha'am, A. (1962) 'The Jewish state and Jewish problem', in H. Kohn (ed.) *Nationalism and the Jewish ethic: basic writings of Ahad Ha'am*, New York: Schocken Books, 66–89 (first published 1897).
Harding, V. (1969) 'New creation or familiar death?', *Negro Digest*, 18 (5), 5–14.
Herzl, T. (1917) *A Jewish state: an attempt at a modern solution of the Jewish question*, New York: Federation of American Zionists (first German edition [*Der Judenstaat*] 1896).
Irele, A. F. (1965) 'Négritude or black cultural nationalism', *Journal of Modern African Studies*, 3 (3), 321–48, doi: 10.1017/S0022278X00006157.
Krings, M. (2003) 'Diaspora: historische Erfahrung oder wissenschaftliches Konzept? Zur Konjunktur eines Begriffs in den Sozialwissenschaften', *Paideuma*, (49), 137–56, available at: www.jstor.org/stable/40315515.

Lee, R. H. (1949) 'The decline of Chinatowns in the United States', *American Journal of Sociology*, 54 (5), 422–32, doi: 10.1086/220396.
Lee, R. H. (1960) *The Chinese in the United States of America*, Hong Kong: Hong Kong University Press.
Legum, C. (1961) 'The roots of pan-Africanism', in C. Legum (ed.) *Africa: a handbook to the continent*, London: Anthony Blond, 541–55.
Lovejoy, P. E. (1973) 'The Kambarin Beriberi: the formation of a specialized group of Hausa Kola traders in the nineteenth century', *Journal of African History*, 14 (4), 633–51, doi: 10.1017/S0021853700013098.
Macartney, C. A. (1934) *National states and national minorities*, London: Oxford University Press.
Métraux, A. (1951), 'L'Afrique vivante en Haïti', in A. Diop et al. (eds) *Haïti: poètes noirs*, Paris: Seuil, 13–21.
Minogue K. (1967) *Nationalism*, London: Batsford.
Paden, J. N. and E. W. Soja (eds) (1969) *The African experience: final report, volume 1*, African Curriculum Project, Evanston, IL: Program of African Studies.
Park, R. E. (1939) 'The nature of race relations', in Edgar T. Thompson, et al. (eds) *Race relations and the race problem: a definition and an analysis*, Durham: Duke University Press, 3–45.
Röhrig, H. J. (1993) 'Diaspora in Römisch-Katholischer Sicht', *Die evangelische Diaspora: Jahrbuch des Gustav-Adolf-Werks*, (62), 81–100.
Röhrig, H. J. (1999) 'Gustav-Adolf-Werk: Diaspora aus evangelischer Sicht', in G. Riße and C. A. Kathke (eds) *Diaspora: Zeugnis von Christen für Christen: 150 Jahre Bonifatiuswerk der deutschen Katholischen*, Paderborn: Bonifatius, 183–202.
Rojas, F. (2007) *From black power to black studies: how a radical social movement became an academic discipline*, Baltimore: Johns Hopkins University Press.
Roman, C. V. (1921) *American civilization and the negro: the Afro-American in relation to national progress*, Philadelphia: F. A. Davis (first edition 1916).
Saint Clair Drake, J. G. (1975) 'The black diaspora in pan-African perspective', *The Black Scholar*, 7 (1), 2–13, doi: 10.1080/00064246.1975.11413763.
Schweinitz, E. de (1859) *The Moravian manual: containing an account of the Protestant Church of the Moravian United Brethren or Unitas Fratrum*, Bethlehem, PA: Moravian Publication Office.
Shepperson, G. (1966) 'The African diaspora – or the African abroad', *African Forum*, 2 (1), 76–93.
Smith, A. D. (1971) *Theories of nationalism*, London: Duckworth.
Sorre, M. (1947) *Les fondements de la géographie humaine: essai d'une écologie de l'homme*, Paris: Armand Colin.
Sorre, M. (1957) *Rencontre de la géographie et de la sociologie*, Paris: Marcel Rivière.
Toynbee, A. J. (1961) *A study of history, volume XII: reconsiderations*, London: Oxford University Press.
Toynbee, A. J. (1965) *Change and habit: the challenge of our time*, London: Oxford University Press.
Toynbee, A. J. (1972) *A study of history*, Oxford: Oxford University Press.
Tromp, J. (1998) 'The ancient Jewish diaspora: some linguistic and sociological observations', in G. Ter Haar (ed.) *Religious communities in the diaspora: new perspectives on past and present*, Leuven: Peeters, 13–35.
Van Unnik, W. C. (1993) *Das Selbstverständnis der jüdischen Diaspora in der hellenistisch-römischen Zeit*, Leiden: Brill.

2
Diaspora studies
Past, present and promise

Khachig Tölölyan

The UCLA sociologist Rogers Brubaker (2005) pointedly titled his critique of the rapid growth of diaspora studies 'The "diaspora" diaspora'. He noted that during the 1970s the word 'diaspora' and its cognates appeared as keywords only once or twice a year in dissertation abstracts; in the late 1980s, they appeared on average 13 times a year; and by the year 2001 alone, nearly 130 times. Brubaker warned that this rapid dispersion of the term into many disciplinary discourses was stretching and diluting its meaning. He identified the journal *Diaspora* as 'a key vehicle for the proliferation of academic diaspora talk', but added that even its editor (that would be me) worried that diaspora 'is in danger of becoming a promiscuously capacious category'.

The first issue of *Diaspora* appeared at the end of May 1991. In my introductory essay for that issue, I wrote that the 'semantic domain' of the term 'diaspora' was being 'share[d]' with such terms as 'migrant, expatriate, refugee, guest-worker, exile, overseas community and ethnic community', and that diasporas had become 'the exemplary communities of the transnational moment'. Old diasporas, like nations, were being reshaped and new ones formed by the accelerating mobility across state borders of people, money and cultural products such as information, ideas, images, music. I also meant that at the same time, scholars working on a wide range of primary materials in many disciplinary fields were finding the category of diaspora an appealing and potentially useful one for organizing their enquiry. Ever since, as scholars ranging from Schnapper and Bordes-Benayoun (2006) to Oliver Bakewell (2008) have noted, we have been observing the further crowding of diaspora's semantic domain. Such crowding is not merely additive, but transformative. Consequently, since the late 1960s, 'diaspora' has come to mean what it does in its imbrication with the terms transnationalism, globalization, migrancy, ethnicity, exile, the postcolonial and the nation. Since the 1980s, the changing meanings of 'belonging' and 'citizenship' have further complicated the conceptual situation. So have digital media, in which networks emerge and nominate themselves as diasporas, not without some grounds, except perhaps in the case of those programmers who, objecting to Facebook's practices in February 2010, fled that social network and established a new digital network named 'Diaspora*'. Here I will focus primarily on a few terms and concepts that have mattered and persisted and that seem to me likely to remain significant as diaspora studies moves forward; in some cases, pairs of these terms have functioned as formative binaries that will help us map the contemporary field of diaspora studies.

Mapping diaspora studies

Dispersion and diaspora

The first and simplest of these pairs of binaries is dispersion and diaspora. If I were establishing the journal now, its subtitle might be 'a journal of dispersion studies'. 'Dispersion' is the more general and inclusive term, whereas 'diaspora' is merely one of several kinds of dispersion so that, in a curious reversal, it has become a synecdoche, the part – diaspora – standing for the whole. Other forms of mobility and dispersion include migration intended to acquire education, jobs, land, settlement, new citizenship, or a combination thereof; there are also mobile traders and itinerant labourers who circulate between homeland and extraterritorial opportunities; there are victims of mass deportations, refugees and asylum-seekers – some choose mobility, others have it thrust upon them; some are uprooted, others uproot themselves. Some eventually return home, many are assimilated, and the remainder may become consolidated into diaspora communities.

Until the 1930s, the social formations known as 'diasporas' consisted of a network of communities, some sedentary and others quite mobile, that lived in often involuntary dispersion from their homelands and that resisted full assimilation or were denied the option of assimilating, or both at the same time. Many of them existed in lamentable and precarious conditions, glorified by no one in an era when the nation-state was the supreme form of polity, and diasporicity could mean second-class citizenship. In this earlier period, scholars confined the term 'diaspora' to just three groups – Jews (the paradigmatic case), Armenians (since the eleventh century) and Greeks.

The ascendance of the term 'diaspora' as a cognate for all dispersions is a complex process, the product of the convergence of several autonomous events. Elsewhere, I have offered my own analysis of this process (Tölölyan 1996, 2007), which I will not recapitulate here except to say that, in my view, the preconditions that enabled this convergence in the USA took place between 1964 and 1968. The most encyclopaedic account of all uses of the term appears in Stéphane Dufoix's 650-page dissertation, published as *La dispersion* (2012), a marvellous synthesis but one whose richness of detail sometimes obscures the relative suddenness of the term's leap into scholarly popularity.

The first event enabling that popularity was the empowerment of black Americans as voters by the civil rights acts of 1964–5 and the subsequent emergence in the USA of the Black Power movement; the renaming of coloured people and negroes first as black, then as African Americans, a terminological ethnicization that took place during the rise of Jesse Jackson as a temporarily plausible presidential candidate around 1984; and the parallel emergence of the term 'African diaspora', first noted at a pan-Africanist conference in Dar es Salaam, in Tanganyika, in 1964 by George Shepperson (1966). While not widely accepted by all African-American laymen, the term 'African diaspora' is now firmly lodged in universities and in the discourse of serious intellectuals and journalists in the USA. The dispersion of the descendants of former African slaves from the USA and Jamaica, to Brazil and the Indian Ocean, to Britain and Colombia is now a 'diaspora' to scholars in history and sociology, in ethnomusicology as well as in literary and cultural studies; in the latter, Paul Gilroy's *The black Atlantic* (1993) had a catalytic, cascade effect rarely witnessed in scholarship.

The second autonomous event that contributed to the renaming of various dispersions as diasporas was the June War of 1967 in which Israel, a state founded by people born in diaspora, spectacularly defeated its Arab opponents and galvanized the already considerable support it had in the Jewish American community into not just a political lobby but a movement in intellectual life. An attendant product of the boom in post-1967 Jewish American discourse was what I call the re-diasporization of ethnicity. Greek, Armenian, Black, Puerto Rican, Cuban, Irish, Indian and Chinese leaders of old and new ethnic groups became animated by new and specifically diasporic commitments. It became possible and even fashionable to develop and advocate translocal commitments to the ancestral homeland and to kin communities in other countries. Community leaders added to the older task of staffing and funding intra-communal ethnic institutions the work of cross-border 'outreach'. Often explicitly working with the Jewish-Israeli model, even when this was inappropriate, notables of ethnic communities engaged in diasporic activities even before accepting the term, striving for the acknowledgement of new self-identifications in universities, public media and lobbies, culture and the arts; indeed, at all sites and events where representations of diasporic groups are formulated and disseminated, or its rights and obligations discussed.

The third event to converge with these above-named factors was the passage by the United States Congress of the Hart-Celler Immigration and Nationality Act of 1965 by a vote of 76 to 18, which enabled non-European immigration to the USA on a global scale. Americans began to take renewed note of the fact that theirs was a country of immigrants who became citizens with full rights long before their cultural assimilation was complete. The two texts that played a key role in this process were President John F. Kennedy's (1964) *A nation of immigrants*, and Nathan Glazer and Daniel Moynihan's (1963) influential account, *Beyond the melting pot: the Negroes, Puerto Ricans, Jews, Italians and Irish of New York City*.

It was in this environment that the American media and then university curricula began to note and ascribe importance to the fact that the major industrial countries of Western Europe had also been taking in new immigrants, starting with Caribbean people in 1948, then labour migrants from Italy and Yugoslavia, Turkey and Portugal since the late 1950s, to whose number Commonwealth and French citizens from the former colonies were added as their homelands were decolonized, starting with Vietnam in 1954, Ghana in 1957, Algeria in 1962, and ending with the disintegration of the Portuguese empire in 1974. The recognition of these immigrations into Europe, accelerated by Enoch Powell's speech of 1968, was coupled with a dim awareness that Canada and Australia were also easing immigration and slowly developing laws and cultural policies advocating tolerance and acceptance that were recast as 'multiculturalism' in the 1970s. Increasing reflection on the new immigration, ethnicity and multiculturalism cleared the ground for the acceptance of the diaspora concept, which made it possible to think of fellow citizens with multilocal commitments, dual citizenship, and participation in transnational networks as something other than dangerous people with divided loyalties whose discontent might someday cause 'rivers of blood' to flow.

Finally, the fourth major development that in my view prepared the ground for the acceptance by scholars of the diaspora concept was the emergence and eventual valorization within university curricula of the notions of identity, difference and diversity as subjects of enquiry. Again, taking the USA as my example, after the costly but remarkable success of the movement for the civil rights of Black Americans, a series of struggles emerged during the later Vietnam War for the rights of women, homosexuals and others. The privileging and celebration of difference led to identitarian claims and turf wars in academe that had and still have problematic consequences; but they also led to an acceptance within much of the educated American elite of the right to difference that would eventually facilitate the acceptance and high valuation of 'diaspora' as a concept and a signifier of identity. This movement, which excoriated exclusion and advocated inclusion without homogenization, was widespread in both theoretical and empirical work. Like intolerant racist, masculinist and heterosexist norms that silenced and excluded others, homogenizing norms of national identity were rejected. Historians formulated research agendas to fill gaps and lacunae, to enable silenced voices to be heard, to let the subaltern speak, in the belief that she could, and should, and would be heard. Diaspora studies was a beneficiary of this wider movement

Together, these steps led to the broad social and scholarly acceptance of dispersion as consequential; it was no longer viewed as merely a preliminary stage of the disappearance of distinct social formations and collective identities, but rather as a first step to their acceptable persistence in the form of consolidated diasporas. In my own practice as a scholar, I call 'diasporas' those communities of the dispersed who develop varieties of association that endure at least into their third generation. But as an editor, I am open to the ideas of colleagues who take other positions concerning transnational networks and social fields, positions shared by many of the referees for the journal.

Objective and subjective

If dispersion and diaspora are one set of formative binaries that bookend conceptual tensions and terminological variations in diaspora studies, 'objective' and 'subjective' mark another persistent contestation. To breathe life into these banal terms, let me cite an essay by the Chinese Canadian literary scholar Lily Cho (2007: 4):

> Diaspora must be understood as a condition of subjectivity and not as an object of analysis. I propose an understanding of diaspora as first and foremost a subjective condition marked by the contingencies of long histories of displacements and genealogies of dispossession. . . . Some diasporic subjects are transnational, but not all. . . . Diaspora emerges as a subjectivity alive to the effects of globalization and migration, but also attuned to the histories of colonialism and imperialism. Diaspora is not a function of socio-historical and disciplinary phenomena, but emerges from deeply subjective processes of racial memory, of grieving for losses which cannot always be articulated and longings which hang at the edge of possibility. It is constituted in the spectrality of sorrow and 'the pleasures of obscure miracles of connection'.

Since I have just been arguing that the popularity of 'diaspora' is due to the convergence of socio-historical and disciplinary phenomena, I can hardly endorse Cho's views in their totality; indeed, no scholar can afford to agree with the notion that diaspora may not be 'an object of analysis', as she puts it. We know too much about diasporas as neighbourhoods and networks, chains of connection and exchange, as weak victims of persecution but also as wealthy practitioners of what I call 'stateless power' in my own work, to agree wholeheartedly with her characterization. And yet her claim is crucial. There is indeed no place called 'diaspora', though there are sites of habitation and memory. There is no legal, juridical, bureaucratic category named 'diaspora', though there are passports and visas and residency permits, legal and illegal aliens, *les dépaysés* and *les sans-papiers*, documented and undocumented aliens, permanent residents, refugees, stateless people but also holders of dual citizenships and the like. Cho's insistence that diasporas are mourners of loss links her to scholars who see individuals gathering into communities of traumatic memory, consisting of victims whose identity and claims to rights are bound to their wounds. Robin Cohen (1997) had introduced the notion of victim diaspora a decade before Cho wrote, and he acknowledged that while no enduring diaspora endures merely through such memory, still much of its life can be organized around commemorative functions and discourses and practices that take the wound as their starting point.

Of course, genocide and ethnocide, rape and dispossession, are nothing if not real. But they are not part of the lived, objective experience of subsequent diasporic generations, who can have no direct and unmediated memories of the horror. Rather, as Marianne Hirsch (2008) argues, later generations inherit or construct what she names 'postmemory' through photographs and narratives, artefacts and exhibits, at conventions and conferences and now online. The subjective is real, though in a different register than the materiality of the objective, and it helps to constitute the diasporic individual subject who is drawn to others sharing the same mediated subjectivity. This is one reason why the study of literature and mass culture, and of the new digital media, must be brought closer to the work of social scientists.

Home and homeland

A third formative binary for diaspora studies is that of home and homeland. The dominant theories claim an orientation towards the homeland as an essential feature of diasporic identity; this position is deeply influenced by a certain view of Jewish history that eventually became Zionism's and is now that of the Jewish state. Many have argued that the Jewish diaspora always lived with the hope of 'next year in Jerusalem', a ritual statement that is taken to figure an unwavering orientation towards the project of return, of *aliyah*. Even today, when not all Jews choose to return to Israel, and when 400,000 Israeli Jews live in a new diaspora, and even when the Jewish diaspora no longer holds quite so dominant a place in the field of diaspora studies as it once did because space has been made for other forms of postcolonial, transnational dispersions, it is still the case that a homeland orientation is usually taken for granted. Only the Roma, or Gypsies, it has been noted, are diaspora as stark dispersion, with no gaze turned towards a homeland, no memory of it, no aspiration to return to that area of what is now the Indian–Pakistani border, which they seem to have left around the eighth century. The Roma exist as a diaspora across borders because their leaders recognize themselves as dispersed and oppressed fragments of a people, fragments that they increasingly work to reconnect.

With this exception, all other dispersions are seen as having a homeland and being oriented towards it. This is so much the prevailing wisdom that one encounters it in the functionaries of homeland governments, which have been persuaded of the importance of reclaiming their diasporas and are busily creating ministries and bureaux of diaspora in Armenia and Italy, in Greece, the Dominican Republic and even the Basque autonomous region of Spain. Serving as a consultant to two of these, I have found it necessary to argue for a slightly different and more productive position, whose foundation I can best illustrate with three linked anecdotes.

In 2002, I attended an international conference in Poitiers, France, at which well-known Israeli scholars routinely spoke of the role of Israel as the homeland of the world's Jews. Eventually, an American associate professor asked to respond. She said: 'I am a Jew and an American. My home and my parents' home is the United States. My grandparents' home was Hungary. Israel is the homeland of my ancestors, not my homeland. After the USA, it is the world's second most important country for me, and its prosperity and security matter a lot to me.' Two months earlier, at an Armenian American event in Watertown, Massachusetts, a college student who identified himself as belonging to the fourth generation of his family born in the USA said much the same thing to a speaker passionate about what he regarded as the audience's 'Armenian homeland'. 'I'm an American', the student said. 'This country has been my family's home for several generations. I understand that Armenia is the homeland of my ancestors and that I have distant kin there, and I'd like to do something to help it be secure from Turkey and less economically miserable than it is.' Part of what he said was virtually identical to the words of the Poitiers speaker.

These sentiments are widespread among the young students I have been teaching for several decades. My next anecdote, which I also narrate elsewhere (Tölölyan 2010), occurred on the first day of my course on 'Diasporas, Transnationalism, and Globalization' four years ago. I asked the 16 students in the seminar to say something about their ethnodiasporic interests, if any. There was a long silence. I turned to a student I had already taught twice and knew well from long conversations and said: 'I know you, I know you're Jewish, you've talked about it, why the silence?' She took her time answering. 'Professor,' she said eventually, 'I know I'm Jewish. You know I am Jewish. The trouble is, the second I admit that, my mother and grandmother also know just what kind of Jew I should be, whom I should date, what I should do. I can't *afford* to be that Jewish.' The remark initiated conversation. A Korean American student whose parents are, as is often the case with recent Korean immigrants to the USA, committed evangelical Protestants, expressed similar reservations about claiming a diasporic identity. In universities and online, a great many of the young who will form the next generation of America's diasporas express the same views. They acknowledge an ancestral homeland and an ethnodiasporic identity, and both matter. But they won't acknowledge fully any diasporic identity that is conceived in relation and subordination to the national and moral authority attributed to the homeland because such consent will confine them and prescribe their behaviour. Immediately after admitting to any form of homeland-bound diasporic identity, they seek distance from its possible claims, pointing out that they have many identities – the usual gender, race, class, sexual orientation, along with ethnodiasporic identity. They desire and aspire to what I would call, in analogy to Aihwa Ong's (1999) *Flexible citizenship: the cultural logics of transnationality*, multiple and flexible identities that they can configure as needed – they want to select from each and all those elements of which they can be proud and whose claims and obligations they are prepared to honour. They are at home in America, while retaining their feeling for the homeland of their ancestors and the more tightly defined and homeland-oriented diaspora of their elders. They have already abandoned exilic nationalism for diasporic transnationalism.

It comes as no surprise that diaspora scholars have begun to use terms like 'contingent community' for long-lived diasporas that are rapidly being altered by the attitudes of their educated young, or that Aram Sinnreich has titled his book on new music *Mashed up: music, technology and the rise of configurable culture* (Sinnreich 2010). He argues that the young demand and celebrate what he calls 'musical "configurability" rooted in a global, networked communications infrastructure'. Sinnreich uses interviews with prominent DJs, music industry executives and attorneys to argue that today's battles over sampling, file sharing, and the marketability of new styles such as 'mash-ups' and 'techno' anticipate even broader social change. 'Music, which has a unique power to evoke collective emotions, signal identity, and bond or divide entire societies' is now also raw material, a resource for reconfiguring identifications as multilocal as diasporas themselves. Gayatri Gopinath's (1995) article on global bhangra music makes a similar case.

My argument has been that we must be careful not to locate the diasporan's home in the ancestral homeland too easily. This is a habit partly shaped by studies of diasporic politics. Michel Laguerre's (1999: 641) remark that 'the nation has outgrown the state because of its diasporic tentacles' is exemplary of the problem: it confuses first-generation Haitian migrants with an established diaspora and attributes to that diaspora the status of a fragment or an extension of the nation. In my view, a collection of transnational migrants becomes a diaspora when its members develop some familial, cultural and social distance from their nation yet continue to care deeply about it not just on grounds of kinship and filiation, but by commitment to certain chosen affiliations. We know that the homeland is reached easily by telephone and video and airplane, and that the transnational social space is the space in which the new immigrants still feel most at home, and they project this characteristic of recent forms of dispersion onto diasporas.

By contrast, after several generations, any one member of a diaspora is no longer committed because of kinship links and personal memories (though both will matter to the extent that they can be revived and invigorated through travel and participation); nor is he or she committed simply because of not being integrated into the host society, as the first and second generations of dispersion often are not. The diasporan not committed through these links is now a citizen in his or her 'new' home country, possesses a hybrid culture and identity or at the very least has developed a comfortable bicultural competence. He or she is a diasporan because of a set of cumulative decisions to continue to remain bi- or multi-local, to care about others in diaspora with whom she shares an ethnodiasporic origin, and also to care in some manner about the wellbeing of the homeland of the ancestors.

Other binaries

Time constraints will not allow me to discuss at similar length other features and formative binaries of diaspora studies. In particular, I regret not having time to explore the debate on the political roles of diasporas and homelands. Other binaries we might consider are the tension between the term 'identity', which risks reification and essentialism, and 'identification', which points to a much more flexible and reversible process. Another binary harks back to a distinction between the emic and the etic, first made by linguistic anthropology in the 1950s. For linguists, the emic, modelled on the phonemic, designates the perspective of the native speaker, the knowledge and fluency of the insider, who neither needs nor knows the etic discourse by which scholars describe the phonetic, grammatical and syntactical features of a language. The analogue of the etic is the scholarly discourse of diaspora studies, which in my view too often fails to understand the emic vocabulary, concepts, representations, dispositions and behaviours by which the members of a diaspora talk about themselves to themselves and perform their identifications for each other, as they study, debate and nurture their own social formation.

The gap between the emic and etic understandings of diaspora has become more apparent in recent years, as homeland governments and international organizations such as the World Bank and the International Monetary Fund (IMF) have quite clumsily sought to develop means to attract more investment and remittances, sell bonds to the diaspora, and generally direct the political and economic capital of diasporas, ranging from the Indian to the Rwandan and the Armenian, Haitian and African.

Conclusion: the politicization of diasporas

This chapter began with a consideration of the enabling social and political conditions leading to the explosive growth of diaspora studies that worried Rogers Brubaker. It then proceeded to a partial typology of conceptual binaries that persistently structure the proliferation Brubaker finds so troubling. While the need to remain vigilant about terminological and conceptual clarity remains, I would like to end by directing our attention to the current, problematic politicization of diasporas and to the role that the relatively autonomous field that is a maturing diaspora studies can play in ameliorating that trend.

Diaspora studies is in danger of becoming a servant to global political forces, as anthropology was once in danger of serving imperialism. The multi-sided politicization of diasporas is due to many factors. As diasporic social formations are consolidated, their own new elites and political entrepreneurs aspire to become leaders, brokers of influence and intermediaries of the diasporas' relations with the governments of their new countries of settlement, as with the governments of former homelands. Inspired by the successes of Israel, India and China in variously attracting diasporic investment and lobbying support, homeland governments are crafting enticements ranging from dual or special citizenship status, to elections for positions in homeland legislatures, as a way of keeping their diasporas productively engaged as subordinates. NGOs, the World Bank and the IMF are now involved in parallel attempts that aim to secure for homelands and their governments more investment, more remittances, more philanthropy, and purchase of diaspora bonds and the like. Finally, the governments and security apparatus of the countries in which new diasporas are emerging, anxious about everything from terrorism to unemployment, are also inclined to reduce the lived complexity of diasporas to a few political platitudes about loyalty and involvement.

Diaspora studies can try to be an antidote to the reductive instrumentalization of the social, cultural and affective complexity of diasporas. As scholars of diaspora studies, we need to foreground, to remind ourselves and others of that amazing complexity, which is the product of diasporic efforts to construct, represent and discuss the quotidian life of local diaspora communities while also attending to the demands of engagement with other diaspora communities and the homeland. The paradoxical combination of localism and transnationalism, the fierce aspiration to achieve economic and social success and the willingness to sacrifice for the community and the homeland, indeed the oscillation between loyalty and sceptical detachment that characterizes the performance of diasporic lives, is in my view an example of the way everyone, including nationals, will have to live in an increasingly heterogeneous and plural world. It is a world in which diasporas have been living for a while. I hope for a diaspora studies that lives up to the complexity of the diasporas, which are both the objects and co-subjects of its analysis.

Acknowledgement

This chapter is drawn from an inaugural lecture launching the Oxford Diasporas Programme at the Holywell Music Room, University of Oxford, on 2 June 2011.

References

Bakewell, O. (2008) 'In search of the diasporas within Africa', *African Diaspora*, 1 (1/2), 5–27, doi: 10.1163/187254608X346024.
Brubaker, R. (2005) 'The "diaspora" diaspora', *Ethnic and Racial Studies*, 28 (1), 1–19, doi: 10.1080/0141987042000289997.
Cho, L. (2007) 'The turn to diaspora', *Topia: Canadian Journal of Cultural Studies*, 17, 11–30, available at: https://pi.library.yorku.ca/ojs/index.php/topia/article/viewFile/13229/22406.
Cohen, R. (1997) *Global diasporas: an introduction*, London: UCL Press.
Dufoix, S. (2012) *La dispersion: une histoire des usages du mot diaspora*, Paris: Editions Amsterdam.
Gilroy, P. (1993) *The black Atlantic: modernity and double consciousness*, London: Verso.
Glazer, N. and D. Moynihan (1963) *Beyond the melting pot: the Negroes, Puerto Ricans, Jews, Italians and Irish of New York City*, Boston: MIT Press.
Gopinath, G. (1995) 'Bombay, UK, Yuba City: Bhangra music and the engendering of diaspora', *Diaspora*, 4 (3), 303–21, doi: 10.1353/dsp.1995.0011.
Hirsch, M. (2008) 'The generation of postmemory', *Poetics Today*, 29 (1), 103–28, doi: 10.1215/03335372-2007-019.
Kennedy, J. F. (1964) *A nation of immigrants*, New York: Popular Library.
Laguerre, M. (1999) 'State, diasporas and transnational politics: Haiti reconceptualised', *Millennium: Journal of International Studies*, 28 (3), 633–51, doi: 10.1177/03058298990280031201.
Ong, A. (1999) *Flexible citizenship: the cultural logics of transnationality*, Durham, NC: Duke University Press.
Schnapper, D. and C. Bordes-Benayoun (2006) *Diasporas et nations*, Paris: Odile Jacob.
Shepperson, G. (1966) 'The African abroad or the African diaspora', *African Quarterly*, 2 (1) 76–93.

Sinnreich, A. (2010) *Mashed up: music, technology and the rise of configurable culture*, Amherst, MA: University of Massachusetts Press.
Tölölyan, K. (1996) 'Rethinking diaspora(s): stateless power in the transnational moment', *Diaspora: A Journal of Transnational Studies*, 5 (1), 3–36, doi: 10.1353/dsp.1996.0000.
Tölölyan, K. (2007) 'The contemporary discourse of diaspora studies' *Comparative Studies of South Asia, Africa and the Middle East*, 27 (3), 647–55, doi: 10.1215/1089201x-2007-040.
Tölölyan, K. (2010) 'Beyond the homeland: from exilic nationalism to diasporic transnationalism', in A. S. Leoussi, A. Gal and A. D. Smith (eds) *The call of the homeland: diaspora nationalisms, past and present*, Amsterdam: Brill, 27–46.

3

Key methodological tools for diaspora studies

Combining the transnational and intersectional approaches

Anna Amelina and Karolina Barglowski

In this chapter, we review the key social science strategies used to examine cross-border linkages and transnational migration and discuss their merits for empirical research on diaspora formation. As Roger Brubaker noted, most early discussions on diaspora 'were firmly rooted in a conceptual "homeland"' and were 'concerned with a paradigmatic case, or a small number of cases' (Brubaker 2005: 2). Today, however, the concept encompasses a proliferation of meanings and applications. Influential thinkers like Paul Gilroy (1993) and James Clifford (1994) have paved the way for a decidedly non-essentialist understanding of diaspora, which focuses on migrants' cross-border linkages, flows and circulation, and practices of establishing social and symbolic ties. Rather than relying on notions of fixed connections to places, identities and cultures, we now see diasporas as communities that are constantly negotiated and constituted (Faist 2010). The negotiations involved reveal that ethnicity is not a stable category, but one that relies on the social practices of people who organize their membership of a group and evaluate their experiences of it according to what they consider to be 'ethnic'. Because understandings of ethnicity vary across time and space, people by no means agree on ethnic sameness and otherness and, although diasporas may bring together individuals and offer them sources of community feelings, not all migrants from the same country of origin are equally included in diasporic life. In a study of Peruvian associations in the United States, Paerregaard (2010) observed that some organizations are open to all Peruvians who want to come together – for example, to play football, dance or engage in traditional folklore – whereas others select their members according to their regional origin or socio-economic status. Thus, it is important to focus more attention on the power relations and inequalities in the countries of emigration and immigration that coalesce in the diaspora.

Intersectional perspectives

In addition, scholars of queer and gender studies have offered numerous empirical examples of the complexities and challenges of diasporic life. More specifically, they have focused on heteronormative notions of heterosexual reproduction and intimate relationships, particularly in relation to those who deviate from the predominant ideas about the ways of life that are common in their communities (Peña 2013). Queer studies that focus on diaspora have provided evidence of the contingent nature and flexible use of categories like ethnicity that are often taken for granted. In some circumstances, 'queer' migrants may emphasize a specific ethnic belonging to maintain membership in a diaspora, whereas in interactions with the non-migrant population, they may emphasize their 'queerness' to avoid racialized resentment (Manalansan 2000). Conversely, they may downplay their sexual belonging to gain access to economic and social resources from the diaspora in which they are living, even if doing so reinforces heteronormativity (Peña 2013). Other scholars have criticized the concept of diaspora for its failure to consider the distinct experiences of women in diasporic communities. Although women fulfil a crucial function in the reproduction of diasporas and 'homeland' attachments, and although they are given a distinct place in the global economy, they are often not represented in diaspora studies, which leads to the normalization of male experiences (Spivak 1996).

The works of these scholars resonate with constructivist notions that social categories and forms of belonging, such as gender and ethnicity, do not necessarily unite people (Anthias 1998; Wimmer 2008). For a study of diasporas in general, and especially an analysis of identity formation, it is thus imperative not to privilege ethnicity and nation over other types of boundaries, such as gender, class and sexuality. The criticism levelled at such approaches relates to the more recent intersectional perspectives that examine the interplay of gender, ethnicity, race, class and other axes of difference on various levels of social life, including the micro level of lived experience, the meso level of social relations and organizations, and the macro level of the social structures in which power and hierarchies are embedded (Amelina 2017; Lutz 2014). Accordingly, research on the formation of diasporas must consider the heterogeneity of the diasporic experiences of actors confronted with attributions relating to 'gender', 'ethnicity', 'race', 'class', 'sexuality', 'disability', 'age', 'generation' and 'space' (see also Bilge and Denis 2010).

This chapter builds on the above-described more nuanced and non-essentialist understandings of diaspora that rely on transnational and intersectional approaches to provide research strategies for studying the complexities of diasporic life. Methodologically, this involves acknowledging three central dimensions of diaspora formation. The first of these is the analysis of the *practices of people* who act together and, as a result, establish temporally stable forms of social and symbolic cross-border ties. This approach does not focus on the boundaries of diasporas, or on an ontology of 'what is a diaspora?', but rather on how actors draw boundaries to construct forms of belonging (Wimmer 2008). Second, these practices may involve *ideologies of a 'homeland'* and of an idealized return (Safran 1991) – an aspect strongly emphasized in the classical understanding of diasporas. More generally, they may also involve dense and continuous cross-border linkages (Faist 2010). Third, practices of 'doing diaspora' are linked to *hierarchies of gender, ethnicity/race, class and other socially constructed axes of difference*, which cannot be known *a priori* but must be studied empirically as social attributions.

This focus on diasporas certainly has its merits, but while it offers new opportunities to understand contemporary social life in an increasingly globalizing world, it also poses challenges and raises important methodological questions about the definition of our empirical field, the sample, and how to conduct our empirical analyses. In this chapter, we provide some guidance on studying the cross-border linkages of diasporas, though without favouring one form of belonging over others. Most importantly, we avoid methodological nationalism and 'ethnic lenses', for they disregard the multiple boundaries that together produce a diaspora. We begin the chapter with some reflections on the methodological challenges involved in researching diasporas, followed by a discussion of the most important research strategies for collecting and interpreting data. The chapter concludes with a closer look at the need to deconstruct the 'groupist' and fixed connotations of the concept of diaspora.

Pitfalls of homogenization: methodological predicaments

In empirical research on diasporas, it is important to guard against viewing diasporic communities as homogeneous. Homogenization occurs when diasporic entities are predefined exclusively by their ethnic or national origin, and/or when cultural similarity among community members is assumed. To overcome this form of naturalization during analysis, scholars must be aware of the challenges of methodological nationalism, the ethnic lens and heteronormative bias, all of which may be implicitly inscribed in their conceptual and empirical research efforts.

Methodological nationalism, which has been common in migration research since its origins (for a counter view, see Amelina et al. 2012; Wimmer and Glick Schiller 2003), addresses nation-states as the main contexts of empirical analysis and as the central frameworks of conceptual work. 'Diaspora studies often trace dispersed populations no matter where they have settled, focusing on the dynamic interconnection, nostalgia and memory and identity within a particular population, relating them to a particular homeland', but sometimes they reproduce elements of a methodologically nationalist position by approaching 'nation' as 'extending across different terrains and places but nevertheless imagined as an organic and integrated whole' (Wimmer and Glick Schiller 2003: 598). Paradoxically, it is exactly this imagination of a territorially unbound (yet homogeneous) 'national body' that makes it difficult to study how 'nation-state building processes . . . impinge upon diasporic populations in its various locations', which in turn makes it impossible to examine concrete ways in which state policies contribute to and shape cross-border diasporic communities (Wimmer and Glick Schiller 2003: 598).

Similarly, the ethnic lens (Glick Schiller and Çağlar 2016) and ethnic groupism (Brubaker 2002) in diaspora research create the risk that diasporic entities are approached as uniform communities characterized by consistent ethnically defined 'cultural' traits. By addressing ethnicity as a personal attribute of individuals, this approach ignores the relational and interactional production of ethnic belonging among those socially designated as members or non-members of diasporic communities (Wimmer 2008), and its essentialist perspective addresses 'cultures' as 'package cultures' whose members have unchangeable values and principles (cf. Amelina and Faist 2012).

The heteronormative bias of studies on diasporas is another aspect of homogenization. Researchers working in the areas of gender and queer studies, for example Manalansan (2000), have criticized this bias in the social sciences for perpetuating the idea that individuals rather than practices build diasporic communities and that migrant men and women (often biologically defined) produce the future generations of diasporans. However, given that both gender studies and the social sciences now commonly accept that gender relations are socially generated (West and Zimmermann 1987), this must be applied to research on diasporas. Instead of naturalizing and biologizing diasporic masculinities and femininities, researchers must ask how gender relations are constituted socially both within a diasporic community and in interactions between a diaspora and its social context.

The challenges posed by methodological nationalism, the ethnic lens and ethnic groupism, and the heteronormative bias in empirical research in the field make it necessary to develop research strategies that increase researchers' sensitivity and reflexivity when studying cross-border diasporic phenomena.

Complexities of diasporic life: methodological tools for empirical research

Research on processes of diaspora formation must involve an analysis of the social practices through which actors establish social and symbolic cross-border ties. Their often-unpredictable practices underlie complex forms of belonging to other individuals and places across the globe. In this section, we discuss social scientific methods of data collection and data interpretation. Our discussion focuses on qualitative methods, for the lower degree of pre-structuring they involve makes them the most suitable methods for approaching the complexity of diasporic life. The most prominent research strategies for data collection we introduce here are multi-sited ethnography, mobile ethnography, matched sampling and open forms of data collection, all of which call into question the sedentary views of social life that normalize immobility.

George E. Marcus's (1995) seminal article 'Ethnography in/of the world system: the emergence of multi-sited ethnography' has had a major influence on research on mobility and transnationality. His main premise is that ethnographic methods should not conceive of their empirical field as having clearly defined boundaries. In the mid-1990s, this view was ground-breaking because cross-border spatiality was still a relatively new concept in the social sciences. Marcus's multi-sited ethnography includes reflections on cross-border spatiality as a distinct dimension of research design, which makes this methodology very useful for studying the complex character of the formation of diasporas that connect a variety of different people and places within and across borders. To allow researchers to identify their field, Marcus (1995) proposed six modes of analysis – 'follow the people', 'follow the thing', 'follow the metaphor', 'follow the plot, story or allegory', 'follow the life or biography' and 'follow the conflict'. These, he argued, provide a more appropriate understanding of the cross-border organization of contemporary social life.

Mobile ethnography, which draws on the modes of analysis that Marcus proposed, places researchers' mobility, as well as their 'object' of investigation, at the centre of their methodological reasoning. For example, Büscher and Urry (2009), who believe that neither mobility nor sedentarism should be regarded as the predominant 'grammar' of social life, argued that these two dimensions are interwoven and that researchers themselves are 'on the move'. 'By immersing themselves in the fleeting, multi-sensory, distributed, mobile and multiple, yet local, practical and ordered making of social and material realities, researchers gain an understanding of movement not as governed by rules, but as methodically generative' (Büscher and Urry 2009: 103–4).

Likewise, the 'matched sample methodology' developed by Valentina Mazzucato takes into consideration that social phenomena may involve various sites (see Mazzucato 2009). Mazzucato is interested in how flows of goods, money, services and ideas between Ghanaian migrants in the Netherlands and the individuals they know back in Ghana are transforming the institutions that shape local economies in the two countries. Mazzucato generally agrees with George E. Marcus that researchers should follow people, things, metaphors and so on, but she is also aware that it can be challenging to synthesize research in the various locations that play a part in the formation of a diasporic community, especially with in-depth and contextualized knowledge about these locations. Instead of following people, things, metaphors and so on, Mazzucato developed a research programme that reflected migrants' simultaneous connections to various localities (usually, though not always, 'home' and 'host' localities) and suggested that researchers should work with scholars in the emigration countries to enable the international research team formed as a result to conduct research in various locations simultaneously.

Scholars must decide how to collect data, regardless of whether they follow people, and so on, or whether they work with scholars in other geographic locations. Quantitative methods such as large-scale surveys do have their merits, but qualitative methods are more useful for studying the formation of diasporas because of their less structured character (on designing semi-structured interviews in multi-sited ethnography, see Barglowski et al. 2015). The methods of data collection used in this area, the most common of which are interviews and participant observation, range from highly structured to highly open. The more open a data collection process, the more likely it will reveal the complexities of diasporic experiences.

An analysis of the social formation of diasporas that avoids a homogenizing view on diasporic communities requires appropriate qualitative tools not only for the collection but also for the interpretation of empirical data. Of importance in this regard are strategies for studying social signification processes, such as transnationally oriented social scientific hermeneutics, biographical approaches and data-interpretation methods inspired by intersectionality.

The focus of transnational hermeneutics is on the reconstruction of the intersubjective knowledge incorporated into the social practices of diasporic communities (Amelina 2010). The aim of this method, which originally emerged in the sociological tradition of the German-speaking research community (Soeffner 2004), is to reconstruct meaning patterns, classifications or cultural beliefs[1] that are incorporated into social practices and, thus, shape social actions.[2] This research strategy can be used to analyse qualitative interviews and participant observations and is usually applied not by one researcher alone but by a team of them. Prior to the data collection stage, the researchers using this strategy conduct a reflexive self-assessment of their own theoretical and individual bias towards the object of their investigation (Shinozaki 2012). After the data have been collected, transcribed and anonymized, the research team identifies the most important parts of the interview (or other) text, usually by means of open coding (Strauss 2010). Then follows a sequence analysis of the most important parts of the interview transcript, which presupposes that 'every sentence and even every word of the selected passage has to be analysed with the aim of extracting the meaning pattern within the text' (Amelina 2010). During this procedure, the research team 'tries to develop as many versions of potential meaning patterns of the respective text parts as possible' (Amelina 2010). In the last step, the researchers discuss their assumptions about the potential meanings identified in the text and focus on the most significant ones. What makes transnationally oriented hermeneutics so useful in this context, then, is that it understands diasporic practices as embedded in situations in which patterns of meaning relating to a similar object or situation may overlap. For example, actors may be simultaneously confronted with two or more understandings of masculinity, femininity and ethnic belonging. This means that in the last step of the hermeneutic analysis, identifying the most significant assumption(s) about the meaning pattern of a particular passage, requires researchers to be sensitive to the potential multiplicity of cultural scripts (concerning the same object or situation) with which mobile actors are potentially confronted. Only then will the researchers be able to identify overlaps of the meaning patterns that often characterize diasporic practices. This data-interpretation strategy is critical for homogenizing and holistic descriptions of diasporic social spaces.

Since biographical approaches have drawn some inspiration from transnational migration studies (for example, Apitzsch and Siouti 2014), transnationally oriented hermeneutics can be fruitfully combined with biographical data interpretation methods. The starting point of transnationally oriented biographical research is its focus on biographies as the 'nodal points' of individuals' multilocal lifeworlds. Narrative interviews, which often represent the initial step in studies using the biographical approach, give scholars an opportunity to reconstruct individuals' experiences of mobility, immobility, long-distance relationships and multilocal life projects retrospectively. Here, the interpreter's work involves two steps – a hermeneutical case reconstruction of life history – that is, the experience lived through the life course – and the reconstruction of the life story – that is, the narrated vision of the life. 'The life story and the life history always come together; they are dialectically linked and produce each other' (Rosenthal 1995: 60, author's translation). The benefit of interpreting biographical interviews by differentiating between an individual's life story (presented by an interviewee) and that individual's life history (reconstructed by a researcher) is that this method can uncover individual experiences and knowledge patterns relating to the interviewees' retrospective perceptions of cross-border diasporic lifeworlds, which may include experiences in the migration-sending, the migration-receiving and any third countries or localities. In addition, this research strategy can also reveal the mutual shaping between individual biographical projects and the structures of diasporic communities (Bilecen and Amelina 2017). In the past, it was applied primarily in French- and German-speaking migration research communities, and it can be used to analyse aspects of diaspora formation, either as a stand-alone method or in combination with other research strategies.

The third data-interpretation strategy draws on one of the most recent approaches of gender studies – intersectionality (Lutz 2014; Walby et al. 2012). The key tenet of this approach is that to analyse processes of domination and social inequalities – in particular, in the context of migration and transnational processes – it is necessary to consider the interplay of various 'axes of difference' that are generated as a result of processes such as 'gender', 'ethnicity'/'race', 'class', 'sexuality', 'health'/'disability', 'age'/'generation' and 'space' (Amelina 2017): 'The overall aim of intersectional analysis is to explore intersecting patterns between different structures of power and how people are simultaneously positioned – and position themselves – in multiple categories such as gender, class and race/ethnicity' (Christensen and Jensen 2012: 110; see also Phoenix 2011).[3] Strategies for interpreting interviews and other data can build on the intersectional perspective by using Mary Matsuda's well-known 'ask the other question' methodology. As she (Matsuda 1991: 1189) explains:

> The way I try to understand the interconnection of all forms of subordination is through a method I call 'ask the other question'. When I see something that looks racist, I ask 'Where is the patriarchy in this?' When I see something that looks sexist, I ask, 'Where is the heterosexism in this?' When I see something that looks homophobic, I ask, 'Where are the class interests in this?'

A major benefit of using the intersectional perspective for data interpretation is that it allows us to address the relational production of power and domination both (1) inside diasporic communities and (2) between diasporic communities and the institutional structures of the sending and receiving countries:

1. By analysing power asymmetries within diasporic communities, scholars can reconstruct dominant and marginalized masculinities and femininities within the diasporas they are studying, as well as their linkages to notions of ethnic/racial, class-specific, (im)mobility-related and other diasporic images and attributions. This enables researchers to reveal dominant and subordinated social positions within diasporic configurations and, thus, to describe diasporas as multifaceted and non-homogenous (Amelina and Faist 2012; Lykke 2011).
2. The focus of intersectionality-inspired data-interpretation strategies on the relations of domination between diasporic communities and the institutional structures of sending and receiving countries offers a better understanding of the relational and complex co-constitution of power relations between the immobile 'majorities' and mobile 'minorities'. In other words, such analysis considers a 'majority-inclusive' principle in the study of diasporic relations (Christensen and Jensen 2012), in that it allows for analysis not only of those conventionally categorized as 'minorities' but also of interrelated 'lives . . . of the more powerful and privileged' immobile actors often overlooked in research because of 'the imagined normality of [sedentary] majority groups' (Christensen and Jensen 2012: 112). Having emerged from the work of the English-speaking research community, the intersectional approach can be fruitfully combined with the analytical strategies mentioned earlier, for it also focuses, at least in parts of the paradigm, on the processes of signification and meaning-making incorporated into inequality-related categorization processes (Amelina 2017).

Conclusion

In this chapter, we proposed a non-essentialist approach to diaspora analysis that offers valuable insights into the complexities of social life both within and across borders. The methodological programme presented here makes it possible to call into question homogenizing views on diaspora formation that are based on an assumed 'sameness' and instead points to the multiplicity of 'axes of difference' involved in the (re)production of diasporic communities. This research agenda certainly has its merits when it comes to gaining a more nuanced understanding of social life, but because conventional research often tends to conceive of diasporas as entities with clear boundaries and taken-for-granted forms of solidarity and trust, it is far from being unchallenged. Empirical research shows that diasporic communities are by no means homogenous, but that they are composed of various subjective experiences and meanings of ethnicity/race, gender, class, sexuality and space, among others, which include notions of migration, mobility and immobility (Amelina 2017; Clifford 1994; Manalansan 2000; Paerregard 2010). We have shown that the criticism of the sedentarist bias in migration research has contributed to the emergence of new social scientific data collection and interpretation strategies that benefit the empirical study of diaspora formation. Research methodologies such as multi-sited and mobile ethnography rest on the assumption that diasporic life involves different sites. We have also discussed important means of data interpretation, including transnationally oriented hermeneutics, the biographical method and interpretation strategies inspired by intersectionality. These methods, and the distinct focus that each represents, make it possible to trace complex significations on the edges of diasporic configurations and, simultaneously, to consider their socially produced spatiality. Hence, we argue that diaspora research requires multi-sited, open research designs to accommodate the wide variety of structures and meanings that exists within and across borders.

Notes

1 The term 'culture' is not used here in its essentialist sense, but rather refers to socially produced and changeable meaning patterns, scripts and schemes that are incorporated into social practices, networks, organizations and institutions (Amelina 2017).
2 Unlike 'objective hermeneutics', social scientific hermeneutics is based on the socio-constructivist premise that social meaning is not stable but historically specific and changeable.
3 This research programme, which goes back to black feminism and involves relational and processual perspectives, highlights often overlooked forms of social inequality that result from the interplay of 'gender'- and 'class'-related categorizations, or of 'ethnicity'/'race'- and 'sexuality'-related categorizations (Amelina 2017; Choo and Ferree 2010).

References

Amelina, A. (2010) 'Searching for an appropriate research strategy on transnational migration: the logic of multi-sited research and the advantage of the cultural interferences approach', *Forum: Qualitative Social Research*, 11 (1), art. 17, available at: http://nbn-resolving.de/urn:nbn:de:0114-fqs1001177

Amelina, A. (2017) *Transnationalizing inequalities in Europe: sociocultural boundaries, assemblages and regimes of intersection*, New York: Routledge.

Amelina, A. and T. Faist (2012) 'De-naturalizing the national in research methodologies: key concepts of transnational studies in migration', *Ethnic and Racial Studies*, 35 (10), 1707–24, doi: 10.1080/01419870.2012.659273.

Amelina, A., D. D. Nergiz, T. Faist and N. Glick Schiller (eds) (2012) *Beyond methodological nationalism: research methodologies for cross-border studies*, New York: Routledge.

Anthias, F. (1998) 'Evaluating "diaspora": beyond ethnicity', *Sociology*, 32 (3), 557–80, doi: 10.1177/0038038598032003009.

Apitzsch, U. and I. Siouti (2014) 'Transnational biographies', *ZQF – Zeitschrift für Qualitative Forschung*, 15 (1/2), 11–23, available at: www.budrich-journals.de/index.php/zqf/article/view/21631/18910.

Barglowski, K., B. Bilecen and A. Amelina (2015) 'Approaching transnational social protection: methodological challenges and empirical applications', *Population, Space and Place*, 21 (3), 215–26, doi: 10.1002/psp.1935.

Bilecen, B. and A. Amelina (2017) 'A network approach to migrants' transnational biographies', Gender, Diversity and Migration series, working paper no. 12, Goethe University Frankfurt am Main.

Bilge, S. and A. Denis (2010) 'Introduction: women, intersectionality and diasporas', *Journal of Intercultural Studies*, 31 (1), 1–8, doi: 10.1080/07256860903487653.

Brubaker, R. (2002) 'Ethnicity without groups', *European Journal of Sociology*, 43 (2), 163–89, doi: 10.1017/S0003975602001066.

Brubaker, R. (2005) 'The "diaspora" diaspora', *Ethnic and Racial Studies*, 28 (1), 1–19, doi: 10.1080/0141987042000289997.

Büscher, M. and J. Urry (2009) 'Mobile methods and the empirical', *European Journal of Social Theory*, 12 (1), 99–116, doi: 10.1177/1368431008099642.

Choo, H. Y. and M. M. Ferree (2010) 'Practicing intersectionality in sociological research: a critical analysis of inclusions, interactions, and institutions in the study of inequalities', *Sociological Theory*, 28 (2), 129–49. doi: 10.1111/j.1467-9558.2010.01370.x.

Christensen, A. D. and S. Q. Jensen (2012) 'Doing intersectional analysis: methodological implications for qualitative research', *NORA – Nordic Journal of Feminist and Gender Research*, 20 (2), 109–25, doi: 10.1080/08038740.2012.673505.

Clifford, J. (1994) 'Diasporas', *Cultural Anthropology*, 9 (3), 302–38, doi: 10.1525/can.1994.9.3.02a00040.

Faist, T. (2010) 'Diaspora and transnationalism: what kind of dance partners?', in R. Bauböck and T. Faist (eds) *Diaspora and transnationalism: concepts, theories and methods*, Amsterdam: Amsterdam University Press, 9–34.

Gilroy, P. (1993) *The black Atlantic: modernity and double consciousness*, Cambridge, MA: Harvard University Press.

Glick Schiller, N. and A. Çağlar (2016) 'Locating migrant pathways of economic emplacement: thinking beyond the ethnic lens', in A. Amelina, K. Horvath and B. Meeus (eds) *An anthology of migration and social transformation: European perspectives*, Cham: Springer, 307–26.

Lutz, H. (2014) 'Intersectionality's (brilliant) career: how to understand the attraction of the concept?' Gender, Diversity and Migration series, working paper no. 1, Goethe University Frankfurt am Main, available at: www.fb03.uni-frankfurt.de/51634119/Lutz_WP.pdf.

Lykke, N. (2011) 'Intersectional analysis: black box or useful critical feminist thinking technology?', in H. Lutz, M. Vivar and L. Supik (eds) *Framing intersectionality: debates on a multi-faceted concept in gender studies*, Farnham: Ashgate, 207–20.

Manalansan, M. F. (2000) 'Diasporic deviants/divas: how Filipino gay transmigrants "play with the world"', in C. Patton and B. Sánchez-Eppler (eds) *Queer diasporas*, Durham, NC: Duke University Press, 183–203.

Marcus, G. E. (1995) 'Ethnography in/of the world system: the emergence of multi-sited ethnography', *Annual Review of Anthropology*, 24, 95–117, doi: 10.1146/annurev.an.24.100195.000523.

Matsuda, M. (1991) 'Beside my sister, facing the enemy: legal theory out of coalition', *Stanford Law Review*, 43 (6), 1183–92, doi: 10.2307/1229035.

Mazzucato, V. (2009) 'Bridging boundaries with a transnational research approach: a simultaneous matched sample methodology', in M.-A. Falzon (ed.) *Multi-sited ethnography: theory, praxis and locality in contemporary research*, Aldershot: Ashgate, 215–32.

Paerregaard, K. (2010) 'Interrogating diaspora: power and conflict in Peruvian migration', in R. Bauböck and T. Faist (eds) *Diaspora and transnationalism: concepts, theories and methods*, Amsterdam: Amsterdam University Press, 91–108.

Peña, S. (2013) *Oye loca: from the Mariel boatlift to gay Cuban Miami*, Minneapolis: University of Minnesota Press.

Phoenix, A. (2011) 'Psychosocial intersections: contextualizing the accounts of adults who grew up in visibly ethnically different households', in H. Lutz, M. Vivar and L. Supik (eds) *Framing intersectionality: debates on a multi-faceted concept in gender studies*, Farnham: Ashgate, 137–52.

Rosenthal, G. (1995) *Erlebte und erzählte Lebensgeschichte: Gestalt und Struktur biographischer Selbstbeschreibungen*, Frankfurt am Main: Campus.

Safran, W. (1991) 'Diasporas in modern societies: myths of homeland and return', *Diaspora: A Journal of Transnational Studies*, 1 (1), 83–99, doi: 10.1353/dsp.1991.0004.

Shinozaki, K. (2012) 'Transnational dynamics in researching migrants: self-reflexivity and boundary-drawing in fieldwork', *Ethnic and Racial Studies*, 35 (10), 1810–27, doi: 10.1080/01419870.2012.659275.

Soeffner, H. G. (2004) 'Social scientific hermeneutics', in U. Flick, E. von Kardorff and I. Steinke (eds) *A companion to qualitative research*, London: Sage, 95–100.

Spivak, G. C. (1996) 'Diasporas old and new: women in the transnational world', *Textual Practice*, 10 (2), 245–69, doi: 10.1080/09502369608582246.

Strauss, A. L. (2010) *Qualitative analysis for social scientists*, Cambridge: Cambridge University Press.

Walby, S., J. Armstrong and S. Strid (2012) 'Intersectionality: multiple inequalities in social theory', *Sociology*, 46 (2), 224–40, doi: 10.1177/0038038511416164.

West, C. and D. H. Zimmermann (1987) 'Doing gender', *Gender and Society*, 1 (2), 125–51, doi: 10.1177/0891243287001002002.

Wimmer, A. (2008) 'Elementary strategies of ethnic boundary making', *Ethnic and Racial Studies*, 31 (6), 1025–55, doi: 10.1080/01419870801905612.

Wimmer, A. and N. Glick Schiller (2003) 'Methodological nationalism, the social sciences and the study of migration: an essay in historical epistemology', *International Migration Review*, 37 (3), 576–610, doi: 10.1111/j.1747-7379.2003.tb00151.x.

4

The social construction of diasporas

Conceptual development and the Rwandan case

Simon Turner

> 'The Rwandan government is targeting the positive diaspora and the negative diaspora.'
> *(Spokesperson of the Rwandan Directorate General for the Diaspora)*

Over the past decades, the term 'diaspora' has found its way from its largely academic use – concerned initially with the Jewish, Armenian and transatlantic African diasporas – to an expression used by the World Bank, sending states and many migrant groups claiming to be diasporas. The World Bank and development agencies in the Global North are particularly concerned with the development potential of diasporas and their role in conflict resolution. Sending states, by contrast, appeal to 'their' diasporas to invest in their home countries, while attempting to diffuse any possible political threats of hostile diasporas. Again, various migrant groups and ethnic minorities are increasingly asserting themselves as diasporas – for example, the Filipino diaspora, the Greek diaspora and the British diaspora. The concept is also used beyond an ethno-national anchoring, as we may now talk of a Muslim diaspora (Werbner 2004) or a queer diaspora (Patton and Sánchez-Eppler 2000). In this chapter, I am concerned with how moral attributes are assigned to particular diasporas or parts of a diaspora, developing my argument both conceptually and with respect to the Rwandan government's construction of diaspora. On the one hand, the Rwandan government does what it can to attract investments and encourage return migration of those abroad who are believed to be supportive of the present regime (its 'positive diaspora'). On the other hand, it also actively works on its so-called 'negative diaspora'; those Hutu who fled with the old regime and allegedly resent the present regime.

Conceptual development

What are the effects of this proliferation of the concept inside and outside academia? It is tempting to claim that this widespread use of the term has resulted in diluting the concept; now diaspora means so much that it has lost any conceptual clarity and hence usefulness as an analytical concept. The task, then, would be to try to salvage the concept and define it clearly according to a set of criteria. This is what scholars like Safran (1991), Sheffer (2003) and Cohen (1997) have done as far back as the early 1990s. The idea is to limit conceptual stretching and hence make it analytically more useful. Gabriel Sheffer (2003: 7) argues that

> Essential aspects of this phenomenon (diaspora identity) are the endless cultural, social, economic, and especially political struggles of those dispersed ethnic groups, permanently residing in host countries away from their homelands, to maintain their distinctive identities and connections with their homelands and other dispersed groups from the same nations. These are neither 'imagined' nor 'invented' communities.

He emphasizes the connection not only with co-nationals but also with their homeland and stresses the hostility that they often encounter. Furthermore, he rejects that notion that diasporas are imagined or invented and hence socially constructed.

Those claiming that diaspora is a social construction take an emic starting point seriously, basing their analysis on how actors define themselves or others as diaspora. Rather than defining what is and what is not diaspora, based on a preconceived set of criteria, we explore the proliferation of the concept. This also entails that we pose different questions to our material. Rather than explore who fits in the category, we may ask *how* certain diasporas are created and contested, what the *effects* are of being labelled diaspora, and *why* the concept has so much traction now. In terms of asking how diasporas are constructed, we may explore the main claims that are made in the name of diaspora, who is in a position to make such claims, and how host and home societies are engaged in the process. In other words, a social constructivist approach asks how the concept is contested and how it has become a battlefield for claiming rights and recognition.

This approach also calls for analyses of the *effects* of the social construction of diaspora. What does the use of the concept do? What happens to relations between nation-states and populations living outside the national territory when the latter claim to be diasporic and/or when the nation-state claims them to be diasporic in certain ways? We may also explore issues of integration and assimilation when migrant groups claim diasporic loyalties to other places. Does this mean that they are less likely to become assimilated into host societies, or can they easily span the two identities? Finally, as a more general question, one may also ask why this particular term has taken such a prominent position as an identity marker at a global scale right now. Are diaspora identities the answer to globalization and possibilities but also the insecurities that it creates? How does the proliferation of diasporic identity claims relate to the present shape of the nation-state? I will return to this question later.

Common to these questions is that they accept that diaspora is not a static concept that can be reeled in and defined once and for all, but a process that is embedded in the social world, constantly evolving and contested, echoing Kleist's (2008) call for perceiving diaspora as 'becoming' rather than 'being'. Along the same lines, I have argued elsewhere that we should move away from diaspora as a noun to *diasporize* as a verb or *diasporic* as an adjective (Turner 2008). To diasporize is an active process towards claiming that a certain community is a diaspora. This process can be active or defensive; diaspora can be worn as a mantel or what Dufoix (2008) has called a 'rallying call', strengthening identity, community and claims-making. As I will show below, outside actors may, however, also force it upon a category of people, as when the Rwandan state claims that a 'negative diaspora' exists, thereby categorizing any Hutu outside the country as part of this diaspora. Finally, as many scholars have cautioned before me, diasporas are not homogeneous (for example, Anthias 1998). Empirically, this is rather obvious; gender, class, generation and so forth affect the identity position of members of a diaspora. Analytically, however, it is interesting because it reminds us that the process of creating a diaspora inevitably involves homogenizing identities. In other words, as in the construction of any common identity and any idea of a community, identities are bent towards each other and identities are contested and disputed in the process. They may be contested by gender (Werbner 2004) or class (Bowman 1994), just as generations construct different diasporic identities (Kublitz 2016). To use the adjective *diasporic* is to accentuate that diaspora cannot stand alone but is always articulated with other identity markers such as community, people, nation – themselves empty signifiers in need of a qualifier such as diasporic.

Hybridity, loss and longing

If we are to find a common element in the social construction of diaspora, it is the emphasis on loss and longing. Often, diasporas are defined by social scientists as having been forcefully removed from a homeland. According to William Safran (1991), they or their ancestors have been dispersed from a specific original 'centre' to two or more 'peripheral', or foreign, regions. Zlatko Skrbiš (1999) also emphasizes 'a sense of banishment and alienation from the homeland' and a 'nostalgic yearning and myth of return' when defining the diaspora. However, his definition is not concerned with whether banishment and alienation actually took place but more with the perceptions amongst members of a given diaspora that it did. Brian Keith Axel (2002) inverts the usual causality between lost homeland and diasporic identity, arguing that place is overemphasized in definitions of diaspora and that the 'diasporic imaginary' is instead the product of violence and creates the idea of a lost home retrospectively. While the 'idea' of a lost place remains strong among diasporas – also in the case he uses, namely the imaginary Khalistan, created by Sikhs across the globe as a response to the violence of the Indian state – it is not the homeland that created the diaspora but vice versa.

A different approach to the study of diaspora comes from postcolonial studies and is more concerned with theoretical discussions of identity-making (Hall 1990), hybridity (Bhabha 1994) and belonging (Gilroy 1993) than with the dispersion of concrete ethnic groups and their relations to a homeland. This approach has run parallel to the other debates on diaspora and the two rarely interact. The emphasis in these theories is on mixing and hybridity rather than ethnic purity, seeing the diaspora position as potentially a privileged position because it challenges the common-sense hegemony of national identities (Bhabha 1994). It is the outsider, the migrant, or someone of mixed heritage who has the potential to reveal the illusion of pure identities. Gilroy (1993) famously claims that we must explore routes rather than roots when searching for identity. One might critique some of these scholars for overemphasizing the playfulness of identity construction or for privileging creolization and hybridization without acknowledging the pain and loss that many postcolonial migrants also feel. This critique is somewhat misplaced, as Stuart Hall and Paul Gilroy do, however, acknowledge loss and longing in diasporic identity. Gilroy, for instance, emphasizes that we have to pay close attention to the specific, historical routes that have created a particular diaspora, and Hall agrees that identity is created around a sense of loss that seeks closure.

In Lacanian terms, identity formation is always built up around a presumed original loss (Žižek 1989). In this sense, creating a migrant community relies on referring back to something lost: the homeland (in Lacanian terms, *l'objet petit a*). This does not need to be a real homeland that was actually lost. Rather, it is construed retrospectively, as Axel (2002) argues, and it is the return of the homeland (which is not the same as the return to the homeland) that promises closure (suture). This presumed lost homeland, created in the diasporic imaginary, is the 'glue' that makes the community stick together. Without the 'glue' of loss, 'the community' would cease to exist and simply become an assembly of individuals from the same country.

In his study of the Palestinian diaspora, Glenn Bowman (1994) argues that Palestine became an 'empty signifier' that was so open and vaguely defined that it managed to encompass all the troubles and tribulations of a diverse, dispersed and heterogeneous population. Whether a member of the educated elite, such as Edward Said, or a poor refugee in a camp in Lebanon, they all dreamed of Palestine and hence felt a common belonging to the diaspora. However, with the Oslo negotiations – when Palestine lost is mythological status and the Palestinian state instead became a concrete, political reality – the diaspora lost its 'glue' and the differences among the diaspora – based on class, geography, gender – surfaced, thus also threatening the idea of a diaspora as such. In other words, diaspora refers simultaneously to mixing and hybridity as emphasized by postcolonial scholars (Bhabha 1994; Gilroy 1993; Hall 1990), and to closure of identity, as we may witness in long-distance nationalism (Anderson 1994; Skrbiš 1999); it is at once rhizomatic and rooted. And this is what makes the concept so attractive.

Rwanda: the making of 'positive' and 'negative' diasporas

In Rwanda, diasporic politics have played a central role in defining the nation, just as the state has been keen to define, contain and control diasporas. Members of the Tutsi diaspora, returning from neighbouring countries, and from Uganda in particular, dominate the post-genocide political and economic elite. They or their parents fled the country following the Hutu revolution in 1959 and the anti-Tutsi violence that followed. They perceive themselves not as victims but as heroes and liberators, seeing as it was them who liberated the country from the Hutu regime and stopped the 1994 genocide. With their moral claims to having stopped the genocide and saved the indigenous population, they epitomize the new Rwanda.

The present regime has a strong commitment to development and to creating national unity after the genocide that tore the country apart along ethnic lines. In order to increase development, the Rwandan state reaches out to its diaspora – in particular, the wealthy and well-educated Tutsi who live in Europe and North America. In 2001, a desk in charge of the diaspora was created in the Ministry of Foreign Affairs and Corporation, and in 2008, the Diaspora Desk was formalized into the Diaspora General Directorate (DGD). The diaspora is seen to be able to contribute to the homeland in three main ways: as agents of economic development, as good ambassadors and representatives, and as a resource of knowledge and skills. The mission and general objectives of DGD are: '*To create a conducive environment enabling Rwandan Diaspora to be a strong cohesive community with a constructive relationship with their motherland aiming at national development of Rwanda.*'[1] In other words, it is important to be able to exploit this human resource and unleash the potentials of the diaspora, first of all to stimulate the creation of a united diaspora; as inside the country, cohesion is seen to be vital. In order for the diaspora to invest money and skills in the homeland, it must feel committed to the homeland, and this cannot be taken for granted.

In most of the policy documents, the diaspora is described in positive terms, the main task being simply to turn the potential of the diaspora into practical action. However, there are cracks in this presentation of the diaspora, mainly because the diaspora does not always act in ways that the sending state desires. In particular, in the old colonial power, Belgium, the Rwandan diaspora is strongly split along ethnic and political lines, and in Congo a Hutu rebel movement has at times threatened national security. Interestingly, the Rwandan government is explicitly aware of what it calls the 'negative diaspora' and has various programmes in place to tackle this challenge. The Rwandan Patriotic Front, in power since 1994, was itself created in exile in Uganda by what might be termed a 'negative diaspora' of disgruntled Tutsi. For this reason, the RPF government is acutely aware of the dangers of having a negative diaspora across the border. After invading Eastern Congo in 1996 and forcing the majority of potentially hostile Hutu back, the government has led a policy of trying to convince the remaining 'negative diaspora' that Rwanda is perfectly safe to return to. One way of doing this is to arrange camps for diaspora youth every summer, so that they may not forget their cultural roots and so that they may experience national unity in practice.

A high-ranking official of the Diaspora General Directorate explained to me that they split the diaspora into three categories: those who are willing to invest time and money in Rwanda, those who need convincing, and a small group of diehard genocide revisionists. The challenge, as he saw it, was to reach out to the second group and to minimize the influence of the third group. This often meant targeting the youth who were not 'stuck in a pre-genocide mind-set'. A more costly, but certainly spectacular, approach has been the 'come and see' programmes. Apparently, they started when President Kagame visited the diaspora in Belgium, where he met a lot of scepticism and criticism from the 'negative', Hutu-dominated diaspora. According to the government narrative, he on the spot invited the most vocal critics to come and see for themselves – all costs paid. This exercise has been repeated several times since, meeting critical members of the diaspora in various countries and inviting them to 'come and see'. According to one of the organizers – himself a Hutu who used to live in Belgium – it is easy in Canada and the UK where most Rwandans support the president, but much more tough in France or Belgium. He is part of a team that goes to France weeks in advance of the presidential visit to convince members of the diaspora to attend the meetings. It is difficult to say who is the audience of this *mise-en-scène*. The primary audience is members of the sceptical diaspora who need to see the country with new eyes. It is, however, also a state spectacle when the state demonstrates its magnanimity towards the Hutu in exile and also demonstrates its sovereignty towards a domestic audience.

The positive and negative diasporas correspond with the Tutsi who fled the Hutu regime before 1994 and the Hutu who fled in 1994, and any critique posed by the Hutu diaspora may therefore be dismissed as being the leftovers of old genocide mentalities. 'They are stuck in a pre-1994 mind-set', I was often told by government officials. What is more troubling for the Rwandan state – disturbing this neat dichotomy of positive and negative diasporas – are the numerous Hutu and Tutsi individuals who have been fleeing the country over the past decade. Many of them have held high-ranking positions in the army or government and have become concerned with the autocratic tendencies of Kagame's regime. These individuals cannot be dismissed as *génocidaires* and cannot be lured back to Rwanda through 'come and see' programmes, as they already have seen the country post-1994. They reveal the limits of the government's attempts to construct the diaspora in specific ways in order to contain and control its potential threat.

The Rwandan case highlights that not only are diasporas socially constructed but that they are highly contentious constructs, and that various actors are actively involved in constructing and challenging them in various ways. The Rwandan government draws on and feeds into global discourses on diasporas as agents of change, promoted by the World Bank, International Organization for Migration and a number of sending states when it sees its diaspora as its 'gold'. Meanwhile, not all Rwandans living abroad feel part of such a supportive diaspora, which means that the Rwandan government has had to readjust its construction of the Rwandan diaspora by distinguishing between a positive and a negative diaspora. In this way, the government is attempting to manage and govern its population outside the territory through naming and categorizing. Naming and categorizing is, however, not enough, and with them come concrete economic and political opportunities and sanctions that have concrete consequences for the different diasporas – negative or positive. Finally, the Rwandan government's attempts to control the diaspora through such social categorizations never fully succeeds, as certain groups remain hostile and resist its attempts to 'rein them in'.

Conclusion

As we have seen, diaspora is a powerful social construction with increasing popularity both in academia and elsewhere (Dufoix 2008: 30–4). Brian Keith Axel (2004: 26) calls it a 'globally mobile category of identification'. While more migrant groups and ethnic minorities claim to be diasporic, sending states also increasingly invoke diasporas, creating ministries and directorates for diasporas, hoping to attract investments and political loyalties and to diffuse hostility. Turner and Kleist (2013: 195) write:

> Not only do the overall societal, policy and academic developments facilitate the identification and definition of certain groups and their activities as diasporas and as diasporic involvement, it also makes it a more attractive position to claim. The diaspora position signals agency, authenticity, responsibility and resources and it might be conducive to getting access to funding or other advantages.

In the case of Rwanda, government consciously bifurcated their construction of the Rwandan diaspora into two segments.

Why has diaspora become such a powerful concept, even if sometimes an empty signifier, across the globe? Perhaps Tölölyan (1991) provides a clue, when claiming some 26 years ago that 'Diasporas are the exemplary communities of the transnational moment'. Diaspora elegantly connects hybridity, flows and mixing with promises of closure of identity, creating the ideal response to the constant and increasing tension between the forces of globalization and the continued hegemony of the nation-state as an ordering principle. In this tension, diaspora gives access to claims to recognition. For a woman whose parents moved from Turkey to Frankfurt to claim to be part of the Kurdish diaspora asks for other kinds of recognition than for her to be a second-generation immigrant in Frankfurt. She can make claims to belonging to a community that transgresses Frankfurt and Germany while still operating within the recognizable paradigm of belonging to a nation. Diaspora operates both as an expression of globalized identities – transgressing national borders, mixing cultural expressions and drawing on dispersed heritages – and an expression of national belonging and cultural closure. In this sense, diaspora is a powerful means for making claims and seeking recognition, neither succumbing to the pressure to assimilate to national identities nor merely claiming to belong to fuzzy ideas of hybridity, cosmopolitanism or global citizenship.

Note

1 www.rwandandiaspora.gov.rw/index.php?id=36 (accessed 18.05.2017).

References

Anderson, B. (1994) 'Exodus', *Critical Inquiry*, 20 (2), 314–27, available at: www.jstor.org/stable/1343913.
Anthias, F. (1998) 'Rethinking social divisions: some notes towards a theoretical framework', *The Sociological Review*, 46 (3), 505–35, doi: 10.1111/1467-954X.00129.
Axel, B. K. (2002) 'The diasporic imaginary', *Public Culture*, 14 (2), 411–28, doi: 10.1215/08992363-14-2-411.
Axel, B. K. (2004) 'The context of diaspora', *Cultural Anthropology*, 19 (1), 26–60, doi: 10.1525/can.2004.19.1.26.
Bhabha, H. (1994) 'Anxious nations, nervous states', in J. Copjec (ed.) *Supposing the subject*, New York: Verso, 201–17.
Bowman, G. (1994) '"A country of words": conceiving the Palestinian nation from a position of exile', in E. Laclau (ed.) *The making of political ideologies*, London: Verso, 138–71.

Cohen, R. (1997) *Global diasporas: an introduction*, Seattle: University of Washington Press.
Dufoix, S. (2008) *Diasporas*, Berkeley, CA: University of California Press.
Gilroy, P. (1993) *The black Atlantic: modernity and double consciousness*, Cambridge, MA: Harvard University Press.
Hall, S. (1990) 'Cultural identity and diaspora', in J. Rutherford (ed.) *Identity: community, culture, difference*, London: Lawrence & Wishart, 225–47.
Kleist, N. (2008) 'In the name of diaspora: between struggles for recognition and political aspirations', *Journal of Ethnic and Migration Studies*, 34 (7), 1127–43.
Kublitz, A. (2016) 'From revolutionaries to Muslims: liminal becomings across Palestinian generations in Denmark', *International Journal of Middle East Studies*, 48 (1), 67–86, doi: 10.1017/S0020743815001476.
Patton, C. and B. Sánchez-Eppler (eds) (2002) *Queer diasporas*, Durham, NC: Duke University Press. www.rwandandiaspora.gov.rw/index.php?id=36 (accessed 18.05.2017).
Safran, W. (1991) 'Diasporas in modern societies: myths of homeland and return,' *Diaspora*, 1 (1), 83–100, doi: 10.1353/dsp.1991.0004.
Sheffer, G. (2003) *Diaspora politics: at home abroad*, New York: Cambridge University Press.
Skrbiš, Z. (1999) *Long-distance nationalism: diasporas, homelands and identities*, Aldershot: Ashgate.
Turner, S. (2008) 'The waxing and waning of the political field in Burundi and its diaspora,' *Ethnic and Racial Studies*, 31 (4), 742–65, doi: 10.1080/01419870701784505.
Turner, S. and N. Kleist (2013) 'Introduction: agents of change? Staging and governing diasporas and the African state,' *African Studies*, 72 (2), 192–206, doi: 10.1080/00020184.2013.812882.
Tölölyan, K. (1991) 'The nation-state and its others: in lieu of a preface', *Diaspora: A Journal of Transnational Studies*, 1 (1), 3–7, doi: 10.1353/dsp.1991.0008.
Werbner, P. (2004) 'Theorising complex diasporas: purity and hybridity in the South Asian public sphere in Britain', *Journal of Ethnic and Migration Studies*, 30 (5), 895–911, doi: 10.1080/1369183042000245606.
Žižek, S. (1989) *The sublime object of ideology*, London: Verso.

5
Diasporas as social movements?

Sharon M. Quinsaat

Early discussions of diaspora emphasize forced and traumatic dispersion, homeland orientation, and strict boundary maintenance as constitutive elements (Brubaker 2005; Bruneau 2010; Cohen 1997; Safran 1991; Tölölyan 1996). Involvement in homeland politics among those coercively displaced does not appear unusual; rather, it is expected since they regard their ancestral homeland as their true and ideal home, to which they or their descendants would eventually return when conditions are suitable. This is because, according to Tölölyan (1996: 13), 'diasporas are displaced but homogeneous and established "ethnies" that, while still in their homeland, were already endowed with protonational social and cultural characteristics'.

Recent literature, however, has foregrounded the process of *becoming* a diaspora through the strategic mobilization of constituencies around a homeland political issue on the basis of shared ideas and collective identities. Scholars critique the failure to engage the question of human agency in migrants' intentions in early works and argue that 'objective' circumstances must include a subjective interpretation in the formation of a diaspora (Faist 2012; Sökefeld 2006). Central to the imagination of community are discourses on shared identity that catalyse or hinder mobilization and, at the same time, are also products of the mobilization process (Amarasingam 2015). Hence, emphasis on becoming avoids the trap of essentialism and recasts the research problem on why and how discourses that become the foundation of a diasporic identity arise among a certain group of people across time and space.

To explain the formation of diasporas through political and social mobilization, scholars have used and advocated the use of social movement theory, which requires examining the interaction and combined influence of the shifting political environment, constellation of actors and organizations, and construction of a diasporic consciousness (Adamson 2012; Fair 2005; Koinova 2013; Landolt 2008; Lyon and Uçarer 2001; Østergaard-Nielsen 2003; Sökefeld 2006; Wayland 2004). This shift in paradigm emerged largely in response to the dominance of the analysis of diasporas as *actors* of transnational processes – from financial donors of armed groups or neutral third parties in the prevention and resolution of violent conflicts, to agents of democratization and development in their homeland through participation in elections (Baser 2016; Byman et al. 2001; DeWind and Segura 2014; Itzigsohn and Villacrés 2008; Lyons and Mandaville 2012; Sheffer 2003; Smith and Stares 2007).

Although these studies have contributed to theory development on the role of diasporas in international relations (Shain and Barth 2003), they have largely understated the *social* construction of a transnational 'imagined community' (Anderson 1991) that is central to the formation of diasporas. Boundary-crossing and dispersal of migrants are insufficient to explain the politicization of identity categories rooted in the homeland (Sökefeld 2006). From a constructivist perspective, exiles and migrants become a diaspora through the discursive and framing processes, often by political entrepreneurs[1] (Adamson 2012; Faist 2010; Koinova 2013).

This chapter analyses the formation of diasporas akin to the emergence and development of social movements. I use the dominant canon of the political process theory, which was primarily based on the reform movements of US citizens in the 1960s onwards. Despite criticisms,[2] the political process theory remains the hegemonic framework in social movement scholarship (Goodwin and Jasper 1999). I also discuss mechanisms and processes that recur across a wide range of contentious politics, in the tradition of McAdam et al. (2001) and other scholars who have advanced the research agenda of *Dynamics of contention*.[3] Due to the limitations of social movement theories in explaining mobilizations that challenge nation-state-based citizenship, I also incorporate ideas from long-distance nationalism and migrant political transnationalism to account for a full range of variations within social movement concepts.

Political process theory

Like its predecessors, such as collective behaviour, Marxist and relative deprivation theories, political process theory proposes that the likelihood a social movement develops along with its subsequent trajectories is contingent upon external and internal variables. External variables, which are often referred to as political opportunity structures, include elites' party affiliations and alliances, existing laws and policies, regime type, and relations among states. Internal variables include collective identity, ideology, financial resources, leadership and organizational structure. I focus on elements in the theory that are central in explaining diaspora formation.

Transnational opportunity structures

The prospects for groups and individuals to advance particular claims, mobilize resources and shape outcomes depend on the political environment in which mobilization unfolds (Kriesi 2004; McAdam 1999; Meyer 2004). Research has identified four elements that are important for the emergence and growth of social movements: the relative openness of the institutionalized political system, the stability of the broad set of elite alignments that typically uphold a polity, the presence of elite allies, and the state's capacity and propensity for repression (Jasper 2012; McAdam 1996; Tarrow 2011). These features of the political opportunity structure remain paradigmatic in social movement studies. Meyer and Minkoff (2004), however, suggest distinguishing between general changes in the political context (for example, state breakdown) and issue- or constituency-specific factors (for example, immigration legislation).

For individuals and groups involved in homeland politics, a distinct type of transnational activism, analyses must take into account the political opportunity structures in the homeland *and* host country and how they interact. As Bauböck (2010: 316) argues, 'analysing diaspora from an agency perspective requires examining not only the group's elites and their projects, but also their opportunity structures shaped by other agents, including governments in the country of settlement and the external homeland'. The political environment in both homeland and host land influence the possibility, nature and trajectory of transnational activism

(Waldinger and Fitzgerald 2004). Issues pertaining to the nature of regimes, for instance, are crucial in the analysis of diaspora mobilization, since incentives and constraints originate from the polity in their host country, often democratic, but the target of their actions is their homeland government, most likely authoritarian.

Homeland states that combine democratic and authoritarian elements may nurture the desirability of armed revolutionary groups because the government has subverted the principles and institutions of democracy through corruption, fraudulent elections and violations of human rights. In this case, migrants may be engaged in two or more forms of political contention, such as funding of alternative political parties, conspiracy for *coup d'état*, and lobbying other states to withdraw support for the regime. They may also choose to fund homeland opposition parties and insurgent movements to help bolster their ability to depose the regime in power (Bolzman 2011; Byman et al. 2001; Fair 2005). In post-conflict situations or transition to democracy, diasporas mobilize to rebuild democratic institutions, strengthen civil society and promote justice, truth and reconciliation (Bercovitch 2007).

Linkages between the host and homeland states constitute an important element of the political opportunity structure for claims-making. Foreign policies can shape diaspora mobilization by identifying a specific target and opening access to the institutionalized political system and elite allies in the host society. The growing literature on state relations and diasporas has focused on the conditions that enable migrants and exiles to influence the policy of their host government towards their homeland through ethnic lobbying. However, Koinova (2014: 1047) observes that state-centric theoretical approaches merely 'capture institutional and policy variation, not their implications for transnational diaspora politics'. Thus, a focus on structures alone cannot explain diaspora formation.

Resource mobilization

Social movements do not develop without linkages between groups and individuals, material resources and larger societal support (Gamson 1975; McCarthy and Zald 1977; Piven and Cloward 1979). The centrality of social construction in the analysis of diasporas prompts an analysis of leadership and brokerage. Like all types of mobilization, the making of a diaspora hinges on the ability of political entrepreneurs to galvanize existing networks of migrants and refugees, and to draw on resources in response to opportunities (Adamson 2004).

In pursuit of a political goal, a key task of these leaders is 'to construct or deploy ideologies and categories that can be used to create new political groups out of existing social networks . . . and frame the experiences of those who have subjectively experienced dislocation and marginalization' (Adamson 2004: 49–50). This is because migration does not entail the mere transfer of identities from the country of origin to that settlement, but rather a recreation in a new context.

To foster mobilization, political entrepreneurs may draw upon highly parochial or particularistic ideas, articulated in the language of national loyalty and attachment to a territorial homeland (Lyons and Mandaville 2012). They may also use universalist frameworks such as liberalism to advance the goals related to their homeland (Adamson 2004; Koinova 2010). For example, both Jewish and Arab Americans have portrayed their commitment to Israel and Palestine, respectively, as an extension of their allegiance to American democratic values and strategic interests (Shain 1994/95).

Another central role of these leaders, especially those from organizations that predated the period of displacement, is the preservation of their political identities, associational life and symbols of resistance, especially in the face of rivalry (Shain 2005). Homeland politics among migrants are not devoid of political divisions and competition, since even those who share common ethnicity or ideology hardly possess a unified agenda. These conflicts often emanate from alliances with different homeland political parties or ideologies. Thus, leaders carefully select mobilizing issues and formulate them in a language that appeals to migrants.

Discourses, strategic frames and collective identity

For members of a group to become engaged in contention, an oppositional consciousness[4] must develop (Morris and Braine 2001), and in the process of collective action and political contestation, social movements 'transform cultural representations, social norms – how groups see themselves and are seen by others' (Polletta and Jasper 2001: 284). This is particularly relevant to social movement organizations among migrants, whose identities were politicized through the experiences of relocation and settlement, and whose culture as a boundary-marker expands and contracts as the community in which they are embedded undergoes transformation. Wald (2008) argues that a politicized ethnic identity is less likely to develop among cohorts or groups formed by voluntary migration in search of economic opportunity, compared to those forced out of their home country by political upheaval.

Incorporating frames and collective identity in the analysis of mobilization for homeland politics prompt us to regard the migrant community as a discursive field for the conflict-riven process of meaning-making by various, often opposed, actors. In particular, migrants interrogate ethnicity and nationality as foundations for collective identity within this field. Discourses pivot not only on their common culture but also on interpretations of national history, especially the social and political forces that have shaped their home society. These discourses are prevalent in everyday conversations in the workplace or the household, ethnic media, myths and narratives passed on to subsequent generations, business transactions and social gatherings.

In the discursive construction of collective identity, exiles and migrants often wrestle with charges of national disloyalty, which generate feelings of anxiety, bitterness and guilt (Glick Schiller and Fouron 1999; Shain 2005). They are compelled to exhibit their standing as national loyalists for strategic mobilization and defence of their continued belonging to the homeland. Through sustained performances of their national identity, they counter the fear of being forgotten and the guilt of becoming too contented in their host country with the passing of time. The difficulty rests on the portrayal of their struggle from afar to depose a native home regime as a patriotic mission, especially since they are detached from the day-to-day suffering of the people whom they claim to represent (Anderson 1992).

Affective bonds, couched in the language of loyalty to the nation, are particularly crucial, not just in homeland-oriented migrant mobilization, but also in day-to-day coping with disenchantment, homesickness and marginalization in the host society, and regret at leaving the homeland. The motherland becomes an 'identity reservoir', a reference to one's earlier life and as 'a source for nostalgia and as an implicit standard according to which one makes sense of values, habits, and life experiences in the context of immigration' (Boccagni 2010: 188). In the context of contentious collective action, socially marginalized and politically disenfranchised individuals feel attracted to the notion of belonging to an ethnic community.

Dynamics of contention

While political process theory explains the conditions and determinants of protest, it neglects to capture mechanisms and processes that link variables to outcomes. To complement variable-based explanations to the emergence, growth and outcomes of social movements, McAdam et al. (2001)

developed a relational approach to contentious politics. Among its arguments is widening the focus of episodes of contention to include multiple social actors, not just challengers and authorities.

Three types of mechanisms combine in complex cycles of contention. One is dispositional, such as the attribution of opportunity or threat. Gamson and Meyer (1996) have argued the importance of movement framing of opportunities in justifying strategic choices. In various phases of contention, diaspora activists may recognize discursive openings and elite cleavages, and interpret threats in ways that emphasize opportunity rather than constraint. Political entrepreneurs can also create rather than wait for opportunities by generating controversy in mainstream mass media to make their issues salient.

Another mechanism is environmental, which include population growth or resource depletion. Generational processes, for example, affect the continuity of diaspora organizations, not only in terms of recruitment and personnel, but also in ensuring political commitment through the internalization of a collective identity across time. Whittier (1997: 775) contends that 'the extent to which cohort turnover produces change within social movement organizations also depends on organizational memory, or the effectiveness of information storage and retrieval that allows later activists to learn from their predecessors' experiences'. As the movement participation of long-time militants declines with biographical change, replenishing the ranks entails cohort replacement, a shift in organizational structure and culture, and intergenerational redefinition of movement identity.

Lastly, relational mechanisms facilitate interaction and establish connections among individuals, groups and networks. For instance, as immigrants undertake tasks related to their involvement in politics in their homelands (i.e., lobbying politicians in their host lands on foreign policy issues, educating their ethnic communities on events 'back home', preparing press releases for mainstream news media), they become more embedded into the host land context (Karpathakis 1999; Miller 2011). Thus, the political activities that migrants or refugees undertake related to homeland politics – such as mobilizations for regime change or participation in elections – are no longer seen as diametrically opposed to their actions to improve their situation in the receiving country. In the process, the meaning of one's ethnicity is continuously interrogated, which allows for the redefinition of belonging in 'imagined communities'.

Conclusion

Like other social movements, diaspora mobilization as a transnational political project stems from the interplay of opportunities and threats, resources in the community, and strategic deployment of ideologies and identities. Diaspora mobilization entails traversing two distinct cultural, economic, political and social systems, with different constructions of citizens' relationship to the nation-state. Using social movement theory, analysis must explain the dynamic interaction of political opportunities and threats in both sending and receiving states; the relocation and reproduction of cultural, political and social resources from the homeland to the host society, as well as their maintenance, and the discursive construction of loyalty to the homeland as a foundation of collective identity.

Unpacking the underlying processes and mechanisms that lead to different pathways and trajectories is also central to the analysis of diaspora formation. A focus on the mechanisms at work allows us to see the connections and interactions among important elements of contention and the processes involving simultaneous actions of multiple actors in overlapping arenas (including the homeland, host land, international state system and transnational social fields). At the centre of analysis of the social construction of diasporas is the strategic choices activists make in interaction with other actors in complex and shifting arenas of contention.

Acknowledgement

A few sections of this chapter have appeared in the author's articles published in *Sociology Compass* and *Ethnic and Racial Studies*.

Notes

1 In collective action, a 'political entrepreneur', often part of a privileged group, is an individual willing to bear the costs of social action irrespective of the position taken by others who are also interested in the action's outcomes (Olson 1965).
2 For a comprehensive critique of the political process model, especially on its static treatment of structures and culture and the lack of focus on dynamic interactions, see Goodwin and Jasper (1999), McAdam et al. (2001) and Polletta (1999).
3 For criticisms of the *Dynamics of contention* project, see 'Book symposium: focus on dynamics of contention' (*Mobilization* 2003). Weaknesses identified include obfuscation of mechanisms and processes by not showing precisely how they worked and the appropriate methods to use in documenting them. A special issue of *Mobilization* (2011) built on the shortcomings of *Dynamics of contention* to further advance a mechanisms-oriented approach in the study of contentious politics.
4 Morris and Braine (2001: 21) defines oppositional consciousness as 'an empowering mental state that prepares members of an oppressed group to act to undermine, reform or overthrow a system of human domination'. Minimally, that mental state includes identifying with a subordinate group, concluding that the mechanisms that have produced at least some of the group's inequalities are unjust, opposing the injustice, and seeing a common interest within the subordinate group in eliminating the injustice. Not all subordinated groups, however, develop oppositional consciousness.

References

Adamson, F. (2004) 'Displacement, diaspora mobilization, and transnational cycles of political violence', in J. Tirman (ed.) *The maze of fear: security and migration after 9/11*, New York: The New Press, 45–58.
Adamson, F. (2012) 'Constructing the diaspora: diaspora identity politics and transnational social movements' in T. Lyons and P. Mandaville (eds) *Politics from afar: transnational diasporas and networks*, New York: Columbia University Press, 25–42.
Amarasingam, A. (2015) *Pain, pride, and politics: social movement activism and the Sri Lankan Tamil diaspora in Canada*, Athens, GA: University of Georgia Press.
Anderson, B. (1991) *Imagined communities: reflections on the origin and spread of nationalism*, New York: Verso.
Anderson, B. (1992) *Long-distance nationalism: world capitalism and the rise of identity politics (CASA Wertheim Lecture)*, Amsterdam: University of Amsterdam Press.
Baser, B. (2016) *Diasporas and homeland conflicts: a comparative perspective*, New York: Routledge.
Bauböck, R. (2010) 'Cold constellations and hot identities: political theory questions about transnationalism and diaspora', in R. Bauböck and T. Faist (eds) *Diaspora and transnationalism: concepts, theories and methods*, Amsterdam: Amsterdam University Press, 295–321.
Bercovitch, J. (2007) 'A neglected relationship: diasporas and conflict resolution', in H. Smith and P. Stares (eds) *Diasporas in conflict: peace-makers or peace-wreckers*, New York: United Nations University Press, 17–38.
Boccagni, P. (2010) 'Private, public or both? On the scope and impact of transnationalism in immigrants' everyday lives', in R. Bauböck and T. Faist (eds) *Diaspora and transnationalism: concepts, theories and methods*, Amsterdam: Amsterdam University Press, 185–203.
Bolzman, C. (2011) 'The transnational practices of Chilean migrants in Switzerland', *International Migration*, 49 (3), 144–67, doi: 10.1111/j.1468-2435.2011.00693.x.
Brubaker, R. (2005) 'The "diaspora" diaspora', *Ethnic and Racial Studies*, 28 (1), 1–19, doi: 10.1080/014198 7042000289997.
Bruneau, M. (2010) 'Diasporas, transnational spaces and communities', in R. Bauböck and T. Faist (eds) *Diaspora and transnationalism: concepts, theories and methods*, Amsterdam: Amsterdam University Press, 35–50.
Byman, D., P. Chalk, B. Hoffman, W. Rosenau and D. Brannan (2001) *Trends in outside support for insurgent movement*, Santa Monica, CA: RAND.

Cohen, R. (1997) *Global diasporas: an introduction*, Seattle: University of Washington Press.
DeWind, J. and R. Segura (2014) 'Diaspora-government relations in forging US foreign policies', in J. DeWind and R. Segura (eds) *Diaspora lobbies and the US government: convergence and divergence in making foreign policy*, New York: SSRC and New York University Press, 3–28.
Fair, C. C. (2005) 'Diaspora involvement in insurgencies: insights from the Khalistan and Tamil Eelam movements', *Nationalism and Ethnic Politics*, 11 (1), 125–56, doi: 10.1080/13537110590927845.
Faist, T. (2010) 'Diaspora and transnationalism: what kind of dance partners?', in R. Bauböck and T. Faist (eds) *Diaspora and transnationalism: concepts, theories and methods*, Amsterdam: Amsterdam University Press, 9–34.
Faist, T. (2012) 'Towards a transnational methodology: methods to address methodological nationalism, essentialism, and positionality', *Revue Européenne des Migrations Internationales*, 28 (1), 51–70, available at: https://remi.revues.org/5761.
Gamson, W. A. (1975) *The strategy of social protest*, Homewood, IL: Dorsey Press.
Gamson, W. A. and D. S. Meyer (1996) 'Framing political opportunity', in D. McAdam, J. D. McCarthy and M. N. Zald (eds) *Comparative perspectives on social movements: political opportunities, mobilizing structures, and cultural framings*, New York: Cambridge University Press, 275–90.
Glick Schiller, N. and G. E. Fouron (1999) 'Terrains of blood and nation: Haitian transnational social fields', *Ethnic and Racial Studies*, 22 (2), 340–66, doi: 10.1080/014198799329512.
Goodwin, J. and J. M. Jasper (1999) 'Caught in a winding, snarling vine: the structural bias of political process theory', *Sociological Forum*, 14 (1), 27–54, doi: 10.1023/A:1021684610881.
Itzigsohn, J. and D. Villacrés (2008) 'Migrant political transnationalism and the practice of democracy: Dominican external voting rights and Salvadoran home town associations', *Ethnic and Racial Studies*, 31 (4), 664–86, doi: 10.1080/01419870701784497.
Jasper, J. M. (2012) 'Introduction: from political opportunity structures to strategic interaction', in J. Goodwin and J. M. Jasper (eds) *Contention in context: political opportunities and the emergence of protest*, Stanford: Stanford University Press, 1–33.
Karpathakis, A. (1999) 'Home society politics and immigrant political incorporation: the case of Greek immigrants in New York City', *International Migration Review*, 33 (1), 55–78, doi: 10.2307/2547322.
Koinova, M. (2013) 'Four types of diaspora mobilization: Albanian diaspora activism for Kosovo independence in the US and the UK', *Foreign Policy Analysis*, 9 (4), 433–53, doi: 10.1111/j.1743-8594.2012.00194.x.
Koinova, M. (2014) 'Why do conflict-generated diasporas pursue sovereignty-based claims through state-based or transnational channels? Armenian, Albanian and Palestinian diasporas in the UK compared', *European Journal of International Relations*, 20 (4), 1043–71, doi: 10.1177/1354066113509115.
Kriesi, H. (2004) 'Political context and opportunity', in D. A. Snow, S. A. Soule and H. Kriesi (eds) *The Blackwell companion to social movements*, Malden, MA: Blackwell, 67–90.
Landolt, P. (2008) 'The transnational geographies of immigrant politics: insights from a comparative study of migrant grassroots organizing', *The Sociological Quarterly*, 49 (1), 53–77, doi: 10.1111/j.1533-8525.2007.00106.x.
Lyon, A. J. and E. M. Uçarer (2001) 'Mobilizing ethnic conflict: Kurdish separatism in Germany and the PKK', *Ethnic and Racial Studies*, 24 (6), 925–48, doi: 10.1080/713766482.
Lyons, T. and P. Mandaville (2012) 'Introduction: politics from afar: transnational diasporas and networks', in T. Lyons and P. Mandaville (eds) *Politics from afar: transnational diasporas and networks*, New York: Columbia University Press, 1–23
McAdam, D. (1996) 'Conceptual origins, current problems, future directions', in D. McAdam, J. D. McCarthy and M. N. Zald (eds) *Comparative perspectives on social movements: political opportunities, mobilizing structures, and cultural framings*, New York: Cambridge University Press, 23–40.
McAdam, D. (1999) *Political process and the development of black insurgency, 1930–1970*, Chicago: University of Chicago Press.
McAdam, D., S. Tarrow and C. Tilly (2001) *Dynamics of contention*, New York: Cambridge University Press.
McCarthy, J. D. and M. N. Zald (1977) 'Resource mobilization and social movements: a partial theory', *American Journal of Sociology*, 82 (6), 1212–41, doi: 10.1086/226464.
Meyer, D. S. (2004) 'Protest and political opportunities', *Annual Review of Sociology*, 30, 125–45, doi: 10.1146/annurev.soc.30.012703.110545.
Meyer, D. S. and D. C. Minkoff (2004) 'Conceptualizing political opportunity', *Social Forces*, 82 (4), 1457–92, doi: 10.1353/sof.2004.0082.
Miller, A. (2011) '"Doing" transnationalism: the integrative impact of Salvadoran cross-border', *Journal of Ethnic and Migration Studies*, 37 (1), 43–60, doi: 10.1080/1369183X.2011.521362.

Mobilization (2003) 'Book symposium: focus on dynamics of contention', *Mobilization: An International Journal*, 8 (1), 107–141.
Mobilization (2011) 'Dynamics of contention, ten years on', *Mobilization: An International Journal*, 16 (1), 1–116, available at: http://mobilizationjournal.org/toc/maiq/16/1.
Morris, A. and N. Braine (2001) 'Social movements and oppositional consciousness', in J. Mansbridge and A. Morris (eds) *Oppositional consciousness: the subjective roots of social protest*, Chicago: University of Chicago Press, 20–37.
Olson, M. (1965) *The logic of collective action: public goods and the theory of groups*, Cambridge, MA: Harvard University Press.
Østergaard-Nielsen, E. (2003) 'The politics of migrants' transnational political practices', *International Migration Review*, 37 (3), 760–86, doi: 10.1111/j.1747-7379.2003.tb00157.x.
Piven, F. F. and R. A. Cloward (1979) *Poor people's movements: why they succeed, how they fail*, New York: Vintage Books.
Polletta, F. (1999) 'Snarls, quacks, and quarrels: culture and structure in political process theory', *Sociological Forum*, 14 (1), 63–70, doi: 10.1023/A:1021688711790.
Polleta, F. and J. M. Jasper (2001) 'Collective identity and social movements', *Annual Review of Sociology*, 27, 283–305, doi: 10.1146/annurev.soc.27.1.283.
Safran, W. (1991) 'Diasporas in modern societies: myth of homeland and return', *Diaspora: A Journal of Transnational Studies*, 1 (1), 83–99, doi: 10.1353/dsp.1991.0004.
Shain, Y. (1994/95) 'Ethnic diasporas and U.S. foreign policy', *Political Science Quarterly*, 109 (5), 811–41, available at: www.psqonline.org/article.cfm?IDArticle=13388.
Shain, Y. (2005) *The frontier of loyalty: political exiles in the age of the nation state*, Ann Arbor: University of Michigan Press.
Shain Y. and A. Barth (2003) 'Diasporas and international relations theory', *International Organization*, 57 (3), 449–79, doi: 10.1017/S0020818303573015.
Sheffer, G. (2003) *Diaspora politics: at home abroad*, New York: Cambridge University Press.
Smith, H. and P. Stares (eds) (2007) *Diasporas in conflict: peace-makers or peace-wreckers*, New York: United Nations University Press.
Sökefeld, M. (2006) 'Mobilizing in transnational space: a social movement approach to the formation of diaspora', *Global Networks*, 6 (3), 265–84, doi: 10.1111/j.1471-0374.2006.00144.x.
Tarrow, S. G. (2011) *Power in movement: social movements and contentious politics*, New York: Cambridge University Press.
Tölölyan, K. (1996) 'Rethinking diaspora(s): stateless power in the transnational moment', *Diaspora: A Journal of Transnational Studies*, 5 (1), 3–36, doi: 10.1353/dsp.1996.0000.
Wald, K. D. (2008) 'Homeland interest, hostland politics: politicized ethnic identity among Middle Eastern heritage groups in the United States', *International Migration Review*, 42 (2), 273–301, doi: 10.1111/j.1747-7379.2008.00125.x.
Waldinger, R. and D. Fitzgerald (2004) 'Transnationalism in question', *American Journal of Sociology*, 109 (5), 1177–95, doi: 10.1086/381916.
Wayland, S. (2004) 'Ethnonationalist networks and transnational opportunities: the Sri Lankan Tamil diaspora', *Review of International Studies*, 30 (3), 405–26, doi: 10.1017/S0260210504006138.
Whittier, N. E. (1997) 'Political generations, micro-cohorts, and the transformation of social movements', *American Sociological Review*, 62 (5), 760–78, doi: 10.2307/2657359.

6
Performing diaspora

Alpha Abebe

> *A confluence of communities*
> *lost and found*
> *dispersed and displaced*
> *are meeting through*
> *maps of my veins.*
> *Bubbling and stumbling*
> *over language and accent,*
> *building new canals of identity.*
> *A city-scape of sediments*
> *of homeland and citizenship*
> *are flowing over this bedrock I call home.*
> *Can you hear this river roar,*
> *as it runs through me?*
>
> 'This River Runs Through Me' by Jyotsana Saha (2017)

Grappling with the complexity of diasporas

'Diaspora', as a categorical and theoretical term, is elusive by design. It describes social groups and phenomena that are inherently fluid and ambiguous. In its traditional biblical usage, the term described the specific dispersal of the Jewish people (Cohen 1997; Tölölyan 1991). However, since then, 'diaspora' has been expanded and abstracted by scholars, policy-makers, artists, community groups and others who have used the term to describe countless population and social movements across and within geographic borders. In contemporary discourse, 'diaspora' is also commonly used interchangeably with 'immigrant' and/or ascribed to entire groups of people who have ancestral ties to one nation-state and currently live in another. This is a functional, often crude, way to categorize people and may or may not align with the way people within these groups identify. Things admittedly get messier when we instead use people's own identifications and social practices as a starting point for analysis; however, what we lose in clarity we gain in insight.

Diasporas can be understood as groups of dispersed people who share symbolic and/or material associations to an idealized homeland, which may or may not take the form of an existing nation-state. These 'associations' bear meaning to the extent that individuals and social groups engage with, interpret and leverage them for various means. Therefore, the substantive nature of a diaspora – beyond its use as a crude demographic category – emerges when one observes and analyses a diaspora *in action*. Sometimes this phenomenon is readily accessible, such as when a group of people forms an organization based on shared ties to a homeland (for example, a hometown association). However, this captures only a fraction of the ways in which dispersed people construct, interpret and instrumentalize relationships with their homelands. Moreover, traditional analytical frameworks and methodological tools are designed to generalize and classify social phenomena, which can serve to mask the complex and fluid nature of diasporic identities and social practices. What is needed to fill this knowledge gap is a way of thinking that is flexible and a form of representation that is nuanced – and this is easily found in the arts.

The arts play a critical role in providing people with a platform from which to make sense of, construct and express their diasporic identifications. In the arts, there is ample space for (re)interpretation and ambiguity, and people are given a licence to *explore* without the expectation that they will necessarily *discover*. Diasporas include individuals who have social, emotional and/or material ties that span across various geographies and histories, and the arts provide the opportunity to engage with these parts of their lives without necessarily laying full claim to them. For social scientists, diasporic artistic practice and products are invaluable both as analytical material and tools. They offer insight into the ways that people negotiate and interpret diasporic identities, and can serve as a lens through which to examine the broader social relations and practices that constitute their lives. Artists developed nuanced and sophisticated ways to express and represent diasporic themes long before social scientists, and many of the early cultural theorists who shaped the direction of diaspora studies utilized the arts to inform their analysis and develop their theoretical frameworks (Gilroy 1993a, 1993b; Hall 1990; Said 1990). When we enter the world of the arts, we are reminded of the interpretive, symbolic and performative nature of social constructs, including diasporas, and we are invited to engage meaningfully with this complexity rather than to mask it.

Theorizing diasporic artistic practice

One can define the term 'art' in many ways that would encompass just about any form of expression. However, for the purposes of understanding its relationship to diasporas, I focus here on art as an intentional form of creative expression through various mediums such as music, theatre, film, photography, illustration, literature, poetry and sculpture. In their practice, artists are often doing many things at once, including deep introspection, social observation and commentary, expressing personal feelings and ideas, and speaking and catering to an external audience. Historically, artists play the role of representing thoughts, feelings and experiences that are otherwise difficult to express in other forms of communication. This is particularly true of themes about pain, loss, love and loneliness, which we feel more intensely than we can usually find the words or courage to express in plain speech. 'It is art, according to the "postmodern primitive", Cherokee artist Jimmie Durham, that is "looking for connections that cannot, may be, should not, be made"' (Chambers 2012: 60). Art creates opportunities for empathy and shared experience. We are drawn into someone else's narrative, and through its abstraction we are given the room to bring our own experiences and interpretations to bear.

The migrant, nomad, traveller, outcast, outsider – these are often the people in society in the best position to see things that others take for granted, and describe them with detail, texture and meaning. As such, diasporas and art have a longstanding and important relationship, and each helps to inform and constitute the other. Diasporic artists are often able to communicate themes that are both specific to their diasporic experience and common to the human condition. As Harney et al. (2003: 19) recount:

> Not surprisingly, artists in the visual, literary, musical and theatrical realms have been at the frontiers of exploring the depths and riches of memory, referencing traces of cultural traditions, reclaiming them as their own and mixing them with new experiences as they create collages of artistic and personal identity. In the works of many visual artists, mythologized, partially remembered motifs serve as markers of belonging within the unfamiliar cultural terrain of the diaspora. However, in the best of these arts, they are never quoted directly but rather incorporated into a highly syncretic aesthetic that draws as much from the experiences of displacement as from nostalgia for home.

The tensions between belonging and exclusion, loss and discovery, tradition and reinterpretation, and real and imagined are highly productive when it comes to the arts, and people who connect with a diasporic experience are often hypersensitive to these boundaries and straddle them on a regular basis.

Stuart Hall (1990: 236–7) drew on Caribbean and black British cinema to theorize on cultural identities, noting that these are not simply reflected in but also constituted through the act of representation.

> We have been trying to theorise identity as constituted, not outside but within representation; and hence of cinema, not as a second-order mirror held up to reflect what already exists, but as that form of representation which is able to constitute us as new kinds of subjects, and thereby enable us to discover places from which to speak. . . . This is the vocation of modern black cinemas: by allowing us to see and recognise the different parts and histories of ourselves, to construct those points of identification, those positionalities we call in retrospect our 'cultural identities'.

Both Stuart Hall and Paul Gilroy refer to the role of music to reinforce this point about the constitutive relationship between art and diasporic identities. Hall (1990) argues that the culture of Rastafarianism and the music of reggae helped to construct and articulate a distinct Afro-Caribbean identity that local and diasporic Jamaicans began to identify with in the 1970s.

In his seminal work on the black Atlantic diaspora, Gilroy (1993a) discusses the convergence of musical traditions, and the power that this had in the emergence of 'blackness' as a distinct social, political and cultural identity in the United States and Britain. Also, drawing on the example of reggae, Gilroy (1993a: 82) argues that

> once its own hybrid origins in rhythm and blues were effectively concealed, it [reggae] ceased, in Britain, to signify an exclusively ethnic, Jamaican style and derived a different kind of cultural legitimacy both from a new global status and from its expression of what might be termed a pan-Caribbean culture.

Through this example, we see how art and culture are shaped, changed and reinforced as they move through transnational social fields. The diasporic identities that are constituted in these fields are also 'constantly producing and reproducing themselves anew, through transformation and difference' (Hall 1990: 235).

Many diasporic artists in North America and Europe come from racialized communities, and before they even have a chance to tell their story are assumed to have connections 'elsewhere' because of their skin colour. This representation as the 'other' can follow them through their artistic practice, including expectations that they will communicate a distinct (and/or essentialized) narrative, image or aesthetic through their work. These expectations can come from a commercial market thirsty for exotic art, from gatekeepers within diasporic communities policing the boundaries of cultural authenticity, or from the artists themselves as they negotiate their own relationships to their heritage and homelands (Laine 2015; Mathur 2011). It is important, however, that the academic analysis of diasporic artistic practice looks past, not through, these parochial lenses. Chambers (2012) implores art historians and critics to appreciate the dynamic relationship between artists' identities and their work. Chambers (2012: i) suggests that the work of Australian aboriginal painter Kathleen Petyarre and black British installation artist Isaac Julien should be viewed as more than 'merely an addition to the existing canon – "aboriginal culture", "black art"'. A more flexible and interpretive lens 'invites us to think less of art and rather more with art; less to passively absorb the history of art and rather to work with art as a history that harbours a critical language still to be announced' (Chambers 2012: i–ii).

Using the example of the late Alexander 'Skunder' Boghossian, a painter of Ethiopian and Armenian descent who resided in the United States, Farrell (2003: 26) demonstrates the differences in these approaches to diasporic art.

> When categorized as an Ethiopian artist, Boghossian may be seen as to have been a vessel, a passive bearer and preserver of culture, on who carried within him the past traditions of his people. As a diasporan artist, on the other hand, he was an active interpreter and reassembler of the ocean of cultural signs from the past as encountered in his travels, for present and future generations.

Many scholars who analyse diasporic artistic practice observe a blend of aesthetics and themes drawn together from various geographic and historical influences. Karetzky (2016) explores the work of contemporary artists in the Chinese diaspora. This art often draws on traditional themes and techniques such as Chinese script, while also utilizing contemporary visual elements through new media, and *speaking* to broader Western and cosmopolitan issues. 'These subjects and materials not only forged a link with their homeland, but they also brought their work to the attention of the West' (Karetzky 2016: 282). The dynamic between authenticity and (re)interpretation is a tenuous one, and diasporic artists either consciously experiment with this relationship or find themselves unwittingly implicated by their subject positions.

Holton (2016) examines young people of Portuguese descent in the United States who have recently 'discovered' the traditional Portuguese musical tradition *fado*. *Fado* music is known for its melancholic sounds and themes of nostalgia and mourning, and its performance serves as an important marker of old-world cultural tradition and authenticity. However, Holton (2016: 224) describes the role that new media has played in inspiring a group of young *fadista*s to learn, perform and broadcast this historical musical tradition:

> The second-generation use of technology also facilitates a shift in *fado*'s traditional ethos. A performative value system that for much of the twentieth century emphasized shrouding, secrecy and mystery has been challenged by a new generation of *fadista*s who participate in a more upfront and direct ethos of self-exposure and self-promotion.

Performing *fado* music resonated with these young people because it offered a link to their ancestry and past, but also because they felt it connected to their own angst and passions as they experienced love and loss. Digital media and YouTube served as both a portal and platform for this cultural artistic practice – sustaining and transforming multigenerational diasporic identities in the process. Just as Anderson (1983) demonstrated the impact of print media on the rise of contemporary nation-states, Appadurai (1996) analysed the social impact that electronic media had, and continues to have, in an age of hyper-globalization and mass migration. 'Such media transform the field of mass mediation because they offer new resources and new disciplines for the construction of imagined selves and imagined worlds' (Appadurai 1996: 3).

Contemporary discourse on diasporas often celebrates and romanticizes the notion of hybrid identities and transnational connections and experiences. The arts provide an especially comfortable space for this discourse, where one can indulge in the romance and melancholy of belonging everywhere yet nowhere at once. However, it is important to note that, like all social practices, diasporic arts are structured and implicated in the power dynamics of the transnational spaces within which they are created and consumed. In an analysis of musical performance in the diaspora, Ramnarine (2007: 11–12) offers the term 'calibration' in place of the more common language used to describe the blended nature of diasporic identities and artistic practice (for example, interculturalism, hybridities and in-betweenness).

> Calibration points to the disjunctures between representations and realities, between the visible and the invisible. It moves away from bipolar models. Instead of trying to work through the complexities of creative 'mixes', it shifts attention to competing claims, theoretical disagreements, and even social and musical realities that might not have much to do with our conceptual models.

Viewing diasporic arts through this framework of 'calibration' reminds us that these practices are not simply the individual artist blending cultural influences within a vacuum, but rather a *social* process of positioning and repositioning oneself in relation to proximate and generalized (imagined) others.

Furthermore, whatever is social is also political. While seemingly innocuous, the arts offer a stage, a platform and a voice – all of which create opportunities to gain or reclaim influence, capital and power. This might manifest in obvious ways, such as the Haitian-American singer Wyclef Jean regularly referring to Haiti in his music and translating his pop culture success in the USA into a presidential bid in Haiti, albeit an unsuccessful one (Jean-Charles 2014). It might also take a more diffuse form, such as Tamil artists in the UK using their art to challenge gender norms in Tamil communities, or fashioning their aesthetics to cater to Western commercial markets that are partial to 'authentic' Tamil imagery (Laine 2015). In each case, there is a lot at stake in the representational politics that shape diasporic artistic practice. Art opens opportunities to reconfigure social spaces, historical narratives, contemporary paradigms, personal identities – and bank accounts! Diasporic art brings these dynamics into a transnational context, with added dimensions and implications for us to consider.

A personal lens into diaspora and art

When I travelled to Ethiopia in 1999, it felt very much like a homecoming. This was odd, because it was my first time ever being there. I was born and raised in Canada to Ethiopian parents. My first encounter with the sights, sounds and smells of Addis Ababa should have been jarring at worst, unfamiliar at best. But it felt like home instead. The family I had come to know so well by name were now the people embracing me. I was walking through the very structures and landscapes that once hung as art on my wall. I had eaten all these same dishes before, just never this good. I would also have numerous encounters and experiences that would serve

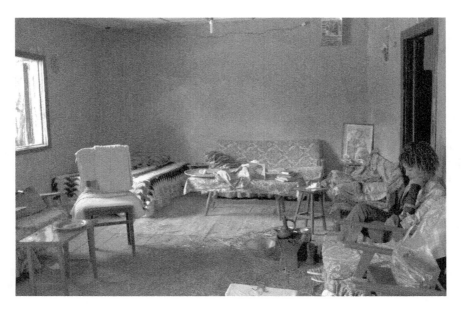

Ethiopia 2013 © Alpha Abebe

to remind me that I did not quite belong. Yes, I was very much connected to this place, but Toronto was also very much my home. However, I learned to live rather comfortably within this ambiguity. It created no existential crisis, it just was.

When we developed the negatives from that first trip to Ethiopia, my mother chastised me on discovering that I had taken very few pictures of myself or other people. She did not

Ethiopia 2009 © Alpha Abebe

Performing diaspora

Ethiopia 2016 © Alpha Abebe

understand why I needed so many pictures of landscapes, architecture and cows. However, that album remains one of my most valued possessions to this day. It is an artefact. I knew I would want to remember what it felt like to be in that exact place at that precise moment, and when memory would fade, those pictures would just have to do. Years later, I would rediscover the storytelling power of photography. It is the tool I use to capture and communicate ideas, experiences and emotions for which I have no other vocabulary. It has been my trusted companion on subsequent trips to Ethiopia, helping me to create memories where there were none, and serving as a repository of moments, encounters and experiences that I knew I would want to remember one day.

As a scholar of diaspora studies (with constructivist leanings), I view my photography as a social practice, and remain attentive to the role it plays in engendering a sense of connection to my country of origin and in shaping my social relations within and outside Ethiopia. Over the years, I have had various opportunities to share my photographs of Ethiopia through exhibitions, social media and academic publications. Each instance is an opportunity to revisit my experiences in and relationship to Ethiopia, and how I might want to represent this personally and to my audience. Heraclitus stated that 'no man ever steps in the same river twice', and this metaphor of fluidity and change helps to describe the different feelings that are evoked and shifts in my focus each time I return to my existing images or head back to Ethiopia with my camera again. What photography has offered me is a mechanism with which to engage with Ethiopia, a language to describe these experiences, and space to (re)imagine who I am in relation to this place and its peoples.

This understanding of photography is useful as a framework for thinking not only about broader diasporic artistic practice, but also about the manner in which diasporic identities are constructed, sustained and shifted. As part of the diaspora, my relationship to Ethiopia is defined by my distance from it as much as my proximity and connection. It took a lot of *work* to transform what could otherwise have been an immaterial ancestral connection into a meaningful and intimate one, and in my case, photography was an important part of that work. For those who are not inclined towards the arts, their *work* might involve launching a charitable project in their country of origin, attending a place of worship with people from the same ethno-national community, engaging in long-distance political projects, or cooking national dishes at home. Like art, each of these is an example of a social practice. They are not expressions of a primordial fixed diasporic identity, but rather processes by which people actively construct and (re)define these identities. It is precisely the act of *identifying* with a homeland, be it a nation-state or otherwise, that points to the conceptual value of 'diaspora' beyond an indication of ancestry or migration. As a framework, it offers a glimpse behind the scenes where identities are constructed and imbued with meaning, and casts a spotlight onto the ways that these identities are represented and performed.

Note

The section on a 'personal lens' contains material first published on the Oxford Diasporas Programme website: www.migration.ox.ac.uk/odp/ethiopia-photo-essay.shtml.

References

Anderson, B. R. O. G. (1983) *Imagined communities: reflections on the origin and spread of nationalism*, London: Verso.
Appadurai, A. (1996) *Modernity at large: cultural dimensions of globalization*, Minneapolis: University of Minnesota Press.
Chambers, I. (2012) *Location borders and beyond*, self-published: CreateSpace.
Cohen, R. (1997) *Global diasporas: an introduction*, London: UCL Press.
Farrell, L. A. (2003) *Looking both ways: art of the contemporary African diaspora*, New York: Snoeck.
Gilroy, P. (1993a) *The black Atlantic: modernity and double consciousness*, London: Verso.
Gilroy, P. (1993b) *Small acts: thoughts on the politics of black cultures*, London: Serpent's Tail.
Hall, S. (1990) 'Cultural identity and diaspora', in J. Rutherford (ed.) *Identity: community, culture, difference*, London: Lawrence & Wishart, 222–37.
Harney, E., J. Donaldson, A. Debela and K. Katchka (2003) *Ethiopian passages: contemporary art from the diaspora*, London: Philip Wilson.
Holton, K. D. (2016) '*Fado* in diaspora: online internships and self display among YouTube generation performers in the US', *Luso-Brazilian Review*, 53 (1), 210–32, doi: 10.3368/lbr.53.1.210.
Jean-Charles, R. M. (2014) 'The myth of diaspora exceptionalism: Wyclef Jean performs *jaspora*', *American Quarterly*, 66 (3), 835–52, doi: 10.1353/aq.2014.0048.
Karetzky, P. E. (2016) 'Contemporary art by Chinese diaspora in a global age', *East Asian Journal of Popular Culture*, 2 (2), 267–85, doi: 10.1386/eapc.2.2.267_1.
Laine, A. (2015) 'Locating art practice in the British Tamil diaspora', *World Art*, 5 (2), 199–222, doi: 10.1080/21500894.2015.1036457.
Mathur, S. (2011) *The migrant's time: rethinking art history and diaspora*, Williamstown, MA: Sterling and Francine Clark Art Institute.
Ramnarine, T. K. (2007) 'Musical performance in the diaspora: introduction', *Ethnomusicology Forum*, 16 (1), 1–17, doi: 10.1080/17411910701276310.
Saha, J. (2017) *The river runs through me*, unpublished work.
Said, E. (1990) 'Reflections on exile', in R. Ferguson (ed.) *Out there: marginalization and contemporary cultures*, New York: New Museum of Contemporary Art, 357–63.
Tölölyan, K. (1991) 'The nation-state and its others: in lieu of a preface', *Diaspora*, 1 (1), 3–7, doi: 10.1353/dsp.1991.0008.

7
Embodying belonging
Diaspora's racialization and cultural citizenship

Taku Suzuki

Avtar Brah (1996: 193), a leading diaspora theorist, asks 'When does a location become home? What is the difference between "feeling at home" and staking claim to a place as one's own?' Many existing studies on diaspora have focused on their ambivalent sense of belonging to the receiving society and the concrete or symbolic connections that they forge and maintain with their ancestral homeland, as well as the transnational processes through which diasporic groups shape their identities or, as Clifford (1997) puts it, their 'roots' and 'routes'. The theme's popularity is unsurprising, considering that the term 'diaspora' refers to those who have left or have been forced to leave their homeland in the 'centre' and dispersed to 'peripheral' locations (Cohen 1997; Safran 1991).

However, once the 'dispersed' peoples have arrived and settled in their destinations, they are viewed as immigrants – newcomers to a pre-established society – by those who already live there. No matter which roots they originally hailed from and which routes they had taken before their arrival, diaspora inevitably become 'locals' under specific historical, political-economic and sociocultural circumstances of the country of their resettlement, a process that produces varying degrees and forms of belonging among them. In examining the process of 'diaspora becoming local', a conventional approach in migration studies has focused on *cultural* transformations that diasporic communities and individuals undergo in their new homes (Glick Schiller et al. 1992). However, more recent inquiries have critically examined 'exactly how identity and belonging are constructed not only culturally but also politically' (Christou 2006: 1044), paying attention to the existing power relations that shape member of a diaspora belonging to the receiving society.

Among the scholars who examine the role of power relations in the process of diasporas becoming local and its consequences on the sense of home and belonging are those who explore the social construction of diasporic bodies as constituting 'a site of enormous symbolic work and symbolic production' (Palumbo-Liu 2001: 82). These studies frequently draw on the concepts of racialization and cultural citizenship. Racialization is typically defined as a social process by which certain physical features or assumed biological characteristics of a particular group come to represent its members' inherent psychological, behavioural and/or moral characteristics (Miles 1989; Omi and Winant 1994). On the other hand, cultural citizenship is loosely defined as 'the production of cultural beliefs and practices necessary for national belonging' (Tsuda 2014: 409).

Two assumptions underpin the concepts of racialization and cultural citizenship. First, individuals are not unified and autonomous beings who exercise free will to position themselves in social relations, economic conditions or cultural climates. Instead, each individual is conceived of as a *subject*, 'a locus in which an incoherent (and often contradictory) plurality of such relational determinations interact' (de Certeau 1984: xi) and whose 'agency is created through situations and statuses conferred on them' (Scott 1992: 34). Diasporic individuals are then deemed to occupy a certain 'subject position', defined as 'a contradictory mix of confirming and contending "identities"' (O'Sullivan et al. 1994: 310; cited in Parreñas 2001: 31). Thus, diasporic individuals' belonging is defined here as contested, with shifting 'subject positions' in which they are placed and place themselves in relation to other individuals and institutions.

In this chapter, I identify several ways in which scholars have examined the actors and the institutions that influence the process of diasporas becoming local through the theoretical lenses of racialization and cultural citizenship to explain diasporas' sense of belonging to their country of resettlement. Scholars have relied on the racialization concept in migration and diaspora studies to highlight the roles played by the receiving states, capital and the labour market in shaping particular subject positions. Similarly, scholars who find the implicit 'methodological nationalism' (Glick Schiller et al. 1992) in migration studies wanting have been drawn to the concept of 'cultural citizenship' as a mode of sociocultural participation (Rosaldo 1994) and a process of subject-making in the complex web of state and capital powers (Ong 1996) to understand the complex and often contested relationships formed by diasporas with the receiving state and its dominant population.

Racialization of diasporas: signifying belonging

Two of the most influential definitions of racialization have been proposed by Miles (1989) and later by Omi and Winant (1994), who have coined the phrase 'racial formation'. Miles (1989: 76) defines racialization as follows:

> a dialectical process by which meaning is attributed to particular biological features of human beings, as a result of which individuals may be assigned to a general category of persons which reproduces itself biologically. . . . The process of racialization of human beings entails the racialization of the processes in which they participate and the structures and institutions that result.

Omi and Winant (1994: 55–6) suggest racial formation as 'the sociohistorical process by which racial categories are created, inhabited, transformed, and destroyed. . . . Race is a matter of both social structure and cultural representation.' Scholars who have attempted to theorize the process of diaspora becoming local, especially those who have examined the experiences that the diaspora from non-European regions undergo in their resettlement destinations with predominantly European-origin populations, have adopted these concepts to explain diasporas' forms and degrees of belonging to the receiving society.

The racialization concept draws on the Foucauldian conceptualization of discursive embodiment, elaborating on feminist and queer theorists' use of the framework. Following Foucault's (1978) propositions on the discursive production of sexual bodies, these theorists have envisioned human bodies not as 'ahistorical, precultural, or natural objects' but as materials for 'corporal inscription', upon which social differences are 'inscribed, marked, engraved' through public discourses (Grosz 1994: 53). Migration and diaspora scholars have attempted to theorize such inscription of meanings onto the bodies of diasporic individuals in the receiving societies.

By refusing to presume the existence of 'raw' (blank, natural or abstract) bodies prior to their social constitutions, the racializing embodiment of diasporic subjects is conceptualized as involving processes in which societal influences inscribe and naturalize certain sociocultural identities onto their bodies (physiques and behaviours), while diasporic individuals accommodate, negotiate or resist these imposed categories through their daily practices.

Among recent studies, some emphasize the macro-scale forces of political-economic structures as shapers of the meanings assigned to diasporic individuals' bodies. Other studies highlight the micro-scale practices of racializing embodiment, such as diasporic individuals' everyday encounters with local residents of the receiving society, as key mechanisms (Yarbrough 2010: 250). In the latter type of studies, theorists often draw on concepts of performance and performativity to capture the profoundly interactive nature of the process of racializing embodiment.

Racial embodiment by state and capital

Sociologists dealing with transnational immigrants have explored racialization by state policies and labour market mechanisms. State-sanctioned or state-perpetrated violence is an example of how the state-imposed racializing embodiment manifests itself. These studies have demonstrated how acts of violence effectively identify, isolate and exterminate 'others' from the 'self', *producing* the racialized self and in-group intimacy by forming 'persons out of what are otherwise diffuse, large-scale labels that have effects but no locations' out of human bodies (Appadurai 1998: 241). Meanwhile, sociological studies about migrant workers in the USA reveal numerous cases of labour market segmentations or 'occupational ghettorization' of non-European immigrants in certain industries, such as domestic service and light manufacturing (Bonacich et al. 2008; Glenn 1981). These scholars view racialization primarily in terms of the labour relationship in a capitalist market, comprising processes that 'involve the use of biological criteria (namely, phenotype, and so forth) to separate people into distinct groups for the purpose of domination and exploitation' (Inwood and Yarbrough 2010: 300). From their perspective, a state that receives diasporic groups, in partnership with capital, 'through its policies and laws, plays a crucial role in the project of racial formation' (Banerjee 2006: 428) of the groups. Banerjee's (2006) study of the *de facto* workplace racial segregation in the US information technology industry, facilitated by the government's H-1B visa issuance, exemplifies this approach.

Numerous scholars have examined the state and capital's influences on such racialized and often gendered labour market segmentations. For instance, Choy and Parreñas reveal how diasporic Filipinas have been systematically produced by the governments of the Philippines and the receiving countries as a 'racialized and gendered' labour force (Choy 2003: 9) in specialized labour markets, such as nursing and domestic work, and as socio-economically and spatially 'dislocated' (Parreñas 2001: 34) from the rest of society in their receiving states. In these studies, diasporic subjects are systematically classified under a racialized (and gendered, nationalized and ethnicized) category through labour market and residential spaces as they become local in the receiving societies.

Racial embodiment through performativity

Macro-scale processes are not the only forces for the racializing embodiment of members of a diaspora when they become locals in the receiving societies. Diasporans' physical bodies are 'vehicles' for individual subjects to exhibit these differences in a series of micro-scale situations in their daily lives (O'Connell 1999). These performances 'actively produce the body as a body of [a] determinate type' (Grosz 1994: x). They draw on Butler's (1990: 140) formulation of performativity, which claims that individuals cultivate (in the Foucauldian sense) their bodies as representations of a certain social identity through the 'stylized repetition of acts' that they consciously or unconsciously perform through gestures, subtle movements and comportment. From this perspective, an individual neither turns from a blank '"subject" before the constitution of a subject' into someone inscribed with a particular social identity, nor is he or she merely a 'puppet of sociocultural processes' (O'Connell 1999: 65). Instead, an individual is always and already *becoming* a certain socially defined subject through everyday performances *vis-à-vis* other members of society.

Many recent anthropological studies have drawn on performativity as a key mechanism of diasporic individuals' subject making by ethnographically portraying their racializing performances in mundane situations (Lundström 2009; Manalansan 2003; Matthews and Nagata 2014; Siu 2005; Suzuki 2010). For instance, the diasporic Japanese in Australia face racialization that legitimizes 'subject-formation, inclusion and exclusion, discrimination, inferiorization, exploitation, verbal abuse, and physical harassment and violence' (Rattansi 1995: 258, cited by Matthews and Nagata 2014: 141). Mathews and Nagata (2014: 151) argue that through frequent reminders of their outsider status in a society that self-identifies as a white nation, the diasporic individuals' '"Japaneseness" is . . . an identification that must be constantly enacted and reenacted, repeated and reiterated'.

The racializing embodiment could also be executed through repetitive performative enactments by the diasporic individuals themselves. Manalansan's (2003) study of gay Filipino dancers and performers in New York City, and Siu's (2005) portrayal of on-stage performances of beauty contestants in the diasporic Chinese community in Panama, demonstrate that the diasporic Filipinoness and Chineseness are represented through their bodily performances that are fuelled by 'the manner in which the [performers'] community asserts belonging in relation to the larger diaspora, to their nation of residence and to the [ancestral] homeland' (Siu 2005: 536). Similarly, some young Latin American diasporans in Sweden, who are keenly aware of their 'non-white marked bodies in the Swedish landscape of race', actively cultivate and display a certain 'Latino image' in public by learning salsa and merengue and frequenting Latin dance clubs (Lundström 2009: 715). Taking advantage of the increasing popularity of Latino music worldwide ('global latinoscape', as Lundström calls it), these diasporic individuals attempt to improve their social status in the receiving society through 'self-tropicalization' or performative self-racialization that 'conflate[s] them with an image of warm climates and tourism created in [the] constant interplay with racialized boundaries of nationhood' (Lundström 2009: 715). These micro-scale studies of everyday discourses and bodily performances by the majority members of the receiving society and the diasporic individuals themselves richly represent the dialectic process of diaspora's racializing embodiment 'through which any diacritic of social personhood – including class, ethnicity, generation, kinship/affinity, and positions within fields of power – comes to be essentialized, naturalized, and/or biologized' (Silverstein 2005: 364).

Cultural citizenship of diaspora

To address the varying degrees and modes of belonging experienced by diasporic individuals in the receiving society, some scholars have expanded the citizenship concept beyond a legal relationship between an individual and the state to 'a more total relationship, inflected by identity, social positioning, cultural assumptions, institutional practices and a sense of belonging' (Werbner and Yuval-Davis 1999: 4). They argue that the receiving society's population is typically divided along the 'impassable symbolic boundaries' between those deemed to truly belong and those who do not, and individual citizens' 'belongingness and otherness' are marked, fixed and naturalized through a 'typically binary system of representation' (Hall 1996: 445). Even diasporic individuals who have acquired legal citizenship in the receiving state may remain excluded from the 'universal citizen' status (Glenn 2002: 20–1), with equal economic, social and cultural rights.

In reviewing the proliferating scholarly discourses on citizenship, Tsuda (2014) lists three conceptualizations. 'Social citizenship' (Park 2005: 2–4) refers to equal social membership and rights of members of a state. 'Cultural citizenship' is 'the right to be different (in terms of race, ethnicity, or native language) with respect to the norms of the dominant national community, without compromising one's right to belong' to a nation-state (Rosaldo 1994: 57). 'Racial citizenship' means 'inclusion in the national community and equal access to social rights despite racial differences' from the dominant population (Tsuda 2014: 409).

These reconceptualizations of citizenship call for more inclusive membership in a state that could accommodate racially embodied diasporic groups who are becoming local. Other scholars (Manalansan 2003; Ong 1999) argue that diasporic subjects may not always single-mindedly pursue the 'universal' (legal, economic, social, cultural and racial) belonging to a nation-state. Instead, they may seek flexibility in their national belonging and contest the very idea of a singular state as a sole anchor of diaspora's belonging. Here, citizenship is envisioned as a two-way negotiation between diasporic individuals and nation-states, a 'dual process of self-making and being made within webs of power', which delineates diasporic individuals' belonging to a receiving state through formalizing and formalized everyday practices (Ong 1996: 738).

Building on Ong's conceptualization of cultural citizenship, Manalansan's (2003) study of diasporic gay Filipinos in New York understands citizenship as a profoundly performative act. Manalansan (2003: 14) suggests that diasporans are not simply partial citizens on their way to complete cultural assimilation to achieve 'universal citizenship' but perform or contest the 'behavior, ideas, and images of the proper citizen' in the receiving state. Through the Indian diaspora's sense of belonging to India, the United States and the United Kingdom, Shukla (2003: 48–9) demonstrates that the ancestral homeland's independence from the British colonizers enabled the diaspora to 'have access to narratives of immigration, particularly those that stressed individual betterment, group legitimacy, and settlement abroad'. My ethnographic study on the Okinawan diaspora in Bolivia and the Okinawan–Bolivian 'return' diaspora in mainland Japan (Suzuki 2010) similarly describes them as actively performing their otherness in front of local residents as a strategic means to enhance their somatically represented symbolic capital, their real or imagined transnational mobility and agency, to counterbalance the precarious socio-economic realities and uncertain futures they face in both locations.

Building on these explorations of diaspora and citizenship, Chariandy (2011: 333), in examining African diasporic identities in Canada, calls for the conceptualization of 'diasporic citizenship', which is 'invested in social change through the ethical *contest* of the "larger political community" . . . a *contest* that emerges through the critical cultivation of diasporic legacies of victimization and struggle'. As Cho (2007: 468) states in her review of scholarly works, decoupling of citizenship from a singular nation-state allows imagining 'the possibility of citizenship in diaspora, of citizenship grounded in cultures whose relation to the nation is complex, circuitous, and uneasy'. Even if the citizenship concept has a problematic legacy of exclusion and discrimination, these innovations of the concept – social, cultural, racial and diasporic – have provided scholars with theoretical tools to comprehend the ambivalent, contradictory and contested belonging of diasporic individuals to their receiving states. By drawing on the concept, scholars can vividly portray the diasporic individuals' belongingness, not as a mere 'product' of the structural forces of state and capital, but as the dynamic 'process' where diasporic individuals actively participate. They daily accommodate, negotiate, resist and perform 'competing ideologies of belonging and citizenship to offset the multiple forms of displacements of life away from the homeland' (Manalansan 2003: 13). Cho (2007: 477) contends, 'To be diasporic is to be marked as culturally alien, and yet for such a subject to claim citizenship is to suspend difference in the name of the universal. . . . [Therefore,] to be a diasporic citizen is to fall headlong into that deliberate oxymoron.' Any critical scholarship on the process of a diaspora becoming local must then attend to this oxymoron to avoid eliding the contradictions inherent in a diaspora's sense of belonging.

Conclusion and prospects

As the studies reviewed in this chapter have shown, a diaspora's sense of belonging and 'home' are shaped and reshaped by structural forces of state and capital, as well as through everyday performative interactions with local residents of the receiving society. Many scholars of diaspora have searched for alternatives to conventional conceptual tools used in nation-state-centric migration studies, such as assimilation, discrimination and acculturation. Such tools presuppose a linear movement of migrants from their ancestral origin to their destination and an irreversible process of cultural and identity transformation from 'nationals' to 'immigrants', where racism and xenophobia are merely roadblocks to the inevitable 'universal citizenship'. In their efforts to make sense of conflicted and ambiguous subject positions and the sense of belonging, two alternatives are racialization and citizenship, both attempting to address the diaspora's everyday experiences of exclusion and inclusion, along with macro-scale impetuses and individual agencies that shape diasporic individuals' subject positions *vis-à-vis* local residents of the receiving state, without erasing the complex web of power spun across the diasporic origin and destination.

A scholar might question the theoretical value of these developments in diaspora studies, claiming that these concepts' definitions are not, on the surface, drastically different from those that have long existed in the sociology and anthropology of migration. What I believe to be the most valuable contribution of these concepts and the studies that embrace them is their effort to resist the nationalistic impetus, scholarly or otherwise, to 'contain' diasporic individuals within predetermined sociocultural and political boundaries of states. This effort could continue our expansion of legal and social categories of citizenship to make states more accommodating to peoples with diverse backgrounds while being critically attentive to both subtle and blatant racialization undergone by the marginalized. By contrast, we could imagine the world beyond the 'national order of things' (Malkki 1995) or the taken-for-granted vision of it as built on a collection of self-contained 'nations' that form 'states' with which all individuals must establish exclusive one-on-one relationships to achieve a proper sense of belonging and home. While acknowledging the exclusionary and violent legacies of the concepts of race and citizenship, I believe that re-imagining these concepts encourages us to embrace the ambiguities, contradictions and contestations as innate aspects of our own home, rather than to seek refuge in an illusionary stability of nation and state in the hope of anchoring our identities.

References

Appadurai, A. (1998) 'Dead certainty: ethnic violence in the era of globalization', *Public Culture*, 10 (2), 225–47, doi: 10.1111/1467-7660.00103.

Banerjee, P. (2006) 'Indian information technology workers in the United States: the H-1B visa, flexible production, and the racialization of labor', *Critical Sociology*, 32 (2/3), 425–45, doi: 10.1163/156916306777835295.

Bonacich, E., S. Alimahomed and J. B. Wilson (2008) 'The racialization of global labor', *American Behavioral Scientist*, 52 (3), 342–55, doi: 10.1177/0002764208323510.

Brah, A. (1996) *Cartographies of diaspora: contesting identities*, London: Routledge.
Butler, J. (1990) *Gender trouble*, London: Routledge.
Chariandy, D. (2011) 'Black Canadas and the question of diasporic citizenship', in A. N. M. Fleischmann, N. Van Styvendale and C. McCarroll (eds) *Narratives of citizenship: indigenous and diasporic peoples unsettle the nation-state*, Edmonton, AB: University of Alberta Press, 323–46.
Cho, L. (2007) 'Diasporic citizenship: inhabiting contradictions and challenging exclusions', *American Quarterly*, 59 (2), 467–78, doi: 10.1353/aq.2007.0035.
Choy, C. C. (2003) *Empire of care: nursing and migration in Filipino American history*, Durham, NC: Duke University Press.
Christou, A. (2006) 'Deciphering diaspora – translating transnationalism: family dynamics, identity constructions and the legacy of "home" in second-generation Greek-American return migration', *Ethnic and Racial Studies*, 29 (6), 1040–56, doi: 10.1080/01419870600960297.
Clifford, J. (1997) *Routes: travel and translation in the late twentieth century*, Cambridge, MA: Harvard University Press.
Cohen, R. (1997) *Global diasporas: an introduction*, Seattle, WA: University of Washington Press.
de Certeau, M. (1984) *The practice of everyday life*, translated by S. Rendall, Berkeley, CA: University of California Press.
Foucault, M. (1978) *The history of sexuality: an introduction*, translated by R. Hurley, New York: Vintage.
Glenn, E. N. (1981) 'Occupational ghettorization: Japanese American women and domestic service, 1905–1970', *Ethnicity*, 8 (4), 352–86, available at: http://files.eric.ed.gov/fulltext/EJ260981.pdf.
Glenn, E. N. (2002) *Unequal freedom: how race and gender shaped American citizenship and labor*, Cambridge, MA: Harvard University Press.
Glick Schiller, N., L. Basch and C. Blanc-Szanton (1992) 'Transnationalism: a new analytic framework for understanding migration', in N. Glick Schiller, L. Basch and C. Blanc-Szanton (eds) *Towards a transnational perspective on migration: race, class, ethnicity, and nationalism reconsidered*, New York: New York Academy of Science, 1–24.
Grosz, E. (1994) *Volatile bodies: toward a corporeal feminism*, Bloomington, IN: Indiana University Press.
Hall, S. (1996) 'New ethnicities', in D. Morley and K. H. Chen (eds) *Stuart Hall: critical dialogues in cultural studies*, New York: Routledge, 441–9.
Inwood, J. F. and R. A. Yarbrough (2010) 'Racialized places, racialized bodies: the impact of racialization on individual and place identities', *GeoJournal*, 75 (3), 299–301.
Lundström, C. (2009) '"People take for granted that you know how to dance Salsa and Merengue": transnational diasporas, visual discourses and racialized knowledge in Sweden's contemporary Latin music boom', *Social Identities*, 15 (5), 707–23, doi: 10.1080/13504630903205340.
Malkki, L. (1995) 'Refugees and exile: from "refugee studies" to the national order of things', *Annual Review of Anthropology*, 24, 495–523, doi: 10.1146/annurev.an.24.100195.002431.
Manalansan, M. F., IV (2003) *Global divas: Filipino gay men in the diaspora*, Durham, NC: Duke University Press.
Mathews, J. and Y. Nagata (2014) 'Pedagogies of the Japanese diaspora: racialization and sexualization in Australia', in G. Tsolidis (ed.) *Migration, diaspora and identity: cross-national experiences*, New York: Springer, 141–55.
Miles, R. (1989) *Racism*, London: Routledge.
O'Connell, S. (1999) 'Claiming one's identity: a constructivist/narrativist approach', in G. Weiss and H. F. Haber (eds) *Perspectives on embodiment: the intersections of nature and culture*, New York: Routledge, 62–78.
Omi, M. and H. Winant (1994) *Racial formation in the United States: from the 1960s to the 1990s*, New York: Routledge.
Ong, A. (1996) 'Cultural citizenship as subject-making: immigrants negotiate racial and cultural boundaries in the United States', *Current Anthropology*, 37 (5), 737–62, doi: 10.1086/204560.
Ong, A. (1999) *Flexible citizenship: the cultural logics of transnationality*, Durham, NC: Duke University Press.
O'Sullivan, T., J. Hartley, D. Saunders, M. Montgomery and J. Fiske (1994) *Key concepts in communication and cultural studies*, London: Routledge.
Palumbo-Liu, D. (2001) *Asian/American: racial frontier*, Durham, NC: Duke University Press.
Park, L. S.-H. (2005) *Consuming citizenship: children of Asian immigrant entrepreneurs*, Stanford, CA: Stanford University Press.
Parreñas, R. S. (2001) *Servants of globalization: women, migration, and domestic work*, Stanford, CA: Stanford University Press.

Rattansi, A. (1995) 'Just framing: ethnicities and racisms in a "postmodern" framework', in L. Nicholson and S. Seidman (eds) *Social postmodernism: beyond identity politics*, Cambridge: Cambridge University Press, 250–86.
Rosaldo, R. (1994) 'Cultural citizenship in San Jose, California', *Polar*, 17 (2), 57–63, doi: 10.1525/pol.1994.17.2.57.
Safran, W. (1991) '*Diasporas* in modern societies: myths of homeland and return', *Diaspora*, 1 (1), 83–99, doi: 10.1353/dsp.1991.0004.
Scott, J. (1992) 'Experience', in J. Butler and J. Scott (eds) *Feminists theorize the political*, New York: Routledge, 22–40.
Shukla, S. (2003) *India abroad: diasporic cultures of postwar America and England*, Princeton, NJ: Princeton University Press.
Silverstein, P. (2005) 'Immigrant racialization and the new savage slot: race migration, and immigration in the new Europe', *Annual Review of Anthropology*, 34, 363–84, doi: 10.1146/annurev.anthro.34.081804.120338.
Siu, L. (2005) 'Queen of the Chinese colony: gender, nation, and belonging in diaspora', *Anthropological Quarterly*, 78 (3), 511–42, doi: 10.1353/anq.2005.0041.
Suzuki, T. (2010) *Embodying diaspora: racializing Okinawan diaspora in Bolivia and Japan*, Honolulu: University of Hawai'i Press.
Tsuda, T. (2014) '"I'm American, not Japanese!": the struggle for racial citizenship among later-generation Japanese Americans', *Ethnic and Racial Studies*, 37 (3), 405–24, doi: 10.1080/01419870.2012.681675.
Werbner, P. and N. Yuval-Davis (1999) 'Introduction: women and the new discourse of citizenship', in P. Werbner and N. Yuval-Davis (eds) *Women, citizenship and difference*, New York: Zed Books, 1–38.
Yarbrough, R. A. (2010) 'Becoming "Hispanic" in the "New South": Central American immigrants' racialization experiences in Atlanta, GA, USA', *GeoJournal*, 75 (3), 249–60, doi: 10.1007/s10708-009-9304-7.

8
Music, dance and diaspora

Ananya Jahanara Kabir

Alma primitiva lejano dolor
Que los negros protestaron con la danza y el tambor
Que los negros protestaron y nadie lo escucho
Hoy es de lamento Chango, hoy es de lamento Chango

(O primitive soul, distant sorrow
which the Blacks resisted with dance and with drum
which the Blacks resisted, and no-one listened to them
Chango is lamenting today, Chango is lamenting today)

In 1970, two 'Nuyoricans' (Puerto Ricans living in New York) created a song about the West African divinity Chango, which described him lamenting the condition of slaves on a Caribbean plantation. An example of the genre since defined as 'salsa', the song, 'Alma primitiva', was meant to be danced to (McMains 2015); it still is, having attained the status of a classic. Here, the slaves protest their dehumanization through dancing and drumming (Fryer 2000), and it is precisely through dancing to the drums that the song was first received in New York and continues to be enjoyed worldwide. On the plantation, the slaves' protests might indeed have been silenced or ignored. But the salsa song's commemoration of those protests transforms trauma into a creative form that generates exhilaration and joy, as well as ensures, through various layers of technological capture, that it is disseminated and memorialized worldwide. The once unheard is now heard wherever someone presses 'play', or clicks on a YouTube link. Chango's laments have not gone in vain.[1]

Catalino Curet, who wrote the lyrics of 'Alma primitiva'; Nacho Sanabría, who first sang it; the musicians in Sanabría's band, Orquesta del Sabor; and all those who danced to the song in New York to the Orquesta's music were diasporic subjects formed out of complex travels between North America and the Caribbean. But they were also inheritors of a more distant diaspora: that of the Africans to the New World during the slave trade. The song evokes that diasporic experience through the phrases 'distant sorrow' and 'primitive soul', which recall the African homeland. Stretching over these spatiotemporal displacements is the divinity Chango, who, like other vodou divinities of West Africa, also made that diasporic journey (Pressley-Sanon 2011). Yet primary

71

and secondary diasporas are linked; as the song progresses, the verb form 'they resisted' (*protestaron*) shifts to 'we resist' (*protestamos*). Linking primary and secondary diasporas, too, are rhythms and body movements of African heritage, manifested in the dancing and the drum that the song is both a product of and references. Moreover, this song is indebted to yet another set of diasporas: the Europeans who migrated to the Americas even as slaves were being transported across the Atlantic: sailors, colonizers, soldiers, missionaries, prostitutes, runaways, pirates. Their sonic and kinetic heritages are sedimented in the European instruments we hear – piano, saxophone, trumpets (Washburne 2008); in its use of the Spanish language; in the reliance on Western notation to arrange the song for the orchestra; and in the partner-hold which dictates the protocol of salsa as a couple dance (Chasteen 2004; Kabir 2013b). In short, it constantly performs a multi-sited and multi-diasporic inheritance.

This chapter uses music and dance forms such as salsa as collective cultural expressions to think through the analysis of diaspora on a global scale. It mobilizes music and dance forms which are demotic and social in origin and contemporary practice – that live on the streets, in the nightclubs, and on the dance floor, even though they may be showcased on the stage. Dance as an embodied and improvised collective practice will complement evidence from diasporic music, which, like all music in modernity, is transmitted through technological capture. The framework of modernity also predicates the chapter's focus on the large-scale displacement of peoples that occurred on a trans-oceanic and trans-continental scale during the formation of global capitalism through expansionism, colonialism, slavery, indentured labour, and, in the postcolonial and neoliberal period, through economic migration (Gilroy 1993; Mbembe 2017). Prominent diasporic populations which emerged out of these historical events are those created by Africans and South Asians to the Americas, in both primary and secondary phases, as well as to Europe. From these groups, I draw examples through which I outline some principles for the study of music and dance in diaspora and to advance methodological propositions, theoretical considerations, and directions for future research. To these ends, the chapter organizes its argument along three sets of paired themes: trauma and *alegria*; embodiment and technology; and authenticity and creolization.

Trauma and *alegria*

Diaspora is frequently experienced, remembered and analysed in terms of trauma. The causes of diasporic migrations range from economic deprivation to political upheaval, and from deceitful enticements – as in the case of indentured labour diasporas (Tinker 1974) – to coercion, violence and the theft of populations in order to convert them into commodities – as in the case of slavery (Baucom 2005; Brown 2008). Even if a diasporic migration had been voluntary, there is always a formative input of some negative affect such as homesickness or nostalgia (Boym 2002). Because of its close and foundational connection to traumatic events, the diasporic condition opens up spaces for reflection on the divergence between official histories and private traumas, including those experiences that have moved from individual to group to become 'cultural trauma' (Eyerman 2001) and 'collective trauma' (Bal et al. 1999), and the intergenerational transmission of traumatic memory as 'postmemory' (Hirsch 1997). Both the moment of departure and the moment of arrival retain immense emotional significance and commemorative potential as nodes where the histories of individuals, families and communities intersect with larger historical process.

Shaped by collective recollection of traumatic departures and arrivals, diasporic communities commemorate the past and remake themselves through cultural and creative practices. Textual explorations of diasporic subjectivity, such as the poem and the novel, fit very well into modern literary preoccupations with alienation, 'unhomeliness' and fragmentation of subjectivity (Kabir 2010). The diasporic writer, conscious of the slippage between origin, belonging and location, is well placed to respond to questions that have vivified modern literature: who am I, and where have I come from? Yet there is another side to diasporic cultural production, best illustrated by music and dance forms: the ability to transform traumatic experiences into modes of resilience, survival and even joy. Although both writing and reading can be profoundly transformative, these remain, typically, solitary experiences of individual epiphanies. On the other hand, diasporic music and dance practices draw overtly on the resources of community, the crowd and the collective, in order to *perform* the transformative power of diasporic experience (Delgado and Muñoz 1997). Carnival celebrations throughout the Americas exemplify this process (Benítez-Rojo 1999; Kabir 2016).

I call the affect generated by such performance *alegria*: a pan-Iberian word for happiness or joy, connotative of a physicality that sometimes evades its English equivalents.[2] *Alegria* is felt in the body. Its transformative force is most apparent in sonic and kinetic responses to the relationship between labour and diaspora, founded on the institution of slavery and perpetrated by the precariousness of post-abolition life and labour migrations. Salsa songs on cane-cutting on Cuban plantations, such as 'Tumba la cana'; funana songs on working the volcanic Capeverdean soil, such as 'Djonsinho Cabral', cited above; sega songs from Mauritius that evolved from the feminine labour of cooking, such as 'Mol mole':[3] these are just some examples of diasporic music genres that transform 'the soundtrack of daily life' into the celebration of labour as a diasporic burden and self-making practice. The transformation of labour into *alegria* is further facilitated through dance practices. Rhythm and melody, call and response, and other structuring features, that once ensured coordinated movement in the plantation and the field, now do so on the dance floor. The 'flow' (Csikszentmihalyi 1996) that dance triggers provides an embodied counterpoint to the memories of labour articulated in the lyrics, converting potentially negative affect generated by those memories to an exhilaration that connects mind and body, individual and crowd.

Embodiment and technology

Building on the insight that the body is a site of memory (Caruth 1996; Nora 1989), my conceptualization of *alegria* shifts attention from negative to positive memory-making through movement, and to the body's ability to transform traumatic memories of diaspora into commemoration through music and dance practices. This capacity derives from the body, and various categories of somatic memory, being the primary carriers of culture in diaspora: food preparation, artisanal crafts, hair braiding, religious chants, ritual practices including drumming techniques, and even rhythms and melodies themselves as abstracted yet embodied forms of knowledge. As we saw in my discussion of 'Alma primitiva', dance and music forms can enfold these embodied practices in different ways: through lyrics about genres of music and dance that sustain community; through instrumentation that plays out modes inherited from different ancestral groups; and through the dancing body that responds kinetically to extract from music its communal, choreographic and performative dimensions (DeFrantz 2004).

Musicians and dancers forge and perpetuate thereby a symbiotic understanding of music and dance as embodied practices that can disrupt the quotidian with an energy both sacred and joyous. As the Cuban classic 'Quimbara' declares: 'the rumba is calling me – even as the bongos speak out, I'm gone' (*La rumba me esta llamando/ bongo dile que me voy*). The call of the drums becomes constitutive of life itself: 'this alone is my life: the beautiful rumba, and the guaguanco' (*mi vida es solo esto/ rumba buena y guaguanco*). The lyrics name two dancers – 'Teresa' and 'Juanito' – who accompany the singing voice, thereby signalling the necessity of community to bring the dance to life. But most importantly, it's a single word, 'quimbara', that we hear over and over again: an apparently meaningless fragment of 'mumbo jumbo' (Reed 1972) which nevertheless signifies 'Africa' through an incantatory function intensified through repetition and semantic opacity. Such incantations link the song and the rumba dance steps, which its rhythm and lyrics predicate, to embodied practices of diasporic religiosity sedimented in different genres of Afro-Cuban dance (Jottar 2009).

Songs like 'Quimbara' are still sung and danced to in Cuba as part of its African diasporic heritage (Moore 2006). At the same time, the dance form that it references, the rumba, is captured and disseminated through music videos that accompany its recent interpretations. Moreover, before the advent of video recording as a technology, the song 'was already a recording' (of a rendition, in fact, by Celia Cruz) 'just as our access to it is made possible only by way of recordings' (Moten 2003: 11). While depending on embodiment to remain meaningful, it is through technologies of reproduction and amplification that diasporic music and dance styles circulate in modernity, including between diasporas and homelands. From the 1930s onwards, radio and records brought Afro-diasporic music to West Africa to give rise to new genres of music such as Congolese rumba (Shain 2002; White 2002) and vodou funk; reggae and hiphop evolve within circum-Atlantic and global circuits. Likewise, music as well as dance styles within Indian labour diasporas were long influenced by popular culture 'back home' through not only radio and records, but also film screenings (Manuel 1998; Servan-Schreiber 2010). Nowadays, the global rise of the music video as a showcase for dance styles draws diasporas and homelands together in ever more complex ways that demand new analytical tools such as what Djebbari (forthcoming) proposes as 'videochoreomorphosis', or the creative impact of music videos on social dancers.

Authenticity and creolization

'Videochoreomorphosis' allows us to acknowledge 'the different ways in which the [music] video medium and popular dance styles are imbricated and mutually agentive' (Djebbari forthcoming: np). We are consequently better able to unpack claims to cultural authenticity and heritage that diasporic musicians and dancers project on to the 'popular screen'. Trinidadian musician Rikki Jai's video 'Mor tor' (2005) opens with a sequence showcasing social interactions between older Indo-Trinidadian women and continues with footage of their younger counterparts 'wining', or moving their hips in an Afro-Caribbean way. This footage is in turn cut with that of an Indo-Trinidadian woman dressed in an outfit for the high-prestige Indian dance Bharatanatyam. While she performs its characteristic hand gestures, her lower body moves in a Caribbean fashion (Kabir 2013a). The song itself is a 'chutney' version of a genre performed by Indo-Caribbean women in female-only pre-nuptial celebrations (Kanhai 1999). In diaspora, these songs have diverged significantly from their more restricted evolution as a marginalized genre within contemporary India (Servan-Schreiber 1999). Whose, then, is the more 'authentic' rendering?

The dialogic relationship between song, choreography and *mise en scène* in Jai's 'Mor tor' video confirms music and dance as being key sites for negotiating cultural capital, belonging and heritage, for diasporic communities as well as those 'back home' (Niranjana 2006). The South Asian folk genre *bhangra* went global through Birmingham's Punjabi diaspora before being claimed back in India through the Bollywood industry but also by Punjabis in Pakistan (Kabir 2011). The entanglement of embodied cultural practices and technologies of reproduction, amplification and, increasingly, digital play, means that memories of memories, cultural retentions and parallel developments of music and dance genres in homeland and diaspora can lead to unexpected cultural alliances. Ghanaian-American singer Azizaa thus launches a feminist diatribe against postcolonial African Christianity through channelling Afro-diasporic spirituality manifested in a circum-Atlantic kinaesthetics of the black body.[4] Spliced together in consonance with a globally comprehensible, postmodern aesthetics of the fragment, her video 'Black magic woman' (2015) manipulates technology to aid the birth of new rituals that augment rather than deplete what Benjamin (1968) once famously called the 'aura' of the work of art.

Worries about technological reproduction are usually linked to fears of the artwork's alienation and loss of authenticity. Instead of asking whether diasporic and diaspora-influenced music and dance are authentic, I propose we analyse them as the results of *creolization*: the propensity to create new cultural products by assembling fragments of pre-existing cultural practices in often unexpected ways. Frequently used to signal specific cases arising from encounter between Europeans and Africans in the Americas as well as Cape Verde (Cohen and Toninato 2010) and the Indian Ocean (Vergès and Marimoutou 2005), this term is arguably appropriate for diasporic dance and music genres in general. For instance, the commonplace designation of Caribbean and Indian Ocean quadrilles (Manuel 2009) and Capeverdian and Antillean mazurkas as 'folklore' obfuscates the relationship between their European and African features, which, however, emerges as constitutive of their status as diasporic products when they are analysed as consequences of creolization. Through this analytical lens, we can calibrate processes whereby dances gain terminology, expand their kinetic repertoire, become commercialized and standardized, and splinter and morph into variations. This approach is especially useful for social dances such as kizomba, which emerged in the 1980s out of the transnational interaction of diasporic (and non-diasporic) groups and their dance-music practices across Angola, Cape Verde, the French Caribbean, Portugal, and France, thus defying classification as being 'authentic' to one group or the other.

The birth of newness from the void of history

In a darkened church in The Hague, an audience hears a voice singing Indian classical music. As the light increases, two black men, dressed identically in neutral tones of grey and beige, rush across the space. Stopping, starting, then moving again, they seek the source of the sound. It is a South Asian man dressed in similar colours, a shawl thrown around his shoulders. He walks towards and past them, still singing. A *tanpura* (a South Asian stringed instrument) occupies the far end of the nave and provides a point of focus for the performers. The two dancers begin adapting their dance to his song through hiphop, other urban dance styles, and capoeira. Movements and voice mesh in a 'trialogue'. The singer plays on *tablas* (South Asian percussion instruments); the dancers contort their bodies around him. He lies down on the floor with the *tanpura*, cradling it as if a lover, while continuing to sing; they also move down low, grappling each other with capoeira-like movements. Their heaving chests and breathing adds another percussive layer as do the unexpected placement of South Asian anklets over their dance trainers. The singer strikes the *tanpura* with a stick as if it were a cello. He sings a melody recognizable to South Asian ears, but the words are Portuguese: *brinca na areia* ('play on the sand'). As his voice soars, the dancers reach a crescendo of exertion, supporting yet challenging each other with their bodies. Beads of sweat catch the light before sudden darkness announces the end. Stray bells from their anklets scatter across the floor like jasmine blossoms.

This performance, *Blood*, is conceptualized and directed by Shailesh Bahoran, Dutch choreographer and hiphop dancer of Indo-Surinamese heritage, and therefore the product of at least two diasporas.[5] The performers are also Dutch: the singer, Raj Mohan, is of Indo-Surinamese heritage, and the dancers, Eddy Vidal and Ramos Sama, are of Angolan heritage. Together, they have created a dance and music piece that draws from the Surinamese preservation of Indian 'classical' music, and urban street dance styles that, although global in their appeal, have an unambiguous Afro-diasporic heritage. The commonalities between different diasporic histories emerge, as well as the difficulties we face in speaking to each other about those shared experiences. Bahoran's profoundly moving piece exemplifies how, through dance and music, we can reach a different understanding of intra-diasporic relationships than that perhaps the written or spoken word can permit. If free from pressures to demonstrate 'authenticity', creolized dance and music forms possess potentially infinite capacities to re-creolize. Indeed, thus freed, they can re-assemble the flotsam and jetsam of modernity through an audacity born under duress and a historical need to improvise. They benefit from the phenomenological amenability of music and dance to technologies and forms of splicing, mixing, layering and sampling. These, together with the characteristics of African-heritage music and dance forms, particularly polyrhythm, syncopation and improvisation (Manuel 2006; Monson 2003; Thompson 1983), enable a range of diasporic music and dance to embrace and juxtapose the inheritances of diverse cultures, including forms developed by other diasporas.

In the words of Wilson Harris (1970: 12) speaking about the limbo dance of the Caribbean: 'this is the dance of the folk – the human limbo or gateway of the gods – which was disregarded or incomprehensible to an intellectual and legal and historical convention'. It is a fitting answer to the question that Salman Rushdie (1988) asked in *Satanic verses* through his character Gibreel Farishta: 'How does newness come into the world?' The novel's answer was itself: an audacious product of diaspora as bewildering, disorienting, alienating, but also unexpectedly creative. This very quote was used by Homi Bhabha (1994) to valorize diasporic cultures through his highly successful theorization of 'hybridity' and 'the third space' of cultural production as a consequence of modernity. For both Rushdie and Bhabha, however, the engagement with diasporic culture remained overwhelmingly textual, bound to Harris's 'intellectual and legal and historical convention'. This preference also characterized the vast majority of those who applied Bhabha's theories to cultural analysis. Consequently, diasporic music and dance forms await sustained examination as 'newness entering the world'. Moreover, discussions of both hybridity and creolization have neglected interactions between diasporic groups which surpass the binary of 'white and non-white'. In drawing attention to these interactions, music and dance born out of diasporic conditions encourages us to break out of a political imaginary that, despite calls for 'South–South dialogue', retains the impress of racialization born out of an inability to think past colonial domination. If 'empire has created the time of history' (Coetzee 1980: 146), from another perspective also left some groups in what Harris (1970) called 'the void' of history. Some of the most demotic, creative and radical ways to step through that void, and to thereby see openings between civilizations, have been through music and dance created through, in and because of diaspora.

Notes

1 Nacho Sanabría, 'Alma primitiva', *El sabor de Nacho* (Borinquen, 1970). The information about this song has been gleaned from several internet sites for salsa history. I thank Leyneuf Tines for her help with transcribing and translating the lyrics. Much of the research underpinning this chapter was undertaken through the resources of the ERC-funded advanced grant 'Modern Moves' (2013–18), which I direct as Principal Investigator.
2 My preference for the Portuguese *alegria* over the Spanish *alegría* derives from the greater transcontinental spread of the contemporary Portuguese-speaking world in comparison to the Spanish-speaking one.
3 For examples of these songs, see www.youtube.com/watch?v=0-8JFz67KR0; www.youtube.com/watch?v=Pdp0y0J-uDk; www.youtube.com/watch?v=qdUgOwMTAYI. Multiple interpretations of each song exist.

4 www.youtube.com/watch?v=bfeGpcmfMBA.
5 *Blood* (dir. Shailesh Bahoran 2017), performed courtesy Korzo Theatre, The Hague, through February 2017. It was also performed at King's College London, as part of the Modern Moves project's annual research showcase, on 24 May 2017.

References

Bal, M., J. Crewe and L. Spitzer (eds) (1999) *Acts of memory: cultural recall in the present*, Hanover: UPNE.
Baucom, I. (2005) *Specters of the Atlantic: finance capital, slavery, and the philosophy of history*, Durham: Duke University Press.
Benítez-Rojo, A. (1996) *The repeating island: the Caribbean and the postmodern perspective*, Durham: Duke University Press.
Benjamin, W. (1936) *Illuminations*, New York: Random House, 1968.
Bhabha, H. K. (1994) *The location of culture*, Abingdon: Routledge.
Boym, S. (2002) *The future of nostalgia*, New York: Basic Books.
Brown, V. (2008) *The reaper's garden: death and power in the world of Atlantic slavery*, Harvard, MA: Harvard University Press.
Caruth, C. (1996) *Unclaimed experience: trauma, narrative, and history*, Baltimore: JHU Press.
Chasteen, J. C. (2004) *National rhythms, African roots: the deep history of Latin American popular dance*, Albuquerque: University of New Mexico Press.
Coetzee, J. M. (1980) *Waiting for the barbarians*, London: King Penguin.
Cohen, R. and P. Toninato (eds) (2010) *The creolization reader*, Abingdon: Routledge.
Csikszentmihalyi, M. (1996) *Creativity: flow and the psychology of discovery and invention*, New York: HarperCollins.
DeFrantz, T. F. (2004) 'The black beat made visible: hip hop dance and body power', in A. Lepecki (ed.) *Of the presence of the body: essays on dance and performance theory*, Middletown, CT: Wesleyan University Press, 64–81.
Delgado, C. F. and J. E. Muñoz (eds) (1997) *Everynight life: culture and dance in Latin/o America*, Durham: Duke University Press.
Djebbari, E. (forthcoming) 'Dance, music videos and screens: intermediality and *videochoreomorphosis*', *Critical African Studies*.
Eyerman, R. (2001) *Cultural trauma: slavery and the formation of African American culture*, Cambridge: Cambridge University Press.
Fryer, P. (2000) *Rhythms of resistance: African musical heritage in Brazil*, Middletown, CT: Wesleyan University Press.
Gilroy, P. (1993) *The black Atlantic: modernity and double consciousness*, Boston: Harvard University Press.
Harris, W. (1970) 'History, fable and myth in the Caribbean and Guianas', *Caribbean Quarterly*, 54 (2), 5–37.
Hirsch, M. (1997) *Family frames: photography, narrative, and postmemory*, Boston: Harvard University Press.
Jottar, B. (2009) 'The acoustic body: *rumba guarapachanguera* and Abakuá sociality in Central Park', *Latin American Music Review*, 30 (1), 1–24, doi: 10.1353/lat.0.0031.
Kabir, A. J. (2010) 'Diasporas, literatures and literary studies', in K. Knott and S. McLoughlin (eds) *Diasporas: concepts, intersections, identities*, London: Zed Books, 145–50.
Kabir, A. J. (2011) 'Salsa/Bhangra: transnational rhythm cultures in comparative perspective', *Music and Arts in Action*, 3 (3), 40–55, available at: www.musicandartsinaction.net/index.php/maia/article/view/salsabhangra/67.
Kabir, A. J. (2013a) 'Calypso and Krishna's flute: the Indo-Caribbean woman's moving body', *Caribbean Review of Gender Studies*, 6, 1–9, available at: http://hdl.handle.net/2139/16301.
Kabir, A. J. (2013b) 'The dancing couple in black Atlantic space', in L. Duran Almarza and E. Delgado (eds) *Gendering the black Atlantic*, New York: Routledge, 133–50.
Kabir, A. J. (2016) 'On postcolonial happiness', in J. G. Singh and D. Kim (eds) *The postcolonial world*, New York: Routledge, 35–52.
Kanhai, R. (ed.) (1999) *Matikor: the politics of identity for Indo-Caribbean women*, Kingston: University of the West Indies Press.
McMains, J. (2015) *Spinning mambo into salsa*, Oxford: Oxford University Press.
Manuel, P. (1998) 'Chutney and Indo-Trinidadian cultural identity', *Popular Music*, 17 (1), 21–42, doi: 10.1017/S0261143000000477.

Manuel, P. (2006) *Caribbean currents: Caribbean music from rumba to reggae*, Philadelphia: Temple University Press.
Manuel, P. (2009) *Creolizing contradance in the Caribbean*, Philadelphia: Temple University Press.
Mbembe, A. (2017) *Critique of black reason*, Durham: Duke University Press.
Monson, I. (ed.) (2003) *The African diaspora: a musical perspective*, New York: Routledge.
Moore, R. (2006) *Music and revolution: cultural change in Cuba*, Berkeley: University of California Press.
Moten, F. (2003) *In the break: the aesthetics of the black radical tradition*, Minneapolis: University of Minnesota Press.
Niranjana, T. (2006) *Mobilizing India: music and migration between India and the Caribbean*, Durham: Duke University Press.
Nora, P. (1989) 'Between memory and history: les lieux de mémoire', *Representations*, 26, 7–24, doi: 10.2307/2928520.
Pressley-Sanon, T. (2011) 'Acting out: performing memory of enslavement in Ouidah, Benin Republic', *The Journal of Pan African Studies*, 4 (5), 57–80, available at: www.biomedsearch.com/article/Acting-out-performing-memory-enslavement/306754338.html.
Reed, I. (1972) *Mumbo jumbo*, New York: Scribner.
Rushdie, S. (1998) *The satanic verses*, London: Vintage.
Servan-Schreiber, C. (1999) *Chanteurs itinérants en Inde du Nord: la tradition oral Bhojpuri*, Paris: L'Harmattan.
Servan-Schreiber, C. (2010) *Histoire d'une musique métisse a l'île Maurice: chutney indien et séga Bollywood*, Paris: Riveneuve Editions.
Shain, R. M. (2002) Roots in reverse: *cubanismo* in twentieth-century Senegalese music, *International Journal of African Historical Studies*, 35 (1), 83–101, doi: 10.2307/3097367.
Thompson, R. F. (1983) *Flash of the spirit: African and Afro-American art and philosophy*, New York: Random House.
Tinker, H. (1974) *A new system of slavery: the export of Indian labour overseas, 1830–1920*, Oxford: Oxford University Press.
Vergès, F. and C. Marimoutou (2005) *Amarres: créolisation india-océanes*, Paris: L'Harmattan.
Washburne, C. (2008) *Sounding salsa: performing Latin music in New York City*, Philadelphia: Temple University Press.
White, B. W. (2002) 'Congolese rumba and other cosmopolitanisms', *Cahiers d'études africaines* (online journal), 168, 663–86, available at: http://etudesafricaines.revues.org/161.

9
Diasporic filmmaking in Europe

Daniela Berghahn

Over the past thirty years, European cinema has undergone an unprecedented transformation as a result of the increased visibility of diasporic filmmakers and a growing interest in the representation of ethnic diversity and multiculturalism on screen. These filmmakers, their parents or grandparents came to Europe as part of postcolonial migrations to the imperial 'mother countries' or as part of labour migration which affected virtually all Northern and Western European countries, irrespective of their colonial past. Others came after the end of the Cold War, when global migration, in particular from the East to the West, intensified. Most recently, Europe has witnessed what has been termed the 'migration crisis', referring to the influx of refugees and asylum-seekers from war-torn Syria and other countries in that region. These diverse migratory flows, the settlement of migrants and refugees, and the gradual emergence of diaspora cultures across Europe have meant that the concept of European identity and nationhood has become ever more fluid and contested. This is not surprising given that transnational mobility and migration belong to 'the key forces of social transformation in the contemporary world' (Castles 2002: 1144) and that public debates over immigration are making media headlines.

Although 'Fortress Europe' has not always been particularly welcoming to strangers clamouring at its gates, over the past three decades the cultural spaces occupied by migrant and diasporic communities have, nevertheless, gradually shifted from the margins to the centre as representations of their identities have begun to assume a more prominent position. In fact, film, alongside music, must be seen as the most influential popular artistic practice with regard to the (self-)representation of migrant and diasporic groups and their experiences and concerns. By foregrounding the experiences of diasporic subjects and by telling stories about the dynamics of cross-cultural encounters and postmodern multiculturalism, diasporic filmmakers living and working in Europe have challenged our understanding of European cinema and what it means to be 'European'. European cinema is no longer exclusively white, nor can it be adequately conceived of as an amalgamation of discrete national cinemas that coexist side by side, separated by geopolitical and linguistic borders.

Defining diasporic cinema

The terms 'transnational', 'migrant' and 'diasporic' cinema are frequently used interchangeably. This is, however, imprecise since the cinemas they denote transcend the boundaries of the nation-state in different ways. Transnational cinema does not refer to the end of national cinema but foregrounds a new perspective that emphasizes 'the cycle of film production, dissemination and reception as a dynamic process that transcends national borders' (Iordanova 2007: 508; see also Ezra and Rowden 2006; Halle 2008; Palacio and Türschmann 2013). Migrant and diasporic cinema can be conceived of as a sub-category of transnational cinema (Higbee and Lim 2010). Its recent emergence as a critical concept is inextricably linked to the postcolonial and labour migrations of the second half of the twentieth century and the beginning of the twenty-first which have 'dramatically changed the social and cultural composition of European [and other Western] societies' (Robins 2007: 152).

The distinction between migrant and diasporic cinema revolves around the different stages of mobility, referenced in the terms 'migration' and 'diaspora', as well as the concept of generation. Migration refers to collective mobility and can be temporary or result in long-term settlement (whether planned or due to the impossibility of returning or of moving on). Migration inevitably constitutes a precondition for the formation of a diaspora, defined as a recognizable and minoritarian social group that preserves its 'ethnic or ethnic-religious identity and communal solidarity' (Sheffer 1986: 9). Diaspora denotes a settler community that has evolved from migration and that is, by definition, dispersed from their original or putative homeland 'to two or more foreign regions' and that is connected by 'a collective memory and myth about the homeland' (Cohen 2008: 17), which may manifest itself in a nostalgic longing to return. Thus, migrant filmmakers can be defined as first-generation immigrants who have themselves experienced migration, leaving their country of birth in search of better economic conditions, a more stable socio-political environment, or for any number of other reasons. Yet rarely are first-generation immigrants in a position to make films, since they are too preoccupied with establishing the material conditions for a new life in a foreign country.

Diasporic filmmakers, in contrast, are typically second- or subsequent-generation immigrants, that is, the children of migrants who were born and raised in the destination country, who have no first-hand experience of migration – and often little familiarity with their parents' country of origin – but for whom the memory of migration and dispersal is mediated through oral history, family photos and home videos, and many other forms of mediation. Broadly speaking, diasporic cinema articulates the memory or postmemory (Hirsch 1997) of migration and the experience of being part of a diaspora. Diasporic documentaries such as *Mémoires d'immigrés, l'héritage maghrébin/Immigrant memories* (Yamina Benguigui 1997), *Wir haben vergessen zurückzukehren/We have forgotten to return* (Fatih Akin 2001) and *I for India* (Sandhya Suri 2005) foreground the construction of migrant memories by dramatizing how these family memories are handed down from one generation to the next.

Most scholars reserve the term for films made by diasporic filmmakers, thereby emphasizing the authenticity of experience and the significance of authorship. Others have criticized the inherent essentialism of this definition and have proposed that diasporic cinema also includes films made by filmmakers of the hegemonic host societies in Europe that lack the kind of deep personal connection constitutive of the postmemory of migration. To bridge this apparent gap Avtar Brah's concept of the 'diaspora space' provides a useful framework, since it disavows the significance of any essentialist notions of origin or of the history of displacement as a prerequisite for partaking in the diasporic experience: 'diaspora space' as a conceptual category is 'inhabited', not only by those who have migrated and their descendants, but equally by those who are constructed and represented as indigenous. In other words, the concept of diaspora space (as opposed to that of diaspora) includes the entanglement, the intertwining of genealogies of dispersion with those of 'staying put' (Brah 1996: 209). Like 'diaspora space', Alison Landsberg's (2004) aptly termed notion of 'prosthetic memory', a type of memory that enables alliances and forms of collective identification that transcend 'natural' belonging to a particular group, race or ethnicity, blurs the boundaries between diasporic and non-diasporic authorship. It assumes that non-diasporic filmmakers can see through the eyes of the other and articulate a collective memory that is not their own and, in so doing, forge alliances and bridge chasms of difference. This wider, non-essentialist definition of diasporic cinema allows the inclusion of films such as *La haine/Hate* (Mathieu Kassovitz 1995) and *Die fremde/When we leave* (Feo Aladag 2011), which centre on protagonists with a migratory background but are created by majority culture filmmakers.[1]

Since the publication of the seminal study *An accented cinema: exilic and diasporic filmmaking* in 2001, Hamid Naficy has been celebrated as a pioneer in the field. He proposes that diasporic cinema, in contrast to exilic cinema, invariably reflects the collective experience of mass migration, dispersal and settlement. In contrast to 'exilic cinema' which 'is dominated by its focus on the there and then in the homeland, diasporic cinema' reflects the filmmakers' dual attachments to the homeland and to the 'diaspora communities and experiences' in the countries of residence (Naficy 2001: 15). Whereas Naficy is predominantly concerned with exilic and diasproic documentaries and experimental films from around the world, his theoretical framework has proved influential for numerous subsequent studies that examine diasporic feature films made and/or set in Europe, including Rueschmann (2003), Loshitzky (2010), Berghahn and Sternberg (2010) and Ballesteros (2015). In addition, there has been considerable scholarly interest in how diasporic filmmaking has transformed national film cultures across Europe. Significant studies include Tarr (2005), Durmelat and Swamy (2011) and Higbee (2013) on Maghrebi French film; Korte and Sternberg (2004) on British Asian and Desai (2005) on South Asian diasporic cinema in Britain and North America; and Hake and Mennel (2012) on Turkish German cinema.[2]

Scholarly debates on diasporic cinema are frequently embedded in other discursive frameworks, notably race (Bourne 2001; Mercer 1988; Pines 1991; Young 1995), postcolonialism (Ponzanesi and Waller 2012), plurilingualism (Berger and Komori 2010), minorities (Johnston 2010) and world and transnational cinema (Durovicová and Newman 2010). Due attention has also been paid to prominent themes in European cinema such as diasporic families (Berghahn 2013), border crossings (Kazecki et al. 2013) and return migration (Prime 2015).

Although the concept has come to prominence relatively recently, diasporic cinema is actually almost as old as cinema itself, yet previously different scholarly perspectives and terminologies have prevailed. For example, film historians usually do not conceptualize Jewish exile and émigré directors, actors and actresses, scriptwriters and producers, many of whom fled Germany when the National Socialists came to power in 1933, seeking refuge in Paris, London and eventually Hollywood, in relation to the Jewish diaspora. Instead, these exiled Jewish filmmakers are generally referred to as 'European émigrés', a term that obliterates their Jewish ethnicity – and for good reason. As film historian Thomas Elsaesser (1999: 99) puts it, 'foreigners in Hollywood' had the choice between either 'disavowing their own homeland and heritage' or 'assimilat[ing] and become 110 per cent American or be European and exotic, but also 110 per cent!' The choice of terminologies draws attention to the filmmakers' different agendas: émigré filmmakers in Hollywood had to calibrate carefully the images they projected, either through strategies of camouflage and assimilation or through promoting their alterity like a brand in order to succeed; for contemporary diasporic filmmakers, a self-conscious engagement with difference is invariably the preferred and expected strategy.

Key features of diasporic cinema

According to Graham Huggan (2001: vii–viii), cultural and ethnic Otherness has become part of a 'booming "alterity industry"', making 'marginality . . . a valuable intellectual commodity'.

Diasporic filmmakers such as Gurinder Chadha, Amma Asante, Fatih Akin, Yamina Benguigui or Abdellatif Kechiche play an important role as brokers of cultural difference, trading their minoritarian experience as a prized commodity. On the international festival circuit, these transnational *auteurs* are vying with their established European counterparts for attention and awards. Their 'double occupancy' as hyphenated-identity subjects (Elsaesser 2005), their 'double consciousness' (Gilroy 1993) and 'diasporic optic' (Moorti 2003) enables them to invigorate and renew the traditions of European cinema by drawing on multi-sited impulses and inspirations. By juxtaposing and fusing stylistic templates, generic conventions, narrative and musical traditions, languages and performance styles from European and world cinema, as well as from Hollywood, in their aesthetically hybrid and innovative films, diasporic filmmakers have made the boundaries between European and world cinema more fluid.

Diasporic cinema is quintessentially concerned with place and displacement; it is characterized by a heightened sense of mobility, a preponderance of journeys of quest and a dominance of transitional and liminal spaces that connote identities in flux. The preponderance of claustrophobic interiors and locations on the urban periphery draws attention to the social exclusion or marginalization experienced by the diasporic subjects in these films.

Diasporic films challenge and frequently disavow borders of all kinds. Their protagonists transcend the borders of the nation-state on account of their dual heritage and typically try to assert their place in the social fabric of the hegemonic host society. As such, it is a cinema of identity politics, probing 'difference along the multiple coordinates of race, colour, ethnicity, nationality, regionality, language, religion, generation, class, gender and sexuality' (Berghahn and Sternberg 2010: 41). It is a cinema in which spatio-temporal and spatio-racial modalities coalesce and converge and whose strategic agenda is the relocation of the margins to the centre, the valorization and, ultimately, 'the redemption of the marginal' (Stam 2003: 35). As an artistic practice that 'underscores the interstice, the spaces that are and fall between the cracks of the national and the transnational as well as other social formations' (Moorti 2003: 359), it is centrally concerned with hybrid identities.

Moving diasporic cinema from the margin into the mainstream

In 1988, Isaac Julien, a black British artist and filmmaker, and Kobena Mercer, an art historian and critic who has written extensively on black British art and culture, wrote the introduction to 'The last special issue on race' in the British film and television journal *Screen*, entitled 'De margin and de centre'. In this essay, Julien and Mercer (1988: 2) identify the 1980s as a significant juncture in the cinematic representation of 'cultural difference, identity and otherness – in a word, ethnicity', which emerged as a key issue of contestation and public debate at the time. With 'The last special issue on race', Julien and Mercer (1988: 2) seek to contribute to the 'break-up and deconstruction of structures that determine what is regarded as culturally central and what is regarded as culturally marginal'. According to their programmatic vision, in years to come cultural discourses and practices on race and ethnicity would no longer be assigned a special issue because that in itself is indicative of their marginalization.

They were not alone in identifying cinema's pivotal role in destabilizing long-established hierarchies in the cultural representation of race and ethnicity. The late Stuart Hall (1997: 34), too, has celebrated the moment when diasporic ethnic minority filmmakers gained access to the means of film production and, thereby, self-representation as 'the most profound cultural revolution . . . [that came] about as a consequence of the margins coming into representation'. In fact, it was Hall who identified cinema as the most important medium through which marginal, diasporic identities are constructed, since identity is

> constituted not outside but within representation ... cinema ... [is not] a second-order mirror held up to reflect what already exists but ... [a] form of representation which is able to constitute us as new kinds of subjects, and thereby enable us to discover places from which to speak.
>
> *(Hall 2003: 245)*

Until the 1980s, it was majority culture filmmakers who represented immigrant and diasporic communities, deploying the conventions of the social problem film and foregrounding racial tensions over the experience of displacement. The term 'British race relations films' deftly captures this important distinction. Prominent examples such as *Sapphire* (Basil Dearden 1959) and *Flame in the streets* (Roy Ward Baker 1961), which were made around the time of the Notting Hill 'race riots' of 1958, voice 'liberal humanist pleas for racial tolerance' in which black characters 'tend to function primarily as catalysts for the expression of white characters' anxieties' (Pines 2001: 179). Similarly, the pessimistic narratives of films about so-called *Gastarbeiter* (guest workers) in West Germany, including Rainer Werner Fassbinder's *Angst essen Seele auf/Ali: fear eats the soul* (1974) or Helma Sanders-Brahms' *Shirins hochzeit/Shirin's wedding* (1976), seek to instil a sense of compassion and moral indignation in majority culture audiences.

Against this background, the moment when the children of post-war immigrants came of age in the mid-1980s and 1990s and gained access to the means of film production and control over their own images, marked the most decisive stage in shifting 'de margin' to 'de centre'. Widely regarded as landmarks of diasporic European cinema, the Maghrebi French film *Le thé au harem d'Archimède/Tea in the harem* (1985), written and directed by the French Algerian filmmaker Mehdi Charef, and the Asian British *My beautiful laundrette* (1985), based on a screenplay by British Asian writer Hanif Kureishi and directed by Stephen Frears, mark a new phase. Charef and Frears's films eschew the overtly political messages of earlier black British films such as *Pressure* (Horace Ové 1976) and *Handsworth songs* (John Akomfrah 1986) and portray ethnic minorities without foregrounding their alterity. They focus on the everyday experiences of diasporic protagonists and on the irreversible hybridization of cultures. Although many diasporic films from the 1980s gained critical acclaim, only a few managed to attract audiences large enough to actually challenge public perceptions of diasporic ethnic minority communities. *My beautiful laundrette* is a notable exception; it attracted more than four million viewers when, after its cinematic release, it was shown on Channel Four television.

It was not until the late 1990s, however, that diasporic filmmakers embraced popular genres such as historical epics, road movies, family melodramas and comedies, thereby capturing large national and international audiences and often achieving remarkable box office success. Especially comedies about diasporic families – *Bend it like Beckham* (Gurinder Chadha 2002), *East is east* (Damien O'Donnell, screenplay Ayub Khan-Din, 1999) and *Almanya, willkommen in Deutschland/Almanya: welcome to Germany* (Yasemin Samdereli 2011) – have proved immensely popular in this respect. They invite majority and minority culture audiences to recognize that families, whether they come from Pakistan, North Africa or some other far-flung place relegated to the margins of our Eurocentric maps, have a great deal in common. Like diasporic films featuring inter-ethnic romance – *Mauvaise foi/Bad faith* (Roschdy Zem 2006), *Nina's heavenly delights* (Pratibha Parmar 2006) – these films promote an integrationist agenda.

Rachid Bouchareb's war film *Indigènes/Days of glory* (2006) illustrates how diasporic filmmakers have effectively used genre cinema to make powerful interventions in public discourses about ethnic minorities in European societies. *Days of glory* appropriates the genre conventions of the Hollywood war movie in order to commemorate the sacrifice of 300,000 soldiers from France's North and West African colonies, who were called upon by de Gaulle in the 1940s to liberate Italy and France from fascism. While the D-Day landings in Normandy and the efforts of the French resistance have all been commemorated, the heroism and sacrifice of the colonial soldiers had been elided in France's official accounts of World War II. Not only did Bouchareb's film rewrite French national history from the margins, it also drew public attention to the inequality in war pensions for colonial veterans and sparked a major debate in France, which eventually resulted in a legislative change that ensured that colonial veterans were granted the same pensions as former white French soldiers, thereby rescinding the injustice of some sixty years.

Concluding note

There is every indication that diasporic filmmaking in Europe has entered its final phase, characterized by the normalization of race and ethnicity. More and more diasporic filmmakers working in Europe have been able to shed 'the burden of representation' (Julien and Mercer 1988: 4), which they have carried since the 1980s. At that time, when access to the means of film production for diasporic ethnic minority filmmakers was scarce, they were 'burdened with an inordinate pressure to be "representative"' (Julien and Mercer 1988: 4) in the sense of having to speak for their ethnic constituencies as a whole. To make films about any other topic was perceived as a wasted opportunity. This precarious situation has begun to change over the past ten years, as prominent diasporic directors, including Fatih Akin and Abdellatif Kechiche, are no longer pigeon-holed as 'migrant', 'diasporic' or 'hyphenated-identity' filmmakers, but are increasingly enjoying the freedom to make films about any subject they like.[3]

Notes

1 Feo Aladag is of Austrian origin; her surname is that of her Kurdish ex-husband.
2 In this entry, I focus on Europe's most established diasporic film cultures and reference only English-language scholarship.
3 Examples include Akin's coming-of-age story cum road movie *Tschick* (2016) based on a best-selling German novel of the same title, and Kechiche's lesbian love story *La vie d'Adèle/Blue is the warmest colour* (2013).

References

Ballesteros, I. (2015) *Immigration cinema in the new Europe*, Bristol: Intellect.
Berger, V. and M. Komori (eds) (2010) *Polyglot cinema: migration and transcultural narration in France, Italy, Portugal and Spain*, Münster: LIT Verlag.
Berghahn, D. (2013) *Far-flung families in film: the diasporic family in contemporary European cinema*, Edinburgh: Edinburgh University Press.
Berghahn, D. and C. Sternberg (eds) (2010) *European cinema in motion: migrant and diasporic cinema in contemporary Europe*, Basingstoke: Palgrave Macmillan.
Bourne, S. (2001) *Black in the British frame: the black experience in British film and television*, London: Continuum.
Brah, A. (1996) *Cartographies of diaspora: contesting identities*, London: Routledge.
Castles, S. (2002) 'Migration and community formation under conditions of globalization', *International Migration Review*, 36 (4), 1143–68, doi: 10.1111/j.1747-7379.2002.tb00121.x.
Cohen, R. (2008) *Global diasporas: an introduction*, London: Routledge.
Desai, J. (2004) *Beyond Bollywood: the cultural politics of South Asian diasporic film*, London: Routledge.
Durmelat, S. and V. Swamy (eds) (2011) *Screening integration: recasting Maghrebi immigration in contemporary France*, Lincoln: University of Nebraska Press.
Durovicová, N. and K. E. Newman (eds) (2010) *World cinemas, transnational perspectives*, London: Routledge.
Elsaesser, T. (1999) 'Ethnicity, authenticity and exile: a counterfeit trade?', in Hamid Naficy (ed.) *Home, exile, homeland: film, media, and the politics of place*, London: Routledge, 97–123.

Elsaesser, T. (2005) 'Double occupancy and small adjustments: space, place and policy in the New European Cinema since the 1990s', in *European cinema: face to face with Hollywood*, Amsterdam: Amsterdam University Press, 108–30.
Ezra, E. and T. Rowden (2006) 'What is transnational cinema?', in E. Ezra and T. Rowden (eds) *Transnational cinema: the film reader*, London: Routledge, 1–12.
Gilroy, P. (1993) *The black Atlantic: modernity and double consciousness*, London: Verso.
Hall, S. (1997) 'The local and the global: globalization and ethnicity', in A. D. King (ed.) *Culture, globalization, and the world-system: contemporary conditions for the representation of identity*, University of Minnesota Press, 19–40, available at: www.jstor.org/stable/10.5749/j.ctttsqb3.6.
Hall, S. (2003) 'Cultural identity and diaspora', in J. E. Braziel and A. Mannur (eds) *Theorizing diaspora: a reader*, Oxford: Blackwell, 233–46.
Halle, R. (2008) *German film after Germany: toward a transnational aesthetic*, Urbana: University of Illinois Press.
Hannerz, U. (1996) *Transnational connections: culture, people, places*, London: Routledge.
Higbee, W. (2013) *Post-beur cinema: North African émigré and Maghrebi-French filmmaking in France since 2000*, Edinburgh: Edinburgh University Press.
Higbee, W. and S. H. Lim (2010) 'Concepts of transnational cinema: towards a critical transnationalism in film studies', *Transnational Cinemas*, 1 (1), 7–21, available at: https://goo.gl/nADZKX.
Hirsch, M. (1997) *Family frames: photography, narrative and postmemory*, Cambridge, MA: Harvard University Press.
Huggan, G. (2001) *The postcolonial exotic: marketing the margins*, London: Routledge.
Iordanova, D. (2007) 'Transnational film studies', in P. Cook (ed.) *The cinema book*, London: British Film Institute, 508–9.
Johnston, C. (2010) *French minority cinema*, Amsterdam: Rodopi.
Julien, I. and K. Mercer (1988) 'Introduction: de margin and de centre', *Screen*, (The last special issue on race), 29 (4), 2–10, doi: 10.1093/screen/29.4.2.
Kazecki, J., K. A. Ritzenhoff and C. J. Miller (2013) *Border visions: identity and diaspora in film*, Plymouth: Scarecrow Press.
Korte, B. and C. Sternberg (2004) *Bidding for the mainstream? Black and Asian British film since the 1990s*, Amsterdam: Rodopi.
Landsberg, A. (2004) *Prosthetic memory: the transformation of American remembrance in the age of mass culture*, New York: Columbia University Press.
Loshitzky, Y. (2010) *Screening Strangers: migration and diaspora in contemporary European cinema*, Bloomington: Indiana University Press.
Mercer, K. (1988) *Black film, British cinema*, London: ICA.
Moorti, S. (2003) 'Desperately seeking an identity: diasporic cinema and the articulation of transnational kinship', *International Journal of Cultural Studies*, 6 (3), 355–76, doi: 10.1177/13678779030063007.
Naficy, H. (2001) *An accented cinema: exilic and diasporic filmmaking*, Princeton: Princeton University Press.
Palacio, M. and J. Türschmann (eds) (2013) *Transnational cinema in Europe*, Münster: LIT Verlag.
Pines, J. (1991) *Representation and blacks in British cinema*, London: BFI Education.
Pines, J. (2001) 'British cinema and black representation', in R. Murphy (ed.) *The British cinema book*, second edition, London: BFI, 177–83.
Ponzanesi, S. and M. Waller (eds) (2012) *Postcolonial cinema studies*, Abingdon: Routledge.
Prime, R. (ed.) (2015) *Cinematic homecomings: exile and return in transnational cinema*, London: Bloomsbury.
Robins, K. (2007) 'Transnational cultural policy and European cosmopolitanism', *Cultural Politics*, 3 (2), 147–74, doi: 10.2752/174321907X194002.
Rueschmann, E. (ed.) (2003) *Moving pictures, migrating identities*, Jackson: University of Mississippi Press.
Sheffer, G. (ed.) (1986) *Modern diasporas in international politics*. London: Croom Helm.
Stam, R. (2003) 'Beyond third cinema: the aesthetics of hybridity', in A. Guneratne and W. Dissanayake (eds) *Rethinking third cinema*, London: Routledge, 31–48.
Tarr, C. (2005) *Reframing difference: 'beur' and 'banlieue' filmmaking in France*, Manchester: Manchester University Press.
Tölölyan, K. (1991) 'The nation-state and its others: in lieu of a preface', *Diaspora*, 1 (1), 3–7, doi: 10.1353/dsp.1991.0008.
Van Hear, N. (1998) *New diasporas: the mass exodus, dispersal and regrouping of migrant communities*, Seattle: University of Washington Press.
Young, L. (1995) *Fear of the dark: 'race', 'gender' and sexuality in cinema*, London: Routledge.

10
Writing in diaspora

Zuzanna Olszewska

In Psalm 137, the Hebrew Bible preserves one of the earliest recorded examples of diasporic literature, and one that has resonated across the ages as emblematic of the sense of loss, nostalgia and longing for the homeland of the diasporic subject:

> By the rivers of Babylon
> we sat and wept
> at the memory of Zion...
> How could we sing a song of Yahweh
> on alien soil?
> If I forget you, Jerusalem,
> may my right hand wither!
> May my tongue remain stuck to my palate
> if I do not keep you in mind,
> if I do not count Jerusalem
> the greatest of my joys.
>
> *(Psalm 137)*

Yet the same scripture, in the voice of God via the prophet Jeremiah, also exhorts the Jewish exiles to 'Build houses, settle down; plant gardens and eat what they produce.... Work for the good of the city to which I have exiled you, since on its welfare yours depends' (both cited in Gruen 2002: 4). This tension between exile and acclimatization to a new home; between old world and new life, belonging and alienation, is often seen as the hallmark of the diasporic subject. As some of the most elemental sentiments of all human beings, they have been expressed in numerous different art forms across the centuries, including literary texts. This chapter will provide a brief and necessarily selective overview of diasporic literature, with a focus on written texts from different times, places and traditions, including fiction, autobiography, poetry, sacred texts and scholarship. I highlight both their remarkable diversity, and two important common elements: their close relationship with the socio-economic situation of diasporic communities, and their important role as a cultural resource in the negotiation of such situations.

Conceptualizing the field

An attempt to delineate the definition and scope of diasporic writing immediately poses the same kind of problems that theorists of diaspora have grappled with for decades. Consider, for instance, that Joseph Conrad (1857–1924) was a Polish exile but worked solely in English, primarily addressing English-speaking readers, and is hailed as one of the giants of modernist English literature. Vladimir Nabokov (1899–1977), who fled the Russia of his birth following the 1917 revolution, was trilingual and lived in several countries, but made his most enduring mark on American literature in English. Is there anything to be gained from considering either author as a member of a diaspora? (I shall return to this question in the case of Conrad below.) Consider also the less well-known Munshi Abdullah bin Abdul Kadir (1796–1854), born in Malacca of Tamil and Hadhrami (Yemeni) descent under British rule, tutor in Malay to British officials, and proficient also in Arabic, Tamil and Hindi. Given that he wrote in Malay and is celebrated as the father of modern Malay literature, should he be counted as a member of the Indian diaspora, or indeed of the great and ancient Hadhrami diaspora that has sailed, traded, settled and intermarried all around the rim of the Indian Ocean for centuries, bringing cultural and religious innovation in its wake (Ho 2006)?

Did these writers have anything in common? Should writing by exiles fall into the same category as that by voluntary migrants or even their descendants removed by several generations? Is a kind of diasporic consciousness, orientation towards the homeland, or sympathy with fellow compatriots a *sine qua non* for this category, which might exclude any of the three writers above at various points in their careers?[1] I suggest that it is probably futile to try to segregate biographies and genealogies as complex as these into those which are more or less authentically diasporic. Rather, I will seek out family resemblances and common themes among different kinds of diasporic writing. Certainly differences need to be noted and distinctions need to be made, but I will begin by following Cohen's (1997) expansive definition of diaspora, which includes victim diasporas, imperial diasporas, trade diasporas, labour diasporas and cultural diasporas.

As a starting point, I posit that whether members of such diasporas write primarily for audiences in their home countries or cultures, their host countries, or fellow diasporans, their writing is of interest to us. They may address political interventions or cultural critiques to their compatriots in the homeland. They may present themselves as authentic representatives of their native culture, whether to affirm or challenge host country narratives about it. They may struggle overwhelmingly, and at any cost, to keep alive a collective identity, a cultural tradition, or a language – or to recover their broken pieces when they have been lost. Their choice of language, genre and style – or the necessity of innovating in any of these – will depend on which, or which combinations, of the above orientations are in play. To make sense of such variety, I have found useful the concept of *positioning*. I base this on Hall's postmodern assertion that 'practices of representation always implicate the positions from which we speak or write' and that identity itself is unstable and an act of positioning, rather than an essence (Hall 1990: 233–4). Thus, writers *position* themselves in relation to homeland and host country, their cultures and politics, based on a plethora of factors including their gender, generation, age, class, race, political stances, and the nature of their literary formation. Seen from this angle, Conrad's, Nabokov's and Munshi Abdullah's orientation *towards* their new homelands and their languages can also be seen as examples of diasporic positionings.

Diverse locations; diverse positions

The burgeoning interest in diasporas in recent decades has led to a proliferation of volumes of criticism or critical anthologies of diasporic writing. This literature is so vast that I can only be very selective here: they encompass the transatlantic African diaspora – or, in Paul Gilroy's terms, the black Atlantic (Gilroy 1993; Davies 1994; Durán-Almarza and Álvarez-López 2014); the Caribbean diaspora (López Ropero 2004); the Muslim diaspora in the West (Ahmed et al. 2012); the Arab diaspora (Al Maleh 2009; Hassan 2011; Salhi and Netton 2006); the Latin American diaspora (Kaminsky 1999); the African diaspora (Cooper 2013); the Iranian diaspora (Karim 2006); the Italian diaspora (Rando and Turcotte 2007); twentieth-century Jewish diasporas (Schachter 2013); and numerous works on East and South Asian diasporas (Hussain 2005; Maxey 2012; Upstone 2010; Zhang 2008, to name but a few). All of these are interested primarily in diasporas in Western countries; in many cases, they represent communities of formerly colonized people now residing in the old colonial metropoles and writing in the latter's languages. Hence, they fit squarely into the frameworks of postcolonial and postmodern theory and have largely been interpreted in this light.

These works often invoke the 'hybrid' nature of diasporic identities and cultures that are forged in interstitial 'third spaces' (Bhabha 1994). A common refrain is creative creolization, duality, liminality, border zones, and the perpetual 'border-crossing and border-redefining' of boundaries in 'space, time, race, culture, language and history' (Zhang 2000: 126). They aver that diasporic counternarratives – such as the African diaspora's Négritude movement of the 1930s – have been central to the experience of modernity (Gilroy 1993); and indeed that 'migrancy' is now a constant feature of reality and intellectual life (Chambers 1994). They reflect an era in which the explosion of previous notions of cultural homogeneity is actively celebrated, or at the very least romanticized. Exile, writes Said, 'is strangely compelling to think about but terrible to experience'; it has been transformed into 'a potent, even enriching, motif of modern culture' (Said 2002: 173). As many of the authors above and the key cultural theorists from whom they take their inspiration (for example, Stuart Hall, Homi Bhabha, Paul Gilroy, Gayatri Spivak) are themselves members of diasporas, it can be argued that the scholarship on diasporic literature and other art forms is itself a form of diasporic writing, historically situated in late twentieth- to early twenty-first-century Western intellectual currents.

One must search a little harder to find scholarly treatments of other kinds of diasporas, especially instances of South–South migration. Examples include Bernards (2015) on writing by the Chinese in Southeast Asia; Ryang (2008) on Koreans in Japan (and the USA); Olszewska (2015) on Afghans in Iran; and Civantos (2005) on Arabs and other minorities in Argentina. Waheed (2012) and Schlote (2013) are all too rare and all too brief commentaries on writing emerging from one of the greatest labour migrations of our times, that of South Asian migrants to the Gulf states. Examples from further back in history, for example of various literary 'Golden Ages' of the Jewish diaspora (Decter 2005; Gruen 2002) also constitute interesting complications of the dominant concepts of postcolonial theory, as I show below.

These examples demonstrate clearly that, given the diverse social, political and economic conditions that produce diasporas, their literatures and the preoccupations that animate them are also necessarily irreducible to any one set of themes or problematics. Bowman, for instance, compares three memoirs by Palestinian authors living contemporaneously but in different geographical and economic situations (a refugee camp in Lebanon; the West Bank; New York) to show that these situations 'give rise to different imaginings of community and . . . create a plethora of distinct strategies for realizing the Palestinian nation' (Bowman 1994: 147). In my own work, similarly, I found distinctly different positionings – expressed in the literary genres and styles of choice, but also in lifestyle and worldview – between the first and second generations of Afghan refugees in Iran (Olszewska 2015).

Returning to the historical example of the Jews, that prototypical 'victim diaspora', we encounter Gruen's assertion that in the Second Temple period (530 BCE–70 CE), much Jewish writing defied both the sentiments of Psalm 137 and of Jeremiah. In this period, many Jews lived in communities across the Greco-Roman world as voluntary migrants who moved freely and did not face persecution. Their writings, including many retellings of biblical stories, contained a strong vein of humour, comedy and mischief that bespoke a 'buoyant and self-confident attitude . . . that welcomed mirth and amusement' (Gruen 2002: 10). Most notably, they did not elaborate a *theory* of diasporic being, suggesting that this was not something that greatly preoccupied them. Gruen concludes that these communities neither pined for Jerusalem, nor felt pressure to assimilate; and they both admired and criticized the Hellenic culture that surrounded them (ibid.) Decter, meanwhile, describes another moment of Jewish literary flourishing in diaspora in the tenth century CE, when Jewish Andalusian poets adapted Arabic verse forms and metres (such as monorhyme) to create new genres in Hebrew, a 'revolution' in Hebrew poetry (Decter 2005: 78–9). Their themes were also frequently borrowed from Arabic poetry: gardens, wine drinking, the unattainable Beloved. The trope of weeping at the sight of the Beloved's abandoned encampment – common in pre-Islamic Arabic poetry – was reconfigured to signify the ruins of the Temple; but a twelfth-century poet, Abraham Ibn Ezra (1089–1164), also wept for the destroyed cities of al-Andalus when he was forced into exile by the Almohad invasion in 1172 (Decter 2005: 83).

But at the other end of the spectrum from Gruen's diasporic ebullience, there are traumatized literatures of enslavement, subjugation and exploitation. At their extreme, they do not exist as *writing* because the very fact of enslavement precludes the existence of the material conditions for the creation and transmission of written texts. They may exist instead as oral storytelling, song and poetry, some of which may eventually also be written down, as in the case of the African-American slave narratives that came to constitute a recognizable genre in the eighteenth to twentieth centuries, important for the abolitionist movement (Davis and Gates 1985). Waheed (2012) describes *Goat Days*, a Malayalam novel by an Indian living in Bahrain, as a contemporary slave narrative. Like many of the African-American slave narratives of centuries past, *Goat Days* is a fictionalized account of a true story recounted to the author, Benyamin, by an Indian man who had escaped from a situation of *de facto* slavery as a goatherd in a remote place in the Saudi Arabian desert. Waheed notes that, in a context in which no pathway to citizenship or its attendant rights exists for South Asian immigrants (as is the case across the Gulf states), the novel is decidedly *not* about identity, belonging or cultural hybridity; instead, it is a tale of a lower-class migrant's dreams and their dashing; of exploitative labour and violence; and of faith, liberation and survival. The author Benyamin, a more privileged migrant, did not experience these things himself, but writing and publication in the home country helped him amplify the experiences of untold numbers of compatriots. It was perhaps this realist resonance that gave the book bestseller status in India and won it literary prizes both in Kerala and (in English translation) internationally.

The expected flow of cultural material *from* a bounded homeland and its elaboration in diaspora is sometimes confounded; the Afghan diaspora is a case in point. Green demonstrates the key difficulty that has complicated attempts to tell a cultural history of the Afghan nation: the 'dilemma . . . of containing and channelling towards national ends a literary culture that has at every step outreached the spatial and ideological confines of the Afghan nation state' (Green 2013: 2). In other words, not only did the literary traditions that are still celebrated in Afghanistan (in Persian, Pashtu and Turkic languages, among others) span a much larger geographical area than the current colonially defined borders of the country, they also predate the formation of the nation-state by many centuries. Furthermore, it was Afghan migrants and exiles who brought back with them (from Europe, the Ottoman Empire, Russia, and so forth) many of the ideas and ideologies that consolidated the nation-state itself from the late nineteenth century onwards. Afghanistan's diasporic writing, then, is the story of 'a fragile emergent state challenged by the smuggling of ideologies through its borders in the saddlebags of literature' (Green 2013: 3).

This complex history of literary movements plays out in other unexpected ways in the contemporary Afghan diaspora. In my work (Olszewska 2015), I have described how Persian-speaking Afghan refugee communities in Iran share a literary heritage that is at least a millennium old with their host country, and many of the luminaries of that tradition were born and lived in what is today Afghanistan. Yet, for most Iranians, nationalism has shoe-horned that history into the category of *Iranian* literature. The prestige still accorded to poets, and refugees' lack of access to other high-status professions, means that poets are among the most influential members of the Afghan refugee community in Iran. While psychically many of them do feel split – betwixt-and-between – because of their lack of access to Iranian citizenship, they are adamant that their literary practice is the reclamation of their rightful place in a shared cultural domain, and *not* one of hybridity or a 'third space'. In form, their poetry echoes many of the developments of modern Iranian literature, with a trend towards blank verse, or genres that are classical in form but contemporary in theme and diction, such as the neoclassical *ghazal*. In literary terms, at least, Afghan refugee poets are well integrated into the Iranian literary scene, and often seek out Iranian audiences. Poetry provides the *only* forum for them to raise complaints about the discriminatory treatment they often receive at the hands of Iranians. Thus, their situation is the obverse of diasporic communities in the West, who may have *legal* citizenship but whose literature reflects the struggle for identity and *cultural* belonging.

Linguistic and political positionings

The political effects of diasporic writing can cut in numerous directions, depending on the authors' attitudes both to their homeland and their host society, and the primary audience they have in mind. (Commercial considerations inevitably play a role as well.) Some authors' primary consideration is to use their claim to authenticity to educate and to correct misconceptions about their culture and their homeland, as is the case with the Arab writers discussed by Omri, faced with widespread Islamophobia in Western countries, for whom 'correction often drives creation' (Omri 2006: 53). Ahmed, Morey and Yaqin also note the danger of Muslim diasporic authors becoming token spokespersons, 'locked into predetermined agendas in which Muslims are always being forced to respond to the charge of disloyalty or threat' (Ahmed et al. 2012: 7).

But sometimes, the situation is reversed and an exilic group's negative feelings towards their home country may align with those of their hosts, as with some post-revolutionary Iranians in the West. Motlagh (2011) considers the popularity of autobiographical narratives of life in Iran in the 2000s, what Ahmed, Morey and Yaqin acerbically call 'Muslim misery memoirs' (Ahmed et al. 2012: 7). Not only was there a publishing boom in such works, many of them became bestsellers in Western countries. Some were memoirs by diasporic Iranians reflecting on their unhappy departures from their homeland after the revolution, for example, Azar Nafisi's *Reading Lolita in Tehran* (2004) and Marjane Satrapi's *Persepolis* (2003); others were narratives of return to Iran by a younger group seeking to reconnect with their homeland, for example, Azadeh Moaveni, *Lipstick Jihad: A Memoir of Growing up Iranian in America and American in Iran* (2005). They met with criticism from other members of the diaspora for their highly subjective narratives, foregrounding the suffering of their social groups while claiming to represent the universal Iranian experience. In the tense atmosphere of American-led wars on Iran's immediate neighbours and the ever-present spectre of an attack on Iran itself, autobiographical narratives of people originating in these countries have been marketed and enlisted as sources of authenticity and legitimacy in calls for regime change (Motlagh 2011: 415).

The use of language is another complex and fascinating aspect of positioning. Even for those who adopt the language of their new home, the effects of bilingualism or the native tongue may be detected as a kind of 'ghost language' or palimpsest that makes its presence felt (Omri 2006). Alternatively, for subsequent-generation diasporans, wrestling with the native tongue as a second or partially known language poses its own challenges. Ryang's discussion of novels by second-generation Korean Japanese describes Korean as a 'lost tongue [representing] the pathos of the lost and hidden self' (Ryang 2008: xxxix). Lee Yangji's (1955–92) semi-autobiographical novel *Yuhi* describes a Korean Japanese woman who goes to study in Seoul, as the author did. The protagonist Yuhi struggles with her Japanese accent as she speaks Korean and is unable to find beauty in the contemporary language, searching for a more authentic Korean in the past (Ryang 2008: xxxi).

Two different linguistic strategies employed by members of the same diaspora, albeit at different times and in very different situations, are explored by Gasyna (2011) in his comparison of the work of the Poles Joseph Conrad and Witold Gombrowicz (1904–69). He argues that a struggle with language lay at the core of both men's exilic writing. Conrad, who left an occupied Poland as a young man, following a spell in exile in Siberia for his father's political activism, settled in Britain after a career on the high seas as a merchant mariner. As he attempted to write great English novels, 'he not only had to make a Herculean effort to undo, or overcome, the influence of his native Polish syntax, but also and more crucially to negotiate his Polish past', particularly in his interrogation of empire, nationalism and revolution (Gasyna 2011: 3). These themes are particularly central in the novel *Nostromo* (Conrad 1904), set in a fictitious South American country that is often seen as a cipher for Poland. Gombrowicz, meanwhile, happened to be visiting Argentina at the outbreak of the Second World War and elected to remain there for 23 years, spending his last years in Germany and France. Yet, having been a published and well-known author before his departure, he insisted on writing in Polish, even when the Polish authorities refused to publish uncensored versions of his texts in Poland. His negotiations with language, then, 'occurred principally on the level of form and style. . . . [He] returned to the Polish language but, remarkably, distill[ed] it in his literary oeuvre to an unprecedented level of formal purity and stylistic severity' (ibid.). Diasporic writing, then, is sometimes also a matter of the critic's perspective. Unlike many others, Gasyna explores both these writers specifically as exilic Poles, with all the ensuing cultural and literary liminality that entails.

Conclusion

As I have shown, the forms and themes of diasporic writing have varied more widely than is often acknowledged, according to the socio-political conditions in which they arose, the nature of the relationship between the host and diasporic communities, the cultural traditions on which they draw or seek to innovate, and the individual creative ambition of the author in question. In all these cases, however, they have proved to be potent reservoirs of cultural knowledge, trenchant critique or simply documentation of experience. Perhaps the most constant common thread that binds them is the necessity of consciously negotiating a kind of 'plurality of vision' that non-diasporans may not so readily possess: a contrapuntal 'awareness of simultaneous dimensions' that can be a source of great originality (Said 2002: 186). After all, in Salman Rushdie's words, 'mélange . . . is how newness enters the world' (Rushdie 1992: 394).

Note

1 These three elements are indeed conceded as 'desiderata' for a definition of diaspora, even the broadest possible one, by Cohen (1997: 23), though with less emphasis than earlier writers. He also argues that assimilation and individual social mobility may disqualify one from diasporic membership (1997: 24).

References

Ahmed, R., P. Morey and A. Yaqin (ed.) (2012) *Culture, diaspora and modernity in Muslim writing*, London: Routledge.
Al Maleh, L. (ed.) (2009) *Arab voices in diaspora: critical perspectives on anglophone Arab literature*, Amsterdam: Rodopi.
Bernards, B. (2015) *Writing the South Seas: imagining the Nanyang in Chinese and Southeast Asian postcolonial literature*, Seattle: University of Washington Press.
Bhabha, H. (1994) *The location of culture*, London: Routledge.
Bowman, G. (1994) '"A country of words": conceiving the Palestinian nation from the position of exile', in E. Laclau (ed.) *The making of political identities*, London: Verso, 138–70.
Chambers, I. (1994) *Migrancy, culture, identity*, London: Routledge.
Civantos, C. (2005) *Between Argentines and Arabs: Argentine Orientalism, Arab immigrants, and the writing of identity*, Albany: SUNY Press.
Cohen, R. (1997) *Global diasporas: an introduction*, London: UCL Press.
Conrad (1904) *Nostromo: a tale of the seaboard*, New York: Harper & Bros.
Cooper, B. (2013) *A new generation of African writers: migration, material culture and language*, Oxford: James Currey.
Davies, C. B. (1994) *Black women, writing and identity: migrations of the subject*, New York: Routledge.
Davis, C. T. and H. L. Gates (1985) *The slave's narrative*, Oxford: Oxford University Press.
Decter, J. (2005) 'Literatures of medieval Sepharad', in Z. Zohar (ed.) *Sephardic and Mizrahi Jewry: from the golden age of Spain to modern times*, New York: New York University Press, 77–100.
Durán-Almarza, E. M. and E. Álvarez-López (eds) (2014) *Diasporic women's writing of the black Atlantic*, London: Routledge.
Gasyna, G. Z. (2011) *Polish, hybrid, and otherwise: exilic discourse in Joseph Conrad and Witold Gombrowicz*, New York: Continuum.
Gilroy, P. (1993) *The black Atlantic: modernity and double consciousness*, London: Verso.
Green, N. (2013) 'Introduction: Afghan literature between diaspora and nation', in N. Green and N. Arbabzadah (eds) *Afghanistan in ink: literature between diaspora and nation*, London: Hurst.
Gruen, E. S. (2002) *Diaspora: Jews amidst Greeks and Romans*, Cambridge, MA: Harvard University Press.
Hall, S. (1990) 'Cultural identity and diaspora', in J. Rutherford (ed.) *Identity: community, culture, difference*, London: Lawrence & Wishart, 222–37.
Hassan, W. S. (2011) *Immigrant narratives: Orientalism and cultural translation in Arab American and Arab British literature*, Oxford: Oxford University Press.
Ho, Engseng (2006) *The graves of Tarim: genealogy and mobility across the Indian Ocean*, Berkeley: University of California Press.
Hussain, Y. (2005) *Writing diaspora: South Asian women, culture and ethnicity*, Aldershot: Ashgate.
Kaminsky, A. K. (1999) *After exile: writing the Latin American diaspora*, Minneapolis: University of Minnesota Press.
Karim, P. M. (ed.) (2006) *Let me tell you where i've been: new writing by women of the Iranian diaspora*, Fayetteville: University of Arkansas Press.
López Ropero, M. L. (2004) *The Anglo-Caribbean migration novel: writing from the diaspora*, Alicante: Publicaciones de la Universidad de Alicante.
Maxey, R. (2012) *South Asian Atlantic literature, 1970–2010*, Edinburgh: Edinburgh University Press.
Moaveni, A. (2005) *Lipstick Jihad: a memoir of growing up Iranian in America and American in Iran*, New York: PublicAffairs.
Motlagh, A. (2011) 'Autobiography and authority in the writings of the Iranian diaspora', *Comparative Studies of South Asia, Africa and the Middle East*, 31 (2), 411–24, doi: 10.1215/1089201X-1264325.
Nafisi A. (2004) *Reading Lolita in Tehran*, New York: Random House.
Olszewska, Z. (2015) *The Pearl of Dari: poetry and personhood among young Afghans in Iran*, Bloomington, IN: Indiana University Press.

Omri, M.-S. (2006) 'Voicing a culture "dispersed by time": metropolitan location and identity in the literature and art of Sabiha al Khemir,' in Z. S. Salhi and I. R. Netton (eds) *The Arab diaspora: voices of an anguished scream*, London: Routledge, 53–75.

Rando, G. and G. Turcotte (eds) (2007) *Literary and social diasporas: an Italian Australian perspective*, Brussels: Peter Lang.

Rushdie, S. (1992) 'In good faith', in S. Rushdie *Imaginary homelands: essays and criticism 1981–1991*, Harmondsworth: Granta/Penguin, 393–414.

Ryang, S. (2008) *Writing selves in diaspora: ethnography of autobiographies of Korean women in Japan and the United States*, Lanham, MD: Lexington Books.

Said, E. (2002) 'Reflections on exile', in E. Said *Reflections on exile and other essays*, Cambridge, MA: Harvard University Press, 173–86.

Salhi, Z. S. and I. R. Netton (eds) (2006) *The Arab diaspora: voices of an anguished scream*, London: Routledge.

Satrapi, M. (2003) *Persepolis*, New York: Random House.

Schachter, A. (2012) *Diasporic modernisms: Hebrew and Yiddish literature in the twentieth century*, Oxford: Oxford University Press.

Schlote, C. (2013) 'Writing Dubai: Indian labour migrants and taxi topographies, *South Asian Diaspora*, 6 (1), 33–46, doi: 10.1080/19438192.2013.828500.

Upstone, S. (2010) *British Asian fiction: twenty-first century voices*, Manchester: Manchester University Press.

Waheed, S. (2012) 'Literature in the oil age: a review of *Goat Days*', *Chapati Mystery* blog, available at: www.chapatimystery.com/archives/homistan/literature_in_the_oil_age_a_review_of_goat_days_.html.

Zhang, B. (2000) 'Identity in diaspora and diaspora in writing: the poetics of cultural transrelation', *Journal of Intercultural Studies*, 21 (2), 125–42, doi: 10.1080/713678940.

Zhang, B. (2008) *Asian diaspora poetry in North America*, London: Routledge.

Part II
Complex diasporas

11
Making and 'faking' a diasporic heritage

Marc Scully

Diasporic heritage is not automatically conferred. To claim diasporic heritage is to disrupt associations between birthplace, nationality and citizenship (Gilroy 1997), and to proclaim political, cultural or affective allegiance to a real or imagined 'homeland' other than the place of current residence. However, such claims are subject to challenge and contestation. Individual claims to diasporic heritage must be rhetorically arranged around some form of 'proof' or justification that stands in for the more 'natural' association between nation and identity. While diasporic identification is fundamentally heterogenous, some common patterns can be drawn as to how such claims are made and defended, and equally how they are positioned as 'fake'. It is my contention that 'authenticity' is central to understanding diaspora – not in terms of whether a transnational population may be considered an 'authentic' diaspora or not, but rather how individual and collective claims to diasporic status are authenticated. This focus on 'authenticity' can address the creative tension in the diaspora literature identified by Brubaker (2005) between boundary maintenance and boundary erosion, or by Werbner (2002) as between ethnicparochialism and cosmopolitanism. Following Werbner, I will illustrate how this tension is not just the stuff of theory, but is a live concern for those in the diaspora.

My focus is primarily on the individual 'diasporan' and how she negotiates an 'authentic' diasporic heritage in relation to real or imagined diasporic communities, and the set of meanings around 'nation' and 'belonging' prevalent in both her 'homeland' and place of current residence. This is particularly pronounced for diasporans who were not themselves members of the migrant generation: my interpretation of 'diasporic heritage' highlights those of the second, third or subsequent generations. Although not exclusively so, such individuals' connection with a diasporic identity needs to be made and remade, not being underpinned by a personal narrative of migration. This focus on the individual and their relationship with wider social meanings of 'belonging' and 'authenticity' is specifically a social psychological one. It allows a consideration of how the supposed emancipatory potential of diaspora to enable hybridization, liminality and deconstruction of hegemonic norms of nation measure up against the realities of diasporic lives as they are lived (Mitchell 1997). Do individuals have agency to articulate 'authentic' diasporic identities as they wish, or are they subject to material and discursive constraints?

In order to investigate such issues, this chapter is divided into two parts, roughly by the length of time that has elapsed since the original migration event. The first part addresses diasporans who are members of relatively identifiable diasporic communities: they may continue to have family or other ties with the country of origin and may be classified as ethnic minorities or as members of a migrant community in the country of residence. For such diasporans, the dilemma of authenticity occurs in expressing a personally relevant diasporic identity, in the context of constraints imposed by the 'homeland', the country of residence and other 'diasporans'. A diasporic heritage is here made and remade through *culture*, defined broadly. The second part addresses diasporans for whom the link with the original homeland has been lost, either through individual or collective trauma, or through the passage of time. For such individuals, 'authenticity' becomes a matter of proving a specific diasporic heritage through *descent*: this section will consider what forms of evidence are considered adequate to create an 'authentic' link.

Heritage and hegemony

The fundamental heterogeneity of diaspora has been highlighted by numerous scholars (for example, Anthias 1998) who have cautioned against eliding such intersectional differences of age, gender, sexuality, class and politics in discussing diasporic identity. I propose an additional difference that is occasionally overlooked – that between those with diasporic orientations and those with transnational orientations (cf. Scully 2012b). This requires a working distinction between transnationalism and diaspora, as they apply to the identifications of individuals. As Brettell (2006) has outlined, there is a lack of consensus as to the relationship between the two concepts, with some arguing that transnationalism is supplanting diaspora, some that transnational individuals form the 'building blocks' of diaspora, and some that transnationalism represents a dual allegiance to host and origin countries, while diaspora represents a broader spread of allegiances. Adopting the latter distinction, it is possible to interrogate the notion of 'dual allegiances' further. Rather than arguing for the superior conceptual utility of either 'diaspora' or 'transnationalism', I argue that the two co-exist as a series of perspectives, identifications and allegiances within which individual lives can be situated. From this perspective, 'transnationalism' represents the extent to which a life is lived in two or more countries simultaneously, whether that be materially, socially, economically or affectively. 'Diaspora', meanwhile, represents the extent to which a 'national' life is lived outside the nation without necessarily reproducing the set of meaning-makings around identity that are hegemonic within the nation.

This has implications for making a diasporic heritage in the following ways. It is not unusual for a diasporic identity to evolve, over successive generations, into something very different from identity in the origin country. For instance, the hegemonic set of meanings around Irish-American identity is quite different to the hegemonic set of meanings around Irish identity in Ireland. At times, this can lead to a contestation of 'authenticity': due to the assumption that the set of meanings around identity in the nation are, *ipso facto*, correct, this can lead to the positioning of diasporic identities as inauthentic. Contestation of the authenticity of such identities may happen virtually, due to increased communication capacity, but may also occur through encounters between diasporic individuals and more recent migrants, who may have more transnational orientations. It can be hypothesized that those who lead transnational lives will orient to the set of meanings around national identity currently hegemonic in the homeland, and are likely to position diasporic forms of identity as 'fake'.

A concrete example of such contestations can be found in the context of 1980s London, where recent Irish migrants encountered both older migrants from the previous 1950s wave of mass Irish emigration, and the children of this cohort, many of whom strongly identified as Irish. The more recent migrants, many from a relatively middle-class background, distanced themselves from the forms of diasporic Irishness they encountered in London, labelling them as inauthentic due to being culturally different from 'what we did at home' (Gray 2004). It has been argued (for example, Campbell 1999; Mac an Ghaill and Haywood 2003) that these relatively middle-class migrants, in distancing themselves from what they perceived as 'old-fashioned' forms of Irishness, embodied transnational understandings of 'modern Ireland'. In particular those of Irish descent who claimed Irishness were positioned as inauthentic by recent migrants: leading to the epithet 'Plastic Paddy' to denote those who were seen as making illegitimate claims on Irishness (Hickman et al. 2005).

Simultaneously, those of Irish descent in English cities began to articulate hybridized city-based identities based on both their diasporic heritage and the specificity of their lived experience, such as London-Irish, Birmingham-Irish, Manchester-Irish, and so on. Such labels can be seen as a rhetorical response to being labelled 'fake' by ceding the ground of unhyphenated Irishness, but they can also be read as a more proactive claim on a more personally authentic identity. In my own research on discourses of Irishness in England (Scully 2012a), I found that more recent migrants would regularly comment on the lack of knowledge of those of Irish descent about current affairs in Ireland as a means of positioning them as not 'properly' Irish. Meanwhile, those of Irish descent spoke of the need for their specific experiences and identifications to be recognized as valid, while admitting that their claims on Irishness were context-dependent. Long-term migrants, on the other hand, based their claims of Irish 'authenticity' on continued involvement in an Irish diasporic community, arguing such communities had preserved 'real' Irish culture, that had been lost in Ireland itself due to modernization. From such accounts, I argue (Scully 2010) that there are three main discourses that can be drawn upon in articulating an ethno-national identity outside the nation:

- authenticity through collective experience and memory;
- authenticity through transnational knowledge and practices;
- authenticity through diasporic claim.

These discourses are not exclusively associated with any one cohort in the diaspora, but are available (subject to constraints) to any individual seeking to proclaim the authenticity of their identity relative to the diaspora. Those not of the original migrant generation can assert the validity of their identities by appealing to the collective experience of their diasporic community, potentially through a kind of 'postmemory' (Hirsch 2008). They may also draw on the discourse of transnational knowledge, perhaps by emphasizing regular visits to the 'homeland'. However, it may become necessary to draw on the discourse of authenticity through diasporic claim, especially as a counter-argument to the assumption that 'authentic' identity resides in the 'homeland'. I have defined this discourse as rhetorical attempts to counter or and deconstruct essentialist discourses of identity as dependant on birthplace and/or accent and instead suggest other means of demonstrating authenticity.

These forms of contestation of authenticity can also be seen in other diasporic groups. For instance, Yeh (2007) has highlighted different takes on authenticity throughout the Tibetan diaspora. She explores how the different routes taken by those of Tibetan heritage to the United States have resulted in cultural and linguistic intra-diaspora differences. The hegemonic understanding of 'authentic' Tibetan culture in the USA is dominated by Tibetans who were exiled following the 1959 rebellion and their descendants: this cohort view themselves as exemplifying an 'authentic' Tibetan culture in exile, due to the subsequent promotion of Chinese language and culture in Tibet itself. However this understanding is challenged by more recent migrants from Tibet who draw on their geographical and experiential knowledge of the contemporary homeland to position their own Tibetan identities as the more authentic.

A third group, who have experienced a hybridized Tibetan–Indian culture in Dharamsala, the home of the Dalai Lama, construct that city as the locus of 'authentic' Tibetan culture. While the political context is different, there are obvious parallels with the case of the Irish diaspora. Yeh uses the concept of 'habitus' to describe how her respondents negotiate the authenticity of their own identities. I would argue that one can also trace how they draw on the three discourses outlined above.

Along similar lines, Mavroudi (2010) looks at contestation of authenticity in the Palestinian diaspora in Greece, along class lines as well as whether individuals have ever lived in Palestine. Mavroudi notes that the burden of proving oneself 'really' Palestinian appears to fall on those born in diaspora, who have not lived in Palestine. Such individuals must make diasporic claims for their authentic Palestinian identity, lacking the transnational knowledge of contemporary Palestine, or the collective experience of those who have lived through refugee camps.

How then, can diasporic claims to authentic identity be made in the context of the discursive constraints placed not only by essentialist associations between nation and identity, but also by competing discourses of authenticity in the diaspora? One tactic is to embrace the postmodernity of diaspora, and to seek to call into question the possibility of an 'authentic' identity. However, in the practice of diasporic lives as they are lived, this does not appear to be quite enough. Rather, individual diasporans seek to authenticate their identities through some form of personally meaningful evidence. This may come in the form of, *inter alia*, evidence of descent (more on which below), material objects (Turan 2010) or some form of cultural practice, which may be individual or collective, for instance participation in parades or festivals, although the authenticity of such events is also subject to contestation (Klimt 2000; Scully 2012a; Yeh 2007).

One of the more personal modes of creating a personally authentic diasporic heritage that has been noted by researchers is through food. This can be through the preparation and consumption of certain meals and foodstuffs linked with the homeland, or through seeking to import various brands of food from the homeland. For instance, Kneafsey and Cox (2002) have illustrated how the diasporic food practices of Irish women in Coventry included purchasing Irish brands of everyday foods, such as Galtee cheese, Tayto crisps, Barry's Tea and Kerrygold butter. Many of these brands have subsequently drawn on their popularity in the diaspora as a promotional tool (McDaid 2014). (Having said that, such brands can often provoke contestations of authenticity in themselves – which of the Northern or Southern variety of Tayto crisp is viewed as 'authentic' is an ongoing debate in the Irish diaspora.)

Mannur's (2007) analysis of culinary nostalgia in Asian diaspora literary studies highlights the role played by food and food preparation in diasporic communities, arguing that a

> collective sense of nationhood, an affective longing for the home, and a fear of 'losing' tradition morphs into a desire to retain viability and visibility through a systematic attempt to ossify the fragments and shards of cultural practices deemed 'authentic'.
>
> *(Mannur 2007: 27)*

Mannur's analysis illustrates how such 'authenticity' only makes sense in a diasporic context – in the idealized homeland, 'authentic' food is just food, and subject to regional variations. Moreover, she highlights that the level of attention to detail needed to ensure an 'authentic' dish can sometimes veer into the absurd – for a dish to be 'authentic', do all of the constituent ingredients need to be sourced from the homeland, or merely the recipe?

In drawing attention to the individual diasporan's need to 'navigate the unwritten codes of diaspora', Mannur highlights the various explicit and implicit constraints on making a personally authentic diasporic heritage. The resources available to make this diasporic heritage are also variable.

In the second half of this chapter, I turn to those individuals and communities who are reliant on explicitly written codes in order to construct a diasporic heritage: those of genealogy, and more recently of DNA.

Descent and DNA

In looking at the making of a diasporic heritage through the 'proof' offered by genealogy and genetics, the focus shifts from those of relatively recent migrant heritage, to those for whom the ancestral migration event is further in the past, and the link to the original homeland is now lost, or largely symbolic. Gans's (1979) concept of 'symbolic ethnicity' has been widely used in this context, although its assumption of assimilation clearly has limitations for those who are more obviously positioned as disadvantaged by their ethnicity. Nonetheless, while those who search for a diasporic heritage through genealogical/genetic means may not entirely identify with the hegemonic national identity of the country they live in, their nationality *per se* is generally not under question. Diasporic heritage is therefore not a given; it must be demonstrated either individually or collectively, through 'hard' evidence. It does not seem sufficient merely to assert a diasporic heritage: it must be in some way accounted for, in order to be 'authentic'.

The use of genealogy to demonstrate an 'authentic' link with a diasporic past has been explored in detail in the American context by Catherine Nash, who has focused on Irish Americans, and Alondra Nelson, whose work concentrates on African Americans. Nash (2008) has demonstrated that for Irish Americans involved in the pursuit of genealogical origins, the focus is often to locate a specific geographical place where their ancestor(s) lived, that this 'authenticates and verifies what was previously a general but unspecific ancestral connection'. (This corresponds with my own findings on the importance of county identity in the Irish diaspora; Scully 2013.) The attraction of the discovery of the ancestral home appears to be the air of legitimacy it lends to diasporic claims on Irishness – allowing Nash's respondents to distinguish themselves from 'temporary and superficial' performances of Irish ancestry in America, such as on St Patrick's Day. To be able to point to the specificity of one's ancestry is therefore a rhetorical device allowing one to assert a more authentic diasporic identity than those who cannot do so: something Nash describes as a culture of 'competitive authenticity' in the diaspora.

Of course, as Nash points out, this is a form of essentialism in itself, and rather undermines theoretical claims for diaspora as a means of allowing for more hybrid liminal understandings of identity. Similarly, in many cases, focusing on a specific line of descent privileges one line of ancestry over others: it is often overlooked that many individuals will be members of several diasporas simultaneously, something that may be viewed as the ultimate occupation of 'diaspora space' (Brah 1996). As states proactively engage with genealogical diasporas for tourism purposes, this raises the prospect of something of a market in persuading individuals that of all the possible diasporas they could potentially identity with, *this* one is the most authentic. However, such engagement must take into account the subtle ways in which diasporic heritage is made: the Irish government's initiative to sell Certificates of Irish Heritage to those who could 'prove' Irish descent (effectively a certificate of authenticity) was widely seen as a failure, and discontinued after four years (Kenny 2015).

In the African-American context, Nelson (2016) traces how the popularity of Alex Haley's *Roots* spurred a genealogy boom. She argues that *Roots*, and by extension genealogy, provides a narrative of black life: that it 'became an urtext of African diasporic reconciliation for a generation of Americans' (Nelson 2016: 70). Perhaps the major attraction of this narrative of diasporic heritage was that it could be *made* and fashioned on a personal and collective level, rather than imposed by slavery and its racist legacy. However, as Nelson illustrates, many individuals who wished to make a specific personalized connection to an African-born ancestor found that they could not do so, due to a dearth of relevant records. As she explains, many of her respondents have subsequently turned to the promise offered by genetic genealogy to provide a link to a personalized African past.

This turn, which has been seen in many diasporic communities, as a means of lending a veneer of scientific legitimacy to the process of making a diasporic heritage, needs to be seen in the context of 'applied genetic history', which is marked by 'novel kinds of mediatisation, commercialisation and personalisation of historical knowledge as products' (Sommer 2012: 226). The use of such 'products' as a means of affiliating oneself to a specific diaspora, has the potential to position shared DNA alongside shared language and culture in defining diaspora as an 'imagined genetic community'. It should, however, be pointed out that many population geneticists are wary about the commercial application of population genetics data, pointing out the problems and lack of nuance inherent in applying population data at an individual level, alongside the fact that such tests tend to focus on only one line of descent (see Jobling et al. 2016 for an overview of such concerns). Therefore, assumptions that DNA can fix a point of origin/'homeland' for individual diasporans looking for specificity should be viewed with caution.

Nelson's (2008, 2016) work on African-American users of genetic ancestry testing services illustrates how many were drawn to such services in the hope of a 'usable past', that would provide confirmation of pre-existing narratives, and a familial origin point in Africa. She traces how negotiating the complexity of genetic results can result in the forging of new, unanticipated links, and create 'alternative social worlds with reimagined kinship arrangements and affiliations' (Nelson 2016: 94). While such social worlds might appear to chime with the more liberatory potential of diaspora, it is also clear that marshalling DNA evidence to articulate diasporic links and identities is subject to contestation. Nelson draws attention to the potential of genetic information to act as a 'diasporic resource', allowing for the 'weaving of a social mesh between African communities and their dispersed members, even in the absence of specific kinship ties' (2016: 145). (One might remark that while such genetic links are scientifically questionable, they are culturally resonant.) She illustrates this through the example of the actor Isaiah Washington, who, following a DNA test that linked his maternal DNA ancestry with Sierra Leone, became increasingly involved with present-day Sierra Leone: establishing a charitable foundation, and ultimately adopting dual citizenship. The identification of a high-profile individual as a member of the 'DNA diaspora' undoubtedly counts as a 'diasporic resource' from the point of view of governments in the putative 'homeland': Nelson gives the example of the eagerness of government officials from Guinea-Bissau to claim Whoopi Goldberg, following a suggestion that she was genetically linked to the Papel and Bayote communities of that country. (Lest it be thought that such claims are confined to African governments, decades of proactive uncovering of US presidents' Irish ancestors arguably reached an apex with the establishment of the Barack Obama Plaza motorway service station near Moneygall, Co. Offaly.)

Such claims are tempered (or perhaps motivated) by the concerns of Africans in Africa about the diasporic claims made by African Americans on African diasporic heritage, arguing that African identity was best authenticated by a commitment to working in Africa, rather than through DNA, which Nelson illustrates through online comments. Returning to my typology of discourses of authenticity, this may be seen as an articulation of the need to demonstrate authenticity through transnational *involvement*, as opposed to the diasporic claim of assumed authenticity through DNA. However, what this example illustrates is the role of power dynamics in articulating an 'authentic' diasporic identity. While my previous work comes from the perspective that the discourse of authenticity through transnational knowledge is generally hegemonic, this is not the case in contestations of 'authentic' identity between Americans and West Africans. Nelson points to the asymmetrical nature of the exchange of this 'diasporic resource'.

DNA therefore represents something of a paradox in discussing diaspora, being both inescapably essentialist (being based on a biological essence), and something that can provoke a great deal of fluidity in the remaking of diasporic heritage. Nash (2015) builds on this paradox in cautioning that while viewing identity through the prism of genetic genealogy renders all of non-African humanity diasporic (in that we all ultimately trace our roots to migration from Africa), this is mediated through contemporary power relations that render the diasporic origins of some individuals (and groups) 'normal' and others problematic.

Does DNA, then, position us all in 'diaspora space', in perhaps a rather different way to Brah's (1996) original conceptualization of the term? Thus far, this discussion of diaspora through descent has focused on two 'prototypical' diasporas in Cohen's (2008) terms: the African and the Irish. The concept of the Viking diaspora, on the other hand, is relatively new to diaspora studies, although increasingly employed by medievalists (Jesch 2015). Recent research by myself and colleagues on the *Impact of Diasporas on the Making of Britain* programme has explored, among other things, how individuals might come to interpret a potential Viking heritage through DNA (Scully et al. 2013, 2016). The concept of being of Viking descent is a popular one in the North of England, particularly centred on York, whose urban identity trades to a major extent on its Viking heritage. As tracing a specific Viking ancestor is next to impossible genealogically, many of the participants in this research saw DNA as a way of authenticating their narratives of Viking descent. Whether this can be classed as making a 'diasporic' heritage depends on how far we are willing to stretch the concept of 'diaspora'. Certainly, responses from our participants that 'proof' of Viking heritage would make them feel more deeply rooted in Yorkshire are not particularly disruptive of hegemonic discourses of nation, identity and belonging. Nonetheless, Scandinavia was positioned in these responses as a point of origin, if not necessarily a 'homeland', and as somewhere respondents felt an affinity with. The 'imagined genetic communities' formed through DNA may therefore be classed as a new form of 'affinity diaspora' (Ancien et al. 2009): a potential resource for states that wish to attract interest and some form of loyalty from overseas, but that are unlikely to challenge hegemonic meanings of national identity.

Conclusion

I began by questioning the levels of agency experienced by individual diasporans in making a diasporic heritage given the constraints imposed by hegemonic understandings of national (and transnational) identity. From the evidence I have presented, paradoxically, it appears to be those 'diasporans' with the most tangential claims on the present-day 'homeland' who have the most scope in fashioning a diasporic identity. Claiming a 'Viking' diasporic identity through DNA falls within the category of recreational genomics: as a 'placeholder identity', it does not pose a challenge to the sets of meanings around being 'Norwegian' and 'Danish' in those modern-day countries. However, where diasporans have a greater stake in having their claims on identity recognized as 'authentic', contestation of this authenticity appears to be more fraught, whether within the diaspora, between diasporic and transnational individuals/communities, or between the diaspora and the 'homeland'. The dilemma of 'authenticity' is thus most pronounced for those who occupy the liminal space of diaspora: if only for acknowledgement that that liminal space may be a personally authentic place to be.

References

Ancien, D., M. Boyle and R. Kitchin (2009) 'Exploring diaspora strategies: lessons for Ireland', unpublished paper, National Institute for Regional and Spatial Analysis, Maynooth University, available at: http://eprints.maynoothuniversity.ie/2054/1/RK_Exploring_Diaspora_Strategies.pdf.

Anthias, F. (1998) 'Evaluating "diaspora": beyond ethnicity?', *Sociology*, 32 (3), 557–80, doi: 10.1177/0038038598032003009.

Brah, A. (1996) *Cartographies of diaspora: contesting identities*, London: Routledge.

Brettell, C. B. (2006) 'Introduction: global spaces/local places: transnationalism, diaspora, and the meaning of home', *Identities: Global Studies in Culture and Power*, 13 (3), 327–34, doi: 10.1080/10702890600837987.

Brubaker, R. (2005) 'The "diaspora" diaspora', *Ethnic and Racial Studies*, 28 (1), 1–19, doi: 10.1080/0141987042000289997.

Campbell, S. (1999) 'Beyond "plastic paddy": a re-examination of the second-generation Irish in England', *Immigrants & Minorities*, 18 (2/3), 266–88, doi: 10.1080/02619288.1999.9974977.

Cohen, R. (2008) *Global diasporas: an introduction*, London: Routledge.

Gans, H. J. (1979) 'Symbolic ethnicity: the future of ethnic groups and cultures in America', *Ethnic and Racial Studies*, 2 (1), 1–20, doi: 10.1080/01419870.1979.9993248.

Gilroy, P. (1997) 'Diaspora and the detours of identity', in K. Woodward (ed.) *Identity and difference*, London: Sage, 301–43.

Gray, B. (2004) *Women and the Irish diaspora*, London: Routledge.

Hickman, M. J., S. Morgan, B. Walter and J. Bradley (2005) 'The limitations of whiteness and the boundaries of Englishness: second-generation Irish identifications and positionings in multiethnic Britain', *Ethnicities*, 5 (2), 160–82, doi: 10.1177/1468796805052113.

Hirsch, M. (2008) 'The generation of postmemory', *Poetics Today*, 29 (1), 103–28, doi: 10.1215/03335372-2007-019.

Jesch, J. (2015) *The Viking diaspora*, London: Routledge.

Jobling, M. A., R. Rasteiro and J. H. Wetton (2016) 'In the blood: the myth and reality of genetic markers of identity', *Ethnic and Racial Studies*, 39 (2), 142–61, doi: 10.1080/01419870.2016.1105990.

Kenny, C. (2015) 'Certificate of Irish heritage abandoned after low uptake', *Irish Times*, 17 August, available at: www.irishtimes.com/life-and-style/abroad/generation-emigration/certificate-of-irish-heritage-abandoned-after-low-uptake-1.2320015.

Klimt, A. (2000) 'Enacting national selves: authenticity, adventure, and disaffection in the Portuguese diaspora', *Identities Global Studies in Culture and Power*, 6 (4), 513–50, doi: 10.1080/1070289X.2000.9962654.

Kneafsey, M. and R. Cox (2002) 'Food, gender and Irishness– how Irish women in Coventry make home', *Irish Geography*, 35 (1), 6–15, doi: 10.1080/00750770209555789.

Mac an Ghaill, M. and C. Haywood (2003) 'Young (male) Irelanders: postcolonial ethnicities – expanding the nation and Irishness' *European Journal of Cultural Studies*, 6 (3), 386–403, doi: 10.1177/13675494030063007.

McDaid, A. (2014) '"Sure we export all our best stuff": changing representations of emigration in Irish television advertising', *Nordic Irish Studies*, 13 (1), 41–56, available at: www.jstor.org/stable/24332392.

Mannur, A. (2007) 'Culinary nostalgia: authenticity, nationalism, and diaspora', *Melus*, 32 (4), 11–31, doi: 10.1093/melus/32.4.11.

Mavroudi, E. (2010) 'Contesting identities, differences, and a unified Palestinian community', *Environment and Planning D: Society and Space*, 28 (2), 239–53, doi: 10.1068/d8608.

Mitchell, K. (1997) 'Different diasporas and the hype of hybridity', *Environment and Planning D: Society and Space*, 15 (5), 533–53, doi: 10.1068/d150533.

Nash, C. (2008) *Of Irish descent: origin stories, genealogy, and the politics of belonging*, Syracuse, NY: Syracuse University Press.

Nash, C. (2015) *Genetic geographies: the trouble with ancestry*, Minneapolis: University of Minnesota Press.

Nelson, A. (2008) 'Bio science: genetic genealogy testing and the pursuit of African ancestry', *Social Studies of Science*, 38 (5), 759–83, doi: 10.1177/0306312708091929.

Nelson, A. (2016) *The social life of DNA: race, reparations, and reconciliation after the genome*, Boston: Beacon Press.

Scully, M. (2010) 'Discourses of authenticity and national identity among the Irish diaspora in England', doctoral dissertation, The Open University, available at: http://oro.open.ac.uk/25474/.

Scully, M. (2012a) 'Whose day is it anyway? St. Patrick's Day as a contested performance of national and diasporic Irishness', *Studies in Ethnicity and Nationalism*, 12 (1), 118–35, doi: 10.1111/j.1754-9469.2011.01149.x.

Scully, M. (2012b) 'The tyranny of transnational discourse: "authenticity" and Irish diasporic identity in Ireland and England', *Nations and Nationalism*, 18 (2), 191–209, doi: 10.1111/j.1469-8129.2011.00534.x.

Scully, M. (2013) 'BIFFOs, jackeens and Dagenham Yanks: county identity, "authenticity" and the Irish diaspora', *Irish Studies Review*, 21 (2), 143–63, doi: 10.1080/09670882.2013.808874.

Scully, M., T. King and S. D. Brown (2013) 'Remediating Viking origins: genetic code as archival memory of the remote past', *Sociology*, 47 (5), 921–38, doi: 10.1177/0038038513493538.

Scully, M., S. D. Brown and T. King (2016) 'Becoming a Viking: DNA testing, genetic ancestry and placeholder identity', *Ethnic and Racial Studies*, 39 (2), 162–80, doi: 10.1080/01419870.2016.1105991.

Sommer, M. (2012) '"It's a living history, told by the real survivors of the times – DNA": anthropological genetics in the tradition of biology as applied history', in K. Wailoo, A. Nelson and C. Lee (eds) *Genetics and the unsettled past: the collision of DNA, race and history*, London: Rutgers University Press, 225–46.

Turan, Z. (2010) 'Material objects as facilitating environments: the Palestinian diaspora', Home Cultures, 7 (1), 43–56, doi: 10.2752/175174210X12572427063841.

Werbner, P. (2002) 'The place which is diaspora: citizenship, religion and gender in the making of chaordic transnationalism' *Journal of Ethnic and Migration Studies*, 28 (1), 119–33, doi: 10.1080/13691830120103967.

Yeh, E. T. (2007) 'Exile meets homeland: politics, performance, and authenticity in the Tibetan diaspora', *Environment and Planning D: Society and Space*, 25 (4), 648–67, doi: 10.1068/d2805.

12
Translanguaging and diasporic imagination

Zhu Hua and Li Wei

Language matters for people on the move. It is part of the identity of diaspora and, in some cases, it can be the only connection one has with the ancestral land from which the community has dispersed. When diasporas move across space and change over time, they have to make decisions about the extent to which they can maintain the heritage language or adopt the language of the new place of residence. Language then becomes a symbolic and mobile resource that diasporic communities utilize for strategic purposes. It is, therefore, not surprising that in the last two decades, migration and diaspora have become important topics for applied linguists who are concerned with real-world issues in which language plays a central role (Brumfit 1995: 27). A number of questions linking language, migration and diaspora have been addressed in some depth by applied linguists. These include, as reviewed in Li Wei and Zhu Hua (2013): How and why do migrants maintain 'old' languages, namely languages of their heritage? How and why do they learn 'new' languages, namely languages of their new place of residence? How do migrants negotiate languages, social relationships, identities and ideologies in the family, the community and the workplace? And how do they choose from their multilingual repertoire to communicate in institutional settings such as schools, health and medical services, legal, social and public service encounters?

The recent publication of the *Routledge handbook of migration and language* edited by Canagarajah (2017) provides an overview of the conceptual and methodological frameworks in the field of multilingualism, migration and diaspora, as well as discussions of the implications for policy and practice. In this chapter, we focus on new ways of understanding of language choices from the perspective of diasporic imagination. We explore how diasporic imagination impacts on the language choices diasporic communities make and, at the same time, how language choices and practices infuse and actualize diasporic imagination. In particular, we discuss examples of translanguaging practices through which migrants negotiate their subjectivity and sense of belonging.

Diasporic imagination and linguistic choice

As migrants bring their languages across borders and come into contact with other languages, deciding which language(s) to speak to whom and when often becomes a contentious issue for diasporic families and communities in different contexts. Traditionally, language maintenance, that is, keeping the heritage language(s) through generations, and language shift, that is, giving up one's heritage language(s) in favour of the languages of present place of residence, are seen to represent the opposite values and senses of belonging. Those who wish to maintain the traditional values and practices of the homeland and to keep close contacts with family and friends there also want to maintain their heritage languages, whereas those who accept the values and ways of life of their new home would want to integrate with the local culture and adopt the languages of the local community. Linguists have documented numerous cases where communities have successfully maintained their languages through generations as well as those who have shifted to the languages of the new homes (for example, Clyde 1982; Fishman 2013; Li Wei 1994).

Increasingly, however, migrants find themselves in a transnational space where both the heritage language and the new language of the locality are necessary and important in their everyday lives. The migrants' transnational experience gives rise to a desire for both synchronic and diachronic connectivities which are at the heart of a new diasporic imagination. For us, diasporic imagination is a conscious, self-reflexive and creative thinking about the potentialities of one's dislocated situatedness. It comes out of one's awareness of the differences between the place of origin and the place of presence, their different histories, traditions, values and, of course, languages. But instead of feeling any sense of loss or bewilderment, the focus is on the multiple realms of opportunities and possibilities and the new social spaces migration opens up for the individuals, their families and their communities. In his study of nationalism, Anderson (1983) put forward the notion of 'imagined communities' to describe how nations as political communities come to be imagined and live in the minds of each member who 'will never know most of their fellow members, meet them, or even hear them' (1983: 6). Translating the notion to the context of diasporas, Cohen (2008) argues that there are 'imagined' homelands where the members of the diasporas have never been before and 'imagined' transnational communities which 'unite segments of people that live in territorially separated locations' (2008: 13). Imagined communities do not mean that these communities are something artificial or created by some sort of 'mental' activities, as Sofos (1996) explained. Instead, it is about forging links between social groups through suppressing or neutralizing past differences and establishing shared contexts and common experiences.

Building on the notion of 'imagined' communities, Appadurai (1996) made the case for envisaging imagination as a social practice and as 'something critical and new in global cultural processes' (1996: 31). Combining memory and desire, imagination is

> no longer mere fantasy (opium for the masses whose real work is elsewhere), no longer simple escape (from a world defined principally by more concrete purposes and structures), no longer elite pastime (thus not relevant to the lives of ordinary people), and no longer mere contemplation (irrelevant for new forms of desire and subjectivity), the imagination has become an organised field of social practices, a form of work (in the sense of both labour and culturally organised practice), and a form of negotiation between sites of agency (individuals) and globally defined fields of possibility.

Diasporic imagination can unite people across time and space and create new possibilities for them. It invites a different perspective on language maintenance and language shift among migrants. In studying the transnational experiences of migrant individuals and communities, applied linguists such as Block (2008) have challenged the appropriateness of the metaphor of 'loss' and called for a move away from the excessively emotive and romanticized stances towards language maintenance and language shift. For many such individuals and communities, it is not what they have lost that occupies their minds in their everyday lives, but what they seek to develop and construct for themselves plays a key role in language choices and related identity-making. This is evident in many empirical studies. Ibrahim (1999), for example, found that the continental African immigrants and refugees in a high school in Ontario imagine and position themselves as 'Black American' and choose to speak 'Black stylized English' which they access through rap and hip-hop. In language classrooms, language learners' actual and desired memberships in imagined communities make differences to their learning trajectories, agency, motivation, investment, as well as resistance in the learning of English (Palvenko and Norton 2007).

A further study by Li Wei and Zhu Hua (forthcoming) closely examines the role imagination plays in whether and how members of transnational families individually and collectively maintain or relinquish their heritage languages and adopt other languages. Families that have kept their heritage languages and those that have given them up were invited to talk about where, what and how they would see themselves in ten years' time, and a selection of them were subsequently interviewed and observed after the ten-year period. Their responses are analysed in terms of their constructed experiences, environments and visions of the future; their perceptions and imaginations of different places and cultures; key moments in re-evaluation, or re-imagining, that led to major behavioural changes; and self-evaluation of their imaginations. Three of the findings are relevant here:

- Imagination is shaped both by the individuals' and the families' past experiences and present circumstances. While many factors play a role in language maintenance and shift, how transnational individuals and families imagine their future was a key factor.
- The same imagination may result in different coping strategies. For example, some families imagined that they would not be staying in Britain very long and therefore they wanted to make sure that their children maintain their Chinese to a high level. Others, however, felt that they should make best use of their (imagined) short stay in Britain and get their English to a good level.
- For all the families, imaginations evolve over time as circumstances change, and there are differences and tensions between the imaginations of individual members of the same family, resulting in different attitudes and behaviours. The imagining and re-imagining help to produce a more dynamic notion of 'heritage' and 'heritage language', as well as a more complex sense of belonging.

The diaspora as a translanguaging space

Diasporic imagination not only underpins language maintenance and shift at a macro-community level, but also influences and explains the way migrants go about their language practices in everyday interaction. Migration creates opportunities for linguistic and cultural contact. Many members of diasporic communities speak multiple languages and, therefore, almost by default, diasporic communication is described as 'multilingual'. The consensus from recent studies in applied linguistics seems to be to emphasize the multilingual language user's capacity to create an apparently seamless flow between language and language varieties to achieve effective and meaningful communication. In doing so, applied linguists have attempted to 'disinvent and reconstitute' (Makoni and Pennycook 2007) languages from discrete systems to connected repertoires.

Translanguaging, as a new way of understanding language and communication, refers to the dynamic meaning-making process whereby multilingual speakers go beyond the conventional divides between languages and between modalities of communication (García and Li Wei 2014). The term was originally coined by Cen Williams (1994, 1996) to describe a pedagogical practice in bilingual classrooms whereby students read and listen in one language and speak and

Translanguaging and diasporic imagination

write in another language. The potential advantages of translanguaging pedagogy in developing the learner's academic language skills in both languages were further discussed in Baker (2006). García (2009: 45) extended the notion of translanguaging to refer to 'multiple discursive practices in which bilinguals engage in order to make sense of their bilingual worlds'. The multiple discursive practices cover multilingual practices which have traditionally been described a code-switching, code-mixing, crossing, creolization, and so on. Li Wei (2011) proposed the notion of 'translanguaging space', a space created by and for translanguaging practices, and a space where multilingual individuals integrate social spaces (including 'language codes') that have been formerly practised separately in different spaces by 'bringing together different dimensions of their personal history, experience and environment, their attitude, belief and ideology, their cognitive and physical capacity into one coordinated and meaningful performance' (Li Wei 2011: 1223).

The notion of translanguaging space helps to understand how language(s) and different semiotic resources are integrated and mobilized to connect people on the move, motivated by diasporic imagination. This can be illustrated through the following two examples collected as part of the *Translation and translanguaging* project (www.birmingham.ac.uk/generic/tlang/index.aspx). E and her husband, T, arrived in the UK from their native Poland in 1997. They originally planned to stay for a few years, save some money and return to Poland, where they had bought a house. In this sense, they belong to the type of Polish immigrants dubbed as 'hamsters', that is, 'migrants who treat their move as a one-off act to acquire enough capital to invest in Poland', tend to cluster in particular low-earning occupations and are often embedded in Polish networks (Eade et al. 2007). The couple used their savings to open a Polish shop in Newham, London. We observed E's interaction with customers in the shop and her (extended) family in London and in Poland in face-to-face contexts or via social media during fourth months' linguistic ethnography. The first example is from social media data. It is a screen shot of her Facebook 'wall' (the section in a profile where friends can write messages) on Halloween night. A Facebook friend posted Halloween wishes there.

In this translanguaging space, the Happy Halloween wish is expressed in a combination of English, Polish (życzę wszysktim meaning 'wish everybody'), and two emoticons. The rest of the 'wall', not shown here, is populated with images, either pasted from elsewhere or in the form of emoticons or stickers made available by Facebook. In one post, E used Polish alphabet phonetic spelling: 'Hapi Hapi Halolin' in place of Happy Happy Halloween. The examples illustrate E's and her friends' approach to their multiple languages and semiotic resources. Instead of choosing one language or one mode over the other, they mobilize all the languages and semiotic resources available to them, and move between and integrate different semiotic and linguistic systems creatively. The immediate communicative goal here is to share the excitements of Halloween, a festival that is not celebrated in Poland, but originated in the Western Christian traditions, having gone through a certain degree of Americanization. Their translanguaging practice and imagination connect groups of people who may have different life trajectories, experiences and beliefs. They also produce a fusion of longing and belonging which

Figure 12.1 Example 1: Happy Halloween

Source: Zhu Hua et al. 2015.

in turn provides a vision and a source of inner strength and conviviality that drives migrants forward in their daily struggles. Immigrants and their families do not simply look back all the time; they also look forward and see the potentialities of their present situation.

The desire to connect and get along with others, and above all, to build conviviality (Wise and Velayutham 2014; cf. Valentine 2008) means that people in 'zones of encounters' (Wood and Landry 2007) are flexible about their language choices. They accommodate others' language choices and tolerate ambiguities and mis- or non-understanding. However, there are also occasions when differences are brought out into the open and boundaries of languages are marked. These processes are illustrated in Example 2.

In service encounters, E and her customers tend to use a range of linguistic and semiotic repertoires, including gestures, eye gaze, and body positioning, to complete transactions (Zhu Hua et al. forthcoming). In the interaction transcribed above, both the opening and closing are in Russian, the customer's native language. However, the rest of the conversation uses a mix of Polish, English and Russian (which are at times impossible to tell apart). In Turn 15, E adopts the role of a teacher and makes an attempt to teach the customer the Polish word for the ham

Table 12.1 Example 2: A service encounter (Source: Zhu Hua et al. 2015)

Context: E is serving a Russian speaker in the shop.

Turn		Transcription	English translation
1	C	**Здравствуйте!**	**Hello!**
2	E	**Здравствуйте!**	**Hello!**
3	C	**Мне нужно у вас** (inaudible) **Так. Ну давай кусочек** (11) Tego. (till)	**I need you** (inaudible). **Yes. Let's have a piece of** (11) This. (till)
4	E	Którą?	Which one?
5	C	Tego.	Of this one.
6	E	Tą?	This?
7	C	Może {tak tez bo to tak} (?)	Maybe {like this because it's so} (?)
8	E	Też taki sam **kусочек**?	Also **a piece** like that?
9	C	Ehh **да** <u>ро/по</u> **кусочку** tak tak.	Uh **yes a piece** <u>each</u> yes yes.
10	E	Dobra. (12, till)	Ok. (12, till)
11	E	Uhum. (till)	Uhum. (till)
12	C	<u>I/**И**</u> **здесь** takiego **мясочка кусочек**.	**And** here a piece of this **meat**.
13	E	Tego?	This one?
14	C	Tak. Tego. Tego.	Yes. This one. This one.
15	E	(laughing) Boczek. *Bacon*.	(laughing) Boczek. *Bacon*.
16	C	*Bacon*. **Tak**. *Bacon*.	*Bacon*. **Yes**. *Bacon*.
17	E	I to wszystko?	Is that all?
18	C	Wszystko.	That's all.
19	E	Dobra. (3, bagging, till) I <u>dwa/**два**</u> **сорок** dwa/**два**. (3) Sześć osiemdziesiąt cztery będzie. (5, bagging) Sześć osiem cztery, sześć osiemdziesiąt pięć. Sześć dziewięćdziesiąt. (4)	Ok. (3, bagging, till) And <u>two</u>-**forty**-<u>two</u>. (3) It will be six eighty-four. (5) Six eight four, six eighty five. Six ninety. (4)
21	E	**Спасибо**.	**Thank you**.
22	C	**Спасибо**.	**Thank you**.

Transcription conventions: In both transcription and translation, Russian is represented in **bold**, English in *italics*, Polish in regular script and ambiguous language <u>underlined</u>. Words in { } represent researcher's best guess. The numbers are the length of pauses between utterances in seconds.

she was buying. The Polish word is no other than the word for the Polish traditional, natural smoked bacon, 'boczek'. She marks or hedges her teaching with a gentle laughter and follows the word *boczek* with its English translation, *bacon*. However, the customer only picks up the English word and repeats it as if she is trying to confirm that she indeed wants bacon. It could be either the case that she misunderstands E's intention or that she deliberately resists her teaching. Nonetheless, she herself uses some Polish words without E's prompting in the conversation. This excerpt suggests that while multilingual speakers move between highly dynamic mixes of language, they are also aware of boundaries between different languages. On one hand, E accommodates the language choices of her customers. She responds to the customer's greeting and opts to close the encounter with 'thankyou' in Russian in the last but one turn. On the other hand, she also encourages them to speak some Polish key words, *boczek* being one of them. The customers seem to adopt this practice and, if they have any knowledge of Polish (as is the case with the Russian customer in this example), they use it in the shop.

Conclusion

Language and the diaspora are closely bound to each other. Language can discriminate and alienate individual and groups who may be seen to be different. But language also connects people with shared histories, experiences and values across time and space. As Green and Power (2005) argue, one's membership, allegiance and sense of belonging to their place or culture of origin and new place of settlement can be enhanced by the transnational experiences and interactions (see also Ong 1999; Ray 2003; Shames 1997; Song 2003; van der Veer 1995). The transnational experiences and interactions create a diasporic imagination that is conscious, self-reflexive and creative. This diasporic imagination helps the migrants to see and seek new opportunities and potentials out of an unstable situation in a contact zone, and to find a sense of situatedness in dislocation.

The transnational experience and interaction also create a translanguaging space for the individuals and their communities to negotiate their language choices. Communication in the diaspora typically involves speakers of different languages, registers, styles and cultural backgrounds, and consequently has been described as multilingual and intercultural. However, the diversity and complexity of the migrants' experience necessitate a radical re-think about the nature of diasporic communication, in particular, the underlying assumption that comes with terms such as 'multi-' and 'inter-', as these terms often suggest 'an *a priori* existence of separate units (language, culture, identity)' (Blommaert 2012). Translanguaging, with its emphasis on the language users' creativity and multi-competence, offers a new lens on language and communication in the diaspora.

References

Anderson, B. (1983) *Imagined communities: reflections on the origins and spread of nationalism*, London: Verso, 1991.
Appadurai, A. (1996) *Modernity at large: cultural dimensions of globalization*, Minneapolis: University of Minnesota Press.
Baker, C. (2006) *Foundations of bilingual education and bilingualism*, fourth edition, Bristol: Multilingual Matters.
Block, D. (2008) 'On the appropriateness of the metaphor LOSS', in P. Tan and R. Rubdy (eds) *Language as commodity: global structures, local marketplaces*, London: Continuum, 187–203.
Blommaert, J. (2012) 'Chronicles of complexity: ethnography, superdiversity, and linguistic landscapes', Tilburg papers in Culture Studies 29, available at: www.tilburguniversity.edu/upload/19fb666f-300e-499b-badf-90204b0e89b1_tpcs%20paper29.pdf.
Brumfit, C. J. (1995) 'Teacher professionalism and research', in G. Cook and B. Seidlhofer (eds) *Principle and practice in applied linguistics*, Oxford: Oxford University Press, 27–41.

Canagarajah, S. (2017) *The Routledge handbook of migration and language*, London: Routledge.
Clyne, M. (1982) *Multilingual Australia*, Melbourne: River Seine.
Cohen, R. (2008) *Global diasporas*, second edition, London: Routledge.
Eade, J., S. Drinkwater and M. P. Gapich (2007) *Class and ethnicity: Polish migrant workers in London*, ESRC end of award report, RES-000-22-1294, Swindon: ESRC.
Fishman, J. (2013) 'Language maintenance, language shift, and reversing language shift', in T. K. Bhatia and W. C. Ritchie (eds) *The handbook of bilingualism and multilingualism*, Oxford: Wiley-Blackwell, 466–94.
García, O. (2009) Bilingual education in the 21st century: a global perspective, Oxford: Blackwell.
García, O. and Li Wei (2014) *Translanguaging: language, bilingualism and education*, Basingstoke, UK: Palgrave.
Green, A. and M. R. Power (2005) 'Social construction of transnational identity', conference paper, Annual Conference of the Australian and New Zealand Communication Association, Christchurch, New Zealand.
Ibrahim, A. (1999) 'Becoming Black: rap and hip-hop, race, gender, identity, and the politics of ESL learning', *TESOL Quarterly*, 33 (3), 349–69, doi: 10.2307/3587669.
Li Wei (1994) *Three generations, two languages, one family: language choice and language shift in a Chinese community in Britain*, Bristol: Multilingual Matters.
Li Wei (2011) 'Moment analysis and translanguaging space: discursive construction of identities by multilingual Chinese youth in Britain', *Journal of Pragmatics*, 43 (5), 1222–35, doi: 10.1016/j.pragma.2010.07.035.
Li Wei and Zhu Hua (2013) 'Diaspora: multilingual and intercultural communication across time and space', *AILA Review*, 26, 42–56, doi: 10.1075/aila.26.
Li Wei and Zhu Hua (forthcoming) *Imagination as a key factor in LMLS in transnational families*.
Makoni, S. and A. Pennycook (2007) *Disinventing and reconstituting languages*, Bristol: Multilingual Matters.
Ong, A. (1999) *Flexible citizenship: the cultural logic of transnationality*, Durham: Duke University Press.
Pavlenko, A. and B. Norton (2007) 'Imagined communities, identity, and English language learning', in J. Cummins and C. Davison (eds) *International Handbook of English language teaching*, New York: Springer US, 669–80.
Ray, M. (2003) 'Nation, nostalgia and Bollywood: in the tracks of a twice-displaced community', in H. Karim (ed.) *The media of diaspora*, London: Routledge, 21–35.
Shames, G. W. (1997) *Transcultural odysseys: the evolving global consciousness*, London: Intercultural Press.
Sofos, S. A. (1996) 'Inter-ethnic violence and gendered constructions of ethnicity in former Yugoslavia', *Social Identities: Journal for the Study of Race, Nation and Culture*, 2 (1), 73–92, doi: 10.1080/13504639652394.
Song, M. (2003) *Choosing ethnic identity*, Cambridge: Polity Press.
Valentine, G. (2008) Living with difference: reflections on geographies of encounter, *Progress in Human Geography*, 32 (3), 323–37, doi: 10.1177/0309133308089372.
van der Veer, P. (ed.) (1995) *Nation and migration: the politics of space in the South Asian diaspora*, Philadelphia, Pennsylvania: University of Pennsylvania Press.
Williams, C. (1994) *Arfarniad o ddulliau dysgu ac addysgu yng nghyd-destun addysg uwchradd ddwyieithog*, unpublished PhD thesis, Bangor: University of Wales Bangor. available at: http://e.bangor.ac.uk/9832/.
Williams, C. (1996) Secondary education: teaching in the bilingual situation', in C. Williams, G. Lewis and C. Baker (eds) *The language policy: taking stock*, Llangefni, UK: CAI, 193–211.
Wise, A. and S. Velayutham (2014) Conviviality in everyday multiculturalism: some brief comparisons between Singapore and Sydney, *European Journal of Cultural Studies*, 17 (4), 406–30, doi: 10.1177/1367549413510419.
Wood, P. and C. Landry (2007) *The intercultural city: planning for diversity advantage*, London: Earthscan.
Zhu Hua, Li Wei and A. Lyons (2015) 'Language, business and superdiversity in London: translanguaging business', Translanguaging and Translation working paper 5, available at: www.birmingham.ac.uk/generic/tlang/index.aspx.
Zhu Hua, Li Wei and A. Lyons (2017) 'Polish shop(ping) as translanguaging space', *Social Semiotics*, 27 (4), 411–33.

13
Multi-religious diasporas
Rethinking the relationship between religion and diaspora

Dominic Pasura

Global migration is contributing to the changing global religious landscape as intra- and inter-religious diversity is gaining traction. As Connor and Tucker (2011: 986) tells us, 'religious diasporas, once a phenomenon within only a handful of countries, are now present in almost every country in the world' (see also Johnson and Bellofatto 2012). From ancient civilization, migration has been integral to people's lives, producing complex cultural outcomes. The movement of people, a recurring phenomenon in this age of globalization, also entails the movement of beliefs, traditions, ideas and practices. The increasingly differentiated migration flows encompass forced and voluntary, skilled and unskilled, documented and undocumented, internal and international, temporary and permanent. This chapter examines the question of how the relationship between religion and diaspora has been theorized. It seeks to provide a nuanced understanding of both the meaning of these categories and their relationship. The chapter contributes to new strands of scholarship that contribute to the dismantling of the dichotomous ways of thinking in the modern world by emphasizing the cross-fertilization between different diasporic cultures and religions as they interact.

What are religious diasporas? There is a lack of theoretical clarity in the notion of religious diasporas. While religion and diaspora are inextricably interwoven, it is not helpful to always think of these concepts as a couple. The chapter extends the analytical gaze to the transnational flows of religious beliefs, practices and symbols, and not just the mobility of people. It explores religious beliefs and practices moving, people moving, and their sometimes moving together, sometimes not. As Johnson (2012: 95) observed, 'religions serve as important carriers of diasporas, even as diasporas extend religions into new places and situations of practice, sometimes invigorating them, sometimes threatening them, always transforming and remaking them'.

To understand what religious diasporas are, we need first to define what is meant by the term 'diaspora'. While the treatment of the concept of diaspora has generated voluminous research, prominent scholars of diaspora under-theorize how religion and diaspora intersect. As Kokot et al. (2004: 7) observe, 'in the context of diaspora, religion has always remained central to paradigmatic definitions, although in current theoretical discussions, the topic of religion seems to have moved into the background'. Diaspora has been used as a typological tool to categorize social formations; the archetypal model was one of forcible expulsion or scattering and usually suggested trauma, as in the Jewish model (Cohen 2008; Safran 1991).

The dominant conceptualizations of diaspora is premised on modernist theories of social formations and often take ethnicity and relationship to the real or imagined homeland as central features. However, diaspora has also come to be associated with unbounded transnational movements of people, goods and ideas. Scholars influenced by postmodernism have appropriated notions such as hybridity, fluidity, creolization and syncretism to alert us of the emergence of new articulations of deterritorialized identities. The new notion of diaspora makes no particular reference to ethnicity, a 'homeland' or a particular place of settlement, but emphasizes hybridity and deterritorialized identities and multiple belonging (Kalra et al. 2005). The debates about marking out the boundaries of diaspora are far from over as more and more 'communities' and 'transnational entities', distant from the classical conception of diaspora, are appropriating to themselves a diasporic label. However, the shift in the conceptualization of diaspora away from defining diasporas as substantive entities towards understanding diasporas as a process, a stance or mode of practice has implications for how religion and diaspora intersect (Brubaker 2005).

By examining the relationship between religion and diaspora, a number of specific approaches can be identified within the literature. For this discussion, I have grouped these into four broad categories: religion prioritized over diaspora, diasporic religions, modernist approaches and multi-religious diasporas – discussed in turn below.

Religion prioritized over diaspora

In this approach, religion is seen as constitutive of diaspora at the same time diaspora is understood as expressive of religion. The links between religion and diaspora have typically been investigated in relation to the Jewish diaspora. The term 'diaspora' was first used in the Greek translation of the Hebrew Bible, the Septuagint, referring to exiled Hellenistic Jews in Alexandria, and then came to be used to describe the plight of Jews outside Palestine (Safran 1991). Hence, most early discussions of diaspora refer to the Jewish diaspora as the concept's defining paradigm. However, Werbner (2004) considers the Jewish model of diaspora, taken as the prototype, as 'misleading' in that the Jewish religion, culture and national political orientation coincide, despite geographical dispersion. The Jewish and Sikh diasporas are exceptions because religion and ethnicity closely intertwine and, thus, among such diasporas, affiliation to the geographical territory extends well beyond the confines of ethnicity *per se* (Rai and Sankaran 2011). The restrictive use of the term 'diaspora' means few candidates can be labelled religious diasporas.

In the parallel field of religious studies, scholars often 'directed their attention to the histories of religion, they have less frequently focused on the religious making of histories' (Johnson 2012: 96). Over the past centuries, Catholic missionaries and religious orders evangelized throughout the world, transforming the religious landscapes of many places. As Rudolph (1997: 1) reminds us, religious communities are 'among the oldest of the transnationals; Sufi orders, Catholic missionaries and Buddhist monks carried work and praxis across vast spaces before those spaces became nation states or even states'. This approach takes an institutional perspective in the study of religions as well as in relation to diasporas.

Diasporic religions

In this approach, rather than focus on 'the histories of religion', a growing body of work explores the lived experience of religion through the prism of diaspora (Garnett and Hausner 2015b). Orsi (1985) provided the impetus for the shift from structural and institutional approaches in the study of religion to the theoretical framing of 'lived religion' which prioritizes religious practice in the study of religion. Tweed (1997, 2009) popularized the term 'diasporic religions' to highlight the portability of religion as people move within and across national borders. As people migrate as students, labourers, refugees, they bring their religions with them to new places of settlement. Tweed's spatial concepts 'dwelling and crossing' provide the foundation for a theory of religion that emphasizes the dynamics of transnational religious practices in and through different scales and spaces. The diasporic religion literature can be divided into two distinct fields – one focused on ethnicity and territorial cultures to explore religious diasporas, referred to here as the modernist approach, the other on multi-religious diasporas.

Modernist approaches

The rise of ethnicity and 'race' paradigms in the 1980s to 1990s within social sciences has tended to privilege the ethnic group and national group as units of analysis. The modernist approaches overemphasize the role of ethnicity and homeland's cohesive functions in the diaspora–homeland relations. There is some reluctance among classical diaspora scholars in applying this concept to world religions (Cohen 2008; Safran 1991; Sheffer 2003). Despite the term diaspora's origin in religious traditions, Rai and Sankaran (2011) correctly observe that the centrality of religion in the classical understanding of the term 'diaspora' was subsumed under categories such as ethnicity and culture. The designation 'religious diaspora' is contentious because

> whereas members of ethnic diasporas regards certain territories as their actual homelands, most members of the global religions, with the notable exception of Judaism, are attached to a spiritual center that is not the actual historical birthplace of forebears of the group.
>
> (Sheffer 2003: 66)

Moreover, religious diasporas derive their source of value and religious identities from the 'transcendental realm'; ethnic diasporic identities are based on primordial cultural sentiments, subjective leanings and instrumental consideration. The major distinction is that, whereas ethnic diasporas are trans-state, other groups are transnational entities (Sheffer 2009). For Cohen (2008), religion provides 'additional cement' to ethnic/national diasporic consciousness. Vasquez (2010) cautions us that the re-creation of religious and cultural lives, practices and institutions is not a mere reproduction of practices in the homeland but incorporates religious and cultural dimensions in the host society.

Within this approach, diasporas are depicted as substantive entities which reaffirm the resilience of racial, ethnic and national homogeneity within the transnational space. Informed by Baumann's (2000: 327) characterization of diaspora as 'the relational facts of a perpetual recollecting identification with a fictitious or far away existent geographic territory and its cultural-religious traditions', Johnson (2012: 104) defines religious diasporas as 'extensions in space of a group whose most salient reference is religious identity rather than ethnic, racial, linguistic, or any other social bond, and whose process of displacement or migration is directly a consequence of that religious affiliation'. This approach emphasizes the deployment of territorial identifications in various transnational religious spaces as well as on bodies, cultural artefacts and imaginaries. Diasporic religions are 'territorial cultures' in that their orientation towards the homeland often relies on ethnic and national markers which set themselves apart from the host society. Yet, as Wuthnow and Offutt (2008: 209) argue, although religion 'exists in local communities and is distinctively influenced by a national cultural and political context, it has connections with the wider world and is influenced by these relations'. We need analytical models that are sensitive to local experiences without losing sight of the structural forces that structure them.

Multi-religious diasporas

Responding to the analytical inadequacies of methodological nationalism in the social sciences (Wimmer and Glick Schiller 2002), the emphasis on hybridity in the theorization of diasporas has produced a corpus of work that explores the multi-religious cleavages of dispersed social groups. Multi-religious diasporas refer to dispersed social groups that simultaneously hold on to conflicting sources of identifications/affiliations (local, national, regional or transnational); what Johnson (2012) refers to as 'multiple diasporic horizons'.

Scholars influenced by the cultural turn, postmodernism and postcolonial studies conceive diasporas as deterritorialized social groups for whom the homeland and ethnicity are less relevant to the reality of the diaspora than orientations and activities within the host land. Diaspora is seen as a process, a form of consciousness rather than a bounded group with members co-habiting multiple places, possessing cross identities simultaneously. Werbner's (2004) notion of complex or segmented diaspora captures how migrants coming from a vast region, divided by nationality, religion and language, can situationally form a homogeneous group in a place of settlement. Citing the examples of South Asians, Latin Americans, Africans, Afro-Carribbeans, Werbner (2004) describes complex/segmented diasporas as those that defy any neat typological theorization of diaspora that looks to ethnic/national historical origins exclusively.

Typological theorization of diaspora, focusing on the historical national or ethnic origins, is challenged by complex diasporas (Werbner 2004). The rise of complex/segmented diasporas has led to a reappraisal of religious diasporas. One of the emerging patterns of Afro-American religions in contemporary times is their expansion across ethnic and national barriers (Frigerio 2004). While Afro-American religions such as the Candomble, Batuque, Cuban Santeria were originally mostly binational, they have diffused and span national boundaries, giving rise to trans-national communities of worshippers. Using the term the 'pan-diasporic' to describe non-ethnic transnational entities, Ben-Rafael (2013) cites the examples of Latin American immigrants in the US who are described as 'Hispanics' and immigrants from Arab countries in Europe who see themselves as part of the Muslim diaspora. Also, as Brubaker (2005) suggests, if we see diaspora as a process, stance or category of practice rather than as a bounded entity, then there is a sense in which we can talk of religious diasporas such as Hindu, Sikh, Buddhist, Confucian, Huguenot, Muslim and Catholic diasporas. Gorman (2011) descirbes the Christian experience of diaspora which was rooted in the Great Command: 'Go therefore and make disciples of all the nations, baptizing them in the name of the Father and the Son and the Holy Spirit, teaching them to observe all that I commanded you' (Matthew 28: 19–20). However, emphasizing hybridity and fluidity aspects of diasporas does not pay sufficient attention to issues of structure and materiality, institutional aspects of diaspora, which shape the ways in which transnational religious identities are constituted.

Through the process of 'hybridization', diasporic cultures and religious practices coalesce into the cultures and religions of the host society (Vasquez 2010). Multi-religious diasporas are a consequence of globalization and global migration, and the inter-religious encounters in super-diverse global cities and mobile societies produce spaces for cross-cultural and cross-faith contact and negotiation. Often, multicultural cities offer spaces where the local, the rooted, the diaspora-specific may co-exist with the translocal, transnational and global. They are also spaces to forge new alliances and affiliations across ethnic and national loyalties. The diaspora is seen as contested space embodying competing for social, cultural and religious elements as well as intensifying the forces of conflict and collaboration. Thus, religion in the diaspora thrives by being both ethnic parochial and cosmopolitan (Werbner 2004). Diasporic identities are then continually reworked through being connected to multiple societies simultaneously. Multi-religious diasporas, by emphasizing variability and change, destabilize fixed ideas of race, ethnicity and religion as well as capture the contradictions and the ambiguity of contemporary life.

Complex intersection

In the introduction, I highlighted the importance of dismantling the dichotomous ways of thinking in the modern world by emphasizing the cross-fertilization between different diasporic cultures and religions as they interact; religion and diasporas as analytically distinct but overlapping categories. As Vasquez (2010: 129) argues, 'to say that religion and diaspora are closely connected does not mean that all religions are equally diasporic or diasporic in the same way'. Religion and diaspora both operate in similar ways in the articulation of individual and collective identities, often buttressing and reinforcing each other (Vasquez 2010). We therefore need to consider the question of the relationship of religion and diaspora at a number of levels, different scales and imaginaries, at the structural, the discursive and the situated levels, as well as pay attention to how the relationship between them is dynamic, historical and context-specific.

At the structural level, the intersection between religion and diaspora is institutionalized through the normative secular and multicultural discourses, restrictive immigration laws and coercive integration policies in most Western societies. Until recently, and because of the secularization thesis (Brown 2001; Bruce 1995), religion had become a fixed dirty category to be contained and confined to the private sphere. However, in this 'age of migration' (Castles et al. 2013), and perhaps to the dismay of secularization theorists, religion's public influence and relevance have not waned but increased. The role of religion in the public sphere has been predominantly framed through debates about national security and terrorism; in particular, the place and role of Islam in shaping and sustaining understandings of cultural and religious difference (Pasura 2012). As the order by President Donald Trump to ban refugees and immigrants from seven mostly Muslim countries from entering the US illustrates (Goodman 2017), the nation-state continues to be a category of great significance in determining the conditions in which religion and diaspora interact through restrictive immigration controls and control over citizenship. The predominance of global security concerns in framing debates over religion and migration produce distortions and oversimplifications. It can be argued that many aspects of how religion and diaspora interact have been shaped through structural and institutional forces over the past decades. For example, it can be argued that both multiculturalism and secularism are deployed as techniques to govern difference.

At the level of discourse, the intersection between religion and diaspora, migration more broadly, has become the object of academic and policy gaze monitoring, categorizing and managing individual subjectivities and collective identities for those perceived as different. The intersection of religion and migration (diaspora) is often approached through the instrumental and reductionist lens. Interest in the intersections of religion, migration and diversity is high on the agendas in the USA and most European countries; however, such questions have been pursued primarily in relation to Islam, and as such are less concerned with religion than with security (Pasura and Erdal 2017). For example, and in the words of Alexander (2002: 564), the Muslim diaspora has become 'the ultimate "Other", transfixed through the racialization of religious identity to stand at the margins: undesired, irredeemable'. The key characteristics of this exclusionary discourse are its hostility to migrants, refugees and asylum-seekers. These expert knowledges have shaped everyday understandings of the intersection of religion and diaspora as fixed, natural, and thus affecting processes of developing integration in Western societies.

At the situated level, the intersection of religion and diaspora is constructed and renegotiated through everyday interactions within structural constraints of the countries of settlement. Diasporic identities are not static but processual, relational, fluid, and migrants are active in the creation of their new 'in-between' worlds. The situated level draws attention to the agency of diasporic subjects in their creation of new worlds, separating itself from prior integration paradigms. These reconfigurations can be strategic, but more importantly demonstrate the level at which transnational identities are formed through their relationship to various points of identification. This strand of literature explores how religion in the diaspora informs subjective and collective religious identities as well as how identity informs location. For instance, Garnett and Hausner (2015a) describe how cross-cultural and cross-faith contact and negotiation have become the everyday social reality in London, and thus 'the claiming, sharing, and contesting of space by diasporic groups living alongside one another within civil society'. This multiple affiliation and belongingness subvert dominant agendas. These different levels – the structural, the discursive and the situated – are not mutually exclusive but interact in multi-faceted ways in the intersection of religion and diaspora. It is imperative to conceive the intersection of religion and diaspora not as an end state but a process with no fixed or determinate destination. For Vertovec (2004), the connections between religion and diaspora are better understood by focusing on 'the patterns of change' that follow migration and minority status at different scales (local, national, regional, transnational and global). These religious changes can take different possibilities or trajectories, going forward, backwards or sideways.

In a culture of intense global migration, the proliferation of religious diasporas (Connor and Tucker 2011) raise new questions about identity, belonging and citizenship. What is needed now is not just an addition to the empirical range of problems that should be addressed, but a conceptual rethinking of the relationship between religion and diaspora. Religion has been both as a factor in forming diasporic social organizations as well as in shaping and maintaining diasporic identities (Kokot et al. 2004). Our understandings of the relationship between religion and diasporas, just as the meanings of these categories, has shifted dramatically over the last two decades. There has been a move away from where religion and ethnicity are closely intertwined, such as in the Jewish and Sikh cases, to a position where there are now complex/segmented diasporas characterized by multiple sources of identifications. While ethnicity and the homeland continue to be central to typologies of diasporic religions, these categories have been partially disrupted and decentred. Multi-religious diasporas, influenced by the postmodern the idea of diaspora, emphasize agency, fluidity, relationality and celebrates deterritorialization and the transgression of national boundaries. Theoretically, this has shifted emphasis from the understandings of religion and diaspora as coherent and stable, towards seeing these as dynamic, relational, complex and situated.

References

Alexander, C. (2002) 'Beyond black: re-thinking the colour/culture divide', *Ethnic and Racial Studies*, 25 (4), 552–71, doi: 10.1080/01419870220136637.
Baumann, M. (2000) 'Diaspora: genealogies or semantics and transcultural comparison', *Numen*, 47 (3), 313–37, doi: 10.1163/156852700511577.
Ben-Rafael, E. (2013) 'Diaspora', *Current Sociology*, 61 (5/6), 842–861, doi: 10.1177/0011392113480371.
Brown, C. G. (2001) *The death of Christian Britain*, Abingdon: Routledge.
Brubaker, R. (2005) 'The "diaspora" diaspora', *Ethnic and Racial Studies*, 28 (1), 1–19, doi: 10.1080/0141987042000289997.
Bruce, S. (1995) *Religion in modern Britain*, Oxford: Oxford University Press.
Castles, S., H. de Haas and M. J. Miller (2013) *The age of migration: international population movements in the modern world* (fifth edition), Basingstoke: Palgrave Macmillan.

Cohen, R. (2008) *Global diasporas: An introduction* (second edition), Abingdon: Routledge.
Connor, P. and C. Tucker (2011) 'Religion and migration around the globe: introducing the Global Religion and Migration Database'. *International Migration Review*, 45 (4), 985–1000, doi: 10.1111/j.1747-7379.2011.00874_3.x.
Frigerio, A. (2004) 'Re-Africanization in secondary religious diasporas: constructing a world religion', *Civilisations. Revue internationale d'anthropologie et de sciences humaines*, 51, 39–60, available at: https://civilisations.revues.org/pdf/656.
Garnett, J. and S. L. Hausner (2015a) 'Introduction: cultures of citizenship', in J. Garnett and S. L. Hausner (eds) *Religion in diaspora: cultures of citizenship*, Basingstoke: Palgrave Macmillan, 1–14.
Garnett, J. and S. L. Hausner (eds) (2015b) *Religion in diaspora: cultures of citizenship*, Basingstoke: Palgrave Macmillan.
Goodman, J. (2017) 'US travel ban: why these seven countries?', BBC News, 30 January, available at: www.bbc.co.uk/news/world-us-canada-38798588.
Gorman, R. F. (2011) 'Classical diasporas of the third kind: the hidden history of Christian dispersion', *Journal of Refugee Studies*, 24 (4), 635–54, doi: 10.1093/jrs/fer045.
Johnson, P. C. (2012) 'Religion and diaspora', *Religion and Society: Advances in Research*, 3 (1), 95–114, doi: 10.3167/arrs.2012.030106.
Johnson, T. M. and G. A. Bellofatto (2012) 'Migration, religious diasporas, and religious diversity: a global survey', *Mission Studies*, 29 (1), 3–22, doi: 10.1163/157338312X637993.
Kalra, V. S., R. Kaur and J. Hutnyk (2005) *Diaspora and hybridity*, London: Sage.
Kokot, W., K. Tölölyan and C. Alfonso (2004) 'Introduction', in C. Alfonso, W. Kokot and K. Tölölyan (eds) *Diaspora, identity and religion: new directions in theory and research*, Abingdon: Routledge, 1–9.
Orsi, R. A. (1985) *The Madonna of 115th Street: faith and community in Italian Harlem, 1880–1950*, New Haven: Yale University Press.
Pasura, D. (2012) 'Religious transnationalism: the case of Zimbabwean Catholics in Britain', *Journal of Religion in Africa*, 42 (1), 26–53, doi: 10.1163/157006612X629069.
Pasura, D. and M. B. Erdal (eds) (2017) *Migration, transnationalism and Catholicism: global perspectives*, Basingstoke: Palgrave Macmillan.
Rai, R. and C. Sankaran (2011) 'Religion and the South Asian diaspora', *South Asian Diaspora*, 3 (1), 5–13, doi: 10.1080/19438192.2010.539030.
Rudolph, S. H. (1997) 'Introduction: religion, states, and transnational civil society', in S. H. Rudolph and J. Piscatori (eds) *Transnational religion and fading states*, Boulder, CO: Westview Press, 1–24.
Safran, W. (1991) 'Diasporas in modern societies: myths of homeland and return', *Diaspora*, 1 (1), 83–99, doi: 10.1353/dsp.1991.0004.
Sheffer, G. (2003) *Diaspora politics: at home abroad*, Cambridge: Cambridge University Press.
Sheffer, G. (2009) 'A reexamination of the main theoretical approaches to the study of diasporas and their applicability to the Jewish diaspora', in E. Ben-Rafael and Y. Sternberg (eds) *Transnationalism: diasporas and the advent of a new (dis)order*, Leiden: Brill, 375–96, doi: 10.1163/ej.9789004174702.i-788.128.
Tweed, T. A. (1997) *Our lady of the exile: diasporic religion at a Cuban Catholic shrine in Miami*, Oxford: Oxford University Press.
Tweed, T. A. (2009) *Crossing and dwelling: a theory of religion*, Cambridge, MA: Harvard University Press.
Vasquez, M. (2010) 'Diasporas and religion', in K. Knott and S. McLoughlin (eds) *Diasporas: concepts, intersections, identities*, London: Zed Books, 128–33.
Vertovec, S. (2004) 'Religion and diaspora'. in P. Antes, A. W. Geertz and R. R. Warne (eds) *New approaches to the study of religion, volume 2*, Berlin: De Gruyter, 275–304.
Werbner, P. (2004) 'Theorising complex diasporas: purity and hybridity in the South Asian public sphere in Britain', *Journal of Ethnic and Migration Studies*, 30 (5), 895–911, doi: 10.1080/1369183042000245606.
Wimmer, A. and N. Glick Schiller (2002) 'Methodological nationalism and beyond: nation-state building, migration and the social sciences', *Global Networks*, 2 (4), 301–34, doi: 10.1111/1471-0374.00043.
Wuthnow, R. and S. Offutt (2008) 'Transnational religious connections', *Sociology of Religion*, 69 (2), 209–32, doi: 10.1093/socrel/69.2.209.

14
Homelessness and statelessness
Possibilities and perils

Barzoo Eliassi

The concept of diaspora has been conceptualized and appropriated from a wide range of perspectives. In the context of globalization, it has been described as a transnational social organization (Wahlbeck 1999) and transnational community (Sökefeld 2006) characterized by a triadic relationship involving the country of 'origin', the country of settlement, and an ethnic group dispersed across different states (Cohen 2008). Because the concept is used indiscriminatingly to label a wide range of migratory experiences and identities as diasporic, it has been contested for lacking boundaries and so losing its semantic, conceptual and analytic power (Brubaker 2005). In a critical response to Werbner (2015: 51), Brubaker argues that diasporas have boundaries but that these are 'defined and highlighted situationally, dialectically and over time, in action, through performance and periodic mobilization'. Others have criticized the concept for essentialization and reifying group identities and failing to provide an alternative to the already knotty concepts within migration studies of race and ethnicity (Anthias 1998; Soysal 2002). Radhakrishnan (2003) maintains that identities are constructions of historical and political contexts and that all essentialist notions of them are deployed strategically to attain specific political goals. It is worth mentioning that the very formation of a diaspora was originally situated within a negative discursive field characterized by destruction of the homeland and dispersion of the Jewish community (Cohen 2008; Kenny 2013). However, this is not to say that we should reduce diaspora to an entity or single experience, but should rather see it as a category of practice in motion.

A diaspora has no life outside history, representations and human agency (Brubaker 2005) and no unambiguous meaning; it is constituted rather through historical challenges, political situations, crises, interests and priorities. Thus, it is important to ask how, why, by whom and for which political purpose different actors use such essentialist identities (Sökefeld 2006: 266). Since the concept of diaspora is intimately linked to ideas of home(land), belonging and dislocations, it is important to take into consideration the political contexts in which the lived experiences and discourses of different migrant groups are situated. As Sökefeld (2006) points out, the notion of diaspora is about dislocation, leaving a specific place and living somewhere else. Accordingly, it provides us with an important perspective on the migratory experiences of dislocation, estrangement, uprooting and resettlement that link the 'three dimension of movement, connectivity, return' (Kenny 2013: 105). It is in this context that I engage in this chapter with narratives about home(land) and belonging across different generations of migrants in diasporic contexts, with a focus particularly on stateless diasporas. It might seem tautological to speak of stateless diasporas when the original ones, for example the Jewish diaspora, emerged in an historical context in which nation-states and national identities did not exist. However, since nationalist thoughts and nation-states are the political standard in our contemporary world, it is analytically helpful to distinguish between stateless and state-linked diasporas (Sheffer 2003), for they are asymmetrically positioned in a world that empowers national belonging and discards stateless people as political outcasts and homeless (Eliassi 2016).

In this chapter, I aim theoretically and empirically to show that while most migrants following forced migration have a complicated relationship with issues of home and belonging, statelessness as an ascribed status and lived experience adds a further dimension to their sense of alienation, aloneness and political otherness. In short, I discuss the possibilities and perils of the search for a political home and sense of belonging among stateless diasporas in an uneven world. Drawing on the experiences of Kurdish and Palestinian migrants in Sweden and England, I illustrate how narratives and experiences of home, statelessness and belonging are framed across different generations and national contexts both at individual and collective levels.

Politics of home and belonging in the diaspora

The questions of home and belonging have gained the passionate and academic attention of many writers with direct and indirect experiences of migration and dislocation (Butter 2015; George 1996). For diaspora studies, it makes sense to engage with the concept of home in the context of dispersal, resettlement and homesickness. Exile and diaspora are often viewed as domains of creativity, but they can also become a place characterized by racism, discrimination and destructive group relations (Cohen 2008). For instance, experiences of ethnic and religious discrimination can create reactive identities in diasporic groups and trigger a search for alternative modes and places of belonging (Eliassi 2013). Home as an idea or place provides a useful framework in which to construct a sense of belonging and security, but it is also a powerful ideological device for creating exclusionary discourses against people who are not viewed as members of the 'core group' that constitutes the nation. Although usually equated with one's place of origin and roots, home and belonging should be conceptualized as having multiple dimensions and scales. While home can include dwelling places such as the private home, local neighbourhood, city, region, nation-state, continent and Earth, belonging can also take on a multidimensional form in which a person can feel that they have a range of placed-based identities.

The sense of belonging to a place, state or group often underpins shared collective identity and social solidarity. Guibernau (2013) views belonging as a key antidote to experiencing alienation and loneliness in the context of existential anxiety and political powerlessness. Anthias (2006) points out that, in our globalized world, people feel destabilized and seek to cope with the experiences of uncertainty, disconnection and invisibility that lead to an obsession with finding and asserting a social space as home, where 'we' as a group, family and nation belong. Moreover, people are often aware of the wide range of places, locales and identities to which they do not want to or are not allowed to belong. In the same vein, Antonsich (2010: 644), inspired by Nira Yuval-Davis (2006), provides an analytical framework in which belonging can be analysed both 'as a personal, intimate, feeling of being "at home" in a place (place-belongingness) and as [a] discursive resource that constructs, claims, justifies, or resist forms of socio-spatial inclusion/ exclusion (politics of belonging)'.

The focus on the territoriality of belonging is what is conspicuous about Antonsich's analytical framework, for he mainly locates feelings, practices and discourses of belonging in geographical contexts (Antonsich 2010: 647). The contexualization he posits, which becomes more tangible in everyday negotiations of place-belongingness, challenges postmodern discourses on the demise or weakening effects of globalization on nation-states and territorialized identities. Few of us escape the recurrent everyday question of 'where are you from?' Although it might appear innocent, or a sign of curiosity about one's personal history, non-white immigrants often interpret it as an act of othering in which the person's immigrant *background* becomes the *foreground* (Eliassi 2016). To be a fully-fledged member of a core group is to belong *without questions* (Skey 2011) or stipulations on the terms of belonging or distribution of rights and obligations. This indicates that, since belonging often concerns boundaries that define 'us' and 'them', privilege and discrimination, inclusion and otherness, it is relational and cannot be reduced to an individual issue. These boundaries are constituted not only between members of different nation-states but also within the territorial framework of the same nation-states, in which there is an ethnonational hierarchy of belonging and non-belonging. Nationalist discourse sets a limit to who can and who cannot belong and excludes certain marked constituents from sharing and making an equal claim to the same social space (Sharma 2014). As a result, the dominant group perceives itself and acts as the governor and master of the nation, thus creating a strong nexus between entitlement and belonging (Hage 2000). Although citizenship is the formal marker of belonging to a nation-state, it is often in everyday life and encounters that people translate their citizenship into rights and are made aware of whether they belong (Eliassi 2016).

Therefore, while the literature suggests that a sense of belonging is central to our comfort, wellbeing and security (Anthias 2006; Guibernau 2013; hooks 2009), it is equally important to create inclusive ways of imagining and constructing home and belonging that do not create new forms of exclusion (Duyvendak 2011). First, across all societies and groups, home is not necessarily a cosy dwelling place; it can be the site of gender-based violence, sexual exploitation and child abuse. Moreover, for stateless diasporas, militarization and authoritarian political regimes can often turn people's homes into dangerous, even lethal, places of violence and destruction, as illustrated in the cases of the Kurds, Palestinians, Assyrians/Syriacs and Tamils. Second, dislocation and experiences of otherness strengthen a homing desire in which the diasporic subject yearns for social inclusion and feelings of home. According to Butter (2015: 355), Salman Rushdie is highly critical of a diasporic obsession with home and believes that longing for home can turn into a dangerous and pathological form of fetishization or monopolization involving rejecting different subjects and groups and obstructing the creation of intimate social relationships with the surrounding individuals and societies. Consequently, when home becomes a fetish, it creates alienation and obstructs the process of making one's home in the present place and time. The Swedish-Kurdish writer Mustafa Can (2006) has captured this issue in a book about his mother's life and death following displacement. Can, who came to Sweden at the age of 6, narrates the story of his family's migration to Sweden from a deprived village in Turkish Kurdistan and of how their longing for home plagued his parents' lives and relationships with their children and grandchildren. In the following passage from his book, Can (2006: 247) describes his own difficult feelings about home in the diaspora and back in the village:

> After three weeks in the village I am missing the Western life-style because I have lived in it for 30 years. I am thirty years Western and six years Eastern. Thirty years of satiation and freedom of expression, six years of hunger and lack of freedom of opinion. Despite this, I still feel more Eastern than Western, regardless of how long I live in Sweden, how much and fast I am spinning in the tumble of integration. Wherever, I find myself, I feel more Kurdish than Swedish, East before West.
>
> No, I know that this equation rhymes badly. I cannot solve this equation. Maybe I do not want to solve it.

Yes! I am Swedish.
No! I am a Kurd.
Yes! I want to live here.
No! I do not want to live here.
Yes! I can live here.
No! I cannot live here.
Yes, no, yes, no, yes, no. . . .

Home is away, away is home. In Sweden, I say home is the village. And in the village, I say home is Sweden. I cannot make these countries change their places. I want to move the social security, the free and open society of Sweden to the village, or move the people of the village, its traditions and fragrances to Sweden.

These contradictions are meeting inside me and I am carrying their blisters. 'Yes' and 'no', 'home' and 'away' are hammering in my head, and increasing my feelings of guilt for not being able to choose a home.

Can provides vivid descriptions of how narratives about home pass from one generation to the next within the same family. When his father asked his grandchildren whether it was time to go back home, they responded, 'home to the village?' What home? We were born and grew up in Sweden. We are already at home (Can 2006: 234). While Can's parents are strongly attached to the village as their place of origin, Can admits that he and his sisters do think about it and miss it, but that the grandchildren would never consider lying awake at night wondering about their neighbours and relatives in the village and yearning for its sounds, fragrances, tastes and long warm seasons. These tensions and ambivalences create dilemmas for first-generation diasporans who feel that they live in a social and cultural vacuum, that they are nameless strangers in a foreign country. Can's father experiences his regular visits to the village as a homecoming, for that is where people understand and respect him, where he has a name and is not treated as a 'wog' (*svartskalle*), as he is in Sweden. Returning thus becomes his way of momentarily escaping otherness, homelessness and homesickness. The longer Can's father, children and grandchildren remain in the diaspora, the less attached they feel to Kurdish culture. His father fears that the final dissolution of his family's link to the village will occur when his grandchildren acquire Swedish names. By encouraging regular visits to the home village, he initiates a strategy of counteracting the process of assimilation that absorbs the younger generation and detaches it from its 'original' cultural identity. 'Losing' one's culture is equated with leaving one's place in the cultural order and complicating the dream of a future homecoming to the village.

Younger generations of Kurdish migrants in the diaspora, particularly young women, constitute a transformative force in defying those parts of the cultural order of Kurdish society that underpin patriarchy, strict social codes and gender oppression. To create a safe and inclusive home, Kurdish women in the diaspora are at the forefront of the struggle for democracy, gender equity and rule of law in the Middle East (Eliassi 2016). Experiences of return are not always rosy but, as King and Christou (2010: 112) write, can be

> marked by confrontations with the social and cultural institutions in the place of origin; these institutions, together with wider behavioural norms and practices of the home society (which for the second-generation resettler becomes a host society), obstruct the political project of homecoming, to the frustration and annoyance of the returnee.

For Kurdish migrants, returning home is complicated, for the political situation is such that the Turkish state systematically oppresses any expression of a Kurdish identity. In fact, the state stipulates assimilation as a condition for belonging and having access to rights. This means that the Kurds are shuttled between the assimilationist processes of both the diaspora and the original homeland. Despite their ambivalence towards Sweden and the UK as their 'homes', many Kurdish migrants are aware that given the precarious political situation in the predominantly Kurdish regions, where people live in the shadow of political oppression and militarization, the state cannot deliver the democratic order, social security and rule of law they experience in Sweden and the UK. Since homecoming becomes a postponed mission, life in the diaspora, at least for the first generation, continues to be held in suspension (Maxey 2006). Generally, younger generations of Kurdish diasporans do not view Kurdistan as their final destination, as where they can eventually rest and undo the existential anxiety they experience because of their sense of in-betweenness and non-belonging (Eliassi 2013; King and Christou 2010).

Political homelessness and statelessness

While writing critically about national identity and the nation-state, Malešević (2013: 156–7) underlines that we are often obliged to represent ourselves in national terms and if you say in response to the question 'where are you from?' that you do not have a nation, 'your answer would not be taken as a serious response. Instead, you would be seen as either a joker, a naïve utopian or a nuisance.' Certainly, this becomes even more problematic for groups that have not attained statehood or that do not want to be subsumed under the universality of the nation-state they inhabit. It is in this context that statelessness becomes a status injury in the world of nation-states (Eliassi 2016; Said 1999). Consider the following quote about statelessness by a 63-year-old Palestinian refugee in Sweden:

> Nothing, you are zero. A people without a state are nothing. Nothing. We are struggling daily to survive because we do not have a state. It is a catastrophe that we do not have a state. Everybody puts you in jail, kills you and nobody cares about you. If a Palestinian is killed, nobody asks about him because he does not have a state to protect him. Many people have states that care about them. But for you as a Palestinian, who cares about you? Israel? An orphan is better than a stateless [person] because you do not exist if you do not have a state. An orphan might have relatives who can take care of him/her but we do not have that and nobody embraces us. A human being without a homeland is nothing. Your homeland is one of the most intimate issues you talk about in your life. If you are stateless, it is like when nobody asks you if you are sick, hungry or thirsty. But when you have a state, you belong to a state that can care about you. Just look at Israel, it can start a war over an Israeli citizen, hundreds of Palestinians are killed, nobody cares. You feel that you are weak. In Sweden, I am nobody but in Palestine I have my roots there and when people pass by my grave, they know that I belong to a rooted Palestinian family and not a rootless person nobody knows about. My family is rooted in Palestine. Our flesh and blood is part of Palestinian soil now. Statelessness means a grave without an address. You are gone.

Thus, statelessness adds a further dimension to the sense of alienation, aloneness and political otherness in the context of migration. This framing of statelessness provided above by the interviewee is best understood as a response to the political oppression and powerlessness that Palestinians experience as a stateless people in the context of the Israeli occupation but also in relation to experiences of ethnic exclusion and otherness in West European contexts. While the interviewee above appreciated his Swedish passport, and expressed his gratitude to the Swedish state for its hospitality towards Palestinian refugees, because of his degraded immigrant background he was unconvinced that Sweden was his homeland. He has been told on several occasions that if he does not like Sweden, he can leave, and that immigrants have destroyed Sweden. Despite the political difficulties and legal hurdles that many Palestinians experience over returning to Palestine, there is also a widespread fear of facing the unpleasant realities of Palestine, even if the possibility of return exists. A 30-year-old Palestinian woman illustrates this condition:

> My Swedish and Palestinian friends often tell me that I speak so beautifully about Palestine although I have never been there. They have told me: 'we give you the advice never to visit Palestine because you will be destroyed after being there.' I tell them that they frighten me and ask them why they say that. They tell me, 'when you go down there, you will see how dirty it is there, you see the corruption, you see the division among Palestinians, you see all the nasty things that you do not want to see in Palestine.' This creates a lot of frustration and these experiences demolish one's worldview of Palestine. I am still living and dreaming about Palestine through my grandparents' words that there is a community; everybody cares about each other, the old Palestinian woman who is preparing *za'atar*, an old man who is picking olives from the olive tree and produces olive oil. I have a very romantic image of Palestine. I do not know if it is the correct image, but it is this image that makes Palestine alive within me.

Acts of forgetting and remembering what they have left behind and yearn for (Ahmed 1999) characterize many migrants' narratives. Although many Palestinians view Palestine as their 'true home', given the political transformation of Palestinian society under Israeli occupation and the intra-Palestinian political rivalries between Fatah and Hamas, it is uncertain that they are familiar with the reality of their ancestral homeland. Romanticized narratives about Palestine passed from older to younger generations of Palestinian migrants can kindle the energies of the younger generation to hold onto the idea of Palestine and continue their struggle against Israeli occupation. Palestinian migrants are aware that it would be virtually impossible to achieve a 'pre-Israel' Palestine. Yet, to avoid the territorial obliteration of their national home, they regard the viability of Palestine as a necessity and central to Palestinians' individual and collective projects. This self-assertion by Palestinians and the process of authenticating their Palestinian identity in the diaspora should be seen in the context of the Israeli denial and belittling of a Palestinian existence and identity.

Conclusion: desiring a home in a world of national homes

It is often difficult for migrants to feel fully at home, whether they are 'here/home' or 'there/away'. Home and away are often interchangeable in diasporic narratives, for they are not dichotomies. In the same vein, Ahmed (1999: 330, emphasis in original) argues that:

> Interestingly, it is the 'real' home, the very space from which one imagines oneself to have originated, and in which one projects the self as both homely and original, that is the most unfamiliar: it is there that one is guest, relying on the hospitality of others. It is this home which, in the end, becomes Home through the very *failure* of memory.

While non-white migrants are often assumed to be homesick, there is also a tendency among 'white natives' across Western Europe to delve into nostalgia about how their homes looked before the arrival of the others. The question of home has become the central device of inclusion and exclusion in contemporary Europe (Duyvendak 2011). Estrangement is a central feature of migration. Whereas it is important to feel at home and to belong, it is equally dangerous to make home a fetish and to turn it into an exclusionary symbolic object, which is denied people who are not viewed as legitimate constituents of 'our societies'. Stateless diasporas often view themselves as lacking a homeland, or they assert that their homelands have been 'stolen' or taken over by other groups. This makes the search for a political home a political imperative in the collective identity projects of many members of stateless diasporas. According to Cocks (2006), stateless people who are injured and oppressed by the national sovereign power often reproduce a nationalist ontology in their own struggle for sovereign power, which assumedly leads to political freedom. Even when they attain this power, there is no political guarantee that the dynamics of majority/minority or oppressor/oppressed will end. On becoming a majority in the new nation-state one has achieved, there is an historical tendency for any new group to become ethnic strangers and a potentially politically threatened and oppressed minority. This makes the nation-state an inherently problematic form of social organization (Cocks 2006). Departing from the Israeli–Palestinian experiences, Cocks (2006: 28) gives a compelling account of how the majority that has left a minority position and achieved sovereignty understands a minority's search for national sovereignty. To escape subjugation, the minority

> embraces the institutional ground of its plight as the antidote for it, hammering itself into a sovereign national majority while shifting the costs of minority status to an even more vulnerable population in its way. The latter's predictable reaction to that shift – anger, indignation, violent antagonism – is interpreted by the former as evidence of the continuation of its own threatened minority plight. Such an interpretation leads the new majority to make greater effort to entrench its sovereign mastery, which multiplies the hostile reaction against it, producing another version of the precarious situation that mastery was meant to end.

While Cocks uses this deconstructive rhetoric to create more inclusive forms of social organization than the nation-state, authoritarian regimes, such as those in the Middle East, often use this discourse to quell the dissent of stateless people struggling for parity in political, social and economic life (Eliassi 2016). For instance, the creation of Israel did not entail an end to the Jewish diaspora, although the ultimate political goal of that state was to bring an end to the suffering of the Jewish diaspora and to create a political home and haven for the Jewish people. Relatedly, Radhakrishnan (2012: 40–1) argues that, in the case of Palestinians who lack a sovereign state, it is difficult to valorize exile when 'exile is the very political ill that has been plaguing the Palestinian people ever since the founding of the state of Israel in 1948'. Ever since expulsion was imposed on the Palestinians, they have been looking to 'sovereign nationalization as an answer to their political homelessness'.

Statelessness as a form of political homelessness is based on a territorial account of belonging. By and large, Palestinian and Kurdish diasporas view statelessness in different ways. Members of the Kurdish diaspora describe themselves as stateless to gain political recognition as an autonomous nation in the international community and to detach themselves from the universal identities of Iran, Iraq, Syria and Turkey. Those in the Palestinian diaspora, however, consider statelessness a dangerous epithet because it somehow legitimizes their absence from (and invisibility in) occupied Palestinian lands and denies them the right to claim Palestine as their national home. Members of the Kurdish and Palestinian diasporas see themselves as different from migrant groups with their 'own states', for they do not have secure national homes to which they can return and express their identities free from ethnic oppression. Kurdish and Palestinian migrants also view the rise of populist right-wing movements in Western Europe as a potential threat to their security and citizenship rights in Sweden and the UK. They wonder where they would go if these groups were to gain power, destabilize liberal democracy and evict them from Sweden and the UK. Palestinians have long experiences of evictions in the Middle East, not only from Israel but also from the Arab countries. Their experiences of otherness in the Middle East and Western Europe have strengthened their desire for national sovereignty, which, ironically, is the source of their collective suffering and banishment. According to Cocks (2006), ethnonationalism often hardens collective identities. The question is how to create new pluralistic political forms that do not reproduce unequal relations between the sovereign and non-sovereign. Without condoning the political oppression of non-sovereign groups, national identity and the search for a national home constitute a major obstacle to the liberation of non-sovereign constituents. Although this vision seems adventurous and might be interpreted as utopian, it is essential to create a political form that nurtures equality and heterogeneity, one in which different constituents can live their lives and identities non-hierarchically. Both stateless and state-linked diasporas have a significant role to play in creating 'a political home for a beleaguered people, now humanly enriched and enlarged' (Cocks 2006: 38) to replace the current choking confines that create destructive political divisions and undermine social solidarity in our world.

Acknowledgement

This study is a component of the research project '(Re)conceptualizing "stateless diasporas" in the EU', and formed part of the Oxford Diasporas Programme, University of Oxford (Leverhulme Trust Grant Number F/08/000/H).

References

Ahmed, S. (1999) 'Home and away: narratives of migration and estrangement', *International Journal of Cultural Studies*, 2 (3), 329–47, doi: 10.1177/136787799900200303.
Anthias, F. (1998) 'Evaluating diaspora: beyond ethnicity', *Sociology*, 32 (3), 557–80.
Anthias, F. (2006) 'Belongings in a globalising and unequal world: rethinking translocations', in N. Yuval-Davis, K. Kannabiran and U. Vieten (eds) *The situated politics of belonging*, London: Sage, 17–31.
Antonsich, M. (2010) 'Search for belonging: an analytical framework', *Geography Compass*, 4 (6), 644–59, doi: 10.1111/j.1749-8198.2009.00317.x.
Brubaker, R. (2005) 'The "diaspora" diaspora', *Ethnic and Racial Studies*, 28 (1), 1–19, doi: 10.1080/0141987042000289997.
Butter, S. (2015) 'No place like home? Conceptualizations of "home" in Salman Rushdie's "At the Auction of the Ruby Slippers" and Roshi Fernando's *Homesick*', in F. Kläger and K. Stierstorfer (eds) *Diasporic constructions of home and belonging*, Berlin: De Gruyter, 349–65.
Can, M. (2006) *Tätt intill dagarna: berättelsen om min mor*, Stockholm: Nordstedts.
Cocks, J. (2006) 'Jewish nationalism and the question of Palestine', *Interventions: International Journal of Postcolonial Studies*, 8 (1), 24–39, doi: 10.1080/13698010500514954.
Cohen, R. (2008) *Global diasporas: an introduction*, second edition, New York: Routledge.
Duyvendak, J. W. (2011) *The politics of home: belonging and nostalgia in Europe and the United States*, New York: Palgrave Macmillan.
Eliassi, B. (2013) *Contesting Kurdish identities in Sweden: quest for belonging among Middle Eastern youth*, New York: Palgrave Macmillan.
Eliassi, B. (2016) 'Statelessness in a world of the nation-states: the cases of Kurdish diasporas in Sweden and the UK', *Journal of Ethnic and Migration Studies*, 42 (9), 1403–19, doi: 10.1080/1369183X.2016.1162091.
George, R. M. (1996) *The politics of home: postcolonial relocations and twentieth-century fiction*, London: University of California Press.
Guibernau, M. (2013) *Belonging: solidarity and division in modern societies*, Cambridge: Polity.
Hage, G. (2000) *White nation: fantasies of white supremacy in a multicultural society*, New York: Routledge.
hooks, b. (2009) *Belonging: a culture of place*, New York: Routledge.

Kenny, K. (2013) *Diaspora: a very short introduction*, Oxford: Oxford University Press.
King, R. and A. Christou (2010) 'Cultural geographies of diasporic migration: perspectives from the study of second-generation "returnees" to Greece', *Population, Space and Place*, 16 (2), 103–19, doi: 10.1002/psp.543.
Malešević, S. (2013) *Nation-states and nationalisms*, Cambridge: Polity.
Maxey, R. (2006) '"Life in the diaspora is often held in a strange suspension": first generation self-fashioning in Hanif Kureishi's narratives of home and return', *Journal of Commonwealth Literature*, 41 (3), 5–25, doi: 10.1177/0021989406068732.
Radhakrishnan, R. (2003) *Theory in an uneven world*, Malden, MA: Blackwell.
Radhakrishnan, R. (2012) *A Said dictionary*, New Delhi: Wiley-Blackwell.
Said, E. (1999) *After the last sky: Palestinian lives*, New York: Columbia University Press.
Sharma, N. (2014) 'Belonging', in B. Andersson and M. Keith (eds) *Migration: a COMPASS anthology*, Oxford: Compass, 166–7.
Sheffer, G. (2003) *Diasporas politics: at home abroad*, New York: Cambridge University Press.
Skey, M. (2011) *National belonging and everyday life: the significance of nationhood in an uncertain world*, New York: Palgrave Macmillan.
Sökefeld, M. (2006) 'Mobilizing in transnational space: a social movement approach to the formation of diaspora', *Global Networks*, 6 (3), 265–84, doi: 10.1111/j.1471-0374.2006.00144.x.
Soysal, Y. (2002) 'Citizenship and identity: living in diaspora in post-war Europe?', *Ethnic and Racial Studies*, 23 (1), 1–15, doi: 10.1080/014198700329105.
Yuval-Davis, N. (2006) 'Belonging and the politics of belonging', *Patterns of Prejudice*, 40 (3), 197–214, doi: 10.1080/00313220600769331.
Wahlbeck, Ö. (1999) *Kurdish diasporas: a comparative study of Kurdish refugee communities*, London: Macmillan.
Werbner, P. (2015) 'The boundaries of diaspora: a critical response to Brubaker', in F. Kläger and K. Stierstorfer (eds) *Diasporic constructions of home and belonging*, Berlin: De Gruyter, 35–51.

15
Diaspora and class, class and diaspora

Nicholas Van Hear

While once a core concept of social science, class lost much of its explanatory appeal in the 1990s, as fundamental changes took hold in the global political economy that seemed to undermine the socio-economic basis of class and its usefulness as a means of analysis. This fading appeal of class as an explanation of social change was reflected in migration and diaspora studies no less than in other fields. Forms of social difference, affinity or allegiance such as ethnicity, gender, generation and religion rather became the key concerns, as questions of representation, identity, 'identification', and identity politics came to preoccupy migration and diaspora researchers. Though class is making a comeback in social science more widely (Bottero 2004; Savage et al. 2013; Wright 2015), this is less evident in migration and diaspora studies than in other arenas of social science enquiry.

I argue for the reinstatement of class as a means of understanding how socio-economic and spatial mobility may combine to shape both diaspora formation and diaspora engagement. It suggests that the form of migration and its outcomes – above all, diaspora formation and engagement – are shaped by the resources that would-be migrants can muster. The capacity to mobilize those resources is largely determined by socio-economic background or class, which, drawing on Bourdieu (1986, 1987), can be conceived in terms of the disposal of different amounts and forms of capital – economic, social, political, cultural, symbolic, and so on. Holding combinations of such capital shapes the routes would-be migrants can take, the channels they can follow, the destinations they can reach, and their life chances afterwards. This in turn shapes both diaspora formation and engagement, considered in this chapter.

Class and the making of diasporas

It is generally accepted that international migration is not typically for the poorest of the poor, but is undertaken by those who can mobilize some level of resources. Putting it simply, there is a hierarchy of destinations that can be reached by migrants, according to the resources – economic and network-based – that they can call upon. As more prosperous and desirable destination countries have tightened their migration regimes, the main factors that determine the ability to reach them have increasingly become cost and connections: more affluent and desirable destinations attract higher premiums both through official channels of entry and in terms of smugglers' and agents' charges if irregular routes are followed. It follows that access to more desirable destinations is easier for better-endowed migrants than for less-endowed ones. Navigating the international migration regime then requires different amounts, forms and combinations of capital. Only those who are endowed with certain volumes of capital in certain compositions, or who can convert other forms of capital into the required forms in the required compositions, can undertake international migration – to more affluent destinations at least. So the capacity for a migrant to navigate the international migration order will be largely shaped by his or her endowments of economic and social capital: in other words, their class.

Some refinement of this framework is needed, for it is obviously not the case that all the well endowed are mobile and the less endowed are not. Mobility can rather cluster at both ends of the socio-economic scale:

> Mobility is greatest at the extreme ends of the socioeconomic spectrum. The mobility of the destitute is a hardship-induced rootlessness: the homeless, refugees, people on the margins of job markets, and people pushed into migration out of need or crisis are all clustered at this end of the mobility curve. At the opposite end of the spectrum are the highflyers (literally and metaphorically). In contemporary societies, increasing wealth is attended by increasing mobility and, reciprocally, increasing mobility increases privileges.
>
> *(Domosh and Seager 2001: 110)*

What counts is the degree of choice in moving or staying put. Sometimes, it may be the privileged who can leave while the less endowed are forced to stay, stuck in involuntary immobility: the well endowed may have the resources to move if they want or need to, while the less endowed may have no choice but to stay put because they have insufficient resources to move across borders. At other times, while the less endowed must leave, the privileged may choose to stay: in challenging circumstances, the well endowed may have the resources to stay put – for example, the means to bribe combatants on both sides of a conflict that they should be allowed to stay on – and it may be that the less endowed have no choice but to move. So in sum, the range of conditions includes 'voluntary' mobility or immobility, on one hand, and 'forced' mobility or immobility, on the other, depending on the possibility and degree of exercising agency or choice. The key point is that the *choice* of whether to move or stay put is shaped by resources or different endowments of capital – class, for short.

This pattern is particularly the case for diasporas generated wholly or in part by conflict – perhaps the predominant form of diaspora formation in recent years. In conflict settings, a common pattern is for most to seek safety in other parts of their country, for a substantial number to look for refuge in a neighbouring country or countries, and for a smaller number to seek asylum in countries further afield, often in other continents. Some of those in neighbouring countries of 'first asylum' may later be resettled further afield, or migrate to new destinations as part of onward movements, joining those who have gone there directly. If exile persists and people consolidate themselves in their territories of refuge, complex transnational relations develop among these different locations of the diaspora: that is, among those at home, those in neighbouring territories (the *near diaspora*), and those spread further afield (the *wider diaspora*). This shapes forms of diaspora engagement considered below.

Turning to the societies that receive migrants, from the perspective of receiving countries in the 'Global North', and increasingly in the 'emerging world', a typical pattern is the arrival of a number of waves of migration from conflict-ridden countries like Sri Lanka, Somalia, Iraq, Syria and Afghanistan to form the wider diaspora. Commonly, the following categories of arrival feature in varying combinations, to some degree reflecting class or socio-economic status:

- Elite and professional migrants who wish to pursue professions in law, medicine or engineering, and/or who anticipate trouble and upheaval in their homelands, are typically among the earliest waves: political exiles may well be among them.
- Alternatively, there may have been earlier labour migration pathways that pave the way for later refugee arrivals.
- Students (particularly those who were political activists) may also arrive as tensions rise before conflict breaks out, especially if their studies are blocked at home.
- As conflict escalates and violence erupts, refugees and asylum-seekers arrive, often again in waves, depending on the intensity of fighting.
- Associated with each of these cohorts of 'primary' arrivals are migrants who come for marriage, family reunion and family formation, and these arrivals may continue long after the conflict ends, depending on the resources that households and families can mobilize.
- As diasporas become established and people find or gain the right to move from their new locations, onward or secondary migration may increase, as families split by forced migration may be able to re-group, again depending on their resources.

As can be seen from this frequently witnessed sequence of migrant cohorts, the people who move from conflict-ridden countries are not all refugees, but include people who move for a variety of reasons, involving varying degrees of force and choice. The co-existence of poverty, lack of income opportunities, inequality and conflict-induced displacement mean that much of the migration in many parts of the world is 'mixed' in nature, both in terms of motivations and the character of the flows: those who flee a country where violence, persecution, discrimination and human rights abuses are rife, for example, may also be trying to escape dire economic circumstances – which themselves feed into such violence, persecution, discrimination and human rights abuses. Moreover, refugees and other migrants often follow the same routes, make use of the same smugglers and agents, and end up in the same host communities. 'Mixed migration' has therefore been salient in recent diaspora formation (Van Hear et al. 2009).

If this is the big picture that we need to grasp, we also need to understand the ground or micro level of individuals, households, families and communities, where these patterns are reflected: we need to comprehend what might be called the extended family picture. Conceivably, we may find within one extended family a range of kinds of dispersal and categories of movement. A given extended family may include people who moved prior to the conflict and who have established themselves abroad, often as professionals; refugees in a neighbouring country of first asylum; and asylum-seekers in affluent countries – some with cases pending, some whose cases have been rejected, and some who have secured refugee status. Such extended families may also include irregular migrants stuck in transit places while trying to get to affluent countries, or those who opt to remain irregular rather than seek asylum, since among other things this would make them visible to the authorities. They may also include people displaced within their own countries, and people who stay put or who cannot move, such as the elderly or disabled. They may include labour migrants who make for oil-rich countries or other emergent economies, and people who move for education against the background of conflict. Finally, such extended families likely include people who migrate for marriage or to reunite with their families – or to escape their families.

In summary, and taking account of both the macro and micro levels, there is commonly a *spread* of people who move within and from conflict-ridden countries: some, typically the less endowed, are dispersed within their own countries as internally displaced people; some find their way to neighbouring countries; and still others, with the resources to do so, are able to move to countries further afield. The migrants include not just refugees, but people who move for a variety of reasons, and with varying degrees of force and choice. With their dispersal comes formation of diasporas, and the establishment of transnational relations and networks among the dispersed groups: it is through these networks and relationships that diasporas can exert influence on their countries of origin.

Diaspora and class between homeland and host land

Confounding class: rags to riches, or rags and riches?

If class helps us to understand how options to move or stay put are shaped, and thereby diaspora formation, does class work as an analytical tool in transnational and diasporic settings that are brought about by migration? In some ways, forms of transnational living seem to confound class. Consider three kinds of migration experience.

In the first, the migrant undergoes a shift from relative poverty in the homeland to betterment in the country of destination – such as the move from poor market trader in the homeland to successful businessperson in the destination country. This is the classic 'rags to riches' story of upward social mobility coming from spatial mobility.

In the second, the migrant moves from relatively wealthy status in the homeland to precariousness in the country of destination – such as the qualified doctor or civil servant in the homeland working as a cleaner or taxi driver in the destination country. This is a 'riches to rags' story of spatial mobility leading to downward social mobility.

The third scenario is one of simultaneity: precariousness or poverty in the destination country while holding substantial wealth in the homeland – as is the case with extended families who divide their time between a substantial house and otherwise well-endowed life for a period in the homeland, while living in inferior housing and on low income in a poor part of a world city like London, New York or Berlin for the rest of the year. This can perhaps be characterized as 'rags and riches', the experience of simultaneous though spatially separate wealth and poverty.

These variants pose challenges to thinking about those living transnational lives in terms of class, for the last in particular shows that a person or household may appear to hold a different class position in different settings. However, it does not follow that class is irrelevant or non-existent, but rather that we need better tools to think about the class position of people who live transnationally.

A potentially useful approach here is the notion of the 'precariat' popularized by Standing (2011). A result of three decades of neoliberal globalization, the precariat for Standing comprises those whose lives and identities are beholden to the vagaries of capital, which considers them part of a flexible labour force, and who are consequently unable to live and pursue livelihoods in coherent and sustainable ways. Such 'precarity' has been accentuated since the onset of convoluted financial and economic crises worldwide from 2008.

Both would-be and actual migrants can be seen as part of the global 'precariat'. Indeed, migration is often seen as a means of moving out of the precariat, even though in practice migrants often find themselves stuck in insecure lives and livelihoods in 'host' countries. In effect, they move out of one section of the global precariat in their homeland to precariousness in their 'host' countries, reflecting some of the trajectories outlined above. Transnational practices by migrants or the diaspora can be seen as a way of overcoming or ameliorating precariousness in both the home and host country – with greater or lesser degrees of success. In some cases, the better-endowed may leave the precariat – and perhaps the diaspora too. Their allegiances to particular diasporic groups weaken, and they may pass into the ranks of footloose cosmopolitans, with similar patterns of consumption, outlooks and perspectives – in short, with similar engagement in global capitalism. Arguably, they become part of the expanding global middle class (Wilson and Dragusanu 2008). By contrast, other diasporans find themselves ineluctably stuck in the global precariat.

Diaspora in itself and diaspora for itself

The subtitle of Standing's book is 'the new dangerous class'; but it is difficult to sustain the argument that the disparate people he characterizes as the precariat constitute a 'class' – at least in the way that social science has conceived of that idea. Standing in fact qualifies the claim implied by his book title: from being a 'new class', we are told 'the precariat has class characteristics' and is 'a class in the making if not yet a class in itself' (Standing 2011: 7, 8).

In the Marxist tradition, a distinction is sometimes made between 'class in itself' and 'class for itself'.[1] 'Class in itself' is seen as a collectivity with certain identifiable attributes and interests in common, while 'class for itself' is regarded as a collectivity that acts in pursuit of those common interests. If we can see elements of 'class in itself' operating in the migration field in terms of shaping the means, routes and destinations of migration, as explored above, are there ways in which 'class for itself' figures in diasporic settings? If class helps us to understand how options to move or stay put are shaped at the individual or household level, how do migration, diaspora and class play out in broader currents of social change and transformation?

In the 1960s and 1970s, classes were seen as agents of change – though there was much debate about which and how. There is a substantial literature dating from the 1970s which considers the class position and activity of migrants in what were then described as advanced capitalist countries (see, for example, Castles and Kosack 1973; Cohen 1987; Sivanandan 1981). Migrants (or at least some of them) were seen as part of the working class – and were indeed often at the forefront of working-class struggles in what later became known as the 'Global North'.

As already observed, the wider social context – the political economy – has since changed profoundly. So too has the intellectual debate. As noted at the outset of this contribution, it has been argued that class has faded has a social force (Bottero 2004; Wright 2015), and with that fading, class has lost its appeal as a subject of study too – though there has been something of a revival in recent years, witness the recent British Social Class Survey and the debate it sparked (Savage et al. 2013). So too, largely though not wholly, has interest in the place of migrants in class and class in migration faded – though there has been a modest revival here too (see, for example, Però 2014; Van Hear 2014).

At the same time, the 'transnational turn' from the mid-1990s and the remarkable uptake of the notion of diaspora in scholarly, governmental and political discourse (Cohen 2008; Van Hear 2011) have to some degree cast diasporas in the role that classes formerly held. From the late 1990s and into the 2000s, diasporas came for some to be seen as the vehicles of change – for example, in the form of lobbying and political action in the 'host' country and/or promoting development or post-war recovery in 'home' countries (Adamson 2012; Kapur 2007). One might say that diasporas implicitly replaced classes as putative vehicles of change. The problem with this argument, though, is that diaspora solidarities are usually inward-looking and exclusive – usually based on ethnicity – rather than outward-oriented and inclusive. Moreover, with the shift in the wider socio-political context, people as a whole – and diasporas are no exception – are more atomized, individualized and entrepreneurial: diasporans are 'neoliberal subjects' like everyone else. Many current allegiances seem to be less universalistic and more particularistic.

Further, although they remain players of global significance, the achievements of diasporas as collectivities akin to classes are somewhat limited – diasporas may *sustain* societies through their role as purveyors of transnational social security (remittances, relief from the effects of war, help for post-conflict recovery, and so on), and this is a vital bastion against the background of neoliberal globalization's predations (Horst 2006; Lindley 2010; Van Hear 2002). But the record of *changing* society is mixed, to say the least. Arguably, diasporas are on the whole 'small c' conservatives rather than social transformers. This is not surprising perhaps, since few diasporans are centrally motivated by the idea of social transformation, but prefer to focus on shifting the balance of power among ethnic groups or other affinities.

If this is the case, to adapt the Marxist formulation, can we speak of 'diasporas in themselves' moving to a condition of 'diasporas for themselves' then, engaging in activity that promotes their own interests? The evidence is not wholly convincing. 'Diaspora in itself' has a somewhat shaky social formation, not least as diasporas are often riven with division – by class, cohort, religion, ethnicity, generation, and so on, as we have already seen. 'Diaspora for itself' is at best ephemeral, in evidence during high water marks of political activity, when diasporans may make common cause. So it is perhaps hard to make a convincing case that diasporas are currently what in an earlier era classes were thought to be – vehicles of social change.

Diasporas and the 'left behind'

The response to the recent rise of populism presents a further twist in the relationships between migration, diaspora, class and globalization. In this discourse, those left out or left behind by globalization are cast in quasi-class terms.

The UK's Brexit vote and the election of Trump in the USA, not to mention the continuing appeal of authoritarian 'strongmen' like Russia's Putin, Turkey's Erdogan and India's Modi, have prompted much discussion about the rise of populism, nativism and illiberal democracies worldwide. One obvious and much-mentioned dimension of this is that the ascendancy of the neoliberal variant of globalization over the last three decades has allowed some to do well while making life harder for many others. Political debate is taking account of this and coming to terms with what are now called the 'left behind', the 'left-out', the 'left-aside', the 'left-over', and so on (Van Hear 2016b). The categories are to some degree seen in class or class-like terms.

But these 'left-outs' and 'left-behinds' are not all the same. We can perhaps identify at least two kinds of globalization's left-outs and left-behinds. On the one hand are those left-behinds and left-outs who do not want to be part of a globalized world. For these people, things are changing too quickly, too profoundly, and in ways that they do not like. On the other hand are those who are left out but who do want to be part of and benefit from the globalized world. For these people, things are not changing quickly enough – or are moving in the wrong direction.

Not long ago, from around 2011, it was the latter kind of 'left-out' who either mobilized against austerity and authoritarianism in the mass upheavals of the Arab Spring, Occupy, the *Indignados* and similar movements, or sought to escape illiberal and stagnating societies by migrating and moving away from them. This set of left-outs were simultaneously seduced by the commodities and services that globalization offers and repelled by the fragmentation and disintegration of community that neoliberal globalization entails. It is this digitally literate socio-economic group, especially in the so-called 'emerging world', that seeks to migrate and/or mobilizes politically – often drawing on transnational or diasporic connections.

In the later 2010s, it has been 'left-outs' of the first kind – those who want no part of globalization – who have come to the fore, mobilizing in support of Brexit, Trump, and leaders like Putin, Erdogan and Modi. It could also be argued that 'left-outism' is a driver of recruitment to other more explicitly violent kinds of illiberal insurgency like al Qaeda, Islamic

State and other sects inspired by resurgent religiosity; though they may rail against aspects of neoliberal globalization, such groups draw on the resources it offers (notably social media) to organize transnationally.

Commenting on the inexorable rise in the number of 'superfluous young people condemned to the anteroom of the modern world, an expanded Calais in its squalor and hopelessness', Indian essayist Pankaj Mishra (2015) has captured the worldview of these different left-outs well:

> Mass education, economic crisis and unfeeling government have long constituted a fertile soil for the cults of authoritarianism and violence. Powerlessness and deprivation are exacerbated today by the ability, boosted by digital media, to constantly compare your life with the lives of the fortunate (especially women entering the workforce or prominent in the public sphere: a common source of rage for men with siege mentalities worldwide). The quotient of frustration tends to be highest in countries that have a large population of educated young men who have undergone multiple shocks and displacement in their transition to modernity and yet find themselves unable to fulfil the promise of self-empowerment.

Where do diasporas and diasporans stand in relation to the 'left-behind' and 'left-out' debate? This takes us back to the discussion above on those stuck in the precariat and those who manage to leave it. Thus we can see some diasporans as left-behind, inward-looking parochials, while others are thrusting, forward-looking cosmopolitans. Put another way, they feature as both Goodhart's 'somewheres' and 'anywheres' (Goodhart 2017): in his analysis of the rise and appeal of populism, Goodhart sees the world as divided between 'anywheres' (liberal, rootless metropolitans) and 'somewheres' (grounded provincial folk deeply committed to place in small towns and the countryside). Just as their transnationalism may confound class categorization, diasporans who lead transnational lives to some extent feature on both sides of the parochial/somewhere/cosmopolitan/anywhere configuration.

Conclusion

In this contribution, I have argued that class, for long a key concept in social science, has been underplayed in migration and diaspora studies in recent years. In particular, consideration of the material conditions that shape socio-economic standing has been neglected in favour of concern with cultural factors that shape identity and identity politics. I suggest that reconsideration of the ways in which social science has addressed socio-economic difference is needed to understand how migration, diaspora formation and diaspora engagement work. Drawing on Bourdieu, I have suggested that considering class in terms of different endowments of capital may be helpful for such understanding. Thinking about class in such ways helps us to understand who is able to move and who cannot, and the hierarchy of destinations that different migrants are able to reach – and thereby diaspora formation.

If class shapes the capacity to move and the destinations that can be reached, the transnational connections that are set in play by migration can complicate the picture because those who lead transnational lives can seem to move between classes, as we have seen. What I called the extended family picture also arguably undermines a class-based analysis – since it suggests that people from a particular extended family hold different class positions, whereas class theory tells us that by and large families tend to hold one class position (though there may, of course, be social mobility over life course and across generations). The idea of using transnational connections and resources to try to manage precarious lives may partly resolve this conundrum and underscores the dynamic character of the interplay between migration, diaspora and class.

The notion of class involves not just socio-economic position, or 'class in itself', but the idea of collective action by those with similar interests – 'class for itself'. While diasporas have come to be seen as agents of change, it is difficult to make a case that they act in class-like ways: while 'diasporas in themselves' may from time to time mobilize as 'diasporas for themselves', such mobilization is ephemeral and its contribution to lasting social change or transformation a matter of argument.

In sum, a case can be made that class plays a significant role in the formation of diasporas. The role of class in diaspora mobilization and engagement is less clear-cut: it is difficult to make a case that diasporas as collectivities act in class-like ways – consistently at least. Given these reservations, one might wonder whether class is the most helpful term to use when considering diasporas – might not 'inequality', 'social difference', 'distinction' or other terms be more appropriate? Whichever term is lighted upon, socio-economic status warrants greater attention in diaspora studies than has featured hitherto.

Note

1 Even if Marx did not explicitly make this distinction in these terms (Andrew 1983).

Acknowledgements

The contribution draws on Van Hear (2006, 2014, 2016a and 2016b), as well as helpful comments from and discussion with Steve Lubkemann, Cathrine Brun, Robin Cohen and many others.

References

Adamson, F. (2012) 'Constructing the diaspora: diaspora identity politics and transnational social movements', in P. Mandaville and T. Lyons (eds) *Politics from afar: transnational diasporas and networks*, New York: Columbia University Press, 25–42.
Andrew, E. (1983) 'Class in itself and class against capital: Karl Marx and his classifiers', *Canadian Journal of Political Science*, 16 (3), 577–84, doi: 10.1017/S0008423900023994.
Bottero, W. (2004) 'Class identities and the identity of class', *Sociology*, 38 (5), 985–1003, doi: 10.1177/0038038504047182.
Bourdieu, P. (1986) 'The forms of capital', in J. Richardson (ed.) *Handbook of theory and research for the sociology of education*, New York: Greenwood Press, 241–58.
Bourdieu, P. (1987) 'What makes a social class? On the theoretical and practical existence of groups', *Berkeley Journal of Sociology*, 32, 1–17, available at: www.jstor.org/stable/41035356.
Castles, S. and G. Kosack (1973) *Immigrant workers and the class structure of Western Europe*, London: Oxford University Press.
Cohen, R. (1987) *The new helots: migrants in the international division of labour*, Aldershot: Gower.
Cohen, R. (2008) *Global diasporas: an introduction*, second edition, Abingdon: Routledge.
Domosh, M. and J. Seager (2001) *Putting women in place: feminist geographers make sense of the world*, New York: Guilford Press.
Goodhart, D. (2017) *The road to somewhere: the populist revolt and the future of politics*, London: Hurst.
Horst, C. (2006) *Transnational nomads: how Somalis cope with refugee life in the Dadaab camps of Kenya*, Oxford: Berghahn.
Kapur D. (2007) 'The Janus face of diasporas', in B. J. Merz, L. Chen and P. Geithner (eds) *Diasporas and development*, Cambridge, MA: Harvard University Press, 89–118.
Lindlay, A. (2010) *The early morning phone call: Somali refugees' remittances*, Oxford: Berghahn.
Mishra, P. (2015) 'How to think about Islamic State', *Guardian*, 24 July, available at: www.theguardian.com/books/2015/jul/24/how-to-think-about-islamic-state.
Però, D. (2014) 'Class politics and migrants: collective action among new migrant workers in Britain', *Sociology*, 48 (6), 1156–72, doi: 10.1177/0038038514523519.

Savage, M., F. Devine, N. Cunningham, M. Taylor, L. Yaojun, J. Hjellbrekke, B. Le Roux, S. Friedman and A. Miles (2013) 'A new model of social class: findings from the BBC's Great British Class experiment', *Sociology*, 47 (2), 219–50, doi: 10.1177/0038038513481128.

Sivanandan, A. (1981) 'From resistance to rebellion: Asian and Afro-Caribbean struggles in Britain', *Race and Class*, 23 (2/3), 111–52, doi: 10.1177/030639688102300202.

Standing, G. (2011) *The precariat: the new dangerous class*, London: Bloomsbury.

Van Hear, N. (2002) 'Sustaining societies under strain: remittances as a form of transnational exchange in Sri Lanka and Ghana', in K. Koser and N. Al-Ali (eds) *New approaches to migration: transnational communities and the transformation of home*, London: Routledge, 202–23.

Van Hear, N. (2006) 'I went as far as my money would take me': conflict, forced migration and class', in F. Crepeau et al. (eds) *Forced migration and global processes: a view from forced migration studies*, Oxford: Lexington, 125–58.

Van Hear, N. (2009) (with R. Brubaker and T. Bessa) 'Managing mobility for human development: the growing salience of mixed migration', UNDP Human Development research paper 20, available at: http://hdr.undp.org/sites/default/files/hdrp_2009_20.pdf.

Van Hear, N. (2011) 'Forcing the issue: migration crises and the uneasy dialogue between refugee research and policy', *Journal of Refugee Studies*, 25 (1), 2–24, doi: 10.1093/jrs/fer052.

Van Hear, N. (2014) 'Reconsidering migration and class', *International Migration Review*, 48 (S1), S100–21, doi: 10.1111/imre.12139.

Van Hear, N. (2016a) 'From new helots to new diasporas: opening remarks', in N. Van Hear, S. Molteno and O. Bakewell (eds) *From new helots to new diasporas: a retrospective for Robin Cohen*, Oxford: Oxford Publishing Services.

Van Hear, N. (2016b) 'The new lefts', Centre on Migration, Policy and Society blog, available at: www.compas.ox.ac.uk/2016/the-new-lefts/.

Wilson, D. and R. Dragusanu (2008) 'The expanding middle: the exploding world middle class and falling global inequality', Goldman Sachs Global Economic paper 70, available at: www.ryanallis.com/wp-content/uploads/2008/07/expandingmiddle.pdf.

Wright, E. (2015) *Understanding class*, London: Verso.

16
Working-class cosmopolitans and diaspora

Pnina Werbner

May we say that the new post-war diasporas are cosmopolitan social formations? The powerful attraction of diaspora for early postcolonial theorists was that, as transnational social formations, diasporas challenged the hegemony and boundedness of the nation-state and, indeed, of any pure imaginaries of nationhood (Clifford 1994; Gilroy 1993; Hall 1991). The creative work of diasporic intellectuals on the margins was celebrated for transgressing hegemonic constructions of national homogeneity (Bhabha 1994). One recent scholarly riposte to this view has highlighted the continued imbrication of diasporas in nationalist rhetoric. Again, while postcolonial theorists challenged simplistic paradigms of diasporas as scattered communities yearning for a lost national homeland, whether real or imaginary (Boyarin and Boyarin 1993; Ghosh 1989; Hall 1991), the growing consensus has been, by contrast, that such imagined attachments to a place of origin and/or collective historical trauma are still powerfully implicated in the late modern organization of diasporas. Diasporas, it seems, are both ethnic-parochial and cosmopolitan. The task remains, however, to disclose how the tension between these two tendencies is played out in actual situations.

The most recent challenge to the cosmopolitan vision of diaspora has come from the post-9/11 emergence of Islamic 'terror' cells apparently embedded within settled post-war diasporas in the West. Although it is questionable to my mind whether the 9/11 Al-Qaida terrorists themselves were 'diasporic', since most were temporary students, other young diasporic men (and some women) have continued to emerge supporting extreme Islamic movements like ISIS that reject all other cultures and are, undoubtedly, anti- or 'counter-cosmopolitan' (Appiah 2006), forming a globalized multinational network, all espousing a singular truth and demonizing other cultures, religions and nations, often violently. Their emergence has led to a critical discourse that accuses Muslim immigrants in particular of isolating themselves socially and leading 'parallel lives' (for a discussion, see, for example, Philips 2006).

Against both the idealism of the postcolonial theorists and the gloomy diagnostics of securitization experts is the mounting evidence of everyday 'banal' multicultural conviviality in places like the UK (Gilroy 2004; Werbner 2013). And not only the UK. A further critical contribution to the cosmopolitan version of diaspora comes from ethnographies that challenge elitist perspectives of diaspora, ones focusing only on a relatively small cohort of diasporic artists, musicians and intellectuals, seen as the cosmopolitan bearers of a new, post-national truth. The tendency to associate cosmopolitanism with intellectuals is, of course, not new, and these days includes also so-called 'capitalist cosmopolitans' whose passports 'bear stamps of many countries' (Calhoun 2002: 87; cf. also Skrbis et al. 2004). Instead, Stuart Hall (2008: 346) speaks of 'cosmopolitanism from below':

> There is a 'cosmopolitanism of the above' – global entrepreneurs following the pathways of global corporate power and the circuits of global investment and capital, who can't tell which airport they're in, because they all look the same, and who have apartments in three continents. This is global cosmopolitanism of a very limited kind but it is very different from 'cosmopolitanism from below' – people driven across borders, obliged to uproot themselves from home, place and family, living in transit camps or climbing on to the backs of lorries or leaky boats or the bottom of trains and airplanes, to get to somewhere else. Both of them are forms of globalization and, in so far as they both interact within the same global sphere, are deeply interconnected with one another. But they don't constitute the basis of a 'global citizenship'.

International migrants, he argues, are living 'in translation'. Indeed, the NHS hospital in central London where he was treated regularly was a cosmopolitan island involving many different nationalities (Hall 2008: 354).

With all this, we still need to consider what it means to be, in some sense or other, at home in the world? Ulf Hannerz proposes a set of useful distinctions between cosmopolitans 'willing to engage with the Other', locals, 'representatives of more circumscribed territorial cultures', and transnationals (Hannerz 1992: 252), frequent travellers (usually occupational) who share 'structures of meaning carried by social networks' (Hannerz 1992: 248–9). Oddly, though, Hannerz lumps together migrant- settlers, exiles or refugees, the formative makers of diasporas, with *tourists* (Hannerz 1992: 248):

> Surrounded by a foreign culture, he [sic] perhaps tries to keep it at arm's length, and guards what is his own. For most ordinary labour migrants, ideally, going away may be home plus higher income; often the involvement with another culture is not a fringe benefit but a necessary cost. A surrogate home is created with the help of compatriots, in whose circle one feels most comfortable.

Implicit in this separation of professional-occupational transnational cultures from migrant or refugee transnational cultures is, I propose, the hidden Eurocentric and class bias already mentioned: transnational cultures are most often centred on the North and occupied by high-status professionals. The transnational cultures of migrants and refugees, by contrast, are centred beyond the North and their occupational profile is (primarily) menial and low-income. This implicitly explains why, for Hannerz, instead of a willingness to 'engage with the Other', diasporics are reluctant to step outside a 'surrogate home'. It remains unclear, however, why migrants and diasporics should be distinguished analytically from occupational transnationals, the oil engineers or foreign journalists who prefer to live in special compounds, or the Hilton, wherever they go.

The confusion points to the fact that the class dimensions of a theory of global subjectivity have remained mostly unexamined. Anticipating later arguments, Jonathan Friedman (1995: 79–80) addresses issues of transnational subjectivity as manifestations of new class formations:

> One might also suggest that there has emerged a global class structure, an international elite made up of top diplomats, government ministers, aid officials and representatives

of international organisations such as the United Nations, who play golf, dine, take cocktails with one another, forming a kind of cultural cohort. The grouping overlaps with an international cultural elite of art dealers, publishing and media representatives, the culture industries, VIPs . . . producing images of the world and images for the world . . . a proliferation of interpretations of the world.

The description highlights the ambiguity of Hannerz's cosmopolitan–transnational distinction. In order to function, in order to market their goods globally, global elites must understand local cultures, must 'engage with the Other', even while they sustain their exclusive transnational networks. In this respect, local 'cultures' are at least in part the products of extra-local constructions. Globalization is, at least in part, a business strategy for adapting one's goods to local conditions (Robertson 1995: 28).

Unlike Hannerz, Friedman proposes that we can now speak of a diasporic global structure as marking a radical break from past historical precedents because of the evident power and influence that contemporary diasporas wield (Friedman 1997: 84–5). Yet diasporas too are differentiated by class. Hence he launches into a trenchant critique against diasporic intellectuals who speak 'in the name of mixture and hybridity, a claim to a humanity so fused in its cultural characteristics that no "ethnic absolutism" is possible' (Friedman 1997: 75–6). The celebration of hybridity, in-betweenness or double consciousness by diasporic poets, artists and intellectuals proves to be a self-interested strategy, divorced from working-class migrants' (or indigenous people's) predicaments and concerns. For the urban poor, he claims, 'class identity, local ghetto identity, tend to prevail', leaving 'little room for the hybrid identifications discussed and pleaded for by cultural elites' (Friedman 1997: 84). Cultural self-identifications are, ultimately, Friedman argues, like those of class or gender, a matter of social position (Friedman 1997: 88). Diasporic elites are in reality as socially and culturally encapsulated in their cocktail-sipping worlds as are ghetto dwellers in theirs.

Moreover, as the Rushdie affair tragically demonstrated, diasporic intellectuals are often alienated from the transnational cultures evolved by compatriot migrant-settlers; their artistic works are directed towards an English-reading international intelligentsia rather than fellow diasporics (van der Veer 1997).

All this would still seem to point to a homology between class position and transnational subjectivity: cosmopolitanism is the claimed prerogative of elites within the newly evolving global ecumene. The present chapter disputes this common-sense connection. It argues that even working-class labour migrants may become cosmopolitans, willing to 'engage with the Other'; and that transnationals – Hannerz's term redefined to encompass migrants, settlers and refugees as well as occupational travellers – inevitably must engage in social processes of 'opening up to the world', even if that world is still relatively circumscribed culturally. Against the globalizing Northern (or Western) thrust of economic goods, technological experts and mediatized images, the chapter considers a counter-trend: the emergence of complex transnational ethnic or religious cultural worlds, created by vast flows of labour migrants.

Working-class cosmopolitans

Working-class cosmopolitans are a sub-category of the cosmopolitanism-from-below global flow. Unlike refugees, they are distinctive in *becoming* cosmopolitans while working on roads, in factories or on building sites, sharing hard physical labour with fellow workers of other nationalities, or getting to know non-nationals through intimate encounters as nurses or carers for the sick and elderly (on this, see Ahmad 2011; Liebelt 2011: 79–104). The United Emirates Republic today (including Dubai and Abu Dhabi in particular) has 2.6 million Indians, 1.2 million Pakistanis, 700,000 Bangladeshis and 700,000 Filipinos. In Saudi Arabia, according to one estimate, there are 1.5–2.2 million Pakistanis, the largest Pakistani diaspora worldwide, and 2.5 million Indians, but the number of other nationals is higher: 1.5 million Filipinos, 350,000 Sri Lankans, 300,000 Nepalese and 250,000 Indonesians. Although many of these are professionals, living in their own (mixed) gated accommodation, the vast majority are workers, sharing inferior living conditions, also gated and separated from the indigenous Arab population.

The case of one Pakistani worker in the Gulf who I got to know in Pakistan, where he was working as a volunteer in the lodge of a Sufi saint I studied (cf. Werbner 2003), exemplifies the 'opening up to the world' that working together can engender. On my recent visit to a saint's lodge in Pakistan in 1991, my local guide and guardian angel, Hajji Suleiman, a villager with relatively little education, explained to me where he had learned his English. 'I learnt it,' he explained, 'while I was working in the Gulf.' 'In the Gulf?' I wondered. 'But didn't you tell me that you were working for a Japanese firm there?' 'Yes,' he answered, 'of course.' 'Well, how did you learn it then?' 'I learnt it from the Japanese', he replied. 'The Japanese? But they also don't speak English. How did you manage?' 'We used dictionaries', he explained, as though this should have been quite obvious.

On another occasion, we were chatting about the saint and the large number of foreign visitors he hosted at the *darbar*. 'The saint', he explained, 'likes to entertain each person according to what he is accustomed to. In your case, for example, he has given you a comfortable bed to sleep in. The Japanese are very interested in Sufism. Once there was a Japanese delegation that came here to talk about Sufism. At that time, I was the *Shaikh*'s *darban*, his gatekeeper. I served the visitors green tea without sugar, exactly as I knew they liked it. They were delighted and amazed. 'Once in the Gulf', he added, 'I cured a Japanese of a very bad headache by blowing *dam* on him' (he is referring here to the custom of 'blowing' Koranic verses as a healing device).

Hajji Suleiman is a cosmopolitan traveller with a good deal of international experience. His first labour migration trip followed an instruction by his Sufi *Shaikh* to go to Dubai to earn money for his family. While in the Gulf, Hajji Suleiman not only learned to speak English. He also learned to speak Arabic and even a little Japanese. His encounters with the Japanese were complex. At one point, he left the firm he was working for in Dubai at short notice after he had obtained a valuable visa permitting him to go on *hajj*. His application to the firm for leave was refused. At the time, he was a supervisor, and both site engineers were away in Japan on leave, so he was responsible for 250 men. The manager told him: 'If I let you go, all the Muslims working here will want to go too.' Hajji Suleiman consulted a Pakistani friend who was working for another company. The friend advised him to 'forget' the money and go on the pilgrimage anyway. 'This is a great opportunity for you to go on *hajj*', he said. 'You may never get another one!' So Hajji Suleiman went off on *hajj* without handing in his notice, for fear that the company might take away his passport. He just left, 20 days before the *hajj*. In Mecca, he stayed with the Pakistani *khalifa*, deputy of the *Shaikh*, who was based permanently in the holy city.

When the *Shaikh* arrived in Mecca for the annual pilgrimage, Hajji Suleiman was terrified he would be angry with him for deserting his job. He did not come forward to greet the *Shaikh* but the latter noticed him hiding behind the door and called him in. Even though the saint knew nothing of his desertion, he said to him: 'Suleiman, you have done the right thing. You preferred God to money. Do not worry. God will look after you.'

Hajji Suleiman was afraid to go back to his company. He spent a whole month searching for another job in Dubai, staying with a fellow member of the order, but to no avail. Then, one night, at the end of the month, the saint appeared to him in a dream. He told him to go back to his old company, to go there at 2.30 pm sharp, just after lunch. He found out later, he told me, that the company was about to strike him off the books the following day, and to have him deported. He arrived at 2.30 and all the workers – Hindus, Bangladeshis, Japanese, etc. – greeted him: 'Hello, Hajji Suleiman' (stressing the 'Hajji' bit). At the office, all the Japanese were there except the manager, who was late. They were pleased to see him, but they advised him to wait in the meeting room so that the manager wouldn't encounter him straight away when he returned, since the manager was, they said, very angry with him. They promised to warn the manager that he was waiting for him in the meeting room.

Finally the manager arrived. He told Suleiman: 'I cannot employ you any longer. You were solely responsible for 250 men, and you abandoned them.' 'But,' Hajji Suleiman explained to me,

> I had the *tasawar*, the picture, image, of the Shaikh in front of me (in my inner vision) and this gave me courage so I answered: 'You refused me permission to go on *hajj* when I already had a visa, and all the Muslim workers were laughing at me.' The manager thought for a while, and told me to wait. Eventually he called me to him and told me his company had just started a new project in Baghdad. He promised to send me there. I knew the Japanese manager of the new site, Mr Cato, who was away for a few days in Japan. When he came back I met him to discuss the move to Iraq. He wanted to put me in a lower position than I had before, under an ex-gang leader of mine who had in the meanwhile been promoted. But I still had the *tasawar* of the Shaikh before my eyes, so I refused. In the end, they gave in. They promoted someone else to assistant engineer and made me a supervisor instead of that man. Then the company paid my wages and sent me back to Pakistan for a month. I came straight here, to the *darbar* (the saint's lodge), to see the *Shaikh*, even before going home.
>
> When I first came in to see him, the *Shaikh* said to me: 'Now you are going to Baghdad – first Mecca, now Baghdad. You are a very lucky man. Your company is located close to Abdul Qadr Gilani's tomb, just one stop by minibus. You will work in the company in the daytime and clean the tomb at night.' You see, the *Shaikh* knew everything, even though he has never been to Iraq. As Iqbal [the great nationalist Punjabi poet] says, 'God's *Wali* (friend) can take two and a half steps and see the whole world.'

While he was in Baghdad, Hajji Suleiman's wife joined him there for a while, and the two of them both worked as volunteers cleaning the shrine of Abdul Qadr Gilani, the revered founder of South Asian Sufism.

Hajji Suleiman does not belong to a landowning caste. One of his sons is a watchmaker in a small Punjabi town. But two of his sons have recently married cousins (wife's sister's daughters) in Amsterdam and have moved to the Netherlands. In 1991, when these conversations took place, they were waiting for their passports to be released, and then they would be allowed to bring their parents over to Holland. Hajji Suleiman regarded these marriages as a blessing granted him by the saint as reward for his labours. One day, discussing the issue of 'promotions' on the Sufi path, I asked Hajji Suleiman whether he did not resent his position as a mere murid, disciple, despite the long years of unpaid service he had put in at the lodge. 'No', he said, 'I have been promoted', and he explained that the saint had given him permission to blow *dam*, the healing breath of Qur'anic verses, for all illnesses, including snake bites.

'But could you not become a *khalifa*, a vicegerent or deputy of the saint?' I persisted. 'After all, you know Arabic and can even lead the prayers.' Hajji Suleiman then revealed to me a secret dream. 'Perhaps the Shaikh will send me to Holland', he said, 'to found a branch of his order there'. 'He did have a *khalifa* there before who was sent over from England, I think, but the man proved to be a failure, and has now left.' So Amsterdam is the only place which is now 'empty', he said (that is, has no branch of the order, despite the large number of Pakistanis living there).

'In addition to Pakistanis, you know, there were lots of Turks and Arabs in Amsterdam.' 'The other *khalifa* did not speak Dutch or Arabic', he told me. 'But what about you? You don't speak Dutch either', I said. 'Dutch is very easy', Hajji Suleiman replied, 'it's just like Punjabi'. At this unexpected reply, I burst out laughing, but I had to admit to myself that for a man who had learned English from the Japanese, as well as fluent Arabic, while working on a building site, learning to speak Dutch was likely to be a relatively small challenge.

Hajji Suleiman is a devoted Sufi and an evidently pious Muslim. He would not have been given his job back had his piety and sincerity not been recognized by his Japanese employers. But his story is also a tale of the transnational dimensions of religious orders in the modern world. He is locked into a transnational network, not of relatives and family but of *pir-bhai*, Sufi brothers. A Sufi brother advises him to seize the opportunity and go on *hajj*. He stays in Mecca with the *khalifa* of the order. He meets the saint he left behind in Pakistan at a recognized meeting point of the cult in Mecca, when the saint comes for the annual pilgrimage. He then lives with another saint-brother while seeking alternative employment. Finally, in Baghdad, along with his wife, he spends the days working for wages and the nights working for the love of God at a saint's shrine.

There is a further dimension to this type of transnationalism: for Hajji Suleiman, 'home' is condensed in the image of the saint whom he musters before his inner eye whenever he needs courage to confront superiors and foreigners. That image is always with him, wherever he is. His experience of overseas travel is thus not one of alienation but of triumphant mastery, rooted in his localized faith in his saint – which is, simultaneously, very much also a faith in Islam as a world religion. Hence, one of the most exhilarating aspects of his migration experience for him is the sense of Islam as a boundary-crossing global faith. His work at the tomb of Abdul Qadr Gilani in pious service to God confirms his identity in his own eyes as a cosmopolitan who is at home everywhere, just as God is everywhere. So too, the pilgrimage to Mecca, which he performed subsequently several more times during his stay in the Middle East, provides him with an experience of membership in a global community. He is determined to share in that experience, even at the risk of losing a valuable job.

Although he is a simple man from a poor background and with little formal education, Hajji Suleiman clearly feels that the experience of labour migration has transformed him. He is competent now in the traditions of others. He knows the Japanese intimately, has observed their minutest customs. By the same token, he has also observed the customs, habits and idiosyncrasies of Hindus, Bangladeshis, Arabs and Iraqis. He appears to have had close cross-cultural friendships. His confidence is such that learning Dutch is regarded by him as a small matter, almost like knowing Punjabi – which is his mother tongue. But when he considers moving to Holland, it is nevertheless from the vantage point of his most valued identity as a Sufi. If he moves to Holland, it will be with the mission to found a branch of his order there. He will utilize the Arabic picked up in the Gulf to create a cross-national Sufi community of Pakistanis, Turks and Arabs. He knows he can do that, since he has lived with Muslims from other countries already. The world is mapped by him in terms of his Sufi order. Holland is an empty place, a void, since there is no branch there. His perspective as a Sufi member of Zindapir's transnational regional cult shapes his cosmopolitanism and provides it with a sense of order.

Conclusion

Migration is a class-related phenomenon, and notions of transnationalism or cosmopolitanism as cultural phenomena are of necessity class related (see Novikowski 1984; Werbner 1990). Working-class cosmopolitanism – a knowledge of and openness to other cultures – while implying the same processual *forms* of hybridization and creolization, do not generate the same cultural hybrids as those evolved by elite cosmopolitans. We need always, as Jan Pieterse warns us, to 'investigate the *terms* of mixture, the conditions of mixing and *melange*' (Pieterse 1995: 57). There are multiple modalities of cosmopolitanism.

When it comes to diasporas, the Muslim religious diaspora is itself stratified and divided according to religious tendency. Sufism, one such tendency, creates its own global landscapes. Rather than a one-way Westernized flow of goods and images, the 'McDonaldization' of the world, we see that processes of globalization, transnationalization and localization are historically and culturally specific and that the economic pathways carrying goods and people criss-cross each other to create complex transnational topographies. Within any single national, regional or territorial community, however, these global networks disrupt, as Homi K. Bhabha (1994) has argued, any neat notions of national boundedness, without denying them. Cosmopolitanism, in other words, does not necessarily imply an absence of belonging but the possibility of belonging to more than one ethnic, religious and cultural localism simultaneously. This is as true of working-class cosmopolitans as it is of third-world intellectual elites who produce the kind of hybrid artistic products – books, films, art – which have so far been the main focus of scholarly attention.

Acknowledgement

This chapter draws on Werbner (1999).

References

Ahmad, A. (2011) 'Explanation is not the point: domestic work, Islamic dawa and becoming Muslim in Kuwait', *The Asia Pacific Journal of Anthropology*, 11 (3), 293–310, doi: 10.1080/14442213.2010.516009.
Appiah, K. A. (2006) *Cosmopolitanism: ethics in a world of strangers*, London: Allen Lane.
Bhabha, H. (1994) *The location of culture*, London: Routledge.
Boyarin, D. and J. Boyarin (1993) 'Diaspora: generation and the ground of Jewish identity', *Critical Inquiry*, 19 (4), 693–725, doi: 10.1086/448694.
Calhoun, C. (2002) 'The Class consciousness of frequent travellers: towards a critique of actually existing cosmopolitanism' in Steven Vertovec and Robin Cohen (eds) *Conceiving Cosmopolitanism*. Oxford: Oxford University Press, 86–109.
Clifford, J. (1994) 'Diasporas', *Cultural Anthropology*, 9 (3), 302–38, doi: 10.1525/can.1994.9.3.02a00040.
Friedman, J. (1997) 'Global crises, the struggle for cultural identity and intellectual porkbarrelling. Cosmopolitans versus locals, ethnics and nationals in an era of de-hegemonisation', in P. Werbner and T. Modood (eds) *Debating cultural hybridity: multicultural identities and the politics of anti-racism*, London: Zed Books, 70–89.
Ghosh, A. (1989) 'The diaspora in Indian culture', *Public Culture*, 2 (1), 73–8, doi: 10.1215/08992363-2-1-73.
Gilroy, P. (1993) *The black Atlantic: modernity and double consciousness*, London: Verso.
Gilroy, P. (2004) *After Empire: melancholia or convivial culture?* London: Routledge.
Hall, S. (1991) 'The local and the global: globalization and ethnicity', in A. D. King (ed.) *Globalisation and the world system*, London: Macmillan Educational, 19–39.
Hall, S. (2008) 'Cosmopolitanism, globalisation and diaspora: Stuart Hall in conversation with Pnina Werbner', in P. Werbner (ed.) *Anthropology and the new cosmopolitanism: rooted, feminist and vernacular perspective*, Oxford: Berg, 345–60.
Hannerz, U. (1992) *Cultural complexity: studies in the social organisation of meaning*, New York: Columbia University Press.
Liebelt, C. (2011) *Caring for the 'Holy Land': Filipino domestic workers in Israel*, Oxford: Berghahn.
Novikowski, S. (1984) 'Snakes and ladders: Asian business in Britain' In Robin Ward and Richard Jenkins (eds.) *Ethnic Communities in Business Strategies for economic survival*. Cambridge: Cambridge University Press, 189–210.
Philips, D. (2006) 'Parallel lives? Challenging discourses of British Muslim self-segregation', *Environment and Planning D*, 24 (1), 25–40, doi: 10.1068/d60j.

Pieterse, J. N. (1995) 'Globalisation as hybridisation', in M. Featherstone, S. Lash and R. Robertson (eds) *Global modernities*, London: Sage, 45–68.
Robertson, R. (1995) 'Globalisation. Time–space and homogeneity–heterogeneity', in in M. Featherstone, S. Lash and R. Robertson (eds) *Global modernities*, London: Sage, 25–44.
Skrbis, Z., G. Kendall and I. Woodward (2004) 'Locating cosmopolitanism between humanist ideal and grounded social category'. *Theory, Culture & Society*, 21 (6): 115–36.
van der Veer, P. (1997) '"The enigma of arrival": hybridity and authenticity in the global space', in P. Werbner and T. Modood (eds) *Debating cultural hybridity: multicultural identities and the politics of anti-racism*, London: Zed, 90–105.
Werbner P. (1990) *The migration process: capital, gifts and offerings among British Pakistanis*, Oxford: Berg Publishers.
Werbner, P. (1999) 'Global pathways: working class cosmopolitans and the creation of transnational ethnic worlds', *Social Anthropology*, 7 (1), 17–35, doi: 10.1111/j.1469-8676.1999.tb00176.x.
Werbner, P. (2003) *Pilgrims of love: the anthropology of a global Sufi cult*, London: Hurst.
Werbner, P. (2013) 'Everyday multiculturalism: theorising the difference between 'intersectionality' and 'multiple identities'. *Ethnicities* 13 (4), 401–19.

17
Transversal crossings and diasporic intersections

Amanda Wise

A classical take on diaspora assumes one great fiction: that cultures remain contained through time, and across geographies. We know, though, that culture travels and culture unravels. This chapter deals with the changes and connections that occur in diasporic contact zones (Pratt 1992) and how these travel as diasporas do. In this chapter, I outline the concept of 'transversal crossing and diasporic intersections', which I employ to describe the everyday practices and associated transformations that occur in situations of lived difference.

Conceptualizing diasporic intersections through everyday multiculturalism

The containerized view of diaspora has been challenged by research since the 1990s. James Clifford's (1997) notion of diasporic 'roots' versus 'routes' orients much of this work, while literature on working-class and everyday cosmopolitans (Werbner 1999) has clearly put this fiction to bed. A thoroughly quotidian lens is required to grasp how the micro-transformations implied by the notion of 'routes' occur in practice. There are many ways into this question. For example, my research on everyday multiculturalism (Velayutham and Wise 2009; Wise 2005) has been interested in understanding the quotidian, situated, dynamics of multi-ethnic co-existence in all its variations and across contexts. Points of concern have included how the rituals of social life are negotiated, improvised and transformed in multi-ethnic settings; how individuals themselves are transformed in their engagements with these settings – including whether they acquire capacities or habits particularly attuned to navigating environments of great cultural complexity, whether they become 'everyday cosmopolitans' in disposition and orientation. I consider the ways in which difference appears and dissolves in mundane spaces of social engagement; how classed, raced, gendered and generational identities interplay with other mediating forces such as socio-economic inequalities, migrant and citizenship status, neoliberalism, and urban environments. I consider how wider atmospheres of nativism, tolerance, racism, hate and fear interplay in mundane spaces of 'getting along'. Much of my research has had a central focus on what makes a 'convivial' – in the sense of 'to live together, shared life' – space of multi-ethnic co-existence, and explores what differentiates communities that manage to 'muddle along' with diversity, where diversity has become mundane, commonplace, unremarkable – from communities and people averse to difference or uneven in their accommodation of difference. This focus on the everyday highlights questions of everyday racism as often as 'rosy' modalities of togetherness. I've thought a lot about 'tipping points' and the dynamics at play when formerly benign co-existence turns to hate and exclusion. Empirical areas of focus have included attention to the micro-sociology of social ritual, modalities of reciprocity and gift exchange, accommodation and exclusion, civilities, scripts, language adaptation and accommodation, the spatial and temporal dimensions and rhythms of encounter, the ways in which food, friendship, festivals, religion, sport, work or school mediate togetherness, how the media shapes everyday relationships. This also involves a focus on how material environments, institutions and other macro forces shape the quotidian cut and thrust of everyday multiculture.

The concept 'transversal crossing' (Wise 2005, 2009) spotlights the people and places that produce transformations and intersections between groups in quotidian situations of lived difference. The concept 'diasporic intersections' points to how these processes come to bear on identity orientations of diasporic individuals and groups. Oriented towards Clifford's 'routes' rather than 'roots', it is intended to conceptualize how encounters in place reshape ties, dispositions and connections, how these encounters leave 'traces' that carry forward to new places, particularly among twice (or more) removed diasporic groups. Rather than describe the nature of these traces, my interest has been in understanding some of the ways in which these intersectional and porous identity transformations come into being.

The concept loosely borrows and adapts Yuval-Davis's (1997, 1999) theorization of 'transversal politics',[1] a transformative strategy for inter-group conflict resolution and reflection aimed at nudging participants beyond singular, oppositional identity positions to find links and commonalities across lines of conflict. Influenced by her thinking about intersectionality, transversality conceives of relations across difference in dialogic relational terms. She highlights the fact that 'people who identify themselves as belonging to the same collectivity or category can be positioned very differently in relation to a whole range of social divisions' (Yuval-Davis 1997: 204), and that these other positionalities may well connect to an 'Other' one previously understood as entirely discrete from and opposed to. The central aspect of a transversal politics is a dialogue centred on the idea of dialogical 'rooting' and 'shifting' (1997: 204), whereby each participant in the dialogue brings with them the rooting in their own membership and identity, while also trying to shift in order to put themselves in a situation of exchange with those who have a different membership and identity. Cockburn (1998: 9) emphasizes that this process of rooting and shifting does not mean discarding one's political and other sources of belonging, but neither should rooting render participants incapable of movement, of looking for connection with those among 'the others' with whom they might find compatible values and goals. As Yuval-Davis argues (2004: 27), 'transversal politics is not only a dialogue in which two or more partners are negotiating a common political position, but is a process in which all the participants are mutually reconstructing themselves and the others engaged with them in it'. My borrowing is a loose one.

In my adaptation, I use variations on the term '*quotidian transversality*' to describe the micro-social practices everyday actors employ to produce and smooth interrelations across cultural difference, whether or not they are conscious of these differences. It signals the process by which local and diasporic modes of inhabitance intersect through momentary cross-cultural transgressions and displacements (Amin 2002) in everyday, mundane situations. Quotidian transversality is different to hybridity or code-switching. Nor is it an assimilationist or integrationist notion of exchange across difference where the 'guest' culture merges with the dominant culture over time. Instead, it highlights how cultural difference can be the basis for commensality and exchange; where identities are not left behind, but made permeable in moments of non-hierarchical reciprocity, and are sometimes mutually reconfigured in the process. The prefix 'quotidian' differentiates it from Yuval-Davis's transversality, which refers to more formal, conscious modes of conflict resolution. Quotidian signals the everyday, situated, nature of transversal exchange which is not necessarily about conflict resolution. It can be about conflict avoidance, conflict prevention, or indeed, not about conflict at all but about interchange that consciously or unconsciously produces permeable borders of being across difference. It is through such practices that identities are not only traversed but reconfigured, and biographies are intertwined.

Quotidian transversality comprises practices, people and places. I call these transversal practices, transversal enablers and transversal places, respectively. In the context of our thinking on 'diaspora', I am interested in how these produce intersections across diasporic cultures, and in turn how these produce porous qualities and identity transformations that 'carry over' as a diaspora travels through space and time. That is to say, the focus is more on the transformations that occur on diasporic 'routes', than containerized 'roots'-based identity claims (Clifford 1997). In the following sections, I provide some illustrative examples of each of these three transversal aspects as they relate to diasporic intersections.

Transversal practices

Transversal practices refer to the everyday activities sociologists and anthropologists have traditionally thought of as establishing and maintaining sociality *within* an ethnically homogeneous socio-cultural group. This includes forms of gift exchange and reciprocity such as the exchange of services, items or food, gestures of kindness and care. It includes, among other things, everyday ritual practices and the maintenance of social ties; micro practices of recognition, ways of talking, gossip, humour, forms of everyday hospitality. We know these things to be central to the maintenance of intra-group ties (cf. Komter 2004). The notion of transversality, however, places the emphasis beyond basic relations of intra-group exchange, to highlight practices of *interchange*, in the sense of enacting community across cultural difference, transversally opening up and reconfiguring identities through the extension of, and sometimes mutual modification of, practices that establish and maintain social ties.

One example is the exchange of food or home-grown produce enabling the establishment and maintenance of ties between neighbours of different backgrounds. In my piece *Hope and belonging in a multicultural suburb* (Wise 2005), I described one such moral economy involving four neighbours, of Italian, Lebanese, Anglo-Celtic and Indian backgrounds, living in neighbouring homes in a diverse Sydney suburb. Each house had a back garden growing a variety of fruit and vegetables such as tomatoes, cucumbers, herbs, figs, chillies, curry leaves and citrus fruit. When their backyard crops bore fruit, the produce would be gifted or exchanged between them. Sometimes the produce was cooked or baked and gifted to the neighbours. Frank, of Lebanese background, made a weekly visit to buy fruit and vegetables from the wholesale markets each Friday and would leave a box on the front doorstep of the other neighbours. These exchanges brought with them a sensory repertoire that came with stories about how to cook and where this or that recipe originated. When we think about diasporic maintenance, we tend to think about stories and foodways from the homeland and the ancestors. The Anglo-Australian tradition of 'bring a plate' to a community gathering also offers opportunities for mixing and sharing of foodways and the stories connected to them. In these transversal exchanges, these diasporic traces interweave among culturally different neighbours, creating new moments of opening and connection. Drawing on Werbner (1999), Komter (2004), Simmel (1950) and others, I described this as a form of moral economy bounded by a ritual set of gift relations that knit people together across lines of cultural difference.

Another example (see Wise and Velayutham 2014) are the gift relations one sees in multi-religious, multi-racial places like Singapore. Singapore has a Chinese majority and sizeable

Malay and Indian minorities and is a nation of religious diversity, with practising Christians, Muslims, Hindus and Taoists co-existing in relative harmony. It is a society that has produced a rich array of diasporic intersections. The red packets (*Ang Pows*) that Chinese traditionally gift to relatives at Chinese New Year are also gifted to Malay and Indian neighbours and employees. The practice has been adapted by Malays who often gift 'green packets' at Hari Raya (*Eid el Fitri*). Likewise, traditional Chinese gifts such as mandarin oranges and sweet pineapple biscuits traditionally exchanged between neighbours, friends and relatives at Chinese New Year are also gifted to Malay and Indian co-workers, friends and neighbours. In turn, the sweets and spicy *muruku* snacks favoured by Singapore Indians to share at Deepavali are gifted to Chinese and Malay friends and neighbours – taking care to adapt the offering to the assumed tastes of the other two groups. Sweets for Chinese friends who traditionally don't like spicy food, and spicy snacks for Malays, who do. These forms of gift exchange sometimes produce interesting adaptations and appropriations. For example, the traditional Chinese pineapple biscuit has gradually become a favourite for both Hindus and Muslims to swap during their festivals. My Singapore Indian mother-in-law brings plastic jars of Chinese pineapple biscuits as gifts when she visits the village back in India. Not only do these forms of exchange knit together new forms of community across difference – in transversal ways that involve retaining one's diasporic orientations while opening out across difference and sometimes borrowing across groups – over time, they come to shape the communities involved.

Micro-practices of religious accommodation have to some extent become second nature in Singapore, in part due to a concerted state campaign to promote multi-racial, multi-lingual and multi-religious respect and recognition, but also in part due to everyday encounters between the Chinese, Malay and Indian diasporas of Singapore. It is normal and quite unremarkable, for example, to see a special *halal* table set up at the wedding buffets of Chinese and Indian Hindu Singaporeans as a gesture of recognition to Malay and Indian Muslim friends attending. These accommodations are also built into the urban fabric, with *halal* designated sections in hawker centres and food courts (Wise and Velayutham 2014).

Transversal enablers and diasporic intersections

While all kinds of everyday people in diverse neighbourhoods engage, consciously or unconsciously, in these transversal practices, there are certain types of people that emerged over and over again in my various research sites who seem to excel at this and take on the task of intersectional work with great determination. I call them 'transversal enablers'. Transversal enablers are individuals in towns and neighbourhoods who go out of their way to create connections between culturally different residents in their local area, workplace or other kinds of micro-publics (Amin 2002: 959). They produce and facilitate opportunities for transversal hospitality and exchange, thread diverse people into a social network by way of what I term 'intersectional gossip', knowledge exchange, and inter-ethnic information networks. They also create opportunities for others to engage in various forms of transversal exchange. They tend to be similarly outgoing, outward-oriented, cheerful personalities. Thinking across my research field-sites, these transversal enablers were mostly women, but occasionally I did encounter such men. Their role went beyond simply creating paths for new networks to establish. It extended to translational and accommodative work aimed at knitting people together across significant cultural or religious differences.

Naser was one such character in research I carried out (with my collaborator Selvaraj Velayutham) on everyday multiculturalism in blue-collar workplaces in Singapore and Australia (Wise 2016). Naser was a bus driver based at a depot in Sydney. The bus depot is a unionized workplace and has a large area for socializing, including a canteen area with tables and chairs, a billiards room and recreation room where drivers and depot workers congregate during their breaks and after shifts. They also have BBQ facilities in the yard which are used for regular social events. The workers at the depot elect a 'social coordinator' and, at the time of our research, this role was held by Naser, a Coptic Egyptian bus driver in his 50s. One of his roles was to coordinate the calendar of regular social BBQs – including sourcing and cooking the food, negotiating dates and menus. He has become extremely adept at adapting and accommodating the multiple religious and cultural food preferences of his multi-ethnic colleagues, and he took this responsibility very seriously indeed.

> Because we're doing barbeques or food activities. . . . I have to deal with vegetarians. Most of them are Indian background. Buddhist as well, they do that. I have to deal with halal food for Muslims. I have to deal with the food for Aussies, which is bacon and egg, what they want . . . I have to deal with the Middle Eastern people. They love their meat. Lamb, and stuff like that. I ask them, first, which day you are fasting? Muslims are fasting on Ramadan, I will not do a barbeque when they're fasting, so I have to shove it in a week before, or a week after, or stuff like that. Same with the Orthodox Christians, the Catholic. The Indians, they have one or two days in the week they cannot eat chicken, so we always have to go to the Friday. Some of them, they're eating vegies only [vegetarian], so I have to go for the special type of burgers, plus I have to put a salad and stuff like that. We have a lot of respect – I mean, you have deal with, around it. Some people, they love the spicy food, so I am providing something spicy. Sausages or stuff like that. So it's different. Then we have Italian people here. They love their sausages.

Naser has developed a fine-tuned awareness of the different ethno-religious requirements and food preferences of his colleagues. Rather than resenting this, he has become extremely creative in making the multiple accommodations required, and in so doing creates many intersections and inter-meshings across these cultural differences. Such acts of micro-recognition create a set of affective relations, or a structure of feelings that scaffold the possibility of an outward-looking, non-bounded form of multi-ethnic community to emerge among these workers (see also Wise 2016). I describe this as 'transversal' as it produces momentary shifts across difference without leaving identities behind, nor assimilating into a pre-existing cultural form.

Another transversal enabler I encountered in earlier research (Wise 2009) was a Maori woman in an Australian country town, married to a second-generation Italian citrus farmer. The town was in a large citrus-growing region and was home to a large community of long-settled Sikhs and Italians, and more recent arrivals from various Pacific Island backgrounds, Taiwan, East Timor and refugees from Iraq, Afghanistan, and South Sudan. This diverse group of residents – a classic 'super-diverse' community from established resident citizens to those on various forms of temporary visa – were drawn to the area to work in the town's chicken-processing factory and as fruit pickers on farms around the region. The Maori woman was one of those people who thrive on making social connections between new people to the town. She hosted a BBQ each Friday for her diverse farm workers, and they would all bring something to share. She also made it her business to spot and gather up new arrivals to the town. She would find out as much as she could about their cuisine and cooking preferences, and what kinds of ingredients their cooking required, and would help new arrivals source these ingredients locally. She would invite random new arrivals home for lunch, such as a group of Sudanese men she spotted in the local pub – in town for the picking season just before Christmas – whom she had decided looked a bit lost and lonely. They were enthusiastically co-opted into her Christmas lunch gathering. She made invitations on a 'bring a plate' basis as a means of establishing a 'sharing' relation and as a way to learn about the newcomers' cuisine, and all visitors to her home were asked to sing a song from their 'culture' – which she described as a Maori tradition.

These stories are very much abridged snapshots. Generally speaking, transversal enablers like Naser and the Maori farmer's wife serve a number of important functions which create threads of connection across cultural difference – for themselves, and for their local communities. They do so by engaging in and facilitating transversal practices involving gift exchange; intercultural knowledge exchange; creating opportunities for the production of cross-cultural embodied commensality; and the production of spaces of intercultural care and trust; as well as establishing loose affiliations of sociability through 'gossip relations'.

Transversal places and diasporic intersections

Certain kinds of places also seem to enhance opportunities for transversal intersections to occur. 'Transversal places' are places whose social, material, symbolic and spatial characteristics offer optimal conditions for transversal intersections to occur.

At the top end of Haldon Street in Sydney's Lakemba sits Warung Ita, an Indonesian takeaway restaurant run by a Sumatran family, all devout Muslims. Lakemba is Sydney's 'Muslim heart', with Muslims representing slightly over 50 per cent of the population. It is home to the city's largest mosque, and Muslims from across the world reside there. While the largest group are Lebanese Muslims, the suburb has evolved over the last decade, settling many new communities from Indonesia, Malaysia, Bangladesh, Pakistan, India, Somalia, the Philippines, Burma, Tonga, Sri Lanka, China, Vietnam, Korea, and many other homelands. This is a super-diverse (Vertovec 2007) zone. Warung Ita's big draw-card is the traditional Sumatran *nasi padang* on offer and the ever-ebullient matriarch Rosmanita who greets all customers with a generous welcome of '*apa kaba*! How are you my darling?!'. Regulars call her 'aunty' and she refers to customers as 'brother' and 'sister'. This could be an eatery in any part of Southeast Asia, with its modest furniture, tiled floors, coloured melamine plates, tissue boxes and a little tray with *kecap manis* (sweet soy) and *sambal* on each table. Rosmanita is a 'type' familiar to anyone with roots (or routes) in Singapore, Malaysia or Indonesia. Lunchtimes draw a diverse clientele, but especially familiar are two groups: those who like spicy food, and those who have called Singapore, Malaysia or Indonesia home – including Chinese and Indian diasporas of those post-colonies. Herein lies a story of diasporic intersections and how they come into being, how these transversal crossings travel and produce new connections in new places.

An Indonesian eatery like this is straightforwardly 'homely' for ethnic Indonesians and Malays from Malaysia and Singapore where versions of *nasi padang* are common and the food is similar. However, Indonesia, Malaysia and Singapore remain home to large Indian and Chinese diasporic populations first established during colonial times, and Warung Ita evokes familiar feelings of home for them too, as these diasporas travel. Chinese and Indians from Malaysia and Singapore are familiar with the 'Malay auntie' that Rosmanita embodies, and have grown up eating *nasi padang* in hawker centres and small eateries like this back home. Diasporic Indians (largely Tamil) from Southeast Asia have the added layer of 'curry affinity' in the spicy cuisine. In Singapore, Indian Muslims will choose Malay food over Chinese, assured by taste and the fact that it is *halal*. Lakemba 'locals' are drawn there too. Across the lane are two South Asian spice stores, run by Pakistanis and Bangladeshis, respectively. Their customers stop into Warung Ita for lunch, enjoying the spicy food – we might call this a 'curry and rice' affinity. And of course, the restaurant is *halal*, so beyond those for whom the food is familiar from previous diasporic links, it offers a local lunch stop for Muslims, but also all those who live in the area: Somalis, Rohingyas from Burma, Pacific Islanders. Warung Ita is a 'contact zone' that threads together 'locals' here and now, with the homely desires and nostalgia of Indonesian 'natives' and their diasporic compatriots.

Warung Ita is what I've described as a 'fragrant' space (Wise 2011) – that is to say, a space of encounter that nonetheless remains firmly rooted in and carrying the fragrance of its cultural roots. Other places I describe as 'low-scent' and 'neutrally scented' and offer a different kind of, perhaps more open, meeting ground for people of different backgrounds. These transversal places are the kinds of spaces that ease intercultural encounters and relationships among those perhaps less comfortable with difference. Their success seems to lie in their non-place character, their in-betweenness or their lack of identification with one group or another. They are, in their own ways, borderlands. Some parks, playgrounds and other public spaces fit this bill, so do the quotidian 'borderlands' of front gardens and residential footpaths. They are often the sorts of public spaces (or parochial places – cf. Wessendorf 2014) that people frequent on a routine basis and develop a level of familiarity with others who use the space. One such space that I think offers 'transversal' qualities for encounter is are the so-called 'void decks' of Singapore's public housing estates. Some 80 per cent of Singaporeans live in government-built high-rise housing known as 'HDB estates'. These high-rise flats usually have a 'non-floor' at the ground level – an undercover open area under the apartments that doubles as a lift foyer and general community gathering space. Typically, this is where banks of letterboxes are located, alongside community notice boards. Void decks offer a cool respite from the sun, and a protected area for play during the rain. Many are furnished with tables and chairs – some have *Majhong* tables built in, and people hold weddings and funerals there – showcasing rituals from Muslim, Hindu, Christian, Buddhist and Taoist traditions. As a multi-racial society, the traditions and rituals of the different religions are on display and openly encountered and experienced by residents of other backgrounds. Some void decks have TVs and chairs lined up where the elderly gather to watch and socialize. It is a parochial space where people of quite different cultural and religious backgrounds encounter one another on neutral ground. Void decks are shared territory – where there is consensus and convention that the space is owned by all and none. Like anywhere, there are sometimes negotiations and struggles over aspects of such sharing – particularly around noise and smell – but by and large, such tensions are managed.

Conclusion

What is diasporic about transversal intersections? In Clifford's view, 'routes' rather than 'roots' foregrounds a diacritical approach to thinking culture (Clifford 1997: 250). Over a decade ago, he argued that conceptualizing culture through travel, rather than residence, brings more sharply into view questions of displacement, interference and interaction (1997: 25). Thus, while the myth of diasporic containment remains – contextually – important to many diasporas, they nonetheless are always shaped by the entanglement and blending of 'homeland roots' with 'routes' of travel (1997: 251). That is to say, shaped both within and without, blending here and there. In some instances, entanglements with the here and now may produce closed and defensive 'roots'-focused identity orientations. In other cases, porosity and permeability lead to identities 'turned outwards' – though again, this can be contextual, momentary and sometimes strategic. Travel can be read as 'big T' travel across centuries and continents, the trans-Atlantic slave trade and colonial ties, or small 't' intermingling in neighbourhoods, workplaces, shops and schools. The transversal people, places and practices described in this chapter are examples of the lived, everyday, mundane 'travelling encounters' that may lead to permeable openings and crossings; that may, in turn, leave traces of encounter among diasporic peoples.

Note

1 Adapted from the earlier work of Felix Guattari, the concept of transversality was eventually developed by Italian feminists in the 1970s and 1980s, and more fully by Yuval-Davis, and then was taken up by academic and peace activist Cynthia Cockburn (1998), who used it in her research with women's groups in conflict zones.

References

Amin, A. (2002) 'Ethnicity and the multicultural city: living with diversity', *Environment and Planning A*, 34, 959–80. doi: 10.1068/a3537
Clifford, J. (1997) *Routes: travel and translation in the late twentieth century*, Cambridge, MA: Harvard University Press.
Cockburn, C. (1998) *The space between us: negotiating gender and national identities in conflict*, London: Zed Books.
Komter, A. E. (2004) *Social solidarity and the gift*, Cambridge: Cambridge University Press.
Pratt, M. L. (1992) *Imperial eyes: travel writing and transculturation*, London: Routledge.
Simmel, G. (1950) *The sociology of Georg Simmel*, K. H. Wolff (ed.), New York: Simon and Schuster.
Velayutham, S. and A. Wise (eds) (2009) *Everyday multiculturalism*, Basingstoke; Palgrave Macmillan.
Vertovec, S. (2007) 'Super-diversity and its implications', *Ethnic and Racial Studies*, 30 (6), 1024–56, doi: 10.1080/01419870701599465.
Werbner, P. (1999) 'Global pathways: working class cosmopolitans and the creation of transnational ethnic worlds', *Social Anthropology*, 7 (1), 17–37, doi: 10.1111/j.1469-8676.1999.tb00176.x.
Wessendorf, S. (2014) *Commonplace diversity: social relations in a super-diverse context*, London: Palgrave Macmillan.
Wise, A. (2005) 'Hope and belonging in a multicultural suburb', *Journal of Intercultural Studies*, 26 (1/2), 171–86, doi: 10.1080/07256860500074383.
Wise, A. (2009) 'Everyday multiculturalism: transversal crossings and working class cosmopolitans', in S. Velayutham and A. Wise (eds) *Everyday multiculturalism*, Palgrave Macmillan, 21–45.
Wise, A. (2011) 'Moving food: gustatory commensality and disjuncture in everyday multiculturalism', *New Formations*, 74 (1), 82–107, doi: 10.3898/NEWF.74.05.2011.
Wise, A. (2016) 'Becoming cosmopolitan: encountering difference in a city of mobile labour', *Journal of Ethnic and Migration Studies*, 42 (14), 2289–308, doi: 10.1080/1369183X.2016.1205807.
Wise, A. and S. Velayutham (2014) 'Conviviality in everyday multiculturalism: some brief comparisons between Singapore and Sydney', *European Journal of Cultural Studies*, 17 (4), 406–30, doi: 10.1177/1367549413510419.
Yuval-Davis, N. (1997) 'Ethnicity, gender relations and multiculturalism', in P. Werbner and T. Modood (eds) *Debating cultural hybridity: multi-cultural identities and the politics of anti-racism*, London: Zed Books, 192–209.
Yuval-Davis, N. (1999) 'What is "transversal politics"?' *Soundings*, 12, 88–93, available at: www.lwbooks.co.uk/soundings/12/what-is-transversal-politics.
Yuval-Davis, N. (2004) 'Human rights and feminist transversal politics', lecture presented at the University of Bristol Series on Politics of Belonging.

18
Intersectionalizing diaspora studies

Marie Godin

Until recently, gender was treated as an appendix in the field of diaspora studies. As pointed out by Morawska (2011: 1031):

> Despite a strong appeal for 'gendering the diasporas' more than a decade ago and repeated at the beginning of the new century [. . .] with the exception of occasional references to the patriarchal dominance of men common in diasporic communities, studies of 'diaspora' diasporas have remained largely genderless.

This chapter addresses how diaspora scholarship has evolved from a 'male-stream' to a gendering lens before discussing how an intersectional approach has become more and more incorporated into the field. Diaspora groups are composed of 'different parts of the same diaspora [which] can and do have different interests, defined among other things by class, gender, generation, occupation and religion' (Smith 2007: 5). It will be argued that a 'transnational intersectional approach' reflects the complex system of power relations in which women and men in the diaspora are socially embedded in different contexts. Social actors – at the individual and collective levels – have different capacities to be reflexive about these intersections of multiple positionalities they experience within, across and beyond the diaspora. The last section addresses how the appropriation of an intersectional lens contributes to extending the conceptual, epistemological and methodological boundaries of diaspora studies.

From genderless to gendering the field of diaspora studies

With the extreme proliferating uses of the term 'diaspora' at the beginning of the 1990s, many scholars started to delineate the field more accurately in tracing conceptual boundaries. At the outset, the attention was mainly to identify social heterogeneities between diasporas. Safran (1991), for instance, establishes a series of criteria that need to be fulfilled in order for a group of people to be considered as a 'true diaspora'. His conception was mainly influenced by the underlying paradigmatic case of the Jewish diaspora emphasizing the notion of forced or otherwise traumatic dispersion as central to the diasporic experience. As a response to this too-narrowed approach, Cohen (1997, 2008) has provided a new typology identifying different 'ideal-types' of diaspora (i.e., victim, labour, trade, imperial and cultural) which, among other features, includes a broader definition with regard to forced *versus* voluntary migration. However, these types of categorization have often been described as too rigid, too essentialist, as well as too homogenizing; viewing diasporas as 'emerging simply out of boundary-crossing processes such as migration, exile and dispersal' (Adamson 2012: 27). In fact, diaspora scholars have been more inclined to look at diasporas to assess whether or not they fit into pre-designed descriptions rather than looking at their internal complexity. But diasporas are chaordic structures characterized by 'multiple discourses, internal dissent, and competition for members between numerous sectarian, gendered or political groups, all identifying themselves with the same diaspora' (Werbner 2002: 123). So, for a very long time, social heterogeneities within diasporas formation were overlooked and theoretical accounts were mainly told in genderless ways, privileging 'the mobility of masculine subjects as the primary agents of diasporic formation, and perpetuating a more general masculinism in the conceptualization of diasporic community' (Campt and Thomas 2008: 2).

Echoing some of the developments in the field of migration studies in the mid-1980s influenced by feminist theory, diaspora scholars also started to engender their analysis. Referring to conflict-induced diasporas, Al-Ali (2007: 51) states how it is important 'to understand the gendering of refugees and diasporas not merely in terms of women, but to think about it also in terms of relations of power and privilege informed by situations of maleness and femaleness'. It is often argued in the literature that the diasporic experience can either provide women with more agencies, departing from a nationalistic and patriarchal narrative to a transnational and liberating experience, or rather increase their social marginalization, not only due to gender dynamics but also due to other factors associated with race and ethnicity (Rao Mehta 2015: 5).

The transition from a genderless to a gendered approach has sometimes overlooked the reshaping of gender relations, roles and identities for both men and women. While still scarce, more studies are looking specifically at the role of masculinity prior to migration, during and after migration. Pasura's (2008) work considers the reshaping of gender identities for both men and women. Men's hegemonic masculinities are often threatened through the migration/diasporic process, with pre-migration gendered and social hierarchies being challenged and contested in the host land. The public/private gender divide is reconfigured in the diaspora, putting men and women in a situation to renegotiate gender roles and relations. Being in the diaspora is here defined as a site of cultural conflicts (Tinarwo and Pasura 2014), where different strategies can develop to resist or accommodate to social transformations. Identities are here perceived as fluid, always in the process of 'becoming' (Hall 1992), with new hybrid forms of masculinities as well as femininities emerging as a result of the diasporic experience.

To capture the inherent changeability of diasporas, Al-Ali (2007: 42) suggests looking at diasporas as an ongoing process rather than a state of being. Similarly, Morawska (2011) argues that representations of their homeland by diasporans are context-dependent, changing over time and across space as well as between genders. She argues that they should be treated as enduring perspectives or standpoints rather than 'entities' (Morawska 2011: 1030). This change of paradigm in conceptualizing diasporas can be related to a feminist standpoint theory which, as defined by Yuval-Davis (2011), claims to account for the social positioning of the social agent and challenge 'the god-trick of seeing everything from nowhere' (Haraway 1991: 189) as a cover for and legitimizing of a hegemonic masculinist 'positivistic' positioning (Haraway 1991: 4). Although a gendered approach has contributed to broader assessment beyond the scope of 'diasporic hegemonies' (Campt and Thomas 2008), hegemonic feminism has itself been challenged by racialized feminists. To counter a gendering approach that has often led to over-generalizations about women and gender relations, a new approach was needed: one that considers gender not as the only analytical lens, but one that captures the multiplicity of social axes of power in the ways they shape the reconfigurations of diasporic identities and relations.

From gendering to intersectionalizing diaspora studies

The intersectionality framework is one that is often considered as the most important theoretical contribution in women and gender studies (McCall 2005: 1771). It is crucial to recall that the framework was first developed by black feminists in the USA reacting to the dominance of white middle-class women in the women's movement, as well as against the dominance of black men in the anti-racist movement (Crenshaw 1991; Hill Collins 1990; hooks 1988). Both movements had failed in their discourses to consider intersectional identities such as 'women of colour' (Crenshaw 1991: 1243). The concept of intersectionality was then first developed to capture the specific socio-economic situation of black women caught in between multiple structures of power and domination, also described as 'interlocking systems of oppression' (Hill Collins 1990) with 'race', class and gender, which needed to be understood in terms of their mutual interactions (Combahee River Collective 1981). This framework has subsequently travelled not only across time and space but also across disciplines (Lutz 2014). Whereas the development of feminist and gender studies has expanded the ways in which diaspora scholars have been considering social heterogeneities within a so-called 'diaspora', at the same time, it can also be argued that the field of migration and diaspora studies has immensely contributed to gender and feminist studies by offering a lens to capture not only the multiplicity of such processes, but also their simultaneity across borders.

In order to grasp the complex interlocking between dominant axes of power when moving across borders and different locales, Anthias (2008) developed the stimulating concept of 'translocational positionality'. This approach defines through an intersectional frame, tending to move away from the idea of given 'groups' or 'categories' of gender, ethnicity and class, which then intersect, but paying much attention to social locations and processes (Anthias 2008: 5). In that respect, diaspora studies needs to be framed

> within a contextual, dynamic and processual analysis that recognizes the interconnectedness of different identities and hierarchical structures relating to gender, ethnicity, 'race', class and other social divisions [based *inter alia* on religion, sex, marital status, generation, nationality] at local, national, transnational and global levels.
>
> *(Anthias 2012: 102)*

It captures how transnationality intersects with simultaneous and interacting systems of oppression in different locales.

An 'intersectional lens' sees both masculinities and femininities as always in flux as well as positioned in relation to changing configurations of power linked to ethnicity, class, religion, political affiliation and, crucially, sexual orientation (Al-Ali 2017: xi). With regard to the latter, gender normativity and contemporary nationalist ideologies have often been reproduced in diaspora studies and are now being reconsidered within a queer diasporic framework (Gopinath 2005). Diasporic experiences are racially and socially gendered in relation to constructions of nationhood, which usually involved specific notions of 'manhood' and 'womanhood' (Anthias and Yuval-Davis 1993). However, being in the diaspora can be a space for sexual independence, a space where sexual identities shaped by patriarchal socio-cultural and religious structures and nationalist discourses can be challenged (Batisai 2016). Reflecting on the case of Zimbabwean women, the author shows how conflicting identities can also find a way to be reconciled with each other.

In this line of thought, the diaspora emerges as a conducive transnational platform, a space for agency, for renegotiating restrictive frameworks that police/d gender and sexuality in immigrant's homeland (Batisai 2016: 177). Similarly, Chikwendu (2013) advocates a renewed dedication to the political origins of intersectional theory. Whereas social actors can be forced to switch from one subject positioning to another as a strategy for daily survival, an experience defined by Crenshaw (1991: 1252) as 'intersectional dis-empowerment', this process can also become 'a tool for empowerment – a tool for redefining, transgressing, and critiquing hegemonic constructions of identity categories' (Chikwendu 2013: 34). To describe this process, the author uses the term *circular consciousness*, which refers to a particular lived understanding of intersectionality and which encompasses the fact that identities can be hierarchized while being experienced at the same time and how it allows for negotiations between racial, national and sexual positioning. In that respect, diasporic subjectivities are the result of a performative nexus of race, gender and sexuality taking place in a transnational social field (Campt and Thomas 2008: 7).

Intersectionality as an approach has often been criticized for promoting a form of 'exclusionary identity politics' (Hill Collins 1990). However, scholars of intersectionality have argued that this stance overlooks the fact that identity continues to be 'a site of resistance for members of different subordinated groups' (Crenshaw 1991: 1297). In any case, it is important not to restrict intersectionality to identity in ways that are politically divisive and 'essentializing' (Bassel 2016: 1441) as well as to recognize that the most critical resistance strategy for disempowered groups is to occupy and defend a 'politics of location' (Crenshaw 1991). The next section addresses the formation of diasporic identities as a means of asserting specific political identities in adopting both a gendered and intersectional analysis.

Gendering and intersectionalizing diaspora politics

Diaspora studies used to be framed – and to a certain extent continues to be framed – on the basis of a certain dominant conception of politics, of what is formal versus informal, of what is public versus private, and with a clear distinction between homeland *versus* host-land politics, on the other hand. In addition, mainstream diaspora politics scholarship often suggests that diaspora men are more involved in public, formal and institutionalized domestic and diasporic networks, whereas women are more involved in private and informal networks either in the host country or in the home country. In sum, men are more visible in what can be called the transnational [diasporic] public sphere, whereas women are present in the transnational [diasporic] private sphere (Mügge 2013). Black feminist and postcolonial feminist scholars have opened the path to a broader definition of what 'politics' means. Bringing in transnational as well as intersectional feminist thoughts in the field of diaspora studies has helped blur the lines, to generally rethink these often taken-for-granted dichotomies. This has allowed researchers to grasp how gender identity and its intersection with race, class and other forms of social divisions have shaped women's (as well as men's) diasporic engagement with politics.

Recently, a growing number of scholars have put gender on the map in the field of intersectional diaspora politics, shedding some light on how women and men are engaging differently in both their country of residence and homeland. Osirim's (2008) research on 'new African women migrants' in the United States shows how women have a greater commitment to building civil society organizations in their country of residence while at the same time engaging transnationally to support their household and extended family. By contrast, their male counterparts have been more interested in supporting community organizations in their homeland. The author argues that women encounter stratification based on intersectionality and, as a result, they have been establishing new ties beyond their respective national/ethnic/diasporic communities, particularly in historically African-American communities, thus illustrating the emergence of a new form of Pan-Africanism. Similarly, Bailey's (2012) study of migrant African women in Nottingham expands the notion of politics to include 'community politics' with solidarity. The organization created by women is defined as a 'home place of belonging' (inspired by the concept of 'home place' as a space of resistance; hooks 1990), as a personal political space to which women give voice. Ifekwunigwe (2016: 337) describes this safe space as an imagined gendered community, delineating the contours of a 'global African diaspora' that 'engenders a sense of belonging and inclusion for recent and settled marginalized migrant women (and men) in Europe and which creates the conditions for resilience and resistance strategies.

Although still scarce, a new range of studies is looking at how different conceptions of peace, conflict resolution and development may emerge from diaspora members. Women (as well as men) in the diaspora are far from forming homogeneous communities. Some studies have tried to understand why some women prefer to mobilize in separate groupings (Al-Ali 2007), whereas other studies have shown that ways of organizing can also be different between first and second generations, who do not necessarily share the same experiences in terms of gender constraints or will to organize on the basis of their gender identities (Garbin and Godin 2013). Other divisions may also occur between those living in the diaspora and those back home. Looking at the case of Somali women who decide to return, Horst (2017) shows that their diasporic identity is a marker of social division that deprives them of their right to participate in public debates back home. Al-Ali (2007) states that existing and changing gender relations during the period of war within the country of origin, as well as in the context of migration and living in the diaspora, are among the major factors to consider to understand differences in the ways women and men engage towards their country of origin. However, gender is not necessarily the most significant factor, and other factors such as class, political affiliation, place of origin, experience of conflict, country of settlement and, finally, sexuality and gender expression may also play important roles (Al-Ali 2007: 58).

Another central discussion in the field is whether (long-distance) nationalism and feminism are compatible with one another or mutually exclusive. This has been a subject of debate among feminist and diaspora scholars. In their study of women's activism in Iraqi Kurdistan, Al-Ali and Pratt have shown that nationalism is not always an obstacle to women's rights, and that an articulation between the two is often more complex, especially in colonial and post/neo-colonial contexts (Al-Ali and Pratt 2011: 338). Godin's (2017) study on Congolese women activists in the diaspora demonstrates how 'motherhood', as a political resource for empowerment and resistance (hooks 1990), is being mobilized, thereby forging a specific form of diasporic political identity. Here, Congolese women in the diaspora position their experiences with politics from the perspectives of political motherhood in the personal sense, as well as of motherhood of the nation, establishing a political comparison between the rape of women in the Democratic Republic of Congo and the rape of the nation and its natural resources. At the same time, women advocate for grassroots diasporic forms of collective action, connecting the politics from below to the politics from above, and in doing so, redefine the political space of peace-making. By contrast, Mügge's (2013) study of women active in Kurdish and Turkish transnational migrant politics over a period of roughly 20 years in the Netherlands, demonstrates that in both transnational programmes, the 'woman question' has been subordinated to a broader political programme, that is, Marxism and Kurdish nationalism. In both cases, gender hierarchies from the homeland are likely to be reproduced rather than challenged, leading the author to conclude that diaspora women, in this case, do not really 'go public' in transnational politics (Mügge 2013: 77).

In fact, it is crucial to analyse in each empirical case what Koinova (2017a) defines as 'diaspora positionality', which captures the power diaspora political agents – both men and women – perceive themselves or are perceived to hold and which are derived from their embeddedness in a system of ties to host lands, homelands, and other global locations where diasporic brethren live (Koinova 2017a: 8). In general, local micro-politics of the diasporic public sphere come to be intertwined with transnational diasporic political activism, and reciprocally (see Werbner 2002). More studies need to reflect on the multivocality of diasporic engagement, which results from simultaneous and multiple intersecting power relations in different contexts. Nevertheless, marginalized voices within the diaspora have started to challenge hegemonic understandings of diaspora politics which tend to present 'the diaspora' as a monolithic body (Baser 2015). Innovative and often less visible 'diasporic critical spaces' in which postcolonial subjects can interrogate the gaze of the other (a space where returning the gaze is possible), have been emerging and steadily occupying a more prominent place in the field of diaspora studies.

Beyond the diasporic lens: crossing boundaries

Some time ago, Anthias pointed out 'that the "diaspora" turns the analytical gaze away from the dimensions of trans-ethnic relations informed by power hierarchies and by the cross-cutting relations of gender and class' (Anthias 1998: 577). In that regard, the ethnic marker or the diasporic marker has often been considered as the most important identity marker – and particularly in the field of diaspora politics – as if it were the main social location defining the individual as well as collective agencies. This 'methodological nationalist bias' has led to a consideration of diaspora as a homogenized diasporic group which gives more space to those who are the loudest, those who have more social power. However, political, cultural, social and economic connections among members of the diaspora often extend beyond the rigid triadic framework between a diaspora group, a homeland and a country of residence. Moreover, 'diaspora communities' interact with their broader environment at different levels: at the local, national, transnational and at the global level. Not only does it seem that there is a need to consider other types of ties and social networks within which diaspora members are embedded, but also those connections are not taking place only in the destination country or in the country of origin but in a globalized and interconnected world. In fact, women and men in the diaspora are embedded in multiple social fields that intersect with one another. This multi-embeddedness in a plurality of social fields can provide political diasporic agents with more or fewer political opportunities and structures to raise their voices. However, diasporic transnational networks are still mainly considered as bounded by a particular national, ethnic or religious identity marker and is implicitly not based on a liberal pluralist identity composed of what is called the 'global civil society' (Adamson 2012: 32). In that perspective, even if they promote liberal values, particular tendencies and stronger connections to other kin and original homelands are still considered as prominent. This way of looking at diasporas still undermines the fact that people have multiple identities as well as multiple senses of belonging that can lead to multiple ways of engaging at the local, national, transnational and global levels. Ethnicity, nationality or religion as identity markers cannot always be decisive, in the sense that there is no fixed hierarchization of these multiple social identities. In adopting a transnational and intersectional approach, different identity markers are fully considered, allowing for 'novel articulations and practices of alternative citizenship in the creation of permeable interethnic networks, and civic engagement within and beyond the diaspora, with members of the wider society' (Fumanti and Werbner 2010: 5).

An intersectional epistemological stance can effectively challenge the ethnic/racial and particularistic bias in which diaspora scholars often constrain diasporic agents, by considering them as members and sometimes political entrepreneurs of broader civic engagement movement (Koinova 2017b). Diaspora actors as political agents can engage into diaspora politics and at the same time, or at different points in time, they can engage in 'transversal politics' (Yuval-Davis 2011) which enable people to grasp or understand 'the other', their standpoints, identities, needs, and where they are coming from. In that regard, the intersectional as well as transnational feminist lens applied in the field of diaspora studies offers the possibility to understand in a more nuanced way complex social dynamics within, beyond and across diasporas.

Conclusion

This chapter has explored how a transnational and intersectional lens has been over the years methodologically, epistemologically and theoretically incorporated in the field of diaspora studies. Still being marginalized in mainstream diaspora studies, a 'transnational intersectional approach' considers simultaneously the interplay between local, national, global and transnational layers (multi-layered), different sites (multi-sidedness) and different social locations based on multiple intersecting power relations (multi-embeddedness). Moving from a genderless to a gendering and then to an intersectionalizing lens, it has opened the way for researchers to grasp multiple and changing complex configurations of power, inequalities and injustices over time and space in which gender is constituted and constitutive of other power relations and hierarchies at specific historical moments and in particular empirical contexts (Al-Ali 2017).

Although there are criticisms about the current overuse of the concept of intersectionality, in particular the risks of its depoliticization as an approach (Erel et al. 2010) where any markers of identity tend to be equal to any other markers. This analysis of differences tends to ignore that 'it is an outcome of power relations through which hierarchies are marked between different groups and actors in the field' (Erel et al. 2010: 57). Still there are ways to stay faithful to the original approach, in, for instance, as suggested by Lutz (2014), 'doing intersectionality'. 'Doing intersectionality' means to adopt a lens to study intersecting oppression and inequalities as well as to understand how individuals and groups 'mobilize or deconstruct disempowering discourses, even undermine and transform oppressive practices' (Lutz 2014: 12).

In fact, an intersectional lens is more than ever needed to capture multiple identities, senses of belongings as well as of politics of belonging – that can be both simultaneously or at different points in time diasporic, non-diasporic and/or mixed – at a time of constant reconfigurations of power relations based on class, gender, race, ethnicity, religion, age, sexualities, as well as other social divisions. Social actors are embedded in these complex transnational and intersectional power structures, but at the same time develop some ways through different forms of intersectional capital (in a Bourdieusian sense), to challenge 'the social order of things'. As diasporic political agents being reflexive with regard to their multi-sited embeddedness, women and men are 'doing intersectionality' as a form of critical praxis (Hill Collins 2015). This allows them to magnify their intersectional voices and navigate different 'scales of contention' (at the local, national, transnational and global level) – in order to challenge, re-articulate and transform some of the dominant narratives. The issue nowadays is not only if 'the subaltern can speak' (Spivak 1988), but also who is listening to them and how (Jean-Charles 2014: 213).

Brah (2014) recently re-affirmed that 'diasporas are inherently intersectional, and that the study of diaspora and intersectionality are intrinsically connected'. Yet, diaspora scholars still need to deal with 'intersectionality's theoretical, political and methodological murkiness' (Nash 2008: 1) in order to continue taking part in the persistent calls to unpack and dismantle diaspora studies. Last but not least, applying a transnational and intersectional lens in the field of diaspora studies is to take part in a project of feminist critical analysis which gives more room for emancipatory projects of knowledge production, transmission and intersectional social justice claims.

References

Adamson, F. (2012) 'Constructing the diaspora: diaspora identity politics and transnational social movements', in P. Mandaville and T. Lyons (eds) *Politics from afar: transnational diasporas and networks*, New York: Columbia University Press, 25–42.

Al-Ali, N. (2007) 'Gender, diasporas and post-cold war conflict', in H. Smith and P. Stares (eds) *Diasporas in conflict: peacemakers or peace wreckers?*', New York: United Nations University Press, 39–61.

Al-Ali, N. (2017) 'Identity and political mobilisation of diasporas: a gendered perspective', in D. Carment and A. Sadjed (eds) *Diaspora as cultures of cooperation global and local perspectives*, Palgrave Macmillan, vii–xvii.

Al-Ali, N. and N. Pratt (2011) 'Between nationalism and women's rights: the Kurdish women's movement in Iraq', *Middle East Journal of Culture and Communication*, 4 (3), 337–53, doi: 10.1163/187398611X590192.

Anthias, F. (1998) 'Evaluating 'diaspora': beyond ethnicity?', *Sociology*, 32 (3), 557–80, doi: 10.1177/0038038598032003009.

Anthias, F. (2008) 'Thinking through the lens of translocational positionality: an intersectionality frame for understanding identity and belonging', *Translocations: Migration and Social Change. An Inter-Disciplinary Open Access E-Journal*, 4 (1), 5–20, available at: www.researchgate.net/profile/Floya_Anthias/publication/281475768.

Anthias, F. (2012) 'Transnational mobilities, migration research and intersectionality: towards a translocational frame', *Nordic Journal of Migration Research*, 2 (2), 102–10, doi: 10.2478/v10202-011-0032-y.

Anthias, F. and N. Yuval-Davis (1993) *Racialized boundaries: race, nation, gender, colour and class and the anti-racist struggle*, London: Routledge.

Bailey, O. G. (2012) 'Migrant African women: tales of agency and belonging', *Ethnic and Racial Studies*, 35 (5), 850–67, doi: 10.1080/01419870.2011.628037.

Baser, B. (2015) *Diasporas and homeland conflicts: a comparative perspective*, Farnham: Ashgate.

Bassel, L. (2016) 'Intersectionality', in N. Naples (ed.) *Wiley-Blackwell encyclopedia of gender and sexuality studies*, Hoboken, NJ: Wiley-Blackwell.

Batisai, K. (2016) 'Transnational labour migration, intimacy and relationships: how Zimbabwean women navigate the diaspora', *Diaspora Studies*, 9 (2), 165–78, doi: 10.1080/09739572.2016.1185236.

Brah, A. (2014) 'Europe, diaspora, and multi-ethnic futures: looking through intersectional lens', *Synergy*, 10 (2), 164–71.

Campt, T. and D. A. Thomas (2008) 'Gendering diaspora: transnational feminism, diaspora and its hegemonies', *Feminist Review*, 90 (1), 1–8, doi: 10.1057/fr.2008.41.

Chikwendu, M. (2013) 'Circular consciousness in the lived experience of intersectionality: queer/LGBT Nigerian diasporic women in the USA', *Journal of International Women's Studies*, 14 (4), 34–46, available at: http://vc.bridgew.edu/jiws/vol14/iss4/4.

Cohen, R. (1997) *Global diasporas: an introduction*, first edition, London: UCL Press.

Cohen, R. (2008) *Global diasporas: an introduction*, second edition, Abingdon: Routledge.

Combahee River Collective (1981) (first published 1977) 'A black feminist statement', in C. Moraga and G. Anzaldua (eds) *This bridge called my back: writings by radical women of color*, New York: Kitchen Table, Women of Color Press, 210–18.

Crenshaw, K. (1991) 'Mapping the margins: intersectionality, identity politics, and violence against women of color', *Stanford Law Review*, 43 (6), 1241–99, doi: 10.2307/1229039.

Erel, U., J. Haritaworn, G. E. Rodríguez and C. Klesse (2010) 'On the depoliticisation of intersectionality talk: conceptualising multiple oppressions in critical sexuality studies', in Y. Taylor, S. Hines and M. E. Casey (eds) *Theorizing intersectionality and sexuality*, London: Palgrave Macmillan, 56–77.

Fumanti, M. and P. Werbner (2010) 'The moral economy of the African diaspora: citizenship, networking and permeable ethnicity', *African Diaspora*, 3 (1), 2–11, doi: 10.1163/187254610X508454.

Garbin, D. and M. Godin (2013) '"Saving the Congo": transnational social fields and politics of home in the Congolese diaspora', *African and Black Diaspora: An International Journal*, 6 (2), 113–30, doi: 10.1080/17528631.2013.793133.

Godin, M. (2017) 'Breaking the silences, breaking the frames: a gendered diasporic analysis of sexual violence in the DRC', *Journal of Ethnic and Migration Studies*, 1–18, doi: 10.1080/1369183X.2017.1354166.

Gopinath, G. (2005) *Impossible desires: queer diasporas and South Asian public cultures*, Durham, NC: Duke University Press.

Hall, S. (1992) 'New ethnicities', in J. Donald and A. Rattansi (eds) *'Race', culture and difference*, London: Sage, 252–9.

Haraway, D. (1991) *Simians, cyborgs and women: the reinvention of women*, London: Free Association Press.

Hill Collins, P. (1990) *Black feminist thought: knowledge, consciousness and the politics of empowerment*, London: Harper Collins Academic.
Hill Collins, P. (2015) 'Intersectionality's definitional dilemmas', *Annual Review of Sociology* 41, 1–20, doi: 10.1146/annurev-soc-073014-112142.
hooks, b. (1988) *Talking back: thinking feminist, thinking black*, Boston, MA: South End Press.
hooks, b. (1990) *Yearning: race, gender, and cultural politics*, Boston, MA: South End Press.
Horst, C. (2017) 'Implementing the women, peace and security agenda? Somali debates on women's public role and political participation', *Journal of Eastern African Studies*, 11 (3), 389–407, doi: 10.1080/17531055.2017.1348000.
Ifekwunigwe, J. O. (2016) 'The difference that transnational and intersectional black feminisms make: a commentary on Tripp', *Politics, Groups, and Identities*, 4 (2), 335–40, doi: 10.1080/21565503.2015.1127830.
Jean-Charles, R. (2014) *Conflict bodies: the politics of rape representation in the francophone imaginary*, Columbus: The Ohio State University Press.
Koinova, M. (2017a) 'Beyond statist paradigms: socio-spatial positionality and diaspora mobilization in international relations' *International Studies Review*, 19 (4), 597–621.
Koinova, M. (2017b) 'Diaspora mobilisation for conflict and postconflict reconstruction: contextual and comparative dimensions', *Journal of Ethnic and Migration Studies*, doi: 10.1080/1369183X.2017.1354152.
Lutz, H. (2014) 'Intersectionality's (brilliant) career – how to understand the attraction of the concept?', working paper series 'Gender, diversity and migration' no. 1, Goethe University Frankfurt, available at: www.fb03.uni-frankfurt.de/51634119/Lutz_WP.pdf.
McCall, L. (2005) 'The complexity of intersectionality', *Signs: Journal of Women in Culture and Society*, 30 (3), 1771–800, doi: 10.1086/426800.
Morawska, E. (2011) '"Diaspora" diasporas' representations of their homelands: exploring the polymorphs', *Ethnic and Racial Studies*, 34 (6), 1029–48, doi: 10.1080/01419870.2010.533783.
Mügge, L. (2013) 'Women in transnational migrant activism: supporting social justice claims of homeland political organisations', *Studies in Social Justice*, (7) 1, 65–81, doi: 10.26522/ssj.v7i1.1055.
Nash, J. C. (2008) 'Re-thinking intersectionality', *Feminist Review*, 89, (1), 1–15.
Osirim, Mary J. (2008) 'African women in the new diaspora: transnationalism and the (re) creation of home', *African and Asian Studies*, (7), 367–94, doi: 10.1163/156921008X359588.
Pasura, D. (2008) 'Gendering the diaspora: Zimbabwean migrants in Britain', *African Diaspora*, 1 (1), 86–109, doi: 10.1163/187254608X346060.
Rao Mehta, S. (2015) 'Revisiting gendered spaces in the diaspora', in S. Rao Mehta (ed.) *Exploring gender in the literature of the Indian diaspora*, Cambridge: Cambridge University Press, 1–15.
Safran, W. (1991) 'Diasporas in modern societies: myths of homeland and return', *Diaspora*, 1 (1), 83–99, doi: 10.1353/dsp.1991.0004.
Smith, H. (2007) 'Diasporas in international conflict', in H. Smith and P. Stares (eds) *Diasporas in conflict: peace-makers or peace-wreckers?*, New York: United Nations University Press, 3–16.
Spivak, G. C. (1988) 'Can the subaltern speak?', in C. Nelson and L. Grossberg (eds) *Marxism and the interpretation of culture*, Champaign: University of Illinois Press, 271–313.
Tinarwo, M. T. and D. Pasura (2014) 'Negotiating and contesting gendered and sexual identities in the Zimbabwean diaspora', *Journal of Southern African Studies*, 40 (3), 521–38, doi: 10.1080/03057070.2014.909258.
Werbner, P. (2002) 'The place which is diaspora: citizenship, religion and gender in the making of chaordic transnationalism', *Journal of Ethnic and Migration Studies*, 28 (1), 119–33, doi: 10.1080/13691830120103967.
Yuval-Davis, N. (2011) *The politics of belonging: intersectional contestations*, London: Sage.

19
Bridging the mobility–sedentarism and agency–structure dichotomies in diasporic return migration

Nanor Karageozian

The past few decades have witnessed a surge of interest in return migration studies. However, the focus has mainly been on short-term return mobilities and/or on the first-, and more recently, second-generation migrants. Long-term diasporic return migration, the subject of this chapter, has remained relatively understudied and undertheorized. After situating this topic within the broad literature on migration and diasporas, I present some distinctive features of long-term diasporic return migration. I propose a conceptual framework inspired by social theory for the examination of diasporic return motivations and experiences. The chapter is based on my research on the immigration to and long-term settlement in post-Soviet Armenia of Armenians from well-established diasporic communities – mostly from Iran, Syria, Lebanon, Iraq, Canada and the USA (Karageozian 2015b).

Return in conceptual debates

Although the memory of and commitment to the homeland, and the desire to return to it, held a central place in traditional definitions of diaspora, return has often been presented as ideologically romantic, and, practically speaking, highly unlikely if not impossible (Safran 1991).

Starting in the 1990s, postmodern or social constructionist scholars (for example, Brah 1996) criticized what they saw as an idealized overemphasis on homeland and on the diaspora's yearning for return. They shifted their analytical focus from the 'roots' orientation to the diasporic experience itself – the 'routes' – highlighting diasporans' multicultural and hybrid identities. Underlying the overemphasis on mobility and the relative neglect of sedentarism in these studies is an over-valorization of human agency and underestimation of the significance of objective structures and collective practices (Tölölyan 2003).

The celebration of mobility and fluidity was further reinforced by the rise of the transnationalism approach in migration and diaspora studies in the 1990s. Despite the increasing interest in 'homecoming projects' in the transnationalism literature, the focus has mainly been on temporary return visits and circular flows of mostly first-, and only more recently, second-generation migrants. In addition, many studies that do address long-term return migration concentrate on the transnational links that returnees maintain with their former countries after return. Thus, the processes and efforts through which returnees look for anchors, become emplaced, and integrate in their new environment are often downplayed.

In terms of the generational differences of returnees, many studies examine first-generation migrants who were born in the countries to which they returned. But what about the return migration of second- and older-generation migrants, (co-)ethnics, or diasporans born and raised outside of the homeland of their parents or ancestors? Such movements have been recognized in works that address not only the emergence and formation of diasporas, but also their 'demise' and 'unmaking,' in the form of '*regrouping* or *in-gathering* of migrant communities or dispersed ethnic groups' that lead to 'reversing the scattering' or 'de-diasporization' (Sheffer 2003; Van Hear 1998). They have also been examined by works on 'ethnic return migration' (Tsuda 2009) or 'migration of ethnic unmixing' (Brubaker 1998). King and Christou (2010) prefer the term 'counter-diasporic migration' to describe such movements. They subdivide them into the return of second-generation migrants to their parental homelands and that of older generations to ancestral homelands. They focus on the former.

In general, a growing number of studies in recent years have dealt with return beyond the first generation, especially second-generation cases (for example, Conway and Potter 2009). *Diaspora: A Journal of Transnational Studies* has also dedicated a recent issue (dated 2008, but published in 2014) to diasporic return. Despite this increasing interest, less emphasis has been placed on theorizing long-term diasporic return migration.

Distinctive features of diasporic return migration

While the term 'diaspora' has increasingly been used to refer to many first- or older-generation migrant groups and ethnic communities, often in an interchangeable manner, I support the argument that what differentiates diasporic communities from other groups is their 'ongoing or re-awakened attachment and loyalty' to the homeland *even after several generations* (Shuval 2000: 46), and their ability to preserve a collective identity – though not entirely uniform everywhere and for everyone – over the *longue durée* (Bruneau 2010: 37, 47). This is largely achieved through the discourse and operations of institutions and elites that often operate transnationally (Tölölyan 2000). Thus, on the one hand, diasporic return differs from other migrant return migrations that have more immediate personal or family memories of and connections with the homeland, because the ancestral homeland is envisioned by many diasporans as 'something sacred and desirable but also symbolic – mythical even – and thus to an extent unknown' (Olsson and King 2008 © 2014: 257).

Because of the organized nature of many diasporas, this leads to a collective 'nostalgic discourse' around the importance of homeland and return that produces strong sentiments of '(be)longing' among their members. In the case of diasporas marked by forced scattering, such as the Armenian, the catastrophe factor also plays a role in the perpetuation of collective memory and commitment toward the homeland. On the other hand, while retaining their homeland orientation, diasporic communities often become autonomous, and the elements of their collective identity sometimes develop in quite different ways over time from those in the homeland (Tölölyan 2007). In addition, because of the longevity that diasporic existence involves, shifts in homeland borders and major transformations in other homeland circumstances are more likely to have happened. Therefore, diasporic migration, and especially diasporic return, differs somehow from other kinds of return migration, because it can occur several generations after the initial scattering from the homeland (which itself evolves not only in people's visions and memories but also in more tangible ways), and it might involve or lead to integration tensions and identity (re)definitions – often more aggravated, complex and emotionally loaded than the return of other, more recent, migrants.

Another difference that Olsson and King (2008 © 2014: 257) point out between diasporic and other migrant return migrations is that the former is motivated less by 'the economics of rational-choice behavior' than the latter, because of the 'shared community-formation' qualities of diasporas.

Reluctant to make such a generalized distinction, I prefer to say that economic and other practical motivations remain important, as my study on the Armenian case has found (discussed below), but rarely can they sufficiently explain all the intricacies involved in return decisions. Moreover, regardless of other motives, affective factors about the homeland usually play an important role.

Finally, immediate social networks (such as family relationships), especially in the homeland, often play a less significant role in the inspiration and implementation of ancestral return projects than of first- and second-generation return, particularly for 'pioneer' returnees. This is largely due, again, to the longevity of diasporans' presence outside the homeland and the organized nature of many diasporic communities around, often large-scale, institutions.[1]

Theoretical springboards and conceptual framework

Because of these distinctive characteristics of diasporic return migration, an analysis of the 'routes' cannot adequately explain diasporic return migration motivations and experiences. It needs to be counterbalanced with an examination of the 'roots', and the various ways mobility and sedentarism co-exist and relate to each other.

There are some threads in the existing literature that recognize the need to follow a balanced approach that acknowledges the co-existence and dynamic interaction of roots and routes in general, and for our purposes, among diasporans and migrants. Such ideas have been advanced by some diaspora theorists (Tölölyan 2005), advocates of the 'new mobilities paradigm' (Ahmed et al. 2003; Sheller and Urry 2006), scholars of 'new cosmopolitanism' (Glick Schiller et al. 2011; Werbner 2008), and studies highlighting the interrelationship between integration and transnationalism (Erdal and Oeppen 2013; King and Christou 2014).

However, less attention has been given to devising conceptual tools that could explain *how* the rooted and routed trends co-exist and *why* one or the other prevail or overlap within specific migrant or diasporic groups. One notable framework has been that of 'generations' (Berg 2012). I argue that we can study these how and why questions by relying on broader social theory, and more particularly, on approaches that strive to integrate and harmonize agency and structure-centred approaches. This way, we can also tackle the agency–structure debate that is interlaced through the routes–roots dichotomy.[2] The next subsections present the main elements of a conceptual framework that could help bring together the contextualities and subjectivities of anchoring and floating in the study of long-term diasporic return.

Building blocks: dimensions of return

For analytical purposes, I have identified two main dimensions of long-term diasporic return migration[3] – envisioning and planning return, and experiencing and performing return. The first dimension covers the factors that motivate returnees to consider relocating to the homeland and subsequently to take a decision in this regard. The second dimension encompasses post-return experiences, practices and emotions – integration processes, and their impact on identity and belonging, including the possibility and planning of re-emigration.

Conceptual tools: insights from Bourdieu and others

Some of the conceptual tools Pierre Bourdieu developed with the goal of transcending the dichotomies of micro/macro, subjectivism/objectivism, free will/determinism, and agency/structure can provide useful analytical lenses when studying diasporic return. One such key tool is his concept of 'habitus' – ways of thinking and behaving that have been internalized over time within every individual through socialization. Bourdieu (1977: 72, emphasis in original) conceived habitus as 'systems of durable, transposable *dispositions*, structured structures predisposed to function as structuring structures'. Habitus plays a key role in defining how a social agent acts and feels. It provides an individual with a 'practical sense' or 'feel for the game', where 'game' is what Bourdieu (1990: 66) called the 'field'. Fields are the different arenas of social life, such as arts, education, politics, law and economy. These multiple fields constitute the social space.

Social actors struggle to occupy dominant positions in each field (and hence the social space), using various forms of 'capital' in their social relations. Specifically, Bourdieu (1997: 47) identified three main forms of capital, which are sources of power, and stressed that one form can be converted into another. 'Economic capital' includes resources that can be easily changed into money. 'Social capital' stems from an individual's social networks. 'Cultural capital' can assume three forms: 'embodied' ('long-lasting dispositions of the mind and body', such as language and accent); 'objectified' (physical objects such as photographs, paintings and books); and 'institutionalized' (for example, academic qualifications). For Bourdieu, social action results from the complex interrelationship between habitus and capital within a specific field. He also used the concept of 'doxa': 'an orthodoxy, a right, correct, dominant vision', which is 'accepted by all [players of the game] as self-evident' (Bourdieu 1998: 56, 67).

Bourdieu's theory and its application to migration studies are not without problems and gaps. One major criticism of his theory is that it is excessively structuralist or determinist, and thus unable to transcend the very dichotomies that it claims to negate (Yang 2014: 1523). Though sometimes exaggerated and misguided, some of these criticisms – especially the overemphasis on structure, routine action and social reproduction – are valid to a certain extent. For this reason, I favour Emirbayer and Mische's (1998: 970, emphasis in original) multilayered conceptualization of human agency as encompassing the '*interplay of habit, imagination, and judgment*' that '*both reproduces and transforms*' structural environments within which actors are engaged temporally and relationally. Thus, Emirbayer and Mische (1998) take into consideration three dimensions and corresponding temporal orientations of agency that co-exist in diverse degrees: 'iteration' or routine (past), 'projectivity' or purposivity (future), and 'practical evaluation' or judgement (present). Emirbayer and Mische do not equate Bourdieusian habitual action with structure. On the contrary, they elaborate on how agency is an inseparable aspect of routine schemas. But going one step further, they also discuss how such recurring patterns of action can be challenged, re-evaluated and revised through the exercise of greater creative imagination and situationally based judgement.

This brings us to the other criticism surrounding Bourdieu's theory – determinism. The possibility of change is not absent from Bourdieu's works (Hardy 2012). Field structures, capital accumulation and habitus all vary over time. Nevertheless, this recognition of gradual change is not elaborated extensively by Bourdieu. This results from the fact that the habitus feels like a 'fish in water' (Bourdieu and Wacquant 1992: 127) when it is well adjusted to the respective field. But what about some more abrupt changes where this balance is disrupted? Bourdieu has recognized such situations too through his concept of 'hysteresis', which has nevertheless remained less developed, known and used. Hysteresis denotes a 'mismatch' or 'disruption in the relationship between *habitus* and the *field* structures to which they no longer correspond' (Hardy 2012: 129, emphasis in original). The potential of hysteresis to lead to innovation and habitus transformation is particularly powerful when it is conceived not as a change in a given social field, but as a situation when people enter an entirely new field (Yang 2014). Migration and, for our purposes, diasporic return migration can be considered one such situation.

Bourdieu's conceptual tools are quite abundant in migration research, though not extensively in studies of return migration. One problem with the way his theory has been applied to migration research is the piecemeal use of his concepts. But the main problem with its application to migration is a continuation of the excessive determinism and structuralism of which his theory has been accused. Most works have thus focused on the durability of migrants' habitus after relocation, and have highlighted the tensions between the migrants' habitus and the new environment, the challenges and emotions they generate, and the dualities they often create in migrant lifestyles and identities. However, the ways in which and the reasons why a migrant's habitus changes, or does not, after relocation have not been studied extensively. Such an approach not only downplays migrants' agentic potential and the interrelationship between habitus and field, but also fails to recognize the changes that happen to the external environment beyond the initial period after migration and independent of the migrant's presence, as well as the evolution that takes place within migrants due to life-course developments, for example. A few migration-related studies have tried to address some of these issues (Bauder 2005; Erel 2010; Kelly and Lusis 2006; Noble 2013; Nowicka 2015; Sagmo 2015). Some of these works apply Bourdieu's concepts selectively or to a very specific aspect of migrants' lives, while those involved in more holistic analyses either do not tackle return migration or focus only on short-term return visits.

Tying return dimensions to theoretical framing

Taking into consideration the potential of, but also some of the gaps in, Bourdieu's concepts and their application to migration studies, this section presents the ways they can help explain the two above-identified return dimensions. Some key findings from my research on the Armenian case inform this discussion.

Regarding the first dimension of return, what emerged from my analysis of Armenian diasporic return is that an all-encompassing and dominant return 'reason' cannot be singled out. Instead, returnees are motivated by various combinations of subjective and objective circumstances, individual and collective memories, aspirations and resources. Existing studies do acknowledge the diversity of micro and macro factors that affect return decisions.[4] Nevertheless, they often do not go beyond a mere listing of main rationales or narratives (King and Christou 2014). How can we move from such listings derived from empirical analyses to a more conceptual level? Informed by insights from broader social theory, I argue that return decisions usually result from the complex interrelationship between habitual dispositions, imaginative and goal-oriented projects, and practical considerations within a specific time and structural environment, reflecting the inseparability of agency and structure. Dispositions and imaginations exhibit two directions – ethnonational/cultural and cosmopolitan. They are mainly related to the shaping of a more intrinsically developed desire to return. On the other hand, practical considerations, which aim at the preservation of existing 'capital' forms (especially economic and social) or creation of new ones, are usually associated with the timing and process of return. They include life-course transitions, job/investment opportunities, family reunification plans, and escape from undesirable or dangerous situations. Regardless of the combination of dispositions, imaginations and practicalities involved in motivating return in the Armenian case, an emotional attachment to Armenia – though expressed differently and with diverse degrees – existed in almost all cases.

The Bourdieusian concepts of hysteresis and capital can be employed to examine the second dimension of return. As the homeland visions, as well as individual and collective expectations, encounter the more mundane pleasures and disappointments of life in the homeland, returnees often find their long-held dispositions in a hysteresis situation, that is, out of sync with the new socio-cultural environment. This habitus–field mismatch challenges some 'doxic' ideas that were previously taken for granted or considered normal. To achieve a more holistic application of various Bourdieusian concepts, it is insufficient just to identify this mismatch, or discuss the level of returnees' integration into the new society. This should be complemented with an analysis of how returnees try to address hysteresis, that is, *how* their habituses are re-evaluated and often reshaped, or not, leading also to (re)definitions of identity and belonging. This is where Bourdieu's concept of capital becomes particularly useful. Returnees use different existing capital forms, or develop new ones, consciously or unconsciously, to adjust or not their habitus, often selectively in different fields, in their new environment. Moreover, the interrelationship between various capital forms, a key point made by Bourdieu, should be examined. In my study of Armenian diasporic return, I identified the following post-return strategies – habitus alteration, habitus reproduction, temporary distancing from the field, altering the future generation's habitus, and field abandonment. My research has shown that in most cases, returnees – whether consciously or unconsciously – reproduce certain elements of their habitus, while retaining some others. This co-existence of fixity and change, of preservation and transformation, is often a continuation of the way many returnees used to live in the diaspora, where they were integrated to a certain extent in the 'host' society, without having lost their distinctiveness.

Finally, the ways returnees define and reconceptualize their personal identity, membership of a 'group', as well as ideas of home and belonging upon relocation, must be addressed. In my study of the Armenian case, I identified four major patterns in the way returnees (re)assess and (re)define their identities and sense of belonging as they try to deal with post-return hysteresis – 'lopsided anchoring', 'oscillation', 'liminal homelessness' and 'cosmopolitan floating' (Karageozian 2015a, 2015b). Most returnees exhibit ambivalent directions, where grounding in Armenia and Armenianness exist together with openness and empathy towards other places and cultures. As in the case of return motivations and post-return integration experiences, sedentarism and mobility co-exist – though in various degrees – in all these patterns. Subjective and objective factors affect the inclination of returnees toward either one of the patterns at a specific point in time. Over time, shifts in patterns may occur within the same person. Such intrapersonal variations also happen with the above-mentioned habitus-positioning strategies. These changes are related to the evolution of the external environment ('field') and/or personal re-evaluations (resulting from life-cycle developments, for example). These dynamic processes can only be studied if the focus is on long-term return migration.

So far, I have discussed the way the proposed conceptual framework is applied to examine how anchoring and floating co-exist and interrelate in the two dimensions of return. But why do we encounter variations among returnees? My study has highlighted the importance of three main factors – the diasporic context from which returnees come, the generation to which they belong, and the stage of their life cycle. These factors impact on the returnees' socialization and integration patterns, as well as capital accumulation, prior to and after return, which in turn affect their dispositions, imaginations and practical considerations when envisioning and experiencing return. Thus, spatial, sociocultural and temporal factors interact in various ways in the manifestation of centrifugal and/or centripetal trends.

Conclusion

This chapter called for the adoption of a balanced approach that accounts for both sedentarism and mobility, both objective and subjective factors when studying various aspects of long-term diasporic return. It proposed a framework relying on Bourdieu's conceptual tools, with some modifications, to examine the various levels and combinations of anchoring/floating – and the ways they vary over time – in the return motivations, post-return integration experiences, and identity (re)definition processes of diasporan returnees. Although this framework inevitably contains gaps, it is hoped that it will point to the importance of exerting greater efforts to theorize better long-term diasporic return migration.

Notes

1 In the Armenian case, this is particularly accentuated because the diasporan returnees usually cannot trace an immediate genealogy in the territory of the present Republic of Armenia.
2 The need to account for both agency and structure in migration theory has been recognized by some scholars (for example, Bakewell 2010).
3 In real life, return experiences are much more multidimensional and multidirectional than these categories might suggest.
4 As a sub-process of international migration, return migration has been examined from the perspective of various, often contrasting, theories that focus on one or more sets of factors (economic/non-economic and micro/macro) (Cassarino 2004).

References

Ahmed, S. et al. (2003) 'Introduction: uprootings/regroundings: questions of home and migration', in S. Ahmed, C. Castaneda and A.-M. Fortier (eds) *Uprootings/regroundings: questions of home and migration*, Oxford: Berg, 1–19.
Bakewell, O. (2010) 'Some reflections on structure and agency in migration theory', *Journal of Ethnic and Migration Studies*, 36 (10), 1689–708, doi: 10.1080/1369183X.2010.489382.
Bauder, H. (2005) 'Habitus, rules of the labour market and employment strategies of immigrants in Vancouver, Canada', *Social & Cultural Geography*, 6 (1), 81–97, doi: 10.1080/1464936052000335982.
Berg, M. L. (2012) *Diasporic generations: memory, politics, and nation among Cubans in Spain*, New York: Berghahn Books.
Bourdieu, P. (1977) *Outline of a theory of practice*, translated by Richard Nice, Cambridge: Cambridge University Press.
Bourdieu, P. (1990) *The logic of practice*, translated by Richard Nice, Cambridge: Polity Press.
Bourdieu, P. (1997) 'The forms of capital', in A. H. Halsey, H. Lauder, P. Brown and A. Stuart Wells (eds) *Education: culture, economy, and society*, Oxford: Oxford University Press, 46–58.
Bourdieu, P. (1998) *Practical reason: on the theory of action*, Stanford: Stanford University Press.
Bourdieu, P. and L. J. D. Wacquant (1992) *An invitation to reflexive sociology*, Cambridge: Polity Press.
Brah, A. (1996) *Cartographies of diaspora: contesting identities*, Abingdon: Routledge.
Brubaker, R. (1998) 'Migrations of ethnic unmixing in the "New Europe"', *International Migration Review*, 32 (4), 1047–65, doi: 10.2307/2547671.
Bruneau, M. (2010) 'Diasporas, transnational spaces and communities', in R. Bauböck and T. Faist (eds) *Diaspora and transnationalism: concepts, theories and methods*, Amsterdam: Amsterdam University Press, 35–49.
Cassarino, J. (2004) 'Theorising return migration: the conceptual approach to return migrants revisited', *International Journal on Multicultural Societies*, 6 (2), 253–79, https://ssrn.com/abstract=1730637.
Conway, D. and R. B. Potter (eds) (2009) *Return migration of the next generations: 21st century transnational mobility*, Farnham, Surrey: Ashgate.
Emirbayer, M. and A. Mische (1998) 'What is agency?', *American Journal of Sociology*, 103 (4), 962–1023, doi: 10.1086/231294.
Erdal, M. B. and C. Oeppen (2013) 'Migrant balancing acts: understanding the interactions between integration and transnationalism', *Journal of Ethnic and Migration Studies*, 39 (6), 867–84, doi: 10.1080/1369183X.2013.765647.
Erel, U. (2010) 'Migrating cultural capital: Bourdieu in migration studies', *Sociology*, 44 (4), 642–60, doi: 10.1177/0038038510369363.
Glick Schiller, N., T. Darieva and S. Gruner-Domic (2011) 'Defining cosmopolitan sociability in a transnational age: an introduction', *Ethnic and Racial Studies*, 34 (3), 399–418, doi: 10.1080/01419870.2011.533781.
Hardy, C. (2012) 'Hysteresis', in M. Grenfell (ed.) *Key concepts: Pierre Bourdieu*, second edition, Durham: Acumen, 126–45.

Karageozian, N. (2015a) 'Dreaming of the mountain, longing for the sea, living with floating roots: diasporic "return" migration in post-Soviet Armenia', in N. Sigona, A. Gamlen, G. Liberatore and H. Neveu Kringelbach (eds) *Diasporas reimagined: spaces, practices and belonging*, Oxford: Oxford Diasporas Programme, 69–73.

Karageozian, N. (2015b) *Long-term diasporic return migration in post-Soviet Armenia: balancing mobility and sedentarism* (unpublished doctoral thesis), Oxford: University of Oxford.

Kelly, P. and T. Lusis (2006) 'Migration and the transnational habitus: evidence from Canada and the Philippines', *Environment and Planning A*, 38 (5), 831–47, doi: 10.1068/a37214.

King, R. and A. Christou (2010) 'Cultural geographies of counter-diasporic migration: perspectives from the study of second-generation "returnees" to Greece', *Population, Space and Place*, 16 (2), 103–19, doi: 10.1002/psp.543.

King, R. and A. Christou (2014) 'Second-generation "return" to Greece: new dynamics of transnationalism and integration', *International Migration*, 52 (6), 85–99, doi: 10.1111/imig.12149.

Noble, G. (2013) '"It is home but it is not home": habitus, field and the migrant', *Journal of Sociology*, 49 (2/3), 341–56, doi: 10.1177/1440783313481532.

Nowicka, M. (2015) 'Bourdieu's theory of practice in the study of cultural encounters and transnational transfers in migration', MMG working paper 15-01, Göttingen, Germany: Max Planck Institute for the Study of Religious and Ethnic Diversity, www.mmg.mpg.de/fileadmin/user_upload/documents/wp/WP_15-01_Nowicka_Bourdieus-theory.pdf.

Olsson, E. and R. King (2008 © 2014) 'Introduction: diasporic return', *Diaspora: A Journal of Transnational Studies*, 17 (3), 255–61, https://muse.jhu.edu/article/552359/pdf.

Safran, W. (1991) 'Diasporas in modern societies: myths of homeland and return', *Diaspora: A Journal of Transnational Studies*, 1 (1), 83–99, doi: 10.1353/dsp.1991.0004.

Sagmo, T. H. (2015) 'Return visits as a marker of differentiation in the social field', *Mobilities*, 10 (4), 649–65, doi: 10.1080/17450101.2014.891860.

Sheffer, G. (2003) 'From diasporas to migrants: from migrants to diasporas', in R. Münz and R. Ohliger (eds) *Diasporas and ethnic migrants: Germany, Israel and post-Soviet successor states in comparative perspective*, London: Frank Cass, 17–31.

Sheller, M. and J. Urry (2006) 'The new mobilities paradigm', *Environment and Planning A*, 38 (2), 207–26. doi: 10.1068/a37268.

Shuval, J. T. (2000) 'Diaspora migration: definitional ambiguities and a theoretical paradigm', *International Migration*, 38 (5), 41–57, doi: 10.1111/1468-2435.00127.

Tölölyan, K. (2000) 'Elites and institutions in the Armenian transnation', *Diaspora: A Journal of Transnational Studies*, 9 (1), 107–36, doi: 10.1353/dsp.2000.0004.

Tölölyan, K. (2003) 'The American model of diasporic discourse', in R. Münz and R. Ohliger (eds) *Diasporas and ethnic migrants: Germany, Israel and post-Soviet successor states in comparative perspective*, London: Frank Cass, 50–66.

Tölölyan, K. (2005) 'Restoring the logic of the sedentary to diaspora studies', in L. Anteby-Yemini, W. Bertomière and G. Sheffer (eds) *Les diasporas: 2000 ans d'histoire*, Rennes: Presses Universitaires de Rennes, 137–48.

Tölölyan, K. (2007) 'The contemporary discourse of diaspora studies', *Comparative Studies of South Asia, Africa and the Middle East*, 27 (3), 647–55, doi: 1215/1089201x-2007-040.

Tsuda, T. (ed.) (2009) *Diasporic homecomings: ethnic return migration in comparative perspective*, Stanford: Stanford University Press.

Van Hear, N. (1998) *New diasporas: the mass exodus, dispersal and regrouping of migrant communities*, London: UCL Press.

Werbner, P. (ed.) (2008) *Anthropology and the new cosmopolitanism: rooted, feminist and vernacular perspectives*, Oxford: Berg.

Yang, Y. (2014) 'Bourdieu, practice and change: beyond the criticism of determinism', *Educational Philosophy and Theory: Incorporating ACCESS*, 46 (14), 1522–40, doi: 10.1080/00131857.2013.839375.

Part III
Home and home-making

20
Unravelling the conceptual link between transnationalism and diaspora
The example of hometown networks

Thomas Lacroix

The transnational approach in migration studies emerged in the early 1990s at a time when a greater attention was paid to non-state actors in the international realm. If both transnationalism and the concept of diaspora display distinct genealogies (the first concept coming from international relations, the second having a much older background), both are related. It is not a coincidence that *Diaspora*, a leading journal in this domain in 1991, is subtitled 'a journal of transnational studies'. Admittedly, diasporas are regarded as a specific form of transnational community; the former concept insisting on identity formation and mobilization, the latter on ties and practices (Faist 2010: 11). And yet, the theoretical link between the two realities remains unclear. How do we shift from a transnational social field to a diaspora group? What is the bearing of collective memory and trauma (two key defining criteria characterizing diasporas) on cross-border ties and practices? This link is all the more complex to unfold as the concept of diaspora is itself evolving and polysemic. There is no widely shared definition of what a diaspora is, even more so since the term has fallen outside of the realm of scholarly debates and has been adopted by policy-makers.

Based on my work on hometown transnationalism, this chapter outlines a theoretical framework addressing the link between both transnational and diaspora approaches. This work focuses on three groups: the Sikhs from Punjab based in the United Kingdom, and Moroccans and Algerian Berbers settled in France. The first group is acknowledged as a fragment of a wider world diaspora (Tatla 1999). By contrast, Algerians can be labelled as a transnational community engaged in face-to-face relation with the sending country, while Moroccans present emerging features of a diasporizing group. The three case studies form an adequate terrain for analysing the relationships between transnational communities and diasporas. This reflexion highlights the importance of identity formation and temporality in the making of transnational linkages and practices, and the importance of geography in their transformation into diasporic configurations.

Diaspora: a review of key features

Diasporic groups can take many different forms. Rather than providing an accurate definition of what a diaspora is, scholars have provided a range of typologies mapping the lay of the diasporic land. For instance, Robin Cohen (1997) distinguished between victim, trade, imperial, labour and cultural diasporas. However, beyond the polymorphism of this object, one commonly distinguishes between two distinct but somehow complementary definitions. The 'classical' understanding dwelt upon the archetypal Jewish, Greek and Armenian models, regarding diasporas as the product of a traumatic dispersion of a group, in the wake of a conflict or persecution. In this regard, the dynamics of diaspora formation are rooted in events that precede the migration process. In contrast, in the late twentieth century, and since the 1980s in particular, a 'modern' conception of diasporas emerged, in part inspired by studies of the slave diaspora (Gilroy 1993). This 'modern' paradigm understands diasporas as travelling communities and as international rhizomes (following Deleuze and Guattari 1980) which are constantly being reconfigured after the initial dispersion has lost its founding character (Chivallon 1997). Followers of this approach regard social and cultural processes that *follow* migration as the central crucible of diaspora-building. Personal research on migration and collective memories distinguishes between two regimes of representation of the past among diasporas (Lacroix and Fiddian-Qasmiyeh 2013). The notion of exilic memory is the term of reference for the classical conception of diasporas and can be seen as a collectively shared representation of the traumatic conditions that led to the dispersion of the group. In contradistinction, diasporic memory is not structured by a narration of the point of origin *per se*, but rather is the outcome of a collective migration trajectory.

Recent research has pointed to a third generative process with the emergence and diffusion in most sending countries of diasporic policies meant to urge expatriates into providing financial or political support to the country of origin (Tabar 2016). This, together with the mobilizing impulse of state discourses (and their associated funding and policies), thereby produce diasporas. These policies have resulted in the proliferation of associations that provide an organizational canvas for cross-border engagements. Those diasporic fields where state and diasporic actors co-exist are the crucible of policy-driven discourses about identity and citizenship. In this perspective, the initial conditions (and traumatic experience) of dispersion appear as contingent. Accounting for the role of state actors in diaspora-building has led scholars to distinguish and understand the relations between *emic* (discourses) and *etic* (practices) conceptions of diasporas.

The literature distinguishes between different generative processes and different forms of diaspora groups. Beyond this plurality of approaches, one can identify basic features characterizing what a diaspora is, compared with a transnational community. And the first of these features is a shared consciousness of belonging to a distinctive cross-border group. Diasporans share a feeling of being part of a social ensemble that is neither the mere transposition of a national group outside of its borders, nor the component of a host society, but a sort of third-party actor whose belonging incorporates and transcends the cultural traits of sending and receiving countries. The making of such sense of belonging can follow different pathways, whether stemming from an initial trauma of dispersion, the rhizomic building of a transnational culture, or through the institutional interactions with public authorities. The generative pathways taken by the different groups lead to distinct forms of diasporas. In this process, geography (dispersion) and time (collective memory) matter. Beyond dispersion, interpolarity, that is to say, the relations maintained between the different places of settlement, is a defining feature of diasporas (Ma Mung 2000). Indeed, these transnational connections that shortcut the mediation of the sending country favour the constitution of a distinctive groupness. Time and the transmission of collective memories to subsequent generations are also considered as key dimensions of diaspora-making.

In any case, diasporas do not pop up out of the mere process of mass emigration. Diaspora-building demands the long-term maturation of a shared identity that comes out of multifarious exchanges, associational mobilization and artistic expression. In this regard, the transnational lens that approaches cross-border phenomena at the scale of individuals and social institutions is a useful tool for approaching this process from below.

Hometown transnationalism: a conceptual framework

Hometown transnationalism is one of the most widespread forms of transnational organizing. It is one of the basic archetypes of long-distance sociality. Hometown transnationalism can be defined as the ties and practices maintained by organizations of expatriate villagers with their place of origin. These organizations (usually referred to as hometown associations) provide a collective framework for the reproduction of community ties in the place of settlement. Hometown organizations can be found among many immigrant groups in the world, whether internal (for example, Igbos in Lagos, Auvergnats in Paris or Berbers in Rabat) or international (for example, Mexicans in the USA, Italians in Europe or Latin America). My research focused on Moroccan and Algerian Berbers in France and Indian Punjabis in Great Britain. I found that their primary aim is to provide support to their members in the place of arrival (to find a job or a place to live). Many of them maintain a collective fund meant to cover the expenses of repatriation in case of the death of one of their fellow members. Their general function is to mediate the relationships between migrants and the village community. During the last two decades, hometown organizations have attracted a great deal of scholarly attention because of their growing commitment to development projects for the benefit of their place of origin. This surge of the so-called collective remittances (building of schools, health centres, town hall refurbishment, and so forth) is observed among many groups around the world. The literature has mostly documented this phenomenon among Latin Americans in the USA and Western Africans in Europe. My research was meant to explain why this common trend occurred in different parts of the world at roughly the same time, that is, since the early 1990s.

This phenomenon is the outcome of a convergence between different dynamics. Liberal reforms in sending countries have granted to local civil societies more leeway of action, including in the domain of development. At the same time, the long-term integration of immigrants who arrived between the 1960s and the 1980s has widened the social, technical and financial capacities of hometown organizations. This dynamic took shape at a moment when the primary aim of hometown groupings was becoming obsolete, and they found in development activities a means to reinvent their legitimacy. A detailed presentation of the results of this research is outside of the remit of this chapter (see Lacroix 2016). However, part of the study focused on the motives that lead migrants to dedicate time and money in transnational endeavours. Transnational engagements are usually explained as a status strategy for migrants who seek to compensate for their underdog condition in the place of arrival with a role of successful philanthropist in the place of departure. This explanation does not fully explain the commitments of hometowners to activities that do not necessarily yield large symbolic benefits. In order to provide a more satisfactory response, I developed a three-pronged theoretical framework.

Plural men/women

Firstly, from a theoretical point of view, transnational actors are best understood as *plural men/women* (Lahire 1998). In this perspective, people's identity is made up of a multiplicity of poles that reflect the various processes of socialization they went through during the course of their lives. This is particularly true for migrants whose initial and current socialization do not take place in the same social environment. Migrants' habitus, to take Bourdieu's term, is composite. But this multiplicity of embedding fragments people's lifeworld and their position in the world.

Identity is a narrative they forge to invent a continuity beyond their composite social life. It fosters a feeling of uniqueness and individuality (Corcuff 1999). Individuation stems from an effort to grapple with the complexity of human existence.

Emergence

Secondly, from this premise unfolds a theory of *emergence* of new practices in the transnational realm. The concept of emergence refers to the production of behaviours that cannot be accounted for by the reproduction of past routines. Collective remittances offer an example of emergence. My contention is that emergence is itself an outcome of the multipolarization of actors' identity. Due to their multiple embedding, actors are confronted with a diversity of constraints and expectations that may be at odds with each other. Emergence, in that regard, can be seen as stemming from what Robert Merton calls a 'contradiction in role-set' (Merton 1957). This entails a process of distancing and a capacity to adapt ideas, claims, skills or modes of being from one context to the other. Against this background, actors endorse innovative behaviours to adjust to their environment. Emergent behaviours can be defined as new patterns of actions undertaken by actors in order to cope with the contradictions posed by their social embedding. Furthermore, following Habermas (1984), emergent behaviours can be seen as communicative actions. This means that migrants, through their engagement, express their views about the world and their own being in the world. In doing so, I contest the scholarly distinction between *emic* and *etic* dimensions of diasporization. Addressing cross-border practices as communicative action shows that what migrants do is in fact a way for migrants to express who they are. I am not convinced by the analytical value of the distinction when it comes to account for grassroots activities of hometown organizations; *etic* is *emic*. Indeed, collective remittances are a form of expression (and thereby of legitimation) of their multiple embedding. Through these development projects, they both express their allegiance to and their capacity to import modernity in the place of origin. What was revealed during my investigation was not merely the will to display a pre-eminent status (this was true only for some of the hometowners, a category I called the 'philanthropists'), but, more broadly, the desire to reinvent their villageness, that is, their identity and associated role towards the village. Indeed, their protracted stay in the country of settlement transformed their family status, professional identity, political ideas and other elements of their lives. In other words, their integration radically transformed their lifeworld. The village itself was radically transformed during their time abroad. Hence the need for migrants to reinvent their position of villager that had become meaningless.

Convergence

Thirdly, most extant theories accounting for migrant behaviours usually stop at the level of individuals. But a given action, as creative as it can be, will never have far-reaching effects if it is not endorsed by a number of people large enough to have structural effects. The coordination of innovative action, that is, *convergence*, is a crucial step that is ignored by common 'structure and agency' approaches. Once again, Habermas' theory of communicative action provides an explanation of this phenomenon through the concept of communicative rationality: an action is possible when it is deemed rational, that is, it conforms to a shared understanding of the world.[1] The communicative process of transnational engagement is thereby a two-way process: through collective remittances migrants assert the transnational nature of their dual positioning, and this assertion is, in turn, acknowledged by the village community. For this communicative process to happen at a collective level, individual behaviours are to be mediated by meso-level organizations.

The concept of *social institutions* is generally perceived either through the functions they achieve or as relatively stable patterns of social structuration that drive human activities. They are generally addressed as black boxes that give shape to the patterning of collective behaviours. Moving away from common approaches, I understand social institutions as places of central importance in communicative dynamics. In this regard, social institutions are understood as arenas in which emergent behaviours are forged and validated by the collective. They are the locus of exercise of communicative rationality. They make convergence possible, namely, they transform individual innovations into collective mobilizations. These dynamics can be addressed at two levels: at the individual level, people seek approval of their innovative behaviours in order to overcome the contradictions of their personal embedding; at the collective level, people endorse emergent behaviours in order to reinvent the membership to the group beyond the growing disparities between members. This has been observed among investigated hometown groups. As time goes by, members follow different professional, class or political trajectories, and they share no more than a common origin and memories. Development is a consensual issue in which people are happy to contribute. It is a domain of involvement that allows them to transcend their discrepant views. The case of younger activists seeking to challenge the traditional authority of elders is an interesting example of convergent dynamics occurring within hometown organizations. Their capacities to interact with host-country authorities and thereby to muster new financial or administrative resources have led this category of actor to play a key function. But the recognition of their role often transforms the functioning of these organizations. They may, for example, change decision-making by introducing secret ballots or strengthen the accountability of their activities by keeping closer track of expenditure.

The liminality of transnationalism and diaspora-building

The analysis of hometown transnationalism opens a window on diasporization processes. Let's go back to the defining features of diasporas highlighted above. The primary aspect is the existence of a specific sense of belonging. One can trace in migrants' transnational engagement the building of a consciousness of belonging to a specific cross-border social entity. Collective remittances represent at the same time a proof of allegiance to the community and the introduction in the place of origin of facilities, equipment and therefore practices they experience in the place of settlement. They are emergent endeavours that solve a tension between who they were (a member of the village community) and who they have become. Collective remittances are thereby the expression of a dual embedding that is a move away of the constituency of the village community. They support the building of a feeling of uniqueness.

We have also seen that diasporization is tightly associated with memory-building. The relationship between the collective undertakings of hometown groups and memory-building is apparent in the vocabulary they use to qualify their involvement. Migrants often summon up terms and expressions drawn from village traditional or religious practices like *Tiwizi* or *touiza* (Berber terms naming collective customary duties), or *Seva* (alms in the Sikh religion). Using customary terms to name development projects is a typical example of reinvention of tradition, but it also translates the need for actors to reassess a collective village memory for present needs. In that regard, collective remittances underwrite a reinvention of a collective memory that inscribes expatriate hometowners into a temporal trajectory linking their present ascription as an 'immigrant' with the past of being part of a perceived village tradition. The reinvention of traditional terms and practices is part and parcel of the memory-building that characterize diasporas.

Another key feature of diasporas is their spatial interpolarity. As mentioned above, hometown organizations are key institutions mediating the relationships with the community of origin.

They also play a key role in mediating relationships between village expatriates, even if, in some cases, they are dispersed in several regions, countries, or even continents. During my field research, I have met Punjabi hometown leaders who went to different parts of England, Canada and West Coast America to collect money for the building of a hospital. More generally, hometown organizations cope with dispersion by opening chapters in different cities or countries. This is the case for a Moroccan association whose main organization is based in Gennevilliers (on the outskirts of Paris) and is linked to a sister institution near Amsterdam, the latter gathering hometowners living in the Netherlands and Belgium. No such cross-border ties linking different places of settlement has been observed among Algerian Kabyles. It is true that the vast majority of them (90 per cent) reside in France. Among the three groups investigated, Punjabis display the widest international outreach. This cross-border diffusion of hometown networks is to be understood against the background of the global ties maintained by the Indian diaspora at large. Religious associations, for which India is one country of operation among others, are a case in point. For instance, the Sikh Human Rights Group is an association focusing on the promotion of rights of Sikh people in the world. They are involved in several development projects and campaigns in Punjab. But they also are involved in the support of Sikh students in France in the wake of the enforcement of the law banning religious signs at school. Another category of organization sustaining interpolar linkages is the one of caste associations whose main role is to serve as a dating agency for members of the same caste around the world. This form of interpolarity is rarely encountered, if not absent from, the two other case studies (Moroccans and Algerians in France). The spatial dispersion of Moroccans in France forms an adequate terrain for this interpolar dynamic to take shape, but it is present only among leftist organizations of refugees who fled the Moroccan regime of Hassan II in the 1960s and 1970s. They may temporarily activate their solidarity networks if need be: in 1985, Moroccan associations from France, Spain, Belgium and the Netherlands participated in the Collectif des Associations d'Immigrés en Europe and later in the Migrant Forum. In 2006, in the midst of a campaign for immigrant voting, the same actors formed the Al Monadara network (see below). But this kind of European interaction remains an exception.

The focus on migrants' practices in this chapter has led me to leave aside the importance of non-migrant institutions. And yet, the policies and associate discourses of public authorities regarding transnational behaviours are of central importance. Hometown organizations have largely benefited from the support of state and non-state actors through the diffusion of migration and development policies. Morocco has a long-standing policy for enhancing remittances. In the 1970s, it created a bank specifically dedicated to the channelling of migrants' remittances. In the early 1990s, it established a ministry for Moroccans abroad and a series of co-funding schemes supporting electrification, water conveyance systems and the building of roads by hometown organizations. Likewise, the Indian government created the Ministry for Overseas Indian Affairs in 2005, which includes a programme supporting philanthropic activities. In France, the co-development policy was conducive to the creation of the FORIM (Forum des Organisations de Solidarité Internationales issues de l'Immigration), a platform of migrant NGOs. Similar initiatives were taken by the British government in the early 2000s. The implementation of such programmes went along with the diffusion of a new discourse about emigrants as agents of development. This contributed to create a favourable context for diasporic mobilization. In turn, migrant organizations used these practice to make new claims. An example of this is the mobilization of Moroccan organizations in Europe to ask for the right to vote from abroad and to enhance parliamentary representation in Rabat. A coalition named as the Al Monadara movement formed in 2006. This right for the diaspora to be represented became part of the constitution in 2011.

Conclusion: from transnational communities to diasporas

Transnationalism can be considered as a liminal process spurred by the contradictions of the condition of immigrant. Transnational linkages, especially when state authorities provide financial and discursive support, constitute a matrix in which can emerge the main components characterizing diasporas: an organizational web, a collective culture and memory and, above all, a diasporic consciousness. And yet, not all transnational communities can turn into full-fledged diasporas. Among the three investigated groups, only the Sikhs from Punjab are commonly regarded as such (Tatla 1999). The focus of their cross-border organizations is much broader than the sending country and encompasses the diaspora as such. Transnational engagement is certainly a necessary but not a sufficient condition for the emergence of diasporas. More research is probably needed to investigate the threshold dynamics leading from one type of social organization to the other. But among the drivers of such a process, the role of conflicts is probably key. Indeed, the formation of interpolar relations within the diaspora gains momentum during times of conflict in the country of origin. Collective mobilizations form around a common cause. This was the case during the political violence that affected Punjab between 1984 and 1992. Khalistani organizations advocating for the independence of Punjab formed networks between the UK, the USA, Canada, Australia, New Zealand or Germany. (Khalistan is the name given by Sikh nationalists for an independent Punjab.) Political strife against the monarchy was also what united Moroccan leftist refugees across Europe. But there is more to conflict than a spur for cross-national mobilization. Times of tensions also trigger a break between expatriates and the government of their sending country. They produce the conditions for heightened identity contradictions, for distancing that leaves a space for the emergence of self-consciousness. Political strife might not be a necessary condition for the formation of diasporas, but they considerably accelerate their emergence. This is what was missing in the Moroccan case, since opposition against Moroccan authoritarianism only involved a small proportion of emigrants. One may therefore talk about partial diasporization.

Algerians could appear as a counter-example. Despite a history of protest and a civil war that divided the country during the 1990s, Algerians did not produce any interpolar organizational framework. I see two reasons for this. The first one is that the wider dispersion of Algerian emigration is very weak (geography matters): 90 per cent of expatriate Algerians live in France. The second reason is that the Algerian government has always managed to control interpolar linkages through the Amicale des Algériens en Europe (Friendship Society of Algerians in Europe) (Scagnetti 2014), an organization active until its dissolution in 1988. The civil war of the 1990s did not give birth to any federal organizations, even if a myriad of human rights and victim support organizations were created. The only diaspora type of organization in which Algerians are particularly active is a Berberist federation, the World Amazigh Congress (created in 1997). But internal divisions considerably limited its influence. The lack of relays in counties of emigration other than France is an obstacle for the deployment of Algerian interpolar relations. This may change in the years to come in so far as one observes a diversification of destinations of Algerian emigrants (especially to the UK, Canada and the USA). Their absence confines Algerian transnational relations to the Franco-Algerian sphere and constrains the development of a diasporic culture and consciousness.

Diaspora studies has largely focused on cross-national configurations and mobilization at a global scale. The transnational lens opens the possibility to enter the everyday construction of diaspora ties, memory and identity through grassroots practices of families, businesses or associations. And this approach is useful to identify the steps and drivers of the transformation of a transnational community into a diaspora. Some of them are well known, such as the occurrence of a conflict in/with the sending country or spatial diffusion. Others remain poorly documented, in particular the mechanisms of transmission of a diasporic *raison d'être* to subsequent generations. This is probably one of the major areas for future research.

Acknowledgements

Interviews with leaders and members of associations were undertaken in London and the Midlands, the Paris areas and southern France (Marseilles), field visits were made in villages in Morocco and India. The research is based on doctoral work carried out between 1999 and 2003; the comparative study was made possible thanks to a Marie Curie postdoctoral fellowship at CRER, University of Warwick, and a research contract at the International Migration Institute at the University of Oxford. The results of this research were published in 2016 by Palgrave under the title *Hometown Transnationalism: long-distance villageness among North Indians and North African Berbers*.

Note

1 Conversely, an action that does not receive this collective validation is deemed divergent. Divergence is context-dependent. An action that is deemed as irrelevant in a given context can be acknowledged in another one. Divergence is part and parcel of a broader dynamic of social change when it hides a process of convergence in another social context.

References

Chivallon, C. (1997) 'Du territoire au réseau: comment penser l'identité Antillaise', *Cahiers d'Études Africaines*, 37 (148), 767–94, doi: 10.2307/4392825.
Cohen, R. (1997) *Global diasporas: an introduction*, London: UCL Press.
Corcuff, P. (1999) 'Acteur pluriel contre habitus? À propos d'un nouveau champ de recherches et de la possibilité du débat en sciences sociales', *Politix*, 12 (48), 157–73, doi: 10.3406/polix.1999.1812.
Deleuze, G. and F. Guattari (1980) *Mille plateaux*, Paris: Les éditions de Minuit.
Faist, T. (2010) 'Diaspora and transnationalism: what kind of dance partners?', in R. Bauböck and T. Faist (eds) *Diaspora and transnationalism: concepts, theory and methods*, Amsterdam: Amsterdam University Press, 9–34.
Gilroy, P. (1993) *The black Atlantic: modernity and double consciousness*, Cambridge, MA: Harvard University Press.
Habermas, J. (1984) *The theory of communicative action, volume 1: reason and the rationalization of society*, Boston: Beacon Press.
Lacroix, T. (2016) *Hometown transnationalism: long distance villageness among Indian Punjabis and North African Berbers*, Basingstoke: Palgrave Macmillan.
Lacroix, T. and E. Fiddian-Qasmiyeh (2013) 'Refugee and diaspora memories: the politics of remembering and forgetting', *Journal of Intercultural Studies*, 34 (6), 684–96, doi: 10.1080/07256868.2013.846893.
Lahire, B. (1998) *l'homme pluriel: les ressorts de l'action*, Paris: Nathan.
Ma Mung, E. (2000) *La diaspora Chinoise: géographie d'une migration*, Paris: Ophrys.
Merton, R. K. (1957) 'The role-set: problems in sociological theory', *The British Journal of Sociology*, 8 (2), 106–20, doi: 10.2307/587363.
Scagnetti, J. C. (2014) *La Wilaya Hexagonale: L'Algérie et son émigration, une histoire d'identités, 1962–1988*, Nice: Université de Nice.
Tabar, P. (2016) 'The Lebanese diasporic field: the impact of sending and receiving states', *Immigrants and Minorities*, 34 (3), 256–75, doi: 10.1080/02619288.2016.1191358.
Tatla, D. S. (1999) *The Sikh diaspora: the search for statehood*, London: UCL Press.

21
Deportees as 'reverse diasporas'

Shahram Khosravi

Detention and deportation – the forced removal of non-citizens – have become the significant sanctions imposed by the current migration regime. Following a growing 'securitization of migration' in the past two decades, migration control is increasingly governed through the techniques and discourses used to regulate, control and remove undesired non-citizens. The removal operation is a transnational enterprise involving authorities from different states, transport companies, private security companies, deportation escorts, international networking, as well as various other private companies.

Deportation involves elements of force and coercion. Deportees have no control over their mobility, where they are taken, when their removal takes place, or how they are deported. Because all of these actions are involuntary and out of the deportees' control, deportation is more a sort of forced movement (Walters 2002). Deportation in Europe is a huge enterprise costing almost a billion euro per year (The Migrants' Files 2015). An infrastructure of deportation has emerged, including carceral spaces and modes of transport. Deportation has gradually become a set of economic relations and market processes (Walters 2016), and thereby a financial and political feature of our age.

In order to facilitate deportation, authorities in deporting countries and authorities in the receiving countries collaborate, with the primary aim of identifying individuals who lack official documents. More and more, the collaboration has become a financial transaction. Countries in the Global South are promised economic aid in exchange for accepting deportees. Needless to mention these deportation procedures often pose high risks for deportees. They may be in even more danger after their deportation than before, this being particularly true for asylum-seekers.

We live in an age of mass deportation. Between 2009 and 2016, almost three million people have been deported from the USA, and several million more are planned to be deported in coming years. Europe is organizing mass deportation of several hundred thousand people. Mass deportation is also growing outside the Global North. During 2016, almost a million Afghans were forcibly returned from Iran and Pakistan. Saudi Arabia has deported hundreds of thousands of migrants every year in recent years. In this age of deportation, not only non-citizens but also citizens are threatened by removal. In recent years, there has been a proliferation of revocation of citizenship followed by deportation from Canada and Norway to Bahrain. Rather than being merely a strategy for immigration control, deportation has increasingly become integrated in larger social and economic global transformations.

Mass deportation has increasingly become part of neoliberal economic restructuring and global capitalism (Golash-Boza 2015). Furthermore, deportation is being incorporated in development policies (Collyer 2017), and has been used instrumentally as a weapon in international relations (cf. Greenhill 2010) to influence and manipulate other states.

Global abandonment

The current deportation regime involves more than a single event, namely, the relocation of a person from the host country to the country of citizenship. Rather, it is a process that spans long periods of time and geographical areas, involving a variety of people and institutions: deportees, their families and communities, state officials, bureaucrats, non-governmental organizations (NGOs), activists, media, and private companies (Drotbohm and Hasselberg 2015). Deportees are excluded through inclusion. Golash-Boza (2015) and Rodkey (2016) demonstrate that deportees who have grown up in the USA and who speak English fluently and are familiar with American society make the optimal workforce for American companies that have moved to the Dominican Republic in search of cheap wage-labour force. Like deportability in the host country (De Genova 2002), the post-deportation condition is profoundly disciplinary in order to make deportees a compliant, docile and cheap labour force. Deportees are spatially expelled from the Global North, to be included in the capitalist system outsourced to the Global South.

Some who have been long-term residents continue to receive retirement pay after deportation from the country they have been deported from. Others are still legally linked to the host country through a re-entry ban or through advocacy groups who work for making their return possible (for example, Peutz 2007). Deportees who used to send remittances are now themselves receivers of remittances sent by their children, wives, husbands or parents. While deportees are spatially relocated afar, they still are in a sort of simultaneity with the host country, meaning that their experiences are profoundly interwoven with what happens and what others do in their previous country of residence. Thus, rather than merely being excluded, deportees are, in Giorgio Agamben's meaning, abandoned, kept in the zone of 'indistinction', where 'life and law, outside and inside, become indistinguishable. It is literally not possible to say whether the one who has been banned is outside or inside the juridical order' (Agamben 1998: 28). This is the sovereign abandonment, including what is excluded, or, in other words, creating an inclusive exclusion. Deportation ethnographies demonstrate this logic of inclusive exclusion through which deportees are positioned on the threshold between *in* and *out*.

Experience of the forcibly returned is often an experience of 'double abandonment' (cf. Lecadet 2013). Their narratives attest multiple abandonments that stretch over several countries, including the country of origin, and over a long period. Rather than experiencing a homecoming, deportees become inhabitants of 'transnational corridors of expulsion' (Nyers 2003).

Accordingly, deportation rarely means returning home to a place of safety and belonging. Deportation often means the forced return to a situation worse than the situation prior to the initial departure; politically, financially and socially. Consequently, adjustment and integration into the country of citizenship is usually uncertain and difficult.

While there are several assisted and reintegration programmes for voluntary returnees (organized in collaboration with IOM, the International Organization for Migration), support for deportees generally does not exist. In stark contrast to those who return 'voluntarily', those who are forcefully returned have not had any opportunity to prepare themselves for their return. The lack of preparedness has a great impact on the possibilities of reintegration in the 'homeland' (Cassarino 2004);

namely, the ways in which individuals find and define their position in society, how they feel about belonging and taking part in society. In the cases of countries in war or armed conflicts, deportees usually find their homes ruined and their lands occupied, they face serious problems with landmines, they lack access to healthcare, and their children have no access to schools. It is not unusual for deportees to join other internally displaced people.

There are multiple factors that make adjustment and reintegration difficult, if not impossible, for the deportees. The major problem is financial insecurity. The cost of the initial migration, often in forms of debt, is often not refunded. The lack of a social network in the country of citizenship means that deportees face serious difficulties in finding employment, housing, or getting psychological support. Younger deportees, who have spent their formative years in the country they were deported from, have more difficulty in finding their place in the society. It is not unusual for those who grew up in the host country to not even master the language assumed to be their mother tongue. Furthermore, a gap between their education prior to deportation and the education system in the country they are deported to prevents them from moving forward. Likewise, skills they have obtained not always are of relevance and the certificates, if available at all, are not always translatable or recognized and therefore not useful after deportation (RSN 2016). Another problem deportees struggle with is family split. Contrary to how repatriation is generally represented as a homecoming, for many individuals, removal from the host country results in separation from their families they leave behind there.

A part of double abandonment is experiencing stigmatization. While in Jamaica deportees are regarded as criminals, and in Guatemala deportees are scapegoats for worsening crime and other social problems (Golash-Boza 2015). In Afghanistan, deportees are seen as being 'culturally contaminated' (Schuster and Majidi 2013). Otherwise they are regarded as failures in their migratory project.

Deportation has a deep impact on the relations between deportees and their country of origin. Deportation undermines citizenship (Boehm 2016). Sometimes undocumented migrants, particularly those who are long-term residents, also become undocumented deportees in their country of citizenship. Not being recorded in the national registration system would lead to a long and complicated process of paperwork in order to obtain ID cards. Meanwhile, the deportee remains in a condition of undocumentedness, with no access to citizenship rights. When deportation impedes the achievement of life goals, a feeling of incompleteness is engendered. 'Double abandonment' is experienced as a result of being regarded as both a 'failed citizen' and a 'failed migrant'. Deportation turns individuals into quasi-citizens, or denizens whose rights can be suspended, rejected, delayed and denied. The representation of deportation as *returning home* neglects the power relation between the deporting country and the country one is deported to, as well as the conflicts and struggles within the country one is sent to. By representing deportation as homecoming, and naturalizing the notion of home(land), the brutality embedded in deportation is masked and thereby depoliticized.

There are some countries where the post-deportation aftermath is not so severe. For instance, in Brazil deportees face no such humiliation and marginalization. This is perhaps because migrants usually return to Brazil (Golash-Boza 2015: 254) and that there is a high expectation of migrants' return among Brazilians.

Returned to exile

For those who migrated as children and became long-term residents, the 'country of origin' is a foreign one. Some groups, for instance many Afghans deported from Europe, were born and grew up elsewhere, such as in Pakistan and Iran. Deported young Salvadorans 'banished from the United States after spending the better part of their young lives in this country – are returned "home" to a place where, in their memory, they have never been' (Zilberg 2004: 761). Therefore, many identify their post-deportation experiences in terms of exile (Hasselberg 2016: 27). Several scholars use exile (Coutin 2016; Moniz 2004) and diaspora (Kanstroom 2012) to describe the condition of post-deportation. To be exiled is to be away and banished from one's home. Ethnographies of post-deportation show that the forced return to the 'country of origin' is often followed by a sense of 'disbelonging', loss, alienation and *estrangement*. The country of origin becomes an exile, and the country one is deported from becomes a place of belonging. The experience of abandonment in the country of citizenship invites the deportees to reassess the notion of home.

Deportees' narratives disclose the multilayered relationship between space and identity, and between territory and belonging (cf. Zilberg 2011). For many deportees, the relationship with the place of belonging is not expressed in the standard question *Where are you from?* but rather in the question *Where are you deported from?* A reverse reference point of belonging would lead to the formation of what Hess (2008) has termed a 'reverse diaspora'. In a reverse diaspora, the deporting country becomes a stable frame of reference and meaning for their identity and memory (Hess 2008), and thereby the notions of home and belonging have indeed become more fluid. Exile designates discontinuity, inconsistency and interruption, all in contrast to the nationalist image of belonging to a home(land). Exile is when one lives in one place and dreams in another. Exile involves a dream of going back home, though imagined. Common among deportees is a desire to return to the country they have been deported from (see Khosravi 2017). Going through post-deportation suffering, namely, unpaid debts, vanished remittances, the shame of failure and stigmatization, for them outweighs the risk of being caught and deported once again.

A UNHCR research paper from 2012 indicates that many people forcibly removed to Kabul quickly attempt to re-migrate (Gladwell and Elwyn 2012). Afghans deported to Afghanistan, a country they never have seen before, cross borders again to Iran or Pakistan to reunite with their families. Thus, deportation is not an end of journey or connection but rather it is only another phase of recirculation. My ethnographic studies among travellers without papers (see Khosravi 2009, 2010, 2016) have been full of migrants who have been living a life shaped by a dialectical interplay between deportation and re-migration. Travellers who are stuck between, on the one side, a powerful transnational apparatus which forcibly excludes and expels them from the Global North, and on the other side, the circumstances and the forces which push them towards emigration from the Global South. While the former attempts to impose a petrifying immobility on them, the latter forces them towards an incessant mobility in the shadows and through cracks of the global order of borders. The dialectical positionality, affected by opposing forces, turns them into both object and subject of the national order of things at the same time. Deportation as a disciplinary measure to deter further migration fails because the structural realities behind why people leave are ignored.

Deportspora

The aforementioned factors make forced return not a *homecoming* but rather an entrance to a transnational space of expulsion, oscillating between re-departure and re-deportation, what Nyers (2003) termed a 'deportspora', an abject diaspora. The notion of diaspora generally denotes a gain of various capitals: success, double inclusion, the establishment of transnational connections and networks, enjoyment of mobility a flexible citizenship offers, and an imagined ancestral and historical homeland. Deportspora denotes an absence of all of these things, whereby members are exposed to multiple uprooting, multiple deportations and re-migrations, stuck in a condition of stretching social abandonment, experienced by being regarded both as failed citizen and migrant before and after deportation.

One function of deportation is to maintain a system of global apartheid that intends to sustain the class and racialized separation between those with the right to free mobility and those exposed to forced immobility. Deportation intends to keep two worlds separated from each other. One cosmopolitan, a world of surplus right of mobility, and the other one a world of checkpoints, borders, queues, gates, detentions and removal.

Deportees, suffering from the shrinking space of citizenship and multi-layered expulsions, are deprived of the promises and possibilities of transnationalism and cosmopolitanism (Boehm 2016: 115). Lack of citizenship or weak citizenship means shrinking access to other rights and possibilities. Unlike diasporic ideas of multiple belonging, deportsporic experiences render spatial and temporal stretching of abandonment and inflexible non-citizenship. While diaspora usually offers its members a surplus of mobility rights, to cross borders gloriously as an honourable act in the spirit of globalism and cosmopolitanism, those of deportspora do it through invisibilizing themselves, becoming some*thing* else, or by not being visible at all – hidden in containers and trucks among commodities, or rather as commodities squeezed among other commodities, to be able to cross borders. The former group sit on seats in cabins, the latter hide themselves in containers, under trains, or in airplane wheel units. They move in dark and shadow. They do not go through gates, but through cracks. They do not pass through borders, they jump over walls, or creep under barbed-wire fences. Others use forged passports. Some irregular migration facilitators use a 'look-alike' strategy, which entails finding a passport whose former owner looks like the client. Interestingly, members of deportspora lacking travel documents usually use passports belonging to members of their co-ethnic diaspora, flexible citizens with the right of mobility. By forging passports, travellers without papers create a trustworthy history of mobility for themselves: 'a history of authorised and regularised movement. The forged passports rearticulate the body, supposed to be immobilized, within the international regime of mobility' (Keshavarz 2016: 168). Faking and performing the privileges of diaspora re-articulate deportspora into the world of access, mobility, speed and flexible citizenship.

Despite mobility restriction, members of deportspora have fragmented and hybrid transnational lives. Like diaspora, deportspora is a transnational formation, a heterogeneous social space stretching over countries, communities and cultures. Multiple uprootings and migratory trajectories have provided them access to several languages and cultural capitals, transnational ties and networks, various lifestyle and social imaginaries. They are forced cosmopolitan subjects, not by choice, by class, or by ethnic privileges, but forcibly by the global deportation regime. They are the embodiment of forced transnationality (Zilberg 2004). Unlike the situation in diasporas, people in deportspora usually are not socially or politically organized to promote identity and culture of the 'home'. Rather than collective celebrations, mobilizations, or activities, deportees deploy individual strategies to articulate their memories of the host society, one they think of as home, and attempt to reinstate a life interrupted by deportation. Deportees' memories tend to revolve around the family life left behind, the community, familiar places and urban geographies, the food, the language, and the climate back in the country they were deported from. By reconstructing images of 'home' which is not homeland or country of origin, but rather the host country, keeps the myth of return alive and assuages the pain of exile. By 'keeping in touch' with the previous country of residence through maintaining transnational ties, parenting from afar, celebrating national festivals, and remembrances, deportees resist how deportation would thwart their life achievements and goals. This strategy of 'resynchronisation' (Cwerner 2001) refers to the sense that one's life rhythm is in accordance with the sociocultural time of the host society. Within what Zilberg (2004) calls a politic of simultaneity, deportees are linked inextricably with the country they have been expelled from.

In her study of deportation of Salvadoran immigrant youth, raised and fully integrated in the American society, Zilberg describes the flow of people, memories, and imaginations between Los Angeles and San Salvador and how 'deported Salvadoran immigrant gang youth oscillate between "home" and "abroad", where both home and abroad are themselves unstable locations' (Zilberg 2004: 774). Through cosmopolitan visions and transnational practices, deportees challenge, resist and survive the removal and the immobility imposed on them by deportation.

Final remarks

The notion of *home* is based on an ideology that naturalizes the nation-state system and is built on the uncritical link between individuals and territory which makes border-crossing pathological and 'uprootedness' an 'unnatural' mode of being. Deportation would restore the 'broken' link between 'nativity' and nationality, between biologic life and political life. Thus, removal of non-citizens can be seen as a worship of nationhood, a nationalist project, or as Walters (2002: 282) describes it, a 'technology of citizenship', a way of ensuring that people are in 'their proper sovereigns'. Deportation does not exclude non-citizens but rather keeps them *in their places* in terms of the racial and class hierarchy.

Racism is embedded in the current deportation regime. Let me give two examples. First, while European states discourage their citizens from travelling to Afghanistan or Iraq due to their high safety risk, Afghans and Iraqis are regularly deported to these countries. The deportation regime demonstrates its 'divine' sovereignty by showing its ability to decide which life is liveable and which is not, which deaths are 'grieveable' (Europeans' deaths) and which are not (Afghans' deaths). The lives of the deportees are not seen as being in danger, injured, or lost, simply because they are not recognized as lives at all. In the second example, in 2014, Somalians constituted the largest group in detention centres in Sweden. However, they were not among the first 20 migrant groups who were deported that year. Somalian migrants were detained even though they were not deportable. The question is how the detaining but not deporting of this specific Muslim and black group can be justified (DeBono et al. 2015).

Mass deportation, integrated in global capitalism, maintains the unequal distribution of the right of mobility. In a global apartheid, 'the relatively rich and disproportionately white of the world are generally free to travel and live wherever they would like or have the means to access the resources they "need". Meanwhile the relatively poor and largely nonwhite are typically forced to subsist in places where there are not enough resources' (Nevins and Aizeki 2008: 184). Deportation, rather than stopping aspirant migrants, contributes to 'the perpetuation of cycles of global inequality and human mobility' (Hiemstra 2012: 307). The mass deportation of almost 80,000 Afghans from Europe, particularly from Germany, helps to maintain a global order in which a German passport-holder can travel to 175 countries without a visa, while an Afghan passport-holder can do the same only to 25 countries.

The so-called refugee crisis and the highest number of forcibly displaced people (refugees, asylum-seekers, internally displaced people, stateless people) since the Second World War indicate a growing deportspora. It is not only that the number of people stuck in the transnational corridor of expulsion is growing, but also these situations of abandonment become more and more protracted.

In this global community of deportees, the customary question *Where are you deported from?* rather than *Where are you from?* hints at their sense of belonging together, not to a territory, but to a deportspora. To be deportsporic is a mode of being in the world characterized by multiple precarities: uprooting, prolonged suspension, imaging a futureless tomorrow, home(land)lessness, intense sense of isolation. Nonetheless, deportsporic practices and claims in the form of re-migration, mobilization of transnational networks, maintaining cultural connections, reveal deportspora as a space of agency and defiance. With their mobility, imagination, stances and claims, they make an intervention in the construction of the global apartheid of mobility. Movements of people who are supposed to be immobile after being deported, repoliticize the concept of borders and deportations that have been naturalized and depoliticized by the nation-state ideology. We owe deportspora this recognition.

References

Agamben, G. (1998) *Homo sacer: sovereign power and bare life*, translated by D. Heller-Roazen, Palo Alto, CA: Stanford University Press.
Boehm, D. A. (2016) *Returned: going and coming in an age of deportation*, California: University of California Press.
Cassarino, J. P. (2004) 'Theorising return migration: the conceptual approach to return migrants revisited', *International Journal on Multicultural Societies*, 6 (2), 253–79, available at: www.unesco.org/shs/ijms/vol6/issue2/art4.
Collyer, M. (2017) 'Paying to go: deportability as development', in S. Khosravi (ed.) *After deportation: ethnographic perspectives*, New York: Palgrave Macmillan.
Coutin, S. B. (2016) *Exiled home: Salvadoran transnational youth in the aftermath of violence*, Durham: Duke University Press.
Cwerner, S. B. (2001) 'The times of migration', *Journal of Ethnic and Migration Studies*, 27 (1), 7–36, doi: 10.1080/13691830125283.
DeBono, D., S. Rönnqvist and K. Magnusson (2015) *Humane and dignified? Migrants' experiences of living in a 'state of deportability' in Sweden*, Malmö: Malmö University.
De Genova, N. P. (2002) 'Migrant "illegality" and deportability in everyday life', *Annual Review of Anthropology*, 31, 419–47, doi: 10.1146/annurev.anthro.31.040402.085432.
Drotbohm, H. and I. Hasselberg (2015) 'Deportation, anxiety, justice: new ethnographic perspectives', *Journal of Ethnic and Migration Studies*, 41 (4), 551–62, doi: 10.1080/1369183X.2014.957171.
Gladwell, C. and H. Elwyn (2012) 'Broken futures: young Afghan asylum seekers in the UK and on return to their country of origin', UNHCR's New Issues in Refugee Research, research paper 246, November, available at: https://goo.gl/Xce4gJ.
Golash-Boza, T. M. (2015) *Deported: immigrant policing, disposable labor, and global capitalism*, New York: New York University Press.
Greenhill, K. M. (2010) *Weapons of mass migration: forced displacement, coercion, and foreign policy*, Ithaca, NY: Cornell University Press.
Hasselberg, I. (2016) *Enduring uncertainty: deportation, punishment and everyday life*, Oxford: Berghahn Books.
Hess, C. (2008) 'What are "reverse diasporas" and how are we to understand them?', *Diaspora: A Journal of Transnational Studies*, 17 (3), 288–315, available at: https://muse.jhu.edu/article/552361.
Hiemstra, N. (2012) 'Geopolitical reverberations of US migrant detention and deportation: the view from Ecuador', *Geopolitics*, 17 (2), 293–311, doi: 10.1080/14650045.2011.562942.
Kanstroom, D. (2012) *Aftermath: deportation law and the new American diaspora*, New York: Oxford University Press.
Keshavarz, M. (2016) *Design-politics: An Inquiry into passports, camps and borders*, Doctoral dissertation, Malmö University, Sweden.
Khosravi, S. (2009) 'Detention and deportation of asylum seekers in Sweden', *Race and Class*, 50 (4), 38–56, doi: 10.1177/0306396809102996.
Khosravi, S. (2010) *Illegal traveller: an auto-ethnography of borders*, New York: Palgrave Macmillan.
Khosravi, S. (2016) 'Deportation as a way of life', in R. Furman (ed.) *Detaining the immigrant other: global and transnational issues*, Oxford: Oxford University Press, 169–81.
Khosravi, S. (2017) *After deportation: ethnographic perspectives*, New York: Palgrave Macmillan.
The Migrants' Files (2015) online resource (discontinued 24 June 2016), available at: www.themigrantsfiles.com.
Moniz, M. (2004) 'Exiled home: criminal forced return migration and adaptive transnational identity, the Azores example', PhD dissertation, Department of Anthropology, Brown University.
Nevins, J. and M. Aizeki (2008) *Dying to live: a story of U.S.: immigration in an age of global apartheid*, San Francisco: Open Media/City Lights Books.

Nyers, P. (2003) 'Abject cosmopolitanism: the politics of protection in the anti-deportation movement', *Third World Quarterly*, 24 (6), 1069–93, doi: 10.1080/01436590310001630071.

Peutz, N. (2007) 'Out-laws: deportees, desire, and "the law"', *International Migration*, 45 (3), 182–91, doi: 10.1111/j.1468-2435.2007.00415.x.

Rodkey, E. (2016) 'Disposable labor, repurposed: outsourcing deportees in the call center industry', *Anthropology of Work Review*, 37 (1): 34–43, doi: 10.1111/awr.12083.

RSN (Refugee Support Network) (2016) 'After return: documenting the experiences of young people forcibly removed to Afghanistan', RSN, London, available at: www.refugeesupportnetwork.org/resources/after-return.

Schuster, L. and N. Majidi (2013) 'What happens post-deportation? The experiences of deported Afghans', *Migration Studies*, 1 (2), 221–40, doi: 10.1093/migration/mns011.

Walters, W. (2002) 'Deportation, expulsion, and the international police of aliens', *Citizenship Studies*, 6 (3), 265–92, doi: 10.1080/1362102022000011612.

Walters, W. (2016) 'The flight of the deported: aircraft, deportation, and politics', *Geopolitics*, 21 (2), 435–58, doi: 10.1080/14650045.2015.1089234.

Zilberg, E. (2004) 'Fools banished from the kingdom: remapping geographies of gang violence between the Americas (Los Angeles and San Salvador)', *American Quarterly*, 56 (3), 759–79, doi: 10.1353/aq.2004.0048.

Zilberg, E. (2011) Space of detention: the making of a transnational gang crisis between Los Angeles and San Salvador, Durham, NC: Duke University Press.

22
Diasporicity
Relative embeddedness in transnational and co-ethnic networks

Takeyuki (Gaku) Tsuda

Instead of trying to define diasporas and then engaging in exclusionary intellectual debates about which migratory ethnic groups are diasporic and which are not, I argue that we should examine diasporicity. Diasporicity refers to the relative embeddedness of dispersed ethnic groups in transnational connections to both their ancestral homeland and to their co-ethnics scattered in various countries around the world. Diasporas are not an objective social state (that exists or does not exist) but a relative condition of diasporicity, where some ethnic groups are more diasporic than others. The concept of diasporicity can therefore be used to compare different diasporic groups as well as examine internal differences in a diaspora based on nationality, gender, or immigrant generation. I will discuss the various factors that explain why certain diasporic groups have higher levels of diasporicity than others. The chapter ends with a brief illustration of how this comparative, analytical framework can be applied to the study of the Japanese diaspora.

Defining diasporas

'What is a diaspora?' This has been one of the most fundamental questions in diaspora studies, and it is likely to be subject to ongoing debate. How we define and conceptualize diasporas determines which migratory groups are included in diaspora studies and which characteristics of these groups are emphasized as emblematic of the diasporic condition.

Numerous researchers have noted a dramatic expansion in the meaning and application of the concept of diaspora in recent decades (Adachi 2006: 2; Brubaker 2005: 2; Butler 2001: 189–90; Faist 2010: 12; Safran 1991: 83; Shuval 2000: 42; Tölölyan 1996: 3). Diasporas are now understood to include not only the forced dispersal of persecuted peoples such as the Jews, Armenians, Palestinians and Africans, but also the voluntary scattering of populations around the world for economic, business, colonial and political reasons (see, for example, Bruneau 2010; Butler 2001: 199; Cohen 1997: 28–9, 180–4; Faist 2010: 12; Tölölyan 1996: 12; Van Hear 1998: 6).

In fact, the concept of diaspora seems to have proliferated to such an extent that it is often used to refer to any territorially dispersed population with a homeland, as a number of scholars have noted (Braziel and Mannur 2003: 2–3; Brubaker 2005: 2; Dufoix 2008: 34). Even some migrant groups that are not widely dispersed but reside predominantly in one or two countries, such as

Mexicans, Cubans and Haitians in the United States, are sometimes understood to be diasporic (for example, Clifford 1994: 312, 314; Laguerre 1998; Safran 1991: 90). There are even references to political, gender and musical diasporas (see Brubaker 2005: 2). Although a broader and more inclusive application of the concept of diasporas is to be welcomed, its over-enthusiastic and somewhat indiscriminate application to almost all migratory groups must be avoided (Braziel and Mannur 2003: 2–3; Brubaker 2005: 2–4; Tölölyan 1996: 10). If everything is ultimately diasporic, then nothing is really diasporic and the term eventually loses its meaning and ability to differentiate between different types of migratory groups (see also Brubaker 2005: 2–4).

A number of scholars have therefore advocated a more restricted and limited definition of the term in order to better distinguish between migrants who are diasporic and those who clearly are not (Brubaker 2005: 2–4; Butler 2001: 194; Cohen 1997: 187; Safran 1991: 83; Tölölyan 1996: 10, 30). However, the original definitions of diaspora offered by Robin Cohen (1997: 22–6), William Safran (1991: 83) and Khachig Tölölyan (1996) consisted of extensive lists of six to nine criteria or characteristics (see also Bruneau 2010: 36–7). Since even the most classic diasporic populations do not meet all these criteria (Clifford 1994: 305–6), we are still left with a conundrum: which (and how many) of these fundamental characteristics must a migratory or ethnic population have in order to be considered diasporic?

More recently, scholars have attempted to whittle down these definitional lists to a few (usually three) essential elements that constitute diasporas. They agree that diasporas are ethnic groups that have dispersed to two or more countries and have retained some actual, imagined or mythical connection to their original homelands (Brubaker 2005: 5–6; Butler 2001: 192–4; Faist 2010: 12–13; Parreñas and Siu 2007: 1; Van Hear 1998: 6). However, beyond migratory dispersal and homeland (which are part of all definitions of diasporas), there is less agreement on what the third essential criterion of diasporas should be. The ones that are mentioned are: (1) transnational social relationships between the geographically dispersed ethnic population across national borders; (2) a collective diasporic consciousness and identity; and (3) marginalization and lack of assimilation to the host society.

So which of these is the third essential component that constitutes diasporas? Any choice we make between these three options seems rather arbitrary and is subject to the preferences and interests of individual researchers. Nonetheless, without a third essential definitional component, the concept of diaspora would remain too vague and apply to most of the world's migrant and ethnic groups, which are often dispersed to more than one nation-state and retain some affiliation to a homeland.

Even if we were to agree on the fundamental characteristics of diasporas, such definitional approaches eventually lead to exclusionary intellectual debates about which migratory ethnic groups are diasporic and which are not, as a number of scholars have noted (Clifford 1994: 304–6; Dorais 2010: 94; Lubkemann 2013). In fact, my previous work argued that Japanese Americans are not part of a Japanese diaspora based on a three-part definition (Tsuda 2012a). However, others claim that Japanese descent communities dispersed across the Americas are diasporic (Adachi 2006; White 2003).

Diasporicity

I suggest that the oft-asked question, 'is such-and-such group a diaspora/diasporic?' is the wrong question to ask. Instead of conceptualizing diaspora as an objective social state (which exists, or does not exist), I advance the idea that we understand it as a relative condition of *diasporicity* where some ethnic groups are more diasporic than others. The diasporicity of an ethnic group is defined by its relative degree of embeddedness in transnational social relations and affiliations with both the ethnic homeland and dispersed co-ethnic communities in the diaspora located in other countries.

In contrast to the definitional approach to diasporas, which is based on multiple meanings, diasporicity is grounded on the most constitutive element of diasporas: migratory dispersal from the ethnic homeland and the transnational communities it subsequently produces as scattered populations develop and maintain social connections and identifications with each other across national borders. Diasporas as transnational communities resemble a wheel with the homeland at the centre and the various overseas diasporic communities on the circumference, with the spokes representing their ties to the homeland and the wheel rim representing their connections to each other. Usually, centripetal homeland connections and attachments of diasporic communities are more prevalent and dense than lateral ones across the diaspora. Nonetheless, such lateral transnational connections between dispersed ethnic groups are an equally important part of diasporic analysis.

My use of 'diasporicity' to refer to the relative strength of a dispersed ethnic group's transnational social connections and identifications is different from how it is employed in the literature, where the term is synonymous with diasporas or the diasporic condition in general (for example, Brubaker 2005: 4; Dorais 2010: 94; Klimt and Lubkemann 2002; Lubkemann 2013). As a theoretical move, diasporicity avoids exclusionary debates about whether or not an ethnic group is diasporic, which in turn is based on the different and multiple definitions adopted by individual researchers and intellectually not very productive. Instead of such either/or propositions, diasporicity assumes that all geographically dispersed ethnic populations are diasporic to some extent and simply assesses their level of diasporicity.

Determinants of diasporicity

It is quite evident that different diasporas have varying degrees of diasporicity, which can also change historically over time. In addition, diasporicity can vary within a specific diasporic group depending on differences in nationality, gender or immigrant generation. The concept of diasporicity therefore enables us to compare different diasporic peoples and ultimately attempt to explain why one is more diasporic than another. In this section, I propose several factors that can influence relative levels of diasporicity. There are undoubtedly other determinants of diasporicity as well.

Members of 'victim diasporas' (created by the forced migration of persecuted peoples) tend to have higher levels of diasporicity because they share powerful historical memories of collective persecution, suffering and traumatic dispersal, which can remain a part of their group consciousness for generations and lead to collective solidarity and even mobilization across borders, such as to establish or support a beleaguered homeland or defend against continued ethnic or religious persecution. In contrast, the historical experiences of 'economic diasporas' (peoples who migrated to various countries voluntarily for economic or business reasons) tend to be less powerful and enduring over time, and are less likely to become the basis for collective diasporic communities and transitional social connections.

Diasporas that share the same culture, language and/or religion will likely be more diasporic than those that do not. Despite being scattered geographically, such cultural commonalities and shared religious faith can produce ethnic solidarity across national borders that produces a stronger collective identification as members of a cohesive diasporic community. They can also facilitate communication across national borders, which is essential to transnational diasporic social relations. Needless to say, diasporic groups characterized by internal cultural, linguistic and religious differences are more likely to have weaker or more fragmented diasporic communities and lower levels of diasporicity.

The amount of marginalization and ethnic discrimination that diasporic peoples experience from host societies may also have an impact on their diasporicity. When displaced ethnic communities face considerable socio-economic and ethnic exclusion or persecution, they may become more diasporic by relying more on their transnational ethnic linkages with the homeland and to others in the diaspora as a means to obtain resources, social status and belonging denied them in the host society. In fact, a number of scholars have emphasized how diasporic peoples tend not to be assimilated and socially integrated in the host society and face social marginalization and discrimination (Brubaker 2005: 6; Cohen 1997: 186; Parreñas and Siu 2007: 13; Safran 1991: 83; Shuval 2000: 44). In contrast, other dispersed ethnic groups have become cultural and socially assimilated to their host countries over time, which can lead to an attenuation of their transnational, diasporic connections to homelands and co-ethnic communities abroad. However, a growing number of studies have also documented how the assimilation of immigrants and their descendants is not necessarily incompatible with their continued transnational involvement in countries of ethnic origin (see Tsuda 2012b for a discussion).

The age of a diaspora can also influence diasporicity, since it is related to many of the factors mentioned above. In general, newer diasporic peoples whose migratory dispersal is recent are more likely to have maintained active transnational social connections with both their homeland and co-ethnics in other countries. Because they tend to be less assimilated to their respective host societies, they are more likely to share a common culture and religion and also develop transnational diasporic ties and affiliations with each other in response to the greater level of discrimination they may face as culturally different ethnic minorities. Finally, they may have more recent memories of their migratory dispersal and other common historical experiences (especially if they are victim diasporas) that cause them to maintain transnational social solidarity as a diasporic community. In contrast, older diasporic communities, which consist of later-generation descendants of immigrants, are more likely to have assimilated to different host countries and experience less ethnic discrimination, especially if they live in ethnically inclusive, multicultural societies. As a result, their transnational ethnic attachments to the homeland and to each other have weakened over time, and they often no longer feel much ethnic and cultural commonality as a diasporic peoples.

Studying diasporicity

Among transnational communities, diasporas are probably the most difficult to study because they consist of people scattered over numerous countries, often in different parts of the world. This contrasts with the more limited geographical scope of most other transnational migrant communities, which usually consist of only two localities (the sending and receiving societies). It is almost impossible to conduct extensive ethnographic fieldwork in all (or even most) of the many countries in which a certain diasporic population is scattered. Therefore, although it is possible to write general historical and contemporary overviews of entire diasporic peoples (for example, see Schulz 2003, Van Hear 1998), extensive ethnographic studies of diasporas are quite rare (Levy 2000: 137).

As a result, most in-depth, fieldwork-based research about diasporas focuses on only a part of the diasporic population that resides in one country instead of examining the population in multiple countries. For instance, we have studies of the 'Korean diaspora in Japan' (Ryang and Lie 2009), the 'Chinese diaspora in Australia' (Collins 2002), or the 'Haitian diaspora in the United States' (Laguerre 1998). Although it is certainly possible to do an extensive study of two communities in a diaspora based on multi-sited fieldwork, there are actually very few studies of this nature (for example, see Lee 2016; Parreñas 2015).

The concept of diasporicity helps researchers overcome the inherent difficulties of conducting in-depth, ethnographic studies about diasporas because it does not require us to do long-term fieldwork in numerous, geographically dispersed communities in different countries. In fact, it is possible to do a diasporic analysis based on fieldwork with only one ethnic community in the diaspora by assessing the relative strength of its transnational connections to the ancestral homeland and to co-ethnics residing in other countries, and then explaining its level of diasporicity by referring to the determinants discussed above (or other historical and contemporary reasons). If researchers conduct multi-sited fieldwork in two of the countries in which a diasporic population resides, they would be able to compare the diasporicity of these two communities and explain differences in their transnational embeddedness in homeland and co-ethnic networks. In this manner, the diasporicity of particular ethnic and migrant groups can be studied as part of the broader diasporic community of which they are a part. An analysis of one segment of a diaspora can therefore illuminate the experiences of the entire diaspora (Butler 2001: 195).

The diasporicity of the Japanese diaspora

In order to illustrate how the concept of diasporicity can be used as an analytical, comparative and explanatory framework, I will briefly examine the Japanese diaspora. The population of the Japanese diaspora has been estimated at three million people worldwide (Adachi 2006: 1), and it is considered to be one of the world's major diasporas (see Brubaker 2005: 3; Butler 2001: 201; Cohen 1997: 22, 28, 178).

Japanese have been emigrating from the homeland for well over a century and have scattered to various countries, primarily in the Americas, mainly for economic reasons (thus, the Japanese diaspora is an economic or labour diaspora) (Cohen 1997: 178). Substantial Japanese emigration to the Americas started around the 1880s, initially to North America (mainly to the United States but also to Canada) and lasted for several decades. Emigration to Latin America began in the early 1900s (predominantly to Brazil but also to other South and Central American countries) and continued into the 1960s. Many of these emigrants were from Japan's rural areas, which were suffering from overpopulation and economic difficulties, and they went to the Americas to fill labour shortages as agricultural workers.

Beginning in the late 1960s, Japanese again started emigrating from a now economically prosperous Japan as businessmen, professionals and students, initially to the United States and Europe, but more recently to other countries around the world as well. However, the post-war emigration of highly skilled Japanese has been relatively limited in number, and a majority of them reside abroad only temporarily. As a result, the Japanese diaspora is now becoming older and mainly consists of Japanese descendants of the second, third and fourth generations (called *nikkei* or *nikkeijin*), who reside primarily in North and South America.

Despite their migratory dispersal from the Japanese homeland to predominantly one part of the world, diasporic *nikkei* communities in the Americas have a relatively low level of diasporicity for a number of reasons. Because they are an older diaspora, their centripetal transnational ties to Japan have generally weakened over time, and they have also not developed notable lateral ethnic connections and affiliations with each other (Tsuda 2016: 261–8; White 2003: 316). Unlike newer, first-generation diasporas, these dispersed populations of Japanese-descent *nikkeijin* are generations old and have assimilated to their respective host societies, which has led to the attenuation of both their homeland diasporicity and their transnational ethnic connections to Japanese descent communities elsewhere in the Americas.

Because of considerable socio-economic mobility since the Second World War, Japanese descendants in the Americas are now part of the highly educated and successful urban middle class and are generally well regarded by majority host populations as 'model minorities'. As a result, they no longer experience significant socio-economic marginalization and ethnic discrimination, and therefore have relatively little incentive to reach out to their ethnic homeland or to diasporic co-ethnics in other countries for transnational ethnic belonging or social and cultural resources.

In addition, as an economic diaspora, the *nikkei* in the Americas do not share a strong historical memory of past persecution and traumatic migratory dispersal (unlike classic victim diasporas), nor has there been any collective ethnic or political mobilization across borders to defend themselves or their homeland from persecution, which would increase their diasporicity and transnational community cohesion. Finally, the weak diasporicity of the Japanese diaspora in the Americas is also the result of cultural differences and fragmentation. The *nikkeijin* do not share a common language and are divided among English, Portuguese and Spanish speakers. Japanese is spoken only by a limited number of first-generation migrants and some second-generation descendants and is rapidly disappearing as a common language that unifies the diasporic community. Likewise, the *nikkeijin* do not have a strong and common religious faith as a basis for ethnic solidarity across national borders. Although some have remained Buddhist, others have been raised as Christians, and a significant portion of the diaspora (especially in North America) are agnostic.

However, despite its generally low diasporicity, there are significant comparative differences in diasporicity between different nationalities in the Japanese diaspora. This was evident when I conducted fieldwork among Japanese Americans in the United States and Japanese Brazilians in Brazil, which are the two largest *nikkei* communities in the Japanese diaspora. Compared to Japanese Americans, Japanese Brazilians have stronger and more significant diasporic connections to the ethnic homeland because of their ethnic return migration to Japan, causing many of them to live in cohesive, transnational communities spanning two countries (see Tsuda 2003: chapter 4). Like other developing countries in South America, Brazil suffered from a severe economic crisis in the late 1980s, causing many Japanese Brazilians to return migrate to Japan as unskilled immigrant workers, where they earn five to ten times their Brazilian middle-class incomes. In contrast, Japanese Americans, living in an economically prosperous country in the developed world, have not migrated to Japan in significant numbers and do so mainly as short-term tourists, exchange students and highly skilled professionals. Such generally brief sojourns do not lead to sustained transnational engagement with Japan (Tsuda 2016: chapter 8).

In addition to their low homeland diasporicity, Japanese Americans do not have any notable lateral transnational ties with Japanese descendants in other countries and have little awareness of them, especially those living in South America (see Tsuda 2016: chapter 8). Because the host country of the Japanese Americans is positioned at the top of the global geopolitical and economic order, they seem to have less interest in Japanese Brazilians and other South American *nikkei*, who are positioned lower in the diaspora (just as Americans in general have less interest and knowledge about South America because of its lower significance for them). In contrast, Japanese Brazilians are much more aware of Japanese Americans because they (like other Brazilians) focus their attention on the United States, which is the most powerful country in the Americas and has a significant impact on the entire region.

In addition, Japanese Brazilians have also developed greater diasporic ethnic relations and affiliations with other Japanese-descent co-ethnics who live in South America. This is partly because they are in closer geographical proximity to these other Japanese-descent communities. However, there are also fewer cultural differences between them and other South American *nikkei* compared to the greater cultural differences between Japanese Americans and South Americans of Japanese descent. Not only do Japanese Brazilians have more cultural commonalities with other South American *nikkei*, they also share a similar and mutually intelligible language (Portuguese and Spanish speakers can communicate with each other to a considerable extent).

Conclusion

I have argued that instead of asking whether a dispersed ethnic group is sufficiently diasporic to qualify as diaspora, we should be asking 'how diasporic are they and why?' This question enables us to first assess the extent to which dispersed ethnic groups are transnationally engaged with each other and with the ethnic homeland. Diasporas are therefore not an absolute state but a relative condition of diasporicity. Instead of being defined in exclusionary ways, they should be positioned on a continuum depending on how diasporic they are in relation to others.

The concept of diasporicity can therefore be used to compare different diasporic groups as well as examine internal differences in a diaspora based on nationality, gender or immigrant generation. There are undoubtedly many reasons why certain diasporic peoples have stronger transnational connections and communities than others, which are related to the causes of their diasporic dispersal, their level of cultural similarity, their marginalization and discrimination from host societies, and the amount of time they have been living in the diaspora. In this way, diasporicity provides a framework for researchers to empirically assess, compare and explain the characteristics of transnational ethnic groups constituted by migratory dispersal.

Acknowledgement

The first two sections of this chapter are taken from Chapter 8 of my book, *Japanese American ethnicity: in search of heritage and homeland across generations* (Tsuda 2016).

References

Adachi, N. (2006) 'Introduction: theorizing Japanese diaspora', in N. Adachi (ed.) *Japanese diasporas: unsung pasts, conflicting presents, and uncertain futures*, London: Routledge, 1–22.
Braziel, J. and A. Mannur (2003) 'Nation, migration, globalization: points of contention in diaspora studies', in J. Braziel and A. Mannur (eds) *Theorizing diaspora: a reader*, Malden, MA: Blackwell, 1–22.
Brubaker, R. (2005) 'The "diaspora" diaspora', *Ethnic and Racial Studies*, 28 (1), 1–19, doi: 10.1080/0141987042000289997.
Bruneau, M. (2010) 'Diasporas, transnational spaces and dommunities', in R. Bauböck and T. Faist (eds) *Diaspora and transnationalism: concepts, theories and methods*, Amsterdam: Amsterdam University Press, 35–50.
Butler, K. (2001) 'Defining diaspora, refining a discourse', *Diaspora: A Journal of Transnational Studies*, 10 (2), 189–219, doi: 10.1353/dsp.2011.0014.
Clifford, J. (1994) 'Diasporas', *Cultural Anthropology*, 9 (3), 302–38, doi: 10.1525/can.1994.9.3.02a00040.
Cohen, R. (1997) *Global diasporas: an introduction*, Seattle: University of Washington Press.
Collins, J. (2002) 'Chinese entrepreneurs: the Chinese diaspora in Australia', *International Journal of Entrepreneurial Behaviour and Research*, 8 (1/2), 113–33, doi: 10.1108/13552550210423750.
Dorais, L. (2010) 'Politics, kinship, and ancestors: some diasporic dimensions of the Vietnamese experience in North America', *Journal of Vietnamese Studies*, 5 (2), 91–132, doi: 10.1525/vs.2010.5.2.91.
Dufoix, S. (2008) *Diasporas*, Berkeley: University of California Press.
Faist, T. (2010) 'Diaspora and transnationalism: what kind of dance partners?', in R. Bauböck and T. Faist (eds) *Diaspora and transnationalism: concepts, theories and methods*, Amsterdam: Amsterdam University Press, 9–34.
Klimt A. and S. Lubkemann (2002) 'Argument across the Portuguese-speaking world: a discursive approach to diaspora', *Diaspora: A Journal of Transnational Studies*, 11 (2), 145–62, doi: 10.1353/dsp.2011.0021.
Laguerre, M. S. (1998) *Diasporic citizenship: Haitian Americans in transnational America*, New York: St. Martin's Press.
Lee, S. (2016) 'Between the diaspora and the nation-state: transnational continuity and fragmentation among Hmong in Laos and the United States', PhD dissertation, University of Oxford.
Levy, A. (2000) 'Diasporas through anthropological lenses: contexts of postmodernity', *Diaspora: A Journal of Transnational Studies*, 9 (1), 137–57, doi: 10.1353/dsp.2000.0008.

Lubkemann, S. (2013) 'Diasporicity and its discontents: Liberian identity arguments and the irresolution of return (1820–2013)', paper presented at the African Studies 56th Association Annual Meeting, available at: https://ssrn.com/abstract=2236902.

Parreñas, R. (2015) *Servants of globalization: migration and domestic work*, second edition, Stanford, CA: Stanford University Press.

Parreñas, R. and L. Siu. (2007) 'Introduction: Asian diasporas—new conceptions, new frameworks', in R. Parreñas and L. Siu (eds) *Asian diasporas: new formations, new conceptions*, Stanford: Stanford University Press, 1–27.

Ryang, S. and J. Lie (2009) *Diaspora without homeland: being Korean in Japan*, Berkeley: University of California Press.

Safran, W. (1991) 'Diasporas in modern societies: myths of homeland and return', *Diaspora: A Journal of Transnational Studies*, 1 (1), 83–99, doi: 10.1353/dsp.1991.0004.

Schulz, H. (2003) *The Palestinian diaspora: formation of identities and politics of homeland*, London: Routledge.

Shuval, J. (2000) 'Diaspora migration: definitional ambiguities and a theoretical paradigm', *International Migration*, 38 (5), 41–56, doi: 10.1111/1468-2435.00127.

Tölölyan, K. (1996) 'Rethinking *diaspora*(s): stateless power in the transnational moment', *Diaspora: A Journal of Transnational Studies*, 5 (1), 3–36, doi: 10.1353/dsp.1996.0000.

Tsuda, T. (2003) *Strangers in the ethnic homeland: Japanese Brazilian return migration in transnational perspective*, New York: Columbia University Press.

Tsuda, T. (2012a) 'Disconnected from the 'diaspora': Japanese Americans and the lack of transnational ethnic networks', *Journal of Anthropological Research*, 68 (2), 95–116, doi: 10.3998/jar.0521004.0068.104.

Tsuda, T. (2012b) 'Whatever happened to simultaneity? Transnational migration theory and dual engagement in sending and receiving countries', *Journal of Ethnic and Migration Studies*, 38 (4), 631–49, doi: 10.1080/1369183X.2012.659126.

Tsuda, T. (2016) *Japanese American ethnicity: in search of heritage and homeland across generations*, New York: New York University Press.

Van Hear, N. (1998) *New diasporas: the mass exodus, dispersal and regrouping of migrant communities*, Seattle: University of Washington Press.

White, P. (2003) 'The Japanese in Latin America: on the uses of diaspora', *International Journal of Population Geography*, 9 (4), 309–22, doi: 10.1002/ijpg.289.

23
Moral comforts of remaining in exile
Snapshots from conflict-generated Indonesian diasporas

Antje Missbach

At present, between two and eight million of a total population of about 255 million Indonesians are living temporarily or permanently outside their home country as migrant workers, expatriates, international students, spouses or refugees. The wide divergence in the estimated number arises because some international datasets relating to migrants only include Indonesian-born people living abroad and exclude subsequent generations and other overseas Indonesians not born in Indonesia (Muhidin and Utomo 2015: 95). Most overseas Indonesians live in Malaysia, Saudi Arabia, the United Arab Emirates, Bangladesh, Singapore, the Netherlands, the USA, Kuwait and Australia. While the Indonesian government has paid little attention to overseas Indonesians in the past, it is now doing so, partly because of dramatic cases of the abuse of female labour migrants by their employers (Palmer 2016). As well as taking greater responsibility for citizens in need of support overseas, the Indonesian government has, since 2010, begun to acknowledge the economic potential of its global diaspora, which could become a valuable national resource in terms of remittances, foreign direct investment and socio-economic developments initiated by returning Indonesians. The Indonesian Ministry of Foreign Affairs has established an Indonesian Diaspora Desk, at ambassadorial level, and diaspora congresses are held annually with the support of political leaders (Muhidin and Utomo 2015). While the economic potential is sought after, and cultural activities might get support as 'soft power' agents, the political activities of distant diasporans wanting to interfere in Indonesian politics are not appreciated at all. Yet, among the many Indonesians overseas, there is a small number who – from a safe distance and with little to lose – aspire to be political spokespersons in international fora on behalf of their co-ethnics back home. Disengaged from the often-complex real politics on the ground, they establish a kind of moral superiority for themselves and, in making their political demands and forwarding their political visions, show little will to compromise and little pragmatism or sensitivity.

Indonesians overseas: drivers of diasporic cohesion

Many Indonesians overseas and their kin maintain links with other Indonesians abroad and frequently form cultural associations and ensembles. However, because they are from a multi-ethnic and multi-faith country, they are inclined to form groups based on ethnic and linguistic links and connections, rather than on their shared citizenship or former nationality. For example, Papuans and Moluccans tend to form their own networks rather than mingle with the Javanese, Indonesia's largest ethnic group. Social and cultural activities not only enhance cohesion among Indonesians in their host countries, but also help them connect with friends and family back home, and, more broadly, with their home country (Dragojlovic 2016; Winarnita 2015). Modern technology has greatly improved long-distance communication and enabled individual and collective transnational activities that connect overseas Indonesians with Indonesians at home. The emergence of affordable new means of communication (fax, email, chat forums) supports new forms of sociality and makes it easier for members of a diaspora to build and maintain bonds across distance and over time. Without this, diasporic long-distance politics would hardly be able to play out.

Most Indonesians living overseas left Indonesia voluntarily, but some are asylum-seekers and refugees from their home country who tend to form political interest groups in the diaspora that seek to influence Indonesian politics. Under certain circumstances, migrant communities can also engage in diasporization, defined here as the formation of communities of solidarity founded on victimization and suffering (Missbach 2011b). Engagement in diasporization has been particularly observable among Papuans, Moluccans, East Timorese and Acehnese, most of whom left Indonesia to escape armed conflict and political persecution. In the provinces that were home to these ethnic groups, there have been secessionist movements and conflict at some point in time. These four groups are examples of 'conflict-generated diasporas', characterized by political features that derive from 'a specific set of traumatic memories' (Lyons 2007: 529). Over the last 60 years, members of these conflict-generated diasporas have sought to further their separatist and ethno-nationalist ambitions from afar by militant and terrorist, as well as diplomatic and peaceful, means. Their activities have been thoroughly documented, for example by Amanda Wise (2004, 2006) and Goodman (2000), on East Timorese in Australia; Richard Chauvel (2009a, 2009b), on West Papuans in Australia and the Netherlands; Antje Missbach (2011a, 2011b), on the Acehnese in Malaysia and Scandinavia; and Hans van Amersfoort (2004) and Fridus Steijlen (2010), on Moluccans in the Netherlands. As conflict-generated diasporas, these groups often exhibit an assertiveness in that they are 'less willing to compromise and therefore reinforce and exacerbate the protractedness of homeland conflicts' (Lyons 2007: 529).

The Moluccan diaspora in the Netherlands deserves special mention here, for it is one of the oldest Indonesian diasporas, has existed for two generations and, more importantly, has been through three stages of diaspora politics. Indonesia declared independence from the Dutch in 1945, a few days after the atomic bombs were dropped on Japan and the unconditional surrender of the Japanese occupying forces during the Second World War, but it was not long before the Dutch sought to re-establish their power there. There were many Christian soldiers from the Moluccas in the Dutch army who had enjoyed special privileges under colonial rule. Although they were better equipped technically, the Dutch lost to the young Indonesian forces in 1949. Dissatisfied with the Indonesian republican victory, the Republic of the South Moluccas was proclaimed in April 1950 on the islands of Seram, Ambon and Buru, only to be defeated by Indonesian forces in November 1950 everywhere except Seram, where armed struggle continued until December 1963. As a reward for their loyalty and to guarantee their personal safety, about 3,500 Moluccan military personnel along with their families (approximately 12,500 people) were taken to the Netherlands in 1951 (Steijlen 2010).

On the assumption that their stay would only be temporary, the Moluccans were housed in camps isolated from the Dutch population. Because of political developments in Indonesia, however, they remained in the Netherlands for much longer than originally anticipated, but were not integrated socially or economically. Longing to return to the Moluccas and marginalized in the

Netherlands, the Moluccan diaspora became increasingly politicized, and its political engagement went through several stages. In 1966, a government in exile was formed in the Netherlands, which still exists. In the 1970s, the diaspora went through a fundamental radicalization and engaged in violent acts to draw attention to the Moluccan cause; for example, in 1970, 33 young Moluccans attacked the residence of the Indonesian ambassador in Wassenaar, killing a policeman and taking hostages for a day; and in 1975, seven Moluccans hijacked a train in the northern Netherlands, taking 54 hostages, to which the Dutch authorities responded with full force. Initially, the Moluccan community supported this radical behaviour, but most Moluccans soon distanced themselves from these 'acts of despair' (Steijlen 2010: 150) and returned to less violent and less radical activism. The second generation of Moluccans in the Netherlands was better integrated socially and politically, and, rather than anticipating a return to an independent Republic of the South Moluccas one day, which always had more support among the diaspora in the Netherlands than among the inhabitants of the Moluccas, they visited Indonesia to gather information first hand and helped channel development funding and donations from the Netherlands to small-scale community projects in the Moluccas. An estimated 42,000–50,000 Moluccans and Dutch of Moluccan descent now live in the Netherlands. Although the Moluccan community is still tightly knit, its activism has in many respects been depoliticized. Similar observations can be made of the East Timorese abroad, who once drove the struggle for independence, with the help of many non-Timorese groups and of the Catholic Church (Wise 2004). Once East Timor seceded from Indonesia, the attention of the East Timorese diaspora turned to the development of the new state (Timor Leste). Politically, the Timorese diaspora lost much of its former influence, not least because many leaders decided to return to Timor. Other Indonesian diasporas, such as the Papuan and the Acehnese, continue their long-distance struggle for the independence of their homelands.

Long-distance nationalism

Long-distance nationalism is not a new phenomenon; it has been attributed to diasporas and described by many writers and observers (Anderson 1998; Schiller 2005; Steijlen 2010; Wise 2004). Benedict Anderson (1994) hinted at the convenience of engaging from afar in this sort of armchair nationalism, which is characterized not only by a lack of accountability but also by living free of harm outside zones of danger and violent retribution. Although there were legal repercussions for Moluccan militant radicals in exile, they did not suffer the same cruelties as their peers in the Moluccas, many of whom were killed by Indonesian military. Rather than risk life and limb in Aceh, Acehnese diaspora leaders issued orders and moral encouragement to the fighters in the jungle.

There are many underlying political ideologies that can drive long-distance nationalism in attempts to create a new ethno-nationalist state. The East Timorese were more left-leaning, feeling ideologically close to newly liberated former colonies in Asia and Africa. After the Portuguese colonizers left and before the Indonesian occupation of East Timor, they wanted to build a socially progressive independent state under a leftist government. The Acehnese, on the other hand, have been more reactionary, at times even favouring the revival of the monarchy defeated by the Dutch at the end of the nineteenth century as the form of government in their independent state. The political visions of an independent state of Papua remain highly ambiguous (Myrttinen 2015).

Many scholars of diasporas and long-distance nationalism have identified only the risks of long-distance involvement, such as peace-wrecking and conflict-mongering. Maria Koinova (2011), in her study of Albanian, Armenian and Chechen diasporas and the conflicts in Kosovo, Karabakh and Chechnya during the 1990s, found that diasporas tend to become radicalized with regards to conflict in their homeland when human rights are gravely violated and when moderate elites in their homeland begin to lose credibility in their ability to achieve a secessionist goal. Over time, however, some scholars have also pointed out the potential for diasporas to become peacemakers in helping to resolve conflict in their home countries (Smith and Stares 2007). There is also a growing literature on other examples of positive involvement and political mobilization of diasporas in post-conflict peace-building, reconstruction and development (Abusabib 2007; Brinkerhoff 2008). Rebuilding the home country is often linked to permanent or temporary return of members of the diaspora. Many prominent diaspora figures returned to newly independent Timor Leste to help build the new state (Wise 2006). The Acehnese diaspora is also very indicative of this (Missbach 2011a) and is worth explaining further.

There are Acehnese diasporans in many places; most live in nearby Malaysia but several hundred resettled as refugees in Denmark, Sweden, Norway, Canada and the USA, or migrated independently to Australia. Malaysia was easy to reach by boat and already hosted many economic migrants from Aceh who had set up rudimentary community structures on which newcomers could rely. Like the Moluccans, the Acehnese were fighting for separation from Indonesia. In 1976, they established a guerrilla movement in Aceh, the Acheh-Sumatra National Liberation Front (ASNLF) or *Gerakan Aceh Merdeka* (GAM), but its attacks were sporadic and the Indonesian military soon quelled the insurgency. Military defeat did not, however, put an end to their secessionist ambitions. The movement's most eminent leaders left Aceh – the Malaysian environment was not conducive to their activities – and formed a government in exile in Sweden. From their cosy diasporic homes, the leaders not only organized the training of Acehnese guerrillas in Libya, which helped the conflict in Aceh to flare up again in the late 1990s, but also organized petitions, lobbied international governments and drew attention to human rights violations (Missbach 2011b). Unlike the Moluccans, the Acehnese did not become involved in kidnapping in the host countries, as they lacked the means to do so, but more importantly such acts were not part of their overall strategy. Rather, they preferred to organize international awareness campaigns and lobbying. While the East Timorese diaspora and its struggle for the independence of their country received international support from solidarity groups and the Catholic Church and benefited considerably from the awarding of the Nobel Peace Prize in 1996 to two of its most prominent leaders, Carlos Filipe Ximenes Belo and José Ramos-Horta, which provided a '"moral" dimension to the resistance' (Wise 2004: 165), the Acehnese diaspora was less able to garner the support of prominent international advocates, partly because they focused solely on their political struggle and did not orient their campaigning to broader cultural values and aspirations shared by other ethnic minorities or oppressed people. The East Timorese turned their fight for ethnic independence into a struggle for 'universal human freedom' (Wise 2004: 170) and won the high-profile support of Nelson Mandela.

At the height of the armed conflict in Aceh in 2004, at least 80,000 Acehnese left Indonesia in search of protection overseas. The Aceh conflict lasted until mid-2005, when international brokers facilitated a Memorandum of Understanding (referred to as the MoU Helsinki), which ended the conflict between the government in exile and the Indonesian government. Unlike East Timor, Aceh remained part of Indonesia, but was granted special regional autonomy. This was not what the government in exile and its supporters in the diaspora had hoped for, but following the tsunami that hit Aceh in late 2004, killing tens of thousands and causing widespread devastation, the government in exile could no longer condone more bloodshed. While the people in Aceh enthusiastically embraced the end of the conflict, the government in exile faced stern criticism from some sections of the diaspora.

Given that the Acehnese diaspora was formed long after the Moluccan one in the Netherlands, when the conflict ended, political leadership was still in the hands of first-generation diasporans.

For these people, because the conflict in Aceh had been the main reason for their exile, many returned to Aceh after 2005. Some were interested in claiming political power, as the East Timorese leaders had been; others were keen to become involved in the very lucrative business of post-tsunami reconstruction. Initially, core members of the Acehnese government in exile delayed their return, as they did not entirely trust the peace process they had helped to create, but they too made their way home to the political and economic options that awaited them, and some even took up Indonesian citizenship once again (Missbach 2011a, 2011b). Once they had left the diaspora, political leadership of the remaining diaspora was taken up by a younger generation, which has brought a flicker of hope for those in Aceh who wish to continue the struggle for independence in the future.

Deciding not to return

The question of whether to return or to remain overseas is for many conflict-generated diasporas crucial and has, therefore, been the focus of considerable academic attention (Kibreab 2002; King and Christou 2011; Long and Oxfeld 2004; Stepputat 1994; Tsuda 2009). While returnees have been most closely studied thus far, the study of the motivations and activities of those who choose to remain in the diaspora also offers new insights.

Among those Acehnese who decided to stay overseas for good, two political trends can be observed. Some of the formerly very vocal and politically engaged diaspora became 'ordinary migrants' and began to consolidate their personal situation in the host country, seeking to improve their careers and living conditions. As Fridus Steijlen (2010) observed among the Moluccans in the Netherlands who set aside their ambitions for an independent state, these Acehnese lost interest in supporting secession from afar, for all sorts of reasons. Some former political actors said that they had lost hope for their cause and saw no chance of independence in the current circumstances. Not only had the former guerrilla fighters in Aceh been disarmed during the peace process, but also many had joined the political machinery of local and national parties that seemed to offer greater promise in furthering their individual political and economic ambitions rather than the welfare of the people in Aceh. In post-conflict Aceh, there was much corruption, as well as a turn towards more conservative religious ideas and politics, including the partial introduction of sharia, which was widely rejected in the diaspora (Missbach 2016).

Thus, while some of the remaining diaspora became more apolitical, concentrating instead on the cultural aspects of community life, others were politically reactivated. After a period of confusion over who would take over from the former government in exile, the most prominent members of which had returned to Aceh, a younger generation of diaspora leaders emerged (Missbach 2011a; UNPO 2016). The new leaders had not witnessed Hasan Tiro's declaration of independence in Aceh in December 1976 and had neither been trained in Libya nor fought in Aceh. They lack martial reputation and gravitas, yet they have quickly learned how to become representatives of ethnic minorities in international fora, such as the Unrepresented Nations and Peoples Organization (UNPO). Although their views are not widely accepted by the people in Aceh, they are very active, online and in the diaspora

Renewed long-distance politics

Although the agents of Acehnese diaspora politics have changed, the narratives and arguments produced and distributed by the diaspora have, by and large, remained the same. Any adjustment to the depiction of Aceh's history of suffering is only in nuance or arising from events since the MoU Helsinki (Ariffadhillah 2016). The depiction of political oppression and economic exploitation by the Indonesian government in Jakarta continues to underpin the demand for independence (Aspinall 2009). Diaspora leaders often pay little attention to factual correctness in their telling of history, which is a history of suffering and unjust defeat that ignores periods of peace and prosperity and the betrayal of the independence cause by Acehnese leaders. Yet, they have managed to create a storyline of events (massacres, human rights violations and impunity) that is, at first sight, convincing. Needless to say, the violence exercised by guerrillas does not feature in that storyline. The MoU Helsinki included a provision to establish a commission for truth and reconciliation, but this has not yet materialized. Lack of political will is not only the fault of the Indonesian government, but is also evident in current local government in Aceh, which consists of many former guerrillas whose enthusiasm is dampened by the complex mixture of political interests and compromise. Far away from such real-political practicalities, diaspora leaders can occupy the moral high ground and 'call on the international communities to support the people of Acheh in its struggles for justice, democracy, self-determination and independence' (Ariffadhillah 2016). At the same time, repeated commemoration of the tragic events of the past reinforces persistent feelings of loss and victimization. A UNPO (2016) report on a recent diaspora event illustrates this persistence:

> The General Assembly spanned across two full days, from morning until evening. The process was emotionally involving, democratic, and dynamic, leaving attendees confronted by a myriad of emotions, namely melancholy, happiness, and gratitude. Participants felt sorrow upon contemplation of all the fallen martyrs who defended Acheh over the last 143 years.

Events and commemorations held in the diaspora are reported back to Aceh. A few overseas Acehnese try to place their writings in local newspapers in Aceh, and, if they cannot, they publish them online. The impact of these press reports on the local readers in Aceh is hard to measure, but a recent field trip to Aceh provided little evidence of any profound impact. Nevertheless, given that many people in Aceh consider they have missed out on the dividends of the recent peace, there is, at least in theory, the possibility that disillusioned people in Aceh might reconnect with their overseas diaspora and its ethno-nationalist ideology and anti-government sentiments (Grayman 2016). Whereas the fortieth anniversary of the declaration of independence was celebrated in most diasporic locations, in Aceh it was only celebrated in the rural peripheries.

Meanwhile, lacking financial means and human resources, the leaders remaining in the diaspora proceed rather pragmatically, piggybacking on events and opportunities to prepare themselves for the future. For example, young members of the diaspora participate in media and lobbying training, through which they become familiar with the basics of public diplomacy, communications and United Nations mechanisms, such as its periodic review of human rights developments in all member states (Serambi Indonesia 2016). Their approach follows the example of the East Timorese leaders, who set up a diplomacy training school in Sydney to teach students how to communicate with high-level politicians and officials (Wise 2006). This renewed activism has already borne fruit; for example, a representative of the Acehnese diaspora delivered a statement at the ninth session of the Human Rights Council Forum on Minority Issues in Geneva in 2016, just before the official representative of the Indonesian government spoke. Yet, while the international fora might be prepared to listen to the concerns of the Acehnese diaspora, the people in Aceh are mainly interested in upholding the current peace in Aceh, so are less eager to hear the call or promote their cause in the media.

Conclusion

This chapter started by noting that Indonesians overseas are not a homogeneous diaspora and that the Indonesian refugee communities, for whom issues of displacement, return and longing for the home country are paramount, differ considerably from those of other Indonesian migrant communities. Conflict-generated Indonesian diasporas are emotionally charged, causing considerable difference in their activities overseas. Although some of these diasporas are too small to be of economic importance in Indonesia, they can uphold utopian projects that can become serious irritants for the government of their home country. As the example of the Acehnese who chose to remain overseas after the conflict had ended in their home country has shown, the prospect of an independent Aceh has become more of a utopian vision of paradise than ever, which has for now spared them from the potential disillusion of return and allowed them to continue holding the moral high-ground (Missbach 2011b). While they continue to avoid the messy reality of real politics within Aceh, the remaining diaspora and its political representatives are free to indulge in an aspirational human rights discourse and utopian visions of a prosperous and independent Aceh. Their insistence on the original goals of the independence movement might not win them immediate success, but it gives them moral comfort and a justification for not returning to their adored home country. Since the end of violent conflict, it is harder for them to explain their continuing absence from Aceh, as the conflict was their main *raison d'être* for living in the diaspora.

Not wanting to appear as ordinary economic migrants who seek to better their individual destinies, the remaining diasporans must demonstrate their commitment to the homeland even more vigorously and insist on an almost impossible ultimatum – independence – as a condition for their return. However, those who remain in the diaspora have no intention of becoming involved in politics in Aceh. To do so would require their return, their candidature in local elections and, if elected, their openness to compromise and bargaining with other stakeholders to establish priorities, which can at times become a very vexed process indeed. By choosing not to get their hands dirty, and by engaging in politics from afar, those who remain in the diaspora concentrate on sterile interventions through the internet, in which they offer sharp critical commentary and document their efforts in holding the moral high-ground in international fora. By not engaging in local politics but criticizing them from afar, the diaspora activists maintain their moral superiority over those who returned to Aceh, as they can demonstrate a kind of purity in their struggle for their political goals – independence without the compromise of such things as special autonomy. Their risk of failure is very much reduced, not only because they campaign for the most pristine version of their political utopia (a just state and a benevolent elite, free from corruption and self-interest), but also because they hold no real potentially corrupting power. Occasionally, local media in Aceh have decided not to report on their activities, leaving social media as their main sphere of engagement, but this may change when frustration with real politics in Aceh grows and the Acehnese might once again look for leadership from afar.

References

Abusabib, M. (2007) 'Sudanese diaspora in Sweden: challenges and prospects for contribution to democratization and reconstruction effort in Sudan', in Ulf Johansson Dahre (ed.) *The role of diasporas in peace, democracy and development in the Horn of Africa*, Lund: Lund University, 117–22.

Anderson, B. (1994) 'Exodus', *Critical Inquiry*, 20 (2), 314–27, doi: 10.1086/448713.

Anderson, B. (1998) 'Long-distance nationalism', in B. Anderson, *The spectre of comparisons: nationalism, Southeast Asia and the world*, London: Verso, 58–74.

Ariffadhillah (2016) 'Human rights in Acheh: implementing the Helsinki agreements', speech by the chairman of presidium at European Parliament, Brussels, 14 June, available at: www.asnlf.se/eng/Chairman_of_Presidium_14_June_2016.html.

Aspinall, E. (2009) *Islam and nation: separatist rebellion in Aceh, Indonesia*, Stanford, CA: Stanford University Press.

Brinkerhoff, J. M. (2008) 'Exploring the role of diasporas in rebuilding governance in post-conflict societies', in R. Bardouille, M. Ndulo and M. Grieco (eds) *Africa's finances: the contribution of remittances*, Newcastle: Cambridge Scholars Publishing, 239–62.

Chauvel, R. (2009a) 'From the ramparts of Fort Victoria: knowing Indonesia through a distant mirror', *Review of Indonesian and Malaysian Affairs*, 43 (1), 165–87.

Chauvel, R. (2009b) *Between guns and dialogue: Papua after the exile's return*, APSNet Policy Forum, 23 April 2009, available at: http://nautilus.org/apsnet/between-guns-and-dialogue-papua-after-the-exiles-return/.

Dragojlovic, A. (2016) *Beyond Bali: subaltern citizens and post-colonial intimacy*, Amsterdam: Amsterdam University Press.

Goodman, J. (2000) 'Marginalisation and empowerment: East Timorese diaspora politics in Australia', *Communal/Plural*, 8 (1), 25–46.

Grayman, J. H. (2016) 'Official and unrecognized narratives of recovery in post conflict Aceh, Indonesia', *Critical Asian Studies*, 48 (4), 528–55, doi: 10.1080/14672715.2016.1224125.

Kibreab, G. (2002) 'When refugees come home: the relationship between stayees and returnees in post-conflict Eritrea', *Journal of Contemporary African Studies*, 20 (1), 53–80, doi: 10.1080/02589000120104053.

King, R. and A. Christou (2011) 'Of counter-diaspora and reverse transnationalism: return mobilities to and from the ancestral homeland', *Mobilities*, 6 (4), 451–66. doi: 10.1080/17450101.2011.603941.

Koinova, M. (2011) 'Diasporas and secessionist conflicts: the mobilization of the Armenian, Albanian and Chechen diasporas', *Ethnic and Racial Studies*, 34 (2), 333–56, doi: 10.1080/01419870.2010.489646.

Long, L. D. and E. Oxfeld (eds) (2004) *Coming home? Refugees, migrants, and those who stayed behind*, Philadelphia: University of Pennsylvania.

Lyons, T. (2007) 'Conflict-generated diasporas and transnational politics in Ethiopia', *Conflict, Security and Development*, 7 (4), 529–49, doi: 10.1080/14678800701692951.

Missbach, A. (2011a) 'The Acehnese diaspora after the Helsinki Memorandum of Understanding: return challenges and diasporic post-conflict transformations', *Asian Ethnicity*, 12 (2), 179–201, doi: 10.1080/14631369.2011.571836.

Missbach, A. (2011b) *Politics and conflict in Indonesia: the role of the Acehnese diaspora*, New York: Routledge.

Missbach, A. (2016) '"That is Jakarta's project": views from the Acehnese diaspora on Shari'a, self-determination and political conspiracy', in M. Feener, D. Kloos and A. Samuels (eds) *Islam and the limits of the state: reconfigurations of practice, community and authority in contemporary Aceh*, Leiden: Brill, 214–40.

Muhidin, S. and A. Utomo (2015) 'Global Indonesian diaspora: how many are there and where are they?' *Journal of ASEAN Studies*, 3 (2), 93–101, doi: 10.21512/jas.v3i2.847.

Myrttinen, H. (2015) 'Under two flags: encounters with Israel, Merdeka and the promised land in Tanah Papua', in M. Slama and J. Munro (eds) *From 'stone-age' to 'real-time': exploring Papuan temporalities, mobilities, and religiosities*, Canberra: ANU Press, 125–44.

Palmer, W. (2016) *Indonesia's overseas labour migration programme, 1969–2010*, Leiden: Brill.

Schiller, N. G. (2005) 'Long-distance nationalism', in M. Ember, C. R. Ember and I. Skoggard (eds) *Encyclopaedia of diasporas: immigrant and refugee cultures around the world*, volume 1, New York: Springer, 570–80.

Serambi Indonesia (2016) 'Empat aktivis kemerdekaan Aceh ikuti pelatihan UNPO di Den Haag', *Tribunnews*, 10 November, available at: http://aceh.tribunnews.com/2016/11/10/empat-aktivis-kemerdekaan-aceh-ikuti-pelatihan-unpo-di-den-haag.

Smith, H. and P. Stares (eds) (2007) *Diasporas in conflict: peace-makers or peace-wreckers?* Tokyo: United Nations University Press.

Steijlen, F. (2010) 'Moluccans in the Netherlands: from exile to migrant', *Review of Indonesian and Malaysian Affairs*, 44 (1), 143–62, available at: http://search.informit.com.au/documentSummary;dn=656533723896697;res=IELIND.

Stepputat, F. (1994) 'Repatriation and the politics of space: the case of the Mayan diaspora and return movement', *Journal of Refugee Studies*, 7 (2/3), 175–85, doi: 10.1093/jrs/7.2-3.175.

Tsuda, T. (ed.) (2009) *Diasporic homecomings: ethnic return migration in comparative perspective*, Stanford: Stanford University Press.

UNPO (Unrepresented Nations and Peoples Organization) (2016) 'ASNLF General Assembly confirms current leadership', 7 April, available at: http://unpo.org/article/19068.

van Amersfoort, H. (2004) 'The waxing and waning of a diaspora: Moluccans in the Netherlands, 1950–2002', *Journal of Ethnic and Migration Studies*, 30, (1), 151–74, doi: 10.1080/1369183032000170213.
Winarnita, M. (2015) *Dancing the feminine: gender and identity performances by Indonesian migrant women*, Eastbourne: Sussex Academic Press.
Wise, A. (2004) 'Nation, transnation, diaspora: locating East Timorese long-distance nationalism', *Sojourn*, 19 (2), 151–80, available at: www.jstor.org/stable/41308170.
Wise, A. (2006) *Exile and return among the East Timorese*, Philadelphia: University of Pennsylvania.

24

Islamic schooling and the second generation

A diaspora perspective

Hannah Höchner

'Five Americans are tantamount to forty Senegalese children!'
Teacher in an Islamic school, Dakar

For my doctoral research, I spent a year doing fieldwork in Kano in northern Nigeria, trying to find out how young boys experience their enrolment in Qur'anic schools there. A major challenge was to make the children open up to me and talk. Wider norms on the appropriate behaviour for juniors encourage children to be bashful and demure in the presence of adults. Collecting data on children's opinions required me to be patient, to have as unobtrusive a presence as possible, to learn from observing, and to find research formats that allowed my research participants to talk to each other rather than to me, for example by conducting tape-recorded 'radio interviews' among each other in my absence.

The situation I encountered in Dakar, Senegal, where I studied Islamic schools receiving children from teachers drawn from the Senegalese diaspora – including many children born and raised in the United States – could hardly have been more different. Here, the ten-year-olds scrambled to be 'selected' for an interview, talked a mile a minute, and were upset when I told them it was time to return to class as we had already overstayed the time their teacher had granted us. Here, the challenge was not to make children talk, but rather to find a breathing pause in their word flow to slip in my questions. 'Five Americans are tantamount to forty Senegalese children!' one of the teachers confided to me exhausted after a day's work of trying to tame the buoyant crowd. Profound cultural differences between children raised in a West African setting and youngsters who had grown up in Western contexts had implications not only for me as a researcher, but also for the teachers dealing with them every day in class.

About a third of the students in the school described here are children from the Senegalese diaspora, mostly from the United States, but also from France, Italy and Belgium, where institutions offering full-time education based on the Islamic faith are both rare and expensive. The rest of the student body is made up of Senegalese middle- and upper-class children as well as children of other nationalities whose parents work in Dakar as diplomats.

The students study secular subjects, modelled on the American curriculum, as well as Arabic, Islamic studies and the Qur'an. Many of the children and youth enrolled could not have received a similar faith-based education in the countries in which they grew up. Yet, this is not the only problem for which this school seeks to provide a solution. Many Senegalese migrant families in Western countries find themselves trapped in the bottled-up social misery of North American inner cities and European *banlieues*. Gang violence and drugs, failing public schools, and experiences of racism and Islamophobia push many Senegalese parents in Western countries to search for alternative ways of bringing up their children. Finally, many are wary of seeing their children become all too Westernized and want to make sure they are taught to respect their elders (see Bledsoe and Sow 2011; Kane 2011; Timera 2002). Religious schools are deemed to be particularly well placed to instil the requisite sense of reverence in children. A growing number of private schools in Senegal respond to migrant parents' demand for 'homeland' education today.

This chapter takes the opening of schools like the one just described as a starting point to explore wider questions about the relationship between a diaspora optic and Islamic education systems. What can a look at the literature on Islamic education tell us about the emergence of such schools, and the experiences of the young people enrolled in them? What insights can the migration and diaspora studies literature contribute? The respective bodies of literature have rarely been made to speak to each other, even though phenomenon like the one described here suggest that there may be important points of contact between them. In this chapter, I explore what integrating a diaspora perspective into the study of Islamic education systems could reveal and, vice versa, what we could learn from anchoring questions about religious learning more thoroughly within the study of migration and diaspora.[1] The next section investigates what points of contact exist between migration, diaspora and Islamic education, and how the existing literature has accounted for these. The second part of the chapter sketches out the additional questions and perspectives that a more thoroughgoing conversation between the literature on Islamic education and that on migration and diaspora could open up.

Migration, diaspora and Islamic educational practices

A growing body of scholarship documents today the diversity in Islamic educational practices and traces their origins. Scholars have documented the 'classical' learning arrangements, associated for example with Sufi Islam, which put personal loyalties, 'esoteric' (Brenner 2001) or 'embodied' (Ware 2014) knowledge, and the acquisition of *adab* or good morals (Starrett 1998) centre stage. Such 'classical' learning arrangements often centre around a mosque, Qur'anic school or scholarly household, are sustained by the personal charisma of an individual teacher, and draw on community resources rather than formal fees or state funds (see Boyle 2004 on Morocco; Ware 2014 on Senegal).

Researchers have also explored the social, political and epistemological changes that led to the emergence of 'modern' Islamic schooling across different regions (for example, Brenner 2001, Umar 2001, Ware 2014 on different parts of West Africa; Boyle 2004 on Morocco and Nigeria; Hefner 2009 on Southeast Asia; see also the edited volumes by Hefner and Zaman 2007 and Launay 2016). This literature illustrates how the massive political and epistemological displacements caused by colonialism, decolonization and the rise of Salafism have altered Islamic educational practices and landscapes (see Hefner 2009; Ware 2014). Organizationally, many Islamic schools have come to resemble Western educational settings more closely as a result of these trends.

Far from homogenizing Islamic learning practices, though, these historical processes have produced highly diverse, fragmented and stratified educational landscapes. 'Classical' learning arrangements have anything but disappeared, but co-exist today with both 'modern' and hybrid institutions which integrate 'modern' elements while preserving long-standing traditions at the same time (see, for example, Ware 2014). Curricula and teaching approaches are hotly debated, as evidenced, for example, by the fervour with which reformist/Salafi-oriented Muslims have denounced 'classical' Sufi-inspired teaching approaches as obscurantist (Ware 2014). Finally, religious education sectors have not been exempt from the commodification processes sweeping the wider educational landscape in neoliberal times (Dilger and Schulz 2013), resulting in stratified access to Islamic knowledge (Brenner 2001; Hoechner 2011).

The literature thus has been attentive to a wide range of forces producing and shaping Islamic educational practices and landscapes. How about the role of migration to non-Muslim lands, and of the Muslim diasporas[2] potentially resulting from them? What place do they have in the study of Islamic educational systems?

It has been argued that as a result of deeper-seated barriers confining scientific analysis to neatly circumscribed disciplinary terrains, scholars have paid insufficient attention to the ways in which Islam articulates with migratory processes to non-Muslim lands. Bava (2011), for example, claims that 'Islam in a migratory context is not a field that has attracted scholars specialized in the study of Islam itself'. Scholars of Islam 'study the "real" Islam in its countries of origin', leaving the study of 'hybrid forms of Islam as they are reshaped through migration' to scholars from other disciplinary horizons. Bava traces this divide back to the longstanding – now highly criticized – tradition within Islamic studies of distinguishing between 'learned, scriptural, orthodox Islam' and 'local expressions of the religion, described as "vestiges of the pre-Islamic age"' (Andezian 2001: 18, in Bava 2011: 498).

These overarching trends notwithstanding, a growing number of Islamic studies scholars explore today how Muslim migrants to the Western world seek to ensure the religious education of their children (Haddad et al. 2009; Mandaville 2007; Zine 2008). Importantly, these studies bring to light how questions of 'belonging' and 'identity' are negotiated through Islamic schooling, thus addressing head on a theme that is central to diaspora studies. Mandaville (2007: 226), writing about Islamic schools in Britain, for example, posits that 'education has emerged as a primary space in which fundamental questions about the societal inclusion and belonging of minority communities are negotiated'. Similarly, Zine (2009: 40) notes about Islamic schools in Canada that 'it is within the nexus of resisting cultural assimilation and engaging cultural survival that the need for Islamic schools emerges'.

Interestingly, the concern Islamic education scholars show for the identities and sense of belonging fostered through religious schooling in Western settings mirrors a trend also apparent within migration scholarship. Studies of religion by diaspora and migration scholars have often focused on its role for 'identity construction, meaning making, and value formation' (Levitt 2003: 851). Levitt et al. (2011b: 468), for example, explore how second-generation Indian Americans in the USA 'create religious selves by combining their imaginings of their parents' religious upbringing with their own real and imagined experiences of religious life in the USA, India, and other salient places around the world' (see also Levitt et al. 2011a; Rytter 2010).

This literature offers valuable insights on how young members of the diaspora draw on elements from various sites and sources as they develop their religious selves, on which I will build in the discussion at the end of this chapter. Yet, as Bava (2011: 501) remarks insightfully, religion is not only relevant for identity formation. It 'is also objectively and/or symbolically constitutive of migratory paths themselves. In fact, religion is not only a burden or a resource (material and spiritual), or a value in which migrants in exile can take refuge. It actually generates specific trajectories.'

This is particularly true for Islamic education. Migration and mobility are long-standing themes in (emic) narratives about Islamic learning, often traced back to the Prophet Mohammed who enjoined believers to 'seek knowledge, even as far as China!' This well-known *hadith* (saying of the Prophet Mohammed) has been mobilized in various contexts (see Fortier 1998: 218

on Mauretania) to talk about the close connections between Islamic learning and mobility. Given the scarcity of scholars in the early days of Islam, in many places, acquiring religious knowledge necessitated moving away from home to live with a renowned scholar in one of the emerging centres of learning. In large parts of West Africa, peripatetic traditions have survived to this day. Few travel as far as China, but Islamic boarding schools (both 'modern' and 'classical') are highly popular with Muslim parents to this day, who justify their school choices by arguing that a child cannot learn well within the comfort of home, and that religious maturation requires leaving behind old routines and familiar faces (see, for example, Ware 2014).

In the present-day Muslim diaspora, too, acquiring religious knowledge may make it necessary to relocate. Van Liempt (2011), for example, describes how a lack of propinquity to religious schools in the Netherlands motivates Somali migrant families to move on to the UK. The trope of religiously required mobility also resurfaces when migrants' children travel – or are sent – 'back'[3] to their parents' homelands for the sake of religious education. Many of the young people in Dakar's Islamic schools are sent 'back' to Senegal explicitly to acquire a religious grounding.[4] Similar phenomena have been noted, for example, by Kea (2016) with respect to Gambian migrant families in the UK, and by Razy (2006, 2010) with respect to Malian Soninké migrant families in France (see also Levitt et al. 2011a with respect to American Indian Muslims).

Of course, migrants' children travel 'back' to the 'homeland' not only for religious study. Bolognani (2013) details, for example, that second-generation British Pakistanis travel to Pakistan, among other things, for 'rehab', to visit family, and to go on 'roots tourism' or simply holidays (vacations). A growing body of literature documents how children are being sent 'back' to their parents' homelands for 'disciplining', to protect them from what are considered to be the morally corrupting or outright physically dangerous influences of Western society, or finally to free up their parents' time to work (see Bledsoe and Sow 2011 on children sent 'back' to various parts of West Africa; Lee 2016 on children sent to Tonga; Tiilikainen 2011 on children sent to Somaliland; see King and Christou 2011 for an overview of second-generation returnees).

Even when Muslim diaspora children travel to the 'homeland' for reasons other than religious education, their return may implicate Islamic schools. My own research in Senegal suggests that often religious school enrolment provides a solution to concerns that extend well beyond purely religious matters. For example, Islamic schools may be sought out for their disciplinary function (cf. Last 2000), even by parents who are not particularly strictly practising Muslims. Also, as many Islamic schools provide boarding facilities, they are an attractive option for parents who send their children 'back' to Senegal for one reason or another, but don't want to entrust them to relatives for the duration of their stay.

A closer dialogue between Islamic education and diaspora

I have explored earlier what points of contact exist between migration, diaspora and Islamic education, and how the existing literature has accounted for these. The remainder of this chapter investigates the additional questions and perspectives that may arise when we better integrate a diaspora perspective into the study of Islamic education systems, and anchor questions about religious learning more thoroughly within the study of diaspora.

A first set of questions concerns migratory pathways. What role does the availability of Islamic education play, for instance, for the decision to 'return' to the 'homeland', or to send children 'back'? How does Islamic education figure in decisions to 'move on' within the diaspora? To date, the literature has paid only scant attention to these questions.

A second set of questions concerns the ways in which diasporic demands for Islamic schooling may affect wider religious educational landscapes in Muslim societies. The most obvious setting to explore are Islamic schools like the one described in the introduction to this chapter. In Senegal – and I dare assume that Senegal is no unitary case – a growing number of Islamic schools unmistakably target diasporic communities with their educational offers. The director of the school where I conducted much of my research – African American herself – maintained close contacts with African diasporic communities in the USA, not least to help spread the word about her school. Other head masters in Dakar told me that they advertise their schools via Senegalese community radios in the USA. Many Islamic schools have shiny internet presences (featuring computer rooms and other paraphernalia of a 'modern' religious education), which appeal to diaspora parents.

Questions to explore in this context concern the teaching agendas and pedagogical approaches these schools pursue. To what extent do parents sending their children 'back' seek continuity with their own schooling experiences, and in which domains do they look for innovation? How does the education market respond to such – potentially contradictory – demands? It would be interesting, for instance, to investigate what approach to physical punishment such diaspora-oriented schools pursue (embracing physical punishment as a crucial element of their 'disciplining' agenda, or eschewing it to please Westernized audiences?), what language policy they adopt (teaching in the local language, or teaching in an 'international' language?), and how they situate themselves within wider sectarian/doctrinal landscapes (see below).

Explicitly diaspora-oriented Islamic schools are not the only schools receiving children from the diaspora. How does the presence of such children affect educational institutions that weren't targeting them in the first place? This is another question worth pursuing. In Senegal, I encountered migrants' children not only in the schools with 'cosmopolitan' aspirations described above, but also – albeit in smaller numbers – in neighbourhood Qur'anic schools, which migrants' children attended, for example during summer holidays. An important question to explore here is how the presence of diaspora children influences the schooling experiences of other children. Does it trigger new migration aspirations? Or does it 'educate' local children and parents about the potentially 'harmful' social and religious implications of migration to the West, for example because diaspora children may be seen to lag behind in terms of their prior religious knowledge, their (local) language skills or their behaviour?

Finally, diaspora demands for Islamic schooling may affect the religious educational landscapes of their 'home countries' remotely, as in the situations described by Aarset (2015). She notes that parents of Pakistani origin in Norway seek out Qur'anic teachers in Pakistan who teach their children the Qur'an via Skype. This opens up a market niche for technology-savvy Islamic scholars in Pakistan, while making Qur'anic lessons easier to slot into the busy days of Norwegian-Pakistani families. Qur'an lessons via Skype are not the only way in which diaspora demands affect Islamic educational landscapes remotely, though. Newman (2016: 216–17) also suggests that diaspora may intervene in the Islamic schooling sector by financing the education of young members of their extended family. Questions to explore in this context concern the characteristics of Islamic teachers sought out by the diaspora, as well as the networks enabling the former to 'capture' this diaspora demand.

A third and final set of questions touch upon the experiences of diaspora children. While some attention has been paid to children who attend Islamic school in their 'host' countries, much less is known about the experiences of children learning about Islam in the 'homeland'. The existing literature has drawn attention to the potentially ambivalent feelings such visits may trigger as young people are taken out of their habitual environment and have to learn a new 'habitus' (Zeitlyn 2012; see also Tiilikainen 2011). What is more, 'homeland' visits may widen cultural divides, as in the case described by Bolognani (2013) when diaspora youngsters come to embrace Orientalist attitudes towards the people in the 'homeland'. It may be revealing to pay closer attention the religious implications of 'homeland' visits. How does the competency of diaspora children in religious matters compare to that of their peers in the 'homeland', and, in case the former fare poorly, does this motivate them to 'catch up' or rather turn them away from religion? Furthermore, how do the religious identities diaspora children acquire in Western contexts fit in with 'local' religious identities? Whose model comes to appear worthy of imitation?

Several diaspora youth I met in Senegal were critical of the mystical practices (such as the veneration of Sufi sheikhs or the use of good-luck amulets) which appeared uncontroversial to many of their Senegalese peers. This pushes us to reflect on the question of doctrinal and sectarian orientations mentioned above. How do 'homeland' visits – and transnational ties more generally – affect such orientations? Levitt et al.'s (2011a) study of second-generation American Indians provides some valuable leads on this question. They suggest the relationship of the second generation to both their parents and religion takes one of three forms. Either parents assert themselves as 'keepers of the religious flame' and exact that their children follow suit, or 'children and parents negotiate together what that flame looks like and how to honor and preserve it', or finally children 'claim authority and authenticity, wresting power either peacefully or with a great deal of tension' (Levitt et al. 2011a: 157).

Yet, little is known to date about how their transnational engagements relate to the pathways both children and entire families eventually pursue. Some authors have suggested that close and continued ties with the 'homeland' serve to smoothe the transmission of religious identities and doctrinal orientations, and ensure intergenerational continuity. This argument has been made particularly to account for the fact that some Muslim 'diasporas' appear to show greater 'immunity' to 'radical' forms of Islam than others (see Lesthaeghe 2002, cited in Levitt 2003: 852–3, with respect to Turkish versus Moroccan youths in Belgium; see Babou 2014 with respect to West African diasporas).

A concluding note

Are things really that neat? Bolognani's (2013) research with second-generation Pakistani youths in Britain suggests that there is no inevitable relationship between fostering transnational connections and religious continuity. Her British-raised informants, upon spending time in the 'homeland', came to regard Pakistani Islam as culturally tainted and inferior to their own version of it, not least because such views allowed them to upgrade their own social position in Pakistan (Bolognani 2013: 114–15). In Senegal, not only time-honoured Sufi-oriented Islamic schools seek to attract migrants' children today, but there is also a comparatively new strand of reformist schools, frequently tagged 'Salafi', with a very different approach to Islamic doctrine, which are also popular with migrants' parents. 'Returning' to the 'homeland' rarely means returning to life and religion exactly as migrants left them behind at the time they emigrated. In brief, the relationship between transnational engagements and diaspora children's religious identities clearly demands more thorough scholarly attention than it has received so far.

In the current context of growing Islamophobia and increasingly aggressive secularism in Western countries, many immigrant parents in the West are hard-pressed to bring up their children as practising and self-respecting Muslims. It would not come as a surprise if Muslim 'homelands' were to gain in importance in the future as places to educate diaspora children. Inevitably, this raises questions about the identities and sense of belonging they develop, especially in a context where anxieties are ripe about the presumed 'radicalization' of the second generation and its alienation from Western secular values. While I have provided inadequate answers to the questions raised, I hope, at least, to have shown the value of asking these questions.

Notes

1 For the purpose of this chapter, I use the term 'diaspora' broadly to refer to Senegalese and other Muslim migrants who more or less fulfil the three overarching criteria identified by Brubaker (2005: 5–6), namely 'dispersion in space', an 'orientation to a "homeland"' and a certain degree of 'boundary-maintenance' or the 'preservation of a distinctive identity vis-à-vis [the] host society'.
2 For a discussion of whether it is appropriate to extend the use of the term 'diaspora' to religious groups, or whether it should be reserved for ethnically defined groups, see Vertovec (2004).
3 King and Christou (2011: 456) write aptly that 'in many respects, second-generation returnees are first-generation immigrants in their homelands'. Being sent 'back' can mean for some second-generation children going to a country they have never been to and that they know only indirectly from their parents' tales, or phone calls with relatives there. Others – which have been called the '1.5 generation' (King and Christou 2011: 459) may have been born in that 'homeland', but have spent their 'formative' years elsewhere.
4 Even in cases when children were sent to a secular or private Catholic school in Senegal (considered to offer the best-quality education locally), this is often motivated by religious considerations. Parents hope that spending time in a Muslim-majority environment, where practising the Islamic religion is both encouraged and respected, would nurture their children's religious selves.

References

Aarset, M. F. (2015) 'Transnational practices and local lives. Quran courses via Skype in Norwegian-Pakistani families', *Identities: Global Studies in Culture and Power*, 23 (4), 438–53, doi: 10.1080/1070289X.2015.1024122.
Andezian, S. (2001) *Expériences du Divin dans l'Algérie Contemporaine. Adeptes des Saints dans la Région de Tlemcen*, Paris: CNRS.
Babou, C. A. (2014) 'Making room for Islam in the West: Senegalese Muslims in Europe and North America', African Studies Centre seminar, available at: www.ascleiden.nl/news/seminar-making-room-islam-west-senegalese-muslims-europe-and-north-america.
Bava, S. (2011) 'Migration-religion studies in France: evolving toward a religious anthropology of movement', *Annual Review of Anthropology*, 40 (1), 493–507, doi: 10.1146/annurev-anthro-081309-145827.
Bledsoe, C. H. and P. Sow (2011) 'Back to Africa: second chances for the children of West African immigrants', *Journal of Marriage and Family*, 73 (4), 747–62, doi: 10.1111/j.1741-3737.2011.00843.x.
Bolognani, M. (2013) 'Visits to the country of origin: how second-generation British Pakistanis shape transnational identity and maintain power asymmetries', *Global Networks*, 14 (1), 103–20, doi: 10.1111/glob.12015.
Boyle, H. (2004) *Qur'anic schools: agents of preservation and change*, New York: Routledge Falmer.
Brenner, L. (2001) *Controlling knowledge: religion, power, and schooling in a West African Muslim society*, Bloomington: Indiana University Press.
Brubaker, R. (2005) 'The "diaspora" diaspora', *Ethnic and Racial Studies*, 28 (1), 1–19, doi: 10.1080/0141987042000289997.
Dilger, H. and D. Schulz (2013) 'Politics of religious schooling: Christian and Muslim engagements with education in Africa. Introduction', *Journal of Religion in Africa*, 43 (4), 365–78, doi: 10.1163/15700666-12341262.
Fortier, C. (1998) 'Le corps comme mémoire: du giron maternel à la férule du maître coranique', *Journal des Africanistes*, 68 (1/2), 197–224, doi: 10.3406/jafr.1998.1169.
Haddad, Y. Y., F. Senzai and J. I. Smith (eds) (2009) *Educating the Muslims of America*, Oxford: Oxford University Press.
Hefner, R. W. (ed.) (2009) *Making modern Muslims: the politics of Islamic education in Southeast Asia*, Honolulu: University of Hawai'i Press.
Hefner, R. W. and M. Q. Zaman (eds) *Schooling Islam: the culture and politics of modern Muslim education*, Princeton: Princeton University Press.
Hoechner, H. (2011) 'Striving for knowledge and dignity: how Qur'anic students in Kano, Nigeria, learn to live with rejection and educational disadvantage', *European Journal of Development Research*, 23 (5), 712–28, doi:10.1057/ejdr.2011.39.
Kane, O. (2011) *The homeland is the arena*, Oxford: Oxford University Press.
Kea, P. (2016) 'Photography and technologies of care: migrants in Britain and their children in the Gambia', in J. Cole and C. Groes (eds) *Affective circuits: African migrations to Europe and the pursuit of social regenerations*, London: University of Chicago Press, 78–100.

King, R. and A. Christou (2011) 'Of counter-diaspora and reverse transnationalism: return mobilities to and from the ancestral homeland', *Mobilities*, 6 (4), 451–66, doi: 10.1080/17450101.2011.603941.

Last, M. (2000) 'Children and the experience of violence: contrasting cultures of punishment in northern Nigeria', *Africa*, 70 (3), 359–93, doi: 10.3366/afr.2000.70.3.359.

Launay, R. (ed.) (2016) *Islamic education in Africa: writing boards and blackboards*, Bloomington: Indiana University Press.

Lee, H. (2016) '"I was forced here": perceptions of agency in second generation "return" migration to Tonga', *Journal of Ethnic and Migration Studies*, 42 (15), 254–79, doi: 10.1080/1369183X.2016.1176524.

Lesthaeghe, R. (2002) 'Turks and Moroccans in Belgium: a comparison', seminar presented at the Center for Population and Development Studies, Harvard University.

Levitt, P. (2003) '"You know, Abraham was really the first immigrant": religion and transnational migration', *International Migration Review*, 37 (3), 847–73, doi: 10.1111/j.1747-7379.2003.tb00160.x.

Levitt, P., M. D. Barnett and N. A. Khalil (2011a) 'Learning to pray: religious socialization across generations and borders', in M. Rytter and K. F. Olwig (eds) *Mobile bodies, mobile souls: family, religion and migration in a global world*, Aarhus: Aarhus University Press, 139–60.

Levitt, P., K. Lucken and M. Barnett (2011b) 'Beyond home and return: negotiating religious identity across time and space through the prism of the American experience', *Mobilities*, 6 (4), 467–82, doi: 10.1080/17450101.2011.603942.

Mandaville, P. (2007) 'Islamic education in Britain: approaches to religious knowledge in a pluralistic society', in R. W. Hefner and M. Q. Zaman (eds) *Schooling Islam: the culture and politics of modern Muslim education*, Princeton: Princeton University Press, 224–41.

Newman, A. (2016) *Faith, identity, status and schooling: an ethnography of educational decision-making in northern Senegal*, doctoral thesis, University of Sussex, available at: http://sro.sussex.ac.uk/60607/1/Newman%2C%20Anneke.pdf.

Razy, É. (2006) 'De quelques "retours soninké" aux différents âges de la vie', *Journal des Anthropologues*, (106/107), 337–454, available at: http://jda.revues.org/1211.

Razy, É. (2010) 'La famille dispersée (France/Pays Soninké, Mali). Une configuration pluriparentale oubliée?', *L'Autre*, 11 (3), 333–41, doi: 10.3917/lautr.033.0333.

Rytter, M. (2010) '*A sunbeam of hope*: negotiations of identity and belonging among Pakistanis in Denmark', *Journal of Ethnic and Migration Studies*, 36 (4), 599–617, doi: 10.1080/13691830903479407.

Starrett, G. (1998) *Putting Islam to work: education, politics, and religious transformation in Egypt*, Berkeley, CA: University of California Press.

Tiilikainen, M. (2011) 'Failed diaspora: experiences of *dhaqan celis* and mentally ill returnees in Somaliland', *Nordic Journal of African Studies*, 20 (1), 71–89, available at: www.njas.helsinki.fi/pdf-files/vol20num1/tiilikainen.pdf.

Timera, M. (2002) 'Righteous or rebellious? Social trajectory of Sahelian youth in France', in D. Bryceson and U. Vuorela (eds) *The transnational family. New European frontiers and global networks*, Oxford: Berg, 147–54.

Umar, M. S. (2001) 'Education and Islamic trends in Northern Nigeria: 1970s–1990s', *Africa Today*, 48 (2), 127–50, doi: 10.1353/at.2001.0043.

Van Liempt, I. (2011) 'Young Dutch Somalis in the UK: citizenship, identities and belonging in a transnational triangle', *Mobilities*, 6 (4), 569–83, doi: 10.1080/17450101.2011.603948.

Vertovec, S. (2004) 'Religion and diaspora', in P. Antes, A. W. Geertz and R. Warne (eds) *New approaches to the study of religion*, New York: Walter de Gruyter, 275–304.

Ware, R. (2014) *The walking Qur'an. Islamic education, embodied knowledge, and history in West Africa*, Chapel Hill: University of North Carolina Press.

Zeitlyn, B. (2012) 'Maintaining transnational social fields: the role of visits to Bangladesh for British Bangladeshi children', *Journal of Ethnic and Migration Studies*, 38 (6), 953–68, doi: 10.1080/1369183X.2012.677176.

Zine, J. (2008) *Canadian Islamic schools: unravelling the politics of faith, gender, knowledge, and identity*, Toronto: University of Toronto Press.

Zine, J. (2009) 'Safe havens or religious "ghettos"? Narratives of Islamic schooling in Canada', in Y. Y. Haddad, Y. Y., F. Senzai and J. I. Smith (eds) *Educating the Muslims of America*, Oxford: Oxford University Press, 39–66.

25
Diaspora and home
Interrogating embodied precarity in an era of forced displacement

Divya P. Tolia-Kelly

The aim of this chapter is to interrogate and situate the conceptualization of 'diaspora and home' within contemporary geopolitics and experience of forced migration. In effect, the aim is to evaluate the conceptualization through the current Syrian refugee crisis. There are currently more than thirteen million Syrians displaced and in search of humanitarian support.[1] Many are refugees in neighbouring countries such as Turkey, Lebanon and Jordan. One million have sought asylum status in the EU. These are Syrian migrants in search of settlement, scattered in response to the erasure of Syrian society, infrastructure, heritage landscapes and homes through systematic bombing. The distinction between diaspora and migration has long been grappled with (see Shuval 2000; Tölölyan 1996), and those attempting to define it agree that 'no diaspora is a monolith' (Brighton 2009: 14) and that definitions can risk being unhelpfully ethno-nationalistic (Butler 2001: 213). Diasporic migrations are attempted in a more and more precarious world (Waite 2009), one where structures of 'home' and 'citizenship' are precarious materialities, post-migration.

The contemporary migrant is situated in the matrices of the *denial of rights* and a *denial of recognition* at the border, resulting in a newly felt politics of a denial of citizenship. These erasures of rights are in breach of international, national and natural laws of respectful engagement with those traversing the borders of the world in a situation of *precarity*. The chapter outlines the political actions that are shaping the possibilities for migrants and the rendering of their 'rights', 'status' and 'access' to safe haven as being continually in flux, and re-made. Waite (2009: 413) suggests that precarity is marked by a 'generalised societal malaise and insecurity'; economic, societal and spiritual. For migrants, precarity is about 'rights' being constantly re-made, re-interpreted and played out without compassion towards others struggling to escape bombardment, the erasure of cities and societies. Forcibly displaced peoples, despite there being no guarantee of settlement, risk death, disconnection and indeed a loss of a 'liveable life' in the process of migration. This everyday situation for millions renders the grammars and theories of diaspora as inadequate and outdated. To outline the ways in which new grammars are conceptualizing diaspora–migration in a precarious world, this chapter ends with an account from artist–activist projects. The projects cited capture the very nature of diaspora-in-process in refugee camps and sites of shelter for refugees coming from Syria. These are intended as examples of the ways in which migration, mobility and the narratives of cultural groups are being engaged with and recorded for posterity. This is an unnecessary, inhumane crisis resulting from a lack of political will, compassion and action. Political interventions by artists situated at refugee camps at Calais (France) and Lesbos (Greece) highlight the dehumanization of forcibly displaced persons (FDPs). The artists cited here are at the vanguard of witnessing a new 'holocaust' of the twenty-first century; one that results from a cultural and political erasure of our responsibilities towards those migrating away from suffering, wars and genocide. In this account, religion is a key element in new social formations (Vertovec 2004); where to be a *Muslim* situates you outside of protected citizenry.

Diaspora, migration and making 'home'

In light of the recent inauguration of new president of the USA, Donald Trump, whose proclamations continue to stoke up racist actions towards migrants internationally, it seems a little anachronistic to be writing a chapter on 'Diaspora and home'. Diaspora rests conceptually on a community linked through identification with an imagined homeland or culture and sometimes connects a group to the material territory of a national home. In this century, millions of migrants have limited options; for those escaping bombing, erasure and/or genocide, migrating to Europe or North America is their only hope for survival. In these circumstances, *home* becomes an ephemeral place, one of memory, one of erasure and a path to finding a refuge. A new *homeland* rests on the generosity and humanitarian goodwill of other nations. *Home*, postmigration, is also reproduced through feeling out of place, exiled or discordant with the current body-politics of one's nation of residence, location and/or citizenship. In the current climate, it has become much harder for migrants (settled or otherwise) to find sanctuary, or indeed a site to call a home, house or space to have a self-determined identity. Much like the Jewish diaspora of the twentieth century, there is a promulgation of forced displacement, migration and exile in an era of 'the war on terror' where to be Muslim means being outside of the citizenship, nation and heritage futures of places of settlement. Anti-Muslim and anti-migrant violence, internationally, have been propelled further by Donald Trump's executive order placed on 27 January 2017, now colloquially called 'the Muslim ban' of entry to the USA (Trump 2017). This is an order that suspends the 'US Refugee Admissions Program' for 120 days. It explicitly calls for stopping the entry to the USA of anyone who has a visa or green card status and arriving from seven Muslim-majority countries – Iraq, Syria, Iran, Libya, Somalia, Sudan and Yemen. The actions of the new president and his rhetoric have been attributed to a white supremacist agenda; this is evidenced in the Trump administration's removal of neo-Nazi groups from the counter-extremism programme (Dearden 2017). The suspension of rights to entry itself breaches the USA's own Immigration and Nationality Act (1965) which states that no person can be 'discriminated against in the issuance of an immigrant visa because of the person's race, sex, nationality, place of birth or place of residence'.

The basis for these new discriminatory policies has been the claim that the ban works against 'those who would place violent ideologies over American law . . . [in order to] protect its citizens from foreign nationals who intend to commit terrorist attacks in the United States', including those who hold green cards and have rights of permanent residency.[2] It is in the very logics of US *homeland* security, and its implementation post 9/11, to engender in American Muslims the feeling of being an 'enemy within', a citizen that is outside of the body politic. Muslim populations who are fleeing US military action in the Middle East, including in Syria, Afghanistan, Iraq and Yemen, are left in geopolitical limbo. Millions of migrants have been left in a zone of bare life, outside (human) rights and territory. As Owens (2009: 568) suggests, for Agamben 'refugees can be seen as the ultimate "biopolitical" subjects: those who can be regulated and governed at the level of population in a permanent "state of exception" outside the normal legal framework – the camp'.

The perceived 'Muslim' body within contemporary border politics is in this situation of hyper-scrutiny and governance. Violence occurs daily against legal freedoms secured by migrants living in the West, which are disregarded (and even normalized) in the current epoch. This violence renders legal residents a status of illegality based on *ad hoc* decisions at the border. There has been a recent increase in anti-Muslim feeling, and enhanced violent attitudes towards 'foreigners' *per se*, inspired by and consolidated through the US government's actions against 'Muslims'. Dominating the media airwaves is an arbitrary account of their being the major risk to US citizens and their security at home. Many diasporic citizens are feeling vulnerable, at risk of racist violence and, despite having legal citizenship, their very 'diaspora' is what they draw upon as a source of hope, but now also of fear. Many diasporic citizens of the West are in the West as a result of forced displacement in deadly circumstances; leaving behind trails of erasure, de-territorialization and loss. Practices of heritage, culture and identity in situations of forced migration are made precarious. In the contemporary world, 'diaspora' or diasporic relationships and networks are concretized and consolidated through experiences of forced displacement. We live in the midst of a continual promulgation of absences, of rights to territory, citizenship, and indeed to life itself. In this space, it is perhaps impossible to retain diasporic networks, continuities and cultural genealogies.

In June 2016, the United Nations Human Rights Council (UNHCR) reported that more than 65 million people are affected by forced displacement, including global and internal displacement. This is an era of violent rupture between people and their territories of belonging, citizenship, and ultimately their spaces of home, and this has resulted in several urgent global challenges. Embedded in the fracturing and erasure of stable societies is the 'systematic eradication of a group's cultural existence' (Nersessian 2005), also considered by the UN, in situations of conflict, as *cultural genocide*. For many transcultural communities barely surviving migration, there is huge challenge in being able to retain cultural identities, values and practices. A loss of connectedness, cultural space and identity is a human rights issue, and can lead to a large-scale problem of thousands of forcibly displaced peoples (FDPs) suffering anomie, alienation, isolation and violent erasure of a possibility of a future for their language, genealogies and cultural practices and heritage. At the heart of human rights is a right to shelter, to a home. 'Home' is the very thing that defines the diasporic imagination; it shapes hope, loss, fear and identities.

Home: making *home* for diasporic communities

As Said (1990: 365) said: 'The exile knows that in a secular and contingent world, home is always provisional.' For Syrian migrants forcibly on the move, there is an impossibility of connecting with a material sense of home. While home remains conceptualized as a static, available safe space in academic thought, 'home' is unsettled and always 'over there' when in mobility. 'Home' thus needs to be refigured through a lens of mobility and displacement; it is an idea that needs refiguring through an alternative theoretical and political lens. 'Home' has been theorized within the social sciences through the lens of feminist accounts of the value of the domestic scene politically, socially, culturally and economically. These accounts have proliferated in the disciplines of geography, anthropology, cultural studies, law and sociology. Contemporary research on the cultural values of home has rested on notions of 'being' and 'feeling' human and at home in the space of 'dwelling' (Heidegger) or 'habitus' (Bordieu).

These are critical philosophical starting points into thinking about the role of 'home' in human consciousness, identity practices and in socio-political economies and networks. However, these notions are squarely based in a Western canon. Thinking about home through diasporic values of 'home' attends to the need within academic research to conceptualize 'home' transculturally and internationally. Being on the move for diasporic citizens is counter to the seemingly staid and parochial notions of home as sites for social reproduction, situating identity, morality and wholesome hearth for the 'family' that provide a culturally and genealogically rooted status (Blunt 1999, 2005; Blunt and Varley 2004; Brickell 2012; Datta 2008; Holloway and Valentine 2001). One of the few critiques of how 'home' is retained discursively in the public realm, despite evidence that 'home' cannot be attained, is Black's (2002) argument that in European policy 'simplistic notions of a return "home" for refugees are maintained', that are based on unjustified claims that this feat can be achieved. Thus, there is a multiplying of the configurations of immaterial 'home' for the refugee; of myth of 'origin' that can be returned to, the 'phantom' of home that is unethically reproduced as a political means to return refugees back out to countries in conflict. The imagined communities of home, however, live on in shards of memory, stories, narratives and fragments of nostalgia. Home is largely inaccessible, immaterial and always elsewhere for migrants who have been displaced.

It is a 'different' kind of connection that diaspora migrants develop. The intangible relationship with home is one that haunts; sometimes as spectre, sometimes as a dream. The cultural and philosophical values of 'home' thus need to be figured through non-Western notions of 'dwelling' and 'habitus' to include postcolonial experiences, and diasporic cultural values which offer different starting points, timescales and relationships between individuals and a sense of belonging, home and heritage. To figure 'home' in non-Western cultures is to acknowledge that there are philosophically different frameworks of time, heritage, territory and 'dwelling' embedded in them. Importantly, 'social' and 'post-human' accounts of human–land relations are critical to rites and notions of social laws of land rights, human rights, appropriation and governance. Home here is understood through varied conceptualizations of 'social territory' (beyond the Western foundations of nuclear family) to include notions of mobility and time that are transcultural. These transcultural paradigms disrupt bounded categorizations of territory, settlement, residence and 'home' usually encountered in academic research.

Home, it seems, has remained locked within a liberal sensibility; always available, static, embedded with entitlement. However, without a home, there are toxic economies at play, including loss of physical and mental health, vulnerability to exploitation, brutality and death. In a study of 7,000 refugees, Fazel et al. (2005) argue clearly that one in ten adult refugees has post-traumatic stress disorder (PTSD), one in twenty major depression, and one in twenty-five has severe anxiety disorders; many of these conditions are multiply experienced by individuals surveyed. Refugees in Western countries are ten times more likely to suffer PTSD, and these numbers are on the increase. The UN principles on internationally displaced persons recognize a loss of habitual residence and recognize a need for their protection in human rights law and practice. More and more these losses of residence have become protracted to include decades spent away at 'refugee' camps. There is a heightened vulnerability and need for a self-determined sense of 'home', a need for a reconnection with spaces for cultural heritage, identity and well-being in new territories post-displacement.

Syrian refugees in diaspora

Wahlbeck (2002) has long called for refugees to be considered through the lens of 'diaspora' communities, beyond the usual statistical or empirical definition and assessment towards a more ethnographical understanding and conceptualization. He argues that all refugees carry with them a *diasporic consciousness*; a feeling of being part of a network that shares identification with a culture, place or territory. Refugees are thus both transnational and diasporic, and can be considered in social research without being reduced to homogeneous ethnic or cultural categories (Wahlbeck 2002: 225). Brubaker (2005: 1) has argued that there is a proliferation of what counts as diaspora, which he terms a '"diaspora" diaspora', a dispersion of the meanings of the term in semantic, conceptual and disciplinary space. He critiques this proliferation as a way of weakening the conceptual power of diaspora and its critical utility.

In the Middle East context, use of the term 'diaspora' for migrants is complicated by the political revolutions and uprisings that have taken place there. The focus of these was to revive and rebuild the countries rather than secure a foothold in Europe (Fargues 2011). However, the post-revolutionary environment and responses by Arab states have led to a desperate exodus, *en masse*. In the Syrian example, there is a process of 'culturecide' that is occurring. There is an erasure of 'homeland' by the daily bombing of infrastructures and networks. There is also simultaneously a fracturing of everyday life. Thus in the case of contemporary migration from Syria, we should consider the connectedness and cultural realm that is co-produced and which rests *between* Syrian migrants on the move as a 'diaspora' that is defined as a category of practice. In this account, the Syrian form of 'diaspora' is defined as a practice, one that enables the migrant community to 'make claims, to articulate projects, to formulate expectations, to mobilize energies, to appeal to loyalties' (Brubaker 2005: 12). In Williams's (1979) terms, everyday culture acts as a reproductive process for diaspora communities, and is for some a process of cultural re-invention (Tsagarousianou 2004: 52).

In 2017, the UNHCR recorded 2.1 million registered Syrians in Egypt, Iraq, Jordan and Lebanon, more than 24,000 Syrian refugees registered in North Africa, and 1.95 million registered Syrians in Turkey (Yazgan et al. 2015). The insecurities of the living situation in Syria do not seem to show signs of abating in the foreseeable future and, as a result, migration will continue. The Syrian crisis has been exacerbated both by military action from within Syria, and responses to Syrians as refugees by the EU member states and by the new US president, who states that: 'I hereby proclaim that the entry of nationals of Syria as refugees is detrimental to the interests of the United States and thus suspend any such entry' (Trump 2017). This order leads us to consider the ways in which the Syrian diaspora subjects sustain everyday life, in the face of abandonment and erasure. In much of the literature, there is a constant account of diaspora citizens as having a 'myth of return' (Safran 1991), where there is a solidarity garnered amongst migrants through an imagined community linked to a 'homeland' of sustenance and nurture (Abdelhady 2008).

The idea that there is a constructed vision of 'home' means that there is a sense of 'not-here to stay' (Clifford 1994: 311). For Clifford, diaspora migrants living in separate places become effectively a single community. Through modern networks of communication and connection, new territorializations emerge through an e-connectedness (Appadurai 1996). In situations of forced displacement, as in modern-day Syria, these global networks are less about cultural connection than about daily survival, in the search for refuge. The search for a place to stay is an extreme circumstance where the layered and sophisticated relationship Clifford describes is not yet attainable. A place to stay is sought in a situation of heightened precarity. For Syrian migrants, the power to change things at 'home' is denied to them, their invisibility is their hope, contrary to Banki's (2013) claim that refugees have an iterative dynamism which brings political opportunities and thus can form into a social movement. The Syrian diaspora in Europe can be traced through their practices post-migration. These are recorded in the media and *ad hoc*-funded projects as a means through which Syrian diasporic cultural identity is consolidated, in mobility. Some of these practices are not situated in cosy, structured and secure homes, but in refugee camps in Jordan, Calais and elsewhere. One oft-cited example is of the value of art in keeping Syrian culture alive (Dunmore 2016). The artist Mamoud Hariri painstakingly recreates models of ruined monuments of Syrian heritage, including Palmyra. As part of a group of artists called Art from Zaatari, Hariri and his fellow artist-migrants have been recreating miniatures of lost worlds and architectures, erased by bombs and bullets. The art exhibitions are a means for Syrian migrants to reconnect with a heritage that is no longer material, or indeed tangible, on the ground. The art produced by the group thus becomes a space for reconnection, accumulation and re-iteration of Syrian practices of cultural identity within a diasporic sensibility, one of longing, connecting and enlivening memories, histories and cultures facing permanent erasure. The collective act of reproducing these landscapes and monuments connects their sense of enfranchisement to 'Syrian' heritage, landscape and to a cultural geography of Syria as a past *home*. Syria as a space from which these artists have travelled and dispersed is compounded with every artistic reproduction. Together, they create a connected collage of key cultural nodes of being and feeling Syrian.

Making home on the move: in Turkey and in France

The cultural consciousness of any diasporic community is dynamic and in process. And as such, the experience of being on the move, and the environmental contexts of resting, eating and expressing cultural identities shapes notions of 'home', 'diaspora' and 'Syrianness'. In Turkey, there is a strong critique of the ways in which the Turkish government has not automatically granted 'refugee status' to Syrians, but instead treat them as 'guests'. At the core of the critique is the notion that 'charitable' accommodation of their community as guests in need of handouts counters their senses of dignity and righteousness. By retaining a charitable approach, Turkey makes the migrants more vulnerable to negative public opinion, as well as less able to command 'human rights'. This de-humanization is also exacerbated by other practices at the border; Syrians without passports who have fled are often shot at whilst traversing dangerous minefields between Turkey and Syria (Özden 2013: 5). These experiences on the route to refuge effect enormously their senses of status and settlement in conditions considered inhuman in the camps themselves (Özden 2013: 6), once within Turkey. Food in the camps has become a source of tension, as supplies and autonomy in producing food are not available. Syrians in the camps have complaints about uneven distribution of food and bias, as well as recorded food poisoning and a lack of options to cook themselves. This is significant in that a simple meal made for a family could be a way of nourishing refugees beyond simply calories needed to survive (Johnston and Longhurst 2012). Food cultures are more than a means of sustenance (Steavenson 2013); culturally, cooking is a means of cultural connection, identity and a source of nurture (Slocum and Saldanha 2016) that can counteract trauma suffered in their plight.

Gideon Mendel, in his recent project 'Representing the Calais "Jungle"' (Mendel 2017), enables us to reflect on the challenges and sensitivities needed to make 'home' in the camp. The pictures he took between May and October 2016 evoke complex stories. Mendel intended to counter the current iconography of the 'refugee crisis', of boats, lines at borders, campfires and shacks. Instead, Mendel focused on the very materials that *made* everyday life; the material catalysts to a liveable existence. Mendel pictures abandoned toothbrushes, soft toys encrusted with sand, burnt children's books, singed clothes, footballs, and muddy sleeping bags. These are remnants and shards of material cultures that have *made* the Syrian diaspora liveable in Calais. These become the architectures of child-rearing, familial relations and creating 'safety' in the camp. The status of refugee cultures pictured through Mendel's account is focused on specific material cultures left behind. The difficulty of cultural sustenance, expression and articulation robs refugees at the camps of a space *to be*. There is an erasure and denial of cultural expression, consolidated through the military, political and moral infrastructures which form European borders.

The artist Ai Weiwei has also focused on the current plight of refugees in the Mediterranean by travelling to the Greek island of Lesbos to respond to, communicate with and intervene in the crisis of refugees dying and surviving their journey to Europe. Recently, The Mobile Lives Forum commissioned Ai Weiwei to work on an exhibition entitled 'The Refugee Project'. The artist states that '(B)y tracing the refugees' origins and following their journeys, I seek to record and analyse the impact of human conditions we face today' (Weiwei 2016). Here, the artist focuses on how refugee identity networks are maintained and re-made. The Refugee Project outlines how diasporic communities in this age of crisis denote connections. The intensities of ties between refugees are shaped by the strength of satellite cell networks, a Wi-Fi signal and access to chargers. 'How, where, when and whom do we assemble through our phones?' Sheller reflects on the co-dependency between connected communities and the connected infrastructure that enables that connectivity to be powered and effective (Logé and Sheller 2016). The fragility of the means of consolidating connections whilst on the move is paralleled by the disconnect felt and lived by refugees. Weiwei argues that in this maelstrom refugees develop their own 'communicative agency' (Sheller 2016). And thus their defining and refining of the nature, shape and definition of diaspora is also on the move. It is a sad and happy situation where the laws that are deemed to protect humanity are made impotent and the work of the artist is the closest in giving humanity and agency to the diasporic migrant. In *Human flow*, Weiwei's (2017) documentary on the refugee crisis, 23 countries are visited, and the spectacle of migration is communicated as a *human* crisis. There is no one country where those in *peace* are not implicated; the refugee could be any one of us. Peacetime is conditional, not infinite.

Conclusion

In of the midst of the current migrant crisis, I have tried to express the problematics inbuilt in the accounts of diaspora foreclosed by previous generations. Memory, visual culture and written narratives are all cultural materials through which memories of past accounts accrue. Signification of identity, history and heritage, through these material cultures, depends upon the continuing dependence on the past for sustenance in the present. Weiwei offers us an archive through which to record the routes and conditions of scattering migrants. Through The Refugee Project, Weiwei's aim is to create an archive of Syrian diasporic mobility, with migrants themselves. However without the speed of recording the crisis, there are seldom collections of heritage narratives that help us understand how networks are made, defined and redefined. Aligned to this is a project of thinking through transnational art and aesthetics formulated in the process of traversing and exile (Werbner and Fumanti 2013). An ethics of diaspora settlement is also about the creative expressiveness that captures the grammars, vocabularies and new cultural formations.

In the wake of Trump's election, the writer Toni Morrison (2015) reminds us that we need to act, to take up the work of the artist and react:

> This is precisely the time when artists go to work. There is no time for despair, no place for self-pity, no need for silence, no room for fear. We speak, we write, we do language. That is how civilizations heal. I know the world is bruised and bleeding, and though it is important not to ignore its pain, it is also critical to refuse to succumb to its malevolence.

By doing nothing, we ourselves are complicit.

Notes

1 http://syrianrefugees.eu/ (last accessed 13 March 2017).
2 See *The Guardian*, 29 January 2017, available at: www.theguardian.com/us-news/2017/jan/29/trump-travel-ban-peoples-stories-from-us-and-around-the-world.

References

Abdelhady, D. (2008) 'Representing the homeland: Lebanese diasporic notions of home and return in a global context', *Cultural Dynamics*, 20 (1), 53–72, doi: 10.1177/0921374007088055.
Appadurai, A. (1996) *Modernity at large: cultural dimensions of globalization*, Minneapolis: University of Minnesota.
Banki, S. (2013) 'The paradoxical power of precarity: refugees and homeland activism', *Refugee Review: Social Movement*, 1 (1), 1–20, available at: https://refugeereview.wordpress.com/working-papers/paradoxical-power-and-precarity/.
Black, R. (2002) 'Conceptions of "home" and the political geography of refugee repatriation: between assumption and contested reality in Bosnia-Herzegovina', *Applied geography*, 22 (2), 123–38, doi: 10.1016/S0143-6228(02)00003-6.
Blunt, A. (1999) 'Imperial geographies of home: British domesticity in India, 1886–1925', *Transactions of the Institute of British Geographers*, 24 (4), 421–40, doi: 10.1111/j.0020-2754.1999.00421.x.
Blunt, A. (2005) 'Cultural geography: cultural geographies of home', *Progress in Human Geography*, 29 (4), 505–15, doi: 10.1191/0309132505ph564pr.
Blunt, A. and A. Varley (2004) 'Geographies of home: introduction', *Cultural Geographies*, 11 (1), 3–6, doi: 10.1191/1474474004eu289xx.
Brickell, K. (2012) '"Mapping" and "doing" critical geographies of home', *Progress in Human Geography*, 36 (2), 225–44, doi: 10.1177/0309132511418708.
Brighton, S. A. (2009) *Historical archaeology of the Irish diaspora*, Knoxville: University of Tennessee Press.
Brubaker, R. (2005) 'The "diaspora" diaspora', *Ethnic and Racial Studies*, 28 (1), 1–19, doi: 10.1080/0141987042000289997.
Butler, K. D. (2001) 'Defining diaspora, refining a discourse', *Diaspora: A Journal of Transnational Studies*, 10 (2), 189–219, doi: 10.1353/dsp.2011.0014.
Clifford, J. (1994) 'Diasporas', *Cultural Anthropology*, 9 (3), 302–38, doi: 10.1525/can.1994.9.3.02a00040.
Datta, A. (2008) 'Building differences: material geographies of home (s) among Polish builders in London', *Transactions of the Institute of British Geographers*, 33 (4), 518–31, doi: 10.1111/j.1475-5661.2008.00320.x.
Dearden, L. (2017) 'Donald Trump administration "wants to cut white supremacism from counter-extremism programme"', *The Independent*, 2 February, available at: https://goo.gl/c0CQJe.
Dunmore, C. (2016) 'How art is helping Syrian refugees keep their culture alive', *The Guardian*, 2 March, available at: https://goo.gl/AzChsx.
Fargues, P. (2011) 'Voice after exit: revolution and migration in the Arab world', *Migration Policy Institute*, online article, 11 May, available at: www.migrationpolicy.org/article/voice-after-exit-revolution-and-migration-arab-world.
Fazel, M., J. Wheeler and J. Danesh (2005) 'Prevalence of serious mental disorder in 7000 refugees resettled in western countries: a systematic review', *The Lancet*, 365 (9467), 1309–14, doi: 10.1016/S0140-6736(05)61027-6.
Holloway, S. L. and G. Valentine (2001) 'Children at home in the wired world: reshaping and rethinking home in urban geography', *Urban Geography*, 22 (6), 562–83, doi: 10.2747/0272-3638.22.6.562.
Johnston, L. and R. Longhurst (2012) 'Embodied geographies of food, belonging and hope in multicultural Hamilton, Aotearoa New Zealand', *Geoforum*, 43 (2), 325–31, doi: 10.1016/j.geoforum.2011.08.002.
Logé, G. and M. Sheller (2016) 'The refugee project', online document, available at: http://artisticlab.forumviesmobiles.org/en/oeuvre/the-refugee-project.
Mendel, G. (2017) 'Representing the Calais "Jungle"', photographic exhibition, 28 January, Rivington Place, London.
Morrison, T. (2015) 'No place for self-pity, no room for fear', *The Nation*, 23 March, available at: www.thenation.com/article/no-place-self-pity-no-room-fear/.
Nersessian, D. (2005) 'Rethinking cultural genocide under international law', *Human Rights Dialogue*, 2 (12), 7–8, available at: www.carnegiecouncil.org/publications/archive/dialogue/2_12/section_1/5139.html.

Owens, P. (2009) 'Reclaiming "bare life"?: against Agamben on refugees', *International Relations*, 23 (4), 567–82, doi: 10.1177/0047117809350545.

Özden, S. (2013) 'Syrian refugees in Turkey', Migration Policy Centre (MPC) research report, available at: www.migrationpolicycentre.eu/docs/MPC-RR-2013-05.pdf.

Safran, W. (1991) 'Diasporas in modern societies: myths of homeland and return', *Diaspora: A Journal of Transnational Studies*, 1 (1), 83–99, doi: 10.1353/dsp.1991.0004.

Said, E. (1990) 'Reflections on exile', in R. Ferguson, M. Gever, T. T. Minh-ha and C. West (eds) *Out there: marginalization and contemporary culture*, Cambridge, MA: MIT Press, 357–66.

Sheller, M. (2016) 'On the maintenance of humanity: learning from refugee mobile practices', *CARGC*, paper 5, (Fall), online article, available at: www.asc.upenn.edu/sites/default/files/documents/CARGC-Paper%205.pdf.

Shuval, J. T. (2000) 'Diaspora migration: definitional ambiguities and a theoretical paradigm', *International Migration*, 38 (5), 41–56, doi: 10.1111/1468-2435.00127.

Slocum, R. and A. Saldanha (2016) *Geographies of race and food: fields, bodies, markets*, New York: Routledge.

Steavenson, W. (2013) 'Remembrance of tastes past: Syria's disappearing food culture', *The Guardian*, 7 December, www.theguardian.com/world/2016/dec/07/syria-refugees-disappearing-food-culture-kibbeh.

Tölölyan, K. (1996) 'Rethinking diaspora(s): stateless power in the transnational moment', *Diaspora: A Journal of Transnational Studies*, 5 (1), 3–36, doi: 10.1353/dsp.1996.0000.

Tsagarousianou, R. (2004) 'Rethinking the concept of diaspora: mobility, connectivity and communication in a globalised world', *Westminster Papers in Communication and Culture*, 1 (1), 52–65, doi: 10.16997/wpcc.203.

Trump, D. (2017) 'Executive order on immigration', *The Guardian*, 27 January, available at: www.theguardian.com/us-news/2017/jan/27/donald-trump-executive-order-immigration-full-text.

Vertovec, S. (2004) 'Religion and diaspora', in P. Antes, A. W. Geertz and R. R. Warne (eds) *New approaches to the study of religion: volume 2*, Berlin: Walter de Gruyter, 275–304.

Wahlbeck, Ö. (2002) 'The concept of diaspora as an analytical tool in the study of refugee communities', *Journal of Ethnic and Migration Studies*, 28 (2), 221–38, doi: 10.1080/13691830220124305.

Waite, L. (2009) 'A place and space for a critical geography of precarity?', *Geography Compass*, 3 (1), 412–33, doi: 10.1111/j.1749-8198.2008.00184.x.

Weiwei, A. (2016) 'The refugee project', online document, available at: http://artisticlab.forumviesmobiles.org/en/oeuvre/the-refugee-project.

Weiwei, A. (2017) *Human flow*, documentary film, Participant Media/AC Films.

Werbner, P. and M. Fumanti (2013) 'The aesthetics of diaspora: ownership and appropriation', *Ethnos*, 78 (2), 149–74, doi: 10.1080/00141844.2012.669776.

Williams, R. (1979) *Politics and letters*, London: New Left Books.

Yazgan, P., D. E. Utku and I. Sirkeci (2015) 'Syrian crisis and migration', *Migration Letters*, 12 (3), 181–92, available at: www.tplondon.com/journal/index.php/ml/article/viewFile/577/417.

26
Diasporas and political obligation

Ilan Zvi Baron

In an essay on the state of political theory, Isaiah Berlin (1969: 7) suggests that 'the most fundamental of all political questions' is 'why should anyone obey anyone else?' Similarly, A. P. d'Entrèves (1959: 3) claims that 'the history of political theory is to me first and foremost the history of the attempts to solve the problem of political obligation'. The problem of political obligation has been called 'the fundamental or central problem of political philosophy' (Dagger 1977: 86). John Horton (2010: 1–2), in his introductory book about political obligation, defines it as the relationship 'between the people and their political community' and 'about whether we can properly be understood to have some ethical bond with our polity, and if so how this manifests itself'.

If we accept the above statements, political obligation is one of the primary questions in political theory; it is concerned not just with why anybody would obey somebody else, but with what it is about the state that makes it possible to oblige its inhabitants, or rather, its citizens. Political obligation is, in short, about the moral bonds that bind people in a distinct way to the state in which they are citizens. However, what about the moral bonds that bind us to our kin abroad or to a homeland? What about the moral bonds that engender a political commitment on behalf of others who belong to the same transnational community? What about the moral bonds of a political nature that inform diasporic political practice? There are multiple ways in which diasporic groups take on political actions that speak to who they are, and these can be felt as both political and obligatory. These may include:

- sending remittances to support community development or families in home countries (Adams, Jr and Page 2005; Barham and Boucher 1998; Goldring 2004; Vertovec and Cohen 1999);
- diasporic peoples 'returning' to fight wars in their homeland – important, as Hockenos (2003) notes, in the Balkan wars of the 1990s;
- the role of diasporas in global politics more generally (Shain 2007; Sheffer 2003); and
- diasporic populations coming to the aid of their kin abroad, as French and British Jews did in the 1840s when Jews in Damascus were being persecuted on blood libel charges (Frankel 1997; Leff 2006).

In what follows, I address such examples by making three interrelated points to emphasize that there is a form of political obligation that is pertinent to the political geography and experiences of diasporic people. First, the way in which the state insists that its citizens are loyal to it is reflected in the disturbingly narrow way that political theory has conceptualized what counts as a political obligation. Second, the idea of a diaspora involves a political understanding about identity that cannot be reduced to the idea of a citizen having to be politically obliged. Third, there is a liminal political space that does not fit into the ostensibly contiguous delimited spatiality of the territorial nation-state, and it is erroneous to assume that there is nothing in between the spaces of the territorial state and cosmopolitan geographies.

A diasporic sensibility for political theory

Although political theory has traditionally 'worked on models of "closed societies" and exclusive loyalties of citizens toward a single state' (Bauböck 2003: 700), a growing body of political theory is rejecting this narrow vision.[1] Correspondingly, although theories of political obligation are, if nothing else, highly exclusive, it does not follow that there is nothing to be gained from using the idea of obligation when thinking about the politics of diasporas. Admittedly, doing so involves a fairly radical revision of how 'political obligation' is traditionally understood. Central to this tradition is A. J. Simmons's (1980) contribution of the particularity principle, which limits the scope of political obligation to the relationship between citizens and the state in which they are citizens. The importance of the particularity principle is demonstrated by George Klosko, one of the foremost contemporary philosophers of political obligation. He (Klosko 2005: 108) writes that 'an acceptable principle of political obligation must account for the strong connection between the individual and a specific political body, of which he is generally a citizen'. As a political theory, political obligation is expected to reveal what it is that makes the bond between citizens and their state so special that it can override other obligations to people in different lands.[2] There is nothing in the political obligation literature to suggest that the idea of political obligation should have any relevance to understanding diasporic politics.

Moreover, it is rare to find discussions about obligation in the literature on diasporas. James Clifford (1994: 322), in an especially insightful passage, notes that 'the empowering paradox of diaspora is that dwelling *here* assumes a solidarity and connection *there*. But *there* is not necessarily a single place or an exclusivist nation.' Solidarity and connection are the descriptive terms of normative significance in this instance, not obligation. Indeed, although the transnational and diaspora literature presumes membership, it does not address the question of obligation, even when diaspora is understood as a form of membership (Maier 2007). In her critique of citizenship, Melissa S. Williams (2007: 228) comes close to moving in the direction of obligation by defining citizenship not in terms of 'shared identity but in terms of "shared fate"'. She notes the relevance of obligation, but only in passing and primarily focuses on who would be considered to belong to the community and could participate in the decision-making processes of this community. The critical citizenship literature also addresses the question of membership and obligation, precisely because at issue is a kind of shared political community and culture across state borders, which invites specific norms of behaviour and commitment that are often geared toward sustaining the community.[3]

Why, one might ask, in the face of such theoretical obstacles and potential theoretical alternatives, would one want to think about diaspora politics through the prism of political obligation? In his book on sovereignty, the political philosopher Jonathan Havercroft (2011: 5) suggests that as political philosophers we ought to return 'to our everyday political practices'. If we follow his good advice, then it follows that there might exist political obligations that are relevant to diaspora groups and that obligate them as members of a diaspora. In this sense, the idea of a political obligation for diasporas has very little in common with the traditional understandings of political obligation, but is concerned rather with those aspects of life in the diaspora that are felt, experienced or somehow understood to be both obligatory and political. Moreover, by broadening our thinking in this way, the traditional dichotomy between the state (communitarian) and a global human community (cosmopolitan) is problematized as a false dichotomy.

The ethical possibility is not between a cosmopolitan or communitarian position – both of which nevertheless find as their point of reference the role of the state and our normative commitments *vis-à-vis* our state-based identity (Hutchings and Dannreuther 1999; Walker 1999). The Janus-faced character of a diaspora demands that we think differently, as do Jonathan and Daniel Boyarin (2002: 9), who write that a 'diaspora is *not* equivalent to pluralism or internationalism. It is egocentric.' In this way, they acknowledge that the idea of a diaspora provides an option other than the cosmopolitan/communitarian dichotomy.[4] This liminal space, of belonging to multiple geographies and communities simultaneously, is not necessarily exclusive to diasporas, but it is important because of how our political geographies encourage political commitments. Arjun Appadurai (1996: 19) expresses this point when he writes that:

> Nation-states, for all their important differences (and only a fool would conflate Sri Lanka with Great Britain), make sense only as parts of a system. This system (even when seen as a system of differences) appears poorly equipped to deal with the interlinked diasporas of people and images that mark the here and now. Nation-states, units in a complex interactive system, are not very likely to be the long-term arbiters of the relationship between globality and modernity.

It is precisely this point that unites the concerns found in the work of Boyarin and Boyarin (2002) and of Stéphane Dufoix (2003), as well as in the ethics of the de-territorialization literature (Campbell 1994). In this regard, when we think of a diaspora's political obligations, we are nevertheless still concerned about sustaining the normative basis of a political geography, which is part of what shapes the domestic political theory account of political obligation. This geography, however, can be understood in a multiplicity of ways that traditional theories of political obligation ignore, but that correspond to the different understandings of diaspora (Cohen 2008: 4–19).

Obligation

There are some *prima facie* reasons why it makes sense to consider the concept of obligation as having currency for our understanding of the politics of diaspora peoples. One of the most important of these is ethical. The idea of there being political obligations that pertain to diaspora peoples is rooted in the empirical observation that diasporas can have compelling reasons to act in ways that associate their political commitments with their people. Importantly, the reason for thinking of this in terms of obligation is to avoid the reference or implicit assumption of loyalty. First, avoiding the concept of loyalty helps overcome the potential for falling into the trap of dual loyalty and the related presumption that minority groups pose a security threat to the state and that as members of any political community we are expected to have only a singular form of political attachment (Baron 2009).[5] Second, but relatedly, thinking in terms of obligation also makes it difficult to conceive of diasporas as being disloyal. Since diaspora politics are, if nothing else, contingent on the normative understanding of diaspora geography and the meaning of diaspora (Dufoix 2003; Gilroy 1993), to presume that diasporas can be either loyal or disloyal renders a crude dichotomy onto the multifaceted characteristics of diaspora life (Clifford 1994; Lyons and Mandaville 2011; Vertovec and Cohen 1999).

For example, in his introduction to the 1986 edited volume about diasporas and international relations, Gabriel Sheffer (1986: 20) writes that

> in the likelihood of [a] contradiction arising between a state's policies and the predilections of a homeland dwelling[,] people will obviously depend in large part on the degree to which the state apparatus identifies itself exclusively with the interests of that people.

Indeed, it is precisely on this issue that he highlights the need for theoretical enquiry: 'the third theoretical focus [in his book] is on the conditions in host countries conducive to the maintenance of diaspora solidarities and loyalties as well as the conditions in homelands likely to trigger or muffle their expression' (Sheffer 1986: 12).

This approach, however, narrows the potential for our normative enquiry into the binaries of loyalty/disloyalty or solidarity/betrayal. If we think of the refusal to take on an obligation, doing so makes sense because of an overriding moral commitment. This is why political obligation and resistance are so closely connected (Walzer 1970). There are cases where a political obligation, such as being conscripted to fight in an unjust war, or having to obey an unjust law, can be understood as legitimately allowing resistance. The same can be said for diaspora politics when the member of a diaspora, or diasporic community, is torn between competing normative commitments to the homeland or kin abroad. The Jewish diaspora provides a good example of the internal tensions that can arise over what it means to support (or have a relationship with) Israel, and of how, across the Jewish diaspora, we find both criticism of and unwavering support for the Israeli government's decisions being the expected obligation for Zionist Jews in the diaspora (Baron 2015; Kahn-Harris 2014).

To explore the idea of diasporas having political obligations is to recognize that their choices follow from a multitude of potentially competing normative commitments and not from some overriding and singular force of sovereignty.[6] The idea of a diaspora's political obligation is not about sovereignty, the law, or the authority of the state, but about the phenomenology of conforming as members of a diasporic community. In hermeneutic phenomenology, this kind of conformity is an important feature of our being-in-the-world (Heidegger 1962).[7] In other words, the pressures we face as members of a society are part of the phenomenological structure of the world and of our ability to function in it (Dreyfus 1991). Because these pressures are ontological, we can understand them as being obligatory,[8] but because we always have a choice in our conforming behaviour, they are also normative.

Politics

What makes the obligation political in our concern about diaspora politics is, among other things, the way in which the expectation of behaviour/conduct and/or belief are tied to the very identity of the diasporic member or community. In other words, whereas political obligation hinges on how our identity as citizens incurs a special bond to our state, the identity of belonging to a diaspora incurs a special bond to one's people.[9] Theorists of political obligation, such as Margaret Gilbert (2006), seek out features of the relationship that render the political obligations legitimate. However, when we consider that, for diasporas, obligations follow out of their diasporic identity (as opposed, for example, to their citizenship), it becomes not the relationship between an agent and some external source that can oblige the said agent who provides the normative grounds, but rather the ethical construction of a diaspora identity itself.

In other words, it is by virtue of one's being-in-the-world as a diaspora that creates the potential for obligations – the pressures of identity and conformity – and what makes them political is that the obligation is directed both toward the normative future of this community (which follows from Hans Jonas's theory of political responsibility) and one's own self-understanding as a member of this community (Baron 2015).

Political obligations follow from membership of and identification with a community, and there can be no theory of diaspora without acknowledging this membership. Even in some of the more metaphorical usages of the term 'diaspora', membership is central to the idea of diaspora.[10] This community, however, is spatially complicated. In her work on Jews, Israel and Zionism, Judith Butler uses the de-territorialized experiences of diaspora as the spatial frame in which to argue for a political ethic of responsibility that is not rooted in the violence of sovereignty.[11] A more detailed spatial theory of this kind can be found in the seminal text of Boyarin and Boyarin (2002), and in the work of the French scholar Stéphane Dufoix (2003: 34), who points to the Janus-faced character of diaspora in that it allows 'dispersion to be thought of either as a state of incompleteness or a state of completeness'. The word 'diaspora', Dufoix (2003: 106) writes:

> nicely fits the changes in the relationships to distance, in view of the quasi-disappearance of time in its relationship to space. The technological possibility of proximity between people who resemble each other in some way – whether religious, national, ethnic, cultural, professional, or other – allows non-territorialized links (networks) to emerge.

This spatial account of diaspora ostensibly opens up the conditions under which non- or de-territoralized accounts of ethics are possible, which is part of what Boyarin and Boyarin (2002: 5) are getting at when they write that 'there may be something gained in thinking about diaspora ... as a positive *resource* in the necessary rethinking of models of policy in the current erosion and questioning of the modern nation-state system and ideal.'[12] This is the power of the idea of diaspora, one that enables a re-thinking of the spatial grounds on which political ethics (and perhaps political responsibility) can be re-conceptualized. Boyarin and Boyarin (2002: 10) argue that the spatial and ethical dimensions are linked:

> Diaspora offers an alternative 'ground' to that of the territorial state for the intricate and always contentious linkage between cultural identity and political organization. Such an alternative ground could avoid the necessarily violent ways in which states resist their own inevitable impermanence. It could also ameliorate the insistence on purity that derives from the dominant, static conception of legitimate collective identity.

Yet, this alternative can only change the spatial framing via an ethical argument if we assume that certain ontological structures can carry normative inferences within them. Because of the is/ought problem, however, when the literature makes this kind of connection, the normative is derived not from our Being as such, which is what Jonas (1985) argues, but rather from the social constructions of our identity, which can change. The formulation that links political practice to identity is addressed in the sociology of Anthony Giddens (1976) and in the literature on ontological security.[13] In an important book in this field, *Defacing power*, Steele (2010) argues that our sense of identity informs our ability to interpret security risks. The general argument is that who we think we are shapes our ability to interpret the world around us in ways that matter for our political decisions. This insight is as relevant for diasporas as it is for anybody else. Yet, when we work out the normative challenges that face a diasporic group, there are competing identities that follow from the ontological condition of a diaspora, which is rooted in multiple identities and geographies simultaneously. Consequently, enquiring into the normative features of diasporic politics involves engaging with this multiplicity.

Conclusion

Although the above is a condensed outline that borrows from a range of literatures – diaspora studies, international theory and political theory – the underlying argument is that there is a way in which we can think of diasporic politics as involving obligations that are political. They are obligatory to the extent that they emerge out of the phenomenological structure of diaspora being-in-the-world, and they are political in that they refer to normative commitments that exist according to the complex geography of a diaspora identity and identification. There are, therefore, three aspects to any theory of diasporic political obligations.

First, diasporic political obligations follow from the ontological character of life in the diaspora, namely that the identity of a diaspora incurs political commitments that may and do conflict because of the multiple facets of a diaspora identity and geography. Second, diasporic political obligations help to reveal the political tensions within a diasporic life. This exposure serves to highlight not what the areas of controversy are, but why they are controversial, and it does so by highlighting the phenomenological (ontological) dimension of life in the diaspora. Finally, diasporic political obligation suggests that the normative commitments of diaspora follow not because of any special relationship between citizen and polity, but rather because of their identity, and this means that it is not loyalty or solidarity that matters in diaspora politics because one's actions will necessarily be consistent with one's self-understanding.

Notes

1 This literature is sometimes called international political theory. See, for example, Beitz (1979), Boucher (1998), Brown (2002) and Lang, Jr (2015).
2 See also Goodin (1988).
3 See, for example, Bader (1997), Balibar (1988), Benhabib et al. (2007), Kymlicka (2003) and Thelen (2000).
4 See also Baron (2014).
5 Admittedly, using the idea of obligation makes it possible to reach similar conclusions; also, presuming a singular form of political attachment is consistent with the political theory of political obligation. Nevertheless, thinking in terms of obligation provides a clearer opportunity for at least considering, if not accepting, that with any obligation comes the accompanying corollary of legitimate resistance and thus of having multiple and competing commitments.
6 This is based on the traditional understanding of sovereignty. See, for example, Bartelson (1995), Bodin and Franklin (1992), Havercroft (2011) and Krasner (1999).
7 Martin Heidegger evokes the concept of *Das Man* to describe this feature of phenomenology.
8 This correlation comes from the argument advanced by Hans Jonas (1985) that our being-in-the-world as humans carries political responsibilities; in other words, normative commitments follow on from our ontological existence.
9 On peoplehood, although more statist than in this context, see Smith (2003).
10 See, for example, Dufoix (2003) and Gilroy (1993).
11 Butler (2012). See also Rose (2005). For a specific critique of sovereignty in this context, see Cocks (2014).
12 Emphasis in original.
13 See especially Steele (2008).

References

Adams, Jr, R. H. and J. Page (2005) 'Do international migration and remittances reduce poverty in developing countries?', *World Development*, 33 (10), 1645–69, doi: 10.1016/j.worlddev.2005.05.004.
Appadurai, A. (1996) *Modernity at large: cultural dimensions of globalization*, Minneapolis: University of Minnesota Press.

Bader, V. (1997) 'The cultural conditions of transnational citizenship: on the interpretation of political and ethnic cultures', *Political Theory*, 25 (6), 771–813, doi: 10.1177/0090591797025006001.
Balibar, E. (1988) 'Propositions on citizenship', *Ethics*, 98 (4), 723–30, doi: 10.1086/293001.
Barham, B. and S. Boucher (1998) 'Migration, remittances, and inequality: estimating the net effects of migration on income distribution', *Journal of Development Economics*, 55 (2), 307–31, doi: 10.1016/S0304-3878(98)90038-4.
Baron, I. Z. (2009) 'The problem of dual loyalty', *Canadian Journal of Political Science*, 42 (4), 1025–44, doi: 10.1017/S0008423909990011.
Baron, I. Z. (2014) 'Diasporic security and Jewish identity', *Modern Jewish Studies*, 13 (2), 292–309, doi: 10.1080/14725886.2013.824231.
Baron, I. Z. (2015) *Obligation in exile: the Jewish diaspora and a theory of international political obligation*, Edinburgh: Edinburgh University Press.
Bartelson, J. (1995) *A genealogy of sovereignty*, Cambridge: Cambridge University Press.
Bauböck, R. (2003) 'Towards a political theory of migrant transnationalism', *International Migration Review*, 37 (3), 700–23, doi: 10.1111/j.1747-7379.2003.tb00155.x.
Beitz, C. R. (1979) *Political theory and international relations*, Princeton: Princeton University Press.
Benhabib, S., I. Shapiro and D. Petranović (2007) *Identities, affiliations, and allegiances*, Cambridge: Cambridge University Press.
Berlin, I. (1969) 'Does political theory still exist?', in P. Laslett and W. G. Runciman (eds) *Philosophy, politics and society (second series)*, Oxford: Basil Blackwell, 1–33.
Bodin, J. and J. H. Franklin (1992) *On sovereignty: four chapters from the six books of the Commonwealth*, Cambridge: Cambridge University Press.
Boucher, D. (1998) *Political theories of international relations: from Thucydides to the present*, Oxford: Oxford University Press.
Boyarin, J. and D. Boyarin (2002) *Powers of diaspora: two essays on the relevance of Jewish culture*, Minneapolis: University of Minnesota Press.
Brown, C. (2002) *Sovereignty, rights and justice: international political theory today*, Oxford: Blackwell.
Butler, J. (2012) *Parting ways: Jewishness and the critique of Zionism*, New York: Columbia University Press.
Campbell, D. (1994) 'The deterritorialization of responsibility: Levinas, Derrida and ethics after the end of philosophy', *Alternatives*, 19 (4), 455–84, doi: 10.1177/030437549401900402.
Clifford, J. (1994) 'Diasporas', *Cultural Anthropology*, 9 (3), 302–38, doi: 10.1525/can.1994.9.3.02a00040.
Cocks, J. (2014). *On sovereignty and other political delusions*, London: Bloomsbury.
Cohen, R. (2008) *Global diasporas: an introduction*, London: Routledge.
Dagger, R. K. (1977) 'What is political obligation?', *American Political Science Review*, 71 (1), 86–94, doi: 10.1017/S0003055400259315.
d'Entrèves, A. P. (1959) *The medieval contribution to political thought: Thomas Aquinas, Marsilius of Padua, Richard Hooker*, New York: Humanities Press.
Dreyfus, H. L. (1991) *Being-in-the-world: a commentary on Heidegger's being and time*, Cambridge, MA: MIT Press.
Dufoix, S. (2003) *Diasporas*, Berkeley: University of California Press.
Frankel, J. (1997) *The Damascus affair: 'ritual murder', politics, and the Jews in 1840*, Cambridge: Cambridge University Press.
Giddens, A. (1976) *New rules of sociological method: a positive critique of interpretive sociologies*, New York: Basic Books.
Gilbert, M. (2006) *A theory of political obligation: membership, commitment, and the bonds of society*, Oxford: Clarendon Press.
Gilroy, P. (1993) *The black Atlantic: modernity and double consciousness*, Cambridge, MA: Harvard University Press.
Goldring, L. (2004) 'Individual and collective remittances to Mexico: a multi-dimensional typology of remittances', *Development and Change*, 35 (4), 799–840, doi: 10.1111/j.0012-155X.2004.00380.x.
Goodin, R. E. (1988) 'What is so special about our fellow countrymen?', *Ethics*, 98 (4), 663–86, doi: 10.1086/292998.
Havercroft, J. (2011) *Captives of sovereignty*, Cambridge: Cambridge University Press.
Heidegger, M. (1962) *Being and time*, Oxford: Blackwell.
Hockenos, P. (2003) *Homeland calling: exile patriotism and the Balkan wars*, Ithaca: Cornell University Press.
Horton, J. (2010) *Political obligation*, Basingstoke: Palgrave Macmillan.
Hutchings, K. and R. Dannreuther (eds) (1999) *Cosmopolitan citizenship*, London: Macmillan.

Jonas, H. (1985) *The imperative of responsibility: in search of an ethics for the technological age*, Chicago: University of Chicago Press.
Kahn-Harris, K. (2014) *Uncivil war: the Israel conflict in the Jewish community*, London: David Paul Books.
Klosko, G. (2005) *Political obligations*, Oxford: Oxford University Press.
Krasner, S. D. (1999) *Sovereignty: organized hypocrisy*, Princeton, NJ: Princeton University Press.
Kymlicka, W. (2003) 'Immigration, citizenship, multiculturalism: exploring the links', in S. Spencer (ed.) *The politics of migration: managing opportunity, conflict and change*, Oxford: Blackwell, 195–208.
Lang, Jr, A. F. (2015) *International political theory: an introduction*, London: Palgrave.
Leff, L. M. (2006) *Sacred bonds of solidarity: the rise of Jewish internationalism in nineteenth-century France*, Stanford, CA: Stanford University Press.
Lyons, T. and P. Mandaville (2011) *Politics from afar: transnational diasporas and networks*, London: Hurst.
Maier, C. S. (2007) '"Being there": place, territory, and identity', in S. Benhabib, I. Shapiro and D. Petranovic (eds) *Identities, affiliations, and allegiances*, Cambridge: Cambridge University Press, 67–84.
Rose, J. (2005) *The question of Zion*, Princeton, NJ: Princeton University Press.
Shain, Y. (2007) *Kinship and diasporas in international affairs*, Ann Arbor: University of Michigan Press.
Sheffer, G. (1986) *Modern diasporas in international politics*, London: Croom Helm.
Sheffer, G. (2003) *Diaspora politics: at home and abroad*, Cambridge: Cambridge University Press.
Simmons, A. J. (1980) *Moral principles and political obligation*, Princeton: Princeton University Press.
Smith, R. M. (2003) *Stories of peoplehood: the politics and morals of political membership*, Cambridge: Cambridge University Press.
Steele, B. J. (2008) *Ontological security in international relations: self-identity and the IR state*, London: Routledge.
Steele, B. J. (2010) *Defacing power: the aesthetics of insecurity in global politics*, Ann Arbor: University of Michigan Press.
Thelen, D. (2000) 'How natural are national and transnational citizenship? A historical perspective', *Indiana Journal of Global Legal Studies*, 7 (2), 549–65, available at: www.repository.law.indiana.edu/ijgls/vol7/iss2/5.
Vertovec, S. and R. Cohen (1999) *Migration, diasporas, and transnationalism*, Cheltenham: Edward Elgar.
Walker, R. B. J. (1999) 'Citizenship after the modern subject', in K. Hutchings and R. Dannreuther (eds) *Cosmopolitan citizenship*, London: Macmillan, 171–200.
Walzer, M. (1970) *Obligations: essays on disobedience, war and citizenship*, Cambridge, MA: Harvard University Press.
Williams, M. S. (2007) 'Nonterritorial boundaries of citizenship', in S. Benhabib, I. Shapiro and D. Petranović (eds) *Identities, affiliations, and allegiances*, Cambridge: Cambridge University Press, 226–56.

Part IV
Connecting diaspora

27
Diaspora and religion
Connecting and disconnecting

Giulia Liberatore and Leslie Fesenmyer

In attempting to understand the migration and settlement of people around the globe, the concept of diaspora has proven crucial, proliferating not only in scholarly discourse but also in public and policy domains. And, as many people move, they bring along their religious beliefs, ideas, practices and objects, prompting renewed efforts to conceptualize 'religion in motion' (Vásquez 2008). Although diaspora first emerged as a religious concept – the Jews, exiled after the Babylonian capture of Jerusalem in the sixth century BCE, constituted the 'prototypical' diaspora (Cohen 2008) – this initial understanding of their entwinement gave way in the 1960s and 1970s to more secular conceptualizations of diaspora. Taking the disentangling of diaspora and religion as its departure point, this chapter considers how the relationship between them has been approached, before turning attention to current conceptualizations both of diaspora and of religion which offer ways to think anew about their relationship. Adopting a processual understanding of both terms, it subsequently engages with the questions of how religious practices, discourses or objects might activate or deactivate diasporas; how they might connect or disconnect diasporic subjects with multiple others around them; and how they might be transformed in the process. These processes are addressed by exploring enduring issues of identification and belonging among diasporic co-religionists, and how they play out spatially and temporally – through practices and claims of territorialization and de-territorialization, and of continuity and discontinuity.

Diaspora and religion as process and practice

Despite the early entwinement between diaspora and religion, the term's proliferation and dispersal across the social sciences from the 1970s onwards contributed to a scholarly disengagement of diaspora from Jewish studies and, therefore, also from other religious elements, practices and discourses. Rather than seeing religion as integral to an understanding of diaspora, the question that preoccupied scholars was in fact the antithesis: do religions (even) constitute diasporas? In Cohen's (1997) typology, diaspora is defined predominantly as an ethno-national construct, bounded territorially to a homeland. Religions are seen to be missing an 'idealization of a homeland and a return movement', which would classify them as diasporas; they are 'extraterritorial rather than territorial'. Cohen (1997: 189) does acknowledge, however, that 'spiritual affinity may generate a bond analogous to that of a diaspora', and in the revised edition of *Global Diasporas* includes 'religious diasporas' in his model as an example of a de-territorialized diaspora with 'atypical' imaginings of 'home'.

Postcolonial and postmodern critiques in the 1990s problematized the relationships between ethno-religious communities and their homeland origins, just as they challenged fixed understandings of diaspora culture (Baumann 1996; Brah 2006; Gilroy 1993; Hall 1990). These critiques coincided with attempts, within religious studies and the social sciences, to deconstruct 'religion' as an essentialized and universal category for cross-cultural comparison. Reflecting on Cohen's model of diaspora, we can see how it relies on a distinction between ethnicity–nationality and religion, which assumes the demarcation of religion as a separate, rationalized, objective and individualized sphere. The cultural and historical specificity of this distinction, premised as it is on a secular and modern understanding of religion dating back to the post-Reformation period (Asad 1993), makes it less applicable to other settings. In Katy Gardner's (1993) famous study of *Desh-Bidesh* (Home and Away), for example, 'homeland' (*desh*) is associated with fertility, spirituality and religiosity, all of which are interconnected and reproduced through the circulation of people, as well as goods, images and ideas between the *desh* and foreign places (*bidesh*) of migration, such as London. For many of Gardner's interlocutors in Sylhet, 'religion' is not singled out as a separate domain distinct from their ancestral, ethnic or national forms of belonging. In her study, diaspora is not solely or primarily an ethno-national construct from which religious and spiritual ideas and practices can be divorced.

Yet within diaspora studies, the question of whether transnational religious traditions can be classified as diasporic, or whether they should be kept analytically distinct, continues to preoccupy scholars. Vertovec (2004: 282) maintains a distinction between diaspora, transnationalism and migration in his discussion of religion, viewing these as separate but interrelated terms. While 'diaspora suggests dispersal from a homeland . . . it should be defined principally in terms of the continuing consciousness of a connection, real or imagined, to that homeland and a distinctive community of co-ethnics in other parts of the world' (Vertovec 2004: 282). This contrasts with transnationalism, which he defines as the 'actual, ongoing exchanges of information, money and resources – as well as regular travel and communication – that members of a diaspora may undertake with others in the homeland or elsewhere within the globalized ethnic community' (Vertovec 2004: 282).

Moving beyond the question of whether religions constitute diasporas, Johnson (2012) attends to how diasporas are made, transformed and activated through religion. He argues for delimiting the use of 'diaspora' by retaining a territorially based definition, and suggests focusing on how diasporic religions include 'territorial invocations made not just through residence or nostalgia, but also through imagination, ritual practice, narratives and the plotting of futures, as well as the summoning of ancestral pasts' (Johnson 2012: 108). Yet his distinction between 'religious diaspora' and 'diasporic religion' – differentiated in terms of whether religious identifications are at the root or are a consequence of emigration – relies on assessing the intensity or importance of religious identification. It curtails an understanding of religion, limiting it to group identity, and allows insufficient space for an understanding of religion as dynamic, as collective and individual, and as embodied and discursive.

Rather than seeking to identify and label the religious element(s) of diaspora, we suggest that it is helpful to follow Brubaker (2005) in thinking about diasporas in processual terms, and as a category of practice. This approach aligns with conceptual shifts in studies of religion from a focus on texts and beliefs to a consideration of religious practices and of how religion is lived (Hall 1997; McGuire 2008; Vásquez 2008). Lived religion allows us to address 'what people *do* with religious idioms, how they use them, what they make of themselves and their worlds with them, and how, in turn, men, women and children are fundamentally shaped by the worlds they are making' (Orsi 2003: 172, emphasis in original). Here, then, conceptualizations of diaspora and religion – as process, practice, claim, idiom, stance and orientation, to name but a few – converge (Brubaker 2005; Tweed 2009). Such an approach, thus, allows us to explore the ways in which diasporas are activated and transformed by religious practices, ideas and experiences. We can also consider how, and to what effect, the 'religious' is claimed, made sense of, constituted, made and re-made in the process.

Universalizing and particularizing, territorializing and de-territorializing

Some religious traditions, like Christianity, Buddhism and Islam, are categorized as having universal or translocal horizons – their spread facilitated by political formations, such as the Umayads and Abbasids in the case of Islam, or Constantine's Roman Empire and the Spanish and Portuguese crowns for the case of Christianity (Vásquez 2010). Others, such as Hinduism, Judaism or African-based religions, are more closely associated with a place or territory (Vásquez 2010). For many Hindus, for example, India constitutes the sacred homeland. These are, however, analytical distinctions that do not necessarily reflect the ways in which diasporic religions are lived in practice. While the question of whether diasporic religions constitute attachments and orientations to particular territories or homelands has troubled diaspora scholars, approaching diasporic religions in more processual terms necessitates that we denaturalize links between identity and belonging, on one hand, and territory and place, on the other. Rather than diaspora or religion referring to existing groups, it is important to study the practices of diasporic co-religionists that constitute senses of belonging and contribute to identifications. Returning then to the question of religions as universal or particular, we can explore universalizing and particularizing as practices and claims that believers adopt in their own self-positioning, as well as in their interactions with and in relation to co-believers and 'others', both religious and non-religious. Accordingly, diasporic believers might invoke or downplay their relationship to particular territories.

Troubling the relationships between religion, home, homeland, roots and exile, for example, Boyarin (2015: 17) describes diasporic religious practices that are not oriented towards the homeland, but create new forms of territorialization in the host country. Building on his previous work with his brother Daniel (Boyarin and Boyarin 1993), he draws on his ethnography of Yiddish culture in New York as 'an alternative to monolithic territorial nationalisms'. Crafted through a process of hybrid linguistic practices and memories, Yiddish culture, he argues, is not based on an absence from the homeland, but on 'fictive kinship' and creative practices of diasporic Jewish immigrants. Yiddish culture is diasporic – yet, despite its assumed orientation towards a homeland, it has become disentangled from a specific territory and has been transformed in a new setting.

While religious practices in Boyarin's case are re-territorialized abroad and enable the formation of new connections among diasporic subjects, religion and diaspora can also orient people in space in multiple, overlapping ways. As Tweed's (1997) ethnography of Cubans in Miami reminds us, religions can at once be locative, translocative and supralocative. More specifically, religions can engage with the territorial location where believers live and contribute to the re-making of home locally, while they may also facilitate the creation of links across space where co-religionists live and transcend homeland and host land (Tweed 1997: 94–5).

The experiences of Somalis in Britain (Liberatore 2017) similarly point to the co-existence of multiple diasporic horizons, and further complicate the distinctions between universalizing and particularizing, and territorializing or de-territorializing processes. Somalis – who migrated in large numbers in the 1980s and early 1990s as civil war spread across the Somali regions – are often described as a global diaspora with strong ties to their homelands as well as extensive transnational connections across the diaspora. Religious memories, narratives and practices have shaped their experience of movement and living abroad, as well as their continued orientations towards a homeland; religious idioms have not only served to connect Somalis to each other, to other Muslims and to the host society, but have also led to intra- and inter-generational fissions. Some of the older generations of Somalis in Britain look back at the past critically, employing global Islamic reformist idioms to reflect on the immorality and corruption of modern socialist Somalia of the 1970s and 1980s. Since moving to the UK and engaging with global reformist discourses, they have begun reading and reasoning about Islamic texts, attending Somali mosques, and adopting new practices – such as the donning of the *jilbab* – that were uncommon prior to the late 1980s. Others are critical of the advent of reformist Islam and of Somalis who have begun to engage more fervently with Islamic teachings and practices. They view this transformation as an 'Arabization' of Somali culture and look back nostalgically at the Sufi practices that were widespread prior to the 1980s, but that have since been largely abandoned or eradicated. Some of the younger generations share similar outlooks, but those who have begun to engage more actively with pious teachings and modes of self-fashioning orient themselves towards the Middle East as their 'religious home' rather than the Somali regions. By joining other Muslims who are part of the global Islamic revival, and participating in a 'transnational Islamic public sphere' (Bowen 2004), they constitute relations to this homeland through visits, study trips and exchanges with scholars in person or online. Some are more interested in moving to the Middle East, or performing *hajj* or *umrah* (holy pilgrimage), rather than returning to the Somali regions. Within the Somali diaspora, therefore, different individuals and generations establish multiple diasporic horizons.

Young pious Somalis, like many young Muslims in Britain, have also begun to adopt an Islamic reformist discourse of 'religion versus culture' that prioritizes a universal 'authentic' Islam over and above the culture of their parents, which they see as particularistic and tied to a place or country. Islam enables young Muslims in Britain not only to connect to a wider transnational *umma* (community of believers), but also to present Islam as a universal tradition that is applicable in all contexts, including Europe. Through this process, they invert political discourses in Europe that present Islam as a reified and homogenized 'culture' incompatible with universal liberal values. Similarly, in the context of republican France, Fernando (2014) describes how young Muslim French men and women contrast a universal Islam with the particularities of republicanism as a strategy for presenting themselves as integrated and as part of the French nation. Yet, in doing so, like Muslims in Britain, they also cast their parents' generation as particularistic, bound by cultural constraints and insufficiently integrated into France. In sum, Islam is crucial to their home-making practices locally, including some and excluding others in the ongoing constitution of morally and emotionally significant communities of belonging. At the same time, their religious affiliations connect them to co-believers around the world, as evidenced by the existence of extensive transnational religious networks (Werbner 2003), while fostering a sense of belonging within the de-territorialized, global religious community of the *umma*.

Continuity and discontinuity

Just as diaspora and religion orient people in space, they also do so in and over time. Given that both terms are often understood as being oriented to the past, and associated with nostalgia and tradition respectively, it follows that questions of continuity and discontinuity are fruitful to consider in relation to diasporic believers. As we know, continuity is not inevitable, but rather necessitates practices to ensure and perpetuate ways of life, values and ideals. As Boyarin (2015: 21) has commented, diaspora might be better understood as 'a shared strategy of survival, continuity, and the production of meaning', rather than about a 'shared predicament of loss'. Accordingly, we can productively explore how diasporic believers imagine and narrate the past to situate the present and engage with the future. They may strive for continuity with the past and constitute their relation to this past in different ways. This is evident, for example, in the Islamic practices of 'embodying' or 'emulating' role models from Islamic history in the processes of making sense of what it means to be a moral person in the present (Deeb 2009). By contrast, in accepting Jesus as their personal saviour, Pentecostals 'make a break from the past' (Meyer 1998), cast off immoral practices and corrupting relations, and are reborn as God's children. Birgit Meyer (1998: 340) highlights that, while this break may be discursively decisive, it is not so easy to effect in practice. Thus, as Pentecostals oscillate between a 'past' identity linked to family and a 'new, individualist identity', the 'past' comes into the present and must continuously be denounced if it is not to undermine their efforts to secure the future. In the diasporic context of London, Kenyan Pentecostals simultaneously make claims of both continuity and discontinuity with the past. Faced with political, economic and social uncertainty in Kenya in the 1990s, many coming of age in that era left their homeland, intent on realizing their aspirations for social adulthood. Yet, once in London, they continued to struggle to realize their ambitions, and it was in this context of thwarted aspirations that many became born again and began attending Pentecostal churches. Like the young pious Somalis described above, Kenyan Pentecostals distinguish between 'religion' and 'culture', particularly *vis-à-vis* their families in Kenya and their ancestral forebears; they selectively retain some values and practices, which they gloss as non-religious, while forsaking others to realize the promise of being God's children (Fesenmyer 2017). Heeding the Bible's call 'to go and make disciples of all nations' (Matthew 28: 16–20), these born-again Christians seek to come together as brothers and sisters in Christ irrespective of race, ethnicity and nationality.

These social relations constitute bonds of what Boyarin (2015) has aptly referred to as 'fictive kinship' with respect to diasporic Jews; the kinship of Kenyan Pentecostals is rooted in the shared experiences of being born again and through the blood of Jesus Christ. These bonds can be read as evidence of their membership in a global Christian community. Accordingly, they envision their return to a 'homeland' in terms of their deliverance to God's kingdom, one that is deferred to the future. At the same time, they claim continuity with Britain's Christian heritage, marking a (re)alignment 'in relation to an extant and imagined Christian history' (Engelke 2010: 179). Their claims of continuity, however, are made in the face of an often hostile reception to their presence in Britain, with tensions playing out along racial lines and, thus, pointing to (implicit) enduring associations of Christianity with a particular race and specific nations. They remind us not to underestimate the salience of the relational context – a global power geometry that locates those born in a poor, geopolitically weak country like Kenya in an inferior position *vis-à-vis* those in Britain (Massey 1993) – for understanding diasporic identifications.

Finally, as religious traditions travel and are reconstituted through the processes described in the examples above, they also mutate and are transformed. Caution must be paid, however, when investigating the changes brought about by diasporization. In making sense of changes and continuities in diasporic religions, it is too often assumed that religious 'traditions' are bounded and fixed prior to movement abroad, and that migration and diasporization constitute the main drivers of change. This is particularly evident in the scholarship on Islam in Europe, which, by emphasizing the ways in which Islam has become more critical, individualized and hence more European (Cesari 2003; Mandaville 2001, 2003), has over-emphasized change and transformation brought about by migration. As Amir-Moazami and Salvatore (2003) have shown, this approach has neglected the 'potential of transformation and reform that originates within Muslim traditions' themselves (Amir-Moazami and Salvatore 2003: 53). Religious traditions are not only shaped by encounters with external factors and circumstances, but are also themselves internally dynamic (Asad 1986), just as individuals are inevitably active agents in processes of change.

Conclusion

We have suggested moving towards a processual approach to diaspora and religion that enables us to explore how diasporas are activated, maintained or transformed and dismantled through religion, but also how religious practices, idioms, objects and imaginaries are shaped in and through individuals, collectivities and projects that present themselves as diasporic. Following Hall (1990), who highlights the ways in which diaspora is used to open up spaces and imaginative possibilities in places of settlement, we can then think of religion as a mode of engagement in diasporic contexts. Diasporas are constituted through engagements with people and places, whether imagined or experienced, affirmative or alienating, proximate or distant, both temporally and spatially. As the examples of Somalis in Britain, Cubans in Miami, Kenyan Pentecostals, and Sylhetis between Britain and Bangladesh illustrate, religious practices create ties between people or, as Cohen has remarked, 'generate a bond analogous to that of diasporas'. Yet, as Boyarin (2015) points out, these bonds are not necessarily oriented towards a homeland or territory, but may take shape and re-territorialize in distinct places in the host society. Religious practices may generate new connections with spiritual homelands that are not necessarily their places of origin – as in the case of young pious Somalis who orient themselves towards the Middle East – or connect co-religionists to a universal 'imagined community' that is not oriented towards a specific place or time. As with young Muslims in Europe, religious narratives of universality, unity and oneness can enable co-religionists to connect with multiple others outside of their faith communities.

At the same time, religious discourses, idioms and practices can also deactivate or fragment diasporic communities or imaginaries. Pentecostals, for example, seek to 'break' with their families and their pasts in the process of entering a new community of co-believers, and young pious Muslims similarly seek to differentiate themselves from older generations to join a universal community of believers. Yet these efforts to disconnect and connect are fluid and dynamic, they require constant effort to sustain, and are never fully achieved in practice. Attachments to, and detachments from, people, places and times are not only enacted in practices and interactions, but also through discourses and the imagination.

In the process, however, religious practices, discourses and idioms are transformed 'in motion'. Rituals are adapted, institutions are transformed, and individuals seek to adapt dynamic religious practices and ideas to new settings and circumstances. Religious practitioners may strive to connect with religious figures from the past in different ways, but this process of bringing the past into the present is always selective and results in the transformation of a religious tradition. Religions and diasporas are inevitably dynamic, transformed through exchange and contestation, as well as through movement and diasporization.

References

Amir-Moazami, S. and A. Salvatore (2003) 'Gender, generation, and the reform of tradition: from Muslim majority societies to Western Europe', in S. Allievi and J. S. Nielsen (eds) *Muslim networks and transnational communities in and across Europe*, Leiden: Brill, 52–77.
Asad, T. (1986) *The idea of the anthropology of Islam*, Washington, DC: Center for Contemporary Arab Studies.
Asad, T. (1993) *Genealogies of religion: discipline and reasons of power in Christianity and Islam*, Baltimore: Johns Hopkins University Press.
Baumann, G. (1996) *Contesting culture: discourses of identity in multi-ethnic London*, Cambridge: Cambridge University Press.
Bowen, J. R. (2004) 'Beyond migration: Islam as a transnational public space', *Journal of Ethnic and Migration Studies*, 30 (5), 879–94, doi: 10.1080/1369183042000245598.
Boyarin, D. and J. Boyarin (1993) 'Diaspora: generation and the ground of Jewish identity', *Critical Inquiry*, 19 (4), 693–725, doi: 10.1086/448694.
Boyarin, J. (2015) 'Reconsidering "diaspora"', in J. Garnett and S. L. Hausner (eds) *Religion in diaspora: cultures of citizenship*, Basingstoke: Palgrave Macmillan, 17–35.
Brah, A. (1996) *Cartographies of diaspora*, London: Routledge.
Brubaker, R. (2005) 'The "diaspora" diaspora', *Ethnic and Racial Studies*, 28 (1), 1–19, doi: 10.1080/0141987042000289997.
Cesari, J. (2003) 'Muslim minorities in Europe: the silent revolution', in J. L. Esposito and F. Burgat (eds) *Modernizing Islam*, New Brunswick: Rutgers University Press, 251–71.
Cohen, R. (1997) *Global diasporas: an introduction*, first edition, London: Routledge.
Cohen, R. (2008) *Global diasporas: an introduction*, second edition, London: Routledge.
Deeb, L. (2009) 'Emulating and/or embodying the ideal: the gendering of temporal frameworks and Islamic role models in Shi'i Lebanon', *American Ethnologist*, 36 (2), 242–57, doi: 10.1111/j.1548-1425.2009.01133.x.
Engelke, M. (2010) 'Past Pentecostalism: notes on rupture, realignment, and everyday life in Pentecostal and African independent churches', *Africa*, 80 (2), 177–99, doi: 10.3366/afr.2010.0201.
Fernando, M. L. (2014) *The republic unsettled: Muslim French and the contradictions of secularism*, Durham: Duke University Press.
Fesenmyer, L. (2017) 'Place and the (un-)making of religious peripheries: weddings among Kenyan Pentecostals in London', in D. Garbin and A. Strhan (eds) *Religion and the global city*, London: Bloomsbury.
Gardner, K. (1993) 'Desh-Bidesh: Sylheti images of home and away', *Man*, 28 (1), 1–15, doi: 10.2307/2804433.
Gilroy, P. (1993) *The black Atlantic: modernity and double consciousness*, London: Verso.
Hall, D. (1997) *Lived religion: toward a history of practice*, Princeton: Princeton University Press.
Hall, S. (1990) 'Cultural identity and diaspora', in J. Rutherford (ed.) *Identity: community, culture, difference*, London: Lawrence & Wishart, 222–37.
Johnson, P. C. (2012) 'Religion and diaspora', *Religion and Society: Advances in Research*, 3 (1), 95–114, doi: 10.3167/arrs.2012.030106.
Liberatore, G. (2017) *Somali, Muslim, British: striving in securitized Britain*, London: Bloomsbury.
Mandaville, P. G. (2001) *Transnational Muslim politics: reimagining the umma*, London: Routledge.
Mandaville, P. G. (2003) 'Towards a critical Islam: European Muslims and the changing boundaries of transnational religious discourse', in S. Allievi and J. Nielsen (eds) *Muslim networks and transnational communities in and across Europe*, Leiden: Brill, 127–45.
McGuire, M. B. (2008) *Lived religion: faith and practice in everyday life*, Oxford: Oxford University Press.
Massey, D. (1993) 'Power-geometry and a progressive sense of place', in J. Bird, B. Curtis, T. Putnam, G. Robertson and L. Tickner (eds) *Mapping the futures: local cultures, global change*, London: Routledge, 56–69.
Meyer, B. (1998) '"Make a complete break with the past": memory and post-colonial modernity in Ghanaian Pentecostalist discourse', *Journal of Religion in Africa*, 28 (3), 316–49, doi: 10.1163/157006698X00044.
Orsi, R. A. (2003) 'Is the study of lived religion irrelevant to the world we live in? Special presidential plenary address, Society for the Scientific Study of Religion, Salt Lake City, November 2, 2002', *Journal for the Scientific Study of Religion*, 42 (2), 169–74, doi: 10.1111/1468-5906.t01-1-00170.
Tweed, T. A. (1997) *Our lady of exile: diaspora religion at a Cuban Catholic shrine in Miami*, New York: Oxford University Press.
Tweed, T. A. (2009) *Crossing and dwelling: a theory of religion*, Cambridge, MA: Harvard University Press.

Vásquez, M. (2008) 'Studying religion in motion: a networks approach', *Method and Theory in the Study of Religion*, 20 (2), 151–84, doi: 10.1163/157006808X283570.
Vásquez, M. (2010) 'Diasporas and religions', in K. Knott and S. McLoughlin (eds) *Diasporas: concepts, intersections, identities*, London: Zed Books, 128–33.
Vertovec, S. (2004) 'Religion and diaspora', in R. Warne, P. Antes and A. Geertz. (eds) *New approaches to the study of religion: textual, comparative, sociological, and cognitive approaches*, Berlin: Walter de Gruyter, 275–304.
Werbner, P. (2003) *Pilgrims of love: the anthropology of a global Sufi cult*, London: Hurst & Company.

28
Digital diasporas

Mihaela Nedelcu

The vibrant expansion of the digital revolution has transformed migration processes, and the new figure of the 'online migrant' (Nedelcu 2009a, 2016) – also termed as 'connected' (Diminescu 2010) or 'co-present' (Nedelcu and Wyss 2016) – embodies a new ideal-type of mobile population in the twenty-first century. This ideal-type refers to migrants intensively engaged in transnational ways of being and ways of belonging, who are developing new transnational habitus and disseminating cosmopolitan values; while simultaneously engaging in reviving and/or reinventing their myths of origin (Nedelcu 2009a, 2012). This transformation reflects a more global process of cosmopolitanization of social life, in which dialogic imagination makes co-existing particularistic and cosmopolitan attitudes and social practices across borders (Beck 2002a; Nedelcu 2012).

At the same time, the multiplication of new social media have allowed the emergence of new agoras and new public spheres that are giving through virtual space a voice to minorities and dispersed populations. Through innovative practices, online migrants are expressing particular identities, forms of multiple political allegiances and a renewed sense of community (Alonso and Oiarzabal 2010; Georgiou 2010; Nedelcu 2009a). Migrant websites, discussion forums and diverse social media environments are creating new possibilities for the expression of diasporic consciousness and engagement, and diasporic groups are multiplying and becoming increasingly visible in the virtual space.

On another level, a double-ended discourse developed in migration studies with regard to the ongoing symbolic and material engagement of migrants over borders. On the one hand, the 'diaspora' debate intensified during the 1990s (Anteby-Yemini et al. 2005; Bruneau 1995; Cohen 1997; Sheffer 1986; among others) and prominent scholars put significant effort to reframe this concept's essential dimensions to extend it over the paradigmatic case of the Jewish diaspora. On the other hand, and simultaneously, transnational studies gained momentum, highlighting how transnationalism, transnationality and transnationalization represent intertwined features of the (post)modern condition (Faist 2010) that characterize societal transformations in the wake of information society and the mobility paradigm; rooted both within *nations unbound* (Basch et al. 1994) and postnational, cosmopolitan social realities (Beck 2002b).

However, the borderline differentiating transnationalism and diaspora is shrinking. Often a similar lens is applied to the study of both phenomena (in terms of identity, socio-economic networks, political loyalty, and so on). Critical voices are finding regrettable the heuristic devaluation of the diaspora concept as a reflection of modern transnationalism, while new attempts of re-theorization have been noticed in the last decade (for example, Bauböck and Faist 2010; Faist 2010). In this context, discussing the heuristic value of the concept of diaspora comes down to understanding its relevance in a social world strongly reshaped by a new phase of globalization reflected in complex transnational (as well as de-nationalized) cultural, economic and political processes accelerated by information and communication technologies (ICTs) (Beck 2002a; Castells 1998; Nedelcu 2012). This also means addressing the questions of what is (still) there at the core of diasporas, what is not (any more), what is new in the digital age?

This chapter discusses to what extent a concept conceived to describe a particular dispersion – that of the Jewish people, which took place more than two thousand years ago – might prove useful in analysing the emergence of new social dynamics spanning borders, embedded within new digital technologies and virtual spaces. In the digital age, have diasporas – as social constructs – seen their original meaning re-shaped? What impact do ICTs have on diasporas' practices? Are ICTs dramatically transforming diasporic dynamics or are 'digital', 'online' or 'virtual' diasporas just matching and/or reinforcing old diaspora patterns? Is the Internet accelerating diasporic processes already inscribed in a *longue durée*, or is it enhancing the emergence of new social forms in diasporas? To answer these questions, we are arguing that ICTs have both conservative and transformative effects on diasporas. They are deepening the quality of ties diasporic groups are developing among themselves and with the country of origin. At the same time, digital diasporas are the reflection of key transformations of diasporic functioning along with at least three aspects: new media enhances a process of actualization of the homeland (memory) on a day-to-day basis; virtual space becomes a new territory replacing the 'non-lieu' (Ma Mung 1994) of diasporas; and ICTs heighten the agency capability of members of the diasporas who can act transnationally in real time. Moreover, we contend that digital diasporas represent the new moment of the diaspora paradigm, as the expression of a particular form of the cosmopolitan condition.

From (forced) dispersion to digital gathering: what is old and what is new

The diaspora paradigm is based on the archetypal case of the Jewish exile and consists of several prominent characteristics: forced dispersion, a strong consciousness of possessing a particular identity embedded with a non-dissimulated loyalty to origins, an aspiration to physical or symbolic return, a dominated position within the host society, as well as a polycentrism of diasporic flows and groups (Bruneau 1995; Cohen 1997; among others). In fact, in its classical definition, a diaspora exists because its members claim that they belong to it, thus actively perpetuating an ancestral memory of the dispersion; both temporality and spatiality representing crucial dimensions of this process (Bruneau 1995; Ma Mung 1999). Cohen (1997) emphasizes the fact that a diaspora space comes into being through a shared sense of belonging, a shared memory of uprooting and a shared longing for the nation of origin. This implies a shared imaginary of communality that spans borders in space and time; a process that is significantly strengthened by, but also renewed through new media environments in the digital age (Georgiou 2006, 2010; Nedelcu 2002, 2009a).

In their attempt to extend this notion's meaning while reinforcing its heuristic consistency, social sciences scholars suggested various typologies of diasporas: stateless diasporas and diasporas based on a state of origin (Sheffer 1986); diasporas qualified as 'victim', 'imperial', 'cultural' or 'economic' (Cohen 1997); as well as 'classic', 'veteran', 'emerging' or 'sleeping' diasporas

(Sheffer 1986). These typologies aim to widen the spectrum of social phenomena analysable through a diaspora approach, extending it to new modern diasporic processes. In the largest sense, maximalist approaches tend towards considering diasporas as ethnic minorities of migrants who maintain strong affective and material ties with their country of origin while living in a host country (Bruneau 1995; Sheffer 1986). But even through such an approach, the dispersion on its own is not enough to form a resource. According to Ma Mung (1999), it becomes 'positive' as soon as it is claimed and valued by the diasporans themselves. Bruneau (1995) follows Sheffer (1993) in arguing that at least three distinctive features are still at the core of a diaspora in modern times. These are (1) a strong claim to a particular ethnic or national identity; (2) the existence of a political, religious or cultural organization of the dispersed group; and (3) the presence of concrete and/or imaginary ties with the territory or the country of origin.

In our times, recently dispersed migrant groups embedded within new migration flows can easily develop ICTs-mediated dynamics that embrace such a diasporic meaning, such as 'in the age of cyberspace, a diaspora can, to some degree, be held together or re-created through the mind, the cultural artefacts and through a shared imagination' (Cohen 1997: 26).

First coined by Stubbs (1999) to analyse the emergence and the role of computer-mediated diasporic public spheres in re-imagining a homeland at war from diverse global sites, in the case of Croatia, the notion of 'virtual diaspora' spread and won recognition in social sciences in the last two decades. ICTs shaped new virtual spaces that are particularly relevant to diasporas, as they are 'decentralized, interactive and transnational by nature'[1] (Georgiou 2002: 10). As a consequence, the growing proliferation of diasporic groups and dynamics in the virtual space raised new interest in the diaspora approach. New terms – such as 'online', 'virtual', 'digital' or 'e-' diaspora – came into existence, along with numerous empirical studies that emphasized new diasporic patterns in which instrumental online dynamics overlap offline material outcomes (Alonso and Oiarzabal 2010; Brinkerhoff 2009; Kiyindou and Pélage 2012; Nedelcu 2002, 2009b; among others).

Early efforts to identify the extent of the diasporas' presence in the virtual space quickly encountered serious methodological bias, due to a strong heterogeneity in the use of the word 'diaspora' on the Internet and an impressive variation related to the content of websites qualified as diasporic (Bordes-Benayoun 2012; Le Bayon 2010; Ma Mung 2002). In fact, different actors compete to occupy the virtual space of diasporas; for instance, African scientific networks stand alongside the diaspora of Cameroon rugby men (Bordes-Benayoun 2012). The first systematic efforts to map diasporas in digital networks were set up through a project entitled 'e-diasporas atlas',[2] which was conducted for a period of over ten years. Using a specific crawling software to extract a particular corpus of diaspora websites, this project archived some 8,000 migrant websites (Diminescu 2012). However, if digital and virtual methods using the Internet as a research site promise to offer a fresh insight into this new facet of the diasporic process, the study of digital diasporas should not be confined to the analysis of the link structures of websites and webographic content, or quantitative surveys of the websites' users and administrators (Kissau and Hunger 2010). It should also comprehensively address the question of who are the new actors of these processes and how new social media and the Internet generate qualitatively new forms of diasporas and boost their capacity to mobilize transnationally (Nedelcu 2009b).

Digital diasporas were defined by Alonso and Oiarzabal (2010: 11) as 'distinct online networks that diasporic people use to re-create identities, share opportunities, spread their culture, influence homeland and host-land policy, or create debate about common-interest issues by means of electronic devices'. They are different from virtual communities and nations by the fact that strong ties with real nations pre-exist the creation or re-creation of the digital community. This suggests that the process of digitalization of the diasporas maintains their essence, which means it contributes in reproducing dispersed migrants' strong relationships with their country, region or territory of origin, and among themselves. Nevertheless, this same process is also transformative. As is argued in the next section, ICTs contribute to re-imagining homeland through new deterritorialized moorings and a day-to-day actualization process that enables a renewed capacity of agency of diasporic groups. Long-lasting commitment combined with ubiquitous long-distance communication and the capacity of instantaneous online mobilizations transform digital diasporas into legitimate actors within a transnational social sphere where nation-state and diaspora interests meet, converge or confront.

Digital diasporas: the new moment of the diaspora paradigm

The actualization of homeland imaginary through satellite media and Internet

The development of new digital compression technologies and the arrival of Ku band satellites raised the possibilities of broadcasting through large numbers of radio and television channels. Since the 1990s, the so-called 'diaspora broadcasting' to minorities and 'delocalized audiences' grew exponentially (Karim 2003). As a result, this expanded access to mainstream mass media (radio, television and newspapers), produced and distributed in both host and homeland countries, contributed to significant cultural changes. In their study of the media and cultural practices of the Turkish diaspora in the United Kingdom, France and Germany, Aksoy and Robins (2003: 93) argued that satellite television systems allow migrants to 'routinely watch television from Turkey, and to be thereby in synchronized contact with everyday life and events in Turkey'. This capacity to actualize ancestral memories and live in synchronic connection with the socio-political reality of the country of origin transforms the ways migrants experience separation and distance. Although some voices fear that such practices might contribute to a greater essentialization of ethnic, national or religious identities and prevent migrants' integration in the host country, Aksoy and Robins (2003) assert that diaspora broadcasting stimulates 'cultural demythologization'. As Rigoni (2001) also remarks, ethnic media plays a key role in updating perceptions of 'territorial, cultural, social, and political belonging' and engenders a kind of 'banal transnationalism'. Consequently, this process has a corrective effect, pushing migrants to reject conservative tendencies and develop criticism with regard to their own cultural heritage.

ICTs-mediated communication strengthens this effect, as online migrants in general benefit from ubiquitous social media in order to keep up to date with public politics and private life events within transnational social fields, which encompass host and homeland countries (Nedelcu 2009a, 2012). In such a context, discussion forums, social networks, instant communication software, and so on, are the communication tools that contribute to a continuous renewal of the cultural and political landmarks of the diaspora's imaginary. This new reality contrasts with, and renders obsolete, the nostalgic approach inherent to 'old' diasporas. Diasporic groups in the digital age have a firm grip on homeland daily events, and this process heightens the traits of a 'global diaspora culture'. It also contributes to the emergence of new 'imagined communities' in the diaspora, by diversifying the mechanisms through which 'diasporic subjects relate to communities' (Georgiou 2010: 30), based less on nostalgia and symbolic ties, and more on hybrid identities and agency.

Re-creating a new territory for diasporas in the virtual space

Although it defines itself by relating to a (mythical) homeland territory, a diaspora is by definition the result of a dispersion and presents itself as an extremely de-centralized, poly-centric or de-territorialized social structure (Bruneau 1995). Its existence is the result of various flows that link diasporic groups together and with the nation-state of origin (when the latter exists). Thus, the diaspora's spatiality is straight away reticular, with a blurring of unfixed boundaries. As Georgiou (2010: 20) notices:

> by thinking through diaspora, we observe the qualities of space as lived and as imagined, as context for identification and struggle, as dependent on memory, experience and ideology of deterritorialization and reterritorialization, of mobility and of contact or interruption of contact with old and new others.

ICTs, and the Internet in particular, as a 'post-geographically bounded global communication system' (Alonso and Oiarzabal 2010: 9), introduce a new lens for discussing diasporas' territorialities and spatialities. Inevitably, they shed a new light on the virtuality of diasporas. Following Foucher-Dufoix and Dufoix (2012), we argue that digital diasporas mirror two complementary dynamics – the 'virtualization of homeland' and the 'homelandization of the virtual'[3] – through which the nation can come into existence in various ways, not just through its territorial embeddedness. Therefore, a 'virtual', 'digital', 'online' or 'e-' diaspora does not oppose a 'real' 'old' one, but reflects the mechanisms through which a diaspora can come into action in the digital age. Digital diasporas take possession of the virtual space to recreate global imagined communities and give sense to common diasporic experiences. In this context, the Internet makes 'territorial particularity less significant and spaces of communication more relevant for identity and belonging' (Georgiou 2010: 32). At the same time, the webosphere and its arenas of communication generate an encompassing space where members of diasporas can express themselves, organize and come together.

Three particular scenarios caught our attention. On the one hand, as shown in the case of the 'Yugoslav diaspora' (Mazzucchelli 2012), the webosphere offered an alternative sociocultural space that compensates for the dissolution of the former political and territorial organization of the Federal Republic of Yugoslavia. Mazzucchelli (2012) studied how 'Yugonostalgic' websites connect diasporic groups still committed to seeing themselves as a national community in order to re-create 'virtual representations' of the 'past-country' and its territory. Once again, virtual dynamics in this context reinforce a sense of belonging set within a strong memory of the past, as a reiteration of the mythical pattern of the Jewish diaspora.

On the other hand, the virtual space can also simultaneously become a territory of (political) struggle and identity claim. Bernal (2005) takes the Eritrean cyberspace as a case in point to analyse 'ordinary people inventing a public sphere that made possible the articulation of ideas and sentiments that could not be expressed elsewhere' (Bernal 2005: 662). 'Eritrea on-line' (Bernal 2005) represents a good example of how digital diasporas contribute to the fabric of the nation from outside its borders. Diaspora websites function as

> an ambiguous and elastic space, which can serve at times to extend the nation and state sovereignty across borders and at other times can be used as an extraterritorial space, safe for civil society and dissent because of its location outside Eritrea and beyond the reach of the state.
>
> *(Bernal 2013: 22)*

A third scenario relates to regional minority identities. This is the case of Breton diasporic webscapes (Le Bayon 2010) and of the Basque online social networks (Oiarzabal 2012) that give visibility to a strong feeling of belonging to a particularistic identity within national territories. In the case of these groups, often considered as dissenting separatist minorities by national governments and authorities, the presence on the web of Breton and Basque expats and associations abroad gives a broad transnational reach to a local culture. The web mapping of the Breton diaspora carried out by Le Bayon (2010) using crawler tools revealed the various roles and territorial (or digital) anchorage of actors making the virtual territory significant for this regional minority.

These are prime examples of the hybrid nature as well as the plasticity of the homeland's borders that are continuously reshaping themselves in the virtual space. Thus, ICTs, and the Internet in particular, bring into existence the '*non-lieu de la diaspora*' (Ma Mung 1994). Local, national and transnational markers of belonging combine together with a strong determination to give a voice to diaspora minorities, and lead to the creation of this new territory of diasporas (Nedelcu 2002). Moreover, the territorial dimension re-emerges within the virtual spaces of diasporas by merging various (regional, national and global) scales.

Digital diasporas as transnational agents of change in the homeland

From a political perspective, the permanent actualization of homeland imaginary and belonging, combined with the emergence of a new territory of political struggle, represent favourable conditions for the enhancement of new agency mechanisms for digital diasporas. Internet and social media become a de-territorialized transnational public sphere in which diasporic groups can voice their claims, mobilize transnationally and effect political change (Nedelcu 2009b).

Numerous studies on digital diasporas reveal the complex dynamics through which nationals abroad can influence homeland politics. In the case of the Eritrean online diaspora, already mentioned above, diasporans' political participation primarily consists of setting up cyberspace forums as free agoras of expression, and thus creating a public sphere that 'has no offline counterpart in Eritrea', but is 'an integral part of Eritrea's national politics' (Bernal 2013: 22). These forums are the result of a 'kaleidoscopic experience' that mingles 'real life (back home in Eritrea), diasporic life (in a foreign land), and virtual life (on Dehai)' (Bernal 2005: 668), and is there to serve a civic engagement by the diaspora for democracy. Thus, civil society that was unable to develop within the homeland territory finds grounds for evolving online.

Such situations multiply in the case of digital diasporas that organize and mobilize themselves in the context of civil wars, political conflicts and lack of democracy. Leaning on empirical studies on US-based virtual diasporas from Tibet, Nepal, Afghanistan, Somalia and Egypt, Brinkerhoff (2009) backs this argument by highlighting the role of cyber-grassroots organizations that have sprung up through the Internet. Although they exist exclusively in cyberspace, these organizations help crystallize a collective hybrid identity and frame the debate on human rights and democracy in the country of origin. According to the author, digital diasporas can in this way actively produce a more inclusive political culture, thus contributing towards enhancing the state's stability and political legitimacy.

The Arab Spring movements followed similar patterns, with the particularity that they benefited from the contributions of diaspora transnational communities organized through the Web, as much as from the connection between free social media communication and the occupation of urban space (Castells 2012).

Such examples suggest that digital diasporas operate as a watchdog of the power-in-place and take on the role of a transnational actor within civil society, with the ability to reinforce democratic attitudes and power in the countries of origin, and become an 'agent of democratization' (Faist 2010: 25). The enhanced agency capacity of diaspora is even more striking when it combines with the nation-state's openness to partnership and collaboration towards development. An interesting case in point are the scientific e-diasporas that represent an alternative response to the brain drain phenomena and return schemes developed by countries of origin (Nedelcu 2009b). The example of the Romanian scientific diaspora illustrates the effectiveness of a transnational virtual network of scholars of Romanian origin in producing significant change to Romanian policies and practices with regard to reforms to the national research and education systems. As a bottom-up initiative of young expatriate scientists, the website www.ad-astra.ro and its related discussion groups generated a vivid dynamic within the Romanian academic field, as it aimed to install good practices and transnational expertise at the core of the reform process. Although the transnational computer-mediated organization and operation of the *Ad-Astra* group represented successful keys for the diasporic project and acted as catalysts within the Romanian scientific community, it was the creation of a registered home-based NGO that allowed this e-diaspora to act as a legitimate actor in the arena of political players within Romanian civil society. Collective expertise and knowledge transfer occurred through a symbiosis between mixed action and interaction dynamics, both virtual and face to face, bringing together migrant and non-migrant scholars in a common effort to influence research reform. The overlapping of online and offline practices and dynamics was at the core of the process in constructing a common vision of education and research reform (Nedelcu 2009b, 2016).

Finally, these examples reveal the ability of digital diasporas to bring about local change transnationally. ICTs create the premises for a process of globalization of domestic policies and these new transnational dynamics point to major social transformations of 'national' realities that increasingly become transnationally/globally constructed; diasporas being definitely legitimate actors in this process.

Digital diasporas and the cosmopolitan condition

The swift development of the Internet towards collaborative social networking platforms and media sharing (what is usually named web 2.0) since the turn of the twenty-first century, as well as more recent evolutions towards even more connected technologies evolving within a third-generation web (web 3.0) are accelerating complex processes of social transformation. Social life and structures are entering a new phase of global change that social science scholars qualified as glocalization, transnationalization and cosmopolitanization (Beck 2002a; Castells 1998; Faist 2010; Nedelcu 2009a; Robertson 1995). These processes reflect into multiple connections through flows and networks of communication between multi-located poles, and generate multifaceted outcomes that involve to the same extent migrant and non-migrant populations. Therefore, in the same way that those diasporic groups continuously update their homeland imaginary, non-migrants use ICTs to enter various transnational dynamics and open their imaginary to the others' otherness, developing a consciousness of global feeling. They also express themselves through virtual, de-territorialized agoras and become part of a global public sphere, thus being able to take action transnationally through what Castells (2012) called 'networks of outrage and hope'. New global social movements such as 'The Indignatos 15-M Movement' or 'Occupy Wall Street' have been made possible by way of a transnational hybrid 'third space' of autonomy, starting in cyberspace to find their material expression through the occupation of urban public spaces (Castells 2012). These movements are not only forms of transnational politics, but they also have a cultural dimension as they 'share a specific culture, the culture of autonomy, the fundamental cultural matrix of contemporary societies' (Castells 2012: 230). By bringing about a sense of togetherness that could not exist before social media communication, the new 'mass-self communication' technologies are also at the core of the emergence of forms of banal cosmopolitanism. They find themselves at the centre of a process of social cosmopolitanization that 'by no means indicates "a" cosmopolitan society, but the interactive relationship of de-nationalization and re-nationalization, de-ethnicization and re-ethnicization, de-localization and re-localization in society and politics' (Beck 2002b: 81). This is not to say that we are all cosmopolitans (or transnationals) nowadays, but that we are all living lives deeply embedded within both local and global social, economic and political realities and dynamics (Beck 2002b; Nedelcu 2009a, 2012).

In light of the foregoing analysis, digital diasporas are undoubtedly one prominent facet of the actual process of cosmopolitanization of world societies. This is not surprising when brought back to the fact that diaspora consciousness 'is also about feeling global' (Clifford 1997: 257). In her analysis of diasporic transnationalism, Georgiou (2010: 21) already stated that 'diaspora can arguably become a metaphor for life and identity in cosmopolitan times' and that 'diasporic people . . . provide the ultimate example of the cosmopolitan condition' (Georgiou 2010: 31).

However, when posing the question of what kind of dance partners are diasporans and cosmopolitans in the digital age – in the same vein as Faist (2010) asked the question of what dance partners are diaspora and transnationalism – the answer should be more nuanced. It recalls a number of dissimilarities that distinguish, according to Faist (2010), diaspora and transnationalism from globalization approaches and world theories. We argue that diasporans still maintain intense connections to a national or a local territory, which is not central to the preoccupations of cosmopolitans. Although digital diasporas deploy and act transnationally through global de-territorialized mechanisms, diasporans do not claim 'a global consciousness', but are strongly guided by a national centrality. Nor do they struggle to defend the global spread of universalistic norms, as cosmopolitans do.

Conclusion

In the light of this analysis, digital diasporas have given a new momentum to the diaspora paradigm characterized by at least three transforming processes: a permanent actualization of the diasporic imaginary enabling criticism and renewing feelings of belonging to the homeland; the emergence of a new virtual territory that materializes the 'non-lieu' of the diasporas and becomes a public space for diasporas' memory and mobilization; and an increased capacity of agency that allows digital diasporas to act as legitimate transnational actors in the processes of globalization of domestic policies.

All these characteristics reflect a new temporality and spatiality that meaningfully differentiate digital diasporas from 'old' diasporas. Instantaneity, ubiquity and synchronism represent the temporal qualities of how 'new' diasporic collectives function, instead of diachronic landmarks proper to traditional diasporas. They are also in keeping with a more general trend of social change that affects modern societies through a process of cosmopolitanization. In this process, migrants' and non-migrants' transnational ways of being and of belonging in the digital age become manifest through a wide variety of 'orientations within a local-global continuum in which local and global are strongly intertwined and overstep home- and host-countries' horizons' (Nedelcu 2012: 1353).

In this context, digital diasporas offer a heuristically valuable perspective for the analysis of social transformations that require opening social sciences research towards a more inclusive 'both. . . and. . . ' epistemological stance (Beck 2002b) that allows us to think about the making of social worlds in the digital age. In a specific sense, they illustrate in an ideal-typical manner how contemporary (national) societies result from the process of intertwining local and global social dynamics, as well as the intermingling of particular identities and common transnational imaginings, in which migrants and non-migrants, locals and diasporans, mobile and non-mobile populations all play significant roles. Because of this, they could give a new sense to, and understanding of, the national project in modern digital times.

Notes

1 In French in the original: '*décentralisé, interactif et transnational par essence*' (Georgiou 2002: 10).
2 The e-diasporas atlas was developed in the framework of the Fondation Maison des Sciences de l'Homme ICT Migrations programme. For more details, see: www.e-diasporas.fr/.
3 In French in the original: '*virtualisation de la patrie*' versus '*«patrialisation» du virtuel*' (Foucher-Dufoix and Dufoix 2012: 60).

References

Aksoy, A. and K. Robins (2003) 'Banal transnationalism: the difference that television makes', in K. H. Karim (ed.) *The media of diasporas*, London: Routledge, 89–104.
Alonso, A. and P. J. Oiarzabal (2010) 'The immigrant worlds' digital harbors: an introduction', in A. Alonso and P. J. Oiarzabal (eds) *Diasporas in the new media age: identity, politics and community*, Reno: University of Nevada Press, 1–15.
Anteby-Yemini, L., W. Berthomière and G. Sheffer (eds) (2005) *Les diasporas: 2000 ans d'histoire*, Rennes: Presses Universitaires de Rennes.
Basch, L., N. Glick Schiller and C. Szanton Blanc (1994) *Nations unbound: transnational projects, postcolonial predicaments, and deterritorialized nation-states*, London: Routledge.
Baubök, R. and T. Faist (eds) (2010) *Diaspora and transnationalism*, Amsterdam: Amsterdam University Press.
Beck, U. (2002a) 'The cosmopolitan society and its enemies', *Theory, Culture & Society*, 19 (1/2), 17–44, doi: 10.1177/026327602128931206.
Beck, U. (2002b) 'The cosmopolitan perspective' in S. Vertovec and R. Cohen (eds) *Conceiving cosmopolitanism: theory, context and practice*, Oxford: Oxford University Press, 61–85.
Bernal, V. (2005) 'Eritrea on-line: diaspora, cyberspace, and the public sphere', *American Ethnologist*, 32 (4), 660–75, doi: 10.1525/ae2005324660.
Bernal, V. (2013) 'Civil society and cyberspace: reflections on Dehai, Asmarino, and Awate', *Africa Today*, 60 (2), 20–36, doi: 10.2979/africatoday.60.2.21.
Bordes-Benayoun, C. (2012) 'La diaspora ou l'ethnique en mouvement', *Revue Européenne des Migrations Internationales*, 28 (1), 13–31, doi: 10.4000/remi.5700.
Brinkerhoff, J. (2009) *Digital diasporas: identity and transnational engagement*, Cambridge: Cambridge University Press.
Bruneau, M. (1995) 'Espaces et territoires de diasporas', in M. Bruneau (ed.) *Diasporas*, Montpellier: GIP Reclus.
Castells, M. (1998) *La société en réseaux. Tome I. L'ère de l'information*, Paris: Fayard.
Castells, M. (2012) *Networks of outrage and hope: social movements in the internet age*, Cambridge: Polity Press.
Clifford, J. (1997) *Routes: travel and translation in the late twentieth century*, Cambridge, MA: Harvard University Press.
Cohen, R. (1997) *Global diasporas: an introduction*, London: University College London Press.
Diminescu, D. (2012) *E-diasporas atlas: exploration and cartography of diasporas on digital networks*, Paris: Maison des Sciences de l'Homme.
Faist, T. (2010) 'Diaspora and transnationalism: what kind of dance partners?', in R. Baubök and T. Faist (eds) *Diaspora and transnationalism*, Amsterdam: Amsterdam University Press, 9–34.
Foucher-Dufoix, V. and S. Dufoix (2012) 'La patrie peut-elle être virtuelle?', *Pardès*, 52 (2), 57–75, doi: 0.3917/parde.052.0057.
Georgiou, M. (2002) 'Les diasporas en ligne, une expérience concrète de transnationalisme', *Hommes et Migrations*, 1240, 10–18, available at: www.hommes-et-migrations.fr/docannexe/file/1240/1240_03.pdf.
Georgiou, M. (2006) *Diaspora, identity and the media: diasporic transnationalism and mediated spatialities*, Cresskill, NJ: Hampton Press.
Georgiou, M. (2010) 'Identity, space and the media: thinking through diaspora', *Revue Européenne des Migrations Internationales*, 26 (1), 17–35, available at: http://remi.revues.org/5028.

Karim, K. (2003) 'Mapping diasporic mediascapes', in K. H. Karim (ed.) *The media of diasporas*, London: Routledge, 1–18.

Kissau, K. and U. Hunger (2010) 'The internet as a means of studying transnationalism and diaspora', in R. Bauböck and T. Faist (eds) *Diaspora and transnationalism*, Amsterdam: Amsterdam University Press, 245–66.

Kiyindou, A. and T. M. Pélage (2012), 'Réseaux virtuels, reconstruction du lien social et de l'identité dans la diaspora noire', *Études de communication*, 38, 189–201, doi: 10.4000/edc.3425.

Le Bayon, S. (2010) 'Sociologie de la composition des collectifs web 2.0: le cas de la diaspora bretonne', doctoral thesis, Université Rennes 2, Université Européenne de Bretagne, available at: https://tel.archives-ouvertes.fr/tel-00551703.

Ma Mung, E. (1994) 'Non-lieu et utopie: la diaspora chinoise et le territoire', *L'espace géographique*, 23 (2), 106–13, doi: 10.3406/spgeo.1994.3280.

Ma Mung, E. (1999) 'La dispersion comme ressource', *Cultures & Conflits*, 33/34, 89–103, doi: 10.4000/conflits.225.

Ma Mung, E. (2002) 'La désignation des diasporas sur internet', *Hommes et Migrations*, 1240, 19–28, available at: www.hommes-et-migrations.fr/docannexe/file/1240/1240_04.pdf

Mazzucchelli, F. (2012) 'What remains of Yugoslavia? From the geopolitical space of Yugoslavia to the virtual space of the Web Yugosphere', *Social Science Information*, 51 (4), 631–48, doi: 10.1177/0539018412456781.

Nedelcu, M. (2002) 'L'instrumentalisation de l'espace virtuel par une communauté des professionnels immigrés: vers une nouvelle forme d'organisation diasporique?', *Autrepart*, 2 (22), 147–65, doi: 10.3917/autr.022.0147.

Nedelcu, M. (2009a) *Le migrant online: nouveaux modèles migratoires à l'ère du numérique*, Paris: Ed. L'Harmattan.

Nedelcu, M. (2009b) 'Du brain drain à l'e-diaspora: vers une nouvelle culture du lien à l'ère du numérique?', *TIC et société*, 3 (1/2), 151–73, doi: 10.4000/ticetsociete.675.

Nedelcu, M. (2010) 'Présentation', Special Issue *on Les migrants connectés, Réseaux*, No. 159, 9–13.

Nedelcu, M. (2012) 'Migrants' new transnational habitus: rethinking migration through a cosmopolitan lens in the digital age', *Journal of Ethnic and Migration Studies*, 38 (9), 1339–56, doi: 10.1080/1369183X.2012.698203.

Nedelcu, M. (2016) 'Online migrants', in H. Friese, G. Rebane, M. Nolden and M. Schreiter (eds) *Handbuch soziale praktiken und digitale alltagswelten*, Wiesbaden: Springer Reference Sozialwissenschaften, 1–8, doi: 10.1007/978-3-658-08460-8_35-1.

Nedelcu, M. and M. Wyss (2016) 'Doing family' through ICT-mediated ordinary co-presence routines: transnational communication practices of Romanian migrants in Switzerland', *Global Networks*, 16 (2), 202–18, doi: 10.1111/glob.12110.

Oiarzabal, P. J. (2012) 'Diaspora Basques and online social networks: an analysis of users of Basque institutional diaspora groups on Facebook', *Journal of Ethnic and Migration Studies*, 38 (9), 1469–85, doi: 10.1080/1369183X.2012.698216.

Rigoni, I. (2001) 'Les medias des migrants de Turquie en Europe', in I. Rigoni and R. Blioneds (eds) *D'un voyage à l'autre. Des voix de l'immigration pour un développement pluriel*, Paris: Karthala, 207–20.

Robertson, R. (1995) 'Glocalization: time–space and homogeneity–heterogeneity', in M. Featherstone, S. Lash and R. Robertson (eds) *Global modernities*, London: Sage, 25–44.

Sheffer, G. (1986) *Modern diasporas in international politics*, New York: St Martin's Press.

Sheffer, G. (1993) 'Ethnic diasporas: a threat to their hosts?', in M. Weiner (ed.) *International migration and security*, Boulder: Westview Press, 263–85.

Stubbs, P. (1999) 'Virtual diaspora? Imagining Croatia online', *Sociological Research Online*, 4 (2), doi: 10.5153/sro.253.

29
Diaspora politics and political remittances
A conceptual reflection

Lea Müller-Funk

The interest in the political role that migrants can play in their home countries and the type of political remittances they are sending back home has been steadily growing over the past two decades. In major conflicts in the last two decades, such as the Balkan wars, the Arab Spring in 2011, and the attempted coup in Turkey in 2016, the role of migrants and refugees as political actors has become increasingly visible. Yet, this phenomenon is not new as such: Polish, Portuguese, Chinese and Lebanese migrants have historically continued to participate in political processes in their countries of origin, as have classical diasporic communities such as Palestinian, Kurdish and Armenian communities.

Research on transnationalism and diasporas has traditionally shied away from putting politics at the centre of the analysis of transnational processes and practices. Generations of migration researchers have perceived immigrants as persons who leave behind their home and country, and face the painful process of incorporation into a different society and culture. In orthodox theoretical approaches to immigration, immigrants who settle abroad are expected eventually to assimilate into the dominant society's sociocultural systems while simultaneously losing their 'old' cultural practices and political loyalties (Guarnizo et al. 2003: 1215). With the emergence of the concept of transnationalism at the end of the 1990s, the long-held assimilation model has been put into question in academia. Basch, Glick Schiller and Szanton Blanc have argued that increasing numbers of immigrants should be understood as 'transmigrants', thus immigrants 'whose daily lives depend on multiple and constant interconnections across international borders and whose public identities are configured in relationship to more than one nation state' (Basch et al. 1995: 48).

However, early theoretical approaches have often neglected different approaches to integration in other parts of the world. For example, in the Middle East, the nexus between migration and politics has been interpreted quite differently. In Middle Eastern societies, migrants' integration has not become a major policy field – neither historically in the Ottoman Empire with tens of thousands Muslim Circassians fleeing from the Russian advance into the Caucasus between 1855 and 1863, nor with the exodus of Palestinians to neighbouring countries after the Nakba in 1948, nor with the contemporary inflow of Asian migrant workers into the Gulf countries. In many cases, the issue of migrant communities has been far more linked to the securitization of political regimes and political alliances within the region than to 'integration' itself: migration issues are often connected to conflicting national narratives attached to ethnic or religious minorities and to political conflicts (Seeberg and Eyadat 2013: 3–4). This has been true for Shia and Persian communities in the United Arab Emirates, Palestinians in Lebanon and Jordan, as well as Syrian refugees in contemporary Lebanon. In all these cases, migrants and refugees have neither been supposed to 'assimilate' into the receiving societies, nor perceived as losing their distinctive features as 'communities'.

One of the results of the transnational paradigm was the birth of 'diaspora politics' as a new field of academic research at the beginning of the new millennium (Guarnizo et al. 2003; Lyons and Mandaville 2012; Østergaard-Nielsen 2003; Sheffer 2003; Smith 2003; Tarrow 2005). These works have studied those political activities of migrants that aim at gaining political power or influence in their homeland while living outside it. In this type of research, the term 'political remittances' gained in popularity, broadly defined as 'a change in political identities, demands and practices associated with migration' (Goldring 2003: 3). Political remittances were originally conceived as being a 'sub-issue' of 'social remittances', hence a concept originally derived from economic remittances in development studies. Levitt extended the concept of economic remittances to social remittances, arguing that migrants remit not only money from sending countries but also 'ideas, behaviours, identities and social capital that flow from receiving to sending countries communities' (Levitt 1998).

In this chapter, I critically discuss the nexus between diaspora politics and political remittances from a conceptual perspective. In doing so, I aim to bringing three streams of literature together – namely, that on the conceptualization of diasporas, on new social movement theory, and on political transnationalism and remittances. I make three main arguments. First, instead of applying a categorical concept of diaspora, which establishes a matrix of criteria to distinguish between 'true' and 'false' diasporas, I suggest interpreting diaspora politics as a space in which diasporic identities are constructed and sometimes contested. Second, I situate diaspora politics within new social movement theory by underlining that diaspora politics forms collective identities and by stressing the importance of political opportunity structures. Third, I argue that political remittances, which are emitted as part of diasporic politics, are multidirectional and are highly influenced by the context in which migrants live and have lived before their migration.

Diaspora politics and the mobilization of diaspora identities

First, I understand diaspora politics as the space in which to mobilize diaspora identities that are linked to migrants' political demands. Instead of using a categorical definition of diaspora, to understand diaspora politics better, I argue for a constructivist perspective following Dufoix's (2008) argument that diasporas are constructed as a social and political practice.

Since the 1980s, several types of definitions have emerged in the social sciences to describe diasporas. On the one hand, there are open definitions that can be used interchangeably with 'migration from country x to country y' or 'ethnic community x in country y'. They include factors such as the origin of the (voluntary or forced) migration; settlement in one or several countries, maintenance of identity and community solidarity, relations between the leaving state, the host state and the diaspora itself (Sheffer 1986). Categorical definitions, on the other hand, try to establish a matrix of strict criteria to distinguish between 'true' and 'false' diasporas: Safran (1991), for example, formulated a close conceptual model that limits diasporas to minority expatriate communities whose members share several of six characteristics: (1) being dispersed from an original 'centre'; (2) retaining a collective memory, vision or myth about the original homeland; (3) sharing a belief that they are not fully accepted in their host societies; (4) idealizing the ancestral home; (5) sharing a belief that all members of the diaspora should be committed to the maintenance or restoration of the original homeland; (6) continuing in various ways to relate to the homeland (Safran 1991: 83–4). Cohen developed Safran's model further by adding additional features: (1) the dispersal from an original homeland, often traumatically, to two or more foreign regions; (2) alternatively, the expansion from a homeland in search of work, in pursuit of trade or to further colonial ambitions; (3) a collective memory and myth about the homeland; (4) an idealization of the putative ancestral home and a collective commitment to its maintenance, restoration, safety or prosperity, even to its creation; (5) the development of a return movement that gains collective approbation; (6) a strong ethnic group consciousness sustained over a long time and based on a sense of distinctiveness, a common history and the belief in a common fate; (7) a troubled relationship with host societies; (8) a sense of empathy and solidarity with co-ethnic members in other countries of settlement; (9) the possibility of a distinct creative, enriching life in host countries with a tolerance for pluralism (Cohen 2008: 17). A third stream of approaches are rooted in the cultural studies and postmodernist theory of the 1980s and are strongly influenced by the works of Michel Foucault. Their visions of diaspora give place to paradoxical identity, the non-centre and hybridity (Clifford 1994; Gilroy 1994; Hall 1990).

Many of the above-mentioned concepts create an illusion of homogeneity within migrant communities and fail to articulate differences within diasporas, particularly the role played by differences in ethnicity, religion, sex and class, which are essential for understanding diaspora politics. They are often also blind to the fact that identities around which migrant communities mobilize might change over time and tend to forget the political aspects of the situation. Given these criticisms, several authors have suggested focusing on constructivist approaches to studying diasporas. Dufoix, for example, suggests looking at diasporas as a social and political practice by analysing many ways of constructing, managing and imagining the relationships between homelands and their dispersed people (Dufoix 2008: 55–6). I claim that, in studying diaspora politics, it is more important to understand who is trying to mobilize a diaspora and for what reason rather than to determine whether a migrant group forms a diaspora or not. In this argument, I follow Adamson, who maintains that diasporas are best viewed as the products or outcomes of transnational mobilization activities by political entrepreneurs engaged in strategic social identity construction (Adamson 2012: 25–6).

Such a constructivist approach highlights that diasporas are of importance to a broad range of interested parties, including states seeking to organize their emigrants into a collectivity they can control and from which they can extract resources, or migrants whose views on their identity do not necessarily correspond with those of the sending state. Diaspora politics is hence often an arena of political contestation between the sending country's homogeneous notion of nationhood and migrant groups who want to break away from its narrow constraints. Diaspora politics often makes the fragmentation of diasporic identities visible. Delhaye (2010), for example, shows that the Egyptian state reiterates the imagery of an unwavering Egyptian unity dating back to the founding moment of Egyptian nationalism when Egyptian Copts and Muslims united in their fight against British occupation, while Coptic groups abroad interpret this matter differently. Özkul's (2017) research in Germany and Australia shows how Alevis, who were initially part of the labour migration movement from Turkey to Germany in the 1960s and 1970s, started to organize around a newly emerging secular cultural identity in the 1980s and 1990s, and around an institutionalized religious/faith-based one in the 2000s. Both stood in contrast to Turkey's attempts to represent and portray its citizens abroad. Jaulin (2006) demonstrates how Lebanese wanting to portray Lebanon as a Christian country evoked the idea of an 'extraterritorial' nation-state. Through this strategy, they were trying to reintegrate Lebanese emigrants – who are largely Christian – into the political life of the country, defending the *jus sanguinis* provision in Lebanon's nationality law.

What do diaspora politics and social movements have in common?

Second, I maintain that two features bring diaspora politics close to new social movement theory – its focus on collective identity construction and political opportunity structures.

Over the past decade, scholars of social movements have expanded their interest from local and national to international and transnational forms of contention (Keck and Sikkink 1998; Tarrow 2005), including diaspora politics. Keck and Sikkink (1998: 30) distinguish between three categories of transnational networks – those with goals that are essentially instrumental (corporations and banks), those motivated primarily by shared causal ideas (scientific groups or epistemic communities), and those motivated primarily by shared principled ideas or values (transnational advocacy networks). Adamson (2012: 32) argues that diaspora politics should be included as a fourth category in the form of 'transnational identity networks', thus those networks defined primarily by a shared collective identity such as an ethnic, national or religious one. She states that the first task of diaspora activists is to 'construct or deploy identity categories that can be used to create transnational identity communities –transnational imaginaries – out of existing social networks' (Adamson 2012: 34).

Most strands of new social movement theory stress the symbolic action of social movements and the processes by which they construct collective identities. Melucci, for example, argues that, in modern society, the plurality of memberships and the abundance of messages combine to weaken traditional points of reference and sources of identity, thereby creating a 'homelessness of personal identity'. This means that the tendency of people to become involved in collective action is tied to their capacity to define and construct an identity in the first place. It also means that the social construction of a collective identity is both an important prerequisite for and a major accomplishment of new social movements (Melucci 1985). Melucci and Avritzer argue that by supplementing the principle of representation with that of belonging, new social movements introduce a complementary form of dealing with politics: 'many contemporary forms of collective action do not demand to have their claims incorporated into the political system but instead propose new values and moral concerns and introduce these into the public culture' (Melucci and Avritzer 2000: 509). They maintain that the public sphere thus constitutes an alternative political space for representation of plural identities, claims and participation.

According to Lyons and Mandaville (2012: 19), the

> processes of diaspora mobilization and identity construction simultaneously look back to old forms of identity rooted in the 'motherland' as expressed in terms of bloodline, while at the same time creating new, hybrid identities and solidarities among people who share certain imaginary connections despite distance.

Thus, diaspora identities thrive and build on difference. They are not only hybridized, but are also constantly in flux. Portes and Zhou (1993) explain that migrants and former migrants often choose to emphasize the identity that most supports their quality of life in the host land. Thus, they may direct their mobilized identity towards the improved quality of life for compatriots in the homeland, for diaspora communities in the host land, or for both. In her study on digital diasporas, Brinkerhoff underlines that for some migrants mobilizing a diaspora identity helps to maintain or acquire power or other resources or even both, while for others, it is based solely on a sense of belonging, arising in response to feelings of marginalization in the receiving societies (Brinkerhoff 2009: 41).

My own research on Egyptian diasporic activism in Vienna and Paris shows that irregular Egyptian migrants in Paris, with no social or political rights in France, mobilized a diasporic identity that focused solely on being an 'Egyptian emigrant', while the idea of construction a more hybrid identity was practically irrelevant to them. On the other hand, interviewees who had been living in Europe for several years and had acquired social capital there mostly mobilized a more hybrid identity construction. The younger generation 'imagined' their identity as significantly different from that of their parents: their identity constructions were often influenced by prevalent discourses on integration and experiences of discrimination, exclusion or inclusion in the origin and receiving countries. My research also demonstrates that in moments of big political upheavals in the country of origin, such as revolutionary events, identity constructions were particularly in flux (Müller-Funk 2016a). A young Austrian diaspora activist whose parents migrated from Egypt to Austria described her identity and the impact of the Arab Spring as follows (personal interview, Vienna, 26 April 2014):

> For me, this was the first contact [with Egyptians] at all. Before, I went to an Austrian kindergarten, primary school, grammar school, university. And I only had Austrian friends. Yes, you knew each other by sight, I took Arabic classes for six years, so you knew people by sight, but I didn't know their names. And all my friends and acquaintances were Austrian. . . . With Egyptians, it only started later. . . . As children, we always thought that there was only Austria on the whole earth. When I was three, I thought German and Arabic was one language, in kindergarten, I always mixed j languages. . . . I feel Austro-Egyptian. I hate the term 'migration background'. As if I had a criminal past. M-i-g-r-a-t-i-o-n b-a-c-k-g-r-o-u-n-d. I don't like it at all [*laughs*]. . . . I like to say that I am Austro-Egyptian. I definitely see myself as Austrian. From the outside I perceive myself as Egyptian, as a southerner, but inside I am Austrian from A to Z, an Austrian Muslim. I almost have nothing of Egyptian culture and tradition. . . . In Egypt, I don't feel like an Egyptian, I feel a bit displaced. If my husband wasn't from there . . . and my grandmother, that is why I go there. . . . I notice that I defend the Egyptians when I am here, and the Austrians there. . . . My husband's mother was sceptical because I am European and because I grew up here. But then she got to know me and changed her opinion completely. Because most girls in Egypt want to finish university to get married and for me, it was not that. She liked that. . . . I always explain too that having a boyfriend in Europe is like being married, you are faithful and you are only with one person, you don't jump from one person to the other. And then, naturally, it is also very respected there [to be from Austria]. Of course. When I go to the Austrian embassy with an Austrian passport, I am the queen [*laughs*]. This is also positive. Then, I always realize how torn I am between here and there.

My second argument in favour of social movement theory is that applying it to diaspora politics helps one to understand regional differences in diaspora politics. Several studies (Jaulin 2014; Koinova 2013; Müller-Funk 2016b; Rother 2009) have underlined that diaspora mobilizations may take different forms in different localities. I argue that a focus on political opportunity structures can be an explanatory factor for such differences. An increasing number of the academic publications that draw on social movement theory are focusing on the influence of the socio-political environment of the country of residence on understanding migrant political organization since the mid-1990s. Central to the social movement paradigm is the concept of a political opportunity structure defined as 'consistent – but not necessarily formal or permanent – dimensions of the political environment that provide incentives for people to undertake collective action by affecting their expectations for success or failure' (Tarrow 1994: 85). The underlying hypothesis of such an approach is that prevailing political conditions are decisive for the self-organization of migrants and that groups from the same country of origin may organize differently in different political settings. As such, a political opportunity structure approach deconstructs methods that try to explain migrant political organization solely through their respective culture of origin and shows that it is often the situation relatedness of migrants that influences their political mobilization, political demands and agenda setting. My research has shown that access to political rights, debates on 'national identity', and the way migrant communities are institutionalized in the receiving countries influence their activism (Müller-Funk 2016b).

Multidirectional political remittances in diaspora politics

My last argument relates to the term 'political remittances' in research on diaspora politics. Unlike earlier conceptions, I maintain that political remittances should be understood not as a unidirectional flow from receiving to sending countries, but rather stress its multidirectional character. In contrast to some overly optimistic voices in research on diaspora politics, I also argue in favour of a neutral use of the term that does not evaluate their effects as necessarily 'democratic', 'liberal' or 'inclusive', as is sometimes presumed. Instead, I suggest one interpret their outcome as heavily dependent on the context in which migrants and post-migrants live and have lived before their migration.

The dominant conceptualization of political remittances is often linked to return migration – in the form of a unidirectional flow of something learned in the receiving country then being transferred to the sending country. This idea was already included in Levitt's conception of social remittances, which she characterized as 'ideas, behaviours, identities and social capital that flow from receiving to sending countries communities' (Levitt 1998). Goldring, for example, makes equally concrete reference to political remittances as 'the political identities, demand[s] and practices of return migrants acquired as a result of their transnational migration experience' (Goldring 2004: 805). Concepts, on the other hand, that emerged in the context of transnational studies put a strong emphasis on the simultaneous embeddedness of migrants' activism in different localities, the multi-directional flows between them, and the institutional factors contributing to transnational political participation. Piper goes in the same direction when she challenges the definition of political remittances as a one-directional flow, and states that political remittances 'are embedded in the social contexts of origin and destination countries' structural and agential histories, shaped by the migration experience and characterized by multiple directions of flow' (Piper 2009: 238). I therefore define political remittances as the flows of political ideas, political behaviours and identities that flow between the communities of both receiving and sending countries. I understand political remittances as fluid, multidirectional flows of political ideas and forms of behaviour that also influence identity constructions.

My second argument related to political remittances is that they are not necessarily positive or democratic as such, but are heavily influenced by the context in which (post-)migrants live and the experiences they have. The concept of political remittances is often linked to the idea of democratic values learned in Western countries being transferred back to the sending countries. We can cite Shain in this respect, who maintains that diasporas contribute to democratic change from abroad by, for example, challenging home governments' efforts to suppress or co-opt its oppositions or by exposing human rights violations (Shain 1999: 70). Others have interpreted transnational links as an emerging form of progressive politics (Keck and Sikkink 1998), while Guarnizo and Smith (1998) see the political actions of migrants as possibly challenging the *status quo* in their home country. Piper equally draws a connection between political remittances and democratization when she defines political remittances as 'the activities, actions, and ideas aimed at the democratisation of the migration process (ranging from pre- to post-migration) via political mobilisation in the form of collective organisations operating in the transnational sphere' (Piper 2009: 238).

I argue that political remittances are more ambivalent than this and should be understood in the context in which they are happening. This claim is supported by a series of recent studies. Lyons and Mandaville, for example, argue that non-democratic patterns of behaviour survive, and sometimes even thrive, in a diaspora and that transnational politics can just as readily advance neo-patrimonial patterns, chauvinistic political agendas, reinforce sectarian divisions, or sustain brutal civil wars (Lyons and Mandaville 2012: 15). Meseguer and Burgess evaluate the results of transnational homeland politics on electoral participation and attitudes toward democracy equally as mostly negative or at least ambivalent. They maintain, however, that non-migrants with connections abroad seem to turn to alternative forms of non-electoral political engagement, with positive implications for the quality of democracy (Meseguer and Burgess 2014: 6). Tabar (2014) argues that his study on the role of Lebanese Australians in the general elections in Lebanon in 2009 is in fact a showcase of an incorporationalist form of political remittances in so far as they suit the needs of the dominant political elites in Lebanon, with little to no regard for the political aspirations of the diaspora. Tabar maintains in his conclusion that political remittances are shaped not only by the country of origin but also by the country of destination and depend to a large degree on the political environment and its development in both the sending country and the country of destination (Tabar 2014: 445). In my opinion, Rother's (2009) interesting study of Filipino migrants in Saudi Arabia, Hong Kong and Japan made an important theoretical contribution towards understanding the phenomenon of political remittances. His study demonstrates that there can be a darker side to the rosy picture of political remittances in the migration context and the 'diffusion of democracy' in general. He argues that democratic structures in the receiving country influence migrants' political attitudes only if they experience their results directly in their personal lives.

Conclusion

Where does this leave us? Or, to put it more polemically, are diaspora politics bad or good? Should we encourage diaspora politics? Instead of answering this binary question, I suggest rather that we see diaspora politics as a natural phenomenon accompanying migration and globalization. It has presumably become more relevant in our modern times of growing interconnectedness and the opportunities that new media provide to maintain links across borders. Simultaneously, it is, however, a minority within migrant communities who do engage in diaspora politics. They are often those who are better educated than their compatriots, better connected, speak more languages and travel more often (Tarrow 2005: 43).

In this short contribution, I decided against evaluating the effects of diaspora politics as either good or bad, but to see it as an additional civil society voice in an increasingly globalized world. Diaspora politics can be understood as one of many ways of giving agency to migrants. It has often been assumed that engaging in diaspora politics automatically means that migrants and their children are less interested in the country in which they are living. Evidence from my own research, however, suggests that engaging in diaspora politics is not negative in this regard. When explaining the rationale for their activism, many interviewees described their dual loyalties to both countries and claimed often to direct their diaspora politics towards influencing public opinion in the receiving country. They often expressed it as an emancipating experience and as a way of participating politically in the receiving country through awareness-raising, appearing in debates and discussion rounds, and connecting with political actors in the receiving country. My neutral stance on political remittances does not mean that diaspora politics cannot have positive effects: in many cases, migrants make use of the greater freedoms of expression and assembly in the receiving country, support democratic values and become an alternative voice to challenge political conditions back home.

Diaspora politics remains a fascinating and relevant subject to study exactly because it emerges at the intersection of many controversial contemporary political and theoretical debates. Linking it to transnationalism, migration and social movement literature might help to understand better the inner dynamics of diaspora politics and reveal the interlinkages between migration policies, the political environment in which they take place and its actors.

References

Adamson, F. B. (2012) 'Constructing the diaspora: diaspora identity politics and transnational social movements', in T. Lyons and P. Mandaville (eds) *Politics from afar*, London: Hurst & Company, 25–42.

Basch, L., N. Glick Schiller and C. S. Blanc (1995) 'From immigrant to transmigrant: theorizing transnational migration', *Anthropological Quarterly*, 68 (1), 48–63, doi: 10.2307/3317464.

Brinkerhoff, J. (2009) *Digital diasporas: identity and transnational engagement*, New York: Cambridge University Press.

Clifford, J. (1994) 'Diasporas', *Current Anthropology*, 9 (3), 302–38, doi: 10.1525/can.1994.9.3.02a00040.

Cohen, R. (2008) *Global diasporas: an introduction*, second edition, London: Routledge.

Delhaye, G. (2010) 'La réponse des États à la dissidence diasporique', in S. Dufoix, C. Guerassimoff and A. de Tinguy (eds) *Loin des yeux, près du cœur: les États et leurs expatriés*, Paris: Presses de Sciences Po, 323–42.

Dufoix, S. (2008) *Diasporas*, translated by William Rodarmor, Berkeley: University of California Press.

Gilroy, P. (1994) 'Diaspora', *Paragraph*, 17 (3), 207–12, doi: 10.3366/para.1994.17.3.207.

Goldring, L. (2003) 'Re-thinking remittances: social and political dimensions of individual and collective remittances', CERLAC working paper, available at: https://pdfs.semanticscholar.org/dc8c/9b9b784fd f113ad3cf53423632fa3d40228a.pdf.

Goldring, L. (2004) 'Individual and collective remittances to Mexico: a multi-dimensional typology of remittances', *Development and Change*, 35 (4), 799–840, doi: 10.1111/j.0012-155X.2004.00380.x.

Guarnizo, L. E. and M. P. Smith (1998) *Transnationalism from below*, London: Transaction Publishers.

Guarnizo, L. E., A. Portes and W. Haller (2003) 'Assimilation and transnationalism: determinants of transnational political action among contemporary migrants', *American Journal of Sociology*, 108 (6), 1211–48, doi: 10.1086/375195.

Hall, S. (1990) 'Cultural identity and diaspora', in J. Rutherford (ed.) *Identity: community, culture, difference*, London: Lawrence, 222–37.

Jaulin, T. (2006) 'Lebanese politics of nationality and emigration', EUI working paper, available at: http://cadmus.eui.eu/bitstream/handle/1814/6225/RSCAS_2006_29.pdf.

Jaulin, T. (2014) 'Géographie du vote à distance: l'élection tunisienne de 2011 à l'étranger', *L'Espace Politique*, 23, online journal, available at: http://espacepolitique.revues.org/3099.

Keck, M. and K. Sikkink (1998) *Activists beyond borders: advocacy networks in international politics*, Ithaca, NY: Cornell University Press.

Koinova, M. (2013) 'Four types of diaspora mobilization: Albanian diaspora activism for Kosovo independence in the US and the UK', *Foreign Policy Analysis*, 9 (4), 433–53, doi: 10.1111/j.1743-8594.2012.00194.x.

Levitt, P. (1998) 'Social remittances: migration driven local-level forms of cultural diffusion', *International Migration Review*, 32 (4), 926–48, doi: 10.2307/2547666.

Lyons, T. and P. Mandaville (eds) (2012) *Politics from afar: transnational diasporas and networks*, London: Hurst & Co.

Melucci, A. (1985) 'The symbolic challenge of contemporary movements', *Social Research*, 52 (4), 789–816, available at: www.jstor.org/stable/40970398.

Melucci, A. and L. Avritzer (2000) 'Complexity, cultural pluralism and democracy: collective action in the public space', *Social Science Information*, 39 (4), 507–27, doi: 10.1177/053901800039004001.

Meseguer, C. and K. Burgess (2014) 'International migration and home country politics', *Studies in Comparative International Development*, 49 (1), 1–12, doi: 10.1007/s12116-014-9149-z.

Müller-Funk, L. (2016a) 'Transnational politics beyond the Arab uprisings: Egyptian activism in Vienna and Paris', PhD thesis, University Vienna/Sciences Po Paris.

Müller-Funk, L. (2016b) 'Diaspora mobilizations in the Egyptian (post)revolutionary process: comparing transnational political participation in Paris and Vienna', *Journal of Immigrant & Refugee Studies*, 14 (3), 353–70, doi: 10.1080/15562948.2016.1180471.

Østergaard-Nielsen, E. (2003) *Transnational politics: Turks and Kurds in Germany*, London: Routledge.

Özkul, D. (2017) 'From social equality to a transnational religious movement: the Alevi diaspora in Germany and Australia', in H. Markussen and B. Can Zırh (eds) *The Alevi identity revisited*, Leiden: Brill.

Piper, N. (2009) 'Temporary migration and political remittances: the role of organisational networks in the transnationalisation of human rights', *European Journal of East Asian Studies*, 8 (2), 215–43, doi: 10.1163/156805809X12553326569678.

Portes, A. and M. Zhou (1993) 'The new second generation: segmented assimilation and its variants', *Annals of the American Academy of Political and Social Science*, 530, 74–96, available at: https://web.stanford.edu/group/scspi/_media/pdf/Reference%20Media/Portes_Zhou_93_Immigration.pdf.

Rother, S. (2009) 'Changed in migration? Philippine return migrants and (un)democratic remittances', *European Journal of East Asian Studies*, 8 (2), 245–74, doi: 10.1163/156805809X12553326569713.

Safran, W. (1991) 'Diasporas in modern societies: myths of homeland and return', *Diaspora: A Journal of Transnational Studies*, 1 (1), 83–99, doi: 10.1353/dsp.1991.0004.

Seeberg, P. and Z. Eyadat (2013) *Migration, security, and citizenship in the Middle East: new perspectives*, New York: Palgrave Macmillan.

Shain, Y. (1999) *Marketing the American creed abroad: diasporas in the US and their homelands*, Cambridge: Cambridge University Press.

Sheffer, G. (1986) *Modern diasporas in international politics*, London: Croom Helm.

Sheffer, G. (2003) *Diaspora politics: at home abroad*, Cambridge: Cambridge University Press.

Smith, R. C. (2003) 'Diasporic membership in historical perspective: comparative insights from the Mexican, Italian and Polish cases', *International Migration Review*, 37 (3), 724–59, doi: 10.1111/j.1747-7379.2003.tb00156.x.

Tabar, P. (2014) '"Political remittances": the case of Lebanese expatriates voting in national elections', *Journal of Intercultural Studies*, 35 (4), 442–60, doi: 10.1080/07256868.2014.913015.

Tarrow, S. (1994) *Power in movement: social movements, collective action and politics*, Cambridge: Cambridge University Press.

Tarrow, S. (2005) *The new transnational activism*, New York: Cambridge University Press.

30
Postcolonial states, nation-building and the (un)making of diasporas

Jen Dickinson

Twenty years ago, national and international policy-makers rarely used the term 'diaspora'. As emigrant groups gained visibility in political and popular cultural domains, the term was appropriated from its academic origins and used as a shorthand to describe emigrants' potential contributions to postcolonial nation-building efforts (Dufoix 2011). Primarily referring to migrant identities as centred on a territorially defined nation-state of 'origin', there is an assumption that members of diasporas have an in-built motivation to assist their 'homeland' because of some primordial cultural or ethnic connection. This assumption underpins a range of policy prescriptions for the way that postcolonial states ought to conduct relations with their emigrants abroad, with the 'tapping' and 'shaping' of homeland diasporic belongings promoted as a key leveraging strategy (Gamlen 2014).

However, it has been widely recognized that the use of the term 'diaspora' to mean a connection to a national 'homeland' proliferates within the context of an ongoing reconstitution of the colonial hierarchies of race and nation, especially at a time of heightened anxiety about migration (James 2016). Arguably, the histories and priorities of Northern societies continue to be manifest in the present spread of global norms around sending states' engagements with diasporas (Raghuram 2009). As I elucidate in this chapter, this is evident in a range of working papers, briefs and initiatives recommending that states adopt policy instruments and structural bureaucratic forms that are conducive to maximizing the assumed interest of diasporas in homeland nation-building. Such promulgations pose important challenges for decolonial scholarship, which aims to move beyond the dominance of Euro-American perspectives in interpreting diasporic identities.

While the broad focus of this chapter is on the revival of uneven global power relations in the light of influential international bodies shaping states, diasporas and nation-building in the global South, one of my key aims is to offer insights into the various local political contexts that also shape diasporic engagement. Adopting the perspective of 'the postcolony' (Comaroff and Comaroff 2006), I position my discussion to develop a nuanced understanding of the multiple types of agencies and knowledges shaping the impact of diasporas on national civic participation, citizenship and inclusion. This is necessary given the tendency in the academic and policy literature to connect the 'success' of diaspora-building strategies to the absence or presence of the institutions and practices of formal statecraft (Pearlman 2014), regardless of the historical and geographical varieties of state forms, the interconnected nature of diasporic identifications and the multiple ways of knowing, reading and interpreting diaspora-building.

Decolonization, diaspora and nation-building in historical perspective

A key feature of the decolonization process was that it conditioned mobility to suit preferred state formations and a national socio-political character (Vigneswaran and Quirk 2015). Emigration flows in the years following independence were informed primarily by the economic and political instabilities associated with the remaking of borders and the political restructuring of citizenship (Akyeampong 2000; Brown 2006). Emigration was also driven by the search for better opportunities in a context of deteriorating economic conditions, the unfair distribution of political and economic resources, changing demographic patterns and the exigencies of the international economy (Adepoju 1994). Unskilled emigration was even encouraged as a perceived 'safety valve' (Wiltshire 1992), while former colonial power practices of recruiting labour from their ex-colonies also shaped patterns of both skilled and unskilled mobility (Byron and Condon 2008).

Inherited colonial political and socio-economic systems of states moulded the geographical production of diasporic communities from the mid-twentieth century onwards. Historical ties to former colonial powers produced sizeable, permanent, diasporic groupings residing in major countries and cities of the Global North. However, most voluntary international migration and/or displacement was intra-regional and shaped by prior histories of cross-border mobilities (Pelican 2013). The latter part of the twenty-first century saw increasing diversification both in terms of the emergence of second- and third-generation descendants, and in the destination and types of subsequent emigrations, with colonial ties diminishing in importance over time (Vezzoli and Flahaux 2016). Such diversity has led some to question whether one can speak of any country as having a singular, easily identifiable 'diaspora'.

The forms of assistance that diasporas gave to decolonizing nation-states long predates state and global policy-makers' policy attention, with remittances from both internal and cross-border migrants historically meeting various household needs from daily subsistence to investments and education (de Haas 2006). Migrants' hometown associations also played an organizational role in remittance-sending, originally in contexts of rural–urban migrations and later in diasporic settings (McGregor 2009), as well as in areas such as political lobbying, conflict resolution and peace-making (Mohamoud 2006).

Despite the historical role played by diasporas in postcolonial national reconstruction, until the early twenty-first century most states adopted a stance of 'benign neglect' (Kapur 2004). In academic and policy circles, the importance of diasporas was for the most part judged primarily in terms of the remittances sent to support individual well-being, family income and social mobility (Kamau and Kimenyi 2012). However, some states actively rejected the attempts of their diasporas to engage in homeland projects and often saw them as traitors or as challenging the postcolonial state's territorial legitimacy and authority (Iheduru 2011).

State and nation-building in global development discourse

Over the past two decades, a range of different processes has ushered in a new, more active partnership between postcolonial states and their diasporas. Broadly, there has been a wide shift in international aid regimes towards championing state transformation and the involvement of grassroots groups as the most efficient ways of promoting development (Raghuram 2009). As migration became associated with 'capital gain' rather than 'brain drain', development policy-makers and academics started to pay more attention to the conditions in the sending state that were enabling the maximization of remittances (de Haas 2010).

Within current international development narratives, the conceptualization of diasporas, as rooted in, but scattered beyond, national borders, has salience because of its powerful imaginary of migrants as highly mobile, progressive agents of globalization (Dufoix 2011). As read against diasporas, their homelands were often understood as sedentary and backward-looking (Bakewell 2008). McGregor and Pasura (2010) argue that such a positioning has been framed primarily by Western donor interests to legitimize shifting responsibility for homeland transformation onto states, communities and individuals and to realize growth prospects predicated on expanding financial remittances.

This narrow concentration on diasporas as a resource for national progression has had considerable influence over the new types of state forms that are emerging. There are now a large and varied number of donor programmes supporting both diaspora groups and sending states in leveraging their financial potential (Boyle and Kitchin 2014). Specific initiatives targeted at sending states include reform of regulatory and banking measures to secure and capture remittances better, and transform the so-called 'unproductive' use of remittances at household scales into what is perceived as more 'productive' investments in public infrastructure and housing. Diaspora ministries coordinating diaspora engagement have multiplied, and are designed primarily to provide an institutionalized framework for managing the homeland macro-economic environment in such a way as to enable diaspora investment (Brinkerhoff 2012).

The international development community has often used successful examples of diaspora engagement to frame blueprints for other countries (Agunias and Newland 2012). Global development forums like the European Union (Sinatti and Horst 2015) or regional agencies such as the African Union (Kamei 2011) are influential in encouraging states to adopt policy frameworks conducive to generating diaspora-friendly governing environments. In addition, think-tanks and private consultancies, often based in the Global North, have flourished as state policy advisors (Boyle and Kitchin 2014). In producing a standardized view of what a 'successful' institutional environment for diaspora engagement should look like, guidance can often fail to take account of the types of diaspora-led engagements best suited to specific social contexts and political economies.

Modifications to legal citizenship are another feature of recent transformations to postcolonial state structures. Global development policy-makers view measures such as dual citizenship as a critical determinant of a state's ability to leverage financial and human resources from the diaspora (Leblang 2017). The precise nature of these modifications can be uneven, with diasporas given the full spectrum of rights and privileges associated with citizenship in some cases, but limited to travel and banking rights in others (Gamlen 2014). Arguably, this differentiation reflects underlying global neoliberal development paradigms, with diaspora citizenship structured primarily to meet economic development objectives.

As a result, geographical hierarchies are emerging over which diasporic groups the home states regard as their wider diasporic nation. Emigrant groups living in wealthy countries in the Global North tend to be ascribed the label of 'diaspora' to denote their prestige (McGregor and Pasura 2010). Some migrant and minority groups, including poor migrants in neighbouring countries of the Global South, irregular migrants, and those who do not have the capital to engage in homeland contributions, can often remain marginalized as potential participants in, and beneficiaries of, diasporic initiatives (Crush et al. 2016). The popular press and artistic forms may constitute some diaspora members as 'worthy' and 'unworthy' co-nationals, depending on the perceived nature of their contribution to national economic growth (Braun 2016).

Despite the exhortations of international agencies, converting templates for state engagements with diasporas has not been straightforward. Even as they represent a solution to development challenges, diaspora financing may in practice sustain inherited socio-economic inequalities and exclusions (Davies 2012). States' ability to realize the economic capacities of diasporas can be hindered by the emotional costs of remitting, specific immigration and financial regulatory environments of host countries, and the nature of diasporic identification (Datta 2009). Complex interconnectivities and relationalities make diaspora engagement successful in some contexts but not others, which is at odds with a focus on encouraging 'sending' states to create structures conducive to the maximization of diasporas' economic potential.

Rethinking state agencies

The emergence of diaspora engagement in many postcolonial states has been shaped not by global development agendas, but primarily by growing cultural and political interest from the diaspora. Arguably, this interest represents a potential stable and cheap source of finance over which Southern states can shape their economic position in comparison with external dependencies on development financing and trade (Datta 2009). In an increasingly integrated global economy where many postcolonial states remain sidelined or marginalized, the tapping or building of diasporic identities can allow states to generate economic support on their own terms (Adamson and Demetriou 2007).

The challenge that diaspora interest can pose to the territorial sovereignty of the postcolonial state has not escaped the attention of elites, who often structure engagement in such a way as to avoid crises of legitimacy or challenges to authority (Iheduru 2011). For instance, Turner (2013) observes that Rwandan state elites control the ambiguous nature of diasporas as both development actors and state challengers by using state spectacles of engagement to perform public categorizations of diaspora into positive and negative elements, thereby enhancing its sovereignty for Rwandans abroad and at home. Such practices allow states to exert 'thin' sovereignty over the construction and mobilization of cross-border political identifications (Turner and Kleist 2013).

Engaging diasporas effectively across these functions requires sustained management of a varied mixture of trade, fiscal, investment, banking and custom policies, as well as negotiating transformations to constitutional, institutional and foreign and security apparatuses (Resende Santos 2016). States should not therefore be considered as monolithic entities operating with overarching agendas in mind, but as composed of a collection of actors, each exerting his or her own agencies over the way diaspora engagement is put together. These actors may have multiple, sometimes conflicting agendas around state engagements with diasporas (Hickey 2015), including consolidations of their own power (Iskander 2010). As Chacko and Gebre (2013) observe in Ethiopia, attempts to institute diaspora engagement there were challenged by competing interests around the equitable distribution of diaspora investment across economic sectors, administrative regions and political parties. Thus, even while particular types of development might in theory have strategic priority over other concerns, in practice, competing interests may stymy consistent applications of this priority across all of the different institutions and bureaucratic aspects of the same state.

In rethinking what is meant by the sending state, we can also find an historical variety of state forms shaping the nature of diaspora engagement. In international governing forums, the state is most often conceptualized as a set of formal, centralized, national institutions with the ability to wield power over domestic diaspora policies. But such a conceptualization elides local and regional political systems such as customary authorities and cultures of neo-patrimonialism, which have long had an impact on the governance of mobility through networks of ethnic, hometown and regional elite associations (Geschiere and Gugler 1998). Associational networks were historically empowered by postcolonial governmental nation-building policies that promoted a politics of primary hometown belonging and patriotism, particularly in contexts of rural–urban mobilities (Nyamnjoh and Rowlands 1998). The retreat of formal institutions from the provision of authority and services, such as education and access to markets, reconstituted associational networks for resource mobilization in diasporic settings often acting as a resource for elite power and resource accumulation (McGregor 2009). Since hometown associational actors are unlikely to view emigrants primarily as members of a national polity (Pearlman 2014), local interests, identities and political dynamics can be prioritized, sometimes generating highly divisive parochialisms working at the expense of inclusionary transformation (Davies 2012).

Diaspora-building also ties into geographically specific articulations of civic inclusion at different scales. While monetary flows embedded in vernacular politics of diasporic belonging may constitute an exclusionary politics in some cases, associational networks also fulfil progressive participatory development functions in others (Mercer et al. 2008). As Hickey (2011) argues, the extent to which hometown associations can build more inclusive meanings of citizenship turns on locally specific definitions of community and attendant rights and obligations. For example, Kleist (2011) observes that the use of diaspora returnees as chiefs in traditional rural authority structures is a mobilization strategy designed to resolve the oppositional nature of tradition and modernity in contemporary Ghana while bringing forms of development grounded in local customs and rituals. This locally adaptive nature of diasporic engagement can promote diverse forms of nation-building, which arguably better capture the multiple and shifting nature of diasporic identities.

Alongside the varied types of political actors shaping diasporic engagement in the context of a variety of state forms, also significant are networks of varied non-state domestic actors, ranging from universities to private entrepreneurs and commercial businesses. Some emerging research (Cohen 2015; Moniruzzaman 2016) documents their role in tapping diasporic knowledge, brokering skilled return migration and facilitating remittance transactions. The proliferation of private enterprises in diasporic engagements can be interpreted as the hegemony of global market mechanisms in neoliberal governance (Larner 2015) and as indicative of a weak or failed state (Pearlman 2014). However, so too can they fulfil progressive civic functions by offering support and services in the wake of collapsed or non-existent financial institutions (Datta 2009). In Somalia, Lindley (2009) finds that the financial infrastructure of money transmitters connects refugee camps, cities and remote areas to diasporas, providing a degree of socially embedded, globally networked stability.

Conclusion

There is now considerable problematization of the global focus on remedying the formal institutions of postcolonial states as a blueprint for maximizing the national economic development potential of diasporas. As this chapter has shown, economic development is just one of the multiple roles that states envision diasporas playing in nation-building, with the shape and form that diaspora engagements take grounded in historically and geographically specific sociopolitical governing structures. Although such engagements can be understood in some cases as (re)producing new problematic structures of inequality, they also offer a range of domestic actors a means of challenging inherited structures of inequality and developing new means of inclusion. The point is that the different modes of engagement conducted through domestic state and non-state actors create multiple spatialities and types of civic belonging each with different effects, but to prioritize the domain of the formal state reproduces a linear and universal view of the connections between diaspora and nation-building.

This raises several implications for decolonial scholars aiming to find alternative ways of interpreting diasporas. First, moving beyond conceptualizing diaspora engagement as the activities of the formal state offers potential for resignifying the term 'diaspora' with the pluriversal meanings that emerge from multiple political practices and ways of living. Vázquez (2011: 41) argues that such a project is necessary for challenging 'the oppressive grammars of power' within the vocabularies of the academy. Yet, even as multiple understandings of diaspora are beginning to be recognized by international development actors (Dufoix 2011), hegemonic ideas continually circulate and are reasserted in various policy forums. Indeed, even in the popular and public domestic imagination, the term 'diaspora' continues to signify a certain cache associated with Western cultural capital and cosmopolitanism (McGregor and Pasura 2010), posing challenges for unlearning its binary associations.

Although the views of people living in a diaspora are outside the scope of this chapter, the globally interconnected nature of diasporic associational networks offers possibilities of finding ways of connecting different forms of diasporic knowledge, a strategy that Connell (2007: 213) argues is at the foundation of challenging generally accepted genealogies of thought. Although the involvement of diasporic individuals in consultation in international and host country forums may offer some possibilities (Norglo et al. 2016), the difficulty is also in findings ways to incorporate those who, as Crush et al. (2016) elaborate, remain marginalized from inclusion in definitions of diaspora. Here, I see important avenues for diaspora scholars to make inroads into this project, especially since academics have already had some role to play in nuancing policy debates about diaspora and development. The multidisciplinary nature of diaspora studies might be best placed to deliver such a possibility.

References

Adamson, F. and M. Demetriou (2007) 'Remapping the boundaries of "state" and "national identity": incorporating diasporas into IR theorizing', *European Journal of International Relations*, 13 (4), 489–526, doi: 10.1177/1354066107083145.

Adepoju, A. (1994) 'Preliminary analysis of emigration dynamics in sub-Saharan Africa', *International Migration*, 32 (2), 197–216, doi: 10.1111/j.1468-2435.1994.tb00152.x.

Agunias, D. R. and K. Newland (2012) *Developing a road map for engaging diasporas in development*, Geneva: IOM.

Akyeampong, E. (2000) 'Africans in the diaspora: the diaspora and Africa', *African Affairs*, 99 (396), 183–215, doi: 10.1093/afraf/99.395.183.

Bakewell, O. (2008) 'Keeping them in their place: the ambivalent relationship between development and migration in Africa', *Third World Quarterly*, 29 (7), 1341–58, doi: 10.1080/01436590802386492.

Boyle, M. and R. Kitchin (2014) 'Diaspora-centred development: current practice, critical commentaries, and research priorities', in S. Sahoo and B. K. Pattanik (eds) *Global diasporas and development*, New Delhi: Springer, 17–37.

Braun, J. (2016) 'The strange case of "John Black" and "Mr Hyde": constructing migrating Jamaicans as (un)worthy nationals', *Nations and Nationalism*, 23 (2), 395–415, doi: 10.1111/nana.12237.

Brinkerhoff, J. M. (2012) 'Creating an enabling environment for diasporas' participation in homeland development', *International Migration*, 50 (1), 75–95, doi: 10.1111/j.1468-2435.2009.00542.x.

Brown, J. M. (2006) *Global South Asians*, Cambridge: Cambridge University Press.

Byron, M., and S. Condon (2008) *Migration in comparative perspective*, London: Routledge.

Chacko, E. and P. H. Gebre (2013) 'Leveraging the diaspora for development: lessons from Ethiopia', *GeoJournal*, 78 (3), 495–505, doi: 10.1007/s10708-012-9447-9.

Cohen, N. (2015) 'A web of repatriation: the changing politics of Israel's diaspora strategy', *Population, Space and Place*, 22 (3), 288–300, doi: 10.1002/psp.1931.

Comaroff, J. and J. Comaroff (eds) (2006) *Law and disorder in the postcolony*, Chicago: University of Chicago Press.

Connell, R. (2007) *Southern theory*, Cambridge: Polity Press.

Crush, J., A. Chikanda and G. Tawodzera (2016) 'The making of a southern diaspora: South–South migration and Zimbabweans in South Africa', in A. Chikanda, J. Crush and M. Walton-Roberts (eds) *Diasporas, development and governance*, Bern: Springer, 221–38.

Datta, K. (2009) 'Transforming South–North relations? International migration and development', *Geography Compass*, 3 (1), 108–34, doi: 10.1111/j.1749-8198.2008.00190.x.

Davies, R. (2012) 'African diasporas, development and the politics of context', *Third World Quarterly*, 33 (1), 91–108, doi: 10.1080/01436597.2012.627237.

de Haas, H. (2006) 'Migration, remittances and regional development in southern Morocco', *Geoforum*, 37 (4), 565–80, doi: 10.1016/j.geoforum.2005.11.007.

de Haas, H. (2010) 'Migration and development: a theoretical perspective', *International Migration Review*, 44 (1), 227–64, doi: 10.1111/j.1747-7379.2009.00804.x.

Dufoix, S. (2011) 'From nationals abroad to "diaspora": the rise and progress of extra-territorial and over-state nations', *Diaspora Studies*, 4 (1), 1–20.

Gamlen, A. (2014) 'Diaspora institutions and diaspora governance', *International Migration Review*, 48 (1), 180–217, doi: 10.1111/imre.12136.

Geschiere, P. and J. Gugler (1998) 'Introduction: the urban–rural connection: changing issues of belonging and identification', *Africa*, 68 (3), 309–19, doi: 10.2307/1161251.

Hickey, M. (2015) 'Diaspora strategies in the sending states of Southeast Asia: rights, skills and questions of value', *Singapore Journal of Tropical Geography*, 36 (2), 147–63, doi: 10.1111/sjtg.12102.

Hickey, S. (2011) 'Toward a progressive politics of belonging? Insights from a pastoralist "hometown" association', *Africa Today*, 57 (4), 28–47.

Iheduru, O. C. (2011) 'African states, global migration, and transformations in citizenship politics', *Citizenship Studies*, 15 (2), 181–203, doi: 10.1080/13621025.2011.549707.

Iskander, N. (2010) *Creative state*, Ithaca: Cornell University Press.

James, M. (2016) 'Diaspora as an ethnographic method: decolonial reflections on researching urban multiculture in outer East London', *Young: Nordic Journal of Youth Research*, 24 (3), 222–37.

Kamau, A. and M. Kimenyi (2012) 'More than just sending money home: engaging the diaspora as a priority for Africa's development', Brookings Institution report: Foresight Africa project, 18 December, available at: www.brookings.edu/research/foresight-africa-top-priorities-for-the-continent-in-2013/.

Kamei, S. (2011) 'Diaspora as the "sixth region of Africa": an assessment of the African Union Initiative, 2002–2010', *Diaspora Studies*, 4 (1), 59–76.

Kapur, D. (2004) 'Remittances: the new development mantra?', *paper prepared for the G-24 technical group meeting*, April, available at: http://unctad.org/en/Docs/gdsmdpbg2420045_en.pdf.

Kleist, N. (2011) 'Modern chiefs: tradition, development and return among traditional authorities in Ghana', *African Affairs*, 110 (441), 629–47, doi: 10.1093/afraf/adr041.

Larner, W. (2015) 'Globalising knowledge networks: universities, diaspora strategies, and academic intermediaries', *Geoforum*, 59, 197–205, doi: 10.1016/j.geoforum.2014.10.006.

Leblang, D. (2017) 'Harnessing the diaspora: dual citizenship, migrant return remittances', *Comparative Political Studies*, 50 (1), 75–101, doi: 10.1177/0010414015606736.

Lindley, A. (2009). 'Between "dirty money" and "development capital": Somali money transfer infrastructure under global scrutiny', *African Affairs*, 108 (433), 519–39, doi: 10.1093/afraf/adp046.

McGregor, J. (2009) 'Associational links with home among Zimbabweans in the UK: reflections on long-distance nationalisms', *Global Networks*, 9 (2), 185–208, doi: 10.1111/j.1471-0374.2009.00250.x.

McGregor, J, and D. Pasura (2010) 'Diasporic repositioning and the politics of re-engagement: developmentalising Zimbabwe's diaspora?', *The Round Table*, 99 (411), 687–703, doi: 10.1080/00358533.2010.530413.

Mercer, C., B. Page and M. Evans (2008) *Development and the African diaspora*, London: Zed Books.

Mohamoud, A. A. (2006) *African diaspora and post-conflict reconstruction in Africa*, Copenhagen: Danish Institute for International Studies.

Moniruzzaman, M. (2016) 'Governing the remittance landscape for development: policies and actors in Bangladesh', in A. Chikanda, J. Crush and M. Walton-Roberts (eds) *Diasporas, Development and Governance*, Bern: Springer, 101–20.

Norglo, B. E. K., M. Goris, R. Lie and A. O. Ong'ayo (2016) 'The African diaspora's public participation in policy-making concerning Africa', *Diaspora Studies*, 9 (2), 83–99, doi: 10.1080/09739572.2016.1183889.

Nyamnjoh, F. and M. Rowlands (1998) 'Elite associations and the politics of belonging in Cameroon', *Africa*, 68 (3), 320–37, available at: www.jstor.org/stable/1161252.

Pearlman, W. (2014) 'Competing for Lebanon's diaspora: transnationalism and domestic struggles in a weak state', *International Migration Review*, 48 (1), 34–75, doi: 10.1111/imre.12070.

Pelican, M. (2013) 'International migration: virtue or vice? Perspectives from Cameroon', *Journal of Ethnic and Migration Studies*, 39 (2), 237–58, doi: 10.1080/1369183X.2013.723256.

Raghuram, P. (2009) 'Which migration, what development? Unsettling the edifice of migration and development', *Population, Space and Place*, 15 (2), 103–17, doi: 10.1002/psp.536.

Resende Santos, J. (2016) 'Cape Verde: rethinking diaspora in development policy', *International Migration*, 54 (2), 82–97, doi: 10.1111/imig.12212.

Sinatti, G. and C. Horst (2015) 'Migrants as agents of development: diaspora engagement discourse and practice in Europe', *Ethnicities*, 15 (1), 134–52, doi: 10.1177/1468796814530120.

Turner, S. (2013) 'Staging the Rwandan diaspora: the politics of performance', *African Studies*, 72 (2), 265–84, doi: 10.1080/00020184.2013.812888.

Turner, S. and N. Kleist (2013) 'Introduction: agents of change? Staging and governing diasporas and the African state', *African Studies*, 72 (2), 192–206, doi: 10.1080/00020184.2013.812882.

Vázquez, R. (2011) 'Translation as erasure: thoughts on modernity's epistemic violence', *Journal of Historical Sociology*, 24 (1), 27–44, doi: 10.1111/j.1467-6443.2011.01387.x.

Vezzoli, S. and M.-L. Flahaux (2016) 'How do post-colonial ties and migration regimes shape travel visa requirements? The case of Caribbean nationals', *Journal of Ethnic and Migration Studies*, 14 (3), 1141–63, doi: 10.1080/1369183X.2016.1228446.

Vigneswaran, D. and J. Quirk (eds) (2015) *Mobility makes states*, Philadelphia: University of Pennsylvania Press.

Wiltshire, R. (1992) 'Implications of transnational migration for nationalism: the Caribbean example', *Annals of the New York Academy of Sciences*, 645, 175–87, doi: 10.1111/j.1749-6632.1992.tb33491.x.

31
The plasticity of diasporic identities in super-diverse cities

Tamsin Barber

In 'super-diverse' cities such as London across the Western hemisphere, an intensification and diversification of migrant groups is having a profound effect upon how diaspora-making is taking place and how diasporic identities are being formed. A wider range of cultural resources and an increasingly complex ethnic landscape is precipitating the dismantling of conventional categories of difference and identity. In Britain, for example, this diversification consists of a transition from a more conventional immigrant and ethnic minority population (large, well-organized African-Caribbean and South Asian communities and citizens originally from Commonwealth countries or former colonial territories), to a 'new migration' from a diverse range of origins mostly relating to places that have no specific historical and colonial links with Britain (Vertovec 2007). Alongside the increasingly diverse make-up of the population, we are also seeing a proliferation in the ways in which people (particularly young people) are expressing their identities (Fanshawe and Sriskandarajah 2010; Vertovec 2012). This emphasis on the 'super-diversity of identities' suggests the enabling of a more open, public and visible expression of social identities (Fanshawe and Sriskandarajah 2010; Valentine 2013). These developments also present new challenges to the way we may categorize and encounter other people (Valentine 2013), as well as potentially presenting new possibilities for identity formation (Barber 2015). A multiplication of diverse identities can contribute to a more complex, fluid and nuanced understanding of 'race' and ethnicity, and therefore diasporic identities. Conceptions of 'super-diversity' are arguably useful in two ways: firstly, they can offer the potential for avoiding essentialisms by focusing on 'processes of identification' rather than points of origin (Wessendorf 2013); and secondly, they hold the potential to open a space to develop more sophisticated notions of ethnicity in urban contexts by extending dominant or traditional conceptions of multi-racial and multi-ethnic contexts beyond 'hypervisible' groups, like South Asian and African-Caribbean migrant-settler populations in the British context (Knowles 2013).

The diasporic community in the host society

If we understand diasporic identity construction as involving a process of negotiation between the homeland and host society (Parennas and Sui 2009), the concept of diaspora and thus processes of diaspora-making must necessarily be understood in relation to how they are shaped by 'race' and ethnic relations (including racisms) in the host society as well as a range of social and economic relations within the diaspora community. This chapter will focus on relations in the host society. Parennas and Siu (2009: 7) have argued that diasporic consciousness and identification 'emerge and grow stronger from local processes of racialisation'. The more traditional black/white binaries shaping identity politics are thus recast by a more diversified cultural and ethnically plural landscape. These two things might have a very particular significance for diaspora-making and diasporic identity construction in that they might open up some of the constraints posed by more rigid traditional power structures of the postcolonial era by the introduction of new forms of difference. By the same token, it may also offer a new and different range of constraints and opportunities for fashioning diasporic identities. So in exploring the potential transformatory effects of super-diverse contexts upon diasporic identity formations, we must also pay attention to parallel processes which reinforce existing social hierarchies, such as the way in which 'old' essentialized racisms often persist under new guises. New diversity discourses have been criticized for hiding inequalities through prioritizing and celebrating more 'acceptable' kinds of diversity by taking an overly superficial and culturalist approach to difference. While certain differences are marked as 'diverse' – those that are largely an aesthetic, politically and morally neutral expression of cultural difference – others become marked as a 'problematic or dangerous difference not grounded in loyalties and marked by unwanted, or morally objectionable practices' (Anthias 2011: 326; Inda 2006). We need to think about how this has the potential to shape and obscure diasporic identity formation and the presentation of difference by diaspora groups.

In order to explore how super-diverse contexts shape diasporic identity formations, I will use a notion of diaspora and diaspora-making as a creative and ongoing process involving relations in the host society, 'homeland' and the international diaspora (Parennas and Siu 2009). As Parennas and Siu (2009) have noted, diaspora is not simply about transnational forces that shape race relations but also the local manifestations of social inequalities such as racism and xenophobia. Likewise, Hall (1996) has argued that diaspora can form a 'positionality' built on a shared experience of racism and political position. Diasporic identification may then be understood as a 'strategy of resistance' which offers a basis for examining larger structures of domination at work, offering a potential for mobilizing cross-ethnic and cross-racial political alliance (Parennas and Siu 2009: 10–11). This means that we need to take into account the social context in which diasporic populations live and how these effect subject formation as well as the kind of positionalities that are created. The following sections of this chapter reflect specifically upon the role of discourses in shaping the experience of groups who are visible but under-represented within the British multicultural imagination and consider whether the notion of super-diversity offers greater opportunities or constraints to negotiating new forms of identity and inclusion. An emphasis will be placed upon whether super-diversity offers a move away from the more constraining effects of more 'fixed' and recognizable diasporic identities and whether diasporic groups and individuals are afforded greater flexibility in fashioning their identities through occupying a more diverse cultural terrain where a wider range of images and labels are available to contest broader structural discourses. With these questions in mind, the chapter interrogates central contradictions and outcomes related to being both visible *and* invisible in super-diverse cities, the role of 'passing', and the role of social context in providing both limits and opportunities for diasporic identity formation.

The complexities of visible and more familiar/invisible difference

Diasporic identities are fashioned in a wide range of ways in super-diverse cities according to nationally specific historical power relations that render 'difference' more or less visible.

The visibilization of difference may relate to processes including colonial legacy, race relations and forms of racialization based on nationally specific models of ethnic incorporation, cultural and religious differences, as well as a representation and recognition in cultural and political debates and discourse (Phillips 1995; Taylor 1992). Yet the processes by which difference becomes legible, familiar or instead overlooked in everyday life becomes arguably more complex in super-diverse cities where an increasing array of visible markers of difference may be present at any one given time. Encounters across difference may also be rendered more complex and multiple (see, for example, Ahmed 2000; Ali 2003; Amin 2002), leading to an obscuring of conventional categories used to understanding difference, and therefore intersubjective negotiations of identity categories. Such complexity, multiplicity and diversity may well obscure the boundaries between groups, leading to a reduced ability to recognize or distinguish between diasporic groups and identities.

While more established diaspora groups (including those with former colonial links to a country) might be more visible in the discourses of a nation, other newcomer groups may occupy 'uncharted positions' within society due to their non-colonial experience, meaning that they are often subject to a 'poverty of categorisations' (Ang-Lygate 1997). Being subject to a poverty of categorizations may work in two ways: on the one hand, it might liberate groups and individuals from crude and fixed forms of stereotyping; or, on the other hand, it might enforce a resorting to even more basic and homogenizing categories. Newer and more 'uncharted' groups (for example, in Britain those from Eastern Europe, East and Southeast Asia, Latin America and the Middle East, or other minorities within conventional commonwealth groups) might also be subject to a more complex positioning – in terms of their recognizability in everyday encounters in society and in public discourse. This may take place at different levels; for example, forms of visible and more familiar difference experienced by British new commonwealth groups of African Caribbeans and Asians might be experienced at both a discursive level (recognition of culture and history) and at an embodied level (recognizability in everyday encounters). This may be constraining due to the inescapability of 'recognizable' categories, while at the same time their recognition of the visibility/ their presence and that of the cultural heritage may enable a more clearly demarcated politics or 'positionality'[1] (Hall 1996). For less recognizable groups, their difference may be either less visible (for example, because of their skin colour) or less familiar (due to perceived 'impenetrability' of cultures; for example, of Southeast Asia). This particular feature of invisibility may be experienced in a range of contradictory ways, as illustrated below using the example of the British Vietnamese and the East Asian category.

In the super-diverse city of London, the lack of familiarity with East and Southeast Asian groups has often led to an inability to distinguish between ethnic groups, leaving individuals to experience a sense of 'not belonging' and to engage in constant identity work in order to mitigate the effects of being invisible or being called upon to give an account of one's embodied presence (Barber 2015; also see Ahmed 2000). The Vietnamese, like other East and Southeast Asians in Britain (including the more established British Chinese population), have tended to remain invisible and 'silent' minorities who rarely feature in debates on British multiculturalism (Parker 1995; Song 2003). Their invisibility has often protected them from the 'worst kinds of racism' such as the direct and 'old' racisms experienced by black Britons; instead theirs is often indirect and often 'positive' racism (see Archer and Francis 2007). On the other hand, forms of visibility were experienced by this group at a cultural and embodied level through their racialized difference which conformed to a tendency to label all East and Southeast Asian groups under the more familiar 'Chinese' category. Like other East and Southeast Asian groups, the Vietnamese are often perceived as Chinese or simply homogenized under the Chinese category (Archer and Francis 2007; Barber 2015). In super-diverse contexts, the inability of others to distinguish between East and Southeast Asian groups leads to an outcome whereby rather than allowing for complexity and diversity within the British East and Southeast Asian category (or a more nuanced appreciation of 'difference'), anyone of East/Southeast Asian origin is classified as Chinese, leading to a homogenizing tendency rather than a proliferation of difference. For the British-born Vietnamese, instances where they are rendered visible tended to be through the highly racialized confines of Orientalist discourse (Said 1978).

The above example illustrates an unexpected outcome of super-diversity upon diasporic identity-making. In everyday encounters, a more fixed, recognizable category becomes adopted by a less visible group to provide an easy and effective way to engage in mainstream society at the superficial level, highlighting the need to resort to easily recognizable categories in superficial/fleeting encounters across diversity, while also avoiding unnecessarily lengthy discussion about ethnic origins. Thus, the homogenization of difference into 'the Chinese' provides a 'workable' category for the Vietnamese in their encounters with others that works effectively, because, like most encounters in cities between strangers, these encounters tend to be fleeting or rare (Amin 2002). Thus, more broadly, the visibility or invisibility of diaspora groups in super-diverse contexts may work on a number of different levels relating to a combination of physical 'difference' and discursive invisibility. The consequences of this exclusion through invisibility and racism (of the more indirect and 'positive' forms) is likely to lead diasporic individuals to engage in practices of transnationalism to seek out meaning and belonging in the 'homeland' (Cohen 1979; Delaney 1990) including forms of 'ethnic authentification' (Barber 2017; Parennas and Siu 2009).

'Passive' and 'deliberative' passing

Processes of globalization have rendered the figure of the 'stranger' more complex in recent decades, and this is supposedly altering our ability to be able to easily distinguish between so-called 'insiders' and 'outsiders' (Ahmed 2004; Rumford 2013). In super-diverse contexts, this process may be further intensified; as argued above, conditions of super-diversity may obfuscate interpretations of, and familiarity with, difference. Diasporic youth, in particular, may be able to actually navigate between group identities and positions to become sometimes more visible and readable, and at other times less visible and categorizable, depending upon the social context. Practices of passing can become ways to mobilize ethnic and class positionalities in order to strategically appeal to notions of 'acceptable diversity' which are embodied within particular versions of more visible ethnic difference. Scholars recognize that passing can take a variety of forms and may serve a range of different purposes and intentionalities, ranging from 'a fleeting momentary experience', 'mistaken identity', 'opportunistic action', to even the 'subversion of structural and/or personal inequality' (Gilbert 2005: 68). Both 'passive' and 'deliberate' acts of passing thus may be used strategically for seeking acceptance within certain contexts, to achieve social mobility or simply to escape stigma. Examples include the avoidance of inter-ethnic entrepreneurial rivalry (Tuan 1998), to passing under more 'acceptable' forms of Asian Americaness (Shah 2008). Passing may offer opportunities for individuals to manage the effects and outcomes of their broader structural positioning within power relations of ethnic and class hierarchies, and to position themselves more 'positively' in the super-diverse city.

Building upon the example of the British-born Vietnamese, the super-diverse context of London has enabled this group to pass as a range of different East and Southeast Asian ethnicities in order to manage the judgement and social expectations of others. The most common form of passing, passive passing, usually occurs through a process of misidentification whereby the Vietnamese (like other East Asian groups; see Archer and Francis 2007; Yeh 2014) are frequently misidentified in their everyday encounters as Chinese, Japanese, Korean, Thai or 'Oriental', because they elude more straightforward processes of ethnic or racial assignment in British race relations (to which these other groups might more recognizably conform). When unchallenged, this process can provide a form of 'convenience passing', because it offers both an easy and effective way to engage in mainstream society at a superficial level, while at the same time enabling the British-born Vietnamese to avoid uncomfortable or lengthy discussions about their ethnic origins (Barber 2015). The second form of passing, deliberate passing, occurs in relation to a range of behavioural and symbolic attempts to creatively engage with, resist or displace negative stigmatizing labels. This kind of passing was more often employed by young working-class men who used 'visibility strategies' such as hairstyling (spiking and dying), dress style and social mixing/participation to avoid Orientalist racisms associated with the stereotype of the 'passive effeminate Asian male' and avoid more narrow associations with cannabis-growing and criminality more recently associated with the Vietnamese in Britain (Silverstone and Savage 2010).

The use of visible embodiment strategies to pass as Japanese, Korean or Thai, and engage with more positive images associated with 'Oriental culture', enabled these diasporic youth to achieve a better status and image within these contexts (Barber 2015). In the super-diverse London borough of Hackney, where numbers of East and Southeast Asians are highest, being accepted in a more positive way within youthful 'super-diverse' contexts (such as 'the street' or local 'club') required the navigation of a complex hierarchy of images of 'East Asianness'. Similar hierarchies have also been observed among American Asians in the USA, where the status of the country of origin (along geopolitical lines) has strongly dictated the perceptions of different groups in the new host country context (Kim 2008). For example, Japanese youth culture has been well received among youth in the European context (Kinsella 1997), and Japanese Manga-style identity has been linked to providing alternative constructions of masculinity by avoiding the hegemonic/subordinate binary (Barber 2014). Japanese hairstyling, for example, has served as a public performance of 'resistant' Vietnamese masculinities by enabling a negotiation of more positive and powerful masculinities in multi-ethnic contexts. The re-appropriation of Japanese hairstyling by the Vietnamese in the context of London was also combined with other embodiment practices creating a new trans-ethnic style, which facilitated the construction of a broader pan-ethnic 'Oriental' identification and consciousness (Barber 2015; Yeh 2014). This opened up access to a greater range of sub-identities from which to 'choose' (Song 2003). Here, a super-diverse context may be seen as encouraging and enabling a masking over of difference to depoliticize identities (working-class Vietnamese masculinities) which are experienced as 'bad diversity'. The structures that allow for this kind of passing depend upon the existence of populations that are not yet seen as part of multi-ethnic Britain and are still relatively unfamiliar.

What a difference context makes

A focus on context, place and locale are central to constructions of identity (Back 1996; Nayak 2004); likewise, social geographers have long understood place and identities as mutually constitutive (Massey 1998; Skelton and Valentine 1998). In the super-diverse setting of London, the transitionary multicultural 'migrant' landscapes characterizing East and Southeast London are of particular note. Eade (1997) has argued how the complexity of living in the global city has given way to new ethnicities and new cultural attachments, the development of some of which has been illustrated in the above sections. While super-diverse contexts have been found to enable forms of convivial culture in public spaces (Wessendorf 2013), other ethnographic work shows how super-diverse contexts can also enable belonging at varying levels, moving beyond insider/outsider distinctions (Hall 2016). Further research finds the convivial encounters in super-diverse spaces to be less straightforwardly progressive and questions the quality and depth of ethnic mixing that takes place (Neal et al. 2015). Super-diversity itself is not uniform across all parts of London, and the extent and nature of the ethnic mix may be variable (Vertovec 2012). While many of the participants in my research lived in East London, not all of them did, and their experiences of other parts of London shaped how they engaged with and performed their identities. For example, aspirations for collective identities tended to emerge in circumstances where issues of power and representation were important. Super-diverse contexts such as 'the club' in the East of London were drawn upon as important identity spheres for these young adults in which to exercise political identity and contest forms of invisibility (see Barber 2015). In other contexts, particularly the mainstream institutions, including the workplace, where white norms still dominate, a less easily categorizable self was seen as more beneficial and enabled Vietnamese women to be read under more ambiguous notions of difference and discourses of the 'exotic'. The notion of the exotic temporarily enabled individuals to escape fixed labels and negative stereotypes, providing agentic opportunities for renegotiating the terms of their interactions and appeal to more 'positive' forms of racialization. The specific power dynamics inscribed in super-diverse contexts were variable; for some participants, belonging and being accepted in sub-cultural club settings were more immediately important than being accepted in mainstream institutions where white norms prevail.

Conclusion: the limits and possibilities of the social construction of identity

While super-diverse contexts may enable greater elasticity in diasporic identity formation due to the greater range of images and affiliations that may be drawn upon, this should not be conflated with an ability to shift the power dynamics of racial discourse. In super-diverse cities, we might find experiences of invisibility becoming more common and holding a range of different outcomes and possibilities for diaspora groups to negotiate labels and categories at a superficial level. This may occur in the following ways. Firstly, there can be 'category confusion' and/or 'category overload' on the behalf of the external onlookers which may extend the range of identity options available to diasporic groups, enabling a switching between and beyond existing categories. Secondly, a wider range of images and discourses become accessible and may render deliberate passing and creative identity-making more possible. Thirdly, more opportunities for becoming less visible and avoiding the worst effects of racism in truly diverse contexts may make forms of strategic negotiation more possible while at the same time reinforcing existing structures of 'good diversity' and 'bad diversity'. However, these strategies are still likely to be heavily tied to residual power dynamics in the host society's race relations.

By assessing the ways in which diasporic identities are positioned and performed in super-diverse cities, a number of further questions are raised about the potential for agency and the plasticity of diasporic identities at the margins of society. The first issue relates to the question of when being visible is desirable and when it is not. When confronted with feeling invisible in super-diverse settings, what are the options and advantages to becoming more visible in intra-ethnic encounters? This question may relate to questions of power that reside in the ability to categorize others or not. We must ask: to what extent do they actually play a part in the multi-ethnic settings they occupy and on what terms? For example, the Vietnamese men in my research were often located on the peripheries of these social scenes, and in their plight to become more visible, they display aesthetic 'presentations of self' as strategies for masculine empowerment. However, these visibility strategies are problematically caught within the confines of highly consumerist and traditionally more 'feminine' modes of asserting power, as the basis for challenging existing narrow stereotypes – so does super-diversity require more superficial performances and claims to identity to become visible and to belong? There are dangers of simply conforming to notions of 'good diversity' rather than confronting or challenging racism. Aesthetic strategies such as hairstyling and performative disruptions through countering Orientalist discourse might create a space for a wider interpretation and variation of images of East and Southeast Asian masculinities in Western societies, but the very strategy of countering racism by becoming more visible is in itself problematic. Caluya (2006) explores the central flaw in 'strategies of visibility' whereby subjects seek to become more visible, noting that they 'fail to recognize that racial visibility is a precondition of racism in the first place' (2006: 4). To the less discerning eye, their subtle strategies and performances of resistance could be read as simply reinforcing existing notions of Oriental discourse, rather than as offering a substantial alternative. As Caluya (2006) suggests, we need to more carefully critique the terms of visibility itself and question 'what' precisely is made visible, in what way and to 'whom'. The risk is that their responses become reliant upon gendered and sexual discursive and visual regimes, and thus become 'trapped in a cultural politics of subversion' (Caluya 2006). With this in mind, it may be concluded that the plasticity in diasporic identity formation does not occur without various costs to the diasporic group and individual, as navigating the images and expectations of the host society inevitably requires some sort of erasure of the self.

Note

1 It should be noted that the variation and difference and fragmentation within these groups is also well documented (for example, Alexander 1996).

References

Ahmed, S. (2000) *Strange encounters: embodied others in post-coloniality*, London: Routledge.
Alexander, C. (1996) *The art of being black: the creation of black British youth identities*, Oxford: Oxford University Press.
Ali, S. (2003) *'Mixed-race', post-race: gender, new ethnicities and cultural practices*, London: Berg.
Amin, A. (2002) 'Ethnicity and the multicultural city: living with diversity,' *Environment and Planning A*, 34 (6), 959–80. doi: 1068/a3537.
Ang-Lygate, M. (1997) 'Charting the spaces of (un)location: on theorising diaspora', in H. S. Mirza (ed.) *Black British feminism: a reader*, London: Routledge, 168–86.
Anthias, F. (2011) 'Moving beyond the Janus face of integration and diversity discourses: towards an intersectional framing', *The Sociological Review*, 61 (2), 323–43, doi: 10.1111/1467-954X.12001.
Archer, L. and B. Francis (2007) *Understanding minority ethnic achievement: race, gender, class and 'success'*, Abingdon: Routledge.
Back, L. (1996) *New ethnicities and urban culture: racisms and multiculture in young lives*, London: UCL Press.
Barber, T. (2014) 'Performing "Oriental" masculinities: embodied identities among Vietnamese men in London', *Journal of Gender, Place and Culture*, 22 (3), 440–55, doi: 10.1080/0966369X.2013.879101.
Barber, T. (2015) *'Oriental' identities in 'super-diverse' Britain: young British-born Vietnamese in London*, Basingstoke: Palgrave Macmillan.
Barber, T. (2017) 'Achieving ethnic authenticity through "return" visits to Vietnam: paradoxes of class and gender among the British-born Vietnamese', *Journal of Ethnic and Migration Studies*, 43 (6), 919–36, doi: 10.1080/1369183X.2016.1274564.
Caluya, G. (2006) 'The (gay) scene of racism: face, shame and gay Asian males', *Australian Critical Race and Whiteness Studies*, 2 (2), available at: www.acrawsa.org.au/files/ejournalfiles/80GilbertCaluya.pdf.
Cohen, E. (1979) 'A phenomenology of tourist experience', *The Journal of the British Association*, 13 (2), 179–201, doi: 10.1177/003803857901300203.
Delaney, C. (1990) 'The *hajj*: sacred and secular', *American Ethnologist*, 17 (3), 513–30, doi: 10.1525/ae.1990.17.3.02a00060.

Eade, J. (ed.) (1997) *Living the global city: globalization as social process*, London: Routledge.
Fanshawe, S. and D. Sriskanadarajah (2010) '"You can't put me in a box": super-diversity and the end of identity politics in Britain', Institute for Public Policy Research paper, available at: www.ippr.org/files/images/media/files/publication/2011/05/you_cant_put_me_in_a_box_1749.pdf.
Gilbert, D. (2005) 'Interrogating mixed-race: a crisis of ambiguity?' *Social Identities*, 11 (1), 55–74, doi: 10.1080/13504630500100621.
Hall, S. (1996) 'Who needs "identity"?', in S. Hall and P. du Gay (eds.) *Questions of cultural identity*, London: Sage, 1–17.
Inda, J. X. (2006) *Targeting immigrants: government, technology, and ethics*, Malden, MA: Blackwell.
Kim, N. (2008) *Imperial citizens: Koreans and race from Seoul to LA*, Stanford: Stanford University Press.
Kinsella, S. (1997) *Adult manga: culture and power in contemporary Japanese society*, Honolulu: University of Hawai'i Press.
Knowles, C. (2013) 'Nigerian London: re-mapping space and ethnicity in superdiverse cities', *Ethnic and Racial Studies*, 36 (4), 651–69, doi: 10.1080/01419870.2012.678874.
Massey, D. (1998) 'The spatial construction of youth cultures' in T. Skelton and G. Valentine (eds) *Cool places*, London: Routledge, 120–9.
Nayak, A. (2004) *Race, place and globalization: youth cultures in a changing world*, Oxford: Berg.
Neal S., K. Bennett, H. Jones, A. Cochrane and G. Mohan (2015) 'Multiculture and public parks: researching super-diversity and attachment in public green space', *Population, Space and Place*, 21 (5), 463–75, doi: 10.1002/psp.1910.
Parennas, R. and L. Siu (eds) (2009) *Asian diasporas: new formations, new conceptions*, Stanford: Stanford University Press.
Parker, D. (1995) *Through different eyes: the cultural identities of young Chinese people in Britain*, Aldershot: Avebury.
Phillips, A. (1995) *Politics of presence*, Oxford: Clarendon Press.
Rumford, C. (2013) *The globalisation of strangeness*, Basingstoke: Palgrave Macmillan.
Said, E. (1978) *Orientalism*, London: Penguin.
Shah, B. (2008) 'Is yellow black or white? Inter-minority relations and the prospects for cross-racial coalitions between Laotians and African Americans in the San Francisco bay area', *Ethnicities*, 8 (4), 463–91, doi: 10.1177/1468796808097074.
Silverstone, D. and S. Savage (2010) 'Farmers, factories and funds: organised crime and illicit drugs cultivation within the British Vietnamese community', *Global Crime*, 11 (1), 16–33, doi: 10.1080/17440570903475683.
Skelton, T. and G. Valentine (eds) (1998) *Cool places: geographies of youth cultures*, London: Routledge.
Song, M. (2003) *Choosing ethnic identity*, Cambridge: Polity Press.
Taylor, C. (1992) *Multiculturalism and 'the politics of recognition'*, Princeton: Princeton University Press.
Tuan, M. (1998) *Forever foreigners or honorary whites?* New Brunswick: Rutgers University Press.
Valentine, G. (2013) 'Living with difference: proximity and encounter in urban life', *Geography*, 98 (1), 4–9, available at: www.geography.org.uk/journals/journals.asp?articleID=1050.
Vertovec, S. (2007) 'Super-diversity and its implications', *Ethnic and Racial Studies*, 30 (6), 1024–54, doi: 10.1080/01419870701599465.
Vertovec, S. (2012) '"Diversity" and the social imaginary', *European Journal of Sociology*, 53 (3), 287–312, doi: 10.1017/S000397561200015X.
Wessendorf, S. (2013) 'Commonplace diversity and the "ethos of mixing": perceptions of difference in a London neighbourhood', *Identities: Global Studies in Culture and Power*, 20 (4), 407–22, doi: 10.1080/1070289X.2013.822374.
Yeh, D. (2014) 'Contesting the "model minority": racialization, youth culture and "British Chinese/oriental" nights', *Journal of Ethnic and Racial Studies*, 37 (7), 1197–210, doi: 10.1080/01419870.2014.859288.

32
Displaced imaginations, bodies and things
Materiality and subjectivity of forced migration

Sandra H. Dudley

What does it feel like to be displaced? What material things are important to people when they have to move, and why? What are the smells, tastes and textures of forced migration and of unfamiliarity, and how does the body and its comportments adapt to new ways of being? Why should such questions be taken seriously? Focusing on forced relocation, this chapter touches on such questions by approaching migration and diaspora as not only culturally inflected, but material, embodied, sensorial and emotional. This perspective foregrounds the ways in which migrants perceive, imagine, engage with, make and re-make their worlds . . . and are made and re-made by them. Not only do refugee groups undergo different migrations, but even within one population, family or even individual, there may be many kinds of experience. Exploring these is valuable in itself; it also enables more nuanced interpretations of displacement's widely attended-to economic, social and political elements. It may also, enhance policy-making and applied work.

There is still relatively little work addressing forced migration through a lens of materiality and/or embodied experience, though outputs framed in slightly different terms sometimes usefully intersect. These are not always in the realm of scholarly research. Objects of significance to refugees in recent global displacements, for example, is a recent theme for a number of photographers, journalists and non-governmental organizations (NGOs) (for example, Agha 2015; Kingsley and Diab 2015; Mollison 2015; Sokol 2013). In Mollison's (2015) images, seven of the thirteen refugees are shown with items that initially appear, from the brief accompanying texts, to be purely functional. Some objects have no associations with the places the refugees have left, so a casual viewer might wonder to what extent these are the title's 'things refugees carry with them' at all. Three young, blanket-wrapped Syrian boys, for example, are shown next to a mostly eaten packet of biscuits that, their mother Shakrea explains, were given to them 'here', just as diabetic Marie from the Democratic Republic of Congo appears with syringes she was given by aid workers. These things are both new and unsentimental in themselves, and essential to the migrating human bodies they sustain and stabilize. Their presence, however, like that of those objects that connect with an individual's past – Syrian Ahmad, with his photo album; Afghan Muhammed, with his family ring – gives us but a small, partial glimpse of the experiences of their owners. Indeed, the people who gaze out from these images, in front of plain white backdrops, appear at best simplified, all their real, messy, complex humanity reduced to one tragic, problematic essence; and at worst, bewildered and decontextualized, rendered as impotent and passive as forced migrants in earlier literature, whose cultural identities and epistemologies had apparently gone permanently astray.[1, 2]

Some of the academic research that can help to bring greater depth to understandings of displacement has been done not primarily on materiality and sensoriality but on place-making and/or 'home' (for example, Bozkurt 2009; Colson 1971; Hoffstaedter 2014; Jean 2015; Turton 2005).[3] In this literature, however, the focus largely remains a spatial one, be it physical or symbolic (cf. Al-Ali and Khoser 2002: 7). While forced migrants themselves may also privilege such a construct, it can be more helpful to examine how (and how successfully) they work to feel at ease wherever they may now be. This is less about 'making home' and 'home' *per se*, than seeking to feel 'at home' (Dudley 2018). Feeling at home is feeling right, an ontological state:[4] it may (in part) be about place, but it need not be; one can also be 'at home' in one's community(s) and self, now and in relation to the past and future. Perhaps this is an existential problem faced on some level by every human being; arguably, however, it is posed most challengingly by migration experienced as enforced.

The environmental and other material changes that result, together with the addition of an emotionally loaded spatial (as well as the more universal temporal) distance between present and past, challenge the 'ontological experiences of authenticity, familiarity, intimacy' (Dobson 2004: 98) that help to bring about feeling right. Put simply, forced migration inevitably makes things different – for migrants' bodies, emotions and imaginations, producing very significant effects. The results may be manifested or interpreted as place- or home-making; but they may also reveal much else that, if we did not pay at least some attention to the material and subjective aspects of dislocation, would not otherwise be known. This might include the many textured shifts in resource availability and environmental conditions, the diversity of migrants' resilience and creativity, and their perceptions of change, vulnerability and adaptation. But it may also encompass more fundamental aspects of refugees' understandings of their experiences and themselves.

There is a small body of work directly addressing refugee materialities and sensoriality. Its recent growth indicates that this area is being taken increasingly seriously. For example, the *Architectures of Displacement* project explores lived experience of temporary accommodation generated by the Syrian crisis (Scott-Smith et al. 2017). A special issue of *Contemporary Archaeology* (Hamilakis 2016) explores materialities, landscapes and traces of forced and undocumented migration more broadly, from the Indian Partition to the present day. Interestingly, much of this and related work focuses on aspects of the migration journey, immediacies of forced displacement or survival strategies and attempts to become 'emplaced' – including the establishment of new materialities and new sensory experiences – in a new country (for example, Holtzman 2006; Marosszeky 2009). Thus, the temporal frames that feature most prominently in this work are the very immediate past, together with the present and the future.

A slightly more established literature, on the other hand, pays considerable attention to the significance, for some forced migrants at least, of the relationships between the present and pre-displacement past, as well as the influence of these on the future.[5] This includes Parkin's (1999) widely cited examination of objects as mementoes that function as stores of culture, stories and even personhood for (often very long) transitional periods between taking flight and resettlement (whatever that the latter might mean in a particular context). Turan, working with Palestinians living in the USA, relatedly discusses 'objects of legacy' (Turan 2010: 43). Kaiser, focusing on Sudanese refugees in 'temporary' camps in Uganda, gives more nuanced insight into the complexities, choices and negotiations that perfuse refugees' relationships with their displaced material worlds. Arguing that 'challenges to socio-cultural, ritual and political identities and activities are just as great as the more tangible challenges to protection and subsistence for refugees' (Kaiser 2008: 375), she demonstrates the role of certain activities and material cultures in place-making and examines the strategies that refugees develop when particular items are unavailable. My own work with Karenni refugees in prolonged encampment on the Thai–Myanmar border has also explored materiality and place-making (for example, Dudley 2010), as well as arguing that here certain material and ritual forms are held onto, re-created and utilized *for themselves* – not just or even because they represent familiar places and ways of 'doing' and understanding the world and connecting with the pre-exile past, but because they offer something nothing else can (Dudley 2015).

The past in the present

Forced displacement is never a homogenous experience, and for some migrants narrating past traumas is unbearably painful, just as being defined in terms of who, where and what one was may be something to avoid. Others, however, make concerted attempts to sustain some material, bodily and/or emotional sense of continuity with the pre-exile past. We need to understand better both how displaced people do this and why it matters. Parkin's analysis of refugee objects as 'storehouses' that 'take the place of interpersonal relations' and objectify 'social personhood' (Parkin 1999: 315) is one approach, but for me gives too reductive a view. Forced displacement impacts social personhood and relations; even *in extremis*, however, it does not negate, objectify or prevent them. As part of refugees' resourcefulness and adaptability, cultural objects could be said to 'store' cultural knowledge and practice but dynamically and in a way that may be repeatedly re-expressed and re-formed in displacement rather than held over until it can be reactivated (cf. Parkin 1999: 315).

The ways in which objects contribute to creating and sustaining a sense of continuity of self and community are actually very complex. Kaiser (2008: 388) shows the multiple layers of continued production of particular, pre-relocation forms and practices, with her detailed discussion of how Sudanese Acholi refugees in a Kiryandongo refugee camp 'accommodat[e] absences and substitute[e] people and objects' in order to conduct familiar 'social activities, institutions and relationships' as far as possible in the context of constraints imposed by 'exile, poverty and uncertainty'. They create elders' headdresses for funeral rituals using wooden frames and black plastic bags, instead of the pre-displacement ostrich feathers unavailable in the refugee camp. This creative substitution of materials enables core artefacts and practices to be sustained in displacement and, as Kaiser points out, there is 'no tendency to simply abandon the attempt to fulfil familiar social and cultural roles and activities' (Kaiser 2008: 388). Karenni refugees too strive to perpetuate important rituals and other customary practices in displacement, even though this may mean having to utilize what they consider poorer-quality materials, miss out structural elements and, as Kaiser also identifies, experience shifts in the social significances of ritual activities and ritual elders. In celebrating *dïy-küw*, the second most important festival of the Karenni year, for example, while the core elements of sticky rice bundles, rice beer and dancing were to the fore, many refugees talked about the important components that were either missing (for example, the divinatory *phü-dïy-khrïy* figure, and a ritual expert knowledgeable enough to make one) or not as good (for example, the rice beer) (Dudley 2010: 113).

Nostalgic reminiscences like Karenni *dïy-küw* conversations enable remembering of the past and lively comparison of pre-displacement practices in different villages (often to great shared amusement). Through such interlinked material and verbal means, refugees mediate the past in the present, remembering and retelling. Material things and cultural practices that in actuality are now absent are not only memorialized but vicariously re-experienced in the imaginations of tellers and listeners alike. And while certain objects (for example, plastic headdresses) are a new, needs-must manifestation, they simultaneously represent a continuous trajectory from the pre-exile past to the displaced present: of a category of object, a cultural practice, elements of social structure and the life cycle. Even if *particular* refugee objects were themselves not physically present in the pre-exile past, others either very like them or on which they are based – albeit possibly now in different materials – were. Their role in the remembering and imagining of the past is metonymical. They also link with the past metaphorically, however. Moreover, these connections with pre-displacement life are not always positive; they may, for instance, be troubling reminders even in the midst of creative and resilient adaptation. Like a wound that will not heal, they do not allow refugees to forget that things are not as they used to be. They can thus become a focus for the expression of feelings of loss and of yearning for what is apparently gone. The same things that metonymically facilitate positive senses of continuity, concurrently become metaphors for upheaval and what has been left behind.

Being reminded of the past, happily or otherwise, does not only – or even principally – lie in conversation and objects, however. Experiences of both the displaced present and the objects and practices that provide some continuity with the past, are fundamentally corporeal. Seremetakis (1994: 9) has argued that the memory and the senses are so enmeshed that '[t]here is no such thing as one moment of perception and then another of memory, representation or objectification. Mnemonic processes are intertwined with the sensory order in such a manner as to render each perception a re-perception'. Amongst the black plastic headdress-wearing Acholi refugee ritual elders (Kaiser 2008), for example, some may previously have known how it felt to wear the ostrich feather forms. Sensory awareness of the post-displacement differences in the headdresses' sound, weight and movement, for both wearers and others, will interweave with the ongoing familiarity of the dance as it is performed in the camp. Not dissimilarly but on a more quotidian level, for most encamped Karenni refugee women, continuing to wear folded skirt-cloths of the same form and materials that were habitual before becoming displaced enables physical, affective and imaginative continuity with the past (Dudley 2010). The cloths enable the retention of a long-established sense of snugly wrapped comfort, intimate connection between skin and fabric, and a reassuringly quotidian access to the range of functions the skirt-cloth can fulfil (like bathing dresses or gathering vessels).

Food and drink also play very important roles in the dynamics between past and present, including becoming the focus of nostalgia about pre-displacement life (Dudley 2010). The centrality of 'the gustatory . . . to the creation of memory' (Holtzman 2006: 367) has been observed amongst a number of diasporic groups (for example, Hage 1997; Seremetakis 1994; Sutton 2005; Taylor 2013). For refugees in immediate crisis situations and in long-term camps, relief agencies provide rations underpinned by the combined rationale of nutritional necessity, financial economy and ease of use. Cultural appropriateness may also underpin the composition of rations, in theory at least, but the extent to which it really does, and how far it assuages or augments senses of displacement, loss and strangeness vary in practice. Karenni refugees in the late 1990s, for example, were provided by the Thai–Burma Border Consortium (TBBC)[6] with a ration of rice, salt, chilli, vegetable oil, and protein comprising yellow beans or fish paste. Refugees inevitably contrasted this core diet with that available prior to displacement. Relief rice was of poor quality by comparison to the rice that could formerly be grown or bought. More specifically, unlike other displaced groups from Myanmar, the Karenni groups traditionally used neither oil nor fermented fish paste; the inclusion of both ingredients in the camp rations, however, meant they were being adopted in the camps. Oil was causing a shift in food preparation methods from dry cooking, boiling, stewing or smoking, to frying. Fish paste was increasingly embraced by most refugees after some time in the camps, even by those from the northern Karenni groups not habituated to it, as the alternative of yellow beans was experienced as very monotonous.[7] For those without financial means, a dull, limited ration could only be varied by what one could grow or gather – which, for many, was reduced to nothing more than a few bananas, bamboo shoots and green papayas. It was not surprising, then, that food in the present and the past became a predominant topic of conversation. In the process, the pre-displacement past became a mythically better time, one that both those born in exile and those who migrated may never actually have lived at all (cf. Graham and Khosravi 1997).

Present traces

The clothes one wears and how one deports oneself, the food one eats and the manner in which one does so, the shelter under which one sleeps and the ways in which that space is structured and personalized – all these apparently basic elements of life strongly influence experiences of forced migration. In part, as we have seen, this may be about remembering what has been lost, holding onto what one still has and trying to reconnect to past times, places, people and selves. Connecting with the past is about re-creating as much as remembering it, however. Karenni women, for example, repeatedly fold, unfold and refold their skirt-cloths as they have always been accustomed to doing. In that sense, the past is not simply something now gone, of which refugees are sensorially, emotionally and imaginatively reminded; it is performed, and in the process repeatedly re-made, in the now (Dudley 2010; cf. Connerton 1989).

But in their ways of life, whether in the course of practising, remembering and continuing past ways of being or in the midst of flight and its immediate aftermaths, people also leave traces in the *present* – on themselves, on others, on their environment. These myriad embodied, social, material and spatial remnants are recycled and reused, becoming part of ongoing continuities and change, creating a new past in the future. What, though, does this mean for refugees? If landscape, for example, 'is constituted as an enduring record of . . . the lives and works of past generations who have dwelt within it, and . . . left there something of themselves' (Ingold 1993: 152), what record is there for refugees? What are the implications, for a society formerly used to doing so, of no longer being able to live in the same way 'amidst that which was made before' (Meinig 1979: 44; cited in Ingold 1993: 154)?

The ramifications certainly do not render displacement a less socially and culturally shaped experience than any other. Nor do they remove resilience and innovativeness from communities and individuals forced to adapt to both rapid and prolonged dislocations. Indeed, the very process of separation from traces in the landscape of current and previous generations can stimulate resourceful and inventive means of coming to terms with new places and new ways of being. As we have seen, these may include extraordinary creativity and flexibility in finding ways to continue cultural forms that were important before displacement. Equally, refugees may need to abandon not only past places but also things and ideas, leaving material traces on the landscapes across which they journey, as they discard unnecessary and unwanted objects *en route* to life elsewhere (for example, Ma 2017; McGonigal 2015). At the same time, they may create new, digital trails, recording and exchanging experiences (for example, Gillespie et al. 2016).

Approaching lived experiences and traces, old and new, material or otherwise, in ways informed by the anthropology of aesthetics and material and sensory anthropology can make significant contributions to comprehending forced displacement. Exploring which sensory experiences and material forms are given particular value, and investigating their possible connections to memory and nostalgia about places left behind, their production and use in the present, and their relationships to future hopes and objectives, may illuminate how refugees strive to cultivate a sense of rightness and familiarity in the present. The extent to which forced migrants work to bring about appropriate combinations of sensory, cognitive and cultural conditions – and their sensitivity to potential tensions therein – shows how far affective engagement with particular objects, spaces and materialized practices is intensified in displacement. Certain material and other cultural forms come to have particular power or resonance as metaphors for displacement, as statements of difference, as physical and temporal connections with the past, and/or as means of beginning anew.

We need to understand these things and processes better if we wish to develop an insight into how it feels to be a refugee. Bringing them to the fore potentially not only enriches theoretical understandings of displacement but also policy-making and applied work with refugee communities. It has been recognized for some decades that facilitating resettlement and minimizing social and individual trauma and distress in the aftermath of forced migration, for example, is not only a matter of enabling economically productive activity and/or providing food aid and housing and, perhaps, psychological or social support (for example, Cernea 1996; Downing 1996). But neither is it enough to ascertain and enable migrants' familiar social structures and cultural patterns, and work with and through them. Sustaining, and when necessary coming to terms with, changes in one's understandings of who, where and why one *is*, underpins how far refugees cope with the immediacy of displacement and feel at ease. These processes fundamentally depend on the kinds of embodied and material experiences discussed in this chapter. The extent to which forced migrants are able to utilize and develop their own agency and creativity in determining the phenomenological and ontological nature of their immediate and later post-dislocation lives is highly influential on subsequent outcomes. Deepening our understanding of this aspect of migration through further research is imperative to scholarship and global exigencies alike.

Notes

1 For a critique of earlier literature on refugees, see, for example, Malkki (1995).
2 Sokol's subjects, in contrast, appear neither lost nor passive (Sokol 2013). His images are both beautiful and tantalizing, evocative of the temporal, material and emotional entanglements in which all forced migrants are, one way or another, enmeshed.
3 This work on the lived experience and making of home differs from more essentialized connections drawn between people and places that have rightly been critiqued as problematic, especially in relation to refugees and 'statist bias in discourses surrounding forced migration' (Taylor 2013: 130; see also Malkki 1992; Turton 1996).
4 It is also discussed in terms of cultural aesthetics (for example, Dudley 2010).
5 The difference in temporal focus between this literature and some of the more emergent work may at least in part be explained by differences in the displaced populations with whom authors have worked (for example, those living in long-term encampment versus those who are rapidly on the move to destination countries, and those travelling together only with members of their own groups versus those crossing international borders in heterogeneous and shifting groups).
6 Now called The Border Consortium (TBC).
7 Without yellow beans, however, if there is also a lack of green leafy vegetables (and for many there is), a deficiency of vitamin B6 – and consequent rise in incidence of beriberi – is more likely (Dr Jaimie, International Rescue Committee, personal communication, 30 January 1997).

References

Agha, S. (2015) 'We asked refugees: what did you bring with you?', Mercy Corps webpage, 15 June, available at: www.mercycorps.org.uk/photoessays/jordan-syria/we-asked-refugees-what-did-you-bring-you.
Al-Ali, N. and K. Koser (eds) (2002) *New approaches to migration? Transnational communities and the transformation of home*, London: Routledge.

Bozkurt, E. (2009) *Conceptualising 'home'. The question of belonging among Turkish families in Germany*, Chicago: University of Chicago Press.
Cernea, M. (1996) 'Understanding and preventing impoverishment from displacement: reflections on the state of knowledge', *Journal of Refugee Studies*, 8 (3), 245–64, doi: 10.1093/jrs/8.3.245.
Colson, E. (1971) *The social consequences of resettlement*, Manchester: Manchester University Press.
Connerton, P. (1989) *How societies remember*, Cambridge: Cambridge University Press.
Dobson, P. (2004) *Cultures of exile and the experience of refugeeness*, Bern: Peter Lang AG.
Downing, T. (1996) 'Mitigating social impoverishment when people are involuntarily displaced', in C. McDowell (ed.) *Understanding impoverishment: the consequences of development-induced displacement*, Oxford: Berghahn, 33–48.
Dudley, S. (2010) *Materialising exile: material culture and embodied experience among Karenni refugees in Thailand*, Oxford: Berghahn.
Dudley, S. (2015) 'Ritual practice, material culture and wellbeing in displacement: *ka-thow-bòw* in a Karenni refugee camp in Thailand', in A. Horstmann and J. Jung (eds) *Building Noah's ark for migrants, refugees, and religious communities*, Basingstoke: Palgrave Macmillan, 101–26.
Dudley, S. (2018) 'Paku Karen skirt-cloths (not) at home: forcibly migrated Burmese textiles in refugee camps and museums', in L. Auslander and T. Zara (eds) *The things they carried: war, mobility and material culture*, Ithaca, NY: Cornell University Press.
Gillespie, M., L. Ampofo, M. Cheesman, B. Faith, E. Iliadou, A. Issa, S. Osseiran and D. Skleparis (2016) 'Mapping refugee media journeys: smart phones and social media networks', The Open University/France Médias Monde research report, available at: www.open.ac.uk/ccig/sites/www.open.ac.uk.ccig/files/Mapping%20Refugee%20Media%20Journeys%2016%20May%20FIN%20MG_0.pdf.
Graham, M. and S. Khosravi (1997) 'Home is where you make it: repatriation and diaspora culture among Iranians in Sweden', *Journal of Refugee Studies*, 10 (2), 115–33, doi: 10.1093/jrs/10.2.115.
Hage, G. (1997) 'At home in the entrails of the West: multiculturalism, "ethnic food" and migrant home-building', in H. Grace, G. Hage, L. Johnson, J. Langsworth and M. Symonds (eds) *Home/world: space, community and marginality in Sydney's west*, Sydney: Pluto Press, 99–153.
Hamilakis, Y. (ed.) (2016) *Journal of Contemporary Archaeology*, special issue, *Archaeologies of forced and undocumented migration*, 3 (2), available at: https://journals.equinoxpub.com/index.php/JCA.
Hoffstaedter, G. (2014) 'Place-making: Chin refugees, citizenship and the state in Malaysia', *Citizenship Studies*, 18 (8), 871–84, doi: 10.1080/13621025.2014.964549.
Holtzman, J. D. (2006) 'Food and memory', *Annual Reviews in Anthropology*, 35, 361–78, doi: 10.1146/annurev.anthro.35.081705.123220
Ingold, T. (1993) 'The temporality of the landscape', *World Archaeology*, 25 (2), 152–74, doi: 10.1080/00438243.1993.9980235.
Jean, M. (2015) 'The role of farming in place-making processes of resettled refugees', *Refugee Survey Quarterly*, 34 (3), 46–69, doi: 10.1093/rsq/hdv007.
Kaiser T. (2008) 'Social and ritual activity in and out of place: the "negotiation of locality" in a Sudanese refugee settlement', *Mobilities*, 3 (3), 375–95, doi: 10.1080/17450100802376670.
Kingsley, P. and S. Diab (2015) 'Passport, jacket, lemons: what Syrian refugees pack for the journey to Europe', *The Guardian*, 4 September, available at: www.theguardian.com/world/ng-interactive/2015/sep/04/syrian-refugees-pack-for-the-crossing-to-europe-crisis.
Ma, A. (2017) 'Chilling photos of what refugees left behind at Lesbos beach', *The World Post*, 5 January, available at: www.huffingtonpost.com/entry/photos-objects-migrants-left-behind_us_56210c50e4b08d94253ec656.
McGonigal, C. (2015) 'What they left behind: items lost on refugees' arduous journey west', *The World Post*, 19 September, available at: www.huffingtonpost.com/entry/photos-show-whats-left-behind-as-migrants-make-their-journey_us_55f82f5de4b00e2cd5e7ef02.
Malkki, L. H. (1992) 'National geographic: the rooting of peoples and the territorialization of national identity among scholars and refugees', *Cultural Anthropology*, 7 (1), 24–44, doi: 10.1525/can.1992.7.1.02a00030.
Malkki, L. H. (1995) 'Refugees and exile: from "refugee studies" to the national order of things', *Annual Review of Anthropology*, 24, 495–523, doi: 10.1146/annurev.an.24.100195.002431.
Marosszeky, A. (2009) 'Displaced and diffused: fashioning in the refugee experience', in E. Rouse (ed.) *Fashion and well-being?*, conference proceedings, London: International Foundation of Fashion Technology Institutes, 665–77, available at: http://hdl.handle.net/10453/12043.

Meinig, D. W. (1979) 'The beholding eye: ten versions of the same scene', in D. W. Meinig (ed.) *The interpretation of ordinary landscapes*, Oxford: Oxford University Press, 33–48.

Mollison, J. (2015) 'What refugees carry with them', webpage: series of 13 diptychs for *Time Magazine*, available at: http://jamesmollison.com/photography/timemagazine/.

Parkin, D. (1999) 'Mementoes as transitional objects in human displacement', *Journal of Material Culture*, 4 (3), 303–20, doi: 10.1177/135918359900400304.

Scott-Smith, T., M. E. Breeze, D. Hicks and R. Kiddey (2017) 'Architectures of displacement', Refugees Studies Centre webpage, available at: www.rsc.ox.ac.uk/research/architectures-of-displacement.

Seremetakis, C. N. (1994) *The senses still: perception and material culture in modernity*, Chicago: University of Chicago Press.

Sokol, B. (2013) 'The most important thing', webpage, available at: http://briansokol.com/.

Sutton, D. (2005) 'Synaesthesia, memory and the taste of home', in D. Howes (ed.) *The taste culture reader: experiencing food and drink*, Oxford: Berg, 304–16.

Taylor, H. (2013) 'Refugees, the state and the concept of home', *Refugee Survey Quarterly*, 32 (2), 130–52, doi: 10.1093/rsq/hdt004.

Turan, Z. (2010) 'Material objects as facilitating environments: the Palestinian diaspora', *Home Cultures*, 7 (1), 43–56, doi: 10.2752/175174210X12572427063841.

Turton, D. (1996) 'Migrants and refugees: a Mursi case study', in T. Allen (ed.) *In search of cool ground: war, flight and homecoming in northeast Africa*, London: James Currey, 96–110.

Turton, D. (2005) 'The meaning of place in a world of movement: lessons from long-term field research in southern Ethiopia', *Journal of Refugee Studies*, 18 (3), 258–80, doi: 10.1093/refuge/fei031.

33
Disconnecting from home
Contesting the salience of the diaspora

Gijsbert Oonk

In the wonderful Hollywood movie *Mississippi Masala*, director Mira Nair portrays an Indian-African family in Uganda. The film starts in 1972 when the Ugandan dictator Idi Amin expelled all the Asians from Uganda. The family spends a few years in England but then moves on to the USA. Here they live with Indian family members who run a chain of motels. The family eldest, Jay, is profoundly homesick. While in the USA, his main aim is to return home. Home is not India or the UK, but Kampala in Uganda. After attending a court proceeding on the disposition of his confiscated Ugandan house, Jay relinquishes his long-nurtured dream of returning to Uganda, the place he considered as home.

In this chapter, I would like to present two conceptions of home in relation to peoples in the diaspora. The first is related to Jay and his daughter. It is the acknowledgement that some people move on without returning to their 'homeland'. It is the process through migration in which people disconnect from their homeland. Parminder Bhachu has coined the expression 'twice migrants' – people who do not move back to their homeland, but move on (Bhachu 1985). Some even move further and may be coined 'multiple migrants' or 'permanent migrants'. Nevertheless, they continue to create a home away from home. And that new home may be inspired culturally by India as well as Africa in this case. There are various reasons why Jay would not resettle in India. Many South Asians in Uganda had left the continent before India was a nation. Jay and his children were born in Uganda, not in India. They had spent their entire lives in Uganda. They were educated in Uganda. They adapted to the local Swahili culture. At the same time, their Indian culture changed in an African context, but remained visibly Indian in terms of food habits, dress habits and marriage patterns. They would intermarry within the Indian community, but caste barriers were less strict than in India. Economically and increasingly culturally, they were oriented towards Africa and the UK (Oonk 2013). In the early 1950s, the Indian government made it clear that overseas Indians should integrate in the local societies, and not rely on the Indian government for help. Many African Indians took that as a definitive 'farewell'. Moreover, due to the complexities of citizenship issues in the colonial world order, many Indian Africans held British passports or were British subjects. During the turmoil in 1972, India opened its borders to a tiny minority who held Indian passports, rather than the entire Indian diaspora in East Africa. A part of the South Asian community in Africa felt betrayed. In short, the institutional setting was not in favour of natural reconnection with the homeland.

In the second conception of home and homeland, we acknowledge that home is not a natural calling. Jay and his family move on to the UK and later to the USA for two major reasons. First, it is an option because – as British subjects in Uganda – there were no special visa restrictions for them to settle in the UK. In other words, it was an option. In addition, they moved there simply because they had family members and friends in the UK and the USA and not in India. In other words, the availability of networks is important, not the homeland as such. Nevertheless, many first- and second-generation people in the diaspora do share a strong connection with the motherland because of family relations, collective memories, and myths and identification with the nation. But what happens if they do reunite with their places of origin and family members? More often than not, after their arrival in their homeland they face ambivalent feelings. It is not the home they expected. It is a home that may be friendly, but different. This ambivalence is experienced not only by the returnee, but also by those who were left behind. We present a few of these examples in this chapter.

These two commencements, twice migrants and returning migrants, may be seen as an addition to the concept of diaspora as it has developed since the 1990s. Most books on diasporas use broad 'checklists' of factors defining the groups in diasporas, including the dispersal to two or more locations, the collective mythology of one's homeland, and alienation from the host nation, among others. The notions of home and a common culture are often seen as among the most attractive features defining a diaspora. Indeed, at first sight, peoples in the diaspora share an umbilical cord with their motherland. Although there are regional variations in their adaptations, in many ways they display a common cultural relationship with their home country. They may wish their children to prosper in their adopted countries, but at the same time they may prefer them to adopt family values and marriage patterns and to share their common culture. In other words, peoples in the diaspora tend to reproduce their culture, values, language and religion as much as possible. Moreover, many peoples in the diaspora are currently trying to reconnect with their homeland, either through modern mass media, the internet or personal visits. These reconnections are often seen as a romantic rendezvous with the historical past and their 'original roots'. These 'natural feelings of connection' are reinforced by governments that share good reasons for promoting this notion for economic and political ends.

The field of diaspora studies has also grown mature in conceptualizing and theory, along with a number of academic journals, and continues to emphasize the variation and patterns in the ways the umbilical cord between the migrant community and the homeland is structured and organized. Those in this field also began wondering how the word 'diaspora' could be useful in understanding migration, migrants and the relationship between the motherland and the host societies. This was highlighted in particular by the establishment of the journal *Diaspora: A Journal of Transnational Studies*, in 1991. The point of departure for the journal was formulated well by its general editor Khachig Tölölyan, who notes that the concept has been related to a growing field of meanings, including processes of transnationalism, de-territorialization and cultural hybridity. These meanings are opposed to more 'rooted forms' of identifications such as 'regions' and 'nations'. This implies a growing interest in the discourse of 'rootedness', changing identities, and the relationship between the local and the global.

At second sight, however, we notice that many migrants may not (wish to) reconnect with their (mythological) homeland and its culture. In fact, over the years, they have integrated or assimilated in a new culture in a new environment. They have built a new home, with new preferences, prospects and outlooks. They may lose their original language skills and adapt to a new language. They may change their dress and food habits and adapt to the host culture. I do not necessarily refer in this chapter to processes of acculturation or even creolization in which 'roots' are increasingly difficult to find. I am referring more specifically to ambivalent relations with 'roots' and 'origins'. In fact, this chapter argues that the umbilical cord is not self-evident. It needs to be nurtured and negotiated, and even then it might disappear. If we can ask: 'When does a migrant belong to a diaspora?', we may also ask: 'When does someone who once belonged to the diaspora disconnect from his or her "homeland" and vanish in the larger flow of migrants, nationals and nations?' The possible answers may not be definitive in the direction of 'connect' or 'disconnect', but they will be more on the path of ambivalence and uncertainty. Jay transformed from an Indian African to an Asian American. While he would acknowledge his Indian background, he initially considered Uganda as his home. His daughter, who is the main character in the film, falls in love with an African American. She considers her love affair as an example of the 'American way of life'.

In general, the field of diaspora studies has grown beyond the initial 'checklist' fixation wherein it seemed that two questions were most important: what is a diaspora, and who belongs to the diaspora? Here, however, I would like to present examples that show the path of ambivalence and uncertainty regarding a migrant's relation to their motherland. They are in line with my previous research (Oonk 2007) but also confirm Brubaker's critique (Brubaker 2005) of the diaspora concept. When using the diaspora concept as an analytical tool, it is essential not to overestimate the centrality of ancestral and biological national background as a basis for self-understanding, self-categorization and group formation. Nowadays, scholars acknowledge that there are major differences and variations in migrants' adjustment. They may remain loyal to their homelands, they may adjust to their host societies, or they may evolve in a hybrid set of attachments. We can find numerous case studies in favour of one of these directions (Esman 2009).

Twice migrants: home away from home

Many people migrate more than once. If we take a generational perspective, we can easily see that Jay's parents migrated from what is now India to what is now Uganda. Jay and his children were born in Uganda. They had never visited India, but they did consider themselves to be Indian Africans in Uganda. They then move to the USA and become 'twice migrants'. In the USA, his daughter falls in love with an African-American man. The movie weaves nicely around the various race issues involved, especially the double standard that Jay has regarding his daughter (she should not marry an African American), and his love for his homeland Uganda. For the sake of the argument, we can see that children of the marriage of his daughter will again have another relationship with India and Uganda. They may grow up as Americans of mixed descent. They will not fit into most definitions of a diaspora. Many of these multiple migrants/twice migrants do not share an idealized alleged ancestral home, nor a commitment to its maintenance or restoration. Neither do they share a collective memory or myth about this homeland.

Let me illustrate this with a few other examples. Tsuda convincingly shows us that Japanese Americans should not be labelled as part of the 'Japanese diaspora'. They have generally lost their social connections to the Japanese homeland over the generations, and neither have they sustained transnational relations with other Nikkei communities in the Americas. He argues that in these cases of older Japanese diasporas in the USA, they 'have become assimilated and incorporated into their respective host countries are no longer really diasporic, but have simply become ethnic minorities which operate in a national context'. In these cases, there is no reflection of 'home in a mythological motherland'. Home is where they were born, in this case America (Tsuda 2012). By the same token, the level of local integration plays an important role in the argument of Agarwal (2016). He argues that twice migrants in Canada, including South Asians, Chinese and Filipinos in particular, were older, were more likely to speak an official

Canadian language, were slightly more educated and were more skilled than direct migrants. A lack of job opportunities in Canada forced many twice-migrant families to split between two countries. Agarwal means between Canada and the countries from which they migrated, not the country of their roots. In other words, the root country is not a safety net nor a cultural yardstick of orientation.

In places where old and new diasporas of the same root meet, studies show that an ambivalent relation occurs. This is the case in the Netherlands. In the 1970s, a small group of Hindus arrived from Suriname, a former Dutch colony. These Surinamese Hindus arrived as indentured labourers in Suriname in the nineteenth century. Some of the descendants of this group eventually arrive in The Hague as twice migrants. They barely intermarry nor interact in daily life with direct migrants from India. However, they might celebrate the same Hindu festivals, like Diwali (Lynnebakke 2007).

Home is not a natural calling

The reconnection with the mother country is one of the key elements in the diaspora literature. It obviously refers to a strong feeling of embeddedness, cosiness, cordiality and the affection of family, friends and like-minded people. Nevertheless, in diaspora literature as well as in family life, homecoming may not be pleasant, joyful or 'natural'. In many cases, second-, third- and further-generation migrants in the diaspora may never have visited their supposed home country. They are born in countries that they call home. Second- or further-generation Jews who are born in the USA may never have visited Israel. Indians born in the UK may never have seen India, and Chinese in Singapore may never have stayed in China. For many of these second- or further-generation migrants, their home country is the country where they are born. If they visit the country from which their (grand)parents came, they encounter a motherland they have never seen. This may be pleasant and ecstatic, but they may also feel bewildered, surprised and disconnected.

Some communities trace their origin to a certain region or country in the world, but they do not uphold any notion of return or a myth to return to that area. This is the case with Roma (Gypsies), for example, who have no interest in gazing at a homeland that once was. Indeed, there is no aspiration to the region that they supposedly left some 1,200 years ago. At the same time, they can claim transnational connections through their leadership. Their history shows many examples of local oppression and fragmentation. Despite their efforts to connect at a transnational level, there is no urge, as in the typical Jewish case, to create myths about a safe haven that once existed in the past (Sutherland 2017).

The Roma are by no means a unique case. The Parsees are another example. The name Parsees means 'Persians'. They are descended from Persian Zoroastrians who were a group of followers of the Iranian prophet Zoroaster. They migrated to India to avoid religious persecution by the Muslims between the eighth and twelfth centuries. Their economic, cultural and political importance was acknowledged by the British in India in the late nineteenth and early twentieth centuries. In those days, they developed an intermediary identity between the British and South Asian society. Nowadays, they live chiefly in Bombay and in a few towns and villages mostly to the north of Bombay, but also in Karachi (Pakistan) and Bangalore (Karnataka, India). Since the late 1980s, many have left South Asia and have settled in the UK, the USA and other countries. Despite their initial flight from Persia, they do not reproduce any myths about returning to that area. Another interesting example is the Khoja Ismailis, especially the Aga Khanis amongst them. Most trace their background to north-west India where they converted from Hinduism to Islam. Many Khojas migrated and settled over the centuries in East Africa, Europe and North America, especially so in the late nineteenth and early twentieth centuries, particularly in the aftermath of the Aga Khan Case in 1866, when their spiritual leadership under the Aga Khan was officially recognized by the British. The Aga Khan was instrumental in the resettlement of Ismailis (and other South Asian communities) after the expulsion of Asians from Uganda by dictator Idi Amin. The Aga Khan is the guiding leader of the Ismailis. He speaks in the United Nations, with the Pope and with the various national leaders in the world – but the issue is never a new home in India, unlike, for example, in the case of the Armenian diaspora (Akhtar 2015; Daftary 2009).

Coming home? Homeland and its ambivalences

Caryn Aviv and David Shneer (2005: 1) describe a telling anecdote in the beginning of their book *New Jews: the end of the Jewish diaspora*:

> Buses whisked a group of Jewish college students from Ben Gurion Airport to the room where the first Prime Minster of Israel signed the Declaration of Independence in 1948. 'Welcome Home!' the trip leader called out to the disoriented and exhausted participants in a Birthright Israel programme. As one of the counsellors on this trip several years ago, I looked around to see how the students would respond. Even as a Jew who felt very strongly connected to Israel, I wondered whether the language of 'at home' reflected my own understanding of the diaspora-Israel relationship. I expected that the young adults wearing baseball caps and sweatshirts with college logos would find this message of homecoming even more bewildering less than two hours into their first trip to the country.

In this case, we see that the new state of Israel wishes to reconnect with its diaspora. This first moment of reconnection with a home that was never home, a 'mother' they had never seen, is thrilling. But although mother and child might embrace each other, they have to build up their new relationship. The reconnection was not 'natural' or self-evident. It needed massage and negotiating. And in some cases, the reconnection may be filled with caution, mistrust and suspicion. For example, there was no mass emigration from Ethiopia by the Beta Israel after the establishment of the State of Israel in 1948, as with other Jewish communities. Until the 1980s, only about 250 Beta Israel managed to reach Israel. However, under pressure from the international community, Israel accepted 7,700 Beta Israel refugees from Sudan under Operation Moses in 1984–5. Finally, the so-called Operation Solomon brought about 15,000 Ethiopian Jews to Israel. Soon, however, it became clear that, for many of those migrants, Israel was not the 'Promised Land'. When the Ethiopian Jews arrived in Israel, these distinctive people faced appalling discrimination, racism and a lack of empathy for their hardships in Ethiopia and during their journey to Israel. Moreover, this was exacerbated by a mixture of bureaucratic insensitivity and incompetence (Hertzog 1999).

We may contrast the ethnic return migration of peoples who have lived in the diaspora for two or more generations with examples of first-generation diasporic people who return to the country where they were born. The examples of the Jewish diaspora above belong in the first category. We may find a good example of the second category in the work of Mario Rutten and Parvind J. Patel (2007). They followed a group of Patidar returnees who retired from their jobs in the UK to resettle in India. Most of them did not resettle in the villages from which they came, but in a neighbouring town. The authors show that the returnees developed special wishes regarding their food (not too spicy), furniture (not sitting on the ground, and air-conditioning). Those who stayed behind felt that the returnees wished to be treated like kings. They also argued that because they were managing the land and houses in India, they should have a larger share of the inheritance than those who had left the country. In response, the returnees argued that their earlier remittances and gifts should be seen as compensation for this. In other words, both parties held different expectations in the reuniting process.

Conclusion

By the 1990s, a very limited number of states had developed governing institutions to engage with their diasporas. Less than three decades later, more than 50 per cent of the countries are active in some sort of institutional reconnecting with their diasporas. Usually these institutions are housed within the foreign ministries, and more often than not, they are connected with numerous NGOs and economic and cultural organizations. Nowadays, states offer positive incentives for diasporas to relate to 'home'. In return, they desire increasing remittances, investments, philanthropy or acquiring knowledge and experience from foreign-educated 'nationals'. At the same time, the governments wish to regulate money transfers, special visa schemes, property rights and social security. The home country thus needs to be involved at the state level. In this chapter, I have argued that the success of these national diaspora schemes needs to be mirrored against the fact that 'homecoming' is not a natural process. In fact, the reason that these diaspora institutions are flourishing reflects the reality that it is not self-evident that people in the diaspora wish to reconnect with their home countries. It needs promoting and nurturing. On the one side of the spectrum, we find people who move on and even disconnect with the homeland. For Jay and his family, it was not 'natural' to resettle in India, where his grandparents came from. And even then, many people move on and slowly disappear from the motherland's radar. On the other hand, we find people who actually do reconnect with the homeland. But contrary to the general belief, they may be received with hostile feelings even from family members. Or the returnees themselves may feel uncomfortable if their home countries do not fulfil economic, political or cultural expectations. Making and unmaking diasporas goes hand in hand with making and unmaking homes.

Acknowledgement

This chapter is based on a paper written as part of the position of an Honorary Affiliate of the Centre for Indian Studies in Africa (CISA), at the University of the Witwatersrand (Wits) in Johannesburg, South Africa.

References

Agrawal, S. K. (2016) 'Twice migrants in Canada: who are they and how do they perform economically?', *Journal of International Migration and Integration*, 17 (3), 669–86, doi: 10.1007/s12134-015-0428-y.
Akhtar, I. (2015) *The Khōjā of Tanzania: discontinuities of a postcolonial religious identity*, Leiden: Brill.
Aviv, C. and D. Shneer (2005) *New Jews: the end of the Jewish diaspora*, New York: New York University Press.
Bhachu, P. (1985) *Twice migrants: East African Sikh settlers in Britain*, London: Tavistock.
Brubaker, R. (2005) 'The "diaspora" diaspora', *Ethnic and Racial Studies*, 28 (1), 1–19, doi: 10.1080/01419 87042000289997.
Daftary, F. (2009) *A short history of the Ismailis: traditions of a Muslim community*, Edinburgh: Edinburgh University Press.
Esman, M. J. (2009) *Diasporas in the contemporary world*, Cambridge: Polity Press.
Hertzog, E. (1999) *Immigrants and bureaucrats: Ethiopians in an Israeli absorption center*, Oxford: Berghahn.
Lynnebakke, B. (2007) 'Contested equality: social relations between Indian and Surinamese Hindus in Amsterdam', in G. Oonk (ed.) *Global Indian diasporas: exploring trajectories of migration and theory*, Amsterdam: Amsterdam University Press, 235–63.

Oonk, G. (ed.) (2007) *Global Indian diasporas: exploring trajectories of migration and theory*, Amsterdam: Amsterdam University Press.
Oonk, G. (2013) *Settled strangers: Asian business elites in East Africa (1800–2000)*, Delhi: Sage.
Rutten, M. and P. J. Patel (2007) 'Contested family relations and government policy: linkages between Patel migrants in Britain and India', in G. Oonk (ed.) *Global Indian diasporas: exploring trajectories of migration and theory*, Amsterdam: Amsterdam University Press, 167–94.
Sutherland, A. H. (2017) *Roma: modern American Gypsies*, Long Grove, IL: Waveland Press.
Tsuda, T. (2012) 'Disconnected from the diaspora: Japanese Americans and the lack of transnational ethnic network', *Journal of Anthropological Research*, 68 (1), 95–116, doi: 10.3998/jar.0521004.0068.104.

Additional reading

Cohen, R. (1997) *Global diasporas: an introduction*, London: UCL Press.
Keith, M. (2017) 'Complicating the conceptional language of the Bengal diaspora', *Ethnic and Racial Studies*, 40 (3), 389–95, doi: 10.1080/01419870.2017.1249498.
Santamaria, U. (1993) 'Ethiopian Jews in Israel', *Dialectical Anthropology*, 18 (3/4), 405–12, doi: 10.1007/BF01303683.
Tölölyan, K. (2010) 'Beyond the homeland: from exilic nationalism to diasporic transnationalism', in A. Gal, A. S. Leoussi and A. D. Smith (eds) *The call of the homeland: diaspora nationalisms, past and present*, Leiden: Brill.
Vertovec, S. (2009) *Transnationalism*, London: Routledge.

Part V
Critiques and applied diaspora studies

Part V
Critique and applied discourse studie

34
Using pragmatism to approach 'diaspora', its meanings and political implications

Carolin Fischer and Janine Dahinden

Calls for more reflexivity in the field of migration, ethnicity and diaspora studies are increasing. They are based on two main concerns: a sedentarist, nation-state- and ethnicity-centred epistemology that informs a large share of research in this domain (Amelina and Faist 2012; Bommes and Thränhardt 2010; Wimmer and Glick Schiller 2003) and a use of 'migrant' as an *a priori* rather than an analytical category. The conflation of common sense and analytical categories – as scholars have demonstrated – contributes to the reproduction of essentialist perceptions of migration and ethnicity. Consequently, differences between migrants and non-migrants appear to be 'natural' (Crawley and Skleparis 2017; Dahinden 2016; Gillespie et al. 2012).

At a first glance, conventional notions of diaspora exemplify such essentialist perceptions, because they emphasize multi-generational rootedness in a national territory. They fuel the assumption that people naturally feel part of a national entity, which is linked to a particular ethnicity, culture and sense of belonging. As a result, persons of certain national origin tend to be seen as representatives of distinct groups marked by specific and clearly identifiable features and characteristics (Brubaker 2015). While reiterating that territory, culture, identity and belonging are often congruent, Cohen (2008: 123–40) also discusses examples of deterritorialized diasporas. However, the recent expansion of diaspora research further amplifies the tendency to subsume individuals of certain (ancestral) origin under the same heading, all supposedly exhibiting shared characteristics. In this way, the notion of diaspora is used to back the idea that Western societies have been infiltrated by foreign groups that cling on to cultures and values deemed incompatible with enlightened civilizations.

We are not alone in developing an epistemological critique and call for more reflexivity. Dufoix (2003), for example, argues that the notion of diaspora incorporates the *illusion* of an essence, of a natural community and of continuity. He therefore proposes a process-oriented approach to diaspora that focuses on changing identifications that result from historical transitions. Later, Rogers Brubaker (2005: 12) famously questioned the usefulness of diaspora as a concept and social denominator. His claim that diaspora should be analysed as a stance or a claim rather than in substantive terms has become a standard reference for those who strive to approach diaspora from a constructivist and non-essentialist perspective. Considering diaspora as a category of practice requires us to situate the notion within wider contexts that are shaped by different historical and political developments and inhabited by various actors, their objectives and narratives

(Alexander 2017). The latter, in turn, form the basis for practices in which the notion of diaspora and its respective connotations are firmly implicated.

Building on these conceptual propositions for non-essentialist approaches to diaspora, this chapter focuses on social practices of 'doing diaspora' by different actors. Afghan migration and settlement outside Afghanistan serves as an illustration. We argue that an approach based on pragmatism in conjunction with a focus on boundary-work and meaning-making enables us to identify and contextualize emic and etic meanings of being Afghan and belonging to a wider Afghan diaspora.

How 'diaspora' is used for relational boundary and meaning-making

We examine how and with what effects certain actors use the notion of diaspora as a category of practice in certain situations, for certain reasons and with what effects. First, following William James's (1906) notion of pragmatism, we ask initially why diaspora may gain currency in public and political debates. This analytical perspective requires us to evaluate ideas according to their effects on social reality, and their impacts on perceptions and social action. Using pragmatism to approach ideas of diaspora would be to examine what individuals or groups do, or intend to do, when using the concept of diaspora as a label. What are the consequences for those using the notion, for those being labelled and for the social context in which they are embedded? What facilitates and impedes these uses?

Second, drawing on a relational and processual approach to collective identities (Barth 1969; Weber 1996), we illuminate instances of internal and external categorization whereby the notion of diaspora is used to mark boundaries between social groups. Such categorization is effectuated by a broad range of actors – including the media and political stakeholders and decision-makers – which are embedded in particular political and power relations (Jenkins 2008; Wimmer 2013). This way, we unpack how the use of diaspora implicitly or explicitly contributes to the drawing or maintenance of social boundaries. When and with what objectives do people speak of themselves or others as 'diaspora'? What are the implications for subjectivities, belonging and positioning, locally or transnationally? Who are the significant 'others' they are positioning themselves against? What kind of boundaries do they aim to establish or dismantle when using 'diaspora'?

We argue that diaspora as a social category of collective identification with a distinctive group is the result of twofold boundary work: first, in terms of individual *self-identification* that holds people together as a cohesive group; and, second, as a category of external classification of 'others' as a diaspora. The examination of situations in which the notion of diaspora is used either for self-identification or for external categorization yields important insights into political objectives and power relations (Jenkins 1996). Third, our analysis also considers how diaspora as a notion is used to give meaning to the world, to life trajectories, to different facets of everyday life, and to social and political issues.

Based on qualitative data collected among persons of Afghan origin living in Germany and the UK, and a media analysis of public references to an Afghan 'diaspora', we apply Jamesian pragmatism to instances of self-identification among, or external categorization relating to, Afghans outside Afghanistan.

Perceptions, meanings and implications of diaspora: Afghan examples

A first glance from the outside suggests that populations of Afghans outside Afghanistan largely correspond to Brubaker's (2005) definition of diaspora as characterized by dispersion, homeland orientation and boundary maintenance. Millions of people of Afghan origin have been traumatically dispersed to adjacent countries such as Iran and Pakistan as well as overseas over the last four decades, as conflict and violence continued in Afghanistan. In their countries of residence, great numbers of persons of Afghan origin have been found to settle in certain regions, cities and neighbourhoods (Oeppen 2010; Olszewska 2015). This suggests that displacement and dispersal led to instances of re-grouping. In addition, there are indicators for some homeland orientation among Afghans living outside Afghanistan. Besides sending monetary remittances, which are mainly directed to family members living in Afghanistan or adjacent countries, groups of Afghans outside Afghanistan have been engaging in a wide variety of humanitarian and development initiatives in Afghanistan (Fischer, 2018). Moreover, there are numerous Afghan associations in both Germany and the UK that hold festive, cultural, religious and educational events. Yet, rather than assuming that engagements are carried out 'in the name of the diaspora' (Kleist 2008), it is important to have a closer look at situations, identifications, intentions and positions at play whenever the notion of diaspora is used.

We identify two instances when diaspora is employed to establish or dismantle perceived boundaries and to position oneself against a significant other. First, among Afghan populations in Germany and the UK, the notion of diaspora can either constitute a category from which those concerned explicitly distance themselves, or of affirmative self-referencing. Second, actors of the majority society use the notion of diaspora for external classification of Afghan migrants. The categories employed in this context are linked to different protection and residence entitlements, which allows insights to the political and governance objectives tied to the use of specific terminology.

Afghans and their positioning beyond 'diaspora'

Most persons interviewed in the context of our empirical study describe multiple situations in which they do not wholeheartedly identify as part of a wider diaspora. While the notion of diaspora tends to serve as a descriptive category, which is employed to acknowledge that Afghans have been scattered across the world as a result of protracted conflict, many research participants represent this dispersed population of Afghan descent as internally heterogeneous. This strongly affects self-identifications as 'being Afghan'. People rarely see themselves or encounter each other as simply 'Afghans' and as members of an overarching 'Afghan diaspora'. Mutual perceptions are filtered through a range of categories, among which family and socio-economic backgrounds, ethnicity and political affiliations feature prominently (Fischer 2017). While acknowledging that they or their ancestors originate from Afghanistan, research participants refuse to accept 'being Afghan' as their primary category of self-identification. Hence, originating from Afghanistan and being part of a globally dispersed population of Afghan descent does not imply that persons identify as 'being Afghan' in the first place. This is also reflected in the social ties that link persons of Afghan origin.

Accounts recorded by Fischer (2015) exemplify acts of self-positioning amidst widely held beliefs about unity and cohesion among persons of Afghan origin by virtue of their common national descent. Identifications vary according to individual backgrounds and experiences, and according to the significant other confronted. Significant others that contribute to shaping peoples' positioning strategies may either be Afghan co-nationals who are perceived in a certain light, or third persons, such as members of the society of settlement, who articulate an essentialist perception of Afghan diaspora(n)s.

The boundaries delineating different configurations of persons of Afghan origin are charged with various meanings. The identification with specific political factions, for example, allows people to preserve their political identity as an important dimension of self. Given the conflict-ridden history of Afghanistan, articulations of political affiliation also constitute a way of positioning oneself *vis-à-vis* other Afghans or international political actors. Conversely, emphasizing the importance of family ties highlights the significance of social environments that are based on trust and intimacy. Configurations that revolve around ethnicity or tribal affiliations may have a similar function. They help people establish a sense of familiarity amidst the unfamiliar, like the receiving society or groups of Afghan co-nationals that are perceived as representing different facets of Afghan society. By explicitly rejecting the notion of diaspora as an etic category of assumed self-identification, people also draw attention to the history and complexity of Afghan society and to the effects that decades of war and protracted violence have had on Afghanistan and its people. The observed boundaries thus need to be situated in the transnational context of political events that shaped the recent history of Afghanistan and affect self-identification and external categorization among Afghan migrants themselves (Fischer 2017; Schetter 2003).

The chosen examples suggest that the notion of diaspora is being contested whenever research participants position themselves *vis-à-vis* other persons of Afghan origin. This way, they reject assumptions that there is a coherent Afghan diaspora that would be objectively existing by virtue of peoples' shared Afghan descent. Taking a distance from diaspora as a category of belonging thus forms an important aspect of self-positioning practices. By rejecting the notion of diaspora as primary mode of identification, research participants also draw attention to the legacy of conflict-induced dispersal.

Conversely, we also find affirmative self-identifications with an (imagined) and more encompassing Afghan population. They revolve around people's perceived attachment to Afghanistan and a desired sense of 'being Afghan', which does not necessarily involve the explicit mentioning of diaspora as an identity category. At the outset, it may seem paradoxical that such perceptions or desires of membership and belonging are articulated by the same persons who reject the idea of membership in an overarching Afghan diaspora. However, articulations of belonging to a wider population of Afghans are tied to different situations, desires, meanings and positionings than statements emphasizing difference and divisions. Phrases such as 'we as Afghans', 'our history' and 'our country' suggest that there is not only an underlying idea of Afghanistan as a wider territorial entity but also an idea of an all-encompassing Afghan people. This imagined Afghan community transgresses political, ethnic and territorial boundaries and constitutes an imagined version of what Faist (2010) defines as transnational social space and Appadurai (1991) calls a 'deterritorialised nation'.

In this context, diaspora is used as a building block of national group-making whenever persons feel negatively confronted with 'national others'. Generalized references to Afghan culture or something 'typically Afghan' are mobilized in different situations and for different purposes. For example, narratives underlining Afghan hospitality or the beauty of Afghanistan or one's desire for peace and inclusiveness are employed to counter widespread images of war-torn Afghanistan and a victimized Afghan society. Ideas of a more encompassing – though dispersed – Afghan nation are tied to the objective to change imaginaries about Afghan and Afghanistan. Diaspora thus forms part of a desire for peace and a spirit of collectiveness as key attributes of an imagined Afghan nation.

Generalizing categories of being Afghan thus tend to be mobilized to counter other generalizing national categories. For example, by identifying with an inclusively defined Afghan people, research participants may seek to transcend the legacy of decades-long conflict and the imprints it has left on the Afghan people. Generalizing notions of an Afghan diaspora are also mobilized to counter the boundaries that prompt the internal division of Afghan populations and protracted tensions between different sub-groups. References to an imagined Afghan community do not necessarily express the desire to be part of a nation as such, but a desire for peace and social justice that is articulated in opposition to widespread negative perceptions and to claim crucial dimensions of self-representation. Diaspora thus constitutes a resource for an identity project. Self-identifications with a broader, diasporic Afghan people may also be employed to challenge perceived boundaries between migrants or certain migrant groups and the host country's majority society.

In short, persons of Afghan origin self-identify as 'being Afghan' in different ways. Depending on the context in which they are embedded, people articulate certain dimensions of their identity. Both affirmative identifications and acts of self-distancing involve instances of self-positioning and boundary work. The inclusiveness or exclusiveness of boundaries is contingent on the meaning people seek to convey and the significant other they confront.

Exploring diaspora as politicized external category

Having examined different ways of using diaspora as an emic category of self-reference, we now shift the focus to how external actors apply diaspora as a social category when referring to Afghans outside Afghanistan. Discussions around the integration of migrants and refugees into Western societies constitute one exemplary context.

In recent years, references to an Afghan diaspora have become more widespread in the context of reinforced out-migration from Afghanistan and the arrival of Afghan refugees across Europe. In international public media, such as broadsheets, national radio channels or web-based outlets, the notion of diaspora has been used to distinguish between an established Afghan diaspora and newly arriving asylum-seekers (Schmeidl 2015; Skodo 2017). According to such distinctions, representatives of an Afghan diaspora are persons who fled Afghanistan during different stages of conflict before the early 2000s. They have been recognized as refugees, and many adopted the citizenship of their receiving country (Koser 2014). Conversely, those arriving in recent years are perceived more sceptically by policy-makers, media voices and the wider public (Oeppen 2016). They are assumed to be seeking a better life abroad rather than fleeing acute threats. Newly arriving persons of Afghan origin tend to be labelled as economic refugees and opportunists, and are not considered as persons in need of protection. This also has repercussions on the legal status and entitlements granted to newly arriving Afghan migrants. Schuster (2011) illustrates this when tracing the post-2001 transformation of Afghan refugees into 'illegal migrants'. The drop in numbers of Afghans granted asylum (*Die Zeit* 2017) and the ongoing deportation of persons who were declined refugee status (Schuster 2016, 2017) across European countries are further consequences of a political and social climate that grows increasingly restrictive.

Conversely, those representing the so-called old and established Afghan diaspora are believed to have good reasons to live outside Afghanistan. Their destiny as political refugees is emphasized (von Burg 2015). Distinctions between an established diaspora and new arrivals refer to the former as well educated and well integrated into their receiving societies. In a recent article that appeared in a Swiss broadsheet, a commentator describes established Afghan immigrants as '*gebildet, fleissig und unauffällig*' (well educated, diligent and unnoticeable) (Wilhelm 2015). Although the label 'diasporas' applied here seems to be charged with positive attributes, it draws a clear boundary between a group of immigrants and the Swiss majority society. The chosen attributes suggest that Afghans constitute a group of strangers that does, however, make efforts to blend in with what is perceived as a genuinely Swiss attribute. Being linked to positive characteristics, the label 'diaspora' underlines that established immigrants of Afghan origin are perceived as meeting the requirements of successful integration. At the same time, the label reflects the principles of migrant integration into Western societies more generally. To a large extent, approaches to integration continue to adhere to assimilationist principles. Consequently, the image of the well-educated, hard-working Afghan migrant, who blends in well with the respective society of settlement, serves as a yardstick to assess more recent immigrants of Afghan origin.

Conversely, newcomers tend to be represented as less well educated and more religious and traditional (Wilhelm 2015). Their entitlement to live outside Afghanistan and be granted protection is more disputed, and the threat of being expelled and deported back to Afghanistan is looming. This is further amplified by the perceived duty of recent Afghan migrants to rebuild their country of origin. Citing voices of the established diasporas may be used to substantiate the perceived difference between diaspora and newcomers. For example, a young Afghan woman who was raised in Germany by refugee parents and who works as a translator for German immigration authorities alongside her university studies, expressed a lack of understanding for the majority of current Afghan asylum applicants. She drew a clear distinction between her parents' generation of 'real' political refugees and recent arrivals, who, according to her, did not leave Afghanistan for reasons of persecution but 'merely' in search for better livelihoods. In addition, she underlined that their generally low level of education impedes a smooth integration of recent Afghan migrants into Western societies (Fischer 2015).

Such examples reveal a juncture of boundary work deriving from internal and external categorizations. The persistent divisions and tensions among Afghans outside Afghanistan are mobilized to justify perceptions of and political measures adopted towards certain groups of Afghan origin. For instance, representations of diasporic voices may be employed to justify current restrictive immigration, asylum and residence policies *vis-à-vis* persons of Afghan origin who arrived more recently. Those who apply the notion of diaspora deliberately restrict it to a certain group of Afghan migrants. This selective use of the notion is tied to political objectives and immigration control rather than a more profound understanding of Afghan populations outside Afghanistan. The above examples thus demonstrate how the use of diaspora is closely linked to policies and practices of border controls.

Conclusion

In line with attempts to overcome sedentarist, nation-state- and ethnicity-centred epistemologies in the study of migration and mobility, our contribution revisits the need for a 'de-diasporization' of research. To retain the usefulness of diaspora as a concept, we propose to apply Jamesian pragmatism to the study of diaspora as a category of self-identification and external categorization. We highlight the processes and objectives at play whenever the notion of diaspora is used as a category of self-identification or external classification. To this end, we scrutinize the teleologies of social actors who employ the notion of diaspora – either in relation to themselves or as a label for a perceived different group of Afghan migrants.

The use of diaspora in relation to Afghans outside Afghanistan necessarily involves boundary work. However, the substance and implications of observed boundaries vary according to the objectives of those mobilizing the notion of diaspora and the meanings the term is charged with respectively. Concerning diaspora as a category of self-identification, we found persons of Afghan origin to draw boundaries between different perceived subgroups based on family ties, ethnicity or political affiliations. Acts of self-distancing from diaspora as an overarching category of identification draws attention to the aspects that structure relations between Afghans outside Afghanistan. These structuring elements in turn need to be situated in the light of the recent history of conflict in Afghanistan. We found references to particularistic identity categories to be employed whenever research participants were eager emphasize their unwillingness to identify as 'Afghan' in terms of an etic catch-all category. The emphasis on fragmented identities also suggests that memory is not necessarily collective but often selective, particularly in circumstances of homeland conflict.

Diaspora as an ambiguous category of self-identification is also used to draw distinctions between established Afghan migrants and recently arrived newcomers. Such differentiations are articulated by both Afghan and non-Afghan actors. Whilst the former draw distinctions between a well-integrated Afghan diaspora and newly arriving opportunity seekers, the latter mobilize the same differentiation to delegate the task of staying put and rebuild Afghanistan to those who have left the country in recent years.

Conversely, a more inclusive and positively charged idea of an (imagined) Afghan people is articulated in situations in which people seek to confront negative connotations of being Afghan or of perceived exclusion or alienation from the society of residence. Here, self-identification is based on positively charged attributes, which are represented as applying to Afghanistan and its people as such. This way, the notion of diaspora may serve the same individual to highlight the consequences of war and violence in Afghanistan and to express his or her desire to transcend this legacy and instead emphasize positive attributes of an imagined Afghan nation. In the latter case, the concept of diaspora is employed to support a collective group-making project that aims to challenge widespread ideas and preconceptions of Afghanistan and being Afghan. In the examples cited, images of war and humanitarian crisis are juxtaposed with ideas of peacemaking and a spirit of solidarity and cohesiveness. Hence 'being Afghan' and part of a wider, diasporic Afghan population represent identifications which people reflexively and consciously use, keeping both the origin and receiving country in mind. Depending on the context and the significant others involved, the notion of diaspora and the type of boundary work it implies are charged with different meanings.

Boundary work also plays an important role whenever diaspora is used as a category of external classification. We demonstrate how the notion of diaspora is employed to distinguish between a well-integrated Afghan diaspora and recently arrived Afghan refugees. The juxtaposition of established diaspora and recent arrivals, in turn, lends itself to support restrictive immigration and settlement policies, which many European destination countries are adopting to deter persons of Afghan origin who are associated with different attributes than those constituting a well-integrated, docile Afghan diaspora. Diaspora thus turns into a means of immigration politics and border control that forms part of contemporary migration regimes. In such contexts, diaspora is used to simultaneously legitimize the presence of a certain group of migrants and to problematize the presence of another perceived group in the same context of residence and settlement.

Our analysis shows that the notion of diaspora constitutes a rich but fluid resource. It can be mobilized for self-identification and positioning and for political ends. Using the notion of diaspora as a flexible tool rather than a fixed category enables us to unpack that applied notions of diaspora often go far beyond the mere classification of a specific migrant population. Notwithstanding our adoption of pragmatism, our analysis reiterates that 'diaspora' is a highly politicized category that powerfully contributes to instances of social inclusion and exclusion.

References

Alexander, C. (2017) 'Beyond the "The 'diaspora' diaspora": a response to Rogers Brubaker', *Ethnic and Racial Studies*, 40 (9), 1544–55, doi: 10.1080/01419870.2017.1300302.

Amelina, A. and T. Faist (2012) 'De-naturalizing the national in research methodologies: key concepts of transnational studies in migration', *Ethnic and Racial Studies*, 35 (10), 1707–24, doi: 10.1080/01419870.2012.659273.

Appadurai, A. (1991) 'Disjuncture and difference in the global cultural economy', in M. Featherstone (ed.) *Global culture. Nationalism, globalization and modernity*, London: Sage, 295–310.

Barth, F. (1969) *Ethnic groups and boundaries: the social organization of culture difference*, Bergen: Universitetsforlaget.

Bommes, M. and D. Thränhardt (2010) *National paradigms of migration research*, Osnabrück: Institut für Migrationsforschung und Interkulturelle Studien.

Brubaker, R. (2005) 'The "diaspora" diaspora', *Ethnic and Racial Studies*, 28 (1), 1–19, doi: 10.1080/0141987042000289997.

Brubaker, R. (2015) *Grounds for difference*, Cambridge, MA: Harvard University Press.

Cohen, R. (2008) *Global diasporas: an introduction*, second edition, London: Routledge.

Crawley, H. and D. Skleparis (2017) 'Refugees, migrants, neither, both: categorical fetishism and the politics of bounding in Europe's "migration crisis"', *Journal of Ethnic and Migration Studies*, online early, doi: 10.1080/1369183X.2017.1348224.

Dahinden, J. (2016) 'A plea for the "de-migranticization" of research on migration and integration'", *Ethnic and Racial Studies*, 39 (13), 2207–25, doi: 10.1080/01419870.2015.1124129.

Die Zeit (2017) 'Flüchtlinge: Afghanen werden seltener als Asylberechtigte anerkannt', *Die Zeit*, Hamburg, 18 July, available at www.zeit.de/politik/deutschland/2017-07/afghanistan-asylbewerber-anerkennung-quoten-abschiebung.

Dufoix, S. (2003) *Les diasporas. Que sais-je?: le point des connaissances actuelles*, Paris: Presses universitaires de France.

Faist, T. (2010) 'Diaspora and transnationalism: what kind of dance partners?', in R. Bauböck and T. Faist (eds) *Diaspora and transnationalism: concepts, theories and methods*, Amsterdam: Amsterdam University Press, 9–34.

Fischer, C. (2015) 'Relations and agency in a transnational context: the Afghan diaspora and its engagement for change in Afghanistan', unpublished PhD thesis, University of Oxford.

Fischer, C. (2017) 'Imagined communities? Relations of social identities and social organization among Afghan diaspora groups in Germany and the UK', *Journal of Intercultural Studies*, 38 (1), 18–35, doi: 10.1080/07256868.2016.1269060.

Fischer, C. (2018) 'Reframing transnational engagement: a relational analysis of Afghan diaspora groups', *Global Networks*, doi:10.1111/glob.12186 Online Early.

Gillespie, A., C. S. Howarth and F. Cornish (2012) 'Four problems for researchers using social categories', *Culture & Psychology*, 18 (3), 391–402, doi: 10.1177/1354067X12446236.

James, W. (1906) 'What pragmatism means', transcribed lecture, available at www.marxists.org/reference/subject/philosophy/works/us/james.htm.

Jenkins, R. (1996) *Social identity*, London: Routledge.

Jenkins, R. (2008) *Rethinking ethnicity*, second edition, Los Angeles: Sage.

Kleist, N. (2008) 'In the name of diaspora: between struggles for recognition and political aspirations', *Journal of Ethnic and Migration Studies*, 34 (7), 1127–43, doi: 10.1080/13691830802230448.

Koser, K. (2014) *Transitions, crisis and mobility in Afghanistan: rhetoric and reality*, Geneva: International Organization for Migration.

Oeppen, C. (2010) 'The Afghan diaspora and its involvement in the reconstruction of Afghanistan', in C. Oeppen and A. Schlenkhoff, (eds) *Beyond the 'wild tribes': understanding modern Afghanistan and its diaspora*, London: Hurst & Co., 141–56.

Oeppen, C. (2016) '"Leaving Afghanistan! Are you sure?" European Efforts to deter potential migrants through information campaigns', *Human Geography*, 9 (2), 57–68, available at: http://sro.sussex.ac.uk/id/eprint/61744.

Olszewska, Z. (2015) *The Pearl of Dari: poetry and personhood among young Afghans in Iran*, public cultures of the Middle East and North Africa, Bloomington: Indiana University Press.

Schetter, C. J. (2003) *Ethnizität und ethnische Konflikte in Afghanistan*, Berlin: Reimer.

Schmeidl, S. (2015) *Afghanistan: Jugend in unruhigen Zeiten*, available at www.boell.de/de/2015/01/20/jugend-unruhigen-zeiten.

Schuster, L. (2011) 'Turning refugees into "illegal migrants": Afghan asylum seekers in Europe', *Ethnic and Racial Studies*, 34 (8), 1392–407, doi: 10.1080/01419870.2010.535550.

Schuster, L. (2016) *Kabul is still not safe – but the EU is deporting people there anyway*, available at http://theconversation.com/kabul-is-still-not-safe-but-the-eu-is-deporting-people-there-anyway-66933.

Schuster, L. (2017) *As violence sweeps Kabul, the rapid pace of deportations from Europe continues*, available at http://theconversation.com/as-violence-sweeps-kabul-the-rapid-pace-of-deportations-from-europe-continues-78956.

Skodo, A. (2017) *How Afghans became second-class asylum seekers*, available at http://theconversation.com/how-afghans-became-second-class-asylum-seekers-72437.

von Burg, C. (2015) *Afghanische Diaspora: Nicht alle freuen sich über mehr Landsleute*, available at www.srf.ch/news/schweiz/afghanische-diaspora-nicht-alle-freuen-sich-ueber-mehr-landsleute.

Weber, M. (1996) 'Ethnic groups', in G. Roth and C. Wittich (eds) *Theories of ethnicity: a classical reader*, Berkeley: University of California Press, 52–66 [originally published in 1922, edited by Werner Sollors, New York: New York University Press, 385–89].

Wilhelm, M. (2015) 'Gebildet, fleissig, unauffällig', *Tages-Anzeiger*, Zürich, 13 November, available at www.tagesanzeiger.ch/schweiz/standard/gebildet-fleissig-unauffaellig/story/31491264.

Wimmer, A. (2013) *Ethnic boundary making: institutions, power, networks*, Oxford studies in culture and politics, New York: Oxford University Press.

Wimmer, A. and N. Glick Schiller (2003) 'Methodological nationalism, the social sciences, and the study of migration: an essay in historical epistemology', *International Migration Review*, 37 (3), 576–610, doi: 10.1111/j.1747-7379.2003.tb00151.x.

35
Why engage diasporas?

Alan Gamlen

In recent years, there has been increasing interest in relations between migrant-sending states and 'their' diasporas, in the form of both empirical research and normative critique. This began with an explosion of literature on political transnationalism (Bauböck 2003; Guarnizo et al. 2003), focusing on both the bottom-up transnational political activities of migrants themselves (Smith and Guarnizo 1998), and the orientation of migrant-sending states towards transnational migration (see, for example, Brand 2006; Cano and Délano 2007; Gamlen 2006; Levitt and de la Dehesa 2003; Smith 2003; Margheritis 2007; Østergaard-Nielsen 2003b). It has evolved into a nuanced literature that compares and theorizes state diaspora relations (see Cano and Délano 2007; Choate 2008; Green and Weil 2007). This research is particularly relevant to policy-makers searching for ways of understanding a world transformed by migration.

Within this literature, there remains a deep tension between studies that criticize states for interfering with their diasporas – and thereby with other groups or states (Basch et al. 1994; Fitzgerald 2006; Glick Schiller and Fouron 1999) – and those who celebrate 'diaspora engagement' (De Haas 2006; Fullilove and Flutter 2004; Ionescu 2006; Kuznetsov 2006; Lowell et al. 2004; Newland and Patrick 2004; Sriskandarajah and Drew 2006; Van Hear et al. 2004). This tension is rarely addressed through systematic normative analysis, and instead these studies tend to remain encased within separate sets of normative assumptions.

The purpose of this chapter, therefore, is to review and evaluate the main arguments for and against diaspora engagement policies. The chapter concludes that better diaspora policies are needed in order to avoid the arbitrary inefficiencies and injustices that commonly characterize state–diaspora relations.

Defining 'diaspora'

The meaning of the term 'diaspora' has been debated extensively since the late 1960s. At one extreme, some scholars have argued that the term should only refer to 'victim' groups dispersed through coercion, who maintain an antagonistic relationship with their host societies (for discussion, see Cohen 1995, 1996 1997; Safran 1991, 1999). At the other extreme, many researchers use the term to refer to any group residing outside its place of origin – and even to any group exhibiting the same characteristic – for example, there have been references to a 'gay diaspora' (Tölölyan 1994, 2000).

The 'homeland' of a diaspora group may be real or imagined, and the group may engage in varying levels of transnationalism (see Snel et al. 2006). Self-ascription is important (Vertovec 2005) in that people who share a characteristic but do not define themselves or each other according to that characteristic should not necessarily be thought of as members of a diaspora. The current consensus seems to be that the essential features of a diaspora group are: dispersion to two or more locations; ongoing orientation towards a 'homeland'; and group boundary maintenance over time (Brubaker 2005; Butler 2001). This definition covers archetypical cases such as the Jews, and also remains relevant to other non-traditional groups (Hugo 2006; Reis 2004). Importantly, it is sufficiently specific to avoid the conceptual inflation often associated with a diminishment in the term's analytical value.

Beyond debating definitions, diaspora research has addressed why these communities emerge and dissipate. Diasporas are not necessarily pre-existing groups with static characteristics that meet or do not meet specific academic criteria (Dufoix 2008). Instead, they can be heterogeneous populations that are imagined and developed into collectivities through the 'projects of states and émigrés' (Waldinger 2008: xiv). Diaspora studies, Dufoix suggests, should spend more time examining how and why this process occurs.

This study therefore approaches 'diaspora' as an umbrella term for extra-territorial groups that, through processes of interacting with their origin state, are in various stages of formation. These include temporary or transnational migrants who may arbitrarily fall into one or other policy category of the origin state. They also include longer-term emigrants settled in another country, and their descendants who may identify as diasporic. This approach emphasizes that, while diasporas are not homogenous entities, the groups captured by this definition share important characteristics in common. Employing 'diaspora' as an analytical unit leads to interesting questions about how and why state policies can *make* heterogeneous extra-territorial populations *into* members of a diaspora who share a state-centric identity. For example, they allow one to examine how state mechanisms apply to different extra-territorial groups, and how this leads to different 'thicknesses' of diasporic membership (Smith 2003). It is also important to ask how states should behave towards people with these shared characteristics of dispersion, group identity, and connection to 'homeland'.

Why engage diasporas?

This chapter defines diaspora policies as state institutions and practices that apply to members of that state's society who reside outside its borders. These range from state-sponsored celebrations for expatriates, to bureaucratic units, to voting rights and bilateral agreements, through to the mechanisms through which origin states extract finances and expertise from their diasporas. In short, they consist of that portion of the state machinery which protrudes beyond its territory. Diaspora policies are most often interpreted as facets of 'external' or 'extra-territorial' citizenship (Barry 2006; Bauböck 1994; Glick Schiller 2005; Itzigsohn 2000; Laguerre 1998; Lee 2004): by incorporating the diaspora into the state, these policies redefine membership to 'national society'.

There have been numerous attempts to taxonomize diaspora policies. Some have drawn distinctions between economic, political and cultural devices of sending states (Barry 2006; Chandler 2006; Østergaard-Nielsen 2003a). Levitt and de la Dehesa (2003) distinguish between bureaucratic reforms, investment policies, political rights, state services abroad and symbolic politics. Gamlen (2006, 2008) identifies two types of diaspora policy: 'community building policies' aimed at cultivating or recognizing diaspora communities, and mechanisms for extending membership privileges and obligations to these communities.

It is important to note, however, that policies affecting diasporas are not novel, rather it is the deliberate coordination of such policies as part of a wider 'diaspora strategy' (Larner 2007) that is substantially new. Until recently, relatively few governments have treated diaspora policy as a distinct issue area, and policy is therefore still for the most part both *ad hoc* and arbitrary, reflecting the interests and historical trajectories of different government agencies with different interests in emigrants and their descendants. For example, because bilateral agreements and consular services are elements of foreign policy, they may impact arbitrarily and unjustly on what might be seen as 'domestic' populations living abroad. In this sense, improving diaspora policies may be a matter of improving the coherence of what is already taking place.

Continuing in this vein, the following section discusses arguments in favour of better diaspora policies at the national and supranational levels. First, it notes the common argument that migrant-sending countries' interests are served by better diaspora policies, drawing attention to the imperatives that transnationalism presents to existing state institutions and policies, and the opportunities arising from the supposed connections between migration and development. Second, it examines the equally common normative argument that migrant-sending states have obligations to treat their diasporas fairly. Finally, it considers the increasingly widespread argument that better 'diaspora governance' is required to enhance international cooperation in the area of migration.

Interests

Those advancing this argument say that the involvement of their diasporas presents sending states with certain policy *imperatives*, and may offer unique *opportunities*. From this perspective, forming better diaspora policies is therefore in the best interests of migrant-sending states.

Imperatives

Increased population mobility leads to transformations in political, economic and social dynamics in migrant-sending states (see Vertovec 2004), and institutions that fail to adapt lose their relevance and legitimacy. For example, increasing extra-territorial political participation influences the composition of legislatures (see Bauböck 2005a; Collyer and Vathi 2007; Rubio-Marín 2006; Spiro 2006). However, because expatriates usually vote for a candidate representing the geographical electorate where they *used to* live, it can be unclear whether elected representatives are adequately serving extra-territorial voters.

In the realm of economic policy, policy-makers have decent data only on inward, and not outward, migration. Furthermore, unless it is obvious (for example, when GDP is reliant upon remittances), the economic impact of diasporas tends to be ignored. Different types of transnational involvement – such as identification with the homeland or political connectedness – interact in ways that economic policy-makers are only beginning to understand.

Similarly, social policy has to address increasingly mobile populations that spread their lives across multiple nation-states and their associated institutions (Lunt et al. 2006). This raises important questions surrounding the provision of public goods such as education and healthcare. For example, (grand)parents who retire abroad carry implications for the demand on public childcare services. Conversely, outflows of young people increase the number of elderly people who require state-provided care. If not applied coherently and consistently, mechanisms such as bilateral agreements on social security and taxation can create incentives to 'free riders'.

In short, the impact of diasporas on existing public institutions and policies is a complex area, one that has traditionally been approached in an *ad hoc* manner, based on one-sided migration data.

Opportunities

It is also now commonplace to hear that diaspora engagement policies can further national interests by enhancing flows of remittances, investments, knowledge transfers and political influence from diaspora groups. The significance of remittances is widely acknowledged: in 2006, global remittance flows to developing countries topped US$ 220 billion. Only foreign direct investment (FDI) flows supply poorer countries with more stable currency than remittances. Remittances may reduce poverty and boost living standards among recipients, and can have a stabilizing effect during periods of upheaval (Goldin and Reinert 2006: 176). As a result, many countries have implemented policies to facilitate remittance flows ranging from increasing competition and access to remittance infrastructure; to matching each dollar remitted through official channels with state funds (as in Mexico's *tres por uno* scheme); to duty-free allowances on remitted goods (as for the Philippines' *balikbayan* boxes).

Many governments, both developing and OECD members alike, now turn to well-connected expatriates to attract FDI. For example, the Irish Development Agency utilized Irish-American business connections and skilled expatriate labour to attract Intel to Ireland. Similarly, New Zealand has set up a 'World Class New Zealander' network of high-profile business people in key markets, hoping to attract wealthy expatriates to invest in the country.

'New Growth' economic theories, which identify knowledge as the engine of growth, have stimulated interest in promoting transfers of knowledge and technologies from abroad through two main types of policy. One is based on facilitating returns of a temporary (or sometimes long-term) nature, by providing consultancy or fellowship opportunities for expatriate researchers. The second aims to cultivate 'diaspora knowledge networks' – dispersed networks of researchers who collaborate on scientific projects in the hope of benefiting their shared home country (Kuznetsov 2006).

In sum, there is in an argument that states face imperatives to adapt to a transnational world through policy-making, and that there may be added developmental advantages to doing so. However, the empirical link between emigration and development in the sending country is not universally accepted, and it is wise to ask whose interests this discourse serves. Is the 'migration and development' case really evidence that national interests can converge over migration, or is it more an argument that nation-states should be open to cooperation for a global collective interest? Furthermore, even if the interests of states are served by diaspora policies, do these interests trump the territorial norms around which politics is – at least in theory – organized? The following section considers these arguments.

Obligations

There are three main normative arguments as to why states should *not* engage their diasporas. *External non-interference* refers to the international norm that one state should not interfere with a population residing within another sovereign state. Diaspora policies may violate this norm – depending on how they are perceived by the other state. There are cases where long-standing ethnic rivalries or territorial disputes engender suspicion of irredentism, but there are also instances where bilateral relations are warm enough to prevent diaspora policies from causing conflict (see Délano 2006). Governments whose resources are stretched by large inflows of migrants may appreciate origin-state efforts to share the burden. For example, local and municipal governments often welcome the provision of health and education assistance by migrant-sending states.

Internal non-interference refers to the liberal norm that someone who does not consent to the authority of the government in one place should be free to leave that place. Diaspora policies are sometimes interpreted as attempts to assert authority over migrants wherever they are. This is fair criticism, but it must be added that in an era of easy international mobility, many diasporas have migrated out of convenience rather than dissent, and it may be problematic to portray them as undeserving of policy attention from their primary homeland. Conversely, if non-residents do wish to escape the reach of their origin state, they usually have the option to naturalize in their host country and avoid contact with homeland institutions, which exercise no jurisdiction where they live.

Non-preference refers to the notion that a state should privilege people within its own territory. When a state grants diasporas rights in the home country, they may be privileging non-residents at the expense of residents. This too is a fair point, although it must be noted that diasporas cannot simply be labelled as 'outsiders'. As populations become increasingly mobile, making contributions in one place and drawing on public resources in others, it is as much a mistake to strictly differentiate between diaspora and domestic populations as to ignore the differences between them. Diasporas often contribute to and draw on public goods in their home countries and therefore there are arguments that they should be considered part of them.

There are two positive arguments that states should intervene in diaspora populations. The first is that migrant-sending states should ensure that people who leave are still fulfilling any outstanding obligations to the country left behind. For example, people who benefit from publicly subsidized healthcare should be obliged to contribute to the economy during their working lives – regardless of their place of residence – and there should be mechanisms to enforce this reciprocity. In short, rights and obligations must go together (Bhagwati 2003).

Second, the reverse argument for diaspora policies is also valid: migrant-sending states inevitably exert some influence over 'their' diasporas – even if just through granting the passport – and therefore states are obliged to treat diasporas fairly. Pension transferability provides a useful example: many countries have national pension plans that discriminate against people who pay taxes during their working lives but are not eligible for full pensions if they decide to retire in another country (Clark 2002). In sum, while there are strong arguments that sending-state policies cannot legitimately apply to extra-territorial populations, such policies do in fact exist, and policy-makers should focus on how to make them more consistent with an evolving set of international norms.

Cooperation

Arguments about national interests and the norms governing relations between states and their citizens abroad assume that moral obligations operate within specific cultural contexts; that members of one's community should be prioritized over others. However, there are also cosmopolitan arguments for engaging diasporas based on the view that all humans belong to a common moral community which should promote the good of all. One strand of cosmopolitan thinking argues for 'global governance' (Rosenau 1999), which promotes multilateral cooperation to address and rectify the current lack of global migration frameworks and regulation (Betts 2008).

There are at least two cosmopolitan arguments for engaging diasporas. First, there is a 'global efficiency' argument that international cooperation over migration brings benefits to all involved, and that it requires the participation of both destination and origin states. Migration policy is usually dictated by destination states, to the exclusion of migrant-sending states – who often feel piqued by the treatment of 'their' emigrants. From this perspective, the formation of diaspora policies and institutions contributes to the capacity of origin states to participate in international cooperation concerning migration. Put differently, diaspora policies are being cast as an element of global migration governance.

Second, there is a 'global multicultural' argument that national communities should govern their own affairs in ways that are compatible with the global greater good. This follows a similar line to Kymlicka's (1995) argument for liberal multiculturalism at the national level, which distinguishes between types of minority cultural practices that states should and should not protect. He argues that states should enforce the liberty of ethnic minorities to pursue their cultural practices without interference from the majority culture. For example, this argument would justify a national law preventing employers from banning turbans in the workplace. Kymlicka also argues, however, that states should not enforce minority cultural practices that restrict the liberty of their members. Translating this line of argument to the global context might mean that states should be allowed to protect the rights of 'their' emigrants, but not to restrict their liberty. Such arguments have emerged prominently in the European debates about 'status laws'. For example, Hungary's Status Law, which extended protection to Hungarian ethnic minorities abroad, fell foul of ethnic nationalists in neighbouring states, who accused Hungary of irredentism. However, the response of the framers of the status law was that, far from harbouring territorial ambitions, their intent was to promote Hungary's integration into a 'multicultural' Europe in which territorial borders were increasingly irrelevant (Ieda 2004).

Summary and implications

This chapter has reviewed and evaluated prominent arguments surrounding diaspora engagement policies, focusing on three main areas: the interests of states, the mutual obligations between states and emigrants, and the cooperation between sending states, receiving states and migrants themselves. It has shown that migrant-sending states are confronted with imperatives and opportunities to pursue their interests through engaging their diasporas, but that these arguments alone do not necessarily override the territorial norm around which world politics are theoretically organized. When a migrant-sending state engages its diaspora, one should ask: Does it violate the sovereignty of the receiving state (external interference)? Does it interfere with the liberty of emigrants to exit the political community (internal interference)? Finally, does it allow outsiders too much say in local affairs (non-preference)?

There are rebuttals to these normative arguments. Firstly, as Délano (2006) has suggested, whether receiving states feel their sovereignty violated by a diaspora engagement policy depends on a wide range of contextual factors within the bilateral relationship. Secondly, not all emigrants have exited the political community: many remain active as members, and their engagement in home country affairs should be considered an ongoing concern. Thirdly, it is simplistic to label diasporas as 'outsiders', and many migrants would be unjustly disenfranchised if excluded from homeland decision-making processes (see Bauböck 2005a).

In addition to these communitarian justifications of diaspora policies, this chapter has highlighted more cosmopolitan arguments advocating better diaspora policies. There is an argument that global efficiency may be promoted by better global migration governance, which involves improving origin-state capacities to manage relations with their diasporas. There is also a 'global multicultural' argument that diaspora policies allow national communities to manage their own affairs in a world where territorial borders are becoming less important.

In concluding, it is important to say that having better diaspora policies does not necessarily mean having more diaspora policies. In some cases, a successful diaspora policy may involve cutting back existing regulation to prevent unwarranted forms of interference. Such interference is more common than might be expected, though not necessarily deliberate: the institutions and policies of sending states typically impact on diasporas accidentally, in arbitrary ways, resulting in outcomes that would not be tolerated in the domestic policy-making sphere, where government action is subject to much stricter oversight. The general point, therefore, is that coherent diaspora policies tend to be better diaspora policies in so far as they may prevent the arbitrary injustices and inefficiencies that currently characterize the ways that states relate to their diasporas in many parts of the world.

Acknowledgements

An earlier version of this chapter was presented at the UNECE (United Nations Economic Commission for Europe) Conference of European Statisticians, held at the OECD in Paris, 12 June 2008. I am grateful for comments from Robert Didham, Jean-Christophe Dumont and Ali Rogers.

References

Barry, K. (2006) 'Home and away: the construction of citizenship in an emigration context', *New York University Law Review*, 81 (1), 11–59, available at: www.nyulawreview.org/sites/default/files/pdf/6_1.pdf.
Basch, L. G., N. G. Schiller and C. Szanton Blanc (1994) *Nations unbound: transnational projects, postcolonial predicaments, and deterritorialized nation-states*, Amsterdam: Gordon & Breach.
Bauböck, R. (1994) *Transnational citizenship: membership and rights in international migration*, Cheltenham: Edward Elgar.
Bauböck, R. (2003) 'Towards a political theory of migrant transnationalism', *International Migration Review*, 37 (3), 700–23, doi: 10.1111/j.1747-7379.2003.tb00155.x.
Bauböck, R. (2005a) 'Expansive citizenship: voting beyond territory and membership', *Political Science and Politics*, 38 (4), 683–87, doi: 10.1017/S1049096505050341.
Bauböck, R. (2005b) 'Stakeholder citizenship and democratic participation in migration contexts', in J. E. Fossum, J. Poirier and P. Magnette (eds) *The ties that bind: accommodating complex diversity in Canada and the European Union*, Oxford: Peter Lang, 105–28.
Betts, A. (2008) 'Global migration governance', Global Economic Governance Programme working paper 2008/43, University of Oxford, available at: www.geg.ox.ac.uk/geg-wp-200843-global-migration-governance.
Bhagwati, J. (2003) 'Borders beyond control', *Foreign Affairs*, 82, 15 June, available at: www.foreignaffairs.com/issues/2003/82/1.
Brand, L. A. (2006) *Citizens abroad: emigration and the state in the Middle East and North Africa (Cambridge Middle East studies no. 23)*, Cambridge: Cambridge University Press.
Brubaker, R. (2005) 'The "diaspora" diaspora', *Ethnic and Racial Studies*, 28 (1), 1–19, doi: 10.1080/0141987042000289997.
Butler, K. (2001) 'Defining diaspora, refining a discourse', *Diaspora*, 10 (2), 189–219, doi: 10.1353/dsp.2011.0014.
Cano, G. and A. Délano (2007) 'The Mexican government and organised Mexican immigrants in the united states: a historical analysis of political transnationalism (1848–2005)', *Journal of Ethnic and Migration Studies*, 33 (5), 695–725, doi: 10.1080/13691830701359157.
Chander, A. (2006) 'Homeward bound', *New York University Law Review*, 81 (1), 60–89, available at: www.nyulawreview.org/sites/default/files/pdf/7_0.pdf.
Choate, M. I. (2008) *Emigrant nation: the making of Italy abroad*, Cambridge, MA: Harvard University Press.
Clark, G. (2002) 'Country of residence and pension entitlement: the arbitrary geography of UK legal formalism', *Environment and Planning A*, 34 (12), 2102–6, doi: 10.1068/a3412b.
Cohen, R. (1995) 'Rethinking "Babylon": iconoclastic conceptions of the diasporic experience', *New Community*, 21 (1), 5–18, doi: 10.1080/1369183X.1995.9976469.
Cohen, R. (1996) 'Diasporas and the nation-state: from victims to challengers', *International Affairs*, 72 (3), 507–20, doi: 10.2307/2625554.

Cohen, R. (1997) *Global diasporas: an introduction*, London: UCL Press.
Collyer, M. and Z. Vathi (2007) 'Patterns of extra-territorial voting', Sussex Centre for Migration Research working paper T22, University of Sussex, available at: www.migrationdrc.org/publications/working_papers/WP-T22.pdf.
De Haas, H. (2006) 'Engaging diasporas: how governments can support diaspora involvement in the development of countries of origin', Oxfam Novib report, June, University of Oxford.
Délano, A. (2006) 'The politics of the migrant-sending state from an international perspective: a study of the Mexican case', presented at the COMPAS Annual Conference 2006: International labour migration: in whose interests?, Center on Migration Policies and Society, Oxford, 5–6 July.
Dufoix, S. (2008) *Diasporas*, Berkeley, CA: University of California Press.
Fitzgerald, D. (2006) Rethinking Emigrant Citizenship. *New York University Law Review*, 81 (1), 90–116, available at: www.researchgate.net/publication/260036588_Rethinking_Emigrant_Citizenship.
Fullilove, M. and C. Flutter (2004) *Diaspora: the world wide web of Australians*, New South Wales: Longueville Media.
Gamlen, A. (2006) 'What are diaspora engagement policies and what kinds of states use them?', *COMPAS* working paper 0632, Centre on Migration, Policy and Society, University of Oxford.
Gamlen, A. (2008) 'The emigration state and the modern geopolitical imagination', *Political Geography*, 27 (8), 840–56, doi: 10.1016/j.polgeo.2008.10.004.
Glick Schiller, N. (2005) 'Transborder citizenship: an outcome of legal pluralism within transnational social fields', in F. von Benda-Beckmann, K. von Benda-Beckmann and A. Griffiths (eds) *Mobile people, mobile law: expanding legal relations in a contracting world*, London: Ashgate, 27–150.
Glick Schiller, N. and G. Fouron (1999) 'Terrains of blood and nation: Haitian transnational social fields', *Ethnic and Racial Studies*, 22 (2), 340–66, doi: 10.1080/014198799329512.
Goldin, I. and K. A. Reinert (2006) *Globalization for development: trade, capital, aid, migration, and policy*, Basingstoke: Palgrave Macmillan.
Green, N. L. and F. Weil (eds) (2007) *Citizenship and those who leave: the politics of emigration and expatriation*, Urbana, IL: University of Illinois Press/Combined Academic (distributor).
Guarnizo, L., A. Portes and W. Haller (2003) 'Assimilation and transnationalism: determinants of transnational political action among contemporary migrants', *American Journal of Sociology*, 108 (6), 1211–48, doi: 10.1086/375195.
Hugo, G. (2006) 'An Australian diaspora?', *International Migration*, 44 (1), 105–33, doi: 10.1111/j.1468-2435.2006.00357.x.
Ieda, O. (2004) 'Post-communist nation building and the Status Law syndrome in Hungary', in Z. Kántor, B. Majtényi, O. Ieda, B. Vizi and I. Halász (eds) *The Hungarian Status Law: nation building and/or minority protection*, Sapporo: Hokkaido University, Slavic Research Center, 3–57.
Ionescu, D. (2006) *Engaging diasporas as development partners for home and destination countries: challenges for policymakers*, Geneva: IOM.
Itzigsohn, J. (2000) 'Immigration and the boundaries of citizenship: the institutions of immigrants' political transnationalism', *International Migration Review*, 43 (4), 1126–54, doi: 10.2307/2675977.
Kuznetsov, Y. (ed.) (2006) *Diaspora networks and the international migration of skills: how countries can draw on their talent abroad*, WBI Development Studies, Washington, DC: World Bank.
Kymlicka, W. (1995) *Multicultural citizenship: a liberal theory of minority rights*, Oxford: Clarendon Press.
Laguerre, M. S. (1998) *Diasporic citizenship: Haitian Americans in transnational America*, Basingstoke: Macmillan.
Larner, W. (2007) 'Expatriate experts and globalising governmentalities: the New Zealand diaspora strategy', *Transactions of the Institute of British Geographers*, 32 (3), 331–45, doi: 10.1111/j.1475-5661.2007.00261.x.
Lee, C. (2004) 'The transnationalization of citizenship and the logic of the nation-state', paper given at the Asian-Pacific Sociological Association 6th Conference on Asia-Pacific Societies in Globalization, Seoul.
Levitt, P. and R. de la Dehesa (2003) 'Transnational migration and the redefinition of the state: variations and explanations', *Ethnic and Racial Studies*, 26 (4), 587–611, doi: 10.1080/0141987032000087325.
Lowell, B., A. Findlay and E. Stewart (2004) 'Brain strain: optimising highly skilled migration from developing countries', Institute for Public Policy Research (IPPR) working paper, available at: www.ippr.org/publications/brain-strainoptimising-highly-skilled-labour-from-developing-countriesworking-paper-3-of-the-asylum-and-migration-series.
Lunt, N., M. McPherson and J. Browning (2006) 'Les familles et whānau sans frontières: New Zealand and transnational family obligations', Families Commission report, Superu, Wellington, available at: www.superu.govt.nz/sites/default/files/BS-les-familles-et-whanau.pdf.

Margheritis, A. (2007) 'State-led transnationalism and migration: reaching out to the Argentine community in Spain', *Global Networks*, 7 (1), 87–106, doi: 10.1111/j.1471-0374.2006.00158.x.

Newland, K. and E. Patrick (2004) 'Beyond remittances: the role of diaspora in poverty reduction in their country of origin' report for the Migration Policy Institute, Washington DC, available at: www.migrationpolicy.org/sites/default/files/publications/Beyond_Remittances_0704.pdf.

Østergaard-Nielsen, E. (2003a) 'International migration and sending countries: key issues and themes', in E. Østergaard-Nielsen (ed.) *International migration and sending countries: perceptions, policies and transnational relations*, Basingstoke: Palgrave Macmillan, 3–32.

Østergaard-Nielsen, E. (ed.) (2003b) *International migration and sending countries: perceptions, policies and transnational relations*, Basingstoke: Palgrave Macmillan.

Reis, M. (2004) 'Theorizing diaspora: perspectives on "classical" and "contemporary" diaspora', *International Migration*, 42 (2), 41–60, doi: 10.1111/j.0020-7985.2004.00280.x.

Rosenau, J. (1999) 'Towards an ontology for global governance', in M. Hewson and T. J. Sinclair (eds) *Approaches to global governance theory*, New York: State University of New York Press. 287–302.

Rubio-Marín, R. (2006) 'Transnational politics and the democratic nation-state: normative challenges of expatriate voting and nationality retention of emigrants', *New York University Law Review*, 81 (1), 117–47, available at: www.nyulawreview.org/sites/default/files/pdf/9.pdf.

Safran, W. (1991) 'Diasporas in modern societies: myths of homeland and return', *Diaspora*, 1 (1), 83–99, doi: 10.1353/dsp.1991.0004.

Safran, W. (1999) 'Comparing diasporas: a review essay', *Diaspora*, 8 (3), 255–91, doi: 10.1353/dsp.1999.0002.

Smith, M. P. and L. E. Guarnizo (eds) (1998) *Transnationalism from below*, (Comparative urban and community research, volume 6), New Brunswick: Transaction Publishers.

Smith, R. C. (2003) 'Migrant membership as an instituted process: transnationalization, the state and the extra-territorial conduct of Mexican politics', *International Migration Review*, 37 (3), 297–343, doi: 10.1111/j.1747-7379.2003.tb00140.x.

Snel, E., G. Engbersen and A. Leerkes (2006) 'Transnational involvement and social integration', *Global Networks*, 6 (3), 285–308, doi: 10.1111/j.1471-0374.2006.00145.x.

Spiro, P. J. (2006) 'Perfecting political diaspora', *New York University Law Review*, 81 (1), 207–33, available at: https://ssrn.com/abstract=876955

Sriskandarajah, D. and C. Drew (2006) *Brits abroad: mapping the scale and nature of British emigration*, London: Institute for Public Policy Research.

Tölölyan, K. (1994) 'Diasporama', *Diaspora*, 3 (2), 235, doi: 10.1353/dsp.1994.0016.

Tölölyan, K. (2000) 'Diasporama', *Diaspora*, 9 (2), 309–10, doi: 10.1353/dsp.2000.0015.

Van Hear, N., F. Pieke and S. Vertovec (2004) 'The contribution of UK-based diasporas to development and poverty reduction', ESRC Centre on Migration, Policy and Society (COMPAS) report, University of Oxford, available at: www.compas.ox.ac.uk/media/ER-2004-Diasporas_UK_Poverty_Reduction_DfID.pdf.

Vertovec, S. (2004) 'Migrant transnationalism and modes of transformation', *International Migration Review*, 38 (3), 971–1001, doi: 10.1111/j.1747-7379.2004.tb00226.x.

Vertovec, S. (2005) 'The political importance of diasporas' Centre on Migration, Policy and Society working paper 13, University of Oxford, available at: www.compas.ox.ac.uk/media/WP-2005-013-Vertovec_Political_Importance_Diasporas.pdf.

Waldinger, R. (2008) 'Foreword', in S. Dufoix, *Diasporas*, Berkeley, CA: University of California Press, xi–xvii.

36
Diaspora mobilizations for conflict
Beyond amplification and reduction

Maria Koinova

In the early twenty-first century, scholarship on conflict processes started identifying diasporas as important non-state actors in world politics. Previously, conflict dynamics had been considered as shaped primarily by majorities, minorities, neighbouring and distant states, and international organizations. Yet the mounting intrastate conflicts of Bosnia-Herzegovina, Ethiopia, Kosovo, Kurdish areas in the Middle East, Nagorno-Karabakh, Palestine, Rwanda, Somalia and Sri Lanka, among others, pointed out that diasporas affect conflicts and post-conflict dynamics by way of durable links to their countries of origin. An influential World Bank study showed that post-conflict polities that have strong links to a US-based diaspora are not likely to resolve conflicts in the long run (Collier and Hoeffler 2000). Diaspora members support their families during warfare, but also raise funds for moderate and radical political factions, lobby foreign governments, stage demonstrations and even take up arms and become part of terrorist networks (Adamson and Demetriou 2007; Brinkerhoff 2011; Byman et al. 2001; Koinova 2014; Shain and Barth 2003; Sheffer 2003). The US 9/11 attacks, together with difficult-to-resolve domestic conflicts such as those in Iraq and Afghanistan, reinforced such negative views. Yet, diasporas have not been simply agents of conflicts but have participated in peace processes (Lyons 2007; Orjuela 2008; Smith and Stares 2007), democratization (Betts and Jones 2016; Koinova 2009) and development (Brinkerhoff 2008). By the late 2000s, the question whether diasporas are 'peace-makers or peace-wreckers' (Smith and Stares 2007) was answered – they could act as both. More productive ways to study this research agenda is to develop better conceptual tools, conduct comparative and quantitative studies and contribute to middle- and large-scale theorizing to bring more sophisticated understanding of diaspora behaviours in conflict and post-conflict processes.

This chapter focuses on concepts and theories illustrated by empirical evidence from different parts of the globe. I briefly discuss the concept of 'diaspora', specifically 'conflict-generated diaspora'. I also look into the concept of 'diaspora mobilization', its operationalizations, and its relationship to 'conflict spiral' and 'contested sovereignty'. Besides drawing theoretical leverage from scholarship on conflict and post-conflict processes, this research agenda uses insights from transnational social movements, foreign policy lobbying and, more recently, sociospatial dynamics. The chapter also discusses the emergence of new theoretical streams to deepen the existing research agenda on diasporas and transitional justice, and on weak and fragile states.

Diasporas and their mobilizations

The definition of the term 'diaspora' has triggered numerous debates in the founding generation of scholars working on diaspora politics, remaining inconclusive. Many scholars agreed that the term entails *dispersal* of populations – as for the Armenian and Jewish diasporas – their scattering across the globe, orientation towards a homeland and its territory, and maintenance of transnational links to that territory (Brubaker 2005; Cohen 1997; Safran 1991; Shain and Barth 2003; Sheffer 2003; Tölölyan 2000). Debates could not resolve whether the term 'diaspora' should incorporate only *historically dispersed* and stateless populations, or also those who are *more recently formed* and have states, while maintaining durable ties with their original homelands. As numerous scholars joined the discussion, working definitions were adopted to conduct a variety of comparative and quantitative analyses. Thereby debates emerged whether diasporas should be considered in *essential* terms and as unitary actors, as in quantitative studies (Collier and Hoeffler 2000), or as *multiple actors* and even *constructed* through a mobilization process, as in many qualitative studies (Abramson 2017; Adamson and Demetriou 2007; Sökefeld 2006). While the debates have split along epistemological and methodological preferences, the need to think comparatively prompted others to disaggregate the term and think how 'diaspora entrepreneurs' constitute diasporas by making claims on behalf of their original homeland (Brinkerhoff 2011; Koinova 2014, 2016; see also Brubaker 2005 and Koopmans et al. 2005 specifically on claim-making).

Conflict-generated diasporas are constituted of refugees and other migrants and their descendants who have escaped individual or collective violence and repression from countries of origin and have been durably socialized with the traumatic experience of violence and dispersal. Such diasporas could be 'long-distance nationalists' (Anderson 1998), maintaining a 'myth of return' to a real or imagined territory (Safran 1991; Sheffer 2003). Their identities could remain 'frozen' in time in remote locations, while embedded in diaspora institutions (Shain 2002), thus reinforcing traumatic memories and creating less eagerness to compromise (Lyons 2007). Lyons, among the first to mention the concept 'conflict-generated diasporas', argued that such diasporas could have a 'prominent role in framing conflict issues and defining what is politically acceptable'. He drew evidence from the Ethiopian diaspora in the USA, which managed to reframe domestic conflicts and eventually contribute to peace-building. Diasporas could nevertheless act in moderate ways, especially when their countries of origin no longer experienced conflicts or contestation of statehood (Koinova 2016).

The concept of *diaspora mobilization* has often been discursively engaged in scholarship on international diaspora politics, indicating the use of specific frames, mobilizing structures, networks and resources, and relating to different opportunities and constraints (Adamson and Demetriou 2007; Brinkerhoff 2011; Koinova 2014; Koopmans et al. 2005; Wayland 2004). The term was also applied differently. Byman et al. (2001) distinguish 'moderate' and 'radical' mobilizations, depending on whether diaspora individuals advocate *violent* tactics to achieve their goals. An alternative way to see such actions is to consider whether diaspora entrepreneurs use *transgressive* or *contained* mobilization in line with categorizations by McAdam et al. (2001). 'Contained' mobilizations channel diaspora interests through existing rules and processes in the state and society, 'transgressive' by challenging and acting outside established rules. Depending on where the target of action is located, diaspora entrepreneurs could pursue their collective interests through different channels, *state-based* or *transnational* (Koinova 2014). Variation also occurs in the *level of involvement*; diasporas could exercise 'direct, or 'indirect' practices to influence stakeholders in the homeland or via host-society channels (Østergaard-Nielsen 2001). Mobilization can have different *duration*, depending on whether efforts to organize are 'sustained' or 'ad hoc' (Koinova 2016), and different *strength*, as activists can engage resources 'materially' or 'symbolically', with intensity depending on their empowerment from the global position from which they organize.

The concept of *conflict spiral* comes from conflict studies and has been applied to diaspora studies according to Bercovitch's (2007) conceptual framework on diaspora intervention in a conflict cycle. Having researched the Armenian, Cambodian, Croatian, Jewish, Palestinian and Tamil diaspora cases, the contributors to a volume applying this framework (Smith and Stares 2007) found that diaspora entrepreneurs act as 'peace-wreckers' during the escalation phase rather than the prevention or termination phases of conflicts. They are more likely to act as 'peace-makers' if their political engagement reinforces their identity and coincides with the political line of the homeland and their aspirations to statehood (Bercovitch 2007; Smith and Stares 2007). This worthy contribution nevertheless does not consider that conflicts could be recurring, be blurred or overlapping, or emerge in succession. The relationship between diasporas and conflicts is therefore not that straightforward.

I have proposed that the relationship between diasporas and the *contested sovereignty* of states to which diasporas are transnationally linked is salient. Building on Krasner's (1999) framework of challenges to domestic and international sovereignty, I developed the framework of the large-scale European Research Council Project 'Diasporas and Contested Sovereignty', considering that the institutional strength or weakness of polities challenged in their domestic sovereignty could condition how diasporas connect and mobilize for them. Diasporas linked to fully sovereign states, even if such states are divided on ethnonational or sectarian grounds (such as Bosnia-Herzegovina versus Iraq), would do so differently from diasporas linked to *de facto* states, seeking international recognition (such as Kosovo, Palestine or Nagorno-Karabakh) or a stateless diaspora such as the Kurdish, linked to multiple states in the Middle East – Turkey, Syria, Iraq and Iran – challenged in both their domestic and international sovereignties (Koinova 2017).

Theories from sociology, international relations and political geography

To go deeper into the factors and mechanisms providing opportunities and constraints for diasporas to amplify or reduce conflicts, scholars have so far employed analytical tools from a variety of literatures: social movements, migration and transnationalism, foreign policy analysis and sociospatial theories.

Scholars in the international politics of diasporas started incorporating insights from classic works on social movements (McAdam et al. 2001; Snow and Benford 1992; Tarrow 2011) to answer *how* diasporas mobilize. Diaspora entrepreneurs act upon local and global *political opportunity structures* (Adamson 2013; Cochrane 2015; Østergaard-Nielsen 2001; Smith and Stares 2007; Wayland 2004); use *mobilizing structures*, the formal organizational forms or networks available to them (Adamson 2013; Wayland 2004); become *transnational brokers* connecting previously unconnected networks (Adamson 2013; Koinova 2014; Wayland 2004); use *framing* of specific contentious issues to reach certain audiences and expand the message to others (Adamson and Demetriou 2007; Koinova 2014; Smith and Stares 2007; Wayland 2004); *cooperate* across borders (Carment and Sadjed 2017); and build domestic or transnational *coalition*s to achieve common goals. They do so though off-line politics, but also increasingly through the Internet and social media (Brinkerhoff 2009; Nagel and Staeheli 2010).

Other literatures have provided alternative explanations about *why* diasporas mobilize in more radical or moderate ways. In migration and integration scholarship, Ireland argued, on the basis of research in Switzerland and France, that if institutional arrangements contribute to the isolation of migrants in the host state, diasporas are more likely to make homeland-oriented claims (Ireland 1994). Homeland-oriented claims could be further shaped by the conjuncture of incorporation regimes, migrants' collective identities and homeland influences (Koopmans et al. 2005). Others asserted that migrants' integration (Lewis 2007), or segmental assimilation into a host society (Morawska 2004; Portes and Zhou 1993), are more likely to foster migrant transnationalism. These studies have remained inconclusive, as socially disengaged individuals embedded in disempowered segments of migrant societies might have more incentives to radical actions, yet not actually act upon them, while highly educated and integrated individuals with no such incentives might rally in transgressive ways. In my own research, for example, while more educated individuals among the Palestinian diaspora would be found to lobby host-land and international institutions, individuals integrated across the economic spectrum could be part of the Boycott, Divestment and Sanctions Movement.

Politically relevant foreign policy factors have also been identified to cause diasporas to amplify or reduce conflicts. Established scholarship on ethnic lobbying in foreign policy has been more interested in capturing specifics about how policy lobbying takes place through state institutions, party systems and trade unions. An old, politically unified, organizationally strong, partly assimilated diaspora, active in foreign policy issues and keen on alliances with other interest groups, is likely to lobby successfully (Mearsheimer and Walt 2007; Rubenzer 2008; Sheffer 2003; Tölölyan 2000). Also important is the convergence of foreign policy and diaspora goals (Haney and Vanderbush 1999). Military interventions could exacerbate diaspora mobilizations, as in the Albanian diaspora for Kosovo independence related to NATO's 1999 military intervention (Koinova 2014), the 2003 intervention in Iraq as in the Iraqi diaspora (Brinkerhoff 2008), and the lack of military intervention in the Syrian conflict and its mobilization in the Syrian diaspora (Moss 2016). A traumatic contentious issue stemming from a failed military intervention, the Dutch UN peace-keeping's failure to protect the Srebrenica enclave during the wars of former Yugoslavia enabled contentious mobilizations among the Bosnian diaspora in the Netherlands, long after the violent conflict was over (Koinova 2016).

Several scholars have shown the detrimental effects on diaspora mobilizations of *critical events* stemming from the country of origin, where events associated with violence play an important role. Construction of a separate Kashmiri diaspora in the UK could be attributed to the rise of anti-Indian insurgency and violence in Jammu and Kashmir in 1989 and diaspora association with Khalistan (Sökefeld 2006: 273). Violent events in Kosovo and Sri Lanka also galvanized their diasporas (Demmers 2007; Koinova 2014), as did the gradual breakdown of the peace process in Sri Lanka (Godwin 2017; Orjuela 2017). The 2009 final battle, which crushed the militant Liberation Tigers of Tamil Eelam (LTTE), also became a critical event for diaspora mobilization (Hess and Kopf 2014). In scholarship so far, these events have been marked in empirical terms, but analysed minimally in theoretical terms. Hanafi (2005) argued that the 'centre of gravity' of the Palestinian movement changed from the diaspora to the West Bank and Gaza with the 1993 Oslo Accords; Brun and Van Hear (2012) spoke of the 'centre of gravity' after the LTTE defeat by the Sri Lankan government.

Taking a long-term perspective of the evolution of the Kosovo and Palestinian independence movements for statehood, I have argued that *critical junctures* – a theoretical tool of path-dependence scholarship – have the capacity to transform international and state structures and institutions, change the position of a strategic diasporic centre pursuing a homeland-oriented goal from 'outside', a homeland territory to 'inside' that territory, and vice versa. *Transformative events* – a theoretical tool of sociology – are less powerful and have the capacity to change diaspora mobilization trajectories to expand or contract (Koinova 2017). For example, the end of communism in 1989–91 and NATO's 1999 military intervention in Kosovo are critical junctures, as the diasporic strategic centre moved from state to exile in 1991, and from exile to state in 1999, in line with changing international regimes and state structures. In contrast, the mass killing of the family of a Kosovo Liberation Army leader in Drenica in 1998 and the mob violence in Kosovo in 2004 are *transformative*, because they expanded the mobilization in the diaspora, but did not change its position *vis-à-vis* the state.

Discussion on critical junctures and transformative events and their systemic effects across the globe belongs to recent emerging conversations about effects of sociospatial embeddedness on diaspora mobilization in international relations. These have been built on larger literature in political geography (Lefebvre 1974; Sassen 2007). As Björkdahl and Buckley-Zistel (2016) have shown, peace and conflict processes could be 'spatialized', with ample evidence demonstrating that agents could mobilize not simply in states but in sub-state units such as border areas, hotels, camps and other spaces. I made an early endeavour to theorize about diaspora *sociospatial positionality* and the power diaspora entrepreneurs derive from their social relationships embedded in different global contexts (Koinova 2012), and continued theorizing in more detail (2014, 2017). The positionality of Bosnian diaspora entrepreneurs in the Netherlands, where the Srebrenica issue is salient in Dutch institutions and society, and there is physical and sociospatial proximity to the International Criminal Tribunal on Former Yugoslavia, conditions diaspora entrepreneurs to be more likely to make contentious claims, especially *vis-à-vis* the claims of other diaspora activists (Koinova 2016). In the UK and Sweden, for example, where the issue of Srebrenica has not been contentious, the Bosnian diaspora was more open to incorporate multicultural perspectives (Koinova and Karabegovic 2017). Adamson and Koinova (2013) have also shown that London as a global city provides specific space for diasporas to mobilize, with the clustering of institutions, networks and resources.

On the basis of different spatialities, authors have started to show that a classic triangular relationship model considering diasporas, home states and host states as the sole actors inducing diasporas to mobilize is no longer valid. Contexts are not simply states as classically considered in international relations, but *sociospatial*, as diaspora entrepreneurs are embedded in relationships with others, and often function in transnational social spaces (Faist 2000; Pries 2001) or transnational social fields (Levitt and Glick-Schiller 2004). Diasporas are linked to different spaces, such as cities, online, refugee camps, supranational organizations, sites of global visibility and spaces contiguous to or distant from the homeland (Adamson 2016; Brinkerhoff 2009; Gabiam and Fiddian-Qasmiyeh 2016; Koinova and Karabegovic 2017; Kok and Rogers 2017; Van Hear and Cohen 2016). Besides *positionality*, authors emphasized the importance of *contiguity* (Koinova 2016; Van Hear and Cohen 2016), *translocalism* (Karabegovic 2017), *scale* (Koinova and Karabegovic 2017), and *multi-sited embeddedness* (Horst 2017). As this research agenda is still in inception, the systematic effects of sociospatial processes on diaspora mobilizations for amplification and reduction of conflicts are still to be analysed.

Diasporas in conflict and post-conflict reconstruction: a conversation

While the initial discussion about whether diasporas are 'peace-makers or peace-wreckers' has been concluded, scholarship is seeking to deepen the conversation along several new theoretical lines. First is a more systematic analysis of the relationship between diasporas and transitional justice. This conversation has been scattered so far, and actual scholarship on transitional justice has not been considerate of the fact that conflict legacies are not confined to the original homelands in a globalized world. Simultaneity of communications allows diasporas to voice their experiences and versions of the past in real time while transitional justice processes unfold on the ground (Koinova and Karabegovic 2017). Diasporas could participate in truth commissions, as in Liberia, Haiti, Sierra Leone or Cambodia (Hoogenboom and Quinn 2011; Young and Park 2009), launch court cases abroad seeking to prosecute dictators, as in the case of Chilean general Augusto Pinochet (Roht-Arriaza 2006) and war criminals, as in the case of the Khmer Rouge in Cambodia (Mey 2008). Diasporas could become involved in the establishment of legal tribunals, as in the special tribunal in Iraq (Haider 2014), or in memorialization and genocide recognition initiatives as in the Armenian, Bosnian and Jewish cases, among others (Koinova and Karabegovic 2017; Tölölyan 2000).

The second line of theory-building is connected to transitional justice, as the latter takes place in post-conflict states, where institutions are weak, and local and central authorities might lack the procedures or political will to engage with diaspora populations. Carment and Calleja (2017) demonstrate that authority, legitimacy and capacity are related not simply to domestic actors within a certain state, but to diasporas engaging from abroad with fragile states. The authors show variations of diaspora engagement regarding states that have experienced recent violent conflicts (Afghanistan, Ukraine, Somalia) and those where intrastate violence has not been prevalent (Ghana, Haiti, India). Conflict narratives could be entrenched in fragmented state institutions and school systems, which leave youth rooted in dominant conflict-based ideologies, as in the case of internally divided Bosnia-Herzegovina (Karabegovic 2017). Crises in weak states will not necessarily create diaspora mobilizations abroad, as durable and long-term instabilities of institutions and processes in the original homeland make diasporas jaded and uninterested in active participation, as in the case of diasporas linked to Greece and Palestine (Mavroudi 2017).

While these lines of scholarship provide some future avenues of engagement, other ways to deepen the knowledge would be to develop quantitative studies to scale up case-based and middle-range generalizations derived from comparative case studies into large-number analysis. Diaspora mobilization studies have developed some initial quantitative studies regarding remittances (Escribà-Folch et al. 2015; Leblang 2017) and sending states' engagement with diasporas abroad (Gamlen et al. 2013; Ragazzi 2014). But the study of diasporas and conflict and post-conflict processes is still lagging, despite Hall's (2016) study on Bosnian diaspora attitudes in Sweden and Bosnia-Herzegovina. A large-scale survey conducted in 2017 within the ERC Project 'Diasporas and Contested Sovereignty' is seeking to address this gap and bring more clarity in the near future.

References

Abramson, Y. (2017) 'Making a homeland, constructing a diaspora', *Political Geography*, 58, 14–23, doi: 10.1016/j.polgeo.2017.01.002.
Adamson, F. (2013) 'Mechanisms of diaspora mobilization and the transnationalization of civil war', in J. Checkel (ed.) *Transnational dynamics of civil war*, Cambridge: Cambridge University Press, 63–88.
Adamson, F. (2016) 'Spaces of global security', *Journal of Global Security Studies*, 1 (1), 19–35, doi: 10.1093/jogss/ogv003.
Adamson, F. and M. Demetriou (2007) 'Remapping the boundaries of "state" and "national identity"', *European Journal of International Relations*, 13 (4), 489–526, doi: 10.1177/1354066107083145.
Adamson, F. and M. Koinova (2013) 'The global city as a space of transnational identity politics', SOAS working paper, available at: http://eprints.soas.ac.uk/id/eprint/17378.
Anderson, B. (1998) *Imagined communities*, London: Verso.
Bercovitch, J. (2007) 'A neglected relationship: diasporas and conflict resolution', in H. Smith and P. Stares (eds) *Diasporas in conflict*, Tokyo: UNU Press, 17–38.
Betts, A. and W. Jones (2016) *Mobilizing the diaspora*, Cambridge: Cambridge University Press.

Björkdahl, A. and S. Buckley-Zistel (eds) (2016) *Spatializing peace and conflict*, London: Palgrave.
Brinkerhoff, J. (ed.) (2008) *Diasporas and development: exploring the potential*, Boulder: Lynne Rienner.
Brinkerhoff, J. (ed.) (2009) *Digital diasporas*, Cambridge: Cambridge University Press.
Brinkerhoff, J. (2011) 'Diasporas and conflict societies', *Conflict, Security, and Development*, 11 (2), 115–43, doi: 10.1080/14678802.2011.572453.
Brubaker, R. (2005) 'The "diaspora"' diaspora', *Ethnic and Racial Studies*, 21 (1), 1–19, doi: 10.1080/0141987042000289997.
Brun, C. and N. Van Hear (2012) 'Between the local and the diasporic', *Contemporary South Asia*, 20 (1), 71–65, doi: 10.1080/09584935.2011.646070.
Byman, D., P. Chalk, B. Hoffman, W. Rosenau and D. Brennan (2001) *Trends in outside support for insurgent movements*, Santa Monica, CA: Rand.
Carment, D. and R. Calleja (2017) 'Diasporas and fragile states: beyond remittances', *Journal of Ethnic and Migration Studies*, forthcoming.
Carment, D. and A. Sadjed (eds) (2017) *Diaspora as cultures of cooperation: global and local perspectives*, London: Palgrave.
Cochrane, F. (2015) *Migration and security in the global age*, London: Routledge.
Cohen, R. (1997) *Global diasporas: an introduction*, London: UCL Press.
Collier, P. and A. Hoeffler (2000) 'Greed and grievance in civil war', World Bank Policy Research working paper 2355, available at: http://documents.worldbank.org/curated/en/359271468739530199/Greed-and-grievance-in-civil-war.
Demmers, J. (2007) 'New wars and diasporas', *Journal of Peace, Conflict & Development*, 11, 1–26, available at: https://goo.gl/PWE5cw
Escribà-Folch, A., C. Meseguer and J. Wright (2015) 'Remittances and democratization', *International Studies Quarterly*, 59 (3), 571–86, doi: 10.1111/isqu.12180.
Faist, T. (2000) *The volume and dynamics of international migration and transnational social spaces*, Oxford: Oxford University Press.
Gabiam, N. and E. Fiddian-Qasmiyeh (2016) 'Palestinians and the Arab uprisings', *Journal of Ethnic and Migration Studies*, 43 (5), 731–48, doi: 10.1080/1369183X.2016.1202750.
Gamlen, A., M. Cummings, P. Vaaler and L. Roussouw (2013) 'Explaining the rise of diaspora institutions', International Migration Institute, Oxford, working paper 78, available at: www.imi.ox.ac.uk/publications/wp-78-13.
Godwin, M. (2017) 'Winning Westminster-style', *Journal of Ethnic and Migration Studies*, forthcoming.
Haider, H. (2014) 'Transnational transitional justice and reconciliation', *Journal of Refugee Studies*, 27 (2), 207–33, doi: 10.1093/jrs/feu002.
Hall, J. (2016) 'Are migrants more extreme than locals after civil war?', *Journal of Conflict Resolution*, 60 (1), 89–117, doi: 10.1177/0022002714540471.
Hanafi, S. (2005) 'Reshaping geography', *Journal of Ethnic and Migration Studies*, 31 (3), 581–98, doi: 10.1080/13691830500058703
Haney, P. and W. Vanderbush (1999) 'The role of ethnic interest groups in US foreign policy', *International Studies Quarterly*, 43 (2), 341–61, doi: 10.1111/0020-8833.00123.
Hess, M. and B. Kopf (2014) 'Tamil diaspora and the political spaces of second-generation activism on Switzerland', *Global Networks*, 14 (4), 419–37, doi: 10.1111/glob.12052.
Hoogenboom, D. and J. Quinn (2011) 'Transitional justice and the diaspora', paper presented at International Studies Association annual convention, Montreal, 16–19 March, available at: http://citation.allacademic.com/meta/p_mla_apa_research_citation/5/0/0/6/2/pages500626/p500626-1.php.
Horst, C. (2017) 'Making a difference in Mogadishu?', *Journal of Ethnic and Migration Studies*, forthcoming.
Ireland, P. (1994) *The policy challenge of ethnic diversity*, Cambridge, MA: Harvard University Press.
Karabegovic, D. (2017) 'Aiming for transitional justice?', *Journal of Ethnic and Migration Studies*, forthcoming.
Koinova, M. (2009) 'Diasporas and democratization in the post-communist world', *Communist and Postcommunist Studies*, 42 (1), 41–64, doi: 10.1016/j.postcomstud.2009.02.001.
Koinova, M. (2012) 'Autonomy and positionality in diaspora politics', *International Political Sociology*, 6 (1), 99–103, doi: 10.1111/j.1749-5687.2011.00152_3.x.
Koinova, M. (2014) 'Why do conflict-generated diasporas pursue sovereignty-based claims through state-based or transnational channels?', *European Journal of International Relations*, 20 (4), 1043–71, doi: 10.1177/1354066113509115.
Koinova, M. (2016) 'Sustained vs. episodic mobilization among conflict-generated diasporas', *International Political Science Review*, 37 (4), 500–16, doi: 10.1177/0192512115591641.

Koinova, M. (2017) 'Diaspora mobilization for conflict and postconflict reconstruction: contextual and comparative dimensions', *Journal of Ethnic and Migration Studies*, forthcoming.
Koinova, M. and D. Karabegovic (2017) 'Diasporas and transitional justice: transnational activism from local to global levels of engagement', *Global Networks*, 17 (2), 212–33, doi: 10.1111/glob.12128.
Kok, S. and R. Rogers (2017) 'Rethinking migration in the digital age: transglocalization and the Somali diaspora', *Global Networks*, 17 (1), 23–46, doi: 10.1111/glob.12127.
Koopmans, R., P. Statham, M. Giuni and F. Passy (2005) *Contested citizenship: immigration and cultural diversity in Europe*, Minneapolis: University of Minnesota Press.
Krasner, S. (1999) *Sovereignty: organized hypocrisy*, Princeton: Princeton University Press.
Leblang, D. (2017) 'Harnessing the diaspora', *Comparative Political Studies*, 50 (1), 75–101, doi: 10.1177/0010414015606736.
Lefebvre, H. (1974) *The production of space*, Oxford: Blackwell.
Levitt, P. and N. Glick-Schiller (2004) 'Conceptualizing simultaneity', *International Migration Review*, 38 (3), 1002–39, doi: 10.1111/j.1747-7379.2004.tb00227.x.
Lewis, P. (2007) *Young, British, and Muslim*, London: Continuum.
Lyons, T. (2007) 'Conflict-generated diasporas and transnational politics of Ethiopia', *Conflict, Security and Development*, 7 (4), 529–49, doi: 10.1080/14678800701692951.
McAdam, D., S. Tarrow and C. Tilly (2001) *The dynamics of contention*, New York: Cambridge University Press.
Mavroudi, E. (2017) 'Deconstructing diasporic mobilisation at a time of crisis: perspectives from the Palestinian and Greek diasporas', *Journal of Ethnic and Migration Studies*, 44 (8), 1309–24
Mearsheimer, J. and S. Walt (2007) *The Israel lobby and foreign policy*, New York: Farrar, Straus and Giroux.
Mey, E. (2008) 'Cambodian diaspora communities in transitional justice', briefing paper, International Center for Transitional Justice, New York, available at: www.ictj.org/sites/default/files/ICTJ-Cambodia-Diaspora-Justice-2008-English.pdf.
Morawska, E. (2004) 'Exploring diversity in immigrant assimilation and transnationalism', *International Migration Review*, 38 (4), 1372–412, doi: 10.1111/j.1747-7379.2004.tb00241.x.
Moss, D. (2016) 'Diaspora mobilization for western military intervention during the Arab Spring', *Journal of Immigrant and Refugee Studies*, 14 (3), 277–97, doi: 10.1080/15562948.2016.1177152.
Nagel C. and L. Staeheli (2010) 'ICT and geographies of British Arab and Arab American activism', *Global Networks*, 10 (2), 262–81, doi: 10.1111/j.1471-0374.2010.00285.x.
Orjuela, C. (2008) 'Distant warriors, distance peace-workers', *Global Networks*, 8 (4), 436–52.
Orjuela, C. (2017) 'Mobilizing for justice', *Journal of Ethnic and Migration Studies*, forthcoming.
Østergaard-Nielsen, E. (2001) 'Transnational political practices and the receiving state', *Global Networks*, 1 (3), 261–82, doi: 10.1111/1471-0374.00016.
Portes, A. and M. Zhou (1993) 'The new second generation', *Annals of the American Academy of Political and Social Sciences*, 530 (1), 74–96, doi: 10.1177/000271629353000106.
Pries, L. (ed.) (2001) *New transnational social spaces*, London: Routledge.
Ragazzi, F. (2014) 'A comparative analysis of diaspora policies', *Political Geography*, 41, 74–89, doi: 10.1016/j.polgeo.2013.12.004.
Roht-Arriaza, N. (2006) *The Pinochet effect*, Philadelphia: University of Pennsylvania Press.
Rubenzer, T. (2008) 'Ethnic minority interest group attributes and US Foreign policy influence', *Foreign Policy Analysis*, 4 (2), 169–85, doi: 10.1111/j.1743-8594.2007.00063.x.
Safran, W. (1991) 'Diasporas in modern societies: myths of homeland and return', *Diaspora: A Journal of Transnational Studies*, 1 (1), 83–99, doi: 10.1353/dsp.1991.0004.
Sassen, S. (2007) *A sociology of globalization*, New York: Norton.
Shain, Y. (2002) 'The role of diasporas in conflict perpetuation and resolution', *SAIS Review*, 22 (2), 115–44, doi: 10.1353/sais.2002.0052.
Shain, Y. and A. Barth (2003) 'Diasporas and international relations theory', *International Organization*, 57 (3), 449–79, doi: 10.1017/S0020818303573015.
Sheffer, G. (2003) *Diaspora politics: at home abroad*, Cambridge: Cambridge University Press.
Smith, H. and P. Stares (2007) *Diasporas in conflict*, Tokyo: UNU Press.
Snow, D. and R. Benford (1992) 'Master frames and cycles of protest', in A. D. Morris and C. M. Meuller (eds) *Frontiers of social movement theory*, New Haven: Yale University Press, 133–55.
Sökefeld, M. (2006) 'Mobilizing in transnational space', *Global Networks*, 6 (3), 265–84, doi: 10.1111/j.1471-0374.2006.00144.x.
Tarrow, S. (2011) *Power in movement*, third edition, Cambridge: Cambridge University Press.

Tölölyan, K. (2000) 'Elites and institutions in the Armenian transnation', *Diaspora*, 9 (1), 107–36, doi: 10.1353/dsp.2000.0004.
Van Hear, N. and R. Cohen (2016) 'Diasporas and conflict: distance, contiguity and spheres of engagement', *Oxford Development Studies*, 45 (2), 171–84, doi: 10.1080/13600818.2016.1160043.
Wayland, S. (2004) 'Ethnonationalist networks and transnational opportunities', *Review of International Studies*, 30 (3), 405–26, doi: 10.1017/S0260210504006138.
Young, L. and R. Park (2009) 'Engaging diasporas in truth commissions', *International Journal of Transitional Justice*, 3 (3), 341–61, doi: 10.1093/ijtj/ijp021.

37
Diaspora and development

Ben Page and Claire Mercer

There are few areas of public policy in which the idea of a diaspora has been applied more instrumentally and extensively than in the international development sector. A cursory perusal of *Developing a road map for engaging diasporas in development: a handbook for policymakers and practitioners in home and host countries*, published in 2012 by the International Organization for Migration (IOM) and the Migration Policy Institute (MPI), reveals the current thinking. The task of governments in the Global South is to get to know their diaspora, to mobilize it and to build the diaspora's capacity to contribute to homeland development. In some cases, the task is even to construct a diaspora if none exists. In this policy-framing, diasporas are a source of remittances to be leveraged, investment to be procured and human capital to be returned. Engage your diaspora to boost your economic growth (Mithra 2016)! This is a topic where the definition of 'diaspora' is a long way from the standard academic definitions that have been used in the past. From the global development industry's perspective, first-generation migrants form the primary group of 'diasporas' with whom they attempt to engage, though any individual can be enrolled as long as they are (or can be encouraged to be) sympathetic to the development of their ancestral homeland.

In this chapter, we start by describing how diaspora has been applied to development practice since the 1990s. We show how the global development industry is attempting to incorporate diasporas into mainstream development interventions, just as it has done in the past with gender, participation or civil society. To do this, we distinguish between the activities of the governments of diaspora home countries, the World Bank's Remittances Team, other development industry actors and the governments of diaspora-hosting countries. This typology is problematic because of the home/host distinction and because it suggests separation where there is often connection, cooperation and overlap. It also deliberately ignores individuals in diasporas themselves, except when they explicitly organize as development-diaspora NGOs. We then provide a more critical analysis of four conceptual terrains where diaspora and development have been brought together: modernization, time/space, belonging/identity and securitization/financialization.

How have diaspora and development been brought together in practice?

The governments of diaspora-sending countries in the Global South are seen as the key actors in this field. They are being encouraged to follow a 'road map' in order to solicit the help of 'their diaspora' for national development (IOM and MPI 2012). Since the turn of the millennium, many of these governments have opened diaspora ministries and sub-ministries (Gamlen 2014; Kleist and Turner 2013). The menu of activities they undertake includes identifying and mapping the diaspora; building trust with the diaspora through initiatives such as extending dual citizenship, holding cultural events and providing services to those abroad; and finally incentivizing individuals in the diaspora to invest in their homeland through information centres, tax breaks, 'diaspora days' and other policy fora. The hope is that, as a result, members of the diaspora will invest both financial and human capital in their countries of origin. This might mean setting up new businesses, or (for the highly skilled) coming home to work on a temporary or permanent basis. Another approach focuses not on entrepreneurs in the diaspora but on diaspora groups with an appetite for philanthropy. This was pioneered by the Mexican government's *Tres Por Uno* programme, which provides matching development funding for diaspora organizations from federal, state and municipal governments (Lopez 2015). These projects have typically been small-scale hometown investments in public goods such as potable water and electrification.

The World Bank's Migration and Remittance Team is also a major player shaping diaspora and development activities in diaspora-sending and diaspora-receiving countries (Ratha and Plaza 2016). Their key interventions seek to maximize formal remittances to developing countries based on the belief that such capital is a major contributor to economic growth in the Global South. This is achieved through four principal routes. First, they disseminate data, knowledge and research on remittances and on their development impacts. Much of this information is made available through the Global Knowledge Partnership on Migration and Development (KNOMAD), funded by the Bank and the Governments of Germany, Switzerland and Sweden. Second, the World Bank provides funding for technical assistance and advisory services to governments that are developing diaspora policies in order to maximize benefits and minimize risks associated with migration. Third, the Bank is at the forefront of attempts to reduce the cost of sending remittances around the world. Finally, the Bank, along with others, has argued for the leveraging of remittances for development by introducing financial products aimed at the diaspora, such as diaspora bonds.

In addition to the above actors, there are a group of institutions that, taken together, constitute that part of the global development industry that is explicitly focused on international migration and diaspora. These include other multilateral development agencies (such as IOM and Global Forum on Migration and Development), NGOs (such as AFFORD), think-tanks (such as the Migration Policy Institute) and migrant lobby groups (such as Migrants' Rights Network). These have been active in a range of migrant issues, including migrant workers' rights, remittance costs and the impact of brain drain. They have most recently organized around getting diaspora-related issues recognized in the 2015 Sustainable Development Goals.

The actors not yet discussed are the governments in diaspora-receiving states. This was the institutional site of many early experiments linking diasporas to international development, such as the co-development policies of Spain, Italy and France in the 1990s (which mostly linked funding from development budgets to return migration). Ultimately, however, many of these interventions are relatively limited in scope. For example, the key diaspora project for the Department for International Development (DFID) in the UK, the Common Ground Initiative, has amounted to only £32 million of funding for African diaspora organizations over 10 years. This initiative provides direct project grants as well as money for capacity-building and research. In the recent past, there has been interest in 'mapping' various diaspora communities within the UK, but less of an idea about how to engage these communities in the development of their place of origin. Since 2016, diaspora issues seem to have slipped down DFID's agenda in the UK and, at the time of writing, there is no explicit diaspora development policy listed on their website at all.

How have diaspora and development been brought together conceptually?

So far, we have described the institutions and activities of the international development industry in relation to the ambition to enrol diasporas in development. In this section, we shift away from what such actors are attempting to *do* in a top-down manner, to identifying, and critiquing, the *concepts* underpinning these diaspora and development initiatives.

First are the traces of the colonial dimension embedded within the concept of *modernization* which echo through the diaspora development field. For example, the Global North is often imagined as the location of more 'developed' values, such as being pro-democracy and gender equality. Diaspora communities, it is implied, absorb these values through a process of social osmosis from the locales in which they now live. The implicit hierarchy in development's reading of 'modernization' justifies a conception of diasporans remitting these more advanced values to their backward homelands through their transnational linkages. However hard more sophisticated theorizations of social remittances seek to emphasize the bi-directional movement of values and the dynamic hybrid qualities of transnational cultures (Levitt and Lamba-Nieves 2011), the idea that modern values move from North to South when migrants return persists in development practice because of the way in which 'development' is imaginatively wedded to those colonial cultural hierarchies. Empirical examples that emphasize the more complex pathways taken by values when people move (for example, JoAnn McGregor's (2008) work on 'African values' in relation to children and education among transnational Zimbabwean families) are problematic for conceptualizations that see diasporas as carriers of modern values. In practice, such examples must either be sidelined by those who build the road maps of diaspora engagement or explained away through the ideological mechanisms of orientalism, which can present African values as the stubbornly persistent quirks of essentialized exotic 'traditional' cultures.

Further, there is also an untroubled confidence in much diaspora development policy about what modernization looks like and how it will be delivered. In this context, development is defined as 'what development professionals trained in the Global North do', and it is distinctly not what non-professionals in the diaspora might imagine it to be (Sinatti and Horst 2014). Of course, there is much overlap in how development professionals and diasporans think of development, but there are also important areas of divergence, for example around which kinds of projects might count as 'modernization'. In our own research with African hometown associations, we have encountered diasporas' energies being channelled into local improvements in the hometown such as refurbishing a mortuary, pursuing land disputes and erecting cultural monuments. These activities were clearly understood by the diaspora as 'developmental' but would not usually find support in development programming by development professionals (Mercer et al. 2008). Assumptions about what counts as the 'productive' uses of remittances are equally problematic, with many of the everyday uses of diasporans' remittances dismissed as unproductive when set against an index of capitalist business. House-building is a good example since it accounts for a large proportion of the money sent home by diasporas, yet such spending is often considered unproductive and even inflationary (despite the fact that house-building has significant local economic effects including the purchase of materials and labour) because it is fundamentally a form of consumption. For those people building these 'modern' houses, however, their projects are unambiguously developmental.

The second set of concepts where diaspora and development meet are those associated with *space* and *time*. In development studies, the geography of diaspora is often imagined as a series of ahistorical binaries such as North/South, developed/developing, host/home, sending/receiving and here/there (Raghuram 2009), which are currently traversed by migrants in order to produce diasporas and then remittances (Datta 2009). As Raghuram (2009) points out, what is missing from this framework is any understanding of the historical 'co-constitution of Europe and the colonies', which was not only central to producing current patterns of inequality but which has also meant that 'the spaces for/of development are already mixed up, that migrants "here" might need development, and that migrants "there" might be agents of development "here"' (Raghuram 2009: 113).

The mixing up of the spaces of development has a long temporal trajectory. For example, the work of Judith Carney (1993) has shown that rice cultivation along the American Atlantic Coast from the mid-eighteenth century was dependent upon the understanding of rice farming among the West African slave diaspora. Although this contribution to the economic development of the American South has been largely ignored or actively denied, Carney argues that

> before the outbreak of the Civil War, an estimated 100,000 slaves were planting between 168,000 and 187,000 acres of wetland rice. The antebellum rice economy included the richest planters of the US South, and the region's capital, Charleston, gloried in one of the greatest concentrations of wealth in the world.
>
> *(Carney 1993: 78)*

This 'development' located in the USA was built not just on diaspora labour, but also on diaspora knowledge. Similarly, the massive transfer of capital from the slave plantations of the Caribbean to the urban infrastructure of Britain in the late eighteenth and early nineteenth centuries illustrates that the industrial revolution and the development that ensued was not so much an illustration of Britain's national genius as a product of forced global population movements. Nor, as Giles Mohan (2002) pointed out long ago, is this process only historical. The development of twenty-first-century Britain is a product of immigration – with new capitalist enterprises, which would not otherwise exist, emerging to serve diaspora populations – as well as of the emigration of the twenty-first-century diaspora of British citizens around the world (MacRae and Wright 2006). American and British development was, and is, co-constituted by its diasporas.

The third conceptual framework where diaspora encounters development circulates around the ideas of *belonging* and *autochthony*. Whilst these ideas have historically been core to debates in diaspora studies, they have been less central in development theory. One of the consequences of connecting development to diaspora has been to give more prominence to these ideas in development studies. This is most easily illustrated through what Oliver Bakewell (2008) has described as the 'sedentary bias' that pervades much of the diaspora and development field and assumes that mobility in and of itself is an aberration because people really belong at 'home' (de Haas 2007). The idea of belonging is used in multiple ways that have fairly unsubtle policy aspirations with obviously political overtones. For example, attempts to use development as a means to eventually stop migration from the Global South to the Global North (de Haas 2007) or as attempts by governments of the Global South to use appeals to patriotism to repatriate capital from their diasporas back to where it belongs at home. In both cases, the idea is that all people *really* belong in some local home. People's affection for their homes becomes both a resource to be used in the effective management of national development and a moral justification for trying to manage who lives where in the world by those who seek to restrict movement.

The sedentary bias is rooted in essentialist understandings of identity which privilege a place of origin, usually a birthplace, as an unchanging home to which diasporas will always be oriented. Indeed, Sinatti and Horst (2014: 137) describe this 'binary mobility bias' as a key part of much diaspora and development policy, in which the assumption is that diasporas will *naturally* wish to contribute to the development of their homeland, and ideally eventually return to it. It is this rootedness in the homeplace – most commonly imagined at the nation-state scale – that is assumed to characterize all members of a given diaspora and to mobilize their action for 'development'. There have been lively debates over many years between those who have emphasized the cosmopolitan character of global diasporas as opposed to those who argue for the universal significance of belonging in a specific place even in an era of global convergence (see, for example, Kibreab 1999 and the subsequent responses), but when these are translated into the policy arena, the idea of 'home' becomes far more instrumental and less nuanced. The point here is not so much about the real and evolving meaning of place in people's lives as the means of using sentiments to pursue quite practical political goals.

The fourth, and final, conceptual area underpinning the development-diaspora field concerns the linked ideas of *securitization* and *financialization*. These are terms that have generally achieved far more prominence in development studies than in diaspora studies thus far (Bracking 2016). In broad terms, securitization is the process of placing increasing ideological and fiscal emphasis on perpetuating state stability by shifting more resources to forms of hard power (military spending, intelligence services) and soft power (diplomacy, deradicalization) in the face of a widespread sense of escalating risks (terrorism, climate change, financial volatility). Critics argue that the sense of risk is exaggerated in order to justify the reduction of civil liberties and the re-orientation of limited public resources towards security. The 'securitization of development' entails not only efforts to manage or end violent conflicts in the Global South (which are seen as a barrier to development at the site of the conflict) but also to end conflicts that are seen to provide sites where global terrorist movements are thought to find sustenance (for example in Syria, Libya, Pakistan, Nigeria or Afghanistan). In a general sense, committing to development in the Global South becomes recast as a strategy for reducing the risks of global insecurity by reducing the spaces where terror can flourish by reforming or replacing ineffective states (Duffield 2005).

Financialization refers to the long history of the growing autonomy and power of finance capital in relation to industrial capital. In the development sector, this initially meant an increased emphasis on financing development from the private sector by encouraging entrepreneurship as well as a growing use of financial instruments like micro-credit or property mortgages to achieve development goals. Following the Addis Ababa Agenda for Action (2015), the financialization of development has moved beyond this to involve much deeper engagement with hedge funds, investment banks, venture capitalists, sovereign wealth funds, and, most particularly, the big global accountancy firms, who often provide the 'kite mark' that reassures other financial actors. Their intent is to deliver development by creating new markets that open up novel ways of investing through creating new products. Government aid budgets are being used to enable this process of financialization. As Mawdsley (2016: 1) puts it '[f]oreign aid is being used to de-risk investment, "escort" capital to "frontier" markets, and carry out the mundane work of transforming objects into assets available to speculative capital flows'. In short, international development as a whole is being transformed simultaneously by securitization and financialization, but the significance for this specific discussion is that diasporas are relevant to both.

The diaspora development field is connected to processes of securitization and finacialization because (a) mobile people in general and some diasporas in particular are seen as a significant security risk, and (b) diaspora remittances and diaspora investment represent one of the major sites for experiments in financialization. One of the central ideas used to promulgate the idea of an ever-present security risk in the West is a sense of the existence of hidden global networks used to enable terrorism. Since diasporas are, often, also global networks (though not really hidden ones), it only requires a short leap of the imagination to cast suspicion on them. As Mark Duffield (2005: 13) puts it when reflecting on this interweaving of development and security:

> the new global danger no longer necessarily lies with the abject poor, who are fixed in their misery: instead, it pulses from those mobile subpopulations capable of bridging and circulating between the dichotomies of North/South; modern/traditional; and national/international.

In this context, the job of development becomes not just to control 'failed states' but also to engage with these mobile sub-populations. So, for example, in the aftermath of the 2001 terrorist attacks on the United States, the FBI intensified their pre-existing enquiry into al-Barakaat's links with al-Qaeda and its leadership. Al-Barakaat was a money transfer company that primarily served the Somali diaspora and operated mainly in the USA, United Arab Emirates, Kenya and Somalia. Though ultimately the FBI were unable to prove any illegal connections and closed the enquiry in 2002, retail banks in the USA and elsewhere started to withdraw services from money transfer companies. They feared major fines from the US government if links between the diaspora remittance companies and terrorist organizations were ever found. While advocates for diasporas drew attention to the negative humanitarian consequences of closing down the remittance corridor (Lindley and Mosley 2014), official development organizations struggled to reconcile the contradictions between the desire for security and the desire to reduce the number of failing states by capitalizing on the flow of diaspora remittances. The development task became finding a way to maintain these flows of diaspora capital into Somalia, but in a secure, transparent, formal way. Meeting this goal illustrates how securitization and financialization are closely connected.

Remittances also form a key focus of financialization efforts addressed to the diaspora by the global development sector – the diaspora's money is being reimagined as an important source of development finance. As Kavita Datta (2017) puts it, the process is taking what was once an 'alternative' form of capital flow and 'mainstreaming' it. The goal is to shift a greater proportion of money transfers into secure 'formal' routes (operated by trusted, regulated bodies such as specialist companies, banks, post offices) and away from 'informal' (such as hand-carries, *hawala* or small corridor-specific operators). This process of making remittances 'safe' simultaneously opens up the possibility of new financial products derived from these capital flows now passing through formal banking channels. The most obvious such products are (confusingly) called securitizations. This is where different assets (often illiquid assets such as mortgages) are pooled together so as to provide a new product that generates interest and can be sold to investors. In the diaspora case, pooled future remittance receipts can be treated as an asset against which a bank can borrow money by selling a bond to investors. In some circumstances (for example where local risks make sovereign borrowing expensive), such products can enable banks in the developing world to raise funds at advantageous rates. Such experiments in development finance are not limited either to diaspora remittances or to securitizations (more direct 'diaspora bond' issues are also much discussed), but they are symptomatic of current debates. A financial discourse is in the ascendant among policy-makers in the development diaspora field.

Conclusion

In this chapter, we have shown how a series of governmental and non-governmental actors have identified specific goals and roles in a process of steering diasporas towards contributing to international development. We have argued that in a matter of a few decades the idea of diasporas being part of the development process has moved from the periphery to the mainstream, largely driven by an interest in remittances. The actors with the greatest interest and responsibility in this process are currently seen as the governments of diaspora homelands, who are increasingly expected to enrol their diasporas into a national development project. In this context, the definition of 'diaspora' is highly instrumental – if an individual is willing to participate in the development of a country they call home, then they are a member of a diaspora.

More critically, we have set out four conceptual areas in this field where the encounter between diaspora and development can generate productive conceptual insights. First, a focus on diaspora reveals the illusion of the way modernity is located in development studies. Second, a focus on diaspora reveals the core historical role of colonies and the slave-trade in the production of the twenty-first-century spaces we call the developed and the developing world. Third, a focus on diaspora reveals the way that the idea of 'belonging' can be treated as an asset to be used by development policy-makers and simultaneously as a moral discourse to underpin a geographical ordering of who belongs where. Finally, we suggest that a focus on diaspora brings broad claims about the securitization and financialization of development into sharp empirical focus. So, in conclusion, it seems that as the diaspora development field has evolved, it has revealed much more about development than about diasporas. Perhaps the time is now right to reverse the question and to ask what forty years of experiments in development practice have taught us about the meaning and character of diasporas?

References

Bakewell O. (2008) '"Keeping them in their place": the ambivalent relationship between development and migration in Africa', *Third World Quarterly*, 29 (7), 1341–58, doi: 10.1080/01436590802386492.

Bracking S. (2016) *The financialisation of power: how financiers rule Africa*, London: Routledge.

Carney J. (1993) *Black rice: the African origins of rice cultivation in the Americas*, Cambridge, MA: Harvard University Press.

Datta, K. (2009) 'Transforming South–North relations? International migration and development', *Geography Compass*, 3 (1), 108–34, doi: 10.1111/j.1749-8198.2008.00190.x.

Datta, K. (2017) '"Mainstreaming" the "alternative"? The financialization of transnational migrant remittances', in R. Martin, and J. Pollard (eds) *Handbook on the geographies of money and finance*, Cheltenham: Edward Elgar, 539–61.

de Haas, H. (2007) 'Turning the tide? Why development will not stop migration', *Development and Change*, 38 (5), 819–41, doi: 10.1111/j.1467-7660.2007.00435.x.

Duffield, M. (2005) 'Human security: linking development and security in an age of terror', in S. Klingebiel (ed.) *New interfaces between security and development: changing concepts and approaches*, Bonn: German Development Institute, 11–38.

Gamlen, A. (2014) 'Diaspora institutions and diaspora governance', *International Migration Review*, 48, S180–S217, doi: 10.1111/imre.12136.

IOM and MPI (2012) *Developing a road map for engaging diasporas in development: a handbook for policymakers and practitioners in home and host countries*, Geneva/Washington: International Organization for Migration/Migration Policy Institute, available at: http://mpi.hifrontier.com/sites/default/files/publications/thediasporahandbook.pdf.

Kibreab, G. (1999) 'Revisiting the debate on people, place, identity and displacement', *Journal of Refugee Studies*, 12 (4), 384–410, doi: 10.1093/jrs/12.4.384.

Kleist, N. and S. Turner (2013) 'Agents of change? Staging and governing diasporas and the African state', *African Studies*, 72 (2), 192–206, doi: 10.1080/00020184.2013.812882.

Levitt P. and D. Lamba-Nieves (2011) 'Social remittances revisited', *Journal of Ethnic and Migration Studies*, 37 (1), 1–22, doi: 10.1080/1369183X.2011.521361.

Lindley, A. and J. Mosley (2014) 'Challenges for the Somali money transfer sector', Rift Valley Institute briefing paper, Nairobi, Kenya, available at: http://riftvalley.net/publication/challenges-somali-money-transfer-sector.

Lopez, S. (2015) *The remittance landscape: the spaces of migration in rural Mexico and urban USA*, Chicago: University of Chicago Press.

McGregor, J. (2008) 'Children and "African values": Zimbabwean professionals in Britain reconfiguring family life', *Environment and Planning* A, 40 (3), 596–614, doi: 10.1068/a38334.

MacRae, M. and M. Wright (2006) 'A model diaspora network: the origin and evolution of globalscot', in Y. Kuznetsov (ed.) *Diaspora networks and international migration of skills*, Washington: World Bank Institute, 201–20.

Mawdsley, E. (2016) 'Development geography II: financialization', *Progress in Human Geography*, online early, doi: 10.1177/0309132516678747.

Mercer, C., B. Page and M. Evans (2008) *Development and the African diaspora: place and the politics of home*, London: Zed.

Mithra, P. (2016) 'Addition by subtraction: how diasporas can boost home-country growth', IMF Direct (blog) available at: https://blog-imfdirect.imf.org/2016/05/18/addition-by-subtraction-how-diasporas-can-boost-home-country-growth/.

Mohan, G. (2002) 'Diaspora and development', in J. Robinson (ed.) *Displacements and development*, Oxford: Oxford University Press, 77–139.

Raghuram P. (2009) 'Which migration, what development? Unsettling the edifice of migration and development', *Population, Space and Place*, 15 (2), 103–17, doi: 10.1002/psp.536.

Ratha, D. and S. Plaza (2016) 'Migration and development a role for the World Bank Group', report available at: http://pubdocs.worldbank.org/en/468881473870347506/Migration-and-Development-Report-Sept2016.pdf.

Sinatti G. and C. Horst (2014) 'Migrants as agents of development: diaspora engagement discourse and practice in Europe', *Ethnicities*, 15 (1), 134–52, doi: 10.1177/1468796814530120.

38
Diasporas and the politics of memory and commemoration

Khatharya Um

If the twentieth century was proclaimed the century of genocide, the twenty-first century is poised to be the century of the globally displaced. According to the United Nations (UN), an estimated 244 million people were living outside their country of birth in 2015, of whom 65.3 million were forcibly displaced, including 21.3 million refugees. That estimate does not include the 10 million stateless people (UNHCR 2015). The numbers of refugees and of the largely unrecognized internally displaced are the highest since the Second World War (UN 2017). This global phenomenon underscores the intellectual and empirical importance of diaspora and the overarching concerns of place, memory and belonging as critical subjects of inquiry. With intensifying interests in migration and the need for more robust theorization, the concept of diaspora has been unmoored from the earlier privileging of the Jewish experience to include various migratory experiences and communities. The increased conceptual elasticity amplifies its explanatory power as it potentially dilutes it.

In this chapter, I examine the relationship between diasporization and memory works, with a particular focus on post-conflict diasporic communities, not as a negation of the applicability to other forms of diaspora, but as an example of one particular form of diaspora. In so doing, I interrogate the conceptual links between diaspora, exile and the politics and performances of remembering as they are informed by the relationships between the sending and receiving countries and the diaspora, and among diasporic communities. If politics is a catalyst of mass dislocation, it also influences remembering and memorialization, a factor that is often lost in the uncritical view of diaspora as a space of subversion and liberation (Mitchell 1997).

Diaspora, forced migration and exile

Theoretical turns and conceptual expansion notwithstanding, discourses about diaspora continue to pivot around some key features, namely dislocation from the ancestral homeland, enduring attachment to the originary source and a longing for return, whether actual, virtual or imagined.[1] In critical ways, these notions are interrelated. The circumstances of displacement inform the ways in which diasporas think about, remember and engage with the ancestral homeland, as well as the possibilities and constraints in negotiating that relationship. They also compel a shift from the unitary view of diaspora towards a more nuanced understanding of the complexities of communities, and the ways in which those complexities inform our understanding of the textures, politics, ethics and economics of diasporic remembering. Without abandoning the potentiality for generalization, historicizing diaspora allows us to recognize the varied responses of the globally dispersed to their conditions of displacement, and their desire for and notions of re-emplacement. It is thus that Clifford argues for the analytic importance of 'rooting and routing' diaspora discourses in 'specific maps/histories' (Carter 2005: 55).

The original conceptualization of diaspora as 'born of catastrophe' (Tölölyan 2007) provides a particularly useful frame for thinking about conflict-engendered diasporas and the politics of remembering. For the forcibly dispersed, migration is a response to the perceived danger of remaining in place, rather than the intrinsic 'pull' of the place of destination. It is, as such, more characteristic of flight from, rather than an intentional movement towards, a chosen country of resettlement. For most, this forced severance accentuates the longing for reconnection. As it is with other migrant communities, conflict-engendered diaspora also reflects internal diversity that is often masked by the foregrounding of the shared experience of forced uprooting. Even under conditions of duress, the experience of flight may differ depending on a host of factors. Some diasporas are able to anticipate the journey, even if only psychologically; for others, departure is abrupt, the movement incremental, and with little certainty about the final destination or the prospect of return. How rupturing that passage is contributes to the liminality that locks diasporas in the backward gaze towards the past.

Differences aside, forced diasporas share the experience of violent severance from the homeland and a sense of 'unfinished business' that such dislocation entails. All things undone, unsaid, unlived constitute diasporic hauntings that nurture the longing for all that the homeland represents, and the hoped-for return. Particularly when the prospect of such eventuality appears bleak because of continued war or disavowal, displacement is tantamount to exile. For those diasporas, the collective identity is informed not only by forced dispersal but also by the denied possibility of return.

Diasporic relationships with home/land/regime

These political and experiential contexts shape diasporas' relationship with the homeland from which they were violently uprooted. Bifurcated by dispersal, memory serves as a vehicle through which the nation is made whole. Inhabiting the space of discontinuities, diasporas, through remembering, can re-insert themselves into familiar frames that reaffirm their histories, genealogies, identities and, above all, sense of belonging. Memory thus is a salve against the ravages of exile. For those disenfranchised in both sending and receiving contexts, it presents a different temporality in which the past, edited and filtered, is not lost but inhabits the present and, in the process, makes the latter more habitable.

Elsewhere a solace, memory can also be a source of pain. Trauma is relived through remembering, with 'thinking too much' identified as one of the leading causes of illness among elderly survivor-refugees of the Cambodian genocide (Handelman and Yeo 1996). For many, the wounding of loss remembered is only matched by the pain of forgetting. This lived tension between remembering and forgetting is part of the texture of diaspora's exilic condition.

Memories of home also nurture long-distance nationalism and spur transnational activism. Where the traumatic history that engenders displacement involves transgression and threat to nationhood, diasporan preoccupation with the homeland acquires a moral dimension, rooted in the self-embraced sense of obligation to speak and act for the silenced nation; diaspora is a space where politically suppressed memories can be made legible in ways not possible at the source. Long-distance nationalism has fostered diasporas' active engagement in oppositional politics that includes raising and remitting funds for homeland political activities, launching transnational resistance movements, forming governments in exile, and returning to participate in post-war national reconstruction (Smith and Stares 2007; Um 2006). It also manifests in micropolitical acts such as participation in family or village-based projects aimed at restoring institutions and practices that were targets of political destruction.

Cultural production in the diaspora as counter-narration of home and history is equally imbued with political significance. Restoring, preserving and transmitting traditions threatened with irretrievable loss are deemed essential to ensuring the nation's survival, hence deeply political. Heritage and language programmes, ceremonies, festivals and everyday socialities are institutionalized practices through which home is remembered and memorialized as acts of resistance against historical erasure. Viewed through the optic of possibilities rather than of bare life, the liminal space of the refugee camp becomes a site of cultural revival and reinvention. There, a new generation of Afghans was retrained in the traditional art of rug weaving, and a surviving handful of Cambodian artists came together to rescue, essentially from memory, the repertoire of centuries-old classical dance from genocidal extinction. In camp markets and eateries in the diaspora, music and food of 'before' are re-introduced in defiance of time, distance and politics. In that sense, Carter (2005: 54) is correct to note that 'diasporas can also reproduce the essentialized notions of place and identity that they are supposed to transgress', something that is often overlooked in the literature. As oppositional positioning, these interventions become part of post-conflict contestations over questions of 'authenticity', loyalty, and ultimately, claims to belonging.

In the interstices of nation-states and the potently liminal cyberspace, technology, with its increasing affordability, is an important vehicle for transnational community-building and engagement, not only between the diaspora and the source country but also among diasporic communities. Teleconferencing and electronic mails facilitate multisite planning and coordination of events and commemorations, while camcorders and mobile phones make it possible for families and communities that are widely dispersed to participate translocally and, in so doing, to affirm their communal identity; 'people of diaspora do not root in place but in each other' (van Gelder 2008: 58). Within the fraught space of transnational politics, the anonymity of the internet mediates against fear of reprisal, and makes political discourse more inclusive. In the absence of physical space, the virtual space of the internet is invaluable for sharing, archiving and transmitting ideas and memories, and serves, especially for younger-generation diasporas, as an indispensible source of information that compensates for the disrupted narratives in the homes.

Diasporic ambivalence

Where history involves an implosion of violence in the form of civil war, ethnic conflict, occupation or self-implicating 'autogenocide', as in the case of Cambodia, diaspora's position towards the homeland is also one of ambivalence (Um 2015). It is of this sense of alienation that Edward Said (1999: 142) wrote:

> Even now the unreconciled duality I feel about the place, its intricate wrenching, tearing, sorrowful loss as exemplified in so many distorted lives, including mine, and its status as an admirable country for them (but of course not for us), always gives me pain.

This ambivalence is also registered among diasporas who are resettled in countries that are implicated in their history of displacement, be it through sponsored war or outright colonization. The 'roots and routes' of diasporic crossing through transitory and permanent places of resettlement are more often than not charted by histories of conquest and ruination, mapped onto the nexus of empire, militarization and refugee-making. These histories of entanglement, tension and contradiction complicate diasporas' relationship with their host land, for 'rescue' in fact is from the rescuer's manufactured rubbles, and the gift of freedom is wrapped in the shroud of historical haunting.

For many forced diasporas, dislocation from the homeland is reinforced by the sense of non-belonging that they feel in the country of resettlement, of being 'of no place', which Bourdieu refers to as *atopos*. Parades held by diasporic groups are ways of not only remembering home but also asserting and making visible their presence in the place of resettlement. It is this alienation of an exilic life lived on the periphery of both nation-states and societies that compels the search for belonging in multiple places, and influences – even distorts – the way the past is remembered. In that sense, the claim to belonging elsewhere, even to a time 'before', helps deflect from the denied belonging in the here and now.

With these entangled and conflicted relationships, understanding of diasporas' engagement with the homeland calls for a decoupling of multiple notions – of home and land, and country and regime. Arguing that distinctions must be made between regime and people, engagement, for some diasporas, is a moral obligation to the nation that is similarly victimized by a regime that bears no accountability to its people, at home or abroad; for others, engagement is complicitous. Likewise, homeland can be further deconstructed to separate the notion of 'home' that may be altered by time and politics, from the 'land', the place of one's ancestral graves to which one remains affectively bound. In that sense, diasporic attachment is in fact to a place that has been made into a 'home' by memories that are sensory, physical, topographical – the mountains, the family *stupas*, or the scent of a new harvest. Even when the country's landscape has been scarred by mass graves, there is a permanency that resists and lives in the diasporic imaginary.

The texture of diaspora

Just as it is important to deconstruct critical concepts and to contest prevailing assumptions about diasporan politics and orientation, it is also important to deconstruct the often-assumed homogeneity of diasporic communities, and to put analytic attention on the internal diversity that exists. Like all communities, forced diasporas are also differentiated along lines of class, gender, generation, religious and ethnic affiliations, timing and experiences of migration and resettlement, and ideology. These internal differences shape diasporas' understanding of their objective conditions, inform their politics, positionalities *vis-à-vis* the sending and receiving regimes, and memories of and relationships with the homeland. Different segments of the community may have different resettlement experiences that buffer against the nostalgic pull of the past, dull the longing for return, and determine the prospect and form of return. The notion of 'homeland' itself is complicated by protracted encampment that produces a whole generation born neither at the originary source nor at the final destination, but in the liminal space of first country asylum. These factors mediate the notions of the homeland, which as Cohen (2007) contends, could vary from 'solid, ductile and liquid'. Diasporic longing thus is not necessarily conceived of in terms of *re-emplacement* but of *orientation*, a turning towards home as a referent, one that may be mediated, diluted or transformed into virtuality depending on temporal, political, demographic and generational shifts.

While diasporic spatiality does extend beyond the confines of the nation-state to include spaces and places in betwixt, diaspora is not unbounded. Diasporic imaginary may be translocal or even virtual, but is also anchored in locality. It is thus that to discount the re-territorializing elements of diasporic practices (Carter 2005: 55) is to overlook the politicized and historicized identities of diasporas that undergird their lived realities. In the negotiations with sending and receiving regimes, diaspora has the potential to be, but is not necessarily, a critique of the nation-state. Rather than contesting or subverting them, diaspora may reinforce or affirm nation-state politics; it may even serve to extend the reach of the nation-state, thus undermining its potential as a space of resistance and hope.

The im/possibility of diasporic remembering

The ability of diasporas to commemorate their histories and collective experiences depends on the triangulated relations between diasporas and the sending and receiving governments, and on the broader political environment. In post-conflict situations, politics intrude, and remembering and commemoration can become a site of affirmation and reconciliation, or of contestation and suppression. Where diasporas' political agendas are aligned with those of the sending country or interested states, commemorative activities are applauded, endorsed, and even financially supported. Where they counter hegemonic discourse, they are vulnerable to the vagaries of national and international politics; while the European Union officially acknowledges the Srebrenica massacre, the Association of Southeast Asian Nations remains silent on the Cambodian genocide.

Like homeland regimes, host land politics also determine the possibilities and limits of diasporic engagement. Where there is alignment of interests, host regimes can amplify forced diasporas' narratives of persecution and loss, if only to shore up their ideology of rescue. Where diasporic activities are perceived as threatening bilateral relations between sending and receiving countries, they are denied public endorsement, and may even be blatantly suppressed, as in the case of the destruction of the boat people memorials by the Malaysian and Indonesian governments, purportedly under pressure from Vietnam (Carruthers and Huynh-Beattie 2011).

Where the diaspora is a locus of homeland politics, ideological tension also registers within the diaspora community. With different and divergent memories, what and how to remember, whether something is to be celebrated or mourned, and who can partake in these commemorative acts can be issues of contention in the diaspora. The recent controversy over the participation of Cambodia's Prime Minister Hun Sen's son in a commemorative event in California points to the laden significance of these performances. In the same vein, remembering and commemoration are also made possible or constrained by endogenous factors, particularly the lack of social and political capital, and proximity to power. The privileging of certain histories and the unequal place that different genocides command in the American consciousness is a manifestation of power differentials; it took over four decades before an exhibit on the Cambodian genocide was installed in the Holocaust museum in Washington. Poverty, decimation of the educated class and corresponding lack of leadership and access to the power structure are features of the political economy of memory works that impact the ability of communities to negotiate and secure the necessary space, both physical and political, for public commemoration. Lack of facility with the English language and limited access to literacy further define how and where memories can be produced and disseminated. Four decades in the aftermath, the production and circulation of memoirs and other commemorative writing by first-generation Southeast Asian refugees remain scarce and largely confined to ethnic *milieux*. These are the 'unequal conditions (that) produce unequal memories' (D'Souza 2016), as Viet Nguyen contends. Despite genocidal loss, the magnitude of destruction levied on Cambodia by the United States, and the long-standing presence of the refugee population, only one single-room memorial currently exists for Cambodians in the diaspora. None exists for Rwandans.

Where spaces for public acknowledgement are absent or delimited, remembering is relegated to other realms. With limited access to literacy, Hmong women embroider their war memories onto story cloths, while old Cambodian folk songs of fanciful journeys are re-mastered with new narratives of displacement. Memories are also narrated through bodily practices – in startles and stutters, in fragments, spontaneous eruptions and ellipses during family conversations. They are registered in quotidian practices and rituals – the lighting of incense on ancestral altars or offering of food during *Pchum Ben*, with significance legible only through certain cultural and experiential optics. They are in the silences that hover in the backdrop of refugee homes. As King-Kok Cheung (1993) eloquently reminds us, silence is articulate and 'can speak many tongues, varying from culture to culture', something that is obscured by Western valorization of speech. It is a silence that is not always about traumatic suppression, but also about agency and resistance, about each generation's desire to shield against and repair the continued fraying of the social fabric. It is its own intervention between disclosure and non-disclosure.

Commemoration and healing

Towards what ends do we commemorate? For many forced diasporas, the historical traumas that engender their uprooting are exacerbated by the absence of acknowledgement. All wars, as Viet Nguyen (2016: 4) observes, 'are fought twice, the first time on the battlefield, the second time in memory'. Commemoration is a form of accountability that makes visible experiences, memories and histories that otherwise would be lost. It is a resistance against historical erasure of self and identity, and in that sense is also reparative. Rituals performed free not only the dead but also the living. This is particularly important for communities in which loss takes the form of disappearances; the denial of the corporality of loss keeps survivors in a liminal state of impaired mourning. In that context, rituals do the 'work of getting the dead to die in us' (Baptist 2010: 305). Processes and practices of commemoration also serve to affirm the collective bind and sense of belonging, even if it is belonging to a community that does not belong.

With the politicization of memory, the relationship between healing and commemoration at the collective level is complicated by the questions of reconciliation and justice. In some post-conflict moments, the emphasis is shifted from remembering and accountability to the prevention of the return to war. In ethnically and politically pluralistic communities in the diaspora, as it is in the source countries, remembering, it is argued, could potential prick open 'old wounds' and undermine internal cohesion and stability. Commemoration is thereby 'sanitized' of controversy; date change and abstraction of commemorative aesthetics are some of the negotiations that diasporas undertake to depoliticize memory, even at the risk of flattening it.

While the relationship between commemoration and healing is not predetermined and may be so individualized as to resist theorization, it is possible to contend, nevertheless, that at the very least, for healing to be possible, commemoration must be culturally legible and accessible to those whose memories are being commemorated. Given the internal diversity and power differentials within the diaspora, public commemoration may, in fact, result in the unequal acknowledgement of memories.

Temporality

In thinking about memory and community, it is imperative to think of shifts and temporalities. The relationship of diasporas with the homeland is not static but reflective of political, generational and other shifts that impact memory works. Time and generational distance destabilize memories of the homeland, that which defines diaspora. Linguistic loss and cultural disconnect interrupt memory transmission, rendering commemorations into performances evacuated of meaning. What is inherited is translated, negotiated, reframed and contested as the younger generations work to fit the past into their present. In the same vein, political changes also impact memory and memorialization. With historical turns such as the collapse of the Soviet empire or the fall of the Suharto regime in Indonesia, change can chisel a new political topography that allows for buried memories to surface. In other instances, one form of subjugation merely replaces another, leaving certain memories buried in the crypt of history.

Conclusion

While scholarly attention on memory has increased, relatively few works have looked at it in the context of migration; where memory is tied to the concept of travel, it is trans-temporal rather than trans-spatial. For diasporas, however, memory negotiations take place across temporalities and geopolitical spatialities. How then do we understand memories in exile and memories that have been exiled? If it is as Pierre Nora contends that memory requires emplacement, how might forced uprooting affect the way we remember the past and the importance that we place on remembering? How do memories inform exile, and how does exile shape our notions of the past, and our place and identity as a people? In post-conflict moments, these issues are amplified, for the fear of erasure is not rooted simply in the physical dislocation but also in the multidimensional ravages engendered by war, occupation and mass death. Remembering thus is not reducible to nostalgia but equally compelled by the need to archive and honour. In this age of unprecedented mass movement, the earlier preoccupation with how societies remember (Connerton 1989) necessarily yields to the broader question of how nations, bifurcated by dispersal, remember, and why.

Note

1 For conceptual discussions of diaspora, see Brah (1996), Clifford (1994), Cohen (2008), Safran (1991) and Tölölyan (2007).

References

Baptist, K. W. (2010) 'Diaspora: death without a landscape', *Mortality*, 15 (4), 294–307, doi: 10.1080/1357 6275.2010.513162.
Brah, A. (1996) *Cartographies of diaspora: contesting identities*, London: Routledge.
Carruthers, A. and B. Huynh-Beattie (2011) 'Dark tourism, diasporic memory and disappeared history: the contested meaning of the former Indochinese refugee camp at Pulau Galang', in Yuk Wah Chan (ed.) *The Chinese/Vietnamese diaspora: revisiting the boat people*, New York: Routledge, 147–60.
Carter, S. (2005) 'The geopolitics of diaspora', *Area*, 37 (1), 54–63, doi: 10.1111/j.1475-4762.2005.00601.x.
Cheung, K.-K. (1993) *Articulate silences: Hisaye Yamamoto, Maxine Hong Kingston*, Joy Kogawa, Ithaca: Cornell University Press.
Clifford, J. (1994) 'Diasporas', *Cultural Anthropology*, 9 (3), 302–38, doi: 10.1525/can.1994.9.3.02a00040.
Cohen, R. (2007) 'Solid, ductile and liquid: the changing role of homeland and home in diaspora', QEH working papers 156, available at: www3.qeh.ox.ac.uk/pdf/qehwp/qehwps156.pdf.
Cohen, R. (2008) *Global diasporas*, Abingdon: Routledge.
Connerton, P. (1989) *How societies remember*, Cambridge: Cambridge University Press.
D'Souza, D. (2016) 'Echoes of tragedy', *Psychology Today*, 7 May, available at: www.psychologytoday.com/articles/201605/echoes-tragedy.
Handelman, L. and G. Yeo (1996) 'Using explanatory models to understand chronic symptoms of Cambodian refugees', *Family Medicine*, 28 (4), 271–6.
Mitchell, K. (1997) 'Different diasporas and the hype of hybridity', *Environment and Planning D: Society and Space*, 15 (5), 533–53, doi: 10.1068/d150533.
Nguyen, V. T. (2016) *Nothing ever dies: Vietnam and the memory of war*, Cambridge, MA: Harvard University Press.

Safran, W. (1991) 'Diasporas in modern societies: myths of homeland and return', *Diaspora*, 1 (1) 83–99, doi: 10.1353/dsp.1991.0004.
Said, E. (1999) *Out of place*, New York: Vintage.
Smith, H. and P. Stares (eds) (2007) *Diasporas in conflict: peace-makers or peace-wreckers?*, New York: United Nations University Press.
Tölölyan, K. (2007) 'The contemporary discourse of diaspora studies', *Comparative Studies of South Asia, Africa and the Middle East*, 27 (3), 647–55, doi:10.1215/1089201x-2007-040.
Um, K. (2006) 'Diasporic nationalism, citizenship, and post-war reconstruction', *Refuge*, 23 (2), 8–19, available at: http://refuge.journals.yorku.ca/index.php/refuge/article/view/21350/20020.
Um, K. (2015) *From the land of shadows: war, revolution, and the making of the Cambodian diaspora*, New York: New York University Press.
UN (2017) 'Take action in response to the refugee crisis', United Nations webpage, available at: www.unglobalcompact.org/take-action/action/refugee-crisis.
UNHCR (2015) 'Global trends', available at: www.unhcr.org/global-trends-2015.html.
van Gelder, L. (2008) *Weaving a way home*, Ann Arbor: University of Michigan Press.

39
At home in diaspora
The Babylonian Talmud as diasporist manifesto

Daniel Boyarin

> It has not yet been sufficiently proven that the preservation of the national character of the Jews outside of their land is connected with the Land of the Jews. On the contrary, in the ancient sources there appear clear echoes of a strong feeling of intellectual and religious non-dependence and independence [תואמצעו אי תלו] which was dominant among the Babylonian Jews.
>
> *(Dimitrovsky 1986: 259)*

In this chapter, I propose to show how the Talmud imagines its own community, how it projects its being in Babylonia, its *raison d'être*, the status of Palestine, and its own status *vis-à-vis* Palestine as well. I will argue that multiple passages in the Talmud add up to a virtual diasporist manifesto, acknowledging that there are other much less sanguine voices to be found also. This controversy is thematized in the Talmud, in the practice and discourse of different Rabbis. Though, at first sight, a study of the Babylonian Talmud may appear a *recherché* exercise, it has profound implications, totally reversing the conventional Zionist narrative that the Jewish diaspora was, and is, a place of exile and loss. Rather, as I show in this chapter, it was imagined by Jews as the locus of a new beginning, even a new Zion. Although this study is in the nature of a case study (thus explicitly violating the brief I was given), I hope that the case is sufficiently evocative so as to be useful nonetheless in re-imagining the possibilities of 'diaspora' as a theoretical concept and diaspora as a form of life.

The Babylonian Talmud is, I propose, the *diasporist* text of the Rabbis, *par excellence*. The Babylonian Talmud itself produces thematically the image of diaspora that would ultimately project it as the text of diaspora throughout later Jewish history. Moulie Vidas (2008: 326) has recently pointed out how the Talmud itself theorizes the diaspora:

> Immigration to Palestine becomes unnecessary as the Talmud legitimizes exile; the hegemony of the Land of Israel as the ultimate destination for Jews becomes irrelevant. The action the Bavli takes with respect to geographical matters is similar to the one it took with respect to ethnic matters: it decentralizes the Jewish world not only genealogically but geographically by allowing multiple communities.

The Babylonian Talmud itself thematizes this perspective in more than one way. Several times we hear tell of a particularly important synagogue in the town of Nehard'ea, called by the somewhat bizarre name, בי כנישתא דשף ויתיב, 'the synagogue that slid and settled.' Already by the early Byzantine era if not before that time, an etymology had been offered for the name of this highly important synagogue, namely that it had slid from its place in Palestine and settled in Babylonia (Lewin 1921: 72–3). With the exile of Jeconia in 597 bc, the Jews took with them stones and sand from the destroyed Temple in Jerusalem and used them to build their synagogue in Babylonia. According, moreover, to the Talmud itself, this synagogue was where the Shekhina dwelled in Babylonia. Babylon replaces Palestine, and this synagogue is the new Temple, albeit a reduced one, a מקדש מעט, which, as Elchanan Reiner is a real entity and not a mere device. A striking text from the late gaonic[1] period evinces this point in the context of an argument of one of the last gaonim for maintaining the absolute primacy of the Babylonian centre over-against the new ones in the West:[2]

> Several matters support this: The legacy of the parents is the merit of the ancestors [the parents leave to their children their own merits; that is, my illustrious ancestors render me worthy to be the leader of the Jews worldwide]. And also the place [where it is said] that the Shekhina removed to Babylonia provides support, as it is said: 'For your sake, I sent to Babylonia' [Isaiah 43: 14], and the Sages interpreted: Beloved is Israel that in any place to which they are removed, the Shekhina is with them. And now she is in Babylonia, standing on her foundation, as it is written: Oh Zion save yourself, O dweller with the daughter of Babylon [Zach. 2:7=11 in Hebrew]. Behold the Talmud testifies to you [when it asks]: In Babylon, where is the Shekhina? Rav said in the Synagogue of Hutzal, and Shmuel said in the synagogue that slid and settled in Nehardea. And don't say it is [only] here or [only] there but sometimes it is here and sometimes there. And there [in Babylon] the Yeshiva is established to augment the Shekhina. They bless always also in the synagogue the Prophet Ezekiel and Daniel the greatly beloved and Ezra the Scribe and Barukh ben Neria and the rest of the Sages of the Talmud [all Babylonian Jewish luminaries], the memory of all of them for a blessing.[3]

One of the last of the *geonim*,[4] the leaders of the Babylonian yeshivas, defends here the proposition that Babylonia is the Holy Land, indeed that the Divine Presence, the Shekhina, came with them to Babylonia, settled there (like the synagogue itself) and established it as a new Holy Land.[5] Zion is now in Babylon, and detaching from Babylon is detaching from the Holy Land. The proof from Zachariah is brilliant. Simply from the fact that 'Zion' personified as the Shekhina is called 'dweller with the Daughter of Babylon', we see that the Shekhina moved with the Jews to that place and dwelt there and made it Holy. He finishes off his peroration by listing a selection of Babylonian Jewish holy men going back to Ezekiel and Jeremiah's scribe and forward to the men who produced the Talmud. In indicating that the Shekhina, the Divine Presence in the world, came with them to Babylonia and established herself in a holy place there, the Talmud and its Babylonian rabbinic tradents[6] are reorienting our sense of what a diaspora is, providing us with a new conception of diaspora, transforming it in our conceptual apparatus from a contrast between centre and periphery, from homeland and exile, to a process of the establishment of ever-new centres and locating it in cultural practice – not ancient trauma or loss. It is the study – the Yeshiva – that augments the presence of the Shekhina in Babylonia. The legend of the building of this synagogue out of actual sand and stones brought by Jeconia from the Temple in Jerusalem renders graphic the status of this building as new Temple.

In a brilliant and riveting analysis of this tradition, as well as another one concerning the synagogue of Ezekiel, Elchanan Reiner has shown that the ideological point of these stories is to separate the founding of the Babylonian Jewish community entirely from the destruction of the Temple. Jeconia the King was captured and brought to Babylonia a decade before the destruction, kept in prison until after the destruction, and then released in Babylonia. Replacing the narrative significance of the destruction of the Temple, we have instead, as Reiner demonstrates, a founding legend in which the trauma of the captivity is separated from that Palestinian trauma and redeemed, as it were, by the release of the King, who then founds the community in Babylonia, together with the Prophet Ezekiel, King and High Priest. The synagogue in Babylonia is thus a new Temple, and the community a new Land of Israel (Reiner 2013).

Prior conceptions

In an influential programmatic essay, Richard Marienstras has distinguished between modern notions of diaspora and that of the Jews:

> But it is only recently that this term has come to describe minority groups whose awareness of their identity is defined by a relationship, territorially discontinuous, with a group settled "elsewhere" (for example: the Chinese diaspora, the Corsican diaspora in Mainland France etc.).

So far, so good, but then he goes on to explicitly exclude the Jews from such definitions: 'Historically the term described the dispersed Jewish communities, that is those not living in *Eretz Israel*.' True enough, but why, then, does he assert that '"Diaspora" presumes that there exists an independent or heavily populated Jewish political centre'? (Marienstras 1989: 120). After all, for most of Jewish history, that is simply and inarguably not the case. Was there no Jewish diaspora from 63 BC until AD 1948? My contention is that the Babylonian Talmud falsifies the very ways that the Jewish diaspora is taken as a positive or negative ideal type of diaspora.

Again, Robin Cohen – along with most authorities – continues to stress the allegedly traumatic nature of a 'victim diaspora', using the Jewish experience as paradigmatic. In writing of the addition of the dispersion of Africans, Armenians and Irish to the Jews in the category of 'victim diaspora', he insists:

> These scarring historical calamities – Babylon for the Jews, slavery for the Africans, massacres and forced displacement for the Armenians, famine for the Irish and the formation of the state of Israel for the Palestinians – lend a particular colouring to these five diasporas . . . their victim origin is either self-affirmed or accepted by outside observers as determining their *predominant* character.
>
> *(Cohen 2008: 4)*

Cohen maintains that whatever criteria we wish to assert for an account of the 'common features of a diaspora', '*the traumatic dispersal from an original homeland* and *the salience of the homeland in the collective memory of a forcibly dispersed group*' (Cohen 2008: 4, original emphasis) are *sine qua nons*.[7] This is, one might suggest, the lachrymose version of what makes a diaspora, precisely that which I have set out to displace here (on this, see also Vertovec 1997: 293). Cohen does seek to supplement this lugubrious view but does not go far enough, in my opinion, in displacing it.

I am not, of course, claiming that such a representation is not to be found among historical Jews. Perhaps the most salient literary model for this depiction of the meaning of diaspora is Psalm 137:

1: By the rivers of Babylon, there we sat down, yea, we wept, when we remembered Zion. 2: We hanged our harps upon the willows in the midst thereof. 3: For there they that carried us away captive required of us a song; and they that wasted us required of us mirth, saying, Sing us one of the songs of Zion. 4: How shall we sing the LORD's song in a strange land? 5: If I forget thee, O Jerusalem, let my right hand forget her cunning. 6: If I do not remember thee, let my tongue cleave to the roof of my mouth; if I prefer not Jerusalem above my chief joy. 7: Remember, O LORD, the children of Edom in the day of Jerusalem; who said, Rase it, rase it, even to the foundation thereof. 8: O daughter of Babylon, who art to be destroyed; happy shall he be, that rewardeth thee as thou hast served us. Happy shall he be, that taketh and dasheth thy little ones against the stones.

This text, it could be said, has been made definitive of modern Zionist understanding of diaspora (including, in at least some quarters, the bloodthirsty ending, especially on the day known today in Israel and other Zionist circles as 'the Day of Jerusalem').[8]

Representations within the diaspora

While this entirely negative representation of dwelling in Babylon certainly holds for certain times and places for the Babylonian diaspora of the Jews, and, of course, for multiple later Jewish diasporas as well, it is hardly the case that this is a universal self-understanding by the Babylonian Jews through the millennium (and more) of their life there, nor has it been the experience of many other Jewish communities.

As Isaiah Gafni (2002: 225) has remarked:

> In rabbinic eyes, however, past and present tend to coalesce, and thus in time the rabbinic community of Babylonia would point to those earliest biblical days of captivity as the first links in an unbroken chain of enhanced Jewish existence "by the rivers of Babylon," claiming that all the requisite trappings of a vital and self-sufficient community were transported from Jerusalem to Babylon even prior to the destruction of the First Temple.

As such, a sense of trauma or even discomfort is falsified as a necessary condition for the existence of a diaspora by the very historical experience of the putatively prototype diaspora, that of the Jews, as a set of universally applicable criteria for the identification of diasporas or the definition of diaspora as a thing. Surely by the time of the Babylonian Talmud, the lachrymosity was a thing of the past.

Even while recognizing that Jews had been sent into exile in Babylon, the Talmud can figure that occurrence as a positive event and even as a homecoming in the following remarkable text (bPesahim 87b):

> And Rabbi El'azar[9] said: The Holy Blessed One only exiled Israel among the nations in order that converts will be added to them, As it says, 'And I sowed her in the land' [Hosea 2:]. Does a person ever sow a peck except to harvest several bushels?

We see here Rabbi El'azar focusing not on the scattering but on the sowing of seeds, the productivity that issues from the scattering of Israel among the nations. This rabbinic view is much closer in sensibility to the views of Jews such as Josephus and Philo who consider the purpose of the diaspora of the Jews not as punishment and not as suffering, but to fulfil their universal task of spreading the knowledge of the One God throughout the world. Babylonia can even be described as the 'motherland' of the Jews:

> Rabbi Ḥanina says, 'It is because their language [Aramaic] is close to the language of Torah [and therefore good for the study thereof].' Rabbi Yoḥanan says, 'Because he sent them to the House of their Mother. Its exemplum is of a man who becomes angry at his wife, to where does he send her? To the house of her mother' . . . 'Ulla said 'it was in order that they will eat dates and be busy with Torah.'

The first speaker in this sequence remarks on the great advantage of Babylonia, namely their Semitic speech, which, since it is close to the Hebrew of Torah, promotes the study of Torah. (Not so incidentally, it is this linguistic fact which made it most consequent for the Babylonian Jews and not the Greek-speaking Jews of the Eastern Roman Empire to 'diasporize' with the Palestinian Rabbis.)[10] The most amazing of all of these explanations for the choice of Babylon as the place of Jewish Exile is, however, Rabbi Yoḥanan who turns the 'Exile' into Babylon into a homecoming to their motherland, the land, after all, from which Abraham is commanded to 'Go forth from your land to the land that I will show you!' The entire notion of 'diaspora' as the act of forced dispersion from a single homeland is exploded by the Talmud at this moment (and by a Palestinian speaker, nay the leader of the Palestinian Rabbis in his day). Indeed, as Isaiah Gafni (1997: 63) points out, this statement reads almost as if it is 'embracing of what is usually considered a uniquely Hellenistic idea, namely that Israel, like other ethnic groups, have a dual homeland (δευτέρα πατρίς).'

Babylonia is portrayed here not only as a second homeland but as the original homeland from which they have come to Palestine! The concepts of homeland and Holy Land are thus, at least for these Rabbis, not coterminous (see Rubenstein 2004). Far from being sent into an oppressive situation, the Jews were brought to a refuge in the place in which they would feel most at home, returning home, as it were, owing to their ancient roots and cultural ties with that place (Gafni 2002: 224).[11] There is, to be sure, ambivalence signified here as well. Even though Babylonia is pictured repeatedly as a place of refuge here, nonetheless, there *is* a sense of exile from the Holy Land that is encoded as well. A bride being sent to her mother's house is, of course, the sign of the at least temporary dissolution of a marriage. This does not mean, then, that the Jews abandoned the ancient hope to be restored to the Holy Land, as well, but, as so poignantly evoked, especially by Jewish liturgy, this was an eschatological hope, for the end of times, for the whole world, and not even a structuring principle for life in the here and now. For the present time, despite having been exiled from the husband's house, we are at home in the mother's safe refuge and warm embrace. There is an amusing doubling of this ambiguity in the statement of

> Ulla too, for after having praised the abundance of Babylonia and the possibility of studying Torah owing to the abundance of food in the form of dates, he goes on to remark that he spent the better part of his first night there on the toilet and wonders how they manage to study Torah at all there! But, nonetheless, asserts the Talmud: 'We [in Babylonia] have made ourselves the equal of Palestine [Gittin 6a].

There are, however, two Talmuds; one that we call Palestinian (Hebrew Yerushalmi, both an anachronism and an anatopism), the other the Babylonian, or Bavli. Each of the Talmuds is diasporic with respect to the other, in the sense that it is made up from materials from its own place and from the place of the others, thus both demonstrating and constructing the diaspora of which I speak. The Babylonian Talmud was, as its name implies, composed by Rabbis who lived in southern Mesopotamia in the province of Āsōristān of the Sasanian Empire.[12] The Palestinian Talmud was formed in that province (Syria Palaestina) of the Roman Empire. Needless to say, perhaps, the Palestinian Sages did not willingly accept the decentring of the Holy Land. There is a highly evocative text in the Palestinian Talmud (Yerushalmi) in which that resistance is made manifest. The context is precisely of a Sage who has left Palestine owing to the persecutions of the Romans to set up a fully independent-functioning rabbinic polity on the banks of the Pakod River in Babylonia:

> Ḥananiah the nephew of Rabbi Yehoshua intercalated (added a leap month to the year to keep the Solar and Lunar calendars synchronized) outside of the Land. Rabbi (Yehuda the Nassi) sent him three letters with Rabbi Yitzḥak and Rabbi Natan: In the first, he wrote 'To his Holiness Rabbi Hannaniah.' In the second, he wrote, 'The kids that you left behind have become billy-goats.' In the third, he wrote, 'If you don't accept [our authority], go out in the wilderness of the bramble, and you be the slaughterer and Neḥunion the Priest who sprinkles the blood.'[13] He read the first and honoured them; the second and honoured them. When he read the third, he wished to discredit them. They said to him, 'You cannot, as you have already honoured us!' Rabbi Yitshak stood up and read in the Torah: 'These are the festivals of Ḥananiah the nephew of Rabbi Yehoshua.' They said to him: 'These are Festivals of The Lord.' He said to them, 'That's *our* version.' Rabbi Natan got up and completed [i.e. read the portion from the Prophets]: 'For from Babylon will go out the Torah, and the Word of the Lord from Nehar Paqod!' They said, 'For from Zion will go out the Torah, and the Word of the Lord from Yerushalayim.' He said, 'That's *our* version.' (PT Nedarim 50a).[14]

This brilliant little narrative practically drips with venomous sarcasm. The Rabbi, having left Palestine during a time of Roman persecution, sets himself up to perform the duty of intercalating the calendar in Babylon, which duty had previously an exclusive prerogative of the Nassi's court in Jerusalem. Rabbi Yehuda the Nassi, hearing of this, sends along some tricky letters and tricky messengers to dissuade him from this rebellious act of setting up a new Zion. The third letter contains the kicker, or rather two kickers. First, he is told that if he persists in his 'rebellion', he should go out into the desert and rule over the brambles and thorn bushes, and then he is compared to another Ḥananiah, Onias who built a Temple in Egypt to compete with the Jerusalem one, an incredibly powerful figure of schism. At this point, Ḥananiah tries to discredit the couriers, but cannot as they have already been credited by him. These now press the attack. Sarcastically and mercilessly parodying the verse 'These are the festivals of the Lord', when one is called up to read from the Torah, he reads it: 'These are the Festivals of Ḥananiah.' In other words, he implies, Ḥananiah's calendar rebels against the calendar of the Lord and replaces it with a human one. The people, not quite getting the point, reply, but the verse says 'These are the festivals of the Lord!', to which Rabbi Yitzḥak returns, 'Yes that's what's written in *our* Torah but apparently in yours (you Babylonians) it says, "The festivals of Ḥananiah".'

The trick is repeated when Rabbi Natan reads the portion from the Prophets and recites, 'For from Babylon will go out Torah and the Word of the Lord from Nehar Peqod' (the place in Babylonia where Ḥananiah was sitting). Once again, the people are tricked into supplying the correct reading and receive the same comeuppance. It is, of course, amazing that by the time of the great French German Rabbenu Tam (as mentioned above), the Babylonian, diasporized Torah tradition had so won the field that he could take this sarcastic parody of the verse and appropriate it, entirely unsarcastically, to mean: indeed the Torah goes out from Bari and the

Word of the Lord from Otranto! Moreover, only a few generations later (in the fourteenth century), both appropriating Rabbenu Tam and referring to Rabbenu Tam and his Rhineland fellow Rabbis, a Sephardic Talmud scholar would declaim: 'For out of Zarephat (France) will go out the Torah, and the Word of the Lord from Ashkenaz (the Rhineland).'[15] The very diasporic adventures of the parodic saying itself mirrors the ways that the Babylonia Talmud produces a diasporic and diasporist culture.

Needless to say, therefore, when the Babylonians tell this very same story, its meanings are quite reversed.[16] In that Talmud, the story appears at Berakhot (63 a–b):

> Rav Safra said: Rabbi Abbahu used to relate: When Ḥanina,[17] the nephew of Rabbi Yehoshua went into the exile, he used to intercalate the years and determine the beginning of months outside of the Land, they sent after him two Sages: Rabbi Yose the son of Kiper and the son of Zekharia the son of Kabutal. When he [Ḥanina] saw them, he said to them: Why have you come here? They said: to learn Torah we have come. He declared about them: These men are the giants of their generation and their fathers served in the Temple! . . . He [Ḥanina] would declare something impure and they declared it pure; he would say that something was permitted, and they would say forbidden. He declared of them: These men are worthless and they are *tohu*! They said to him: You have already built; you may not tear down. You have already fenced in; you may not break down the fence. He said to them what is the reason that what I declare impure, you declare pure and what I declare forbidden, you declare permitted. They said to him, because you intercalate years and determine months outside of the Land. He said to them, but didn't Aqiva the son of Yosef [the great Rabbi Aqiva] intercalate years and determine months outside of the Land?! They said to him: Leave Rabbi Aqiva aside, for he had not left behind him in the Land of Israel anyone as great as he was. He [Ḥanina] said: Also I have not left behind me in the Land of Israel as great as I. They said: the kids you have left behind have become billy-goats with horns, and it is they who sent us after you, and they said to us go and say to him in our name. If he obeys it is good, and if not, he will be excommunicated. And say to our brothers in the Exile [that they should reject Ḥanina if he does not obey them]: if they obey it is good, and if not, they should go up to a mountain where Aḥia [their leader] will build an altar, Ḥanina will play the harp, and all will apostatize and say they have no portion in the god of Israel!
>
> All of the people began to low and cry and said: God forbid; we do have a portion in the god of Israel! And why all this fuss [on the part of the Palestinians], because it says 'for from Zion will go out Torah and the word of the Lord from Jerusalem!'.

We can see that the story is the same story but it has been subtly manipulated in its transfer from Palestinian to the Babylonian Talmud. The Palestinians still 'win', as it were, but a crucial ideological difference is inscribed. The crux is in the phrase: 'The kids that you left behind have become billy-goats.' In the Palestinian Talmud, this is a compliment to Rabbi Ḥannaniah: those young pupils whom you trained have become great Talmud scholars, which Rabbi Ḥannaniah accepts as a compliment and then realizes that this means that he has approbated these very hostile emissaries. In the Babylonian Talmud's version, it means something quite else. Now it is a contest of where the greater Torah-scholars are to be found, in Babylonia or in Palestine, and the emissaries from Palestine are made to claim that those young students whom he left behind there have become great scholars and, therefore, his claim to be able to intercalate in Babylonia (as the greatest scholar in the world) is invalid. Now the ideological point is that the Palestinians are made here to admit, as it were, that should it be the case that the greater

Talmudic scholarship is, indeed, in Babylonia, then Babylonia is now the new Zion (*Ṣiyyon*), the place where Torah study is excellent (*meṣuyyan*), just as the Babylonian Rabbis have claimed in many of the texts that I have cited in this chapter, while according to the Palestinian Talmud's version of the story, Palestine is always and forever the only Holy Land and sole centre of authority: 'For from Zion will go out Torah and the word of the Lord from Jerusalem' – no metaphors, no transfers, no diaspora.

Editorial note

The notes and references in this chapter reflect Talmudic conventions.

Notes

1 Geonim [ge'onim] (also transliterated 'gaonim') were the presidents of the two great Babylonian, Talmudic Academies of Sura and Pumbedita, in the Abbasid Caliphate, and were the generally accepted spiritual leaders of the Jewish community worldwide from the eighth until the early eleventh century.
2 See Boyarin (2015: chapter 1) for documentation on the move of Talmudic centres from East (Babylonia) to West (Europe and North Africa).
3 This quote is drawn from Schechter (1903: 123) and Poznánski (1904: 5). I owe these references to my friend, Prof. Elchanan Reiner.
4 Schechter conjectured that the author of the letter was Rabbi Shmuel ben Hofni (d. 1034), the last Gaon of Sura (Schechter 1903: 121). This attribution is not, however, proven.
5 For discussion and further bibliography, see Reiner (2013: 52–4).
6 Tradents examine and process traditions for their own time. Thus, as James A. Sanders (1998) argues, 'all scribes, translators, commentators, midrashists and even preachers are tradents'.
7 Thus, even when Cohen contests (rightly) the overly negative representation of diaspora on the part of Safran, he does so only after the fact, as it were, recognizing some positive effects of diasporic existence without contesting the traumatic nature of that existence or of its origins (Cohen 2008: 7).
8 I do not wish to suggest that this negative understanding of Jewish life in Babylonia disappeared from Talmudic culture entirely. See, for example, Shabbat 33a.
9 As pointed out correctly by Isaiah M. Gafni (1997: 36 n. 27), this is surely the correct reading and not Rabbi Eli'ezer. This Rabbi El'azar, of Babylonian origin, went to Palestine to study with Rabbi Yoḥanan and ended up his successor.
10 Compare the entirely different formulation of this in Unnik (1993: 55). Lietzmann was right when he wrote: 'Das Talmudjudentum hat seine Griechisch redende Schwester getötet, ihre Stätte zerstört und den Pflug darüber geführt.' It would be equally just to claim, I suppose, that it was the Church that murdered Diaspora Judentum by absorbing it.
11 See also the illuminating pages in Gafni on the identification of biblical sites with local late-antique Babylonian ones and the cultural role of these identifications (Gafni 2002: 228–30).
12 It seems important to note that Babylonia itself was *not* a term used by the Sasanians to indicate a province, although the Jews, of course, continued its usage. Naming the local place with its Hebrew name and refusing its current local name, itself manifests the people as diasporic. For the fourth-century Ammianus Marcellinus, all this area was simply called Assyria in his time (Bainbridge 2012: 5).
13 Following interpretation of Qorban Ha'edah, ad loc.
14 I want to thank Tal Chybowski-Hever for reminding me of this text.
15 Teshuvot HaRiva"sh, no. 376.
16 As brilliantly shown by Gafni (1997: 116).
17 This is the Babylonian form of the Palestinian Ḥananya.

References

Bainbridge, R. G. (2012) 'Ammianus Marcellinus: description of the 18 provinces of Sasanian Empire', available at: www.sasanika.org/wp-content/uploads/AMMIANUS-MARCELLINUS-Province-of-Sasanian-Iran.pdf.
Boyarin, D. (2015) *A traveling homeland: the Babylonian Talmud as diaspora*, Philadelphia Penn Press.

Cohen, R. (2008) *Global diasporas: an introduction*, London: Routledge.
Dimitrovsky, H. Z. (1986) 'Do the Jews have a Middle Ages?', in Moshe Bar Asher (ed.) *Meḥkarim Be-Mada'e Ha-Yahadut*, Jerusalem: Hebrew University, 257–65, in Hebrew.
Gafni, I. M. (1997) *Land, center and diaspora: Jewish constructs in late antiquity*, Sheffield: Sheffield Academic Press.
Gafni, I. M. (2002) 'Babylonian rabbinic culture', in David Biale (ed.) *Cultures of the Jews: a new history*, New York: Schocken Books, 223–66.
Lewin, B. M. (ed.) (1921) *Iggeret Rav Sherira Ga'on*, Haifa: no publisher. In Hebrew.
Marienstras, R. (1989) 'On the notion of diaspora', in Gérard Chaliand (ed.) *Minority peoples in the age of nation-states*, translated by Tony Berrett, London: Pluto Press, 119–25.
Poznánski, von S. (1904) *Schechter's Saadyana*, Frankfurt: J. Kauffmann.
Reiner, E. (2013) '"Knesset", "Bet Hakkneset", and holy place', unpublished manuscript, Jerusalem.
Rubenstein, J. (2004) 'Addressing the attributes of the land of Israel: an analysis of Bavli Ketubot 110b–112a', in Isaiah M. Gafni (ed.) *Center and diaspora: the land of Israel and the diaspora in the Second Temple, Mishna and Talmud periods*, Jerusalem: Merkaz Zalman Shazar le-toldot Yisrael, 159–88.
Sanders, J. A. (1998) '"Spinning" the Bible', available at: http://fontes.lstc.edu/~rklein/Documents/spinningbible.htm.
Schechter, S. (ed.) (1903) *Saadyana: Geniza fragments of writings of R. Saadya Gaon and others*, Cambridge: Deighton & Bell.
Unnik, W. C. van (1993) *Das Selbstverständnis der jüdischen Diaspora in der hellenistisch-römischen Zeit*, Leiden: Brill.
Vertovec, S. (1997) 'Three meanings of "diaspora," exemplified among South Asian religions', *Diaspora*, 6 (3), 277–99, doi: 10.1353/dsp.1997.0010.
Vidas, M. (2008) 'The Bavli's discussion of genealogy in Qiddushin IV', in G. Gardner and K. L. Osterloh (eds) *Antiquity in antiquity: Jewish and Christian pasts in the Greco-Roman world*, Tübingen: Mohr Siebeck, 285–326.

Wider reading

Brody, R. (2003) 'Pirqoy Ben Baboy and the history of internal polemics in Judaism', in Mordechai A. Friedman (ed.) *Jewish culture in Muslim lands and Cairo Geniza studies, vol. III*, Tel Aviv: Tel Aviv University Press, 7–31. In Hebrew.
Fishman, T. (2011) *Becoming the people of the Talmud: oral Torah as written tradition in medieval Jewish cultures*, Jewish Culture and Contexts, Philadelphia: University of Pennsylvania Press.
Gundry, R. H. (1964) 'The language milieu of first-century Palestine: its bearing on the authenticity of the gospel tradition', *Journal of Biblical Literature*, 83 (4), 404–8, doi: 10.2307/3264174.
Kalmin, R. (2006) *Jewish Babylonia between Persia and Roman Palestine*, Oxford: Oxford University Press.
Widengren, G. (1987) ĀSŌRISTĀN: name of the Sasanian province of Babylonia', *Encyclopedia Iranica*, online research tool, available at: www.iranicaonline.org/articles/asosristan.

40
Diasporas building peace
Reflections from the experience of Middle Eastern diasporas

Bahar Baser and Mari Toivanen

In almost every conflict around the world today, diasporas are identified as critical stakeholders (Geukjian 2014; Probst 2016: 2; Shain 2002). Indeed, the growing importance of diasporas in contemporary world politics has brought more intense scrutiny to them. A bourgeoning literature has thus arisen on their role as contributors to (and spoilers of) peace processes, as agents for post-conflict development, and as bridges between third parties and homeland political actors (Baser and Swain 2008; Cohen 2008; Pande 2017: 5). Although until recently diasporas were portrayed as victims of conflicts and/or as passive recipients of the politics of both homeland and host country, they are now more and more also seen as purposive and capable agents. This reality is being increasingly recognized by academics, as well as by NGOs and key political actors in both the homeland and host countries. As Cohen (1996) rightly put it over two decades ago, yesterday's victims have become today's vocal challengers to existing political mechanisms and processes, both at home and abroad. If migration and refugees remain highly charged and visible topics in contemporary politics, diasporas will also continue to receive ample scrutiny and will surely attract greater attention in the future.

Diasporas from the Middle East

Diasporas from the Middle East were, globally speaking, the largest diasporic movements to form during the twentieth century. Whereas earlier migration movements from the region were more closely linked to outward labour migration, in the late twentieth century humanitarian migration resulting from inter- and intra-ethnic conflicts rose in importance. In scope and intensity, the migrations from Turkey, Lebanon, Syria, Iraq, Iran and Palestine (among other countries) have been tightly linked to societal and political developments within these countries. Middle Eastern diasporas today therefore constitute something of an amalgam of both labour (voluntary) and conflict-generated (largely involuntary) waves of historical migration. This has meant that, across the globe, the engagement of diasporic communities with homeland affairs has been neither homogenous nor straightforward. The 'politicized ethnic identities' (Wald 2009: 1304) of those in the diaspora whose migration has been conflict-generated have tended to sustain loyalties to the homeland. Establishing mature organizations and actively transmitting identities, traumas and experiences from generation to generation has allowed diasporas to have a range of capacities for mobilization and action. The environment of continual insecurity and crisis in the Middle East also perpetuates these migration flows and, with each emerging new calamity or conflict, the existing diasporas acquire new members.

An abundant body of empirical research shows how different diasporic groups from the Middle East participate in peace-making efforts in their conflict-ridden home countries. The types of Middle Eastern diasporic participation on which case studies have been based include establishing advocacy networks (Mavroudi 2008), lobbying policy-makers in the host state (Baser 2015; Toivanen 2014), participating politically through external voting (Tabar 2014), taking part in conflict resolution (Geukjian 2014), investing and providing development support (Brinkerhoff 2008), and supporting reconciliation and justice-seeking endeavours (Bamyeh 2007). Mobilization has also occurred online, thanks to the new communication technologies and easy access to homeland media outlets (Alinejad 2011; Ben-David 2012; Helland 2007). The most commonly studied cases are the Palestinian, Lebanese, Jewish, Kurdish and Egyptian diasporas. Some, such as the Egyptian diaspora in the UK (Underhill 2016), have only recently mobilized following a crisis in the homeland. Others, due to statelessness and constant oppression – notably the Palestinian and Kurdish diasporas – have maintained consistent mobilization over time (Baser 2015; Mason 2007; Toivanen 2014). The Armenians of Lebanon (Geukjian 2014) and the Coptic diaspora from Egypt (Yefet 2017) are also widely studied, providing insights into diasporic groups that are religious minorities in their respective homelands. The newly emerging Syrian diaspora is also receiving a lot of attention in the literature, especially from NGOs and think-tanks offering humanitarian assistance in the region, for they see its members as providing a useful conduit to the local communities there (Svoboda and Pantuliano 2015).

Such examples demonstrate the multiple ways in which different diasporic groups and their members participate in homeland affairs, as well as the internal heterogeneity of diasporas themselves (Van Hear and Cohen 2016). They also speak volumes about the contradictory effects that diasporic activism can have on perpetuating a conflict instead of providing a means for peace-building. As Probst (2016: 2) argues, 'the role of diasporas is not unconditionally positive or negative', for they have multifaceted roles to play in conflict. The debate on whether diasporas are 'peace-wreckers or peace-makers' (Smith and Stares 2007) has dominated discussions on the role of diasporas for the last decade. Most of the literature has been based on case studies of a specific country, and findings have been highly context-dependent. For instance, scholars studying security or terrorism have focused on how diasporas prolong conflicts by giving material and non-material support to terrorist organizations, in the context of increasing suspicions about diasporic engagement. The dominant perspective has been that diasporas have been involved in non-transparent actions that were potentially altering political situations in their homelands and that a better understanding of the mechanisms they were using to prolong conflicts while undermining the surveillance mechanisms of the host countries was needed (Hoffman et al. 2007).

Scholars from a social movement background have underlined that diasporas mobilized similarly to advocacy networks and that their actions could be better understood from a social movement perspective, with its focus on mobilizing resources and social capital (Biswas 2004). Another strand of research has focused on the positive impact that diasporas can have on homeland conflicts and specifically highlighted their role in post-conflict reconstruction and development, whether it be through investing in the homeland economy or by acting as a third party between donors and homeland governments (Cochrane et al. 2009; Kent 2006). The ongoing debates, despite multiple approaches, have all concluded that diasporas are multifaceted and not at all homogenous. Therefore, within a diasporic group, there could be multiple clusters of different ideological, religious, ethnic or economic backgrounds and with varying agendas for the homeland and host country. For instance, McAuliffe (2007) clearly shows how first- and second-generation members of the Iranian diaspora are divided across religious lines, even as both maintain their transnational links with the theocratic Iranian state. The Alevite diaspora from Turkey has also set up separate associations from those established by Sunni Muslim groups coming from the same country (Sökefeld 2006). Moreover, a diasporic group can alter its strategy during a conflict – a stance towards a homeland struggle is not static. Diasporic identities are fluid, and so are their political aims and goals (Smith and Stares 2007).

All these points have left scholars pointing to the significant dilemma host countries face when addressing the question of 'how, when and who to engage' among their local diasporas in conflict resolution in their homelands. Since clearly 'diasporas matter', the questions that follow are 'what impact' do they have and 'under what conditions'? – questions that still remain to some extent unaddressed in the literature. Original case-study-based research offers the prospect of gaining significant insight into these questions, although the jury is still out on whether diaspora's role in conflicts is positive or not.

What conditions the resolution and prolongation of conflict?

Not all diasporas from the Middle East wish to engage in homeland affairs (Asal and Ayres 2017). Those that do adopt different means of exercising their influence in homeland and host country politics. Moreover, the overall impact will depend on the political and societal contexts of the homeland, as well as of the host country, not to mention the diaspora's ability and motivation for engagement. The political opportunity structures in the sending and receiving countries, diplomatic relations between them, and the robustness of transnational channels (networks and institutional structures) are factors that influence a given diaspora's impact on homeland peacemaking or peace-wrecking (Baser 2015; Sökefeld 2006; Yefet 2017).

Acquiring an independent role as a political actor in peace-building necessitates as a first step a political opportunity structure in the host country that facilitates diaspora lobbying, para-diplomacy and advocacy work towards host-state political actors (Baser 2015; Geukjian 2014). Even where the host country is open to this kind of activism, diasporic groups may not be particularly successful. Yefet (2017: 1207) argues that, although the Coptic diaspora in the USA has been successful in terms of lobbying Congress and effectively raising White House awareness of the plight of the Copts, they have had little influence on shifting US foreign policy towards Egypt in a direction that would favour their agenda. Extensive political opportunities in the host country have in this case been superseded by other factors that have limited the diaspora's impact. The compatibility of the national interests of both homeland and host country is thus a highly pertinent factor in the equation. Resource attributes – particularly levels of education, integration and financial heft – are also major determinants of a diaspora's success. For instance, Skulte-Ouaiss and Tabar (2015: 160) have found that the presence of these resources has been crucial to the ability of the Lebanese diaspora in Australia, Canada and the USA to affect homeland affairs in Lebanon. Moreover, growing Islamophobia and securitization since 9/11 have placed significant obstacles in the way of diasporic groups from the Middle East (Howell and Shryock 2003). Often, discussions on terrorism dovetail with the migration issue and the question of refugees and diasporas (Schmid 2016). Where a diaspora is portrayed as sympathizing with groups listed on the US and EU list of terrorist organizations, the prospect of being criminalized and having severe restrictions on self-representation and activism/mobilization is ever-present.

Also, the homeland–diaspora relations are not always rosy. When debates about homeland affairs between homeland political actors and diasporas erupt into conflict, the latter may find themselves in a challenging situation. First, there may be a fundamental disconnect between local political actors and the diaspora over expectations of how the latter will contribute, participate and/or exercise influence in the homeland. As Khachig Tölölyan notes in relation to the diaspora–homeland nexus in the Armenian case: 'they want service and money from diasporans, not thoughts or opinions' (cited in Shain 2002: 104). Second, the homeland might consider the diaspora a threat to its own security or interests. The Kurdish diaspora in Europe and elsewhere has often contested the Turkish state's sovereignty from abroad, resulting in considerable diplomatic tension between European countries and Turkey (Baser 2015; Østergaard-Nielsen 2003).

As mentioned, diasporas are not merely victims of surrounding circumstances; they also exercise agency and make use of their capacities to shape and influence events proactively (Geukjian 2014). The diaspora's *capacity and motivation* to influence a homeland conflict (Freitas 2012: 5) is immensely important in terms of determining the scope of its actions. Some groups may have higher levels of motivation but less capacity to influence peace outcomes, while others might proceed with caution despite having significant resources at their disposal. Some might have adverse aspirations about the conflict yet lack the capacity to act as saboteurs, while in other cases the capability will be present but the group may remain indifferent. In many cases, the diaspora's impact remains solely philanthropic (Yefet 2016: 1210). More importantly, different political orientations, cross-cutting loyalties, as well as, among other factors, ethnic and religious backgrounds, can cause diasporas to have divided interests among themselves (Probst 2016: 6). The actions of their members are hindered by divisions that mirror existing cleavages in the homeland, or emerge from newer rifts because of shifting conditions in the host country. Developing projects for diasporic engagement will be complex for home and host countries, as well as for third parties, unless these facts are considered.

Diasporic engagement in peace-building at various stages of a conflict

Literature on peace-building and conflict resolution in different states or regions that are politically unstable, and/or in the process of democratic transition, is abundant (Cochrane et al. 2009). This research shows that diasporic involvement is dependent on the stage of the conflict and the various other factors mentioned above. As Bercovitch (2007) has noted, each phase of the conflict – from conflict prevention to the post-conflict scenario – generates different diasporic behaviour, offering varying options for intervention.

Diasporas can play versatile roles when there is an ongoing conflict in the homeland. They can lobby host governments, push for economic sanctions and organize advocacy networks (Bercovitch 2007: 30). Transnational space provides an excellent platform for diasporas from the Middle East – especially for those who form a minority in the homeland – to mobilize and voice their demands without oppression or fear of persecution. That is why Kurdish and Palestinian diasporas, as the two largest stateless nations of the world, use this space to protest and contest the sovereignty of their respective states, which have undermined their identity, culture and even their right to exist. While the conflict endures in their homeland, they continue to lobby supranational institutions as well as host states to put leverage on their oppressors. For instance, Arab states encourage Arab diasporas all around the world to boycott Israeli products (Bercovitch 2007: 31). The Kurdish diaspora, on the other hand, puts a lot of pressure on the European Union to admonish Turkey for its human rights violations against the Kurds (Baser 2015).

Diasporans can also organize media campaigns, massive demonstrations, petitions and awareness drives to make their voices heard during a conflict. The Kurdish diaspora from Iraq organized widespread marches and hunger strikes during Saddam Hussein's Anfal campaign, which killed thousands of Kurds in the late 1980s. Moreover, during the invasion of Iraq, the Iraqi

Kurdish diaspora was highly supportive of US involvement, and even provided political consultancy and intelligence to foreign governments during the war. However, the general Iraqi diaspora's reaction to the US invasion was much less focused and homogenous. Diasporans also quickly react to critical junctures in their homelands. During the so-called 'Arab Spring', they played an especially vital role in transmitting messages from the homeland to a wider Western audience (Breuer et al. 2015). During the Gezi protests, the Turkish diaspora also reacted immediately and created awareness in Europe, the USA and Australia when the media in Turkey were heavily censured (Baser 2015).

Advocacy and lobbying are among the activities that diasporic groups can undertake during an ongoing conflict, for their efforts during this phase are more visible and detectable. However, when it comes to the actual peace process, a diaspora's engagement is more limited and its potential to make an impact on the ongoing process is minimal. One reason for this is that most peace processes are private and take place behind closed doors. This secrecy isolates third parties, including diasporas, unless the talks are explicitly designed to encompass them. Although they are designated actors for advocacy, their agency might be undermined during peace processes. Their inclusion/exclusion also depends on how crucial they are to the negotiating parties and how much leverage they have on each actor involved in the process. Diasporas can, in short, sabotage or accelerate a peace process depending on their own agenda and how compatible it is with that of the homeland actors. Moreover, diasporic inclusion in these processes prompts a question about representation. Diasporas are not elected by any constituency; they are merely mobilized (and often highly vocal) people claiming to represent a certain group. Therefore, their inclusion complicates the process. For instance, as Gertheiss (2015) has noted, both Jewish and Palestinian diasporas have had hawkish and dovish factions, each with varying agendas for a potential solution to the Israeli–Palestinian conflict.

Diasporans are also becoming influential actors in transitional justice mechanisms, for more and more state actors are perceiving them as stakeholders in that process. They participate in truth commissions, testify in courts and support homeland actors and third parties in bringing human rights violations to the fore. Moreover, where transitional justice does not formally take place, diasporas invest in commemoration events that not only strengthen their ties to their kin in the homeland but also keep traumatic events on the agenda. For instance, the Iraqi Kurdish diaspora has been investing significant amounts of money and energy into achieving recognition of Saddam Hussein's Anfal campaign as a genocide in various European parliaments. With the help of the Kurdistan Regional Government's official representations in European countries, they have been successful in this in Sweden, Norway and the UK (Baser and Toivanen 2017). Assyrians from Turkey have also lobbied the Swedish parliament to recognize the atrocities perpetrated against them during the Ottoman era as genocide. Kurds from Turkey also demand transitional justice and truth commissions in Turkey and constantly feed information to the local Kurds about other truth commissions around the world.

Scholars have provided rich documentation on how Middle Eastern diasporas, among others, contribute to homeland development via economic and social remittances, long-distance political participation and return migration. For instance, in 2016 the economic remittances that migrants from developing countries sent back home amounted to three times the official aid flows and constituted more than 10 per cent of GDP in 25 developing countries (World Bank 2016). Economic remittances to the Middle East have been growing steadily, with Egypt becoming the top recipient in 2015 (World Bank 2016). An IOM (2010) study found that the Egyptian diaspora's economic remittances are employed not only to meet the daily household expenses of migrants' families back home but also for investment purposes. Studies such as Tabar's (2014) research on the Lebanese diaspora in Australia show the impact and relevance of long-distance voting to homeland political processes in post-conflict situations. On the other hand, the return of diasporans after conflicts has previously been considered a precondition for post-conflict reconstruction. However, in a case study on Iraqi Kurds in Sweden, Emanuelsson (2008) shows that transfer of knowledge and expertise can also take place via partial return or transnationally without necessitating a permanent return. The development of digital technologies in the form of 'mobile money' accounts and electronic money transfers via smart phones enable low-cost and cross-border money transfers to be made to sending regions that can then support post-conflict reconstruction processes and development initiatives back home.

Studies have also shown that there is a continuum between peace-building and development activities once the homeland conflict has subsided (Horst et al. 2010). The engagement of diasporas in development activities can, in a post-conflict situation, become part of the reconstruction process. However, what shapes diasporic engagement in post-conflict reconstruction is the way the conflict has ended. For instance, Van Hear and Cohen (2016: 4) list three possible outcomes of a conflict that shape such activities: (1) stalemate (Afghanistan and Palestine); (2) negotiated peace and settlement (Lebanon); and (3) military victory by one side (Iraq). The result of the conflict shapes not only the motivations of diasporans to engage in post-conflict reconstruction – for instance, if they are on the losing side – but also their possibilities of doing so.

One factor to hinder diasporic engagement in homeland development and post-conflict reconstruction through official channels can be a lack of trust towards local institutions and financial instruments. Paasche's (2016) study on Kurdish return migrants in Iraqi Kurdistan, and their experiences of corruption in the context of post-conflict peace, is an illustration of this point. A recent report by Malouche et al. (2016) shows that the members of Middle Eastern diasporas are more attached to their cities and immediate networks of family and relatives than to their countries of origin. The transfer of political, economic and social remittances often takes place via these more informal channels and personal networks. As a general trend, the study also shows that Middle Eastern diasporas are motivated to contribute towards their homeland development, regardless of their country of residence.

Conclusion

Diasporas are contemporary non-state actors whose importance has been acknowledged but whose influence has yet to be fully understood. They are stakeholders in virtually every conflict today, and there is growing interest in exploring the intricacies of engaging them in conflict resolution. As they are not homogenous, their size, motivation and capacity differ, and their networks are sometimes not evident; they constitute a complex partner for the home and host countries that seek to engage them in such processes.

Diasporas from the Middle East are a particularly challenging for policy-makers and third parties to discern. They usually come from countries in conflict, and most of these groups are abroad because they are being oppressed or undermined by their respective states. In addition, they often actively contest the sovereignties and political legitimacy of these states at home and abroad. There are also groups in the diaspora that support the policies of their home state, and this contributes to the multilayered nature of their interests and agendas. Although we have provided plenty of examples above, it is difficult to talk about a monolithic 'Middle Eastern experience', for each diaspora's capacity to exercise impact in the homeland varies according to the opportunity structures, foreign policies and other political, economic and social factors in host states. Also, the openness of a home state to its diaspora's influence makes each diaspora's manoeuvring space very different.

What is demonstrated here is that diasporas from the Middle East continue to show interest in their homeland; they engage in various repertoires of action to influence policy-making in both home and host country, and they will continue to do so – perhaps with even more rigour as their agency keeps getting recognized by political actors. The importance of Middle Eastern diasporas in homeland peace-building and conflict resolution will only increase with the so-called 'refugee crisis' and their rising numbers in Western societies. However, with the growth of Islamophobia, xenophobia and the general rise of right-wing parties in the host countries, they might also face more suspicion and more limited opportunities to intervene. Given such pressing conditions at home and abroad, diasporas are yet to carve out their spaces of representation.

Acknowledgement

The authors are listed in alphabetical order; they contributed equally to this chapter.

References

Alinejad, D. (2011) 'Mapping homelands through virtual spaces: transnational embodiment and Iranian diaspora bloggers', *Global Networks*, 11 (1), 43–62, doi: 10.1111/j.1471-0374.2010.00306.x.

Asal, V. and R. W. Ayres (2017) 'Attention getters: diaspora support for ethno–political organizations in the Middle East', *Studies in Conflict and Terrorism*, online article, 1–15, doi: 10.1080/1057610X.2017.1283194.

Bamyeh, M. A. (2007) 'The Palestinian diaspora', in H. Smith and P. Stares (eds) *Diasporas in conflict: peace-makers or peace wreckers?* Tokyo: United Nations University Press, 90–105.

Baser, B. (2015) *Diasporas and homeland conflicts: a comparative perspective*, Farnham: Ashgate.

Baser, B. and A. Swain (2008) 'Diasporas as peacemakers: third party mediation in homeland conflicts', *International Journal on World Peace*, 25 (3), 7–28, doi: 10.2307/20752844.

Baser, B. and M. Toivanen (2017) 'The politics of genocide recognition: Kurdish nation-building and commemoration in the post-Saddam era', *Journal of Genocide Research*, 19 (3), 404–26.

Ben-David, A. (2012) 'The Palestinian diaspora on the web: between de-territorialization and re-territorialization', *Social Science Information*, 51 (4), 459–74, doi: 10.1177/0539018412456769.

Bercovitch, J. (2007) 'A neglected relationship: diasporas and conflict resolution', in H. Smith and P. Stares (eds) *Diasporas in conflict: peace-makers or peace-wreckers?* Tokyo: United Nations University Press, 17–38.

Biswas, B. (2004) 'Nationalism by proxy: A comparison of social movements among diaspora Sikhs and Hindus', *Nationalism and Ethnic Politics*, 10 (2), 269–95.

Breuer, A., T. Landman and D. Farquhar (2015) 'Social media and protest mobilization: evidence from the Tunisian revolution', *Democratization*, 22 (4), 764–92, doi: 10.1080/13510347.2014.885505.

Brinkerhoff, J. M. (2008) 'Exploring the role of diasporas in rebuilding governance in post-conflict societies, in R. Barbouille, M. Ndulo and M. Grieco (eds) *Africa's finances: the contribution of remittances*, Newcastle: Cambridge Scholars Publishing, 239–62.

Cochrane, F., B. Baser and A. Swain (2009) 'Home thoughts from abroad: diasporas and peace-building in Northern Ireland and Sri Lanka', *Studies in Conflict and Terrorism*, 32 (8), 681–704, doi: 10.1080/10576100903040716.

Cohen, R. (1996) 'Diasporas and the nation-state: from victims to challengers', *International Affairs*, 72 (3), 507–20, doi:10.2307/2625554.

Cohen, R. (2008) *Global diasporas: an introduction*, London: Routledge.

Emanuelsson, A.-C. (2008) 'Transnational dynamics of return and the potential role of the Kurdish diaspora in developing the Kurdistan region', special series report, Defence Academy of the United Kingdom, available at: www.files.ethz.ch/isn/98210/2009_03_transnational.pdf.

Freitas, A. (2012) *Diaspora groups in peace processes: lessons learnt and potential for engagement by the EU*, EU Institute for Security Studies, Africa briefing report, available at: www.iss.europa.eu/uploads/media/OA_Diaspora_Briefing_Report.pdf.

Gertheiss, S. (2015) *Diasporic activism in the Israeli–Palestinian conflict*, Abingdon: Routledge.
Geukjian, O. (2014) 'An ignored relationship: the role of the Lebanese Armenian diaspora in conflict resolution (1975–90)', *Middle Eastern Studies*, 50 (4), 554–67, doi: 10.1080/00263206.2014.886570.
Helland, C. (2007). 'Diaspora on the electronic frontier: Developing virtual connections with sacred homelands', *Journal of Computer-Mediated Communication*, 12 (3), 956–76.
Hoffman, B., W. Rosenau, A. J. Curiel and D. Zimmermann (2007) 'The radicalization of diasporas and terrorism: a joint conference by the RAND corporation and the Center for Security Studies', Santa Monica: RAND Corporation, available at: www.rand.org/pubs/conf_proceedings/CF229.html.
Horst, C., R. T. Ezzati, M. Guglielmo, P. Mezzetti, P. Pirkkalainen, V. Saggiomo, G. Sinatti and A. Warnecke (2010) '*Participation of diasporas in peacebuilding and development: a handbook for practitioners and policymakers*', Peace Research Institute report, available at: www.prio.org/Publications/Publication/?x=7305.
Howell, S. and A. Shryock (2003) 'Cracking down on diaspora: Arab Detroit and America's "War on Terror"', *Anthropological Quarterly*, 76 (3), 443–62, doi: 10.1353/anq.2003.0040.
IOM (International Organization for Migration) (2010) 'A study on the dynamics of the Egyptian diaspora: strengthening development linkages', IOM report, available at: www.eip.gov.eg/Upload/Publications/study.pdf.
Kent, G. (2006) 'Organised diaspora networks and homeland peacebuilding: the Bosnian world diaspora network as a potential development actor', *Conflict, Security and Development*, 6 (3), 449–69, doi: 10.1080/14678800600933639.
McAuliffe, C. (2007) 'A home far away? Religious identity and transnational relations in the Iranian diaspora', *Global Networks*, 7 (3), 307–27, doi: 10.1111/j.1471-0374.2007.00171.x.
Malouche, M. M., S. Plaza and F. Salsac (2016) *Mobilizing the Middle East and North Africa diaspora for economic integration and entrepreneurship*, Washington, DC: World Bank Group.
Mason, V. (2007) 'Children of the "idea of Palestine" 1: negotiating identity, belonging and home in the Palestinian diaspora, *Journal of Intercultural Studies*, 28 (3), 271–85, doi: 10.1080/07256860701429709.
Mavroudi, E. (2008) 'Palestinians in diaspora, empowerment and informal political space', *Political Geography*, 27 (1), 57–73, doi: 10.1016/j.polgeo.2007.06.009.
Østergaard-Nielsen, E. (2003) 'The politics of migrants' transnational political practices', *International Migration Review*, 37 (3), 760–86.
Paasche, E. (2016) *Return migration and corruption: experiences of Iraqi Kurds*, Oslo: University of Oslo.
Pande, A. (2017) 'Role of diasporas in homeland conflicts, conflict resolution, and post-war reconstruction: the case of Tamil diaspora and Sri Lanka', *South Asian Diaspora*, 9 (1), 51–66, doi: 10.1080/19438192.2016.1236458.
Probst, M. (2016) 'Diasporas as catalysts for dialogue: the cases of Laos and Papua', Oslo Forum papers no. 5, available at: www.css.ethz.ch/content/dam/ethz/special-interest/gess/cis/center-for-securities-studies/resources/docs/Diasporas-as-catalysts-for-dialogue-the-cases-of-Laos-and-Papua.pdf.
Schmid, A. P. (2016). 'Research on radicalisation: topics and themes', *Perspectives on Terrorism*, 10 (3), 26–32.
Shain, Y. (2002) 'The role of diasporas in conflict perpetuation or resolution', *Sais Review*, 22 (2), 115–44, doi: 10.1353/sais.2002.0052.
Skulte-Ouaiss, J. and P. Tabar (2015) 'Strong in their weakness or weak in their strength? The case of Lebanese diaspora engagement with Lebanon', *Immigrants and Minorities*, 33 (2), 141–64, doi: 10.1080/02619288.2013.877347.
Smith, H. and P. Stares (2007) *Diasporas in conflict: peace-makers or peace-wreckers?* Tokyo: United Nations University Press.
Sökefeld, M. (2006) 'Mobilizing in transnational space: a social movement approach to the formation of diaspora', *Global Networks*, 6 (3), 265–84, doi: 10.1111/j.1471-0374.2006.00144.x.
Svoboda, E. and S. Pantuliano (2015) 'International and local/diaspora actors in the Syria response: a diverging set of systems', Overseas Development Institute (ODI) working paper, available at: www.odi.org/sites/odi.org.uk/files/odi-assets/publications-opinion-files/9523.pdf.
Tabar, P. (2014) '"Political remittances": the case of Lebanese expatriates voting in national elections', *Journal of Intercultural Studies*, 35 (4), 442–60, doi: 10.1080/07256868.2014.913015.
Toivanen, M. (2014) 'Political transnationalism as a matter of belonging. Young Kurds in Finland', in P. Ahponen, P. Harinen and V. S. Haverinen (eds) *Dislocations of civic cultural borderlines – methodological nationalism, transnational realities and cosmopolitan dreams*, Heidelberg: Springer.

Underhill, H. (2016) 'Learning in revolution: perspectives on democracy from Egypt's UK-based diaspora activists', *Contemporary Levant*, 1 (1), 25–37, doi: 10.1080/20581831.2016.1149357.

Van Hear, N. and R. Cohen (2016) 'Diasporas and conflict: distance, contiguity and spheres of engagement', *Oxford Development Studies*, online article, 1–14, doi: 10.1080/13600818.2016.1160043.

Wald, K. D. (2009) 'The diaspora project of Arab Americans: assessing the magnitude and determinants of politicized ethnic identity', *Ethnic and Racial Studies*, 32 (8), 1304–24, doi: 10.1080/01419870701722356.

World Bank (2016) *Migration and remittances factbook 2016*, third edition, Washington: World Bank Group.

Yefet, B. (2017) 'The Coptic diaspora and the status of the Coptic minority in Egypt', *Journal of Ethnic and Migration Studies*, 43 (7), 1205–21.

Index

Aarset, M.F. 210
abandonment, deportees 182
Abdullah bin Abdul Kadir 87
Abebe, A. 55–62
academic uses of *diaspora* 16–17; *see also* universities
Acehnese diaspora 198, 199, 200–3
activism: Acehnese diaspora 201–3; Moluccan diaspora 199; transnational 48–9; women's 158
Adamson, F. 49, 159, 253, 254
'affinity diaspora' 103
Afghan diaspora 184, 186, 294–9
Afghanistan 295, 296, 298
Afghan literature 89–90
African Americans 17–19, 23, 101–3
'African diaspora' 23
African migrants, Ontario 108
Afro–American religions 116
Afro–Caribbean identity 57
Aga Khan case 287–8
Agamben, G. 182, 215–16
Agarwal, S.K. 286–7
agency–structure dichotomy, 163–70
Ahmed, S. 125
Aksoy, A. 244
Al-Ali, N. 155, 156, 158, 160
Al-Barakaat 325
alegria (joy) 73
Alevis 253
Algerian Berbers 173, 175–7, 178, 179
alienation 330, 331
'Alma primitiva' (song) 71–2
Alonso, A. 243, 245
ambivalence towards homelands 288–9, 330–1
Amelina, A. 4, 31–9
American Indians 211
Amin, A. 149, 271
ancestral homes 101
Anderson, B. 107, 199
Anthias, F. 156, 159
Antonisch, M. 121–2
'anywheres'/'somewheres' 135
apartheid, global 185, 186

Appadurai, A. 59, 107, 225
Arab Americans 49
Arab Spring movement 246, 255, 349
Armenia 26
Armenian diaspora 164, 167, 168, 348
art/artists 55–62, 218–19, 220
Art from Zaatari 219
'ask the other question' methodology 36
Aspinall, E. 202
assimilation 123, 192
Australia 149–51
Austria 255
Austro–Egyptians 255
authenticity: 'competitive authenticity' 101; contestation of 98–100; identity 97–105; music 74–5
autobiographical narratives 90–1
autochthony, development 323
Aviv, C. 288
Axel, B.K. 42
Azizaa 75

Babylonian Talmud 336–44
Bahoran, Shailesh 75
Bailey, O.G. 158
Bakewell, O. 323
Banerjee, P. 65
banking 325
Baptist, K.W. 333
Barber, T. 268–75
Barglowski, K. 4, 31–9
Baron, I.Z. 7, 223–30
Basch, L. 251
Baser, B. 7, 9, 159, 345–53
Basque social networks 245–6
Batisai, K. 156–7
Bauböck, R. 48, 224
Bava, S. 208
Beck, U. 248
Belgium 44
belonging 97, 121–4, 174, 177, 184; development 323; embodiment of 63–70; and exile 331; sedentary bias 323–4

Index

Berbers, Algerian 173, 175–7, 178, 179
Bercovitch, J. 313
Berghahn, D. 79–85
Bernal, V. 245, 246
Beta Israel 288
Bhabha, H. 76
Bhachu, P. 284
bhangra (South Asian folk genre) 74
Bible 13, 86
bilingualism 108–9
biographical data 35–6
black cinema 57
'black diaspora' 17–19
'Black magic woman' (music video) 75
Black, R. 217
Block, D. 107
Blood (dance and music piece) 75–6
boat people memorials 332
Boccagni, P. 50
Boehm, D.A. 185
Boghossian, Alexander 'Skunder' 58
Bolivia 67
Bolognani, M. 209, 211
border controls 299
Bosnians 314, 315, 316
Bouchareb, Rachid 83–4
boundary work 294, 298, 299
Bourdieu, P. 165–8
Bowman, G. 43, 88
Boyarin, D. 225, 227, 235, 336–44
Boyarin, J. 225, 227, 235, 237, 238
Brah, A. 62, 80, 103, 160
brands 100
Braun, J. 262
Brazil 183, 194
Breton diaspora 245–6
Brinkerhoff, J. 254, 262
Britain *see* England; United Kingdom
British Pakistanis 209, 211
'British race relations films' 83
British Vietnamese 270–2, 273
broadcasting 244
Brubaker, R. 3–4, 22, 28, 120, 218, 293
Bruneau, M. 164, 243
Burgess, K. 257
Büscher, M. 34
Butler, J. 227
Butler, K. 193
Byman, D. 312

Calais "Jungle" 219
'calibration', diasporic arts 59
Calleja, R. 316
Caluya, G. 274
Cambodia 332–3
Canada 208, 286–7
Can, M. 122–3

capital: Bourdieu 166, 167, 168; international migration 129, 130; racial embodiment 65
'capitalist cosmopolitans' 139
Caribbean, limbo dance 76
Carment, D. 316
Carney, J. 323
Carter, S. 329, 330, 331
caste associations 178
Castells, M. 247
categorization, external 294, 297–8, 299
Catholic missionaries 114
cell phones 330
Chambers, I. 56, 58
Chango (West African divinity, also Shango) 71
Charef, Mehdi 83
Chariandy, D. 67
Cheung, K.-K. 333
Chikwendu, M. 157
children, 'homeland' visits 210–11
Chinatowns 17
Chinese diaspora 19, 58, 66, 151
Chinese gifts 149
Cho, L. 25
Choy, C.C. 65
Christian diaspora 116
Christianity 14, 237
cinema 57, 74, 79–85
circular consciousness 157
cities, super-diversity 268–75
citizenship 63–4, 66–8, 183, 185, 224, 262, 264
Clark, G. 306
class 129–37, 139–44; 'class in itself'/'class for itself' 133–4, 136; migration experience 132–3; self-interest 134; working-class cosmopolitans 140–4
Clifford, J. 6, 7, 63, 146, 147, 152, 218, 224, 329
clothing 279, 280
Cockburn, C. 147
Cocks, J. 126, 127
Cohen, A. 19–20
Cohen, R. 1–10, 25, 41, 87, 103, 107, 115, 174, 190, 233–4, 238, 242–3, 253, 293, 331, 338, 345
collective identities 50, 254, 294
collective memory 177
colonialism 261, 270, 322
comedy films 83
commemoration 332, 333
'commercial diasporas' 19
Common Ground Initiative 321
'competitive authenticity' 101
complexities of diaspora 5–6, 29, 33–6, 55–6
conceptualization of diaspora 3–4, 8, 40–2, 114, 173–4, 189–90, 252–3, 285, 312
conflict 130, 131, 312, 313, 333; diaspora mobilization 311–19; Indonesian diaspora 197–205; Middle East 345–53; *see also* violence

355

Index

conformity 226
Congolese diaspora 158
Connerton, P. 334
Conrad, Joseph 87, 91
consciousness 217
'contained' mobilizations 312
contention/contestation: dynamics of 50–1; identity authenticity 98–100
continuity, religion 237–8
convergence, transnationalism 176–7
Copts 347
cosmopolitanism 138–45, 185, 247–8, 306–7
Crenshaw, K. 157
creolization 74–5, 76
cultural citizenship 63–4, 66–8
cultural genocide 216
cultural identities 57
cultural objects 278–9
cultural production 330
cultural self-identification 140
'culturecide' 218
Cwerner, S.B. 185

Dahinden, J. 8, 293–301
Dakar, Islamic schools 206–7, 209, 210
dance 71–8
data collection 34, 35
data-interpretation strategies 35–6
Datta, K. 263, 325
Days of glory (Bouchareb, dir.) 83–4
decolonization 261
Decter, J. 89
definitions of diaspora 19–20, 189–90, 233, 252–3, 302–3, 312
DeFrantz, T.F. 73
deliberate passing 272
Democratic Republic of Congo (DRC) 158
Department for International Development (DFID), UK 321
deportation/deportees 181–8, 297
'deportspora' 184–7
de-territorialization 235–6
development 261–3, 320–7; *see also* remittances
development agencies 321
DFID *see* Department for International Development
DGD *see* Diaspora General Directorate
Diaspora: A Journal of Transnational Studies 22, 173, 285
diaspora: complexities of 29, 33–6, 55–6; conceptualization of 3–4, 8, 40–2, 114, 173–4, 189–90, 252–3, 285, 312; definitions 19–20, 189–90, 233, 252–3, 302–3, 312; etymology 13; first use of term 114; limitations of term 261; preconceptual history 13; typologies 242–3; usefulness/uses of 13–21, 114, 293, 294
diaspora engagement: diaspora policy 302–10;

Global South 320–1, 323; nation-building 260–7; peace-building 348–51
Diaspora General Directorate (DGD), Rwanda 43, 44
diaspora mobilization: conflict 311–19; peace-building 345–53
diaspora policy 302–10
'diaspora space' 80, 101
diaspora studies 1–10, 22–30, 31–9
diasporic 42
diasporic consciousness 217
diasporic intersections 146–53
diasporicity 7, 189–96
diasporize 41
Dickinson, J. 260–7
difference, visibility of 269–71, 273–4
digital diasporas/media 58–9, 241–50, 330; cosmopolitanism 247–8; definition 243; re-territorialization 244–6; transnationalism 246–7
Dimitrovsky, H.Z. 336
'disbelonging' 184
discontinuity, religion 237–8
discrimination 121, 192, 215–16; *see also* racism
dispersion and diaspora 23–5
displaced persons *see* refugees
diy-küw festival 278
DNA, genetic genealogy 101–3
documentary films 80
Domosh, M. 130
'doxa' concept 166
DRC *see* Democratic Republic of Congo
drums 73
'dual allegiances' 98
Dubai 141
Dubnow, S. 15, 16
Dudley, S.H. 276–83
Duffield, M. 325
Dufoix, S. 1, 4, 13–21, 23, 41, 227, 245, 252, 253, 293

Eade, J. 272
East Timorese 198, 199, 200, 202
economic development 261–3
'economic diasporas' 191
economic policy 304
e-diasporas *see* digital diasporas
Egypt 253, 347
Egyptian migrants 254–5
Eliassi, B. 5, 120–8
elites 131, 263
Elsaesser, T. 81, 82
El Salvador 186
embodiment: of belonging 63–70; dance and music 73–4; deliberate passing 272; precarity 214–22; racial embodiment 65–6
emergence, transnationalism 176

emic perspective 2, 28
Emirbayer, M. 166
empirical research tools 33–6
engagement *see* diaspora engagement
England: Irishness in 98–9; Viking diaspora 103; *see also* United Kingdom
English language 108
entrepreneurs 313
Erel, U. 160
Eritrean online diaspora 245, 246
essentialism 99, 120, 293
ethics 220, 227
Ethiopia 59–62, 263, 288
Ethiopian diaspora 312
Ethiopian Jews 288
ethnicity 24, 31, 82, 101, 115
ethnic lobbying 314
ethnic media 244
ethnography 34, 192–3
etic perspective 2, 28
etymology of *diaspora* 13
Europe: cinema 79–85; deportation of migrants 181, 186; immigration 24; 'migration crisis' 79
exile 13–16, 86, 88, 121, 126, 328–9, 331; cinema 81; deportees 183–4; Indonesian diasporas 197–205; memory 174
extended families 131, 135
external categorization 294, 297–8, 299
external non-interference, diaspora policy 305–6

Facebook 109
fado (Portuguese music genre) 58
Faist, T. 241, 248
faith-based schools 206–13
Fanon, F. 18
Farrell, L.A. 58
FBI (Federal Bureau of Investigation) 325
FDI *see* foreign direct investment
FDPs (forcibly displaced persons) *see* refugees
feminism 155, 156
Fernando, M.L. 236
Fesenmyer, L. 8, 233–40
festivals 149, 278, 341
'fictive kinship' 237
fieldwork-based research 192–3
Filipinas, racialized labour markets 65
Filipino migrants 257
film/filmmakers 57, 74, 79–85
financial insecurity 183
financialization, development 324–5
Fischer, C. 1–10, 293–301
food culture/sharing 100, 148–9, 150–2, 219, 278, 279–80
forced migration: diversity of communities 331; and home 214–22; materiality and subjectivity 276–83; memory 328–35; *see also* refugees

foreign direct investment (FDI) 305
foreign policy 314
Foucault, M. 64
France: Algerian Berber migrants 173, 175–7; Calais "Jungle" 219; Egyptian migrants 254–5; Moroccan migrants 173, 175–7; World War II 83–4
Frears, Stephen 83
Freedman, M. 19
Freitas, A. 348
Friedman, J. 139–40
future diasporas 2–3

Gafni, I. 339, 340
galuth (exile) 13, 14, 15, 16
Gamlen, A. 2, 9, 260, 262, 302–10
Gamson, W.A. 51
Gans, H.J. 101
Gardner, K. 234
gender 6, 31–2, 154–62
genealogy 101–3
generational processes 51
genetic genealogy 101–3
Gennadius Scholarius 14
genocides 316, 332, 349
geonim (leaders of Babylonian Talmudic academies) 337
Georgiou, M. 243, 245
Germany 14–15, 45
Gerring, J. 3
Giddens, A. 3
gift relations 148–9
Gilbert, D. 271
Gilroy, P. 23, 31, 42, 57, 88
Ginsberg, Asher (Ahad Ha'am) 15
global apartheid 185, 186
'global efficiency' 306–7
globalization 134–5, 140
Global North: deportation of migrants 184; 'developed' values 322; migration to 130–1
Global South, diaspora engagement 320–1, 323; *see also* remittances
Godin, M. 5, 154–62
Golash-Boza, T.M. 182
Goldring, L. 252, 256
Gombrowicz, Witold 91
Goodhart, D. 135
Google searches 4
governments in exile 199, 200, 201
Grayman, J.H. 202
Greece 100, 220
Greek language 14
Green, N. 89–90
Gruen, E.S. 89
Guarnizo, L.E. 251
guerrilla movements 200, 202

Index

Guinea-Bissau 102
Gulf States 141

Ha'am, Ahad 15
Habermas, J. 176
habitus concept 165–7, 168
hairstyling 272
Haiti 59
hajj (pilgrimage to Mecca) 141, 143
Halloween 109
Hall, S. 42, 57, 82–3, 87, 139, 269
Hamilakis, Y. 277
Ḥannaniah, Rabbi 341, 342
Hannerz, U. 139
Harding, V. 19
Hariri, Mamoud 218–19
Harney, E.J. 57
Hausa 19
Havercroft, J. 224
Hayley, Alex 101
headdresses 279
healing, refugees 333
Hebrew Bible 13, 86
hegemony 98–101
heritage 97–105; food practices 100; genetic genealogy 101–3; and hegemony 98–101; languages 107, 108
hermeneutics, transnational 35
Hertzog, E. 288
Herzl, T. 15
Hess, C. 184
heteronormative bias 33
Hickey, S. 264
Hickman, M.J.S. 99
Hirsch, M. 26, 80
Höchner, H. 7, 206–13
Hoffman, B. 346
Hollywood 81
Holton, K.D. 58
Holy Land 337, 340, 341
home 6–7, 26–8, 121–4, 125; critiques of 217; disconnection from 284–90; fetishization of 122, 126; and forced migration 214–22
homecoming 123–4
homeland/s 6–7, 8, 26–8, 42, 234; ambivalence towards 288–9, 330–1; deconstruction of concept 331; 'imagined' homelands 107; Jewish 340; and mass media 244; 'nostalgic discourse' 164; politics of 47, 48–9, 51, 347–8; refugees 329–31; reintegration in 182–3; religion 235; transnationalism 246–7; virtualization of 245
homelessness 120–8
home-making 6–7, 216–17
hometown associations/networks 264, 322
hometown transnationalism 173–80
homogenization 33, 42, 271
Horton, J. 223
host societies, identity formation 268–75
Hua, Z. 5, 106–12

Hungary 307
Hussein, Saddam 348, 349
Hutu 43, 44
hybridity 42–3, 76, 140
hysteresis, Bourdieu 166, 167, 168

ICTs *see* information communication technologies
identity: authenticity 97–105; 'category confusion'/'category overload' 273; collective identities 50, 254, 294; construction of 42, 254–5, 268–75; cultural identities 57; diasporic heritage 97–105; essentialism 99, 120; formation of 42, 254–5, 268–75; gender 155; genetic genealogy 101–3; heritage 97–105; identitarian movement 24–5; 'identity reservoirs' 50; misidentification 270–2; multiplicity of 27, 159, 175; passing 271–2; and politics 252–3; regional minorities 245–6; sexual identities 156; social context 272–4; super-diversity of 268–75; visibility of 269–71, 273–4
imagination 106–8
'imagined communities' 107, 244
'imagined' homelands 107
immigration politics 117, 299
India 178, 284, 286, 287
Indian diaspora 151, 284
Indonesia 197
Indonesian diasporas 151, 197–205
information communication technologies (ICTs) 241–50
insecurity, financial 183
intellectuals, cosmopolitanism 138–9, 140
internal non-interference, diaspora policy 306
international development 261–3, 320–7
international relations 313–15
Internet 243, 244, 245, 247
interpolarity, spatial 177–8
intersectionality 31–2, 36, 160; diaspora studies 154–62; transversal crossings 146–53
interviews 35–6
investment 321; *see also* remittances
Iran 181, 184
Iranian diaspora 347
Iranian literature 90
Iraq 142, 348–9
Iraqi Kurdish diaspora 348–9, 350
Iraqis, deportation of 186
Ireland, P. 313–14
Irish Americans 98, 101
Irish identity 98–9
Islam 143, 236, 237, 238; *see also* Muslims
Islamic education 206–13
Islamist movements 138
Ismailis 287–8
Israel 15, 23–4, 26, 125, 126, 288

Jai, Rikki 74
Jamaican diaspora 57
James, W. 294
Japanese 141, 142, 143, 193–4
Japanese Americans 194, 286
Japanese Brazilians 194
Japanese hairstyling 272
Javanese 198
Jewish Americans 49
Jewish diaspora 114, 126, 226, 242, 288, 349; Babylonian Talmud 336–44
Jewish filmmakers 81
Jewish literature 88–9
Jews 1, 9, 13–16, 18, 19, 26, 27, 86, 288
Johnson, P.C. 113, 234
Julien, I. 58, 82
justice, transitional 315–16, 349

Kabir, A.J. 71–8
Kagame, President 44
Kaiser, T. 277–8
Karageozian, N. 5, 163–70
Karenni refugees 278, 279, 280
Karetzky, P.E. 58
Karim, K. 244
Kashmiri diaspora 314
Kenyan Pentecostals 237
Khoja Ismailis 287–8
Khosravi, S. 6, 181–8
King, R. 164
Kiryandongo refugee camp 278
kizomba 75
Kleist, N. 41, 45, 295
Klosko, G. 224
Koinova, M. 9, 49, 158, 199–200, 311–19
Kokot, W. 113, 118
Korean Japanese novelists 91
Korean language 91
Kosovo 314, 315
Kurdish diaspora 45, 122–4, 126–7, 348–9, 350
Kuznetsov, Y. 305
Kymlicka, W. 307

labour market, racialization 65
labour migration 131, 141
Lacroix, T. 6, 173–80
Laguerre, M. 27
Landsberg, A. 80
language: boundaries of 110–11; imagination 106–8; linguistic choice 106–8; multilingualism 141–3; translanguaging 106–12
Larner, W. 304
'lateral connections' 7
Latin America 66, 193–4; *see also individual countries*
Latino music 66
Lebanese Australians 257
Lebanon 253, 257

Lee, R.H. 16–17
'left-outs'/'left-behinds' 134–5
Lesbos 220
Levitt, P. 7, 208, 211, 252, 256, 303
Liberatore, G. 8, 233–40
limbo dance 76
Lindley, A. 264
linguistic choice 106–8
linguistic positioning 90–1
literature 73, 86–93
lobbying 321
London: Irish diaspora 98–9; Kenyan Pentecostals 237; multiculturalism 118; super-diverse context 272–3; Vietnamese diaspora 270–2
longing 42–3
Los Angeles 186
loss 42–3
loyalty 225–6
Lundström, C. 66
Lunt, N. 304
Lutz, H. 160
Lyons, T. 198, 254, 257, 312

McAuliffe, C. 347
McGregor, J. 264
McNeill, W.H. 1
Malay literature 87
Malays 149, 151
Malešević, S. 124
Ma Mung, E. 243
Mandaville, P. 254, 257
Mannur, A. 100
Maori 150–1
Marcus, G.E. 34
marginalization 262
Marienstras, R. 338
masculinities 272
Massey, D. 237
mass media 244
'matched sample methodology' 34
material culture, refugees 276–83
Matsuda, M. 36
Mavroudi, E. 100, 316
Mawdsley, E. 324
Mazzucato, V. 34
media 244
Melucci, A. 254
memorials 332
memory 174, 177, 328–35
Mendel, G. 219
Mercer, C. 320–7
Mercer, K. 82
Merton, R. 176
Meseguer, C. 257
methodological nationalism 33
Mexico 321

Index

Meyer, D.S. 51
Middle East 218, 251, 345–53; *see also individual countries*
migrant cinema 80
migrant lobby groups 321
migration: capital 129, 130; collective identity construction 50; established/recent migrant differentiation 297–8, 299; experience of 132–3; Islamic education 207–9; religion 117, 207–9; return migration 163–70; 'twice migrants' 284, 285, 286–7; *see also* deportation/deportees; refugees
'migration crisis' 79, 186, 214–15
Miles, R. 64
military interventions 314; *see also* conflict
Minogue, K. 20
minorities, sovereign nationalization 126
Mische, A. 166
Mishra, P. 135
Missbach, A. 7, 197–205
missionaries 14, 114
Mississippi Masala (Nair, dir.) 284–5, 286
Mitchell, K. 328
Mithra, P. 320
mobile ethnography 34
mobile phones 330
mobility–sedentarism dichotomy 163–70
mobilization *see* diaspora mobilization
modernization, development 322
Mollison, J. 276
Moluccans 198–9
money transfer companies 325
Morawska, E. 154, 155
Moroccan associations 178
Moroccan diaspora 173, 175–7, 178, 179
Morocco 178
Morrison, T. 220
'Mor tor' (music video) 74
motherlands, 'identity reservoirs' 50
Motlagh, A. 90, 91
movies 57, 74, 79–85
Mügge, L. 158
Müller-Funk, L. 7, 251–9
multiculturalism: in 1970s 24; Australia 149–51; diasporic intersections 146–51; meeting-places 151–2; and the state 307
multilingualism 108–11, 141–3
multi-religious diasporas 116–17, 118
Munshi Abdullah 87
music 27, 57, 59, 71–8; authenticity 74–5; embodiment 73–4; intra-diasporic relationships 76; Latino music 66; salsa songs 71, 72, 73; and trauma 72–3; videos 74
Muslims 90, 117, 138, 144, 215–16, 236, 238, 251; *see also* Islam
Myanmar 279
Myrttinen, H. 199

Nabokov, Vladimir 87
Naficy, H. 81
Nair, Mira 284
narrative interviews 35–6
Naser (Sydney bus driver) 149–51
Nash, C. 101, 103
Natan, Rabbi 341
National Health Service (NHS) 139
nationalism 2, 20, 33, 107, 199–201, 329–30
national sovereignty 126, 127, 313
nation-states *see* the state
Native Americans 211
Nedelcu, M. 241–50
'negative diasporas' 40, 43–4
Nelson, A. 101–3
neoliberalism 134–5
Nersessian, D. 216
Netherlands: Moluccan diaspora 198–9; South Asian Sufism 142–3; Surinamese Hindus 287
'New Growth' economic theories 305
New Testament 14
New York 71
Nguyen, V.T. 333
NHS (National Health Service) 139
Nikkei communities 193–4, 286
non-interference, diaspora policy 306
North America 193–4
Norway 210
'nostalgic discourse' 164
Nottingham 158
Nyers, P. 182, 184

objectivity, diaspora studies 25–6
obligation, political 223–30
O'Connell, S. 65, 66
Oeppen, C. 297
Offutt, S. 115
Oiarzabal, P.J. 243, 245
Okinawan diaspora 67
Olsson, E. 164
Olszewska, Z. 86–93
Omi, M. 64
Omri, M.-S. 90
Ong, A. 67
online diasporas *see* digital diasporas
Ontario 108
Oonk, G. 8, 284–90
oppression, political 126, 202; *see also* persecution
Orientalist racisms 272, 274
Orsi, R.A. 235
Osirim, M.J. 157–8
othering/otherness 58, 122

Paasche, E. 350
Paden, J. 18
Page, B. 320–7
Pakistan 141, 181, 184, 209

Index

Pakistani diaspora 141
Palestine 125, 336, 342, 343
Palestinian diaspora 43, 88, 100, 314, 348, 349; statelessness 126–7; in Sweden 124–5
Palestinian Talmud 340, 341, 342
Palmer, W. 197
Papuans 198
Parennas, R. 269
Paris 254–5
Parkin, D. 277, 278
Park, R.E. 16
parliamentary representation 178
Parreñas, R.S. 65
Parsees 287
particularization, religion 235–6
passing, 'passive' and 'deliberate' 271–2
passports 185
Pasura, D. 5, 113–19, 155
Patel, P.J. 288
Patidar returnees 288–9
peace-building 345–53
pensions 306
Pentecostals 237, 238
performance 55–62, 72–3; *see also* dance; music
performativity, racial embodiment 65–6
persecution 192, 198; *see also* political oppression
Peruvian associations 31
Petyarre, Kathleen 58
philanthropy 321
photography 60–2, 219
Pieterse, J. 144
Piper, N. 256–7
'Plastic Paddy' epithet 99
poetry 90
Poland 91
policy, diaspora 302–10
Polish immigrants 109–11
Polish language 91, 109–11
political activism *see* activism
political geography 315
political obligation 223–30
political oppression 126, 202; *see also* persecution
political positioning 90–1
political remittances 7, 251–9
political theory 48–50, 223–30
politics: gendering of 157–9; homeland politics 47, 48–9, 51, 347–8; and identity 252–3; immigration politics 117, 299; intersectionalizing of 157–9; of memory 328–35; political obligation 223–30; politicization of diasporas 28–9; remittances 7, 251–9; and social movements 254–6
population genetics data 102
populism 134
Portes, A. 254
Portuguese culture 58
positionality 158–9, 270, 315

positioning 87–91, 295–7
'positive diasporas' 43–4
postcolonial states, diasporic engagement 260–7
postcolonial studies 42
post-conflict reconstruction 315–16
post-traumatic stress disorder (PTSD) 217
poverty 131
power relations 36, 63, 156
pragmatism 293–301
precariat 132, 133, 135, 214–22
Probst, M. 346
'prosthetic memory' 80–1
'Protestant Diaspora' 14–15
Psalm 137 86, 338–9
PTSD *see* post-traumatic stress disorder
public housing estates 152
Puerto Ricans 71
Punjab 179; *see also* Sikh diaspora

qualitative methods 34, 35
quantitative methods 34
queer studies 31–2
'Quimbara' (song) 73–4
Quinsaat, S.M. 4–5, 47–54
quotidian transversality 147–8
Qur'anic schools 206–13

rabbinic views of Jewish diaspora 339–43
race, cultural representation of 82
racial citizenship 67
racialization 63, 64–6, 68, 273
racism 68, 186, 269, 270, 272, 273, 274; *see also* discrimination
Radhakrishnan, R. 126
radio 74, 244
Raghuram, P. 261, 323
Rao Mehta, S. 155
refugee camps 279, 330
'The Refugee Project' exhibition 220
refugees: commemoration 332, 333; continuity with pre-exile past 278; cultural objects 276–83; de-humanization of 219; diversity of communities 331; embodied precarity 214–22; food culture 279–80; global number of 216, 328; homeland, relationships with 329–31; material culture 276–83; memory 328–35; 'migration crisis' 79, 186, 214–15; post-traumatic stress disorder 217; remembering 329, 332–3; subjectivity of 276–83; *see also* Afghan diaspora; Indonesian diasporas; Kurdish diaspora; Palestinian diaspora; Sudanese Acholi refugees; Syrian refugees
reggae 57
regional minority identities 245–6
Reiner, E. 338
relational approach/mechanisms 51, 294
relief agencies 279

361

Index

religion 5, 8, 13–15, 113–19, 191, 194, 233–40; continuity and discontinuity 237–8; diasporic religions 114–15; dynamic processes 238; and ethnicity 115; and migration 117; modernist approaches 115; multi-religious diasporas 116–17, 118; territorialization and de-territorialization 235–6; universalization and particularization 235–6
religious associations 178
religious schools 206–13
remembering 329, 332–3
remittances 176, 177, 182, 261, 262, 295, 305, 321; aid comparison 349; financialization and securitization 325; importance to developing countries 349; political remittances 7, 251–9; 'productive' uses of 322; social remittances 256, 322
removal of migrants 181–8, 297
research 33–6, 192–3
resource mobilization 49–50
'resynchronisation', deportees 185
re-territorialization 235, 244–6, 331–2
return migration 163–70, 288–9, 350
'reverse diaspora' 184
rice farming 323
Robins, K. 244
Rodkey, E. 182
Roma 26, 287
Roman, C.V. 18
Romanian scientific diaspora 247
Romans 341
'rooting', transversal politics 147
Roots (Hayley) 101
Rosenthal, G. 35
Rother, S. 257
rumba 73
Rushdie, S. 76, 91, 122
Russian language 110, 111
Rutten, M. 288
Rwanda 40, 43–4, 263
Ryang, S. 91

Safran, W. 41, 42, 154, 190, 252–3
Saha, Jyotsana 55
Said, E. 88, 91, 271, 330
Salafism 208, 211
salsa songs 71, 72, 73
Salvadoran diaspora 186
San Salvador 186
Satanic Verses (Rushdie) 76
satellite television 244
Saudi Arabia 141, 181
Scandinavia 103
scientific e-diasporas 246–7
Scully, M. 5, 97–105
Seager, J. 130
Second World War 83–4

secularization 117
securitization 324–5
sedentarism 163–70, 323–4
self-identification 294, 295–7, 298–9, 303
self-interest 134
'self-tropicalization' 66
Senegal 206–7, 209, 210
Senegalese diaspora 206–7, 211
Septuagint 13
Seremetakis, C.N. 279
sexual identity 156
Shain, Y. 256
Sharma, N. 122
Sheffer, G. 41, 80, 115, 226
Shekhina (Divine Presence) 337
Sheller, M. 220
'shifting', transversal politics 147
Shneer, D. 288
Shuval, J.T. 164
Sikh diaspora 114, 173, 175–7, 178, 179
Sikh Human Rights Group 178
Simmons, A.J. 224
Singapore: food culture 151; gift relations 148–9; public housing estates 152
Sinnreich, A. 27
Siu, L. 269
Six Day War (1967) 23
skirt-cloths 279, 280
Skrbiš, Z. 42
Skype 210
slaves 89, 323
Smith, A.D. 20
Smith, R.C. 303
social categorization 297–8
social citizenship 67
social class *see* class
social constructivism 4–5, 40–6, 48
social context 272–4
social institutions 177
social media 109, 241, 247
social movements 47–54, 247, 254–6
social policy 304
social remittances 256, 322
socio-economics, class 129–37
sociospatial positionality 315
Soja, E. 18
Sökefeld, M. 120
Somalia 264
Somali diaspora 236, 238
'somewheres'/'anywheres' 135
songs 71, 72, 73–4, 75
Sorre, M. 19
South America 193–4; *see also individual countries*
South Asians, Uganda 284
sovereignty 126, 127, 313
spatial interpolarity 177–8
Srebrenica 314, 315

Sri Lanka 314
Stam, R. 82
Standing, G. 132, 133
the state: and diasporas 2, 3, 260–7, 289; economic development 261–3; homeland states 48–9; multiculturalism 307; nation-building 261–3; political obligation 224; postcolonial states 260–7; racial embodiment 65; sovereignty 126, 313; violent conflict 316
statelessness 124–7
Status Law, Hungary 307
Steele, B.J. 227
Steijlen, F. 198, 199, 201
stigmatization 183
structure–agency, return migration 163–70
students 131
subjectivity: diaspora studies 25–6; refugees 276–83
Sudanese Acholi refugees 278
Sufism 141, 142, 143, 208, 211, 236
Suleiman, Hajji 141–3
super-diverse cities 268–75
Surinamese Hindus 287
Sutherland, A.H. 287
Suzuki, T. 63–70
Sweden: Kurdish migrants 122–4, 350; Latin American migrants 66; Palestinian refugees 124–5
sweets 149
Sydney, food culture/sharing 148, 151–2
'symbolic ethnicity' 101
Syria 314
Syrian refugees 214, 216, 217–20

Tabar, P. 174, 257
Talmud 8–9, 336–44
Tamil artists 59
tampura (South Asian stringed instrument) 75
Tarrow, S. 255, 257
Tayto crisps brand 100
technology, music 74
television 244
temporality, memory 333–4
territoriality, belonging 121–2
territorialization, religion 235–6
terrorism 138, 347
'This River Runs Through Me' (Saha) 55
Tibetan diaspora 99–100
Timor Leste 199, 200
Toivanen, M. 7, 9, 345–53
Tolia-Kelly, D.P. 6, 214–22
Tölöyan, K. 22–30, 47, 163, 164, 285, 348
Toynbee, A.J. 1–3, 17
'trade diasporas' 19
transformative events 314–15
transitional justice 315–16, 349
translanguaging 106–12

translocational positionality 156
transnational activism 48–9
transnational cinema 80
transnational communities 179–80, 191
transnational cultures 139
transnational hermeneutics 35
transnationalism 98, 107–8, 135, 163, 234, 248; diasporicity 189–96; digital diasporas 246–7; hometown networks 173–80
transnationality 156
transnational migrants 27
transnational networks 159, 254
transversal crossings 146–53
transversal enablers 149–51
transversal places 151–2
transversal politics 147
transversal practices 148–9
trauma 72–3, 89, 217, 329, 339
travel documents 185
tribunals 316
Trump, D. 215, 218
truth commissions 316
Tsuda, T. 7, 67, 189–96, 286
Turkey: Alevis 253; and Kurdish diaspora 124, 348, 349; Syrian refugees 219; television 244
Turner, S. 4, 40–6, 263
Tutsi 43, 44
Tweed, T.A. 115, 235
'twice migrants' 284, 285, 286–7

UAE *see* United Arab Emirates
Uganda 284, 286, 288
Um, K. 9, 328–35
umma (community of believers) 236
United Arab Emirates (UAE) 140–1
United Kingdom (UK): British Pakistanis 209, 211; 'British race relations films' 83; Common Ground Initiative 321; ethnic landscape of 268; Islamic schools 208; Muslims in 236; Sikh diaspora 173, 175–7; slavery 323; Somalis in 236, 238; Tamil artists 59; Ugandan Asians 285; *see also* England
United States (US): and Cambodia 332; deportation of migrants 181, 182; discriminatory policies 215–16; homeland security 215; immigration 24; Iraq invasion 349; Japanese diaspora 193–4; Peruvian associations 31; slave economy 323; Tibetan diaspora 99–100; 'twice migrants' in 286; US Refugee Admissions Program 215
universalization, religion 235–6
universities, identitarian movement 24–5; *see also* academic uses of *diaspora*
Unrepresented Nations and Peoples Organization (UNPO) 201, 202
Urry, J. 34
US Refugee Admissions Program 215

363

Index

Van Hear, N. 5, 129–37, 314, 350
Van Liempt, I. 209
Vasquez, M. 116, 117
Vázquez, R. 265
Vertovec, S. 118, 234
'victim diasporas' 191, 338
Vidas, M. 336
'videochoreomorphosis' 74
videos, music 74
Vietnamese diaspora 270–2, 273
Viking diaspora 103
violence 122, 131, 199, 202, 216, 316; *see also* conflict
virtual diasporas *see* digital diasporas
visibility of difference 269–71, 273–4
'void decks', public housing estates 152

Waheed, S. 89
Waite, L. 214
Wald, K.D. 345
Walters, W. 181
Walzer, M. 226
warfare *see* conflict
war films 83–4
Washington, Isaiah 102
websites 243, 245–6
Wei, L. 5, 106–12
Weiwei, A. 220
Werbner, P. 5, 116, 138–45, 155
Wessendorf, S. 272
West Africa 74

West Germany 83
Whittier, N.E. 51
Wilhelm, M. 297, 298
Williams, C. 108
Williams, M.S. 224
Winant, H. 64
Wise, A. 5, 146–53, 200
women: activism 158; in diaspora studies 32; Kurdish migrants 123; Zimbabweans 156–7
working-class cosmopolitans 140–4
World Bank 321
World War II 83–4
writing *see* literature
Wuthnow, R. 115

Yang, Y. 166
Yefet, B. 347, 348
Yeh, E.T. 99–100
Yehuda the Nassi, Rabbi 341
Yiddish culture 235
Yoḥanan, Rabbi 340
York 103
Yugoslav diaspora 245
Yuval-Davis, N. 147

Zhou, M. 254
Zilberg, E. 184, 185–6
Zimbabwean women 156–7
Zion 337, 341, 343
Zionism 15–16